Who Saved Antarctica?

Andrew Jackson

Who Saved Antarctica?

The Heroic Era of Antarctic Diplomacy

Andrew Jackson ⓘ
University of Tasmania
Hobart, Tasmania, Australia

ISBN 978-3-030-78404-1   ISBN 978-3-030-78405-8   (eBook)
https://doi.org/10.1007/978-3-030-78405-8

© The Editor(s) (if applicable) and The Author(s), under exclusive licence to Springer Nature Switzerland AG 2021
This work is subject to copyright. All rights are solely and exclusively licensed by the Publisher, whether the whole or part of the material is concerned, specifically the rights of translation, reprinting, reuse of illustrations, recitation, broadcasting, reproduction on microfilms or in any other physical way, and transmission or information storage and retrieval, electronic adaptation, computer software, or by similar or dissimilar methodology now known or hereafter developed.
The use of general descriptive names, registered names, trademarks, service marks, etc. in this publication does not imply, even in the absence of a specific statement, that such names are exempt from the relevant protective laws and regulations and therefore free for general use.
The publisher, the authors and the editors are safe to assume that the advice and information in this book are believed to be true and accurate at the date of publication. Neither the publisher nor the authors or the editors give a warranty, expressed or implied, with respect to the material contained herein or for any errors or omissions that may have been made. The publisher remains neutral with regard to jurisdictional claims in published maps and institutional affiliations.

Cover credit @ Andrew Jackson

This Palgrave Macmillan imprint is published by the registered company Springer Nature Switzerland AG.
The registered company address is: Gewerbestrasse 11, 6330 Cham, Switzerland

PREFACE

mining deep inside the rock of the peripheral mountains of Antarctica will proceed throughout the long winter months ... hollowed out of the rock, irradiated with simulated sunshine generated electrically from nuclear power, the mining townships will be independent of surface weather conditions and shift work will proceed around the clock ... housewives will cook and tend their infants ... and all the busy activity of a normal township will proceed in this human ant hill ... treatment plants will reduce the ores of zinc, lead and silver to concentrates and to separate the gold ... heavy tractor trains will haul the concentrates of minerals and experimental trials of giant hovercraft ore carriers will be made ... ships will work through the short summer season to load the cargoes of mineral concentrates from Antarctic mines. (Phillip Law, Australia, speaking in 1964)

the daring, perhaps heroic, decision by leaders of countries like Australia and France, we must admit, led to something better. (Evan T. Bloom, United States, speaking in 2016)

Hobart, Tasmania, Australia   Andrew Jackson

ACKNOWLEDGMENTS

As a diplomatic history, this book necessarily relied on the documentary evidence of events. Tracking it down was greatly assisted by many. Access to records at the National Archives of Australia was facilitated by Barrie Paterson, Bruce Kay, Christina Beresford and John Wallace. I am also grateful to Australian Antarctic Division staff, including Amy Young, Gill Slocum, Jason Mundy, Malcolm Swingler, Megan Cooper, Phil Tracey, Sandra Hodgson and Tess Egan, for supporting the research and facilitating access to records held there. Bill Bush, long regarded as a wise expert in the field, generously donated his remarkable personal collection of Antarctic documents and interpretations of them. Professor Marcus Haward at the Institute for Marine and Antarctic Studies gave patient support. Other colleagues past and present provided timely encouragement in many other ways, as did family and friends—you know who you are. Meagan Simpson and Anisha Rajavikraman at Palgrave Macmillan provided invaluable guidance in the publication of this work.

Actually, this history was made by the countless brilliant diplomats, lawyers, government officials, politicians, scientists, environmentalists and journalists whose efforts have been sewn together to tell this story. Excerpts from their words and writing appear, and I have simply provided the segues. Unfortunately, as this history is based on documents, there is insufficient space to tell their full story and, because of the necessary word limits, it is impossible to include everybody who deserved it. Every one of these people will have their own memories of their place in these events, and I regret that I cannot include all their impressions of this unforgettable episode in Antarctic affairs.

EXPLANATORY NOTES

This book regularly refers to the 'Antarctic Treaty System' (ATS). This is not a formal name, but it is commonly used to describe the Antarctic Treaty in conjunction with its associated instruments and institutions. The term appears to have been coined in 1973.

References to 'Article IV' and 'Article VI' refer to key elements of the Antarctic Treaty. Article IV accommodates differences over Antarctic sovereignty. Among other things, it prohibits new territorial claims or the extension of existing ones, and provides that no action taken while the Treaty is in force can be used as a basis to assert, support or deny a claim. Article VI specifies the Treaty's area of application and, relevant to this book, ensures that the Treaty does not prejudice the rights of states under international law relating to the high seas.

This book refers to two kinds of consultative meeting, the formal meetings held under Article IX of the Antarctic Treaty. They are the Antarctic Treaty Consultative Meeting (ATCM—the default primary forum) and Special Antarctic Treaty Consultative Meeting (SATCM). Relevant to this book, the latter addressed the regulation of marine living resources, mineral resources, establishment of an environmental regime and consideration of Parties' assertion to have met the requirements for Consultative Party status. Until 1991, biennial Preparatory Meetings were held, usually to agree on issues to be placed on the agenda of the full ATCM. The last such meeting was in April 1991, after which the ATCM was held annually with the agenda adopted provisionally at the end of the preceding ATCM.

During the period covered by this book, the composition of Parties to the Antarctic Treaty changed. There were new accessions, a dissolution (the USSR), a reunification (Germany) and the elevation of non-Consultative Parties to Consultative status. The list of Parties and relevant dates are provided by the Antarctic Treaty Secretariat. What has not changed, of course, is the number of original signatories (12) or claimant states (7). The Antarctic Treaty Consultative Parties (ATCPs) are distinguished by their entitlement to participate in decision-making at a consultative meeting.

The book refers to various forms of international legal instruments (such as *treaties, conventions* and *protocols*). Such instruments will be *adopted* or *concluded* at the end of negotiations when agreement is reached on the form and content of the instrument. A *Final Act* may be signed to record that agreement and possibly some interpretations of its provisions. A state may *sign* the instrument showing it intends to proceed to *ratification*, a formal process by which a state consents to be bound by the instrument. *Entry into force* occurs when sufficient states have ratified in accordance with the instrument's provisions. A state that has not signed the instrument may later *accede*. The *Depositary* is the state which takes on the obligation of receiving ratifications and notices of accession and recording the status of the instrument. In the period which is the subject of this book, the measures adopted by the ATCMs usually took the form of Conventions or Recommendations.

References to government departments and agencies, and the titles of ministerial positions, have in many cases been simplified to indicate the policy responsibility relevant to this narrative (for example, for obvious reasons Australia's Department of the Arts, Sport, the Environment, Tourism and Territories is reduced to 'Environment Department'). Apart from saving space, such abbreviation is also done to avoid the confusion created by the changes to departmental names and ministerial titles.

Some liberty has been used when referring to minerals activities. Reflecting the political nature of the debate, it proved convenient for environmentalists, journalists and officials (and therefore this book) to simply say 'mining'. In this book, 'mining' should be taken to embrace all the stages of prospecting, exploration and development (terms which are defined in CRAMRA).

The reader should also note that in the records there is inconsistent use of Australia/France; France/Australia; Australian-French; Franco-Australian, and so on. In many cases, the records refer to the Australian initiative, rather than point out that it was jointly run with France (and, later, Italy and Belgium—in which case the short-hand 'Four Powers' was often used).

USE OF ARCHIVAL SOURCES

Research for this book used records of the Australian government. Many of these were previously inaccessible, largely as a result of the operation of the *Archives Act* 1983. Under the act, records become publicly available by default 20 years after the creation of the records, although the records of many of the government agencies involved in the events discussed have not yet been lodged with the National Archives of Australia (NAA). As noted in the text, some documents are available in ATADD, a documents database hosted by the University of Tasmania (https://www.utas.edu.au/library/atadd). This book quotes from numerous documents including diplomatic cables, other government records and contemporaneous meeting notes. Unless presented as transcripts, the quotations used are from documents, not individuals.

Contents

About the Author

Andrew Jackson's interest in Antarctic geopolitics stems from a long career in the Australian Antarctic Division as a policy specialist. In that role he advised on policy options, including during the negotiation of the Madrid Protocol and subsequent development of polar law. He regularly participated in Antarctic Treaty Consultative Meetings, meetings of experts and related forums as a member of Australian delegations. He has visited Antarctica by sea and by air on many occasions including as an expedition leader, an inspector under the Antarctic Treaty and a lecturer and guide on tourist visits. He is currently a postdoctoral research fellow at the Institute for Marine and Antarctic Studies at the University of Tasmania. In addition to research in Antarctic geopolitics, he encourages appreciation of the importance of the Antarctic region's natural and political environment. Dr Jackson completed this work as part of the Australian Research Council Discovery Grant (DP190101214) on *Geopolitical change and the Antarctic Treaty System*.

Abbreviations

4P	Shorthand for 'Four Powers' (Australia, France, Belgium, Italy)
AAD	Australian Antarctic Division
AAE	Australasian Antarctic Expedition 1911–1914
AAT	Australian Antarctic Territory
ABC	Australian Broadcasting Corporation
ACF	Australian Conservation Foundation
ACT	Australian Capital Territory
A-G's	Attorney-General's Department (Australia)
AHC	Australian High Commission
ALP	Australian Labor Party
ANARE	Australian National Antarctic Research Expeditions
ASOC	Antarctic and Southern Ocean Coalition
ATADD	Antarctic Documents Database (hosted by the University of Tasmania)
ATCM	Antarctic Treaty Consultative Meeting
ATCP	Antarctic Treaty Consultative Party
ATS	Antarctic Treaty System
AWJ	Andrew Jackson (used in context of document sources)
BAS	British Antarctic Survey
BMR	Bureau of Mineral Resources (Australia)
CCAMLR	Convention on the Conservation of Antarctic Marine Living Resources 1980
CCAS	Convention for the Conservation of Antarctic Seals 1972
CEP	Committee for Environmental Protection
CIA	Central Intelligence Agency
COMNAP	Council of Managers of National Antarctic Programs

CRAMRA	Convention on the Regulation of Antarctic Mineral Resource Activities 1988
DASETT	Department of the Arts, Sport, the Environment, Tourism and Territories
DFAT	Department of Foreign Affairs and Trade (Australia)
EPA	Environment Protection Authority (United States)
FCO	Foreign and Commonwealth Office (United Kingdom)
Four Powers	Australia, France, Belgium, Italy
FRG	Federal Republic of Germany
GOSEAC	SCAR Group of Specialists on Environment and Conservation
HOD	Heads of Delegations
IDC	Inter-Departmental Committee (Australia)
IGY	International Geophysical Year 1957–1958
IP	Information paper (used in Antarctic Treaty forums)
IUCN	International Union for the Conservation of Nature
Kiel 5	Argentina, Norway, the United Kingdom, the United States, Uruguay
MERT	Ministry of External Relations and Trade (New Zealand)
MFA	Ministry of Foreign Affairs (France) – also known as the Quai d'Orsay
MFAT	Ministry of Foreign Affairs and Trade (New Zealand)
NAA	National Archives of Australia
NCP	Non-Consultative Party (Antarctic Treaty)
NGO	non-government organisation [environmental]
OPEC	Organization of the Petroleum Exporting Countries
PM&C	Department of the Prime Minister and Cabinet (Australia)
Quai d'Orsay	Ministry of Foreign Affairs (France)
SATCM	Special Antarctic Treaty Consultative Meeting
SCAR	Scientific Committee on Antarctic Research
SCM	Shorthand for 'Special Antarctic Treaty Consultative Meeting' (SATCM)
TNA	The National Archives (United Kingdom)
UN	United Nations
UNCED	United Nations Conference on Environment and Development 1992
UNCLOS	United Nations Convention on the Law of the Sea 1982
UNGA	United Nations General Assembly
USG	United States Government
WG	Working Group (used in Antarctic Treaty forums)
WP	Working paper (used in Antarctic Treaty forums)
WWF	World Wildlife Fund (now known as Worldwide Fund For Nature)

CHAPTER 1

Introduction

"Now that, folks, is legacy!", declared Sophie Taylor-Price in 2019 at the memorial for her grandfather, Bob Hawke. That legacy was the outcome of Hawke's campaign against mining in Antarctica.[1] To widespread applause she had highlighted an achievement that Hawke claimed as one of his greatest.[2] She may also have been hoping to draw a line under debate about who was responsible for saving Antarctica.

Four years earlier, media had reported on the annual release of archived Cabinet records. An *Australian* article headed 'Cabinet papers 1988–1989: hot under collar at who saved Antarctica' suggested that the issue of Antarctic mining had been added to arguments over the legacy of past Australian prime ministers Bob Hawke and Paul Keating.[3] If there is a

---

[1] 13 June 2019, Sophie Taylor-Price, memorial service for the late Bob Hawke, Prime Minister of Australia (broadcast on ABC TV, starting at approx. 1:23).

[2] 17 May 2019, Michelle Grattan "The golden bowl is broken—tributes to the nation's loved larrikin leader" https://theconversation.com/the-golden-bowl-is-broken-tributes-to-the-nations-loved-larrikin-leader-117281 (accessed 3 February 2021). 24 May 2019, interview with Leigh Sales "Blanch d'Alpuget on the late Bob Hawke" *ABC TV 7:30*.

[3] 1 January 2015, Troy Bramston "Cabinet papers 1988–1989: Hot under collar at who saved Antarctica" *The Australian*. Debate about the Hawke and Keating legacies is covered in: Troy Bramston, *Paul Keating: The Big Picture Leader* (Scribe, 2016). Bob Hawke and Derek Rielly, *Wednesdays with Bob* (Macmillan, 2017). Blanche d'Alpuget, *Bob Hawke: The Complete Biography* (Simon & Schuster, 2019).

question over saving Antarctica, why would it involve only Hawke and Keating? Indeed, was Antarctica saved? If so, saved from what?

AUSTRALIAN POLITICS MEETS FOREIGN DIPLOMACY

Antarctic affairs thrive on shared commitment to the Antarctic Treaty's fundamentals and consensus governance. Consensus cemented key measures to protect flora and fauna, and to conserve seals and marine living resources. In June 1988, the Treaty Parties adopted the Convention on the Regulation of Antarctic Mineral Resource Activities (CRAMRA).[4] It ended many years of informal discussion and six years of difficult negotiation. Consensus on mining was achieved even though there were no known economic minerals.[5]

In May 1989, less than a year after Australia had agreed to the text of the Convention, the Antarctic Treaty Parties were shocked when Hawke announced his Cabinet's decision not to sign it. Australia, a strong defender of the Treaty, had broken the precious norm of consensus. Rather than trying to make CRAMRA more palatable, the government proposed banning mining and establishing an Antarctic wilderness park.[6] Instead of being praised for its bold initiative, Australia was blamed for destabilising the Treaty.

Two years later, after intense negotiations, the Treaty Parties adopted the 1991 Protocol on Environmental Protection to the Antarctic Treaty (the Madrid Protocol).[7] Mining was prohibited and comprehensive environmental rules were adopted. There would be no 'wilderness park' as advocated by Australia, nor the 'world park' demanded by environmentalists—Antarctica was designated a 'Natural Reserve, Devoted to Peace and

---

[4] "Convention on the Regulation of Antarctic Mineral Resource Activities," https://documents.ats.aq/recatt/Att311_e.pdf. (accessed 26 March 2020).

[5] Neal Potter, "Economic Potentials of the Antarctic," *Antarctic Journal of the United States* 4, no. 3 (1969). The absence of economic resources was regularly pointed out by John Behrendt between 1981 and 1991, for example: John C. Behrendt, "Geophysical and Geological Studies Relevant to Assessment of the Petroleum Resources of Antarctica," in *Antarctic Earth Science*, ed. R. L. Oliver, P. R. James, and J. B. Jago (Australian Academy of Science, 1983). In this book, resources are only 'economic' if they provide a return in a commercial market able to operate freely.

[6] 22 May 1989, Prime Minister "Protection of the Antarctic environment" http://pmtranscripts.pmc.gov.au/sites/default/files/original/00007607.pdf (accessed 3 February 2021).

[7] "Protocol on Environmental Protection to the Antarctic Treaty," https://documents.ats.aq/keydocs/vol_1/vol1_4_AT_Protocol_on_EP_e.pdf. (accessed 26 March 2020).

Science'. Between one Antarctic Treaty Consultative Meeting (ATCM) and the next, the Parties had gone from regulating the mining of resources whose existence was unknown, to a ban on mining them whether they existed or not. By 1998, with consensus restored and the Protocol in force, political tensions had dissipated. The turnaround on mining was a pivotal moment in Antarctic history.[8]

The Treaty treasures consensus, even if getting there involves vigorous disagreement.[9] Political scientists tell us that "after unanimity, consensus is the most demanding decision rule there is".[10] Consensus has benefits and disadvantages—benefits when there is harmony; disadvantages in that it can be extraordinarily difficult to achieve. *Blocking* consensus is easy—just one Party can do it.[11] Australia did that when it reneged on CRAMRA. But *creating* consensus is far more difficult as one Party cannot insist that reluctant others adopt a new proposal.[12] Thus, the Protocol could not have been achieved by Australia alone. Had it tried, Australia's actions may well have backfired, entrenching mining as legitimate. Indeed, it may have *precipitated* mining as the then moratorium on minerals activities was contingent on CRAMRA's 'timely entry into force'.[13] With CRAMRA gone, the moratorium was removed. A 'gold rush' was avoided but, nevertheless, Australia's actions seriously challenged the status quo.

This book provides an account of Antarctic politics and diplomacy: painstaking achievement of consensus, its loss and its ultimate restoration. It examines Australia's support for CRAMRA, its change of heart and CRAMRA's demise. It examines how consensus was rebuilt around an

---

[8] Christopher C. Joyner, *Governing the Frozen Commons* (University of South Carolina Press, 1998), 178–80.

[9] Brian Roberts, "International Co-operation for Antarctic Development: The Test for the Antarctic Treaty," *Polar Record* 19, no. 119 (1978): 119.

[10] Arild Underdal, "One Question, Two Answers," in *Environmental Regime Effectiveness: Confronting Theory with Evidence*, ed. Edward L. Miles, and others (MIT, 2002), 25.

[11] In ATS forums, consensus is taken to mean the absence of formal objection, rather than positive consent—a crucial difference. Erik Jaap Molenaar, "CCAMLR and Southern Ocean Fisheries," *International Journal of Marine and Coastal Law* 16, no. 3 (2001): 470. Andrew Jackson, "Politics, Diplomacy and the Creation of Antarctic Consensus," *Yearbook of Polar Law* 9 (2018).

[12] Stuart Kaye, Michael Johnson, and Rachel Baird, "Law," in *Australia and the Antarctic Treaty System: 50 Years of Influence*, ed. Marcus Haward and Tom Griffiths (UNSW Press, 2011), 101–02.

[13] Harlan K. Cohen, *Handbook of the Antarctic Treaty System*, 9th ed., 2 vols. (US Department of State, 2002), 434.

alternative vision for the Antarctic, how it was achieved and who participated. This book shows it involved many more than Hawke and Keating.
It included other politicians, diplomats and their advisers, non-government
organisations, scientists and the media. Their roles are placed in the context of external factors, including calls for an Antarctic 'world park' and
what seemed to be serendipitous events.

A CONTEXT FOR CONTEST

CRAMRA was developed between 1982 and 1988.[14] It was replaced by
the 1991 Madrid Protocol.[15] It is often said that CRAMRA was defeated
by the decisions of Australia and France, two of the Parties essential for its
entry into force.[16] Those decisions have been described retrospectively as
"daring, perhaps heroic".[17] In Antarctic affairs, the term 'heroic' is usually
applied to the early exploratory expeditions in the first two decades of the
twentieth century. In the context of Antarctic diplomacy, it could be
argued that the negotiation of the Treaty itself, which accommodated differences over sovereignty, was 'heroic'. This book will help explain why
'heroic' can equally be used to describe decisions about Antarctic mining
and the environment.

The view that Antarctica is contested in the legacies of Bob Hawke and
Paul Keating is not new.[18] It was repeated in recent biographies.[19] The

[14] Ibid., 384–436.

[15] Ibid., 18–36 and 471–75.

[16] See, for example: Olav Schram Stokke and Davor Vidas, eds., *Governing the Antarctic* (Cambridge University Press, 1996), 162–65. Sanjay Chaturvedi, *The Polar Regions* (Wiley, 1996), 125–26.

[17] 30 May 2016, ATCM39 AD010 (25th Anniversary Symposium) Evan T. Bloom "Remarks on the history, vision behind and impact of the protocol on environmental pro-tection" https://documents.ats.aq/ATCM39/ad/ATCM39_ad010_e.pdf (accessed 26 March 2020).

[18] See, for example, Andrew Jackson and Peter Boyce, "Mining and 'World Park Antarctica'," in *Australia and the Antarctic Treaty System: 50 Years of Influence*, ed. Marcus Haward and Tom Griffiths (UNSW Press, 2011), 251–52. Tim Bowden, *The Silence Calling: Australians in Antarctica 1947–1997* (Allen & Unwin, 1997), 410–14. Richard Woolcott, *The Hot Seat: Reflections on Diplomacy from Stalin's Death to the Bali Bombings* (HarperCollins, 2003), 215.

[19] Bramston, *Paul Keating: The Big Picture Leader*, 317–19. David Day, *Paul Keating: The Biography*, First printing, 1st ed. (HarperCollins, 2015), 321–23. The 2015 pulping of the first printing of Day's biography was not connected with the Antarctic references: 9 May 2015, Mark Kenny "Keating biography to be pulped" *Canberra Times*, 1.

Keating claim contrasts distinctly with Hawke's view, which has been canvassed widely by his biographer and some of his other colleagues.[20] The problem with making credit for Australia's actions a binary choice between Australian politicians is that it dismisses the prospects of joint or collegial responsibility, especially as others came up with the idea first that Antarctica's environment deserved special protection.[21] Some writers avoid the issue of individual responsibility.[22] Lobbyists played an important role, including prominent individuals such as "celebrity environmentalist" Jacques Cousteau.[23] This book argues that responsibility rests not with individual people or nations but with all of the then 26 Antarctic Treaty Consultative Parties (ATCPs) because, in a system relying on consensus, only collective action can secure a decision. So, the question is one of how these events came about and who, be they individuals or nations, can claim responsibility. The answer is found in multiple players and a plethora of parallel events.

This book presents the story of *what* occurred in the mining/no mining debate in an uninterrupted historical narrative. It is done from a distinctly Australian perspective made possible by access to government records. The internal record helps overcome the Treaty's sometimes obscure internal workings which need to be taken into account.[24] This is because, as one diplomat noted, "much of the record is not public" and

---

[20] Barry Jones says of Hawke that saving Antarctica was "all his own work". d'Alpuget, *Bob Hawke: The Complete Biography*. Susan Ryan and Troy Bramston, eds., *The Hawke Government: A Critical Retrospective* (Pluto Press, 2003). Hawke and Rielly, *Wednesdays with Bob*, passim. Craig Emerson, *The Boy from Baradine* (Scribe, 2018), 186–97.

[21] New Zealand is often reported to have proposed a world park in 1975, an idea later seized on by environmentalists. B. E. Talboys, "New Zealand and the Antarctic Treaty," *New Zealand Foreign Affairs Review* 28, no. 3 and 4 (1978): 32–33. In 1964, the Treaty Parties designated Antarctica as a 'Special Conservation Area'. See Antarctic Treaty, Recommendation III-VIII https://ats.aq/devAS/Meetings/Measure/35 (accessed 26 March 2020).

[22] Gareth Evans and Bruce Grant, *Australia's Foreign Relations in the World of the 1990's* (Melbourne University Press, 1992), 156–58.

[23] Shortis argues that Cousteau's role is underappreciated, even though he seemed unaware of the development of CRAMRA until 1988. Emma Shortis, ""Who Can Resist This Guy?" Jacques Cousteau, Celebrity Diplomacy, and the Environmental Protection of the Antarctic," *Australian Journal of Politics & History* 61, no. 3 (2015).

[24] Lorraine M. Elliott, *International Environmental Politics: Protecting the Antarctic* (Macmillan, 1994), 53 and 126. Francesco Francioni, "The Madrid Protocol on the Protection of the Antarctic Environment," *Texas International Law Journal* 28, no. 1 (1993): 51, at footnote 15. Jeffrey D. Myhre, *The Antarctic Treaty System: Politics, Law, and Diplomacy* (Westview, 1986), 40–43.

"in any case, the proceedings of the Consultative Meetings are not recorded except in their final reports".[25]

The existing accounts of the events had scant access to government records.[26] Conservationist Geoff Mosley tells some of the story from an environmentalist's perspective, but for such an important period of Antarctic and environmental history, there are few other 'insider' accounts.[27] In 2002 and 2017, Malcolm Templeton provided a rare exception with an engrossing New Zealand perspective.[28] Seeking to dispel what he called 'mythology', he pointed to some 'rewriting of history' after the change in attitude to CRAMRA was announced in 1990. Templeton observes that "when and if the archives of the principal participants are eventually opened, some of the speculation about their motives may need to be revised".[29] This book uses recently opened Australian documents to shed light on the commonly accepted story that in Paris, in 1975, New

---

[25] The ATCM final reports record decisions made, but not the process by which they were achieved. J. R. Rowland, "The Treaty Regime and the Politics of the Consultative Parties," in *The Antarctic Legal Regime*, ed. Christopher C. Joyner and Sudhir K. Chopra (Martinus Nijhoff, 1988), 11.

[26] Other accounts include: Anthony Bergin, "The Politics of Antarctic Minerals: The Greening of White Australia," *Australian Journal of Political Science* 26, no. 2 (1991): 216–39; Lorraine M. Elliott, *Protecting the Antarctic Environment: Australia and the Minerals Convention*, Australian Foreign Policy Papers (Australian National University, 1993). *International Environmental Politics: Protecting the Antarctic*. W. M. Bush, ed. *Antarctica and International Law: A Collection of Inter-State and National Documents (Looseleaf Volumes)* (Oceana, 1994–2003), Vol IV, Booklet AU88–89, 11–33. Margaret L. Clark, "The Antarctic Environmental Protocol: NGOs in the Protection of Antarctica," in *Environmental NGOs in World Politics*, ed. Matthias Finger and Thomas Prince (Routledge, 1994). W. M. Bush, "Australia, Antarctica, the Minerals Convention and Environmental Protection," Antarctic and Southern Ocean Law and Policy Occasional Paper 7 (Faculty of Law, University of Tasmania, 1995). Bowden, *The Silence Calling: Australians in Antarctica 1947–1997*, 408–18. Joyner, *Governing the Frozen Commons*, 147–80. Tom Griffiths, *Slicing the Silence: Voyaging to Antarctica* (UNSW Press, 2007), 286–89. Chavelli Sulikowski, *France and the Antarctic Treaty System* (PhD thesis, University of Tasmania, 2013). Runyu Wang, *International Law on Antarctic Mineral Resource Exploitation* (Peter Lang, 2017), 87–98, 142–49. Alessandro Antonello, *The Greening of Antarctica* (Oxford University Press, 2019), 77–107.

[27] J. G. Mosley, *Saving the Antarctic Wilderness* (Envirobook, 2009).

[28] Malcolm Templeton, *Protecting Antarctica: The Development of the Treaty System* (New Zealand Institute of International Affairs, 2002). *A Wise Adventure II: New Zealand and Antarctica after 1960* (Victoria University Press, 2017).

[29] *A Wise Adventure II: New Zealand and Antarctica after 1960*, 126. This author applauds that view and also calls for access to other relevant archives.

Zealand proposed an Antarctic world park—a claim for which Templeton, relying on New Zealand documents, suggests no written record exists.[30] There may well be no record of it in New Zealand, but there *is* one in the Australian archives. Even New Zealand's 1975 ambitions had their roots elsewhere. Thus, the idea of continent-wide protection of the Antarctic environment easily pre-dates Hawke's initiative. Clearly, there is more to the story than we have been led to believe. The official documents help fill the gaps and show that the process was much more complex than so far reported.[31] Access to government records allows assumptions to be challenged and helps dispel misunderstandings about what Australia did.[32] For example, this book shows that Australia and France did not always act in harmony despite many accounts lumping Australia and France together as though they were one.[33] This book reveals the differing domestic political imperatives, internal policymaking processes, and the very real challenges faced by officials seeking to translate political decisions into practical international law.

Some commentators suggest that Antarctica was at imminent risk of destruction, that an outright mining ban was the only solution and that environmental harm is now prevented—all wrong. In addition, successful conclusion of the Madrid Protocol was by no means a foregone conclusion, and many objectives set by Australia in May 1989 were not achieved. In fact, several complementary and contradictory proposals were considered, pointing to how compromise is essential in consensus decision-making and to how 'victory' is characterised. Distilled to its extremes, the story contrasts pursuit of free access to Antarctic minerals versus establishment of a world park. Ultimately, neither option won.

The title of this book picks up two of the many themes that are explored—the idea that it is possible to identify someone responsible for a

---

[30] Ibid., 90–92 and 334 fn42.

[31] For example, resolving the issues required much more than three Treaty meetings. Catherine Redgwell, "Antarctica: Wilderness Park or Eldorado Postponed?" *Environmental Politics* 1, no. 1 (1992): 137–38.

[32] See, for example, the idea that Australia *signed* CRAMRA but refused to *ratify*. D. W. H. Walton, "The Scientific Committee on Antarctic Research and the Antarctic Treaty," in *Science Diplomacy: Antarctica, Science, and the Governance of International Spaces*, ed. Paul Arthur Berkman, et al. (Smithsonian Institution, 2011), 81–82.

[33] See, for example: Elliott, *International Environmental Politics: Protecting the Antarctic*; Chaturvedi, *The Polar Regions*; Joyner, *Governing the Frozen Commons*; Adrian Howkins, *The Polar Regions: An Environmental History* (Polity, 2016).

decision to ban Antarctic mining and that their actions were in some way heroic. Despite depictions of the Protocol as Australia's moment of victory, Australia did not act alone or with confidence. Even for the part played by Australia, no single individual was responsible and resolving an argument between two political figures does not adequately explain what occurred. The actions of politicians were an essential catalyst, but not enough in isolation. This book shows that insufficient weight has been placed on the alignment of other events difficult to predict and impossible to orchestrate. So:

- Who came up with the idea to change the future use of Antarctica from a regime that facilitated mining to one that prohibited it?
- What political, diplomatic, legal and community circumstances made that decision possible?
- Can Australians take credit for this outcome?
- Why was serendipity important?
- From what was Antarctica 'saved'?

This book tries to answer such questions. What it does not do is find a single 'hero' of Antarctic environmental protection, nor will it identify a single defining event that made the outcomes inevitable—the story was far more complex. It tells the story of a turning point in the development of Antarctic governance, particularly the question of mining and environment protection. It does this through the lens of the political arguments and diplomatic negotiations, rather than the legal substance of the issues being discussed. It adds to Antarctic history more generally, but also diplomatic history, international environmental history and understanding of environmental politics on a continental scale.

STRUCTURE OF THIS BOOK

The history is told essentially in narrative form. Chapter 2 introduces the minerals problem, starting with the early interest in Antarctic minerals precipitated by the discovery of flecks of gold during the Shackleton and Mawson expeditions. It discusses how the imagined prospect of valuable resources amplified existing friction over the Antarctic territorial claims and how the states involved developed environmental measures, overcame their reluctance to discuss resources and put in place a temporary mining moratorium while protecting their own national interests. Early ideas of environment protection are revealed.

Chapter 3 examines the mining debate, including the six years of exhausting negotiations. Argument over political, legal and environmental issues ended in June 1988 with consensus on the Antarctic mining convention, even in the absence of known economic minerals. It sets the scene for the eruption of doubts about the agreement and the question of Antarctica's future.

Chapter 4 describes how in 1989 the Australian and French governments, impelled by others, turned their backs on what had just been agreed. The objections are juxtaposed with 1980s domestic and international environmental politics, amplified by the sublime timing of polar disasters which shaped what was to follow.

Chapter 5 tells the story of the 1989 Antarctic Treaty meeting in Paris, which was shaken by international shock and anger at the unprecedented developments. The initiation of a diplomatic campaign is covered, as well as the breaking of once-strong bonds between traditional allies and Australia's formation of an improbable alliance with France, whose environmental reputation was in tatters with years of nuclear testing in the Pacific and the bulldozing of penguin habitat in Antarctica.

Chapter 6 reveals the diplomatic manoeuvres as nations tried to settle their disagreements before they had to meet again. It plots the course of changing attitudes around the world as diplomats worked hard to re-establish fractured relations and keep the Treaty intact. New Zealand's shift in position marked a turning point.

Chapter 7 takes the narrative into 1991 when the bulk of a new environmental regime, which tackled the mining issue, was rapidly developed and on the verge of being adopted. With negotiations at risk of failing, the USSR's well-timed insertion of an ellipsis into the draft saved the day.

Chapter 8 will recount how last-minute problems intervened, including the refusal of the United States to agree. The Parties moved to adopt the Madrid Protocol in October 1991, marking the restoration of consensus just in time to head off growing concern in the United Nations and a much-feared review of the Treaty itself.

In Chap. 9, historiographic techniques and concepts of international regime formation provide a theoretical explanation of what occurred. It explains how pre-existing circumstances and serendipitous events propelled change, and assesses the roles of politicians, diplomats, scientists, environmentalists, the media and others whose leadership influenced the events.

The final chapter seeks to answer the question 'who saved Antarctica?' and considers from what Antarctica was 'saved'. It puts in context the competing claims of prime ministers, presidents and others (and there are many) from the international community whose roles have remained hidden. It shows that no single individual or single event precipitated the turnaround in attitudes and concludes that *how* change was affected turned out to be as important as *who* did it.

THE LIMITATIONS OF DIPLOMATIC HISTORY

This book considers domestic politics and policy processes, diplomacy and decision-making processes within the Antarctic Treaty System (ATS), and domestic politics in Australia and other key Parties where they are revealed in Australian government records. The book does not use the archival records of environmental campaigners.[34] However, it does rely on the author's own involvement in many of the events covered.[35] Another Antarctic historian argues that, generally, legitimacy is conferred on historians who have actually visited the places they write about which, in this case, are Antarctica and various Antarctic policy forums.[36] This author has done both on many occasions and brings understanding of bureaucratic dynamics, negotiation experience within the ATS and access to personal records and observations.[37]

If this was just a story about mining, it could be told in terms of geological knowledge, economic imperatives, engineering challenges and logistic problems. However, even the most ardent Antarctic geologists

[34] Archives of non-government organisations are not generally available. Records of the Greenpeace Antarctic campaign have been lodged with the National Library of Australia. https://trove.nla.gov.au/work/34271882 (accessed 3 February 2021).

[35] The assumption that "being an insider offers a distinct advantage" is examined in Robert V. Labaree, "The Risk of 'Going Observationalist': Negotiating the Hidden Dilemmas of Being an Insider Participant Observer," Qualitative Research 2, no. 1 (2002).

[36] Adrian Howkins, "'Have You Been There?' Some Thoughts on (Not) Visiting Antarctica," Environmental History 15, no. 3 (2010): 514–15.

[37] While not one of the 'bureaucratic elite' to which Elliott refers, the author's 'insider' perspective helps unravel the working of the various forums: Elliott, *International Environmental Politics: Protecting the Antarctic*, 125–26. The value of inside information is also reflected in: Patrick G. Quilty, "Looking South: Australia's Antarctic Agenda," *Polar Record* 44, no. 4 (2008): 379.

recognise that it cannot be told without reference to the Treaty, regulatory options, environmental impacts and Antarctica's legal and political circumstances.[38] This is a diplomatic history, a form of history dealing with more than two states and the relations between them, and typically uses official archives to do so. This requires selective choice of evidence, even though almost "any historical object can sustain a number of equally plausible descriptions or narratives".[39] In this case, the author expands on existing accounts that bypassed important data because archival material was not available. In particular, the book seeks to reveal more about the circumstance and events described, and encourage a richer understanding of them by drawing on the internal records of government (mostly from Australia). As a result, it is hoped that any sense of Australian triumphalism is moderated by a fuller appreciation of how Antarctic consensus operates.

To help unravel the conflicting perspectives and congruent (or incongruent) events, this history was helped by applying two analytical tools available in the academic literature. It was found practical to apply Robert Mark's characterisation of the circumstances which precipitate historical events as being:

- *Contingency*—the necessary prior conditions, that is, the circumstances upon which later developments depend.
- *Conjuncture*—the interaction of otherwise independent developments to create a unique historical moment.
- *Accident*—circumstances that erupt to influence events.[40]

The narrative shows that each of these forms of event was instrumental in what occurred. As to the influence of individual players, the author has drawn on Oran Young's typology of leadership styles[41]:

---

[38] Maarten J. De Wit, *Minerals and Mining in Antarctica: Science and Technology, Economics and Politics*, Oxford Science Publications (Oxford, 1985). John F. Splettstoesser and Gisela A. Dreschhoff, eds., *Mineral Resources Potential of Antarctica*, vol. 61, Antarctic Research Series (American Geophysical Union, 1990).

[39] Marc Trachtenberg, *The Craft of International History: A Guide to Method* (Princeton University Press, 2006), 7–8.

[40] Robert B. Marks, *The Origins of the Modern World*, 3rd ed. (Rowman & Littlefield, 2015).

[41] Oran R. Young, "Political Leadership and Regime Formation: On the Development of Institutions in International Society," *International Organization* 45, no. 3 (1991): 288–302.

- *Intellectual leaders*—individuals who produce intellectual capital to shape the perspective of participants. They are the thinkers who rely on the power of ideas, and use their wits to make their ideas felt.
- *Entrepreneurial leaders*—individuals who foster negotiation and put together deals that would otherwise elude participants. They are agenda-setters who use negotiating skills to broker interests.
- *Structural leaders*—individuals occupying positions of power that can be used to achieve bargaining leverage. In a diplomatic context, they typically promote institutional arrangements suited to the states or interest groups they represent.

Each form of leadership is demonstrated by the narrative's various players, with some exercising influence in more ways than one. The result is that the circle of influence far exceeds the narrow scope of Australian politicians and, in many cases, preceded by many years the roles played by the celebrated figures. Several individuals (particularly diplomats) keep appearing in the narrative, evidence of the sustained influence of certain states and the exceptional people representing them.

Historian and diplomat Ted Carr encourages historical study that depends on identifying suitable documentary evidence to tell a story. A particular caution is necessary in using archival material.[42] With specific reference to diplomatic records, Carr cautions that "no document can tell us more than what the author of the document thought". Documents have no meaning until deciphered by the historian. Thus, the historian is engaged in an iterative process of fitting facts to the interpretation, and interpretation to the facts.[43] The reader will note that this book relies principally on Australian governmental archival records and commentary by other authors, even if their commentary was itself limited by lack of access to the archival material. In the view of Tom Griffiths, historians "always have at least two stories to tell: what we think happened, and how we

---

[42] Christopher Darnton, "Archives and Inference: Documentary Evidence in Case Study Research and the Debate over US Entry into World War II," *International Security* 42, no. 3 (2017/2018): 84–85.

[43] E. H. Carr, *What Is History?* 2nd ed. (Penguin, 2008), 16–18, 29. In Carr's analogy, facts are like fish in a vast ocean. They are caught partly by chance, which in turn is determined by the choice of ocean fished and the fishing tackle employed—usually the historian will get the facts they want: ibid., 23.

know what we think happened".[44] This book goes into the Antarctic archive to tell those two stories.

It is not an exhaustive history, giving just a taste of the dynamism of the Antarctic Treaty System. Nevertheless, important lessons come from the recurring themes that emerge: potential benefit from Antarctic resources, public interest in the world's special places, stewardship of Antarctica to protect its environmental values, assertion of territorial claims as a source of influence and cause of stress, and, above all, commitment to the integrity of the Antarctic Treaty. The book ends with some observations about Antarctica's future: whether there will ever be mining in Antarctica or whether Antarctica will ever be a world park—both options remain open.

REFERENCES

Antonello, Alessandro. *The Greening of Antarctica*. Oxford University Press, 2019.
Behrendt, John C. "Geophysical and Geological Studies Relevant to Assessment of the Petroleum Resources of Antarctica." In *Antarctic Earth Science*, edited by R L Oliver, P R James and J B Jago, 423–28: Australian Academy of Science, 1983.
Bergin, Anthony. "The Politics of Antarctic Minerals: The Greening of White Australia." *Australian Journal of Political Science* 26, no. 2 (1991): 216–39.
Bowden, Tim. *The Silence Calling: Australians in Antarctica 1947–1997*. Allen & Unwin, 1997.
Bramston, Troy. *Paul Keating: The Big Picture Leader*. Scribe, 2016.
Bush, W M, ed. *Antarctica and International Law: A Collection of Inter-State and National Documents (Looseleaf Volumes)*: Oceana, 1994–2003.
———. "Australia, Antarctica, the Minerals Convention and Environmental Protection," *Antarctic and Southern Ocean Law and Policy Occasional Paper 7*, (1995): 39-86.
Carr, E H. *What Is History?* 2nd ed.: Penguin, 2008.
Chaturvedi, Sanjay. *The Polar Regions*. Wiley, 1996.
Clark, Margaret L. "The Antarctic Environmental Protocol: NGOs in the Protection of Antarctica." In *Environmental NGOs in World Politics*, edited by Matthias Finger and Thomas Prince, 160–85: Routledge, 1994.
Cohen, Harlan K. *Handbook of the Antarctic Treaty System*. 9th ed. 2 vols.: US Department of State, 2002.
"Convention on the Regulation of Antarctic Mineral Resource Activities." https://documents.ats.aq/recatt/Att311_e.pdf.

---

[44] Tom Griffiths, "History and the Creative Imagination," *History Australia* 6, no. 3 (2009): 74.8.

d'Alpuget, Blanche. *Bob Hawke: The Complete Biography.* Simon & Schuster, 2019.

Darnton, Christopher. "Archives and Inference: Documentary Evidence in Case Study Research and the Debate over US Entry into World War II." *International Security* 42, no. 3 (2017/2018): 84–126.

Day, David. *Paul Keating: The Biography.* First printing, 1st ed.: HarperCollins, 2015.

De Wit, Maarten J. *Minerals and Mining in Antarctica: Science and Technology, Economics and Politics.* Oxford Science Publications. Oxford, 1985.

Elliott, Lorraine M. *International Environmental Politics: Protecting the Antarctic.* Macmillan, 1994.

———. *Protecting the Antarctic Environment: Australia and the Minerals Convention.* Australian Foreign Policy Papers. Australian National University, 1993.

Emerson, Craig. *The Boy from Baradine.* Scribe, 2018.

Evans, Gareth, and Bruce Grant. *Australia's Foreign Relations in the World of the 1990's.* Melbourne University Press, 1992.

Francioni, Francesco. "The Madrid Protocol on the Protection of the Antarctic Environment." *Texas International Law Journal* 28, no. 1 (1993): 47–72.

Griffiths, Tom. "History and the Creative Imagination." *History Australia* 6, no. 3 (2009): 74.1–74.16.

———. *Slicing the Silence: Voyaging to Antarctica.* UNSW Press, 2007.

Hawke, Bob, and Derek Rielly. *Wednesdays with Bob.* Macmillan, 2017.

Howkins, Adrian. "'Have You Been There?' Some Thoughts on (Not) Visiting Antarctica." *Environmental History* 15, no. 3 (2010): 514–19.

———. *The Polar Regions: An Environmental History.* Polity, 2016.

Jackson, Andrew. "Politics, Diplomacy and the Creation of Antarctic Consensus." *Yearbook of Polar Law* 9 (2018): 243–61.

Jackson, Andrew, and Peter Boyce. "Mining and 'World Park Antarctica'." Chap. 11 In *Australia and the Antarctic Treaty System: 50 Years of Influence*, edited by Marcus Haward and Tom Griffiths, 243–73: UNSW Press, 2011.

Joyner, Christopher C. *Governing the Frozen Commons.* University of South Carolina Press, 1998.

Kaye, Stuart, Michael Johnson, and Rachel Baird. "Law." Chap. 4 In *Australia and the Antarctic Treaty System: 50 Years of Influence*, edited by Marcus Haward and Tom Griffiths, 97–117: UNSW Press, 2011.

Labaree, Robert V. "The Risk of 'Going Observationalist': Negotiating the Hidden Dilemmas of Being an Insider Participant Observer." *Qualitative Research* 2, no. 1 (2002): 97–122.

Marks, Robert B. *The Origins of the Modern World.* 3rd ed.: Rowman & Littlefield, 2015.

Molenaar, Erik Jaap. "CCAMLR and Southern Ocean Fisheries." *International Journal of Marine and Coastal Law* 16, no. 3 (2001): 465–500.

Mosley, J G. *Saving the Antarctic Wilderness.* Envirobook, 2009.

Myhre, Jeffrey D. *The Antarctic Treaty System: Politics, Law, and Diplomacy.* Westview, 1986.

Potter, Neal. "Economic Potentials of the Antarctic." *Antarctic Journal of the United States* 4, no. 3 (1969): 61–68.

"Protocol on Environmental Protection to the Antarctic Treaty." https://documents.ats.aq/keydocs/vol_1/vol1_4_AT_Protocol_on_EP_e.pdf.

Quilty, Patrick G. "Looking South: Australia's Antarctic Agenda." *Polar Record* 44, no. 4 (2008): 378–79.

Redgwell, Catherine. "Antarctica: Wilderness Park or Eldorado Postponed?". *Environmental Politics* 1, no. 1 (1992).

Roberts, Brian. "International Co-Operation for Antarctic Development: The Test for the Antarctic Treaty." *Polar Record* 19, no. 119 (1978): 107–20.

Rowland, J R. "The Treaty Regime and the Politics of the Consultative Parties." In *The Antarctic Legal Regime*, edited by Christopher C Joyner and Sudhir K Chopra, 11–32: Martinus Nijhoff, 1988.

Ryan, Susan, and Troy Bramston, eds. *The Hawke Government: A Critical Retrospective*: Pluto Press, 2003.

Shortis, Emma. ""Who Can Resist This Guy?" Jacques Cousteau, Celebrity Diplomacy, and the Environmental Protection of the Antarctic." *Australian Journal of Politics & History* 61, no. 3 (2015): 366–80.

Splettstoesser, John F, and Gisela A Dreschhoff, eds. *Mineral Resources Potential of Antarctica* Vol. 61, Antarctic Research Series: American Geophysical Union, 1990.

Stokke, Olav Schram, and Davor Vidas, eds. *Governing the Antarctic*: Cambridge University Press, 1996.

Sulikowski, Chavelli. *France and the Antarctic Treaty System.* PhD thesis, University of Tasmania, 2013.

Talboys, B E. "New Zealand and the Antarctic Treaty." *New Zealand Foreign Affairs Review* 28, no. 3 and 4 (1978): 29–35.

Templeton, Malcolm. *Protecting Antarctica: The Development of the Treaty System.* New Zealand Institute of International Affairs, 2002.

———. *A Wise Adventure II: New Zealand and Antarctica after 1960.* Victoria University Press, 2017.

Trachtenberg, Marc. *The Craft of International History: A Guide to Method.* Princeton University Press, 2006.

Underdal, Arild. "One Question, Two Answers." In *Environmental Regime Effectiveness: Confronting Theory with Evidence*, edited by Edward L Miles, and others, 3–43: MIT, 2002.

Walton, D W H. "The Scientific Committee on Antarctic Research and the Antarctic Treaty." In *Science Diplomacy: Antarctica, Science, and the Governance of International Spaces*, edited by Paul Arthur Berkman, Michael A Lang, D W H Walton and Oran R Young, 75–88: Smithsonian Institution, 2011.

Wang, Runyu. *International Law on Antarctic Mineral Resource Exploitation.* Peter Lang, 2017.

Woolcott, Richard. *The Hot Seat: Reflections on Diplomacy from Stalin's Death to the Bali Bombings.* HarperCollins, 2003.

Young, Oran R. "Political Leadership and Regime Formation: On the Development of Institutions in International Society." *International Organization* 45, no. 3 (1991): 281–308.

CHAPTER 2

Antarctic Mining Might Be Possible: From Finding Gold to 1982

EARLY PROSPECTS

In his Adelaide laboratory sometime around 1940, Mr Trevett William Dalwood of the Assay Department of the South Australian School of Mines discovered Antarctic gold. He had analysed samples collected by Douglas Mawson's 1911–14 Australasian Antarctic Expedition (AAE). Dalwood was meticulous.[1] Before him was a minute concentration—but it was indeed gold. As Mawson commented, "though this is an exceedingly small content of gold, it is an important determination as constituting the first record of gold in the Antarctic".[2] Perhaps claiming to be first was important as specks of gold had also been suspected in a marine sediment sample taken from the Ross Sea on 17 November 1915.[3] The AAE also found other minerals including copper, arsenic and silver—also in trace amounts—and a common thread in the report was that nothing of commercial value was detected.

Mawson, a mining engineer, had gone to Antarctica with Shackleton in 1907, the expedition which discovered coal. Mawson returned captivated

---

[1] "Trevett William Dalwood—obituary" http://www.users.on.net/~idalwood/myfamily/trevett-w-obit.html (accessed 3 February 2021).

[2] Douglas Mawson, "Record of Minerals of King George Land, Adelie Land and Queen Mary Land," *Australasian Antarctic Expedition 1911–14. Scientific Reports. Series A* Vol IV, no. 12 (1940): 373–74.

[3] Ernest Shackleton, *South* (William Heineman, 1919), 325–26.

and, understanding Australia's geological contiguity with Antarctica, used the prospect of minerals to plead support for an expedition of his own.[4] It was argued that "there will be great advantages, and material advantages, from the exploration of the mineral wealth that lies in the Antarctic".[5] Mawson wanted to take possession of the land for the British Empire, implicitly linking sovereignty with ownership of resources. But he was not the first to pursue Antarctic geology. In 1899, Carsten Borchgrevink had discovered quartz reefs near Cape Adare: "minerals of value occur in this vicinity, justifying the belief that, in time to come, exploration will receive much support from commerce."[6] 'Heroic era' expeditions between 1895 and 1918 made many discoveries.[7] However, finding minerals was a quite different proposition from extracting them. On his 1909 return from Shackleton's expedition, Professor T. W. Edgeworth David poured cold water on Antarctic mining.[8]

Mawson returned to Antarctica for his 1929–31 British, Australian and New Zealand Antarctic Research Expedition, with scientific aims complemented by claiming territory. As a result, the Australian Antarctic Territory (AAT) was asserted in 1933.[9] Australian Attorney-General John Latham lauded resources as a benefit of the new territory.[10] It appeared that the rush was on—not for precious metals, but for possession in case they were found.[11] The United States did not make a territorial claim, but the US

[4] Douglas Mawson, "The Australasian Antarctic Expedition," *Geographical Journal* 37, no. 6 (1911): 610–12.

[5] Ibid., 619.

[6] C. E. Borchgrevink, "The 'Southern Cross' Expedition to the Antarctic, 1899–1900," *The Geographical Journal* 16, no. 4 (1900): 390.

[7] Robert J. Tingey, "Heroic Age Geology in Victoria Land, Antarctica," *Polar Record* 21, no. 134 (1983): 453.

[8] 8 June 1909, Press Association "Mining in Antarctica. Not a promising outlook" *Poverty Bay Herald* (New Zealand), 5. https://paperspast.natlib.govt.nz/newspapers/PBH19090608.2.33 (accessed 3 February 2021).

[9] Order in Council of 7 February 1933 in: W. M. Bush, ed. *Antarctica and International Law: A Collection of Inter-State and National Documents* (Oceana, 1982), Vol II, 144–45. This Order in Council was given effect by the *Australian Antarctic Territory Acceptance Act* 1933 and proclaimed on 24 August 1936. Ibid., 151–52.

[10] Attorney-General John Latham invoked the case of Alaska to illustrate the advantages of acquiring territory. 26 May 1933, House of Representatives Hansard, 1949–1958.

[11] Adrian Howkins, "Science, Environment, and Sovereignty: The International Geophysical Year in the Antarctic Peninsula Region," in *Globalizing Polar Science—Reconsidering the International Polar and Geophysical Years*, ed. R. D. Launius, J. R. Fleming, and D. H. DeVorkin (Palgrave Macmillan, 2010), 245–49.

Antarctic Service had the objective of surveying the region's natural resources.[12] While not motivated solely by resources, by 1946 seven claims had been formalised with all subject to possible counterclaim.[13]

IGY AND THE ANTARCTIC TREATY

Although the 1957–58 International Geophysical Year (IGY) was focused on geophysical phenomena, UK officials "fully expected" the Antarctic component to reveal if there were resources. Others saw the IGY as an economic survey.[14] No minerals of value were found, but the potential remained. In 1958, states that had been active in Antarctica during the IGY accepted a US invitation to discuss future cooperation. The resulting Antarctic Treaty set aside disruptive argument about sovereignty and jurisdiction.[15]

Starkly absent from the Treaty was any mention of minerals, but not because Antarctic states were unconcerned. In January 1947, Chilean Foreign Minister Raúl Gomez had defended Chile's interest by noting, "the Antarctic soil itself contains important riches … coal, petroleum and 141 different minerals". A decree reserved to Chile the exploitation of all uranium deposits found in its territory.[16] Chile's Antarctic station was

---

[12] 7 July 1939 "United States Antarctic Service" (AU-ATADD-1-BB-US-69).

[13] The claims are, in order of being asserted: Great Britain 1908; New Zealand 1923; France 1924; Australia 1933; Norway 1939; Chile 1940; Argentina 1946. One sector, between 90° West and 150° West, is unclaimed. The United States and the Russian Federation asserted the basis of a possible future claim. Brian Roberts, "Territorial Claims in the Antarctic," (UK Foreign Office Research Department, 1945). Bush, *Antarctica and International Law: A Collection of Inter-State and National Documents*, passim. Klaus Dodds, *Geopolitics in Antarctica* (John Wiley, 1997). Marie Kawaja and Tom Griffiths, "'Our Great Frozen Neighbour': Australia and Antarctica before the Treaty, 1880–1945," in *Australia and the Antarctic Treaty System: 50 Years of Influence*, ed. Marcus Haward and Tom Griffiths (UNSW Press, 2011).

[14] Howkins, "Science, Environment, and Sovereignty: The International Geophysical Year in the Antarctic Peninsula Region," 251. *The Polar Regions: An Environmental History*, 139.

[15] How the 1959 Treaty emerged has been addressed by others, including: Bush, *Antarctica and International Law: A Collection of Inter-State and National Documents*. F. M. Auburn, *Antarctic Law and Politics* (Hurst, 1982). Peter J. Beck, *The International Politics of Antarctica* (Croom Helm, 1986). Arthur Watts, *International Law and the Antarctic Treaty System* (Grotius, 1992). H. Robert Hall, *International Regime Formation and Leadership: The Origins of the Antarctic Treaty* (PhD thesis, University of Tasmania, 1994).

[16] Bush, *Antarctica and International Law: A Collection of Inter-State and National Documents*, Vol II, 334–67. Gómez specifically mentioned silver, zinc, gold, iron, copper,

named Soberania (sovereignty), an unambiguous statement of its intentions. In assessing Antarctic territorial claims, the United States pointed to the prospects for coal, and indicated the potential for copper, magnesium and molybdenum and, possibly, petroleum and "fissionable minerals".[17] New Zealand argued that "exploitation of the resources of the Antarctic continent must be related also to questions of sovereignty".[18] This echoed speculation about the motives for national expeditions: "the continent may be likened to a Christmas cake, in which there is always the chance of finding a three-penny bit."[19] In 1953, Australia proclaimed rights to sea-bed minerals on the continental shelf, including off the AAT.[20] In February 1954, Australia established Mawson, the first permanent station south of the Antarctic Circle. External Affairs Minister Richard Casey justified this on the basis that "many valuable and useful minerals are known to exist … the possibility of finding uranium in this region must be borne in mind".[21] Casey would have been pleased: within two months of establishing Mawson, a coded telegram reported the discovery, not of a three-penny bit, but of the radioactive element thorium.[22] The External Affairs Department noted the importance of Antarctica's possible resources and the Australian Defence Committee assessed the strategic importance of "the exploitation of natural resources which are unpredictable at present".[23] Uncertainty over Antarctica's mineral potential had not deterred bold pre-

antimony and molybdenum. 9 June 1947, Memorandum from Australian Legation Santiago, "Chilean Activities in the Antarctic 1947" (NAA: A3300 541A).

[17] 3 October 1947, US State Department, Office of Intelligence Research Report no. 4296 "History and current status of claims in Antarctica". (AU-ATADD-1-BB-US-30), iii–iv.

[18] 16 May 1951, "Mineral resources of the Antarctic: Statement by Minister of External Affairs" (AU-ATADD-1-BB-NZ-30)

[19] W. L. S. Fleming, "Contemporary International Interest in the Antarctic," *International Affairs* 23, no. 4 (1947): 557.

[20] Commonwealth of Australia, 10 September 1953. Proclamation claiming sovereign rights over the continental shelf of Australia and its territories, reproduced in: Bush, *Antarctica and International Law: A Collection of Inter-State and National Documents*, Vol II, 172–74.

[21] R. G. Casey, "The Establishment of a Scientific Research Station on the Antarctic Mainland: Statement by the Minister for External Affairs, the Rt Hon R G Casey, 20th March 1953," *Current Notes in International Affairs* 24, no. 3 (1953): 170.

[22] Un-numbered file "Geology Antarctic" retrieved from AAD Library Special Collection (probably a file held by Phillip Law, ex-Director of the AAD).

[23] August 1954 "Article on the Australian Antarctic Territory (extract)" (AU-ATADD-1-BB-AU-14). 23 July 1957, Memorandum from Australian External Affairs Office London, "The strategic importance of Antarctica" (TNA: DO/35/6984). The Committee was

dictions by US Rear Admiral George Dufek (Commander of Operation Highjump and Operation Deepfreeze), who even countenanced the idea of using a hydrogen bomb to expose the bedrock minerals.[24]

In 1956, Walter Nash, then New Zealand Opposition Leader, advocated abandoning sovereignty and placing Antarctica under United Nations (UN) trusteeship.[25] The United Kingdom also contemplated ceding its claim, although not before the conclusion of IGY in case "materials of strategic value are discovered".[26] Ceding claims would not have been considered had valuable resources been found.[27] During IGY, the United Kingdom was even more cautious because "the chance of a lucky strike may bring news of an important geological discovery. The sooner we reach some kind of general settlement the better".[28] The Colonial Office noted presciently that "it would be less difficult to reach an agreement before a sensational discovery is made".[29] When Douglas Mawson died in October 1958, he may have been rather relieved that his visions of Antarctic resources, and a privileged place for Australia, were safe.

The nexus between sovereignty and resource benefits is indissoluble.[30] That minerals were not addressed in the Treaty did not suggest their irrelevance—on the contrary, tackling it head-on may well have derailed negotiations entirely.[31] Instructions to Australia's delegation to the 1959 Washington conference were "to accept only with extreme reluctance … any phrase likely to encourage consideration of the exploitation of natural

relieved that "there is no apparent economic justification for the establishment of a Communist base in Antarctica".

[24] 4 November 1955 "Why the race to the Antarctic: Interview with Rear Adm George J Dufek" (AU-ATADD-5-BB-GE-37), 86–87.

[25] 25 January 1956, "Call for UN control of Antarctica", *The Times*. 15 October 1959, "New Zealand statement at the Conference on Antarctic in Washington" (AU-ATADD-1-BB-NZ-104).

[26] 5 March 1957, Ministry of Defence, Draft report "United Kingdom strategic interests in the Falkland Islands and Antarctica" (TNA: DO/35/6984).

[27] Howkins, *The Polar Regions: An Environmental History*, 139.

[28] 15 July 1957, Colonial Office Memorandum, "Antarctica: Joint note by the Foreign Office and the Colonial Office (TNA: DO/35/6984).

[29] 26 June 1957, Colonial Office, file note (TNA: DO/35/6984).

[30] A. Bell, "Economic Analysis of Territorial Sovereignty," in *Economic Analysis of International Law*, ed. Eugene Kontorovich and Francesco Parisi (Edward Elgar, 2016), 85.

[31] See 18 October 1960, ministerial statement in the House of Representatives, reproduced in: Bush, *Antarctica and International Law: A Collection of Inter-State and National Documents*, Vol I, 288.

resources".[32] Such was the sensitivity of minerals that the Treaty did not even flag it for future discussion.[33] The chief US negotiator regarded minerals as "unfinished business", requiring attention "long before they reach the point of controversy".[34] After settling sovereignty, there was little appetite for upsetting the new-found harmony, and, in the absence of known resources, the matter lay dormant. It was also left ambiguous. As the Treaty did not prohibit mining, it could be argued that, being a peaceful use, mining complied with Article I.[35] Perhaps that is why in 1960, before the Treaty entered into force, George Dufek was speculating again. Among other things, he anticipated that by 2000 Antarctic nuclear energy would be used to heat air currents to redirect rainfall to deserts; families would occupy buildings made from locally won ores and wear suits heated by portable nuclear energy cells. Antarctic mail would arrive by guided missiles from other continents, although only third-class mail because some flights would inevitably miss their target (a naval commander's surprising lack of confidence in US Cold War missile technology).[36] Dufek's credibility was only slightly tarnished by his remarkable assertion that Antarctica held reserves of brass, a human-made alloy.[37] All this assumed there were viable minerals, an idea dismissed in simultaneous advice to the US Senate by Antarctic geologist Laurence McKinley Gould.[38] Nevertheless, the prospect that resources might be discovered, and the

[32] October 1970, "Sixth Antarctic Treaty Consultative Meeting, Brief for the Australian Delegation" (NAA: B1387 1991/640 PART 3).

[33] Article IX of the Antarctic Treaty lists several areas for possible measures, but omits mineral resources.

[34] Paul C. Daniels, "The Antarctic Treaty," *Bulletin of the Atomic Scientists* 26, no. 10 (1970): 15.

[35] R. H. Wyndham, "Report of the Working Group on Legal and Political Questions," in *Antarctic Resources: Report from the Informal Meeting of Experts 30 May-9 June 1973*, ed. Finn Sollie (Fridtjof Nansen Foundation, 1974), L10. 12 June 1975 "United States statement on claims to sovereignty and the exploitation of Antarctic mineral resources" in Bush, *Antarctica and International Law: A Collection of Inter-State and National Documents*, Vol III, 489.

[36] 'Antarctica in the year 2000' in: George J. Dufek, *Through the Frozen Frontier* (Brockhampton, 1960), 171–86.

[37] Deborah Shapley, *The Seventh Continent: Antarctica in a Resource Age* (Resources for the Future, 1985), 124.

[38] US Senate, 14 June 1960 "The Antarctic Treaty", Hearings before the Committee on Foreign Relations, 77 at: https://babel.hathitrust.org/cgi/pt?id=uc1.$b643287;view=1up;seq=5 (accessed 3 February 2021). Gould had earlier advised "that the Antarctic has coal reserves second only to those of the United States": 3 October 1947, US State Department,

challenges if they were, exercised the minds of Australians during the nascent years of the Antarctic Treaty.[39]

1964: The Antarctic Becomes a Special Conservation Area

In the Treaty's early years, the Parties attended to easier things, including cooperation between Antarctic programs, identifying historic monuments and conserving Antarctic wildlife—at issue because past use of the region's resources had targeted seals.[40] At the first ATCM, in Canberra in 1961, there were more papers on conserving fauna and flora than any other topic. Chile and the United States proposed codes of conduct while the United Kingdom wanted a separate convention. The Scientific Committee on Antarctic Research (SCAR) proposed that Antarctica "be recognised internationally as a nature reserve".[41] Australia, cautious about jurisdiction and the ownership of resources, sought only a voluntary code of conduct.[42] The voluntary rules adopted to preserve living resources foreshadowed principles to be reflected in subsequent measures, and rules precluding the taking of fur seals set a precedent for absolutely prohibiting the exploitation of certain resources.[43]

At ATCM II in 1962, the United Kingdom revised its proposal, suggesting the label 'Nature Reserve' for areas worthy of special protection—a term not to gain traction for another 27 years.[44] The United Kingdom

Office of Intelligence Research Report no. 4296 "History and current status of claims in Antarctica" (AU-ATADD-1-BB-US-30), iii–iv.

[39] 18 October 1960, House of Representatives Hansard, 2108–2111.

[40] R. K. Headland, *A Chronology of Antarctic Exploration* (Quaritch, 2009), 105–35. Whaling was already regulated under the 1946 International Convention for the Regulation of Whaling.

[41] 10 July 1961, meeting paper Sec. Paper/8 "Suggested form of measures to promote conservation of nature in the Antarctic—SCAR document" https://documents.ats.aq/ ATCM1/sp/ATCM1_sp008_e.pdf (accessed 26 March 2020). This reflected earlier thinking: Robert Carrick, "Conservation of Nature in Antarctica," *Polar Record* 10, no. 68 (1961): 534.

[42] June 1961, Antarctic Treaty First Consultative Meeting, "Brief for the Australian Delegation" (AAD: B13/178).

[43] Antarctic Treaty, *Report of the First Consultative Meeting, Canberra, July 10–24 1961* (Commonwealth Government Printer, 1961), 8–9.

[44] 17 July 1962, ATCM II WP003 "Draft Convention on the Conservation of Wild Life in the Antarctic" at: https://documents.ats.aq/ATCM2/wp/ATCM2_wp003_e.pdf (accessed 26 March 2020).

was seeking a convention (a form that in 1990 it would reject) as it was compatible with internationalising Antarctica under the United Nations (a stance it would also decisively reverse). Chile and Argentina, ever cautious on sovereignty, stopped talk about such things. Such sensitivities foretold another concern—that one country's objections could be used "to prevent the raising of contentious issues".[45] Antarctic Division director Phillip Law worried that "if contentious issues are to be struck off the agenda … nothing of real value will be achieved".[46] Years later, Law himself was far less comfortable with such issues being raised.

In early preparation for the third ATCM, the United Kingdom's Brian Roberts wrote to Australia supporting a USSR proposal to declare the Treaty area an 'international nature reserve' and promoting a wildlife convention, a regulatory framework that later became particularly problematic.[47] ATCM III concentrated its effort on conserving fauna and flora but rejected the convention model.[48] The United States argued that if it were a convention, other measures might be seen as less important and, in any event, Article IX of the Antarctic Treaty referred only to 'measures'. The semantic problem was resolved by adopting Recommendation III-VIII containing the "Agreed Measures for the Conservation of Antarctic Fauna and Flora".[49] The Agreed Measures called the region a 'Special Conservation Area'. In further compromise, it was agreed to capitalise this term in the English text (at the insistence of the United Kingdom), and *not* capitalise it in Spanish and French versions.[50] Such is the art of achieving consensus.

[45] 9 August 1962, Savingram 13,955 "Antarctic Treaty Second Consultative Meeting" (NAA: B1387 1989/365 PART 2).

[46] 28 December 1962, Telegram 342 Law to Rowland (NAA: B1387 1989/365 PART 2). The Antarctic Division later became the Australian Antarctic Division (AAD). Phillip Law was the first director of the Division. Kathleen Ralston, *A Man for Antarctica: The Early Life of Phillip Law* (Hyland House, 1993), 109–218.

[47] 14 August 1963, UK Foreign Office, letter from Roberts to Law (NAA: B1387 1989/365 PART 2).

[48] June 1964, W. R. Crocker, "Report of the Australian Delegation on the Third Consultative Meeting of the Antarctic Treaty" (AAD: B13/180), p. 12.

[49] Antarctic Treaty, Recommendation III-VIII https://ats.aq/devAS/Meetings/Measure/35 (accessed 26 March 2020).

[50] "Report of the Australian Delegation on the Third Consultative Meeting of the Antarctic Treaty", 4. It was also capitalised in Russian.

SOVEREIGN RIGHTS

Along with jurisdiction, other issues relating to sovereignty were avoided. Science, however, proceeded enthusiastically, including geology across the continent.[51] While no one was finding economic resources, that did not stop lively speculation. Dufek's imaginative visions in 1955 and 1960 may well have stimulated Phillip Law's equally ambitious 1962 predictions that Antarctic "may lay bare a second Kalgoorlie, Ballarat or Broken Hill".[52] In 1964, he answered the "interesting and persistent question" he had posed to the Institution of Engineers.[53] His answer: within 20 years his audience would be marvelling at Antarctic families living in underground townships irradiated with 'simulated' sunshine generated from nuclear power and transporting zinc, lead, silver and gold to the coast using giant hovercraft.[54]

Dufek and Law were implausibly optimistic, but it was a space-age world where anything seemed possible—possible, that is, if Antarctic minerals actually existed. But maybe Law's prediction was not so odd. Australia's Antarctic policy interests in 1961 included maintaining the AAT and achieving "benefit from any possible worthwhile economic exploitation of the Antarctic". Law may have been motivated by government objectives emphasising the AAT's mineral resources potential.[55] Nevertheless, in those early years of cordial Antarctic relations, Law seemed oblivious to the political problems that would erupt if his prediction had come true. Such a vision being realised in 1984 would have become a major headache by 1991 when a Treaty review conference could have been called. Instead, a later Australian generation would stoke that fire.

[51] See, for example, compilations of research in: Y. Tolstikov, ed. *Atlas Antarktiki* vol. 1 (Glavnoe Upravlenie Geodezii i Kartografii, 1966). Campbell Craddock, *Geologic Maps of Antarctica*, vol. 12, Antarctic Map Folio Series (American Geographical Society, 1970).

[52] August 1962, Phillip Law "Resources and uses of Antarctica" 37th ANZAAS Congress, Geographical Section (AU-ATADD-5-BB-GE-308).

[53] June 1962, Phillip Law "Possible future developments in Antarctica" (AU-ATADD-5-BB-GE-307).

[54] Phillip Law, *Antarctica 1984*, Sir John Morris Memorial Lecture 1964 (Adult Education Board of Tasmania, 1964), 9–12.

[55] May 1961, Submission to Cabinet by J. G. Gorton, Minister Assisting the Minister for External Affairs. In informal folder in AAD Library "Revised Cabinet Submission 17 May 1961—spare copies". R. A. Swan, *Australia in the Antarctic: Interest, Activity and Endeavour* (Melbourne University Press, 1961), 369. Law later urged Australia to relinquish the AAT to facilitate agreement on mining. Antarctic and Southern Ocean Coalition, "Law Says 'Abandon Claim'," *ECO* XXVIII, no. 3, 22–31 May 1984 (1984).

Antarctica's commercial potential did not stop at minerals. Tourists had first visited in 1956, and managing tourism appeared on the ATCM agenda for the first time in 1966. Tourism became entrenched when Lindblad Travel Inc. commissioned a purpose-built Antarctic cruise ship. To help steer discussions, John Heap, recently recruited to the UK Foreign Office, sought information on Lindblad's intentions but, with curious coyness, did so under the pseudonym 'John D Spicer' posing as a potential client (he received a reply simply urging that he make a reservation "right away"!).[56] From the fourth ATCM, tourism became a perennial agenda item. Heap went on to wield considerable personal influence in Antarctic policy, completing his Treaty career in 1991 with the question of how to regulate tourism still contentious, even under the environmental Protocol.

Hovering over the 1968 ATCM were continuing tensions between those favouring immediate internationalisation (the United States and the USSR), those prepared to surrender their claims (the United Kingdom, New Zealand and possibly Norway) and those unwilling to change anything (Argentina, Australia, France and Chile). Since the early 1950s, the United Kingdom had doubted the usefulness of its claim as "Antarctica had no value whatsoever except in respect of science", and in 1959 New Zealand contemplated relinquishing its claims in return for an international arrangement.[57] Both later had a significant change of heart. Argentina objected to anything that threatened its sovereign interests—including a Treaty secretariat. It even objected to a National Geographic map depicting Islas Malvinas as the Falkland Islands.[58] The secretariat issue was not settled until 2003 and the latter tensions never resolved. Jurisdiction remained sufficiently sensitive that it was suggested it "should not even be directly mentioned". Australia observed that "if any one factor is likely to endanger the Treaty, it is this".[59] Such issues provided important backdrops

[56] 29 July 1966, Memorandum from New Zealand High Commission London to External Affairs Wellington, "Antarctic Treaty, Fourth Consultative Meeting (NAA: B1387 1989/366 PART 1). 17 June 1966, letter Lindblad Travel Inc. to "John D Spicer, Stevenage, Herts" (NAA: B1387 1989/366 PART 1).

[57] Bush, *Antarctica and International Law: A Collection of Inter-State and National Documents*, Vol III, 77–79. 18 November 1968, "Antarctic Treaty Fifth Consultative Meeting" (AAD: B13/182), 7–10. Malcolm Templeton, *A Wise Adventure: New Zealand in Antarctica 1920–1960* (Victoria University Press, 2000), Ch V.

[58] 21 November 1966 "Report of the Australian Delegation to the Fourth Consultative Meeting of the Antarctic Treaty" (NAA: B1387 1989/366 PART 3).

[59] Antarctic Treaty Fourth Consultative Meeting "Brief for the Australian Delegation", 2. Australian Delegation brief "Antarctic Treaty Fifth Consultative Meeting, 6.

for forthcoming debates. Sovereign benefit from minerals would bring into sharp focus differing positions—but that had to wait as more productive discussions were progressing on another commercial resource: seals.

The 1964 Agreed Measures applied only to the land and ice shelves, leaving a gap with respect to seals which inhabit the waters and floating pack ice.[60] The United Kingdom drafted a sealing convention in 1968 but, being a high seas issue and thus outside the Treaty, the 1970 ATCM referred sealing to separate discussions. The resulting 1972 Convention for the Conservation of Antarctic Seals (CCAS) became the first new instrument separate from, but linked to, the Treaty.[61] CCAS created a precedent for regulating a resource not under pressure from industry, and confirmed the distinction between Antarctica and the high seas.[62] Despite fleeting industry interest in the mid-1980s, CCAS remains dormant.[63]

Meanwhile, Antarctic geology was increasing. Australia targeted the Prince Charles Mountains to assess previously discovered coal and iron deposits and the USSR extended surveys in the same region.[64] Coincidence or not, the Australian government received "several applications for mining rights". Despite such interest, quantification of Antarctic minerals was nowhere near Law's breathless assessment. The Soviet Union anticipated diamonds, gold, iron, mica, coal, lead, tin and copper. Other assessments pointed out that the minerals found so far came from moraine deposits "with no hope of tracing them back to outcrops". It concluded that Antarctica might have minerals but, to be economic, they would have to be "of very high tenor, contain large quantities of ore, and be in one of the few small areas with relatively good access".[65] The difference between the simple *presence* of minerals and the presence of *economic* minerals was a defining consideration, but outside the Treaty this distinction was blurred.

[60] Bush, *Antarctica and International Law: A Collection of Inter-State and National Documents*, Vol I, 147.

[61] 19 March 1970, Memorandum Australian Embassy Washington to External Affairs "Sixth Antarctic Treaty Consultative Meeting" (NAA: B1387 1991/640 PART 1). The text of the Convention is at: https://documents.ats.aq/keydocs/vol_1/vol1_13_CCAS_CCAS_e.pdf (accessed 26 March 2020).

[62] Bush, *Antarctica and International Law: A Collection of Inter-State and National Documents*, Vol I, 246–47.

[63] Templeton, *A Wise Adventure II: New Zealand and Antarctica after 1960*, 40–41.

[64] 22 July 1968, Department of External Affairs Brief to minister "Australian activities in Antarctica" (NAA: B1387 1991/637 PART 1), 2.

[65] Neal Potter, *Natural Resource Potentials of the Antarctic*, American Geographical Society Occasional Publication No. 4 (1969), 16–17, 30.

1969: Emerging Interest in Minerals

New Zealand also reported approaches from mining companies and suggested an "airing of views" between Parties so that it could respond.[66] In late 1969, New Zealand noted with some understatement that "the problems will not simply go away if they are ignored" and "it would be better to try to solve them on a multilateral basis rather than unilaterally".[67] Thus, New Zealand breathed life into an issue controversial enough to have been avoided for a decade.

Australia did not take the expressions of interest particularly seriously and justified staying silent at February 1970's ATCM Preparatory Meeting because "none of the applications so far received bear any evidence of serious intent".[68] However, pressure rose when Henry Francis of the United States also reported corporations seeking advice on how to "gain best advantage". Applicants were told that leasing sites was out of the question because the United States did not recognise sovereign claims. Aware that when New Zealand tackled the matter "head on", it had been rebuffed by Argentina, the United States considered "the subject posed delicate problems" best dealt with by considering the impacts on science and conservation. Francis proposed that Parties agree not to enter into any licensing without first conferring with other Parties.[69] This was the embryonic restraint that later morphed into the moratorium that lasted until replaced by the prohibition over 20 years later.

At the fifth Preparatory Meeting, the United Kingdom's Brian Roberts sought to put the issue on the ATCM agenda arguing that, because Parties had received prospecting applications, it was necessary to face up to the minerals problem and find a way of "delaying mineral exploitation without inhibiting exploration".[70] Argentina, however, argued that minerals were

---

[66] 17 December 1969, I.128467 "Antarctic Treaty Sixth Consultative Meeting, First Preparatory meeting" (NAA: B1387 1991/640 PART 1).

[67] 19 December 1969, Third Person Note, New Zealand Embassy Tokyo "Mineral prospecting in Antarctica" (NAA: B1387 1991/640 PART 1). Being informal, Preparatory meetings allowed matters of great substance to be canvassed. Preparatory meetings were held until 1991.

[68] 18 March 1970, Memorandum External Affairs to Department of Supply "Sixth Antarctic Treaty Consultative Meeting—Minerals" (NAA: B1387 1991/640 PART 1).

[69] 19 March 1970, Memorandum Australian Embassy Washington to External Affairs "Sixth Antarctic Treaty Consultative Meeting" (NAA: B1387 1991/640 PART 1).

[70] 8 July 1970, Memorandum AHC London "6th Antarctic Treaty Consultative Meeting October 1970" (NAA: B1387 1991/640 PART 2).

altogether "outside the scope of the Treaty".[71] There was still no evidence of economic minerals.[72] Even so, New Zealand predicted diamonds and platinum being found within the year.[73] Chris Beeby of the Foreign Ministry offered to raise the issue at the ATCM.[74] However, at the following Preparatory Meeting it was clear that several Parties were prepared only to have it mentioned under "Other Business".[75]

1970: "TELL THE FIRMS CONCERNED NOT TO BE SILLY"

In October 1970, delegations arrived in Tokyo ready for a minerals discussion, even if not prepared to admit publicly it would occur—after all, it was not formally on the agenda. Australia wanted to avoid a "too legalistic approach" and "create, by indirect means, an international regime for the Antarctic". This is ironic given Australia's later push for an environmental convention. Australia might well have been nervous: the United Kingdom still supported internationalisation of Antarctica; the United States wanted some kind of condominium arrangement; and New Zealand was willing to forego its claim altogether. Thus, Australia found itself closer to Argentina and Chile, which, having competing claims, were the strongest defenders of territorial interests. Australia's position was awkward. It had approached the 1959 conference hesitant about "any phrase likely to encourage consideration of the exploitation of natural resources". At the 1970 ATCM, it wished to preserve Australia's territorial claims and access to resources. The delegation was instructed only to participate in discussions if "necessary to lessen the risk of an undesirable proposal being adopted", but it

---

[71] 3 August 1970, Memorandum Australian Embassy Buenos Aires to External Affairs "Sixth Antarctic Treaty Consultative Meeting October 1970" (NAA: B1387 1991/640 PART 2).

[72] Donald D. Runnells, "Continental Drift and Economic Minerals in Antarctica," *Earth and Planetary Science Letters* 8, no. 6 (1970).

[73] 7 April 1970, "Diamonds and platinum finds are expected in Antarctica" *The Evening Post* (New Zealand).

[74] 14 April 1970, Memorandum AHC Wellington "Antarctica: Mineral exploration" (NAA: B1387 1973/17). Beeby, acting head of the Ministry of Foreign Affairs Legal Division, led New Zealand delegations from ATCM XI and chaired the minerals negotiations from 1982 to 1988.

[75] 2 July 1970, Australian Delegation reporting "The Fifth Preparatory Meeting for the Sixth Antarctic Treaty Consultative Meeting" together with "Provisional United Kingdom views" (NAA: B1387 1991/640 PART 2).

seemed safer simply to instruct the delegation to "take note of what others have to say".[76]

As it turned out, at ATCM VI minerals did not overwhelm other objectives. Nevertheless, by 23 October the issue was being canvassed informally—so informal that Australia brokered a deal that, as all the Parties were exchanging views bilaterally anyway, it would be much more convenient if such exchanges were done with all the others present! The USSR capitulated, provided it was done without a Chair! Despite (or because of) this, "proceedings were orderly", covering a range of what became perennial concerns—the difference between science and prospecting, the implications for scientific data exchange, whether or not commercial activities were open to Treaty inspection, and mining impacts on other activities.

Various ways were considered to deflect inquiries from companies interested in prospecting, such as unresolved jurisdiction and the absence of national laws.[77] With little hope of economic resources being found anyway, Australia's response had been simply to "tell the firms concerned 'not to be silly'". The Tokyo discussions concluded with no decision, but an understanding that the issue would have to be revisited to find a multilateral approach. So concluded the first "airing of views" on a crucial issue, but one that was not on the agenda and that had no meeting papers, and for which no mention appears in the meeting report.[78]

Such coyness did nothing to stop external interest. Parties were becoming alarmed that Antarctica's potential minerals might be rolled into United Nations consideration of resource scarcity and the developing concept of the common heritage of humankind.[79] Maintaining unity was key. So successful was this strategy that, ultimately, it contributed to significant growth in Treaty membership during the 1980s minerals negotiations.

[76] October 1970, "Sixth Antarctic Treaty Consultative Meeting" (AAD: B13/183), 17.

[77] 8 February 1971, letter A. S. Cooley, Supply to Australian Mining Industry Council "Petroleum and other mineral exploration and exploitation in Antarctica" (NAA: B1387 1973/17).

[78] Antarctic Treaty. Report of the Sixth Consultative Meeting, Tokyo, 19–31 October 1970   https://documents.ats.aq/ATCM6/fr/ATCM6_fr001_e.pdf   (accessed   26 March 2020).

[79] 26 February 1971, I.23059 "Committee on Natural Resources" (NAA: B1387 1973/17). Beck, The International Politics of Antarctica, 272–83. Common heritage of humankind concepts arose in a 1967 proposal by Malta's UN Ambassador Arvid Pardo seeking to resolve deep seabed issues. James B Morell, The Law of the Sea: An Historical Analysis of the 1982 Treaty and Its Rejection by the United States (McFarland & Company, 1992), 18–21.

1972: THE ATCM DISCUSSES MINERALS

At the March 1972 first Preparatory Meeting for ATCM VII, the United Kingdom, South Africa and the United States each had proposals on minerals.[80] Australia hesitated because the question of exploration licences would trigger a sovereignty debate. In the absence of Cabinet guidance, existing policy prevailed: that is, avoid such issues. As vetoing debate was unrealistic, Australia preferred to limit discussion to the effects of exploration on science and the environment.[81] The situation was complicated— the government had received seven applications for exploration in the AAT (in one case, over the entire territory), and five around Heard Island.[82] In addition, Soviet scientists enthusiastically reported "large deposits of iron ore" of up to 50% pure iron, in beds of ore stretching tens of kilometres and up to 400 m thick.[83] All of these were in the AAT.

In August 1972, at the third Preparatory Meeting, pressure on Australia increased with proposals to put minerals on the formal ATCM agenda.[84] The United Kingdom suggested that Parties defer considering prospecting applications, for the first time giving practical form to voluntary restraint. France went further, calling for a "prohibition of any exploitation of mineral resources ... for a limited period of the order of 10 to 15 years".[85] More pragmatically, Norway proposed an informal conference

---

[80] 10 March 1972, Seventh Antarctic Treaty Consultative Meeting, Wellington 1972 "Informal Minutes of the First Preparatory Meeting" (NAA: B1387 1989/363 PART 1).

[81] 26 July 1972, Memorandum Department of Foreign Affairs to Department of Supply "Seventh Antarctic Treaty Consultative Meeting, Expanded Preparatory Meeting" (NAA: B1387 1991/462 PART 3).

[82] With respect to the AAT: AOG Minerals Pty Ltd.; A G Fisher Associates Ltd.; David O Parsons XLX NL; Crusader Oil; Shell Development; Amdex Mining Ltd.; and Australian Aquitanic Petroleum Pty Ltd. With respect to Heard Island: Hunt International Petroleum Co; Beaver Exploration Australia NL; Raymond H Levy; Phillips Australian Oil Co; and Shell Development (Australia) Pty Ltd. (AAD: B13/184).

[83] 8 June 1972 "Exploring the Antarctic" TASS News, transcribed in: 23 June 1972, Memorandum Australian Embassy Moscow to Department of Foreign Affairs (NAA: B1387 1981/348 PART 1).

[84] Papers from the United Kingdom (23 June 1972), South Africa (26 July 1972) and the United States (2 August 1972) (AAD: B13/184).

[85] 31 July 1972, ATCM VI Preparatory Meeting paper PP 3/6 "Note by France" (NAA: B1387 1991/462 PART 2).

the following year.[86] Reluctance to formally discuss minerals was overcome, and the issue was now barely camouflaged—the agenda item would be "Antarctic Resources: *Effects* of Mineral Exploration".

WHAT ABOUT A WORLD PARK?

Then, without warning, on 27 September 1972 an entirely new direction was proposed at Yellowstone in an unrelated forum: the Second World Conference on National Parks. It recommended establishing "the Antarctic continent and the surrounding seas as the first world park, under the auspices of the United Nations".[87] Although not binding, it was significant having been endorsed by a meeting which included representatives of the Antarctic Treaty Parties. The proposal came from US delegate Nicholas Clinch, who argued that "Treaty nations were already adhering very closely to the world park concept".[88] What inspired Clinch was not revealed, but Ricardo Luti of Argentina later said that Argentina had made "a proposal of this sort" at a Treaty meeting.[89] Possibly Clinch had been influenced by the 'nature reserve' suggestion of Australian biologist Robert Carrick ten years before at Seattle's First World Conference on National Parks.[90] Or perhaps he was inspired by Robert Cushman Murphy's 1967 proposal for an Antarctic 'international park'.[91]

In October 1972, Australia decided to emphasise a multilateral approach to ensure Parties not get out of step. Australia would support French or UK proposals to defer exploitation because major countries that did not

[86] August 1972, Minutes of the Third Preparatory Meeting (NAA: B1387 1991/462 PART 2), 4.

[87] H. Elliott, "Recommendation 5: Establishment of Antarctica as a World Park under United Nations Auspices," in *Second World Conference on National Parks 1972*, ed. H, Elliott (IUCN, 1974), 260, 443–44.

[88] "International Park," *Antarctic (New Zealand Antarctic Society)* 6, no. 8 (1972). Clinch, president of the American Alpine Club, led the 1966 first ascent of Antarctica's highest peak, Mount Vinson. Damien Gildea, *Mountaineering in Antarctica* (Editions Nevicata, 2010), 15–16.

[89] 30 September 1974, Department of Environment and Conservation memorandum "Antarctic world park" (NAA: B1387 1991/667 PART 1). No evidence has been found of such an Argentine proposal.

[90] Robert Carrick, "Conservation in the Antarctic," in *First World Conference on National Parks*, ed. Alexander B. Adams (US National Park Service, 1962).

[91] Robert Cushman Murphy, "Antarctica: The Urgency of Protecting Life on and around the Great Southerly Continent," *Natural History* 76, no. 6 (1967): 22.

recognise Australian sovereignty, such as the United States, had greater technological capacity.[92]

As ATCM VII approached, the United Kingdom's Roberts sought to frame the debate in a paper consolidating several Parties' proposals. It called for early action even if resources were unlikely to be discovered and argued that unilateral action would harm the Treaty and discussions should not canvass jurisdictional issues. Its draft recommendation proposed developing "agreed measures concerning commercial exploration for mineral resources" and that, meanwhile, a moratorium be put in place.[93] Australia's delegation had arrived in Wellington with no position—its briefing said only that: "at the time of preparing this brief, this matter was before ministers".[94] The Australian delegation, led by Dame Annabelle Rankin, had no guidance until four days into the ATCM when it received its instructions by telephone: support the United Kingdom.[95]

1972: ATCM VII, Wellington

Any hoped-for ambiguity dissolved in a fraught discussion as meeting papers took different directions. Both Latin American Parties were acutely concerned, Argentina warning "delicate and serious problems ... may endanger and even finally destroy the Treaty".[96] Chile agreed: this was "an extremely grave problem that could put an end to the Antarctic Treaty [and] bring to light once more the troubles over sovereignty".[97] Fearing

[92] October 1972, Draft Cabinet Submission "Australian Antarctic Policy" (NAA: B1387 1991/462 PART 3).

[93] 11 October 1972, letter from FCO to AHC London "Seventh Antarctic Treaty Consultative Meeting, Antarctic Resources—effects of mineral exploration" (NAA: B1387 1991/462 PART 3). 18 October 1972, ANT VII ANT/17 (UK) "Antarctic resources: Effects of mineral exploration" https://documents.ats.aq/ATCM7/wp/ATCM7_wp017_e.pdf (accessed 22 March 2020). A simplified version also failed to gain traction. See https://documents.ats.aq/ATCM7/wp/ATCM7_wp017_rev1_e.pdf (accessed 22 March 2020).

[94] October 1972, Brief for the Australian Delegation, Seventh Antarctic Treaty Consultative Meeting (AAD: B13/184).

[95] 3 November 1972, telegram Styles from Hunt confirming telephone call (NAA: B1387 1989/363 PART 1).

[96] 31 October 1972, ATCM VII ANT/37 (Argentina) "Mineral resources, effects of prospecting for minerals" (accessed 22 March 2020).

[97] 2 November 1972, ATCM VII ANT/44 (Chile) "Antarctic resources: Effects of mineral exploration" https://documents.ats.aq/ATCM7/wp/ATCM7_wp044_e.pdf (accessed 22 March 2020).

impacts on high seas rights in parallel Law of the Sea negotiations, the United States would accept only a two-year moratorium and flatly opposed any restraints on its citizens. To Australia, this issue was "the most contentious of any Consultative Meeting for some years" with "several days of fruitless discussion". In partial explanation was the absence of "old hands" familiar with the ATCM. Escape from the impasse came from Tore Gjelsvik, Norway's deputy delegation head, who suggested the Nansen Foundation host less formal discussions. Participation would be by personal invitation to experts in relevant legal, conservation, economic or technical matters—and they would speak personally, not as government representatives. The report would be circulated before the following ATCM (which Norway would also host), but not made public.[98]

Despite stark differences, minerals had made it to an ATCM agenda. There is no record of the debate in the report beyond an important Recommendation which acknowledged the concerns and recognised a responsibility to protect the environment. The sole operative paragraph was that the matter would "be carefully studied and included on the agenda of the Eighth Consultative Meeting".[99] 'Carefully studied' was code for informal discussions to take place in Oslo at the Nansen Foundation. And, while unsaid, another objective was achieved: to demonstrate that the Treaty was addressing the subject and thus discourage other forums "stepping into an assumed vacuum".[100] Thus, ATCM VII ended: Wellington had hosted the 1972 start of intense discussions on Antarctic minerals and, 16 years later, it would host the concluding negotiations.

While it was intended to contain the minerals debates, nothing could be done to keep quiet that sea-floor drilling was underway. The 28th segment of the Deep Sea Drilling Project visited Antarctica. While scientifically motivated, the appearance was different when an unexpected discovery generated considerable interest. Traces of methane and ethane (which indicate hydrocarbon reserves) were detected at three Ross Sea sites. As *Glomar Challenger* was not equipped to prevent blowouts,

---

[98] November 1972, "Report of the Australian Delegation to the Seventh Antarctic Treaty Consultative Meeting, Wellington, New Zealand 1972" (AAD: B13/184), 30C.

[99] Antarctic Treaty, Recommendation ATCM VII-6 "Study and discussion of the exploitation of Antarctic mineral resources" https://ats.aq/devAS/Meetings/Measure/97 (accessed 22 March 2020).

[100] November 1972, Brief to minister on outcomes of ATCM VII, comments on Recommendation VII-6 (NAA: B1387 1991/462 PART 4).

drilling was suspended.[101] The resources have never been subsequently proved, but that did not stop the discovery being used as evidence of Antarctic oil.[102] The Kilroy Company of Texas approached Australia about petroleum exploration off the AAT, a request deflected as there was no legislation in place.[103] For the miner, exclusive permits were essential lest a competitor muscle-in.[104] Moscow sounded another alarm: Soviet geological surveys in the AAT continued "for the first time on such a large scale".[105]

1973: Experts Meet in Oslo

Meanwhile, Parties pondered who to send to the Nansen Conference. Australia relaxed its hesitations about the forum but, with three weeks to go, still dithered over whether to send two experts, one or none.[106] At the last minute two Australians went: Norman Fisher, a Department of Minerals and Energy geologist, and Hugh Wyndham, a Foreign Affairs lawyer.[107] The conference would cover many issues—the outline ran to five pages. Just four days before the start, Fisher was briefed: the minerals question was pressing, and Antarctica was no longer "a sanctuary for scientists".[108] Wyndham already had Antarctic background having attended

[101] Richard D McIver, "Hydrocarbon Gases in Canned Core Samples from Leg 28 Sites 271, 272, and 273, Ross Sea," *Deep Sea Drilling Project Reports* XXVIII, no. 28 (1975). "Sites 270, 271, 272," *Deep Sea Drilling Project Initial Reports* XXVIII, no. 8 (1975): 214.

[102] Antarctic waters were estimated to contain up to 45 billion barrels of oil, at least half of that recoverable from offshore Alaska: Deborah Shapley, "Antarctica: World Hunger for Oil Spurs Security Council Review," *Science* 184, no. 4138 (1974). *The Seventh Continent: Antarctica in a Resource Age*, 124–25.

[103] 12 March 1973, letter N. S. Currie Supply to B. L. Short Kilroy Company of Texas (NAA: B1387 1973/17).

[104] 14 February 1973, J. P. Lonergan, note for file "Antarctic matters" (NAA: B1387 1991/370), 3.

[105] 7 April 1973, TASS News, transcribed in: 15 May 1973, Memorandum Australian Embassy Moscow to Department of Foreign Affairs (NAA: B1387 1981/348 PART 1).

[106] 14 February 1973, J. P. Lonergan, Note for file "Antarctic matters" (NAA: B1387 1991/370), 1–2. 9 May 1973, Fridtjof Nansen Foundation circular "Preliminary list of participants" (NAA: B1387 1991/370).

[107] 25 May 1973, Department of Science, brief to minister "Exploitation of the Antarctic—Nansen Foundation Conference" (NAA: B1387 1991/370). Wyndham had many further connections with Antarctic diplomacy until the conclusion of the Madrid Protocol.

[108] 29 May 1973, Note for file, P. B. Free Department of Science "Meeting of the Nansen Foundation" (NAA: B1387 1991/370).

the two previous ATCMs. Each of the 12 Parties sent experts, 29 in all, split equally between technical and legal areas.

The conference ran from 29 May to 10 June 1973, as many days as a full ATCM. It was hoped that run privately, with statements not personally attributed, the conference would encourage frank exchanges. Chairing was Norwegian Ambassador Edvard Hambro, whose opening address set the tone: growing interest in Antarctic resources raised territorial claims "with a new and pressing urgency". Unregulated exploration could "jeopardise the primary principle that the Antarctic is to be used exclusively for peaceful purposes" and rules should be in place *before* development occurred. Hambro stressed the need "to suspend any exploration and exploitation activities until we have at least established a rudimentary framework".[109] The conference divided into two Working Groups, one for scientific and technical matters and the other the legal and political questions. Hambro chaired the latter, with Wyndham appointed rapporteur.[110]

Scientists and technical experts identified a long list of minerals, including traces of offshore hydrocarbons, the widespread presence of coal (although poor in quality), and an iron ore deposit 120 km long and 100 m deep in the AAT's Prince Charles Mountains "large enough to meet present world consumption for 200 years". The group also examined technical and environmental challenges. Initial interest would be in offshore oil and gas because of the known limits of other reserves. That said, Antarctica's contribution "would, in all probability, be small" and the risks "so great as to be out of proportion to the small gain of energy". The group urged that Parties "as soon as possible establish regulatory measures" unless they decide that exploration "be completely prohibited".[111] The latter option was years ahead of its time.

Meanwhile, policy and legal experts examined the Treaty's emphasis on peaceful use, its protections for science and cooperation, and interactions with the developing Law of the Sea. By employing the 'Chatham House

---

[109] 29 May 1973, "Prepared remarks by Ambassador Edvard Hambro" (NAA: B1387 1991/370).

[110] Finn Sollie, ed. *Antarctic Resources: Report from the Informal Meeting of Experts 30 May-9 June 1973* (Fridtjof Nansen Foundation, 1974), 2–3.

[111] Richard Willett, "Report of the Scientific and Technical Working Group," in *Antarctic Resources: Report from the Informal Meeting of Experts 30 May-9 June 1973*, ed. Finn Sollie (Fridtjof Nansen Foundation, 1974).

rule', for the first time it was possible to discuss jurisdiction.[112] This included distinctions between jurisdiction based on territory, citizenship or operator origin—aspects to become important in future minerals and liability negotiations. Views were split on whether mining was compatible with the Treaty: some arguing that it was not, because of the operation of Article IV. Others argued that as mining was a peaceful use and not prohibited, it could proceed if consistent with any Treaty Recommendations in force.[113] The experts considered fishing required more urgent attention—there was no such pressure for minerals but arrangements should be settled before anyone sought to explore. An interim moratorium had broad support. The group concluded that as CCAS had shown it possible "for the first time in history" to establish a regime *before* exploitation started, it should be possible for minerals as well.[114]

1973: The Global Oil Shock

The Nansen conference cracked open a vexed issue, even if the report was not made public.[115] It was nevertheless timely coming within months of the *Glomar Challenger* drilling and the continued expansion of terrestrial surveys. More fortuitously, it took place before the 1973 OPEC oil embargo. While not eliminating Treaty anxieties, it helped limit the immediate impact of the oil crisis on speculation about Antarctic prospects.[116] The conference usefully prepared the ground for discussion to resume, again in Oslo, at ATCM VIII. None of the issues had been solved, but now the Treaty Parties might not be quite so reluctant to discuss them.

[112] The 'rule', originating in the United Kingdom's Royal Institute of International Affairs at Chatham House, provides that information obtained during a meeting can be reported but not attributed.

[113] In 1993, the term 'Recommendation' was replaced by 'Measure', 'Resolution' or 'Decision' in order of decreasing legal intent.

[114] Wyndham, "Report of the Working Group on Legal and Political Questions," L1–L20. There is useful commentary in: Bush, *Antarctica and International Law: A Collection of Inter-State and National Documents*, Vol I, 283–94.

[115] Publication was never intended, and it was not sent to relevant governments until 1974. See September 1974, Document XIII-SCAR-34 "Report of the meeting of the meetings of the Group of Delegates 4, 5 & 6 September 1974 (NAA: B1387 1989/362 PART 1).

[116] The genesis of the 1973 "oil crisis" is examined in: Roy Licklider, "The Power of Oil," *International Studies Quarterly* 32, no. 2 (1988).

In 1974, the Parties exchanged views on how to proceed. France was concerned about a possible "split within the club" if non-Parties sought to "share the cake".[117] Japan wanted to "avoid controversy at all costs", opposed any exploitation (a position it later changed) and supported a moratorium because it did not possess polar mining technology.[118] The United Kingdom argued that an open-ended moratorium would be "an admission of failure".[119] The United States thought "the spectre of potential wealth" increased the risk of disputes if exploitation became feasible.[120] Chile worried that it was "unable to defend its claims and lacks the technology to exploit any economic discoveries" and feared that other countries might be encouraged to make their own claims, which is why in 1972 it had opposed even airing the issue.[121]

Australia was assessing its policy.[122] Potential benefits still motivated sovereign interest including "access to the resources of the Antarctic … and an equitable share in the exploitation thereof", notwithstanding "uncertainty of what these resources are and where they lie". Until then, asserting sovereignty had been a game of positioning stations, issuing postage stamps, assigning place names and designating historic monuments. With something much more tangible at stake, Australia appeared out of step with the United Kingdom's aim for "a situation where national claims will be irrelevant and will no longer be pressed", and New Zealand's willingness to renounce its claim altogether. To Australia, protecting the

[117] 10 July 1974, Memorandum 873, Australian Embassy Paris "The Antarctic" (NAA: B1387 1989/362 PART 1).

[118] 2 July 1974, Memorandum 881, Australian Embassy Tokyo "Japan: The Antarctic" (NAA: B1387 1991/667 PART 1). 18 July 1974, Memorandum 951, Australian Embassy Tokyo "Japan: Preparations for the 8th Antarctic Treaty Consultative Meeting" (NAA: B1387 1989/362 PART 1).

[119] 25 July 1974, Memorandum 2039, AHC London "The Antarctic" (NAA: B1387 1989/362 PART 1).

[120] 19 July 1974, Memorandum 1799, Australian Embassy Washington to Department of Foreign Affairs "The Antarctic" (NAA: B1387 1989/362 PART 1). This memorandum was prepared by John McCarthy, who later led Australia in concluding the Protocol.

[121] 26 September 1974, Department of Foreign Affairs "Draft briefing: Antarctic Preparatory Meeting: Antarctic resources—effects of minerals exploration" (NAA: B1387 1991/667 PART 1).

[122] 23 September 1974, SC620 "Preparatory Meeting—Antarctic" (NAA: B1387 1991/531 PART 1).

Treaty preserved its interests.[123] Thus, tension was inbuilt: the need to balance the sovereign right to resources against the need to support the regime which protected sovereignty itself.

1974: LAW OF THE SEA ISSUES

Lurking under the surface was another confounding issue—the Law of the Sea conference raised the fundamental questions of the area actually regulated by the Antarctic Treaty. Antarctic hydrocarbons could be outside the minerals discussion if Article VI of the Treaty put the seafloor out of scope. Here was a threshold issue: Would the Antarctic sea floor be covered by a minerals regime? Australia's strong view was that the waters off the AAT were hardly beyond national jurisdiction and, therefore, should not fall under the common heritage concepts of the Law of the Sea.[124] Refusal to cede Antarctica's continental shelf to the Law of the Sea would, years later, help ensure its protection from seafloor exploration.

The United Kingdom was also keen to quarantine Antarctica from the Law of the Sea and, in readiness for the October 1974 ATCM Preparatory Meeting, drafted a minerals protocol to show that the Treaty Parties "have the matter in hand" and forestall any UN attempt "to take our Antarctica".[125] The United Kingdom was equally keen, however, that its paper not be attributed to them.[126] The proposal allowed for exploration and exploitation, including on the continental shelf. Applications would be assessed by the ATCM and, if agreed, jurisdiction and any financial benefit would fall to the Party granting the permit.[127] Discussion on the proposal gained no traction—Chile "saw doubts on every page". The USSR was concerned about environmental impacts. Japan wanted only a

---

[123] 5 August 1974, Cabinet Memorandum "Australian Antarctic policy" (NAA: B1387 1991/667 PART 1), 3.

[124] 9 August 1974, Brief to Minister for Science "Law of the Sea—Implications for Antarctic waters" (NAA: B1387 1991/531 PART 1). Australia had entered the Treaty having already asserted rights to an Antarctic shelf. Bush, *Antarctica and International Law: A Collection of Inter-State and National Documents*.

[125] 9 October 1974, LH19027 "Preparatory meeting: Antarctic" (NAA: B1387 1989/362 PART 1).

[126] 10 October 1974, LH19123 "Preparatory meeting: Antarctic" (NAA: B1387 1989/362 PART 1).

[127] 10 October 1974, Memorandum AHC London covering "Unofficial and Informal Draft Recommendation for Discussion October 1974" (NAA: B1387 1989/362 PART 1).

moratorium.[128] And the United States just wanted progress. It didn't get it. In any event, a protocol was ahead of its time because it appeared to amend the Treaty—unthinkable to many. The discussion concluded that something as ambitious as a draft protocol should not be circulated further lest it "get into the wrong hands in Geneva" (host to Law of the Sea negotiations). Thus sank the first attempt at a minerals regime. Equally unproductive was Australia's attempt to test the world park idea aired in Yellowstone in 1972.[129] In 1974, even the conservation movement was ambivalent about a world park. The Australian Conservation Foundation (ACF), for example, did not oppose mining, asking only that it "not be allowed to endanger the … environment of Antarctica".[130]

FEBRUARY 1975: FROM "TENTATIVE POLICY TO NO POLICY AT ALL"

Back in Canberra, an Inter-Departmental Committee (IDC) debated how to approach ATCM VIII. The IDC lamented, with unremarkable logic, "that the problem would not be quite so complex if the US, USSR and Japan recognised claims in the Antarctic" as it would be easier to keep the International Seabed Authority (ISA) out of "our area". At risk were both Australia's interests in the continental margin and the continent itself. The Department of Foreign Affairs proposed that Australia's approach should be just to take note of others' positions, state that we could not accept a protocol, and avoid going into detail. Henry Burmester of the Attorney-General's Department (A-G's) summed it up incisively: "we seemed to have moved from at least a tentative policy to no policy at all!"[131] The world park concept was briefly considered on the premise that any UN

[128] 24 July 1974, Department of Foreign Affairs record of conversation "Antarctica: Economic exploration" (NAA: B1387 1973/17). Edvard Hambro, "Some Notes on the Future of the Antarctic Treaty Collaboration," *The American Journal of International Law* 68, no. 2 (1974).

[129] October 1974, "Eighth Antarctic Consultative Meeting, Preparatory Meeting. Oslo 14–19 October 1974, Report by Australian Participant" (NAA: B1387 1989/362 PART 2), 6–8.

[130] 14 October 1974, letter J. G. Mosley (ACF) to Minister for Science (NAA: B1387 1991/531 PART 1).

[131] 18 February 1975, "Minutes of Antarctic IDC 18 February 1975" (NAA: B1387 1991/667 PART 1). Henry Burmester went on to have an extended role in Australian international legal policy, including in the minerals and environment debates.

interest in Antarctica might dissipate if the focus was on the environment rather than on resources, but the delegation would be instructed not to initiate discussion on this.[132] This position was later dramatically reversed.

The second ATCM VIII Preparatory Meeting, in Oslo in February 1975, focused on the dilemma of the parallel Law of the Sea negotiations. The Parties were united in protecting the Treaty, but not on high seas rights—in particular the continental shelf and the jurisdiction of the mooted ISA. The United States rejected the view that Antarctica could generate a territorial sea, economic zone or continental shelf and threatened it "might not be able to remain silent" on this in Geneva. Such language incited strong reactions from Argentina and Chile. However, all were determined to keep Antarctica out of the Geneva discussions and avoid any signals of disunity. It was agreed *not* to commit Parties' views to paper lest it encourage Law of the Sea negotiators to look more carefully at Antarctica. If necessary, the Parties would consult further.[133] Some of the claimants became alarmed at possible new challenges to their interests, and France suggested that claimants develop a common approach, foreshadowing what was to emerge as an influential bloc on resource questions.[134]

Australia's IDC embarked on a policy review covering science, the environment, resources, sovereignty, sea law and international relations.[135] Some positions seemed counter-intuitive: the Bureau of Mineral Resources (BMR) talked *down* the prospect of minerals while the Foreign Affairs Department talked them *up*; the Environment Department was lukewarm on the environmental option of a world park.[136] At the same time, a divergence between the non-claimants emerged: the USSR argued for minerals discussions to be deferred, while the United States argued for progress

[132] February 1975, Brief for the Preparatory Meeting "Antarctic World Park" (NAA: B1387 1991/531 PART 2).

[133] 7 March 1975, Keith Brennan, Memorandum 113 covering "Second Preparatory Meeting, Report of the Australian Representative" (NAA: B1387 1989/362 PART 3). Antarctica *did* get raised in Geneva—NGOs specifically referred to Antarctic waters as part of the Common Heritage. 29 April 1975, GE11002 "Law of the Sea—Antarctic" (NAA: B1387 1991/667 PART 2).

[134] 28 February 1975, BE902 "Antarctic Treaty and Law of the Sea" (NAA: B1387 1989/362 PART 2).

[135] See NAA: B1387 1989/362 PART 2; NAA: B1387 1989/362 PART 3; and NAA: B1387 1991/667 PART 2.

[136] 23 April 1975 "Minutes of Meeting of Antarctic IDC" (NAA: B1387 1991/667 PART 2).

towards a regime.[137] The State Department had cited the absence of agreed rules to refuse an exclusive ten-year permit for a US corporation to "develop the mineral or other resources of the Ross and Weddell Seas".[138] "Off the record", John Heap revealed that the United Kingdom was "well on the way to a firm policy" with low "likelihood of any dramatic British initiatives".[139] There was a hint that UK pursuit of internationalisation might diminish. Heap thought that the ATCM might agree to informal inter-sessional work. After all, there was some common ground: Antarctica should be kept out of Law of the Sea discussions, exploitation of minerals should not disrupt the Treaty and the environment should be protected. On this basis, Prime Minister Gough Whitlam signed off on Australia's approach: do nothing to prejudice the AAT and rights to the marine areas, strengthen the Treaty and maintain "influence over decisions affecting Antarctica".[140]

9 JUNE 1975: ATCM VIII, OSLO

ATCM VIII convened in Oslo in June 1975 with agenda Item 17 "Antarctic Resources: Effects of Mineral Exploration". Camouflaging the item was now unnecessary, and coyness evaporated as opening statements tackled the resources challenge. With gendered hyperbole the United Kingdom warned that the lure of minerals "would bring large numbers of men swarming into the continent and such an unregulated invasion could be chaotic, strife ridden and dangerous".[141] The debate revealed fewer tensions, in part because of a change of personnel in key delegations and because Hambro allowed for "set pieces in plenary" and informal working groups "with neutral chairmen to sort out problems".[142] Thus, Item 17

[137] 18 April 1975, Department of Foreign Affairs record of discussion "Antarctic consultative meeting" (NAA: B1387 1991/667 PART 2). 21 April 1975, Department of Foreign Affairs note "Antarctic policy: Stresses on the present regime" (NAA: B1387 1989/362 PART 2).

[138] 12 May 1975 "Department of State letter concerning exclusive permit to explore and develop the Weddell and Ross Seas" (AU-ATADD-BB-US-46).

[139] 14 May 1975, Telex 2936 London to Wellington "8th Antarctic Consultative Meeting" (NAA: B1387 1991/667 PART 2).

[140] 27 May 1975, Submission to the Prime Minister "Australian Antarctic policy" (NAA: B1387 1991/667 PART 3).

[141] Antarctic Treaty, *Report of the Eighth Consultative Meeting, Oslo, 9–20 June 1975* (Ministry of Foreign Affairs (Oslo), 1975).

[142] 16 June 1975, ST1277 "Antarctic meeting" (NAA: B1387 1991/531 PART 2).

headed to subgroups chaired by Ambassadors Keith Brennan and Pierre Charpentier, respectively, of Australia and France—two Parties at that time enjoying a perceived neutrality.

12 June 1975: New Zealand Proposes a World Park, or Something

Mid-meeting reporting referred to what became New Zealand's often-cited 'world park' proposal. An Australian cablegram records that New Zealand put forward the suggestion that "ideally the area should be reserved as an international park in perpetuity".[143] This had occurred in Brennan's subgroup on the morning of 12 June 1975. An Australian delegate recorded the much fêted, ill-fated moment:

> *NZ raises question whether right course might not be to refrain from spoiling this continent's unique characteristics (e.g., the only continent not inhabited by man, unique influence in control of weather etc). Urgent action is required of the Treaty Parties. Antarctic should be preserved as an international reserve, but NZ aware that long term moratorium not acceptable to many.*

This was the world park proposal subsequently referred to during the environment debate.[144] Proposing a complete mining prohibition would seemingly sidestep the minerals issue altogether. The idea had been endorsed in 1975 by New Zealand Labour Prime Minister Bill Rowling and possibly came from the 1972 Second World Conference on National Parks (1972).[145] It may also have drawn on ideas put forward in 1956 by

---

[143] 16 June 1975, ST1276 "Antarctic meeting-mineral resources" (NAA: B1387 1991/531 PART 2). July 1975, "Report of the Australian Delegation, Eighth Antarctic Treaty Consultative Meeting, Oslo 9–20 June 1975" (AAD: B13/185). At the time the term 'world park' was avoided—the proposal was for an 'international park' or 'international reserve'. The nomenclature seemed confused—after the ATCM, Brennan reported New Zealand as preferring a 'national park'. See July 1975, "Report of the Australian Delegation, Eighth Antarctic Treaty Consultative Meeting, Oslo 9–20 June 1975" (AAD: B13/185), 19.

[144] This quote, possibly the only record of New Zealand's proposal, comes from the personal notes of an Australian delegate (probably AAD Director Dr Ray Garrod) in a document headed "12.6.75 (1) A.M." (AAD: B13/185). Templeton reports that "no record survives of the New Zealand statement". Templeton, *A Wise Adventure II: New Zealand and Antarctica after 1960*, 334, fn42.

[145] Ibid., 89–90. Rowling's comments are reported in 9 June 1975 "New Zealand, Announcement of Prime Minister concerning the Antarctic policy" (AU-ATADD-1-BB-NZ-58).

Labour's Walter Nash, who, addressing proposals to internationalise Antarctica, had suggested that Antarctica should be "an area that ought to belong to all the world, and be free to all the world".[146]

Whatever its genesis, New Zealand's park idea launched into turbulent waters. Being an informal proposal, there was no obligation for other Parties to respond, but it appears they did. And the idea sank without trace. Whether scuttled by a subtly raised eyebrow in the meeting room or torpedoed by a volley of more forthright objections in the tea break (or both) is not recorded. In the Antarctic Treaty context, it was provocatively premature. It has been reported that Charles Craw, New Zealand's Head of Delegation who spoke to the proposal, subsequently observed with an equally apposite analogy that "if the phrase 'a lead balloon' was ever applicable, it was on this occasion".[147] It was later that the reserve idea was described as a world park. A world park, however, turned out to be no more acceptable.[148]

A Moratorium Is Put in Place

The USSR, Argentina and Chile continued seeking a moratorium but the United States rejected even a limited pause as it would become hard to lift and argued for immediate work on rules it saw as inevitable within 15 years.[149] It took the "united efforts of the other Parties" to persuade the United States and the United Kingdom to accept any restraint, the US delegation conceding after telephoned instructions arrived in the last hour of the meeting. The resulting passages were "marginally better than nothing [and] on this basis they were approved".[150] Thus, the first minerals discussions ended with a Recommendation recognising "the need for restraint while seeking timely agreed solutions". The operative paragraphs looked simple: "Antarctic Resources: the question of mineral exploration and exploitation" would be fully studied "in all its aspects" at a Special

---

[146] *A Wise Adventure: New Zealand in Antarctica 1920–1960*, 167–68. Nash's idea did not preclude the use of Antarctic resources. In 1956, Nash was Opposition Leader of the New Zealand Labour Party—he became Prime Minister in 1957.

[147] *A Wise Adventure II: New Zealand and Antarctica after 1960*, 91.

[148] Talboys, "New Zealand and the Antarctic Treaty," 33.

[149] 17 June 1975, ST1291 "Antarctic meeting" (NAA: B1387 1989/362 PART 4). 18 June 1975, ST1292 "Antarctic meeting" (NAA: B1387 1991/531 PART 2).

[150] 3 July 1975, Savingram BU1262 "Eighth Antarctic Consultative Meeting" (NAA: B1387 1989/362 PART 4).

Preparatory Meeting in 1976, and the issue would be revisited at the next ATCM.[151]
Achieving this in Oslo had been complicated. One solution was France's offer to host inter-sessional consultations. Calls for SCAR to assess environmental aspects were aimed at keeping Antarctica out of the United Nations. A moratorium, however, was the most problematic issue with protagonists wanting time to catch up technologically; opponents concerned about preventing activities legal under the Treaty; and UK concerns that a moratorium diminished sovereign rights. The Recommendation was seen as a reasonable "expression of intent" even if not a "robust declaration of policy". As Brennan reported, "while the text on the moratorium may not be entirely satisfactory, it was gratifying … to agree on a course of action which required substantial modifications to traditional stands."[152] This was an important lesson—discussions in 1975 were among the Treaty's original 12 Parties already wedded to cooperation. As more states joined, consensus would require even greater effort.

1975: Preparations for a Preparatory Meeting

The ATCM VIII Recommendation's restraint was short-lived. Within ten days the USSR proposed a new station, Druzhnaya, "mainly to prospect for minerals".[153] Establishing it near the Weddell Sea possibly indicated interest in offshore oil.[154] Argentina was alarmed it was within their territory. New Zealand feared similar action by the United States and Japan.[155] In Moscow, meanwhile, the foreign ministry disclaimed all knowledge of the proposal.[156]

---

[151] Antarctic Treaty. Recommendation ATCM VIII-14 "Antarctic resources—effects of mineral exploration" https://ats.aq/devAS/Meetings/Measure/114 (accessed 2 March 2020).
[152] July 1975, "Report of the Australian Delegation, Eighth Antarctic Treaty Consultative Meeting, Oslo 9–20 June 1975" (AAD: B13/185).
[153] 30 June 1975 "Antarctic prospectors: Moscow plans 50-man minerals hunt" *Sydney Morning Herald*, 5.
[154] 21 July 1975, WH21159 "Antarctic—USSR activity" (NAA: B1387 1996/861).
[155] 18 July 1975, WL3465 "Antarctic minerals" (NAA: B1387 1973/17). 15 July 1975, BA2146 "Antarctic minerals" (NAA: B1387 1973/17).
[156] 12 July 1975, MS2056 "Antarctic minerals" (NAA: B1387 1973/17). Ambiguous Russian reporting re-appeared 25 years later: Kira Lebedeva and Sergei Petukhov, "Russia Decides to Return to the Antarctic with Serious Intentions and for Long," *Commersant* 8 (2003).

Draft terms of reference for the Special Preparatory Meeting suggested environmental questions would "figure more strongly", even the option of prohibiting mining completely.[157] Given that the Paris ATCM could study the minerals question 'in all its aspects' there was opportunity to be frank. The diversity of attitudes had not abated and preparation for the 1976 discussion elicited different aspirations.

In Australia, the Antarctic IDC faced the contradiction that the Australian government "has a moral duty … to the Antarctic itself to see that it is not ransacked", while retaining "a free hand to exploit the AAT at will".[158] New Zealand addressed similar conundrums: it wished to maintain its sovereignty, and "if oil was there, they wanted it". On the other hand, it was "in no position to enforce exclusive rights" and "eventually the whole question of claims would fall apart". Ultimately, however, New Zealand wanted to stay on side with both the United States *and* Australia, even though this would require Australia "to move much further to accommodate the American position than did New Zealand".[159] The United Kingdom had internal differences: Brian Roberts, about to retire, proposed settling the issues before exploitation actually began.[160] Two months later, his successor, John Heap, considered the Treaty "a temporary expedient" pending the inevitable internationalisation of Antarctica as "interest in exploitation would likely make the retention of national sovereignty difficult".[161] On minerals, he imagined "a common access regime based on suspended sovereignty", but ultimately took a low-key role as the United Kingdom would chair the forthcoming ATCM.[162] South Africa declined internationalisation, but argued "a jointly administered condominium was urgently necessary to prevent exploita-

[157] 10 September 1975, Aide memoire "Some thoughts on the Antarctic Treaty Special Preparatory Meeting to be held in Paris, Summer 1976" (NAA: B1387 1991/697 PART 2).

[158] 24 October 1975, Department of Foreign Affairs "Working Paper" (NAA: B1387 1991/697 PART 2).

[159] 23 February 1976, Memorandum 146, AHC Wellington "New Zealand Antarctic policy" (NAA: B1387 76/176 PART 2). Several factors were at play for New Zealand, including maintaining the ANZUS alliance and its dependence on US logistics support in Antarctica.

[160] 13 November 1975, Memorandum AHC London "Antarctica" (NAA: B1387 1991/697 PART 2).

[161] 21 January 1976, Memorandum AHC London "Antarctic Policy" (NAA: B1387 1996/864 PART 1).

[162] 30 April 1976, LH51694 "Antarctic preparatory meeting" (NAA: B1387 1991/708 PART 1).

tion by one country at the expense of others".[163] Norway agreed and was determined that Antarctic decisions not undermine its Arctic interests.[164] The USSR also opposed internationalisation and thought it "necessary to extend participation in the Treaty by admitting more States", which Australia suspected meant Soviet Bloc partners.[165] Belgium considered Antarctica's continental shelf to be the province of the Law of the Sea.[166] Argentina disagreed.[167] Chile appeared concerned "that the Americans might try to dump the claimants" and pondered using the Svalbard Treaty as its model.[168] Under this, claimants would retain sovereignty, with others allowed to exploit minerals on agreed terms.[169]

The United States' intent was ambiguous. The State Department's Theodore Sellin insisted that progress on minerals "be made in the Treaty context.[170] This was despite fundamental differences of view over sovereignty including "the prospect of claimant states, like Australia, seeking recognition of economic zones if these are established by the Law of the Sea".[171] On the one hand, the United States was treading carefully, seeking an equitable solution rather than a quick one.[172] On the other hand, it was not clear whether the United States wanted "to speed it up or to slow

[163] 5 February 1976, Memorandum 44, Australian Embassy Pretoria "Antarctica policy" (NAA: B1387 1991/708 PART 2).

[164] 19 January 1976, Memorandum Australian Embassy Stockholm "Antarctic policy" (NAA: B1387 1991/708 PART 2). 4 March 1976, ST2065 "Antarctic policy" (NAA: B1387 1991/708 PART 1).

[165] 1 March 1976, Memorandum 222, Australian Embassy Moscow "Antarctic policy" (NAA: B1387 1991/708 PART 2).

[166] 16 January 1976, Memorandum Australian Embassy Brussels "Antarctic policy" (NAA: B1387 1991/708 PART 2).

[167] 12 January 1976, Record of conversation, Australian Embassy Buenos Aires with Antarctic and Malvinas Division Argentine Ministry of Foreign Affairs (NAA: B1387 1991/708 PART 2).

[168] 11 March 1976, New Zealand cable Santiago to Wellington "Chilean Antarctic policy" (NAA: B1387 1991/708 PART 2). 7 April 1976, UN5371 "Antarctic" (NAA: B1387 1991/708 PART 1).

[169] https://www.jus.uio.no/english/services/library/treaties/01/1-11/svalbard-treaty. xml (accessed 3 February 2021).

[170] 27 January 1976, Memorandum 146, Australian Embassy Washington "United States Antarctic policy" (NAA: B1387 1991/708 PART 2).

[171] 24 March 1976, Memorandum 494, Australian Embassy Washington "United States views on Antarctica" (NAA: B1387 1991/708 PART 1). The Memorandum was annotated that the United States might prefer "to deal with a claimant than with a seabed authority".

[172] 15 April 1976, Memorandum New Zealand Embassy Washington to Wellington "Antarctic Treaty: Special Consultative Meeting" (NAA: B1387 1996/864 PART 1).

it down or to do the latter while attempting to preserve the appearance of aiming for the former" and that its purpose was to "be doing no more than going through the motions of seeking a solution within the Antarctic club while looking for a quite different solution".[173] In further complication were rumblings within the Non-Aligned Summit led by Sri Lankan diplomat Christopher Pinto.[174] Not only was the exploitation of minerals on the table, but potentially the future of the Treaty itself.

JUNE 1976: THE PARIS SPECIAL PREPARATORY MEETING

Three months before the Paris meeting, these questions were being addressed in Canberra in a series of IDCs. The environment department's Peter Crawford reminded participants that environmental protection was essential.[175] A subsequent paper catalogued the risks to "the least polluted of all ecosystems in the world"—risks so great that "the area should be left unexploited". It noted that Australia had not yet considered the 1972 world park proposal, and one option was to declare "all of the Australian Antarctic Territory as a national park".[176] The issues triggered a frank discussion—frank enough for Henry Burmester to observe wryly that the introduction to a Foreign Affairs paper was "more comprehensive than the content".[177] BMR updated its assessment of the AAT's minerals, concluding that they were uneconomic and "most would not warrant further investigation if they occurred elsewhere", before admitting that insufficient research had been done.[178] The absence of a common view was to

[173] 4 May 1976, New Zealand cable from New York "Antarctic Treaty: Special Preparatory Meeting" (NAA: B1387 1991/708 PART 2).

[174] Developing states were urging Antarctic states to take greater account of the international community. Beck, *The International Politics of Antarctica*, 277–81.

[175] 18 March 1976, Interdepartmental Committee Meeting, "Draft Minutes" (NAA: B1387 1991/697 PART 1).

[176] 29 March 1976, IDC paper "Australia's environmental interests in Antarctica" (NAA: B1387 1991/697 PART 1).

[177] 30 March 1976, Interdepartmental Committee Meeting, "Draft Minutes" (NAA: B1387 1991/697 PART 1).

[178] 11 May 1976, BMR paper "Known mineral resources onshore" (NAA: B1387 1991/708 PART 1). 14 May 1976, BMR papers "Past and present geological and geophysical work onshore" and "Future geological work" (NAA: B1387 1991/708 PART 1).

become an even stronger factor in future.[179] The IDC grew to ten departments and contemplated what to put to Cabinet. One thing was certain:
national interests included pursuing resources. The science department
argued that sovereignty was not an end in itself, "but a means of safeguarding or realising objectives".[180] Eli Lauterpacht of Foreign Affairs
agreed: "the most crucial point in the whole matter, namely that the
essential content of sovereignty for Australia is the economic benefits to be
derived therefrom".[181] That was even if the benefits were unknown. It
took three more IDCs to finalise Australia's position: strengthen the
Treaty, maintain sovereignty, protect the environment and continue
restraint on minerals exploration.[182] The resources issues had precipitated
the most intense analysis of Australian objectives for years, with a vigour
not repeated until the other end of the minerals debate.

One day before the Paris meeting, Chile caucused with the Southern
Hemisphere claimants—the first of many such gatherings. Australia,
Argentina and Chile agreed to be "spokesmen of claimant state interests".
All agreed to resist US demands for free access to Antarctic resources. All
were committed to the Treaty's Article IV and balancing claimant and
non-claimant interests—a simple 'without prejudice' statement would be
unacceptable.[183] Finding that balance would prove immensely difficult.

In Paris, the Special Preparatory Meeting had SCAR's draft report on
environmental risks, and a reminder on the absence of firm data on minerals.[184] Nevertheless, the United States predicted the offshore area

[179] 21 April 1976, Interdepartmental Committee Meeting, "Draft Minutes" (NAA: B1387
1991/697 PART 1).

[180] 29 March 1976, Department of Science commentary (NAA: B1387 1991/697
PART 1).

[181] 14 May 1976, Interdepartmental Committee Meeting, "Draft Minutes" (NAA: B1387
1991/697 PART 2).

[182] 31 May 1976, Department of Foreign Affairs draft Cabinet Submission "Australian
policy in the Antarctic" (NAA: B1387 1991/697 PART 2).

[183] July 1976, "Report of the Australian Delegation to the Special Preparatory Meeting of
the Antarctic Treaty Consultative Parties on the Exploration and Exploitation of the Mineral
Resources of Antarctica" (AAD: B13/197).

[184] 28 June 1976, RPS-9 (UK) "Scientific Committee on Antarctic Research of the
International Council of Scientific Unions: Antarctic resources—effects of mineral explora-
tion", in: 10 July 1976, "Final Report of the Special Preparatory Meeting for the Ninth
Consultative Meeting of the Antarctic Treaty, Paris 28 June to 10 July 1976"
(AU-ATADD-3-BB-AQ-296).

yielding "oil in the order of magnitude of tens of billions of barrels".[185] It argued that progress should "not be delayed indefinitely by requests for further studies" and only supported "voluntary restraint on exploitation provided that this is accompanied by visible progress". The United Kingdom now hinted it was "moving towards a more claimant posture".[186] With growing attention outside the Treaty, Parties feared that control of the issue would be lost if they did not act. Most problematic was the intersection with sovereignty. The United States wanted non-discriminatory access to all areas; others demanded claimant interests be satisfied.[187] Brennan was forthright. Sovereignty was not negotiable and Australia "would not accept an arrangement under which the substance of sovereignty was traded for its shadow .... we do not seek to destroy the positions of others, but in return should not be asked to concur in the destruction of our own". Brennan reported that "for all its candour and vigour, the speech was accepted by the Americans as a fair statement of position".[188] The discussion was robust: "our position was being rejected in terms as flat as those in which it was being asserted."[189] Similarly, Argentina and Chile were not prepared to acquiesce if "they were left with the trappings of sovereignty while losing its substance". New Zealand, however, appeared prepared to "accept some abatement of sovereignty".[190]

Brennan also pushed hard on environment protection.[191] Australia's paper proposed impact assessments in advance of mining and restoration of affected areas "to approximate the original conditions".[192] This was the

[185] 28 June 1976, RPS-10 (US) Annex C "Antarctic mineral resources", in: July 1976, "Report of the Australian Delegation to the Special Preparatory Meeting of the Antarctic Treaty Consultative Parties on the Exploration and Exploitation of the Mineral Resources of Antarctica" (AAD: B13/197).
[186] 30 June 1976, PA23566 "Antarctic preparatory meeting" (NAA: B1387 1991/708 PART 2).
[187] 1 July 1976, PA23639 "Antarctic preparatory meeting" (NAA: B1387 1991/708 PART 2).
[188] 1 July 1976, PA23640 "Antarctica" (NAA: B1387 1996/865 PART 2).
[189] 9 July 1976, PA23900 "Antarctic Preparatory Meeting" (NAA: B1387 1991/708 PART 3).
[190] July 1976, "Report of the Australian Delegation to the Special Preparatory Meeting of the Antarctic Treaty Consultative Parties on the Exploration and Exploitation of the Mineral Resources of Antarctica" (AAD: B13/197).
[191] 28 June 1976, "Statement by the Leader of the Australian Delegation", in: Report of the Australian Delegation (NAA: B1387 1991/708 PART 4).
[192] 28 June 1976, RPS-11 (Australia) "Establishment of environment protection arrangements for Antarctica", in: 10 July 1976, "Final Report of the Special Preparatory Meeting

first time a mandatory environmental assessment scheme was proposed and later became defining features of the minerals regime and the subsequent Madrid Protocol. New Zealand was even more ambitious, outlining a regime with a regulatory committee able to veto developments, and zones excluded from any mining. While "designed to steer a middle course ... it found critics on all sides" describing it as going "far beyond its purported objective" and an "effort to reconcile the irreconcilable".[193]

Such concerns revealed the complexities. Fundamental issues had been exposed: the importance of environment protection; technology; licensing, revenue and taxes; area of application; equitable access; prospects for a moratorium; international expectations; and even the future of the Treaty itself. Lurking behind it all was sovereignty. As Brennan remarked: "unresolved sovereignty issues which were set aside when the Treaty was concluded have now surfaced and will not disappear."[194] Such debate was to be repeated as polarised positions played out. Adding complexity was the issue moving into the public domain with exaggerated headlines.[195]

1976: AN "IMBROGLIO OF POLICY REVIEWS" IN AUSTRALIA

The Paris meeting had examined "political and legal issues in greater depth than had hitherto been attempted" but with "little agreement about what should be done".[196] Back in capitals, the Parties reflected. In Canberra, the meeting was considered valuable because attitudes "were expressed more clearly ... than has ever been done since the signing of

for the Ninth Consultative Meeting of the Antarctic Treaty, Paris 28 June to 10 July 1976" (AU-ATADD-3-BB-AQ-296).

[193] 28 June 1976, RPS-14 (NZ) Informal Working Paper "Declaration by Consultative Parties to the Antarctic Treaty", in: 10 July 1976, "Final Report of the Special Preparatory Meeting for the Ninth Consultative Meeting of the Antarctic Treaty, Paris 28 June to 10 July 1976" (AU-ATADD-3-BB-AQ-296). 5 July 1976, PA23705 "Antarctic Preparatory Meeting: Legal and political working group" (NAA: B1387 1991/708 PART 3).

[194] 12 July 1976, I.PA23975 "Antarctic Preparatory Meeting" (NAA: B1387 1991/708 PART 3).

[195] 13 August 1976, Department of Science briefing to ministerial adviser "Parliamentary briefing note" (NAA: B1387 1991/708 PART 3). 29 July 1976, Arthur Gavshon "Can peace be kept in Antarctic?" *The Mercury.* 20 December 1976 "Polar race to uncover mineral riches" *The Australian.*

[196] July 1976, "Report of the Australian Delegation to the Special Preparatory Meeting of the Antarctic Treaty Consultative Parties on the Exploration and Exploitation of the Mineral Resources of Antarctica" (AAD: B13/197).

the Treaty"; sovereignty would not be ignored; and support for the Treaty remained strong. The delegation report triggered a "fresh rethink", despite lamenting "we have an imbroglio of policy reviews out of which we must create some order".[197] Brennan advised that Australia had become de facto leader of the claimants.[198] The IDC set up working groups to examine the options.[199] Key issues were protecting claimant interests and the stability of the Treaty. Concern for the environment "would provide cogent reason for looking towards a moratorium".[200] Despite recognising it "highly unlikely that oil can be extracted", a moratorium "to the year 2000 or for at least 10 years" would be desirable. Global oil demand, however, made a world park option unrealistic.[201] New Zealand agreed, now describing permanent protection of Antarctica as a "hopeless task".[202]

"THE REAL STUFF OF SOVEREIGNTY"

Year 1977 would see another ATCM, this time in London. The Special Preparatory Meeting had exposed the tensions: claimants remained firm; the USSR and Japan wanted to defer the issue; and the United States wanted immediate action, but only on their terms. Progress would depend on reconciling Parties' attitudes. Brennan was "worried about the 'snail's pace' of Treaty negotiations" and thought that "not even the vaguest form of a solution will emerge" from the ATCM.[203] In the United States, the State Department would commission an environmental assessment of possible mineral development (ostensibly to reduce the lead time in case

[197] 16 September 1976, Department of Science "Antarctic policy: Post Paris meeting reappraisal" (NAA: B1387 1991/697 PART 3).
[198] 16 November 1976, "Draft Minutes of IDC on Antarctica" (NAA: B1387 1991/697 PART 2).
[199] 8 October 1976 and 19 October 1976, submissions to Minister for Science (NAA: B1387 1991/697 PART 2 and NAA: B1387 1991/748).
[200] 19 November 1976, "Record of Legal and Political Working Group on Antarctica" (NAA: B1387 1991/748).
[201] 14 January 1977, Department of Environment, Housing and Community Development "Antarctica: Environmental policy" (NAA: B1387 1991/697 PART 3).
[202] 23 March 1977, Memorandum 258, AHC Wellington "NZ: Cabinet Submission on Antarctic Policy" (NAA: B1387 1991/697 PART 3). 18 March 1977 "Exploitation of Antarctic seen as certain" *New Zealand Herald*, 12.
[203] 12 January 1977, "Note for file" (NAA: B1387 1991/748).

of a future legislative requirement).[204] The CIA was predicting that "pressure for new petroleum sources will begin to mount sharply from 1980".[205]

The USSR and Japan argued that nothing be done which could reactivate the claims—anathema to Australia as it implied that the Treaty had somehow *deactivated* them.[206] Australia considered sovereignty the "threshold question". The claims were a reality, and a solution based on an Article IV no-prejudice approach would be inadequate in a minerals context.[207] To Brennan, it was "only the existence of claims which provides any justification … for treating resources other than part of the common heritage of mankind".[208] With uncertainties in the parallel consideration of the marine living resources issue, Third World attitudes and Law of the Sea negotiations, ministers decided that any discussion of Antarctic minerals should be done "without commitment".[209] Brennan was blunt: there were two tensions—"between the activists and the passivists", and "between the claimants and the non-claimants". For the latter, "an acceptable solution … cannot end in a victory for one side or the other. It must end in a draw".[210] This was a concession from a defender of claimant interests who took the view that Article IV applied only to matters addressed in the Treaty—therefore *not* minerals, and thus a claimant could pursue exclusive benefits.[211]

New Zealand was sanguine. Accepting that exploitation was inevitable, and exclusive claimant rights were "unrealistic", it hoped to bridge the "divergent views held by the United States on the one hand, and Australia on the other". The issue was how to "preserve the most important aspects of the Treaty" and achieve a "political accommodation" which included

---

[204] 28 February 1977, WH44953 "Antarctic resources" (NAA: B1387 77/177).
[205] 9 May 1977, BU3211 "Antarctica—non-living resources" (NAA: B1387 77/177).
[206] 10 June 1977, UN 8444 "Antarctica" (NAA: B1387 77/176 PART 1).
[207] 26 June 1977, UN8498 "Antarctica" (NAA: B1387 77/176 PART 1).
[208] 21 July 1977, BU3427 "Antarctica—ANZUS meeting" (NAA: B1387 77/176 PART 1).
[209] 19 July 1977, CH544512 "Antarctica: Australian policy" (NAA: B1387 77/176 PART 1).
[210] 11 August 1977, Memorandum 376, Australian Embassy Berne to Department of Foreign Affairs "Antarctica—the Ninth Consultative Meeting 19 September to 7 October 1977—resources issues" (NAA: B1387 77/176 PART 2).
[211] Philip W Quigg, *A Pole Apart: The Emerging Issue of Antarctica* (New Press, 1983), 196–97. Jonathan I. Charney, *The New Nationalism and the Use of Common Spaces* (Allanheld, Osmun), 186–87.

special recognition of the claimants' interests.[212] Foreign Minister Brian Talboys wrote that "what we are interested in is not a sterile legal claim, but a share in the real stuff of sovereignty" but, with some safeguards, "it is timely for the claimants to make some compromise".[213] It was this crucial compromise that the minerals discussions sought to achieve, with New Zealand leading with the principles it took to London.[214]

SEPTEMBER 1977: ATCM IX, LONDON

The Parties met in London for a three-week ATCM. Now 13 Parties were around the table as there was a new Antarctic Treaty Consultative Party (ATCP): Poland, the first to be added since the Treaty's entry into force.[215] There were two major issues: marine living resources and minerals. Mining's legal and political aspects were separated from the scientific, technical and environmental.[216] SCAR had finalised its report with pessimism about the prospect of economic minerals and frank advice on environmental risks.[217] SCAR's work was the basis for a Group of Experts, led by the United Kingdom's Martin Holdgate, which concluded that further work was required on environmental issues and a decade would pass before exploration could be contemplated. A Working Group on legal and political matters followed. Gradual movement towards a regime became evident, with a sticking point the form of any moratorium—the USSR seeking an "absolute moratorium", and the United States and Japan seeking only "voluntary restraint" while progress was made. Australia proposed that governments refuse exploration until progress had been made

---

[212] 14 July 1977, CH542725 "ANZUS: Antarctica" (NAA: B1387 77/176 PART 1).

[213] 13 August 1977, letter from Brian Talboys, Minister for Foreign Affairs, Wellington to Andrew Peacock, Minister for Foreign Affairs, Canberra (NAA: B1387 77/177).

[214] 9 September 1977, Memorandum, New Zealand High Commission "Ninth ATCM" (NAA: B1387 77/176 PART 2). See also opening address: https://documents.ats.aq/ATCM9/wp/ATCM9_wp067_e.pdf (accessed 26 March 2020).

[215] Antarctic Treaty, *Report of the First Special Consultative Meeting, Held at London 25, 27 and 29 July 1977* (Her Majesty's Stationery Office (London), 1979). A state can achieve ATCP status by conducting substantial Antarctic research.

[216] *Report of the Ninth Consultative Meeting, London 19 September–7 October 1977* (London: Foreign and Commonwealth Office, 1977), 6–8.

[217] Scientific Committee on Antarctic Research, *A Preliminary Assessment of the Environmental Impact of Mineral Exploration/Exploitation in Antarctica (EAMREA)*, ed. J H Zumberge (SCAR, 1977).

on environmental arrangements.[218] The United Kingdom and New Zealand supported only a two-year moratorium as otherwise "any sense of urgency would be lost". The perennial polarisation on claimant rights continued. Australia, Argentina and Chile insisted that sovereignty be addressed. New Zealand was more relaxed. The United Kingdom appeared as "a reluctant claimant" with Norway "similarly ambivalent". The United States, however, was less "even handed" with respect to such issues than it was in parallel marine living resources discussions. This divergence led to "many hours of protracted and confused debate" resulting in a "somewhat unsatisfactory formulation".[219] Brennan thought the wording "a secondary matter compared with the unambiguous and unanimous acceptance of the principle" of no-prejudice to the claims.[220] While there were still stark differences, the ATCM adopted Recommendation IX-1, which kept minerals on the agenda, restated the principles agreed in Paris and reiterated the protections of Article IV. The moratorium remained, although sufficiently controversial that far more oblique wording was required—an understanding to "refrain from all exploration and exploitations" while there was "progress towards the timely adoption of agreed solutions".[221]

MARINE LIVING RESOURCES

Despite advances on minerals, ATCM IX saw a far more tangible outcome: progress on conserving marine living resources. These discussions were chaired by Keith Brennan, who considered this "perhaps the most significant step taken by the Consultative Parties since 1959".[222] Brennan successfully steered the meeting towards a regime to conserve resources, protect the ecosystem as a whole and extend north of 60° South.[223] He

[218] 3 October 1977, ANT/IX/78 "Draft recommendation on Antarctic mineral resources" https://documents.ats.aq/ATCM9/wp/ATCM9_wp078_e.pdf (accessed 5 March 2020).
[219] September 1977, "Report of the Australian Delegation to the Antarctic Treaty Ninth Consultative Meeting, London, 19 September-7 October 1977" (AAD: B13/186), 16.
[220] 10 October 1977, BU3609 "Ninth Antarctic Consultative Meeting—round up" (NAA: B1387 76/176 PART 4).
[221] Antarctic Treaty, Recommendation IX-1 "Antarctic Mineral Resources" https://ats. aq/devAS/Meetings/Measure/117 (accessed 26 March 2020).
[222] September 1977, "Report of the Australian Delegation to the Antarctic Treaty Ninth Consultative Meeting, London, 19 September-7 October 1977" (AAD: B13/186).
[223] Antarctic Treaty, Recommendation IX-2 "Antarctic Marine Living Resources" https:// ats.aq/devAS/Meetings/Measure/118 (accessed 26 March 2020). "Conservation" was

noted that "the atmosphere of the meeting was surprisingly good given the frankness of the exchanges". On sovereignty, delegations were "forced to face up to the necessity of dealing with issues which have rested submerged since 1959". There were commitments to further work on minerals, two meetings on marine living resources and one on telecommunications—all before the 1979 ATCM. The agenda was full. Brennan again: "Australia will become even more pre-occupied with Antarctic questions than has been the case even in the recent past."[224] On one issue, marine living resources, Australia had been handed the leadership role.[225]

Pressure came off minerals as marine living resources went on to occupy three years of negotiations. Brennan chaired two sessions of the second Special Antarctic Treaty Consultative Meeting (SATCM II) and informal consultations in Berne. The result was the Convention on the Conservation of Antarctic Marine Living Resources (CCAMLR), adopted in Canberra on 20 May 1980.[226] It was a major advance in governing Antarctic resource issues and accommodating differences over sovereignty.[227] However, Australia's special influence on marine living resources was to be severely tested when it came to the next Antarctic resources problem, minerals.

The familiar issues simmered. Although living resources could "be exploited without regard to zones claimed", for minerals it would still be necessary to give claimants special recognition.[228] Brian Talboys lamented that avoiding the problem in a world park had "proved unacceptable".[229] Sovereignty was front of mind for Australia, which was about to proclaim

---

defined as including rational use: Antarctic Treaty, *Report of the Ninth Consultative Meeting, London 19 September-7 October 1977*, para 10.

[224] 8 October 1977, LH87624 "Ninth Antarctic Consultative Meeting—round up" (NAA: B1387 1976/33 PART 1).

[225] 12 October 1977, AAP "Australia successful at Antarctica conference" *The Canberra Times*, 9.

[226] https://www.ccamlr.org/en/organisation/camlr-convention-text. CCAMLR entered into force on 7 April 1982.

[227] CCAMLR's operation is examined in: Joyner, *Governing the Frozen Commons*, 122–46. Olav Schram Stokke, "The Effectiveness of CCAMLR," in *Governing the Antarctic*, ed. Olav Schram Stokke and Davor Vidas (Cambridge University Press, 1996), 120–51. Stuart Kaye, Marcus Haward, and Robert Hall, "Managing Marine Living Resources, the 1970s-1990s," in *Australia and the Antarctic Treaty System: 50 Years of Influence*, ed. Marcus Haward and Tom Griffiths (UNSW Press, 2011), 164–80.

[228] 14 February 1978, UN10534 "Antarctic policy" (NAA: B1387 1989/362 PART 2).

[229] 26 April 1978 speech reproduced in: Talboys, "New Zealand and the Antarctic Treaty."

a 200-nautical-mile fishing zone off the AAT.[230] Such issues resurfaced in Washington in July 1979 as Parties met again to prepare for that year's ATCM X. The meeting was "revealing in the way delegations trod carefully and, for the most part, tried to avoid mere repetitions of entrenched positions" and agreed that any regime would determine if mining was acceptable and, if so, how to govern it.[231] In Australia, Foreign Affairs argued that the non-claimant view that the Treaty "freezes territorial claims" should be challenged because, if accepted, it would misrepresent the intent of Article IV.[232] The timing of an academic article characterising Antarctica as "common space" was unhelpful to claimants.[233] Even less helpful was an Australian own goal—Alan Renouf, recently retired secretary of Foreign Affairs, argued that Australia had "selfishly declined" to support internationalisation of Antarctica, and should relinquish its claim and forgo its resources.[234]

1979: ENVIRONMENTALISM COMES TO ANTARCTICA

As Parties softened attitudes to a minerals regime, further complications emerged. Despite the restraint Parties had agreed, press reports disclosed Japan's plan for prospecting oil in Antarctic waters using *Hakurei Maru*, including in the Ross Sea where methane had been encountered in 1975. Japan stressed no decision had been made and the destination was a matter of speculation.[235]

At the same time, Australian interest groups were engaging in Antarctica's future. In 1978, the Barton Federal Electorate Council of the Australian Labor Party (ALP) decided that "the Antarctic region should be preserved as a wilderness" and put the idea to Liberal Prime Minister

---

[230] 9 May 1978, Department of Science, brief to minister (NAA: B1387 1991/697 PART 4).

[231] 6 July 1979, WH79254 "Antarctica: Minerals: Meeting on legal and political issues" (NAA: B1387 1991/897 PART 1).

[232] June 1979, briefing material "Meeting to consider legal and political aspects of mineral resource issues" (NAA: B1387 1991/897 PART 1).

[233] Edward E. Honnold, "Thaw in International Law? Rights in Antarctica under the Law of Common Spaces," *The Yale Law Journal* 87, no. 4 (1978): 807–29. 15 August 1979, Department of Science, note for file "Thaw in international law" (NAA: B1387 1991/748).

[234] Alan Renouf, *The Frightened Country* (Macmillan, 1979), 526. 21 August 1979, "Antarctic territory" *Canberra Times*, 2.

[235] 13 September 1979, TK11781 "Antarctica—Japanese oil survey" (NAA: B1387 1991/822).

Malcolm Fraser.[236] In 1979, the Antarctic Defence Coalition lobbied Science Minister James Webster to ban Antarctic oil.[237] Friends of the Earth called on Foreign Minister Andrew Peacock to make Antarctica "the first world preserve" and nominate the AAT as "world natural heritage".[238] Peacock rebuffed Australian Conservation Foundation (ACF) director Geoff Mosley's bid to join Australia's ATCM delegation, but promised that ACF views would be "taken into account in formulating Australian policy".[239]

There was less sympathy for Earthscan which, Brennan said, "consistently works against claimant state interests".[240] Even though a decision on the Australian Fishing Zone (AFZ) had not actually been made, the issue became very public and not just domestically. A pre-ATCM Earthscan seminar stoked interest when Brennan was asked whether Australia would pool title to Antarctic resources. His comment that "Australia had jurisdiction over the mineral resources of the continental shelf off the AAT" provoked a response that Australia's claim as "amazing and invalid".[241] It also created startling headlines. Brennan was quoted as saying that "the oil belongs to Australia" and that OPEC "does not share the proceeds of their oil, there are few precedents for it, and we have no intention of starting one".[242] During the ATCM, Brennan reported media interest "as greater than anything we have experienced previously" and observed glumly that "I fear we may be getting rather too much publicity".[243] By coincidence, while the ATCM was underway, Australia's governor general proclaimed all the waters for 200 nautical miles around Australia and its

[236] 2 June 1978, letter Martin Peebles (ALP) to Senator Webster (NAA: B1387 1991/633 PART 2).

[237] 1 August 1979, letter from Antarctic Defence Coalition "Re: Antarctic Treaty signatories 10th Consultative Meeting" (NAA: B1387 1991/897 PART 2).

[238] 3 August 1979, letter from Friends of the Earth (NAA: B1387 1991/897 PART 3).

[239] 12 September 1979, letter from Peacock to Mosley (NAA: B1387 1991/897 PART 2).

[240] 5 September 1979, BU5406 "Antarctica" (NAA: B1387 1991/897 PART 2).

[241] 19 September 1979, WH81714 "Antarctica: Xth ATCM" (NAA: B1387 1979/46 PART 2).

[242] 19 September 1979, Graeme Beaton "Australia's claim angers diplomats" *The Australian*.

[243] 21 September 1979, WH81826 "Antarctica: Xth ATCM: Media coverage" (NAA: B1387 1979/46 PART 2). 22 September 1979, WH81825 "Antarctica: Xth ATCM: Media coverage" (NAA: B1387 1979/46 PART 2).

external territories for the purposes of the *Fisheries Act*.[244] It is not clear whether the news made it to the ATCM, but its timing was potentially awkward given the US sensitivity to overt demonstrations of sovereignty. However, any doubts about the AFZ proclamation were resolved six weeks later when a separate one excepted the waters off the AAT.[245]

1979: ATCM X AND "A SLIGHTLY ELLIPTICAL DRAFT"

Recommendation IX-1 in 1977 had called for intensified minerals consultations but they "had not really taken place" because of the pre-occupation with marine living resources.[246] At ATCM X in Washington, minerals discussions could resume, informed by inter-sessional progress in the Group of Experts and updated advice from SCAR.[247] Any sense of harmony was qualified by caveats that proposals were "personal opinions" given on a "non-committal basis". Nevertheless, there was optimism that, if marine living resources negotiations were concluded, minerals could be referred to a SATCM in 1980.[248] For the first time, the discussions produced "a discernible framework for a mineral resources regime" with a tacit recognition it should not weaken the positions of claimants or non-claimants.[249] The ATCM X report explained little of what had transpired, but the fulsome Recommendation X-1 captured it all (well, almost all: it made no mention of the moratorium). The decision was to continue consultations and review progress before the 1981 ATCM XI.[250]

[244] Bush, *Antarctica and International Law: A Collection of Inter-State and National Documents*, Vol II, 202–03.

[245] This proclamation reflected Australia's position in the marine living resources discussions, not the minerals debate. Ibid., Vol 2, 208–09. Kaye, Johnson, and Baird, "Law," at endnote 49.

[246] June 1979, briefing material "Meeting to consider legal and political aspects of mineral resource issues" (NAA: B1387 1991/897 PART 1).

[247] 20 September 1979, ANT/X/20 "The Report of the Group of Ecological Technological and Other Related Experts on Mineral Exploration and Exploitation in Antarctica" (AU-ATADD-2-BB-AQ-46). James H Zumberge, ed. *Possible Environmental Effects of Mineral Exploration and Exploitation in Antarctica* (Scientific Committee on Antarctic Research, 1979).

[248] 1 October 1979, WH82131 "Antarctica: X ATCM roundup" (NAA: B1387 1979/46 PART 2).

[249] 10 October 1979, UN15450 "Antarctica: Xth ATCM" (NAA: B1387 1979/46 PART 2).

[250] Antarctic Treaty, Recommendation X-1 "Antarctic Mineral Resources" https://ats.aq/devAS/Meetings/Measure/123 (accessed 2 March 2020).

The moratorium, central though it was, did not get included as debate polarised between those seeking political advantage in restating the moratorium and those, led by the USSR, arguing that reiterating the moratorium implied doubt about its integrity. In compromise, the Recommendation simply requested that governments "take note of progress made" towards the timely adoption of a regime. Language often holds the key to progress in Antarctic affairs. This would not be the only time that obscurity, bifocalism or creative ambiguity would facilitate consensus. On this occasion, it was aptly described as a "slightly elliptical" solution.[251]

1980: "WE ARE NOT TRYING TO STOP THIS ANYMORE"

Elliptical or not, the Washington outcome created momentum and the following month, November 1979, New Zealand offered to host a meeting in 1980. This proved premature as marine living resources negotiations were still underway, but New Zealand's enthusiasm paid off handsomely in 1982.[252] It would be timely to give full attention to minerals as the United States had proposed an ocean drilling program involving eight companies and with Antarctica to "get early attention".[253] Such developments, coinciding with CCAMLR's conclusion, precipitated further calls for a "world preserve" and demands for a public inquiry.[254] Japan, too, stoked public interest with *Hakurei Maru's* planned 1980–81 surveys.[255] Such surveys would be relevant to "determining the likelihood of oil being found", although Japan denied it was actually a "search for oil" in breach of the moratorium and officials were "confident that the

---

[251] 11 October 1979, UN15456 "Antarctic: Xth ATCM: Summary" (NAA: B1387 1979/46 PART 2). The ellipticity relied on the 1977 "moratorium" which depended on "progress towards timely adoption".

[252] 15 November 1979, CH857295 "Antarctica: Mineral resources meeting" (NAA: B1387 1991/822).

[253] 5 March 1980, CH877176 "Antarctica: Mineral resources" (NAA: B1387 1991/822). Participating companies were to include Exxon, Phillips, Conoco, Mobile and Chevron.

[254] 24 March 1980, Marine Action Centre, Ross Burton and Michael Kennedy letter to Prime Minister Fraser (NAA: B1387 1991/822). It was co-signed by 16 other environment groups.

[255] 24 November 1980, Alan Goodall "Japan joins the rush for a slice of the ice" *The Australian*, 10.

scientific data would be publicly available".[256] Despite such reassurances, "some eyebrows were raised".[257] Meanwhile, in anticipation of a minerals regime, the US State Department commissioned its environmental impact statement, not for exploration and development, but for the regime that would regulate it—a distinction easily missed.[258]

The Parties returned to Washington in December 1980 for the meeting called for in ATCM Recommendation X-1. Claimants caucused on a "shopping list" of objectives including demands for preferential treatment—the free access arrangements just agreed for marine living resources were "not an appropriate model".[259] A further incentive for progress emerged. The chair, Morris Busby of the State Department, warned that Antarctic minerals could soon be raised in the UN General Assembly (UNGA).[260] Chile optimistically suggested concluding the regime in 1981. The USSR's Vladimir Golitsyn was frank: "we are not trying to stop this anymore, we gave that up in 1977."[261] Haste, however, would not solve the perennial sticking point—consensus was impossible if it extinguished sovereignty.[262] For Australia, "any solid, substantial concession on the part of claimants needed to be matched with a solid, substantial movement by non-claimants". But to the United States, being prepared just to embark on a regime showed it had already moved. The United States and the USSR reminded Parties that their bases of claim were specifically reserved in Treaty Article IV, essentially asserting freedom to act both as

---

[256] 24 November 1980, CH929482 "Antarctic minerals" (NAA: B1387 96/893) and 27 November 1980, TK18052 "Japanese geological survey of Antarctic" (NAA: B1387 81/676). It was understood that if data was shared the activity would not be subject to the moratorium as, by its nature, exploration would demand commercial confidentiality. 10 December 1980, WH98180 "Antarctic mineral meeting: Report of the first two days" (NAA: B1387 96/893).

[257] 19 March 1981, "Antarctica: Japanese survey of the Bellingshausen Sea" (NAA: B1387 81/676).

[258] 22 September 1980, Memorandum WH8539 from Australian Embassy Washington "Antarctica: Mineral resources regime" (NAA: B1387 1991/822).

[259] 9 December 1980, WH98121 "Antarctica—mineral resources" (NAA: B1387 96/893).

[260] The predicted UNGA debates are summarised in: Rohan Tepper and Marcus Haward, "The Development of Malaysia's Position on Antarctica: 1982 to 2004," Polar Record 41, no. 2 (2005).

[261] 11 December 1980, WH98220 "Antarctica—mineral resources—USSR attitudes" (NAA: B1387 96/893).

[262] 10 December 1980, WH98180 "Antarctic mineral meeting: Report of the first two days" (NAA: B1387 96/893).

non-claimants *and* claimants.[263] The need to accommodate differences was clear, but how to achieve it was not as non-claimants would make no move towards middle ground if it gave any recognition to the claims.[264] What was achieved, however, was consolidation of a method of work that would characterise the minerals discussions, the Protocol and, later, the liability debate: a Chair producing a 'personal report', without obligation, as a basis for the next round.[265]

1981: "Evidence of a Serious Intention"

Year 1981 would see ATCM XI in Buenos Aires and a February Preparatory Meeting set the scene. The claimants caucused and unity would be key.[266] In contrast to earlier internationalisation ideals, the reversal of UK attitudes appeared complete by displaying "a deeply entrenched claimant state position". Brennan, leading again for Australia, argued that any claimant flexibility on sovereign rights had to be reciprocated—a "small-print Article IV type disclaimer on the back" would be insufficient. The United States offered a glimmer of hope: while it "might not answer the question in exactly the form it was posed" the claimants "would find the answer helpful".[267] South Africa and Norway emphasised the difference between recognising that sovereignty claims *existed* and recognising the sovereignty claims *themselves*, pointing to a "political solution … without changing the legal position".[268] Despite this, the United States and the USSR still insisted the regime provide equal access to resources with "no distinction between claimants and non-claimants". Brennan warned that any state issuing licences to exploit within the AAT "would find itself in serious international dispute" but the United States retorted that Australia could not object as Article IV.2 served to prevent such disputes, a poten-

[263] 12 December 1980, WH98237 "Antarctica: Mineral resources" (NAA: B1387 96/893).

[264] 13 December 1980, WH98296 "Antarctica—minerals discussions—round-up" (NAA: B1387 96/893).

[265] 16 January 1981, Memorandum BU2609, Australian Embassy Berne "Antarctica—mineral resources—meeting in Washington 8–12 December 1980" (NAA: B1387 81/681).

[266] 23 February 1981, BA12202 "Antarctica: Preparatory Meeting-meeting of claimant state delegations" (NAA: B1387 1981/399 PART 2).

[267] 24 February 1981, BA12217 "Antarctica: Preparatory Meeting"; and 3 March 1981, BA12285 "Antarctica XI-ATCM Preparatory Meeting" (NAA: B1387 81/681).

[268] 25 February 1981, BA12229 "Antarctica: Preparatory Meeting" (NAA: B1387 81/681).

tially alarming response.[269] While the meeting appeared to make little progress, Busby's 'Friends of the Chair' group produced a draft Recommendation.[270] Brennan, disappointed that it made no mention of the claims, reflected optimistically that "in many ways, the extreme caution of the non-claimants is evidence of a serious intention" to negotiate.[271] Japan was also disappointed, but for different reasons: *Hakurei Maru's* survey of the Bellingshausen Sea had found "no useful petroleum or mineral deposits".[272] The minerals discussions were still about hypothetical activities.

Pre-ATCM XI consultations revealed discomfort with the 'Friends of the Chair' draft, some arguing that ignoring sovereignty was "a crucial defect". The four Southern Hemisphere claimants rallied around this issue, but were wary of engaging the United Kingdom, France and Norway prematurely lest it be perceived as creating a bloc.[273] While Heap was disappointed, he rather surprisingly admitted that "the UK did not attach much importance to Recommendations", and, in any event, there were differences within Whitehall and the United Kingdom was involved "in some difficult soul-searching".[274] Belgium argued that it could not be required "to recognise today what it refused to recognise in 1959".[275] The USSR could not even accept a reference to "the national interests of all Parties", precipitating the understated French reaction that these "were not grounds for optimism".[276] So, the difficulties remained obvious—and this was not on the substance of a minerals regime, it was only on a Recommendation for further work.

---

[269] Most interpretations were that Article IV does not *prevent* actions such as issuing licences, just that such action cannot later be used to substantiate a sovereign claim. The reporting cablegram was annotated "this is why an Article IV type of solution is dangerous". 3 March 1981, BA12279 "Antarctica—minerals regime—USA/New Zealand/Australia discussions" (NAA: B1387 81/681).

[270] 3 March 1981, BA12281 "Antarctica—mineral resources" (NAA: B1387 81/681).

[271] 3 March 1981, BA12285 "Antarctica XI—ATCM Preparatory Meeting" (NAA: B1387 81/681).

[272] 21 April 1981, WH2769 "Antarctic: Mineral resources" (NAA: B1387 96/894).

[273] 5 June 1981, CH966835 "Eleventh Antarctic Treaty Consultative Meeting: Mineral resources" (NAA: B1387 96/895).

[274] 11 June 1981, LH2540 "Eleventh Antarctic Treaty Consultative Meeting: Mineral resources" (NAA: B1387 96/895).

[275] 11 June 1981, BS5508 "Eleventh Antarctic Treaty Consultative Meeting: Mineral resources" (NAA: B1387 1980/448 PART 1).

[276] 11 June 1981, MS13988 "Eleventh Antarctic Treaty Consultative Meeting: Mineral resources" (NAA: B1387 1980/448 PART 1). 18 June 1981, PA90085 "XIth Antarctic Treaty Consultative Meeting—mineral resources: French approach" (NAA: B1387 96/895).

1981: ATCM XI, BUENOS AIRES

In mid-winter 1981, the Parties gathered in Buenos Aires for ATCM XI, 20 years to the day since the Treaty's entry into force. With 14 ATCPs, claimants no longer held a majority.[277] Starting on a minerals regime appeared inevitable, and New Zealand delegation head Chris Beeby offered to host negotiations the following year.[278] Focusing on the 'Friends of the Chair' draft terms of reference, the debate became a dogged re-run of rhetoric on the principles and dogmatism on the details.[279] While the meeting report devoted only two paragraphs to the subject, Recommendation XI-1 contained three carefully negotiated pages reaffirming the moratorium while establishing a minerals regime. It would maintain the Treaty, provide the means to assess the impact of mining and its acceptability, and protect the environment.[280] Sovereignty problems were handled with "a conscious ambiguity", which Brennan considered "satisfactory". Claimants conferred daily, with New Zealand as spokesperson, and "Beeby carried the heavy burden of negotiation skilfully".[281] Leading Australia for the last time, Brennan was praised "for his untiring and effective efforts which were instrumental in obtaining the Recommendation".[282] The same could be said for his role in CCAMLR. Thus, as one leader in Antarctic diplomacy left, another would emerge as Beeby went on to chair the minerals SATCM, hoping to engineer a consensus on minerals. Little did he know how long that would take.[283]

As arrangements for SATCM IV emerged, so did complications. Japan's search for hydrocarbons was raising concerns about the stability of the moratorium, especially given involvement of the Japan National Oil

[277] In March 1981, the Federal Republic of Germany achieved ATCP status, taking the total to seven non-claimants and seven claimants.
[278] Antarctic Treaty, *Report of the Eleventh Consultative Meeting* (Ministry of Foreign Affairs and Worship (Buenos Aires) 1981), 37–39.
[279] 1 July 1981, BA13057 "Antarctica—XI ATCM—mineral resources" (NAA: B1387 96/895).
[280] Antarctic Treaty, Recommendation XI-1 "Antarctic mineral resources" https://ats.aq/devAS/Meetings/Measure/133 (accessed 11 March 2020).
[281] 7 July 1981, BA13118 "Antarctica-XI ATCM" (NAA: B1387 1980/448 PART 2).
[282] July 1981, C. G. McCue "Report on attendance at 11th Antarctic Treaty Consultative Meeting" (NAA: B1387 1980/448 PART 2).
[283] New Zealand had expected minerals negotiations to conclude in 1983. Templeton, *A Wise Adventure II: New Zealand and Antarctica after 1960*, 148 and 51.

Corporation.[284] The Bellingshausen Sea findings remained hidden and Japan was now eyeing the Weddell Sea. To add suspicion, it was unclear what Japan would do with its data—it was arguing that the Treaty obligation to share scientific data did not require providing *all* of it.[285] If hydrocarbons were found and the fact concealed, the whole tenor of the debate would change.[286]

Adding complication was an International Union for the Conservation of Nature (IUCN) resolution. It called for Antarctica to be given "a designation which connotes worldwide its unique character" and that there be no mineral regime "until such time as full consideration has been given to protecting the Antarctic environment completely".[287]

Then the dispute erupted between Argentina and the United Kingdom over the Islas Malvinas/Falklands Islands. Argentina's use of force, and the United Kingdom's robust response, brought conflict to the edge of the Treaty area.[288] The discovery of oil between Tierra del Fuego and the disputed islands might have been a factor behind Argentina's actions.[289] The dispute's implications for the minerals discussions were not immediately clear. Proceeding with formal negotiations would only make sense if all Parties participated. For the claimants, unity was "of crucial importance" but now at risk.[290] Important for all the Parties, including those engaged in hostilities, was to keep the conflict quarantined.[291] Ahead were

---

[284] 21 November 1981, Alan Goodall "Japan cool on oil exploration" *Weekend Australian*. The article provocatively said that an icebreaker was slipping quietly out of Tokyo Bay on a mission Japan was not anxious to talk about.

[285] 12 December 1981, CH1559 "Antarctica: Japanese offshore surveys" and 17 December 1981, TK24182 "Japan—Antarctic surveys" (NAA: B1387 81/676).

[286] The survey produced unremarkable results. K Kimura, "Geological and Geophysical Survey in the Bellingshausen Basin, Off Antarctica," *Antarctic Record of the Japanese Antarctic Research Expedition* 75 (1982).

[287] Resolution XII at the 15th General Assembly of the IUCN, 11–23 October 1981, reproduced in: Bush, *Antarctica and International Law: A Collection of Inter-State and National Documents*, Vol I, 515.

[288] Beck, *The International Politics of Antarctica*, 83–85.

[289] 23 April 1982 "Argentinians report S Atlantic oil find" *The Age*. Christopher C Joyner, "Anglo-Argentine Rivalry after the Falklands/Malvinas War: Law, Geopolitics, and the Antarctic Connection," *University of Miami Inter-American Law Review* 15, no. 3 (1984): 496–97.

[290] 8 April 1982, CH27582 "Antarctic minerals meeting—Falkland Islands" (NAA: B1387 1981/342).

[291] 5 May 1982, WH16686 "Falklands—implications for Antarctica" (NAA: B1387 1981/342). US insistence on "business as usual" prevailed, as did US refusal to relay through Palmer Station any military messages on behalf of the United Kingdom.

multiple difficulties to manage—to this point, all discussion of Antarctic minerals had been informal. Now the Parties were to embark on formal negotiations.

REFERENCES

Antarctic and Southern Ocean Coalition. "Law Says 'Abandon Claim'." *ECO* XXVIII, no. 3, 22–31 May 1984 (1984): 8.
Antarctic Treaty. *Report of the Eighth Consultative Meeting, Oslo, 9–20 June 1975.* Ministry of Foreign Affairs and Worship (Buenos Aires) 1981.
———. *Report of the Eleventh Consultative Meeting.* Ministry of Foreign Affairs and Worship (Buenos Aires) 1981.
———. *Report of the First Consultative Meeting, Canberra, July 10–24 1961.* Commonwealth Government Printer, 1961.
———. *Report of the First Special Consultative Meeting, Held at London 25, 27 and 29 July 1977.* Her Majesty's Stationery Office (London), 1979.
———. *Report of the Ninth Consultative Meeting, London 19 September-7 October 1977.* London: Foreign and Commonwealth Office, 1977.
Auburn, F M. *Antarctic Law and Politics.* Hurst, 1982.
Beck, Peter J. *The International Politics of Antarctica.* Croom Helm, 1986.
Bell, A. "Economic Analysis of Territorial Sovereignty." In *Economic Analysis of International Law,* edited by Eugene Kontorovich and Francesco Parisi, 76–98: Edward Elgar, 2016.
Borchgrevink, C E. "The 'Southern Cross' Expedition to the Antarctic, 1899–1900." *The Geographical Journal* 16, no. 4 (1900): 381–411.
Bush, W M, ed. *Antarctica and International Law: A Collection of Inter-State and National Documents:* Oceana, 1982.
Carrick, Robert. "Conservation in the Antarctic." In *First World Conference on National Parks,* edited by Alexander B Adams, 281–86: US National Park Service, 1962.
———. "Conservation of Nature in Antarctica." *Polar Record* 10, no. 68 (1961): 532–40.
Casey, R G. "The Establishment of a Scientific Research Station on the Antarctic Mainland: Statement by the Minister for External Affairs, the Rt Hon R G Casey, 20th March 1953." *Current Notes in International Affairs* 24, no. 3 (1953): 169–71.
Charney, Jonathan I. *The New Nationalism and the Use of Common Spaces.* Allanheld, Osmun, 1982.
Craddock, Campbell. *Geologic Maps of Antarctica.* Antarctic Map Folio Series. Vol. 12: American Geographical Society, 1970.

Daniels, Paul C. "The Antarctic Treaty." *Bulletin of the Atomic Scientists* 26, no. 10 (1970): 11–15.

Dodds, Klaus. *Geopolitics in Antarctica*. John Wiley, 1997.

Dufek, George J. *Through the Frozen Frontier*. Brockhampton, 1960.

Elliott, H. "Recommendation 5: Establishment of Antarctica as a World Park under United Nations Auspices." In *Second World Conference on National Parks 1972*, edited by H Elliott, 260, 443–44: IUCN, 1974.

Fleming, W L S. "Contemporary International Interest in the Antarctic." *International Affairs* 23, no. 4 (1947): 546–57.

Gildea, Damien. *Mountaineering in Antarctica*. Editions Nevicata, 2010.

Hall, H Robert. *International Regime Formation and Leadership: The Origins of the Antarctic Treaty*. PhD thesis, University of Tasmania, 1994.

Hambro, Edvard. "Some Notes on the Future of the Antarctic Treaty Collaboration." *The American Journal of International Law* 68, no. 2 (1974): 217–26.

Headland, R K. *A Chronology of Antarctic Exploration*. Quaritch, 2009.

Honnold, Edward E. "Thaw in International Law? Rights in Antarctica under the Law of Common Spaces." *The Yale Law Journal* 87, no. 4 (1978): 804–59.

Howkins, Adrian. *The Polar Regions: An Environmental History*. Polity, 2016.

———. "Science, Environment, and Sovereignty: The International Geophysical Year in the Antarctic Peninsula Region." In *Globalizing Polar Science: Reconsidering the International Polar and Geophysical Years*, edited by R D Launius, J R Fleming and D H DeVorkin, 245–64: Palgrave Macmillan, 2010.

"International Park." *Antarctic (New Zealand Antarctic Society)* 6, no. 8 (1972): 285.

Joyner, Christopher C. "Anglo-Argentine Rivalry after the Falklands/Malvinas War: Law, Geopolitics, and the Antarctic Connection." *University of Miami Inter-American Law Review* 15, no. 3 (1984): 467–502.

———. *Governing the Frozen Commons*. University of South Carolina Press, 1998.

Kawaja, Marie, and Tom Griffiths. "'Our Great Frozen Neighbour': Australia and Antarctica before the Treaty, 1880–1945." Chap. 1 In *Australia and the Antarctic Treaty System: 50 Years of Influence*, edited by Marcus Haward and Tom Griffiths, 9–47: UNSW Press, 2011.

Kaye, Stuart, Marcus Haward, and Robert Hall. "Managing Marine Living Resources, the 1970s-1990s." Chap. 7 In *Australia and the Antarctic Treaty System: 50 Years of Influence*, edited by Marcus Haward and Tom Griffiths, 164–80: UNSW Press, 2011a.

Kaye, Stuart, Michael Johnson, and Rachel Baird. "Law." Chap. 4 In *Australia and the Antarctic Treaty System: 50 Years of Influence*, edited by Marcus Haward and Tom Griffiths, 97–117: UNSW Press, 2011b.

Kimura, K. "Geological and Geophysical Survey in the Bellingshausen Basin, Off Antarctica." *Antarctic Record of the Japanese Antarctic Research Expedition* 75 (1982): 12–24.

Law, Phillip. *Antarctica 1984.* Sir John Morris Memorial Lecture 1964. Adult Education Board of Tasmania, 1964.

Lebedeva, Kira, and Sergei Petukhov. "Russia Decides to Return to the Antarctic with Serious Intentions and for Long." *Commersant* 8 (22 January 2003).

Licklider, Roy. "The Power of Oil." *International Studies Quarterly* 32, no. 2 (1988): 205–26.

Mawson, Douglas. "The Australasian Antarctic Expedition." *Geographical Journal* 37, no. 6 (1911): 609–20.

———. "Record of Minerals of King George Land, Adelie Land and Queen Mary Land." *Australasian Antarctic Expedition 1911–14. Scientific Reports. Series A* Vol IV, no. 12 (1940).

McIver, Richard D. "Hydrocarbon Gases in Canned Core Samples from Leg 28 Sites 271, 272, and 273, Ross Sea." *Deep Sea Drilling Project Reports* XXVIII, no. 28 (1975): 815–17.

Morell, James B. *The Law of the Sea: An Historical Analysis of the 1982 Treaty and Its Rejection by the United States.* McFarland & Company, 1992.

Murphy, Robert Cushman. "Antarctica: The Urgency of Protecting Life on and around the Great Southerly Continent." *Natural History* 76, no. 6 (1967): 18–31.

Potter, Neal. *Natural Resource Potentials of the Antarctic.* American Geographical Society Occasional Publication No. 4. 1969.

Quigg, Philip W. *A Pole Apart: The Emerging Issue of Antarctica.* New Press, 1983.

Ralston, Kathleen. *A Man for Antarctica: The Early Life of Phillip Law.* Hyland House, 1993.

Renouf, Alan. *The Frightened Country.* Macmillan, 1979.

Roberts, Brian. "Territorial Claims in the Antarctic." UK Foreign Office Research Department, 1945.

Runnells, Donald D. "Continental Drift and Economic Minerals in Antarctica." *Earth and Planetary Science Letters* 8, no. 6 (1970): 400–02.

Scientific Committee on Antarctic Research. *A Preliminary Assessment of the Environmental Impact of Mineral Exploration/Exploitation in Antarctica (EAMREA).* Edited by J H Zumberge. SCAR, 1977.

Shackleton, Ernest. *South.* William Heineman, 1919.

Shapley, Deborah. "Antarctica: World Hunger for Oil Spurs Security Council Review." *Science* 184, no. 4138 (1974): 776–77, 79–80.

———. *The Seventh Continent: Antarctica in a Resource Age.* Resources for the Future, 1985.

"Sites 270, 271, 272." *Deep Sea Drilling Project Initial Reports* XXVIII, no. 8 (1975): 211–303.

Sollie, Finn, ed. *Antarctic Resources: Report from the Informal Meeting of Experts 30 May-9 June 1973*: Fridtjof Nansen Foundation, 1974.

Stokke, Olav Schram. "The Effectiveness of CCAMLR." In *Governing the Antarctic*, edited by Olav Schram Stokke and Davor Vidas, 120–51: Cambridge University Press, 1996.

Swan, R A. *Australia in the Antarctic: Interest, Activity and Endeavour.* Melbourne University Press, 1961.

Talboys, B E. "New Zealand and the Antarctic Treaty." *New Zealand Foreign Affairs Review* 28, no. 3 and 4 (1978): 29–35.

Templeton, Malcolm. *A Wise Adventure II: New Zealand and Antarctica after 1960.* Victoria University Press, 2017.

———. *A Wise Adventure: New Zealand in Antarctica 1920–1960.* Victoria University Press, 2000.

Tepper, Rohan, and Marcus Haward. "The Development of Malaysia's Position on Antarctica: 1982 to 2004." *Polar Record* 41, no. 2 (2005): 113–24.

Tingey, Robert J. "Heroic Age Geology in Victoria Land, Antarctica." *Polar Record* 21, no. 134 (1983): 451–57.

Tolstikov, Y, ed. *Atlas Antarktiki* Vol. 1: Glavnoe Upravlenie Geodezii i Kartografii, 1966.

Watts, Arthur. *International Law and the Antarctic Treaty System.* Grotius, 1992.

Willett, Richard. "Report of the Scientific and Technical Working Group." In *Antarctic Resources: Report from the Informal Meeting of Experts 30 May-9 June 1973*, edited by Finn Sollie, 1–18: Fridtjof Nansen Foundation, 1974.

Wyndham, R H. "Report of the Working Group on Legal and Political Questions." In *Antarctic Resources: Report from the Informal Meeting of Experts 30 May-9 June 1973*, edited by Finn Sollie, L1–L20: Fridtjof Nansen Foundation, 1974.

Zumberge, James H, ed. *Possible Environmental Effects of Mineral Exploration and Exploitation in Antarctica*: Scientific Committee on Antarctic Research, 1979.

CHAPTER 3

Negotiating a Minerals Convention: June 1982 to June 1988

JUNE 1982: SPECIAL ANTARCTIC TREATY CONSULTATIVE MEETING IV, WELLINGTON

Special Antarctic Treaty Consultative Meeting (SATCM) IV opened in Wellington on 14 June 1982, a decade since the Parties, also in Wellington, had first discussed minerals. New Zealand's Chris Beeby chaired. Before him were delegates from all 14 Parties, several having been involved in Antarctic affairs for many years. Argentina and the United Kingdom were at the table, while their armed forces were at war. Beeby outlined key elements: the work's urgency, compatibility with the Treaty and the need to cover Antarctica and adjacent offshore areas other than the deep seabed. The regime had to regulate all stages of minerals activity, consider involvement by non-Treaty states, cooperate with other international organisations and identify research necessary to inform management decisions.[1] Reflecting New Zealand policy, Beeby insisted that environment protection was fundamental.[2]

---

[1] June 1982, "Chairman's summary of the most significant elements of agreement recorded in Recommendation XI-1" (NAA: B1387 1982/230 PART 2).

[2] Emphasis on the environment became a hallmark of New Zealand policy. Templeton, *A Wise Adventure II: New Zealand and Antarctica after 1960*, passim.

© The Author(s), under exclusive license to Springer Nature Switzerland AG 2021
A. Jackson, *Who Saved Antarctica?*,
https://doi.org/10.1007/978-3-030-78405-8_3

Beeby's task was formidable, and to canvass views he circulated a ques-
tionnaire.[3] The USSR urged a simple convention with details to be developed later. The United States offered a more complex approach that
would divide Antarctica into four regions with activities decided by
regional panels. Each Party could participate in two panels (helpful to
Australia as the AAT straddled two of the proposed regions), and none
hold a veto. This was received poorly by many, while others said it was
"not beyond redemption".[4] The USSR's "obstructive tactics" were countered by a US threat to "reconsider its policy of voluntary restraint".
Claimants reiterated their sovereign interests, with none well received.
Australia's delegation had been instructed to make an ambit claim starting
"from a maximum position of sovereignty".[5] Its hard-line proposal, that
claimants control activities in their territories, "caused one of the sharpest
reactions … Japan and South Africa were particularly caustic".[6] Such prov-
ocation was unproductive because, to that point, "non-claimants have not
indicated any concessions … as it is fundamentally easier for claimants
than non-claimants to concede points". At their informal meeting in
Canberra the previous month, the claimants had agreed "to maximise the
benefits from their sovereignty" and to act in concert, at least in objectives
if not in tactics.[7]

Environmental ideas proved more promising. Despite the USSR
describing it as a "distraction", emphasis was put on environment protection "to a degree unprecedented elsewhere in the world".[8] Side discussions chaired by the United Kingdom established the principle that

[3] June 1982, "Chairman's proposal for a structure for the discussion of Agenda Item 5 on
the elaboration of a regime" (NAA: B1387 1982/230 PART 2).

[4] 19 June 1982, WL12807 "Antarctic mineral resources" (NAA: B1387 96/896).

[5] June 1982, "Australian negotiating position" (NAA: B1387 89/592).

[6] June 1982, AMR/SCM/7 (Australia) "Summary of a regime for Antarctic mineral
resources" (NAA: B1387 89/592). 23 July 1982, Antarctic Division minute to Deputy
Secretary "Items of interest of the 4th Special Antarctic Treaty Consultative Meeting on
Antarctic Mineral Resources" (NAA: B1387 89/592). Templeton, *A Wise Adventure II:
New Zealand and Antarctica after 1960*, 130.

[7] 22 June 1982, Minute Department of Science and Technology "Antarctic minerals meeting and discussions with the Australian Mining Industry Council" (NAA: B1387 89/592).

[8] 14 July 1982, Memorandum from Department of Science "Evolution of draft paragraphs
for inclusion in the report of the First Session of the 4th Special Antarctic Treaty Consultative
Meeting" (NAA: B1387 89/592).

environmental and economic considerations had to carry equal weight.[9] There was little appetite for mining prohibition options for which proposals were emerging.[10] The meeting outcomes therefore included agreement that "protection of the unique Antarctic environment and its dependent ecosystems should be a basic consideration".[11] Little else was agreed in Wellington other than to meet again in 1983. Beeby circulated 'without prejudice' the outline of a possible regime comprising no more than a list of headings, initially presented as a skeleton, then as a schema.[12] Half of the meeting had been on just one aspect: debate "on the *form* of the regime took up almost all of the second week". Unexpected meeting dynamics emerged. The USSR, the United Kingdom and the United States were the most active; Australia, Belgium, Japan and Poland the least. The anticipated divide between claimants and non-claimants did not occur: the split appeared to be the "USSR and Poland versus the rest". The content and form of a regime had not been agreed, and the moratorium remained intact. Australia thought that Beeby had done "a wonderful job".[13] There was, however, a long way to go.

Early agreement appeared elusive but did not signal lack of interest. At least the scope of a regime was emerging. It would include all stages of minerals activities; the area of application; its relationship to the Treaty and other agreements; compliance and enforcement; essential institutions; the Parties' rights and obligations; environmental measures; and dispute settlement. An intriguing new element arose when Argentina suggested

[9] 18 June 1982 and 21 June 1982 "An Antarctic minerals regime: Environmental aspects. Note by John Heap on a discussion held between interested members of delegations" (NAA: B1387 1982/230 PART 1).

[10] 12 May 1982, David Evans "Campaign for world park in Antarctica", *The* Australian, 5. James N Barnes and Eliot Porter, *Let's Save Antarctica!* (Greenhouse Publications, 1982).

[11] 25 June 1982, AMR/SCM/21 Rev.1/Corr.1 "Report of the First Session of the Special Consultative Meeting on Antarctic Mineral Resources, Wellington, 14–25 June 1982" (AU-ATADD-4-BB-AQ-1).

[12] 23 June 1982, AMR/SCM/10 "Skeleton for an instrument on Antarctic mineral resources" (NAA: B1387 89/592). "Schema for an instrument on Antarctic mineral resources" in: 25 June 1982, AMR/SCM/21 Rev.1/Corr.1 "Report of the First Session of the Special Consultative Meeting on Antarctic Mineral Resources, Wellington, 14–25 June 1982" (AU-ATADD-4-BB-AQ-1), Annex B.

[13] 23 July 1982, Antarctic Division minute to Deputy Secretary "Items of interest of the 4th Special Antarctic Treaty Consultative Meeting on Antarctic Mineral Resources" (NAA: B1387 89/592).

ice be treated as a mineral.[14] Like so many details, that would not be resolved until June 1988. Eleven formal sessions, and countless informal discussions, still lay ahead.

Preoccupation with minerals precipitated an echo of the Nansen Foundation conference almost a decade earlier. For the first time, a meeting would be in Antarctica. The Conference on Antarctic Resources Policy, organised by the University of Chile, was held at Teniente Marsh in October 1982. Ostensibly an academic event, some of the most influential players in Antarctic diplomacy attended.[15] The conference was timely, providing for informal exchanges during preparations for the second session of SATCM IV. While it was the first conference in Antarctica, it was not the last to provide a relaxed space for serious consultation between diplomats and lawyers (for example, another was held in Kiel the following year[16]), albeit without interpreters.

JANUARY 1983: SATCM IV SECOND SESSION, WELLINGTON

Wellington hosted the second session of SATCM IV in January 1983, with Chris Beeby's role continuing and cooperation between Parties healthier. A key product was the Chair's 'Antarctic mineral resources regime: draft articles'.[17] The paper (later known as 'Beeby I') included possible articles on regulatory committees (comprising the relevant claimant, sponsoring state and the two superpowers) and a technical committee. Including the United States and the USSR in *every* regulatory committee was tantamount to treating them as claimants, potentially upsetting others not given that privilege. Nevertheless, it was a pragmatic

---

[14] June 1982, AMR/SCM/8 (Argentina) "Legal nature of Antarctic ice" (NAA: B1387 1982/230 PART 2).

[15] Participants included Chris Beeby (NZ), Keith Brennan (Australia), Tore Gjelsvik (Norway), Roberto Guyer (Argentina), John Heap (UK), Tucker Scully (US) and Fernando Zegers (Chile). Francisco Orrego Vicuña, ed. *Antarctic Resources Policy: Scientific Legal and Political Issues* (Cambridge University Press, 1983).

[16] Rüdiger Wolfrum and Klaus Bockslaff, eds., *Antarctic Challenge: Conflicting Interests, Cooperation, Environmental Protection, Economic Development: Proceedings of an Interdisciplinary Symposium, June 22nd-24th, 1983* (Duncker & Humblot, 1984), 8.

[17] January 1983, meeting document ANT (83) MR/17. 29 March 1984, "Informal personal report of the Chairman of the Working Group on Antarctic Mineral Resources" (AU-ATADD-4-BB-AQ-244), in which 'Beeby I' was presented alongside 'Beeby II'.

way to get US and USSR support.[18] Even the Antarctic and Southern Ocean Coalition (ASOC, an NGO umbrella group), which advocated no mining, recognised Beeby's "genius in providing a political solution" to the problems.[19]

The technique of a respected Chair guiding discussions with personal drafts became well-used as negotiations advanced. No Party was seen to be controlling the meeting's work. The downside was that it promoted argument over drafting rather than principles. The only diversion, and a short-lived one, was mention by the United Kingdom of the South Atlantic dispute. With Argentine naval vessels reported in the Treaty area, Arthur Watts had been instructed to state that "this development coincided with consistently bellicose statements relating to the recovery of unspecified territory". Argentina's Carlos Blanco immediately provided assurance that the vessels were supporting science. At that, "the meeting returned to its previous debate".[20] Such bilateral stresses were to continue in the background, bubbling up years later to delay establishing a permanent Antarctic Treaty secretariat.

Meanwhile, across the Tasman Sea, protesters were active on the Franklin River in Tasmania's South West wilderness, drawing attention to an issue that would play a role in changing the federal government and establish the environmental credentials of a new prime minister.[21] On 5 March 1983, the Australian Labor Party was elected with Bob Hawke as leader. Hawke had no inkling that an Antarctic environmental issue would also help to define his prime ministership. That was still to come after SATCM IV had completed its work, again in Wellington, several years later.

---

[18] Beeby's thinking is in: Templeton, *A Wise Adventure II: New Zealand and Antarctica after 1960*, 132–33.

[19] Antarctic and Southern Ocean Coalition, "Antarctic Minerals Regime: Beeby's Slick Solution," *ECO* XXIII, no. 1, 11–22 July 1983 (1983).

[20] 21 January 1983, WL14882 "Antarctica—reported military activity" (NAA: B1387 1981/342).

[21] Lloyd Robson, *A History of Tasmania (Volume 2)* (Oxford University Press, 1991), 555–79. Greg Buckman, *Tasmania's Wilderness Battles: A History* (Allen & Unwin, 2008), 56–61. Gareth Evans, "The Background Politics of the Tasmanian Dam Case," in *The Tasmanian Dam Case 30 Years On*, ed. Michael Coper, Heather Roberts, and James Stellios (Federation Press, 2017). *Wilderness: Celebrating Australia's Protected Places* (The Wilderness Society Tasmania, 2018), 25–28.

JULY 1983: SATCM IV THIRD SESSION, BONN

In preparation for the SATCM's third session, Australia reviewed its position. Cabinet was reminded how little was known about Antarctic minerals. Nevertheless, given the regulatory gap it would be "easier to negotiate a regime before the pressure from commercial operators or developing countries intensified".[22] Cabinet supported Chris Beeby's emphasis on "economic rationality and operational practicability" with "stringent environment protection provisions".[23] 'Beeby I' was the starting point when the Parties met in Bonn in July 1983.[24] The debate followed a familiar format with Beeby steering negotiations issue-by-issue and allowing Parties to put their views without commitment. Germany noted that "the device of non-papers was frequently found convenient", and thus there was "a narrowing of differences". Some issues were referred to subgroups chaired by the United Kingdom's John Heap and by Douglas Guppy of Australia. Considerable time was devoted to institutional arrangements, including decision-making and the role of consensus versus qualified majority.[25] Unknown at the time, the decision-making mechanisms to be adopted would pave the way for the whole regime to founder.

When the Parties returned to Canberra for a full ATCM in September 1983, the only mention of minerals was a simple note about satisfactory progress being made.[26] ATCM XII also briefly considered the question of iceberg towing.[27] Reduced anxiety over minerals was replaced by concerns over developments in the UN which had a profound impact on the Treaty,

---

[22] 20 June 1983, Cabinet Submission 250 "Australian objectives in Antarctic minerals negotiations" (NAA: A13977, 250).

[23] 13 July 1983, Cabinet Decision 923 "Australian objectives in Antarctic minerals negotiations" (NAA: A13977, 250).

[24] For the Bonn meeting, the paper was re-numbered as meeting document ANT 83/IV SCM 2nd Sess/2.

[25] July 1983, ANT 83/IV SCM 2nd Sess/7 "Report of the second formal session of the Special Consultative Meeting on Antarctic Mineral Resources, Bonn 11–22 July 1983" (AU-ATADD-4-BB-AQ-3). Despite its title and numbering, this report relates to what became referred to as the third session, the distinction between formal and informal sessions having been removed.

[26] Antarctic Treaty, *Report of the Twelfth Consultative Meeting, Canberra, 13–27 September 1983* (Australian Government Publishing Service, 1983), 18–19.

[27] Iceberg harvesting had become subject to serious speculation. A. A. Husseiny, ed. *Iceberg Utilization* (Pergamon, 1978). Peter Schwerdtfeger, "On Icebergs and Their Uses," *Cold Regions Science and Technology* 1, no. 1 (1979).

positive and negative.[28] Ultimately, UN interest played a role in how CRAMRA was replaced. By the time of ATCM XII, non-Consultative Parties (NCPs) were being invited to meetings to improve transparency, and, following the elevation of Brazil and India, the number of ATCPs had grown to 16. Spain and China had also recently acceded, marking the start of increasing accessions coinciding, perhaps unsurprisingly, with progress on minerals.[29]

In parallel was the inclusion of environmentalists in some delegations.[30] This reflected increasing public interest in Antarctic issues which, in turn, reflected a growing global environmental consciousness. On 2 June, Australia's Senate agreed to Australian Labor Party Senator Edward Robertson's motion to hold an inquiry into the exploitation of AAT resources and the adequacy of environmental measures.[31] In Antarctica, meanwhile, an environmental issue was erupting. France had commenced flattening ice-free islets to form an airstrip at Dumont d'Urville. This seemed perplexing: the islets were colonised by seabirds, and the station had been sited there to give biologists access to them.[32] The development triggered direct action by Greenpeace and worldwide publicity. Greenpeace had widened its environmental agenda beyond campaigns against nuclear weapons testing and was becoming increasingly interested in Antarctica.[33]

In Canberra, proposals at September's ATCM XII sought improved environmental measures. The United Kingdom outlined a system for assessing activities having "more than transitory or minor impact".[34] An Australian paper went further, suggesting "an integrated convention for the protection of the Antarctic environment" that would subsume

[28] M. G. Haward and D. Mason, "Australia, the United Nations and the Question of Antarctica," in *Australia and the Antarctic Treaty System: 50 Years of Influence*, ed. Marcus Haward and Tom Griffiths (UNSW Press, 2011).

[29] Ibid., 216.

[30] Australia was one of the early delegations to do this, including Annette Horsler of Fund for Animals.

[31] 2 June 1983, Senate Hansard, 1154.

[32] 17 January 1983, "French in Antarctic: Airstrip plans called threat to wildlife" *Canberra Times*. 17 June 1983, PA11845 "Antarctica: French airstrip" (AAD: 81/346–1).

[33] John May, ed. *The Greenpeace Book of Antarctica* (Child & Associates, 1988), 136–37.

[34] 12 September 1983, ANT/XII/1/REV 1 (Australia) "Agreed measures for the protection of the Antarctic environment: Interim guidelines—draft UK recommendation" https://documents.ats.aq/ATCM12/wp/ATCM12_wp001_rev1_e.pdf (accessed 17 March 2020).

previous measures.[35] Unknown at the time, this foreshadowed Australia's far more controversial proposal in 1989. The United Kingdom and the United States opposed replacing existing instruments, a rehearsal of the debate over comprehensive environmental measures to come after CRAMRA's demise.

JANUARY 1984: SATCM IV FOURTH SESSION, WASHINGTON

The United States hosted the fourth session of SATCM IV in January 1984. Chris Beeby continued to reflect the thrust of discussions in a personal document highlighting areas needing attention. As a result of the Washington session, Beeby added a provision to minimise prejudice to the claims; included environmental principles; and inserted a requirement that applications for minerals activities not be considered until an area was opened. Not addressed was the crucial question of how to make such decisions. 'Beeby II' emerged on 29 March.[36] At the time, what got Australia's attention were the implications of 'Beeby II' for claimant interests. The United Kingdom had similar concerns: the claimants would have to stick together as "several elements were involved ... each pulling in different directions".[37]

Negotiations were accelerating, and, on the eve of the fifth round, Australia reviewed its position. Cabinet was alerted to mounting scrutiny in UNGA and domestically. Some environmentalists were urging a complete mining ban, others calling for better regulation of *all* activities.[38] Cabinet chose the latter. Australia would seek an influential role in the regime, stringent environmental measures and a right to tax earnings from mining in the AAT.[39] Such ambitions were to become sorely tested, but there was comfort in the absence of known economic minerals.

[35] 26 September 1983, ANT/XII/6/CORR 1 "Man's impact on the Antarctic environment" (AU-ATADD-3-BB-AQ-644). This Australian proposal was not for a world park—see 4 October 1983, House of Representatives Hansard, 1321.

[36] 29 March 1984, MR/17 Revision "Informal personal report of the Chairman of the Working Group on Antarctic Mineral Resources" (AU-ATADD-4-BB-AQ-244).

[37] April 1984, "Summary record of discussions between British and Australian officials on Antarctic minerals negotiations, Canberra 11–12 April 1984" (NAA: B1387 1981/351C).

[38] 3 May 1984, Cabinet Submission 746 "Australian objectives in Antarctic minerals negotiations" (NAA: A13977, 746).

[39] 7 May 1984, Cabinet Decision 3180 "Australian objectives in Antarctic minerals negotiations" (NAA: A13977, 746).

May 1984: SATCM IV Fifth Session, Tokyo

In May 1984 the Parties met in Tokyo for the fifth session of the SATCM, with 'Beeby II' still the focus. New elements of the regime were tentatively attempted, and delegations cautiously considered the "practical realities of how an operator would go about mining". Some delegations were more open on the political issues: Norway was "no longer embarrassed by being labelled a claimant". But clear differences emerged on how to structure negotiations: some preferred to drip-feed their positions, and others, wary of surprises, thought they should "not begin to horse-trade until all the cards were on the table". Continuing the equestrian analogy, Argentina was reported as "riding both horses ... seeing itself as both a developing country and a claimant state". With all this prancing going on, New Zealand predicted that discussions would soon be in a "perpetual Heads of Delegation mode". Others had "got to the point where they were prepared to make compromises".[40] Little headway was made.

Desultory progress in Tokyo led to determination for progress in 1985, "or the whole system would become vulnerable to pressures and criticisms from outside" and "possible failure of the moratorium". This was a problem as the United States and Federal Republic of Germany considered "prospecting to be indistinguishable from scientific activity" and therefore not regulated.[41] This, however, ignored the implications for data disclosure. Meanwhile, prominent geologist John Behrendt was adamant "there are no known petroleum resources in Antarctica".[42] The prospects for finding them were nevertheless being talked up: "Antarctica may fool us all and yield some real whopper oil field. You never know until you look."[43]

The possibility of a weak regime alarmed environmentalists. ASOC, while preferring no minerals activities, for the time being would seek stronger environmental provisions in the regime.[44] ASOC's Cath Wallace

[40] 18 June 1984, WL19815 "Antarctica minerals meeting" (NAA: B1387 1981/343 PART 2).

[41] 21 September 1984, brief to Minister for Science and Technology "Antarctic minerals regime—informal discussions 17–20 September 1984" (NAA: B1387 1981/351C).

[42] John C. Behrendt, "Are There Petroleum Resources in Antarctica?" in *Antarctic Politics and Marine Resources*, ed. Lewis M. Alexander and Lynne Carter Hanson (University of Rhode Island, 1985), 191.

[43] John N. Garrett, "The Economics of Antarctic Oil," ibid., 190.

[44] Antarctic and Southern Ocean Coalition, "Beeby II: On the Right Track? But in the Wrong Direction?" *ECO* XXVIII, no. 2, 22–31 May 1984 (1984). Templeton, *A Wise Adventure II: New Zealand and Antarctica after 1960*, 185.

decried 'Beeby II' as "unacceptable and unworkable" because prospecting would be unregulated and "destroy major areas of the Antarctic". Because the regime's commission had no veto, she argued that Antarctica should have wilderness status with no exploitation.[45] New Zealand Prime Minister David Lange, equally robust, rebutted the idea that negotiations were "in some sense evil".[46] The issue was not that environmental issues would be ignored (on the contrary, far-reaching principles were being developed under UK leadership[47]); the deeper issue was how decisions implementing the principles would be made. Also antagonising conservationists were reports of environmental problems at Australia's Antarctic stations and uncertainty about French intentions with the Dumont d'Urville runway. Bob Brown (the high-profile Tasmanian environment campaigner) accused France of flouting the Treaty, and promised massive demonstrations if they resupplied in Hobart.[48] Management of Antarctica was rapidly becoming a public relations problem.

JANUARY 1985: DISCUSSIONS ON ICE

Year 1985 began with another intense conference—genuinely in tents, under canvas on the Beardmore Glacier. Holding it in inland Antarctica was ambitious.[49] It was also symbolic, comprising 57 representatives from ATCPs, acceding states, environment groups, industry and the media from 25 countries. It was also remarkable because of participation by countries outside the Treaty—it included two from Malaysia at a time of heightened UN attention to Antarctica. Following the Nansen Foundation, Teniente Marsh and Kiel precedents, participants would exchange views in a personal capacity. Modestly describing himself as "fairly closely involved", Chris Beeby gave a frank account of the minerals issue and the problems

---

[45] 24 October 1984 "Antarctic draft 'unworkable'" *New Zealand Herald.*

[46] 31 October 1984, WL21304 "Antarctica: New Zealand" (NAA: B1387 1981/343 PART 2).

[47] 26 September 1984, letter from John Heap to Department of Foreign Affairs "Antarctic minerals: Objectives and principles" (NAA: B1387 1984/481 PART 1). This is an early example of a Correspondents' Group letter.

[48] 10 February 1984, "Australia neglecting Antarctic environment" *Canberra Times,* 9. 31 October 1984, CH236857 "Antarctica: Airstrip at Dumont d'Urville" (NAA: B1387 88/159).

[49] This was done, in part, to demonstrate the difficulties of working in Antarctica. *Antarctic Treaty System: An Assessment* (National Academy Press, 1986), 3–4.

ahead. This precipitated frank exchanges on Antarctic politics, the need for external engagement and the technical and legal issues confronting negotiators.[50]

FEBRUARY 1985: SATCM IV SIXTH SESSION, RIO DE JANEIRO

Brazil hosted the March 1985 sixth round of SATCM IV negotiations in Rio de Janeiro. Australia's objectives were essentially unchanged, although with more flexibility provided "the environment will be thoroughly protected". More telling was recognition that some "brinkmanship" might be necessary because "the superpowers are non-claimants and the claimants stand to lose more".[51] While there were few differences over environmental principles, even this area for optimism was put at risk when John Heap made "a tactical error" by pushing "too hard". Another hurdle was discussion being "on an absolutely no-commitment basis" and the US and USSR delegations not carrying instructions. The claimants remained worried that their concerns might not be accommodated, while the USSR dismissed their interests as "scarcely realistic". The Federal Republic of Germany's Kurt Messer suggested that "it was now perhaps time for everyone to swallow the package" that was emerging. This was premature as significant difficulties remained, not least the question of the regime's form and Australia's insistence on preventing unfair economic practices. A significant development was including the non-Consultative Parties (NCPs) as observers for the first time.[52] This saw the inclusion in New Zealand's delegation of ASOC representative Alistair Graham amid concerns that meeting documents might be leaked.[53] They weren't, although opening the meeting in this way while keeping documents closed was an unresolved contradiction. More problematic was "breaking the log jam over the minerals negotiations" without striking "at the heart of the sovereignty claims".[54] Beeby sought to address this after the meeting by secretly circulating to ATCPs a personal note summarising his consulta-

[50] Ibid., 269–302.
[51] February 1985, "Brief for the Australian delegation to the Special Consultative Meeting on Antarctic Minerals, Rio de Janeiro 26 February to 8 March 1985" (AAD: B13/190).
[52] 15 March 1985, LO14743 "Antarctic minerals negotiations" (NAA: B1387 91/262).
[53] 26 March 1985, WL2285 "Antarctica: Minerals meeting in Rio de Janeiro" (NAA: B1387 91/262).
[54] 15 April 1985, LE26482 "Antarctica: Minerals negotiations" (NAA: B1387 91/262).

tions with Heads of Delegations. It was embossed with caveats: an unofficial document; not to be attributed to the Chair; not representing any agreements made; and was only an aid to discussion on a no-commitment basis.[55] And this was regarded as progress. Bill Mansfield of New Zealand neatly summed up what was occurring—negotiations were driven not by resource economics but by political arguments aiming "to preserve the stabilising regime of the Antarctic Treaty". That meant finding a way to accommodate the differences over sovereignty.[56]

MAY 1985: "A MARKED PETROLIFEROUS SMELL"

The proposals in Beeby's 'non-paper' raised eyebrows in Paris at the April 1985 Preparatory Meeting for that year's ATCM. Some aspects appeared acceptable, but not the whole package. Particularly upsetting was claimants losing their veto in Regulatory Committees, coupled with a membership formula leaving them disadvantaged compared to the United States and USSR who qualified for all committees.[57] Chris Beeby had accommodated US and USSR objections to a veto. A claimant caucus agreed that "the time had come for them to take a firm stand" and that the non-paper should not shape the discussions. If a concession on the veto was required, relevant claimants had to be "given a decisive role in drawing up the management scheme". This was "perhaps more important than a veto as such—it was a disguised veto". Echoing Australia's call for a claimant's share of revenue, Chile's Fernando Zegers added that a taxing right for claimants was "simply not negotiable".[58] At least Beeby had achieved his aim of triggering discussion.

A further trigger was discovery by Germany's *Polarstern*, operating in Bransfield Strait, of methane and hydrocarbons with "a marked petroliferous smell".[59] While this still did not prove economic resources, media

---

[55] 27 March 1985, Department of Foreign Affairs memorandum M.CH215981 "Antarctic minerals" (NAA: B1387 91/262).

[56] 25 April 1985, William Mansfield "Who has the right of exploitation, and the right to prevent exploitation, of the minerals of Antarctica?" Address to the American Society of International Law (AU-ATADD-4-BB-AQ-18).

[57] 19 April 1985, Department of Foreign Affairs memorandum M.CH217324 "Antarctic minerals: Chairman's non-paper on key issues" (NAA: B1387 91/262).

[58] 25 April 1985, BS20920 "Antarctic minerals" (NAA: B1387 91/262).

[59] M. J. Whiticar, E. Suess, and H. Wehner, "Thermogenic Hydrocarbons in Surface Sediments of the Bransfield Strait, Antarctic Peninsula," *Nature* 314, no. 6006 (1985).

observed that "the report brings substantially closer the day when a critical decision must be made".[60]

In Australia, preparations were underway for the next round. IDCs were convened, and consultations held with NGOs. The latter were harmonious, unlike fractious debates in the former. An IDC on 1 July 1985 considered a Science Department paper proposing a new mechanism for protected areas. It was supported by Hugh Wyndham of Foreign Affairs but met "fierce opposition from the Departments of Treasury and Resources and Energy" whose officials "launched a concerted attack on the paper" arguing its incompatibility with environmental measures in the minerals regime.[61] Thus began internal arguments which coloured Australian attitudes: a distinctly pro-resources view versus a priority for environmental protection. Differences *between* the Antarctic Treaty Parties would not be the only area needing compromise—domestic disagreements also needed accommodation.

SEPTEMBER 1985: SATCM IV SEVENTH SESSION, PARIS

The September 1985 seventh session of SATCM IV was in Paris, back-to-back with October's ATCM XIII in Brussels. The Parties had a full ATCM agenda and intractable differences in the SATCM. John Heap lamented that "for the last fifteen years I have been hoping every year for things to be easier ... my hopes have been totally confounded!".[62] It was not just the agenda's complexity—multiple additional factors were to frustrate progress on minerals. In New York, the stand-off in UNGA continued over Malaysian-led demands that Antarctic minerals be regarded as the common heritage of humankind.[63] In Antarctica, Greenpeace was planning a visit to Dumont d'Urville station to campaign against the airstrip or, as the French put it, "to question a few penguins" about the project.[64] Greenpeace also contemplated establishing an Antarctic base—an

[60] 22 May 1985 "Antarctic oil deposits pose treaty problem" *Financial Review*.

[61] 2 July 1985, Department of Science minute "Antarctic IDC on protected areas" and 5 July 1985 "Note for file" (NAA: B1387 85/997).

[62] 1 August 1985, John Heap letter to Hugh Wyndham, Department of Foreign Affairs (NAA: B1387 85/997), 2.

[63] Tepper and Haward, "The Development of Malaysia's Position on Antarctica: 1982 to 2004," 115.

[64] 17 September 1985, PA41352 "Antarctica" (NAA: B1387 85/997), para 5.

unprecedented proposal demonstrating considerable independence and resourcefulness.[65]

In October, China and Uruguay achieved ATCP status. France feared the "danger of unwieldiness creeping in" if Treaty membership were "expanded willy nilly". It is not clear which of China and Uruguay was willy and which was nilly, but with surprising frankness, the Foreign Ministry's Christian Bernier criticised Uruguay's elevation based on "three Sergeant-Majors on a visit to the Antarctic with a thermometer".[66] Such disparagement could not undo the shifting balance of influence. Australia had its own issues with the newly established 'Antarctic Wilderness Group' calling for a conservation convention.[67] This was followed by the December 1985 Senate inquiry into Antarctic resources which barely mentioned minerals but recommended numerous environmental protection measures.[68]

MARCH 1986: INFORMAL DISCUSSIONS IN WHANGAROA

To tackle the many blockages, Chris Beeby arranged informal discussions at a remote fishing lodge in Whangaroa Harbour in early March 1986.[69] It involved key players (including Argentina, Australia, Chile, New Zealand, the United Kingdom and the United States). The USSR was left out.[70] Immediately afterwards, the claimants met in Canberra over two days. Facing implacable opposition, it was clear they might have to give ground. Because a minerals regime implied derogation of absolute sovereignty, it was considered that they should demand a special benefit influenced, in part, by Australia's view on revenue sharing.[71] Claimants also

---

[65] 1 August 1985, John Heap letter to Hugh Wyndham, Department of Foreign Affairs (NAA: B1387 85/997), 5.

[66] 17 September 1985, PA41352 "Antarctica" (NAA: B1387 85/997), para 3.

[67] 4 October 1985, Roger Green "Antarctic proposals to be considered" *Canberra Times*, 6. The proposal was advocated by Lyn Goldsworthy, who championed Antarctic issues for many years.

[68] Senate Standing Committee on National Resources, "The Natural Resources of the Australian Antarctic Territory," Parliamentary Paper No 495/1985 (AGPS, 1985).

[69] Templeton, *A Wise Adventure II: New Zealand and Antarctica after 1960*, 178–79.

[70] This oversight would be remedied in the second Whangaroa session in September when, instead, Australia was not invited.

[71] This is not to be confused with a share for developing states under the Law of the Sea common heritage of humankind concept.

agreed not to operate as a bloc on all issues. This would be tested in April 1986 when the Parties met in Hobart for the eighth round.

APRIL 1986: "NEGOTIATIONS SEEM TO HAVE BEGUN IN EARNEST"

Barry Jones, Australia's Science Minister, opened SATCM IV's Hobart meeting. Unlike stereotypically benign welcome speeches, this one was unusually forthright: "Australia is concerned that its interests be adequately reflected", he said, "and Australia looks to a role in the future management of minerals activity within its claimed area and a special share of revenue". Finding a workable instrument could be difficult, but "you must not allow the negotiating process to become becalmed".[72] Beeby also implored progress, citing pressure in UNGA. This may have had some impact as the meeting began to seek "possible compromise ... at last, the negotiations seem to have begun in earnest". The first week was "characterised by a willingness on the part of Parties to address the nitty gritty issues".[73] Such nittiness and grittiness, however, did not extend to the compromise Jones implored—the United States flatly ruled out a special revenue share for claimants. Australia pursued its case as "to do otherwise would be tactically misguided and naïve". The meeting advanced a number of issues, including on environmental protection, although "some rewiring of Beeby II is necessary".[74] This is indeed what happened and, after Hobart, Beeby prepared a revision. ASOC's impassioned plea for the world park option was ignored.[75]

While negotiations were warming up, inter-departmental friction was also generating heat. The Department of Resources and Energy sought to build enthusiasm for Antarctic minerals. It pointed out that while the United States was the most likely to exploit them, France, Japan and the USSR also seemed keen. Australian industry wanted to participate on

---

[72] 14 April 1986, "Opening address by the Hon Barry O Jones" (NAA: B1387 1985/889 PART 2).

[73] 21 April 1986, ZZ012 "Antarctic minerals meeting (4)" (NAA: B1387 1985/889 PART 2).

[74] 26 April 1986, ZZ021 "Antarctic minerals meeting (7)" (NAA: B1387 1985/889 PART 2).

[75] 21 April 1986, ANT SCM/8 ASOC Paper no. 4 "The World Park option for Antarctica" (NAA: B1387 1985/889 PART 2).

equal terms.[76] Meanwhile, the Department of Science talked up environ-mental safeguards including strict liability but, on that, Resources and Energy would accept only "soft measures which will encourage mining". Ultimately, when other departments entered the discussion, they sup-ported a liberal approach.[77] Science, having "primary responsibility for all aspects of Antarctic administration", was determined not to defer to Resources and Energy matters that were "properly our concern".[78] On the eve of October's negotiations, the IDC could not resolve such differences, precipitating the Australian Antarctic Division's (AAD's) last-minute observation that the delegation was not united as the "brief for the Tokyo meeting is not fully agreed".[79]

Inter-departmental disagreements were not unique to Australia. From 1986, differences between domestic agencies became increasingly trou-blesome for New Zealand, with problems compounded by what were seen as increasingly hostile local NGOs.[80] France, too, had such challenges—its displeasure with Greenpeace prompted calls to exclude NGOs from the minerals regime's institutions.[81] But not all NGOs created headaches. Ecofund Australia offered a draft Antarctic Conservation Convention which avoided the minerals issues altogether, while the Australian Conservation Foundation reassured that "a world park won't lock up min-erals forever".[82]

[76] 11 June 1986, letter from Gareth Evans to Barry Jones (NAA: B1387 1985/21 PART 1).

[77] 24 July 1986 and 1 August 1986, Antarctic Division internal minutes (NAA: B1387 1987/16C PART 1).

[78] 15 August 1986, briefing paper "Department of Science Objectives in Antarctica" (NAA: B1387 1987/16C PART 1).

[79] 23 October 1986, letter from Rex Moncur (AAD) to Ian Nicholson, Department of Foreign Affairs (NAA: B1387 1987/16C PART 1).

[80] NGOs were accused of being "intellectually bankrupt", defamatory and libellous. Templeton, *A Wise Adventure II: New Zealand and Antarctica after 1960*, 180–81 and 97.

[81] Ibid., 207.

[82] August 1986, Ecofund Australia "Antarctic Conservation Convention, Second Draft" (AU-ATADD-5-BB-GE-456). 1986 ACF Briefing Paper "Antarctic—the world park and world heritage options" (AU-ATADD-5-BB-GE-174), 3–4.

OCTOBER 1986: SATCM IV NINTH SESSION, TOKYO

In October 1986, the Parties returned to Tokyo for the ninth session. 'Beeby III' comprised draft articles for a convention—the first time the form of regime had been proposed.[83] The session was described as "the most intensive" so far.[84] As in Hobart, subgroups set up by Beeby examined exploration and development (chaired by Norway's Rolf Andersen); legal issues (the Federal Republic of Germany's Rüdiger Wolfrum); data confidentiality (Norway's Olav Orheim); anti-subsidy provisions (Australia's Ian Nicholson), and environmental measures (New Zealand's Harry Keys).[85] While a structure was emerging, there were many sticking points. One stuck point was Australia's proposal to prevent governments subsidising uneconomic mining. Nicholson presented it as "a make-or-break issue". It broke: he was "received in attentive silence".[86] The proposed special share of revenue similarly foundered. The United States "simply could not accept that", and the USSR was dismissive, saying that since it had a basis of claim it, too, wanted a share "throughout all of Antarctica, including the unclaimed sector".[87] Such "attempts to weaken claimant positions" disappointed the claimants who had caucused confidently in Santiago, but seemed to be running out of influence. Adding pressure was Beeby's plan to complete negotiations in just two more sessions: one in Montevideo in May 1987, another in Wellington in 1988. In preparation, Beeby asked delegations to "seek new instructions" on the sticking points and come "equipped to handle two or three issues at the same time".[88]

---

[83] 19 September 1986, "Chairman's informal personal report: MR/17 REV II. Draft articles for an Antarctic mineral resources convention (Beeby III)" (AU-ATADD-4-BB-AQ-245).

[84] 14 November 1986, TK53824 "Antarctica: Ninth Session Minerals Negotiations—Report No 14" (NAA: B1387 1987/16 PART 2).

[85] 13 November 1986, TK53803 "Antarctica: Ninth Session Minerals Negotiations—Report No 11" (NAA: B1387 1987/16 PART 2).

[86] 14 November 1986, TK53821 "Antarctica: Ninth Session Minerals Negotiations—Report No 13" (NAA: B1387 1987/16 PART 2). Australia feared subsidies undermining its lucrative mineral exports.

[87] 12 November 1986, TK53776 "Antarctica: Ninth Session Minerals Negotiations—Report No 9 (NAA: B1387 1987/16C PART 1).

[88] 14 November 1986, TK53824 "Antarctica: Ninth Session Minerals Negotiations—Report No 14" (NAA: B1387 1987/16 PART 2).

February 1987: "Battle Lines Are Only Now Being Drawn Up"

Achieving new instructions would be tricky for Australia where departmental disagreements continued. Treasury argued that "a special share in revenue will be the only economic benefit" for claimants who are "entitled to a precise and unambiguous answer from non-claimants on this basic issue". Treasury's optimism appeared boundless: "the strength of opposition [was] a measure of the importance of the issue", and claimants could "finalise this issue now when their negotiating leverage is greatest".[89] Department of Resources and Energy proposals on exploration and development were dismissed by the Antarctic Division's David Lyons as "propaganda".[90] In turn, both Resources and Energy and the Treasury objected to liability proposals from Science, the Attorney-General's Department and the Department of Arts, Heritage and Environment.[91] The Department of Trade insisted on anti-subsidy measures.[92] This put Australia "on a collision course with the USA", which insisted on "assured access to strategic resources". The United States refused to countenance a special revenue share, for which "battle lines are only now being drawn up".[93] Complicating such arguments in Australia were traditional bureaucratic squabbles over legislative responsibility: the Department of Resources and Energy demanded control as it would be a mining regime, while Department of Science insisted it was responsible for Antarctic matters. It was hard enough just getting agreement on who would take the issue to Cabinet, let alone what to recommend.[94] Treasury was seeking the

[89] 1987 undated and untitled briefing document at folio 167 (NAA: B1387 1987/25 PART 1).

[90] 1987 undated IDC notes "Brief for Montevideo" (NAA: B1387 1987/25 PART 3).

[91] 20 February 1987, brief to minister "Antarctic minerals negotiations—Australian position on liability provisions" (NAA: B1387 89/417).

[92] 9 March 1987, CH418333 "Antarctic minerals negotiations: United States/Australian difficulties" (AAD: 84/360-1).

[93] 23 February 1987, brief to minister, "Antarctic Treaty minerals negotiations" (NAA: B1387 1987/25 PART 1). The United States argued that certain minerals, such as cobalt, would be sought "irrespective of the costs of production". 11 December 1987, CE465165 and 18 December 1987, WE7705 "Antarctic minerals: Anti subsidy article" (NAA: B1387 87/720 PART 1).

[94] 11 March 1987, brief to minister, "Antarctic Treaty minerals negotiations—proposed Cabinet submission". 17 March 1987, letter from Minister for Science to Minister for Foreign Affairs (NAA: B1387 1987/25 PART 2).

revenue share it saw as a sovereign right. Trade persisted with anti-subsidy provisions. Unlike Australia's previous position, Resources and Energy pushed for a practical regime that would relax Beeby's draft and promote mining, even if it conflicted with claimant interests. Resources and Energy was also working to weaken liability provisions so as to make mining more attractive.[95]

Ultimately, Australia's proposed position was settled a week before the delegation departed for Montevideo. Cabinet agreed to seek a special role for claimants in the regulatory committees; stringent environmental protection measures; a right to tax activity in the AAT; a substantial share of revenue expressed as a high fixed percentage; a provision against subsidised mining; strict and unlimited liability with few defences; and support for a final meeting in 1988.[96] These were ambitious positions, especially as many had already been dismissed. Beeby was dismayed by the demand for a special share of revenue for claimants, an option previously rejected during negotiations, and suggested it be pursued in the management scheme for each development. Even other claimants disagreed with Australia, arguing that overt assertion of sovereign rights was guaranteed to be counterproductive. Beeby considered Australia "even further into cloud-cuckoo land than he had thought".[97]

MAY 1987: SATCM IV TENTH SESSION, MONTEVIDEO

A further draft had been circulated by the time Parties arrived in Montevideo in May 1987 for the tenth session of SATCM IV.[98] 'Beeby IV' represented a significant consolidation of issues discussed in Tokyo. It had been produced after a March invitation-only session to "do some additional drafting", again at Whangaroa, and held without publicity lest it provoke demonstrations from environmentalists.[99] With the notional 1988 deadline looming, and increasing interest in UNGA, the Montevideo negotiations were as intense as any before. Discussions were again in sub-

[95] 21 April 1987, brief to minister "Antarctic minerals negotiations—Cabinet submission" (NAA: B1387 1987/25 PART 2).

[96] 27 April 1987, Cabinet Minute, Submission 4757 "Australian objectives in Antarctic minerals negotiations" (NAA: A14039 4757).

[97] Templeton, *A Wise Adventure II: New Zealand and Antarctica after 1960*, 188–90.

[98] 2 April 1987, "Antarctic mineral resources. Chairman's informal personal report: MR/17 REV III" (AU-ATADD-4-BB-AQ-246). This was 'Beeby IV'.

[99] 25 March 1987, John Kennedy "Envoys talk strategy on Antarctic mining" *The Age*, 7.

groups, one handling political and legal issues and the other more practical matters. Delegation member Gillian Triggs reported that the Australian team was "being swept along by the logic that a convention is inevitable … the pressure to compromise is strong".[100] She also made a key observation: differences between Departments were obvious to other delegates, and "there seemed to be no collegiate sense of what it is that Australia hopes to achieve".[101] Acute internal differences were later seized on by other Parties to explain Australia's dissatisfaction with CRAMRA. Triggs also pointed to a paradox: the environmental standards of the proposed convention were tantamount to a moratorium, and "a strong minerals regime can achieve many of the objectives of supporters of a world park concept".[102] A similar outcome came from Chile's suggestion for an 'Antarctic Treaty Park', possibly reflecting Fernando Zegers' concern that the regime would erode Chilean sovereignty.[103]

In Montevideo, the Parties endorsed a final session the following year.[104] To assist this, Beeby arranged further consultations in Auckland in November 1987 as part of the "necessary preparatory work" for the final negotiations. These would be informal 'Whangaroa-type' discussions, but this time all delegations would be invited. In either brinkmanship or exasperation, Beeby catalogued the raft of still unresolved matters, including rules for exploration and development; liability; inspection; area of application; jurisdictional questions; dispute settlement; financial and economic issues; and institutional decision-making.[105] The big political issues, including claimant demands, would be left to the final negotiations when the 'package' could be examined as whole. Australia still insisted on a special share of revenue because of the draft's perceived derogation of claim-

---

[100] May 1987, Gillian Triggs "Antarctic Treaty minerals negotiations, Uruguay 1987: Report to the Minister for Science" (AAD: 87/805), 7. Triggs, then senior lecturer in law at the University of Melbourne, participated as an observer at the request of the Minister for Science, Barry Jones.

[101] Each Australian delegate was free to pursue the objectives of their department.

[102] May 1987, Gillian Triggs "Antarctic Treaty minerals negotiations, Uruguay 1987: Report to the Minister for Science" (AAD: 87/805), 18.

[103] Antarctic and Southern Ocean Coalition, "Let's Hear It for an Antarctic Treaty Park," *ECO* XXXXI, no. 2, 19 May 1987 (1987): 1.

[104] 6 October 1987, ANT/XIV/INF/17 "Report of Chairman of Fourth Special Consultative Meeting on Antarctic Minerals" https://documents.ats.aq/ATCM14/ip/ATCM14_ip017_e.pdf (accessed 25 March 2020).

[105] 3 August 1987, letter from New Zealand High Commission (NAA: B1387 1987/25 PART 4).

ant interests: "the right to tax is a fundamental sovereign right" and claimants need to know the "specific percentage" of their share.[106] Fearing a robust reaction from the USSR delegate Iouri Rybakov, the United Kingdom's Arthur Watts urged Australia to soften its language, if not its position.[107] However, Australia pressed forward with an aide-memoire seeking to counter the chair's 'Rio Palace Package' (developed on the side of the October 1987 Fourteenth ATCM), which had "shifted somewhat against claimant interests".[108] Australia insisted this "was not a 'tit for tat'" for the position of others—the issue was of "basic importance".[109] On the eve of final negotiations, Australia was putting itself on a collision course with other Parties.

OCTOBER 1987: AUSTRALIAN INTERNAL SQUABBLES

A collision closer to home was also imminent: this time, argument over who should represent Australia in Beeby's Auckland consultations was proxy for the deeper departmental disagreements. With delegations limited to three, Environment Minster Graham Richardson implored Foreign Minister Bill Hayden to include an Environment Department official to provide balance: after all, his department was responsible for Antarctica.[110] Hayden refused, pointing out that balance would be achieved because Environment's prime antagonist (Primary Industry and Energy) would also not be represented, neglecting to mention that the equally pro-mining Treasury *would* be. To add injury, in a separate letter on the same day, he asked Environment to relax its attitude to liability.[111] Differences between departments erupted. With two days to go before departure for Auckland, the IDC's discussion of a ten-page Environment Department proposal to strengthen environmental provisions "didn't even get off page 1" on day

---

[106] 29 September 1987, CE427853 "Antarctic minerals: Claimants' meeting and share in revenue" (NAA: B1387 1987/25 PART 4).

[107] 9 October 1987, LH27179 "Antarctic minerals claimants meeting/share in revenue" (NAA: B1387 1987/25 PART 4).

[108] 16 October 1987, CE436555 "Antarctic minerals: Claimant interests" (AAD: 87/592).

[109] 16 October 1987, CE436557 "Antarctic minerals: A special share in revenue for claimants" (AAD: 87/592).

[110] 9 October 1987, letter from Graham Richardson to Bill Hayden (NAA: B1387 87/720 PART 1).

[111] 21 October 1987, letters from Bill Hayden to Graham Richardson (NAA: B1387 87/720 PART 1).

one.[112] As Environment Department representative Jon Stanhope reported, at times the debate was reduced to personal attacks with "objection at some level, in many cases total" from Primary Industry and the Treasury "to almost every suggestion" in the paper. A fundamental issue was stake, whether the convention would be driven by mining or the environment.[113] It was a sign of things to come in the deteriorating relations between Australian departments.

Heeding Beeby's exhortation to "search for the middle ground", the Auckland consultations resulted in "over 20 new and improved articles" for an updated chair's draft. Small groups advanced the issues, with Beeby himself hosting the liability discussion in his personal apartment. The vexed area of application was solved by a "break-through" UK proposal for which "Watts' draft was widely acknowledged by all as ingenious".[114] The principle of revenue sharing appeared to be accepted, provided it was in neutral language, although claimants noted "the large task ahead". The meeting had advanced "some long-standing controversial" issues, and, "while progress had been encouraging", much was left to do.[115] Beeby recognised the challenge and, in presenting 'Beeby V', proposed what would be the penultimate negotiations to be held in Wellington in January the following year.[116] Time was short if a final session were to convene in mid-1988.

JANUARY 1988: SATCM IV 11TH SESSION, WELLINGTON

Despite the urgency, the 11th session had a slow start. 'Beeby V' was discussed article by article (in a group led by Norway's Andersen), with smaller groups tackling unresolved matters. To compile a text for May's final session, Beeby also proposed a drafting committee comprising just

[112] 4 November 1987, handwritten minute "Minerals IDC" (AAD: 87/592).

[113] 12 November 1987, J. D. Stanhope minute "Antarctic minerals regime IDC" (NAA: B1387 87/720 PART 1).

[114] Watts' ingenuity was to define the area of application by reference to the outer limits, rather than extending from problematic territorial baselines. 3 December 1987, Australian delegation report, Auckland consultations (NAA: B1387 87/720 PART 1).

[115] 21 November 1987, AU3646 "Antarctic minerals: Chairman's Auckland consultations" (NAA: B1387 87/720 PART 1).

[116] 26 November 1987, "Antarctic mineral resources. Chairman's informal personal report: MR/17 REV IV" (AU-ATADD-4-BB-AQ-247). This became known as 'Beeby V'.

five members: the chair, plus one for each of the four Treaty languages. His hopes were dashed when Germany refused to accept a group where three of the five were claimants. Five became nine. More problematic for Australia was fracturing claimant solidarity on revenue sharing, some arguing this was less important than early conclusion of the convention. Even so, "no progress was made in bridging the gulf between claimants and non-claimants". Equally difficult was subsidised mining: "polite probing" of Australia resulted in opposition from France, Japan and the United Kingdom and the "deep scepticism of the Americans". Some of the smaller groups made headway "in a realistic atmosphere [although] less progress was made on other key issues and some were not discussed at all". Despite the observation that "the FRG delegation was again instrumental in wasting much time", the Parties believed that they should complete negotiations in May 1988, accepting that "the hardest key issues will only be settled in a final package". A claimants meeting agreed "to consult closely between sessions on tactics and proposals".[117] The room for compromises was narrow, and the room for disappointments large.

Although negotiated behind closed doors, there was enough knowledge of what was happening to provoke public interest. Donning penguin suits, ASOC members welcomed delegations with 'no mining' placards and decried the draft regime for being "quick and dirty"—Antarctic governments would probably have been surprised by at least the former of those two criticisms. ASOC also called for a 50-year moratorium and examination of world park proposals.[118] Others spruiked mining, including the prospects of oil and gas deposits "just offshore from Australia's Davis and Mawson bases".[119] Ultimately, ASOC's view would prevail, but that was still to come. It would require completion of the convention, and much more hyperbole, before public attention in Australia could be drawn away from higher profile events: the bicentenary of Australia's settlement by non-indigenous people, the World Expo in Brisbane and the opening of a new Parliament House.

[117] 29 January 1988, WL32479 "Antarctic minerals—Wellington meeting" (NAA: B1387 87/720 PART 2).
[118] 19 January 1988, "Penguin protest on Antarctic mining" *The Dominion* (New Zealand). 30 January 1988, "Mining talks hailed: Ice park sought" *The Dominion* (New Zealand).
[119] 8 March 1988, Bob Beale "Antarctica is a goldmine of minerals, scientists believe" *Sydney Morning Herald*, 3.

Returning from Wellington, the AAD's David Lyons reported that the Australian delegation was more harmonious than in 1987. Differences of opinion were "easily cleaned up and good team spirit prevailed", buoyed by the fact that "daily delegation meetings were constructive and not too long-winded".[120] Such optimism was short-lived as, back in Canberra, Australian agencies prepared for final negotiations. 'Beeby VI' had been distributed.[121] Officials were developing a Cabinet Submission to underpin delegation instructions and departments were again polarised. At one end, Primary Industries and Energy proposed that unless revenue sharing and anti-subsidy measures were protected, Australia "should not hesitate to adopt a strong stance, even though this might result in the postponement" of a convention.[122] Treasury considered the pressure on claimants overstated: "claimants have undoubted leverage" because a breach of the moratorium was theoretical rather than practicable, and mining companies needed the security of title afforded by a convention. Unexpectedly, Treasury suggested proposing "national park status" for the AAT—but only "as a negotiating tactic" to secure a better revenue share. Such an implausible tactic was not picked up by Environment, which only sought stronger liability rules. The Environment Department considered the convention "workable, although very complex" and that it should administer the implementing legislation, directly contrary to Primary Industries and Energy's ambitions.[123] Cabinet accepted that failure to settle a convention would be serious. It decided that compromise on a revenue share issue might be necessary "to facilitate agreement" and that flexibility might have to be shown on liability. The final decisions would require consultation between ministers including on "as a last resort, the question of precipitating in appropriate company, a postponement of the negotiations in order to secure our essential objectives".[124]

---

[120] 1 March 1988, AAD internal minute "Antarctic minerals meeting—Wellington, January 1988" (NAA: B1387 87/720 PART 3).

[121] 3 February 1988, "Antarctic mineral resources. Chairman's informal personal report: MR/17 Rev. V" (AU-ATADD-4-BB-AQ-250). This is also known as 'Beeby VI'.

[122] 24 March 1988, AAD brief to minister "Antarctic minerals convention—Cabinet Submission" (NAA: B1387 87/720 PART 2), Attachment 1, 41.

[123] 24 March 1988, AAD brief to minister "Antarctic minerals convention—Cabinet Submission" (NAA: B1387 87/720 PART 2).

[124] 28 March 1988, Cabinet Minute 10,819 "Antarctic minerals convention" (NAA: A14039 5558).

APRIL 1988: NEGOTIATIONS "CONDEMNED TO SUCCEED"

In April 1988, the Parties received a copy of a revised 'Beeby VI' produced by the chair's Drafting Committee.[125] Australia made a concentrated push for support on revenue sharing and anti-subsidy measures. The circulation to other Parties of a letter from Foreign Minister Hayden made no impact, probably because of its built-in contradiction of tackling head-on the most sensitive claimant interests while simultaneously calling for a "serious commitment to negotiate a final text".[126] Engaging a politician to argue the case appeared futile. The response from the US State Department "gave no sign that the US was willing to move", and, besides, "if the convention were not concluded now it would get harder to do so later".[127] Even UK foreign secretary Geoffrey Howe's positive response that "when I read your message I nodded vigorously in agreement at certain passages" was immediately countered by "I shook my head" at others.[128] Fellow claimant France would only support Australia on a revenue share, not on anti-subsidy provisions. More optimistically, France considered that the Wellington negotiations were "condemned to succeed".[129]

MAY 1988: SATCM IV TWELFTH SESSION, WELLINGTON

Representatives of the 20 ATCPs headed to Wellington's extended twelfth and final negotiations.[130] Australia had a large delegation: 11 now-familiar names from key departments, plus one NGO. They were led by Foreign Affairs' lawyer John Brook. In their briefcases were 104 pages of briefing, including all relevant Cabinet decisions since 1982. It had conflicting aims: it sought to "conclude a convention", but only "subject to the attainment of its principal objectives". Accordingly, the delegation was exhorted to "exercise considerable discretion and flexibility on matters of

---

[125] April 1988, "Antarctic mineral resources. Chairman's informal personal report: MR/17 Rev. V/Corr. 1" (NAA: B1387 87/720 PART 3).
[126] 14 April 1988, CE523881 "Antarctic minerals negotiations: Message from Mr Hayden" (NAA: B1387 87/720 PART 2).
[127] 19 April 1988, WE11004 "Antarctic minerals negotiations" (NAA: B1387 87/720 PART 2).
[128] 26 April 1988, LE69174 "Antarctic minerals negotiations: Message from Mr Hayden" (NAA: B1387 87/720 PART 3).
[129] 28 April 1988, PA67337 "Antarctic minerals negotiations—French views" (AAD: 81/346-2).
[130] The German Democratic Republic and Italy had achieved ATCP status in October 1987.

detail" but that "judgement will need to be exercised to ensure that we are not manoeuvred to an unacceptable package". The delegation was urged to seek support from within the claimants who would "need to meet frequently". With such flexible instructions, the delegation had room to move. However, that created a vulnerability: "the delegation will need to be closely coordinated and to present a united front on all issues. It is vitally important that we keep each other informed of developments, discuss proposals and pool all papers obtained."[131]

23 MAY 1988: BEEBY IMPLORES "A RESULT THAT IS TOLERABLE TO ALL"

Beeby's objective was to adopt a convention and the SATCM's symbolic Final Act. Plenary sessions would be minimised; Andersen would chair a main committee; and small groups would address key issues under Beeby. Wolfrum would assist drafting. Beeby called for "self-restraint by delegations in not submitting proposals which had no chance of securing consensus". Discussion was hijacked when the Federal Republic of Germany "proceeded to wreck Beeby's work program" supported by the USSR, German Democratic Republic, Italy and France.[132] It was not a good omen. The pace was being "set largely by the FRG and United States, both of whom are seeking to overturn text which has emerged from earlier sessions". Progress appeared possible on some outstanding issues including decision-making mechanisms, area of application and liability but, despite that, it was a "disappointingly slow start".[133] Such dismal reporting from the delegation was not sufficiently self-aware to admit that Australia's intransigence was frustrating progress. Less controversial matters were completely settled, including acceptance of Australia's proposal for the convention's title. Sweden had proposed amending the instrument's title to include the environment. It was reported that "there were a few chuckles around the room at the Swedes' idea". In hindsight, failing to mention the regime's environmental priorities was a tactical misstep which was to

[131] May 1988, "Brief for the Australian Delegation to the Special Consultative Meeting on Antarctic Minerals, 12th Session, Wellington 2 May-2 June 1988" (NAA: B1387 87/720 PART 3).

[132] 3 May 1988, WL33315 "Antarctic minerals: 12th session: Report no 2—opening plenary and work program" (NAA: B1387 87/720 PART 3).

[133] 9 May 1988, WL33372 "Antarctic minerals" 12th session: Report no 3—round-up of week one" (NAA: B1387 87/720 PART 4).

contribute to the convention's complete rejection a year later.[134] By the end of week one, delegations had submitted over 50 documents.[135] A sense began to creep in that the negotiations could be concluded. Even environmentalists recognised the inevitable, dropping calls for a world park and, instead, addressing perceived weaknesses in the convention. In particular, ASOC proposed stricter liability rules, thus strengthening its 'plug the gaps' strategy.[136]

At meeting mid-point the penultimate draft, 'Beeby VII', was circulated.[137] The chair convened Plenary to review progress. Concerned about the ground to be covered in the ten days remaining, Beeby appealed for cooperation. He noted that the convention would not represent any delegation's preferred position: "the most we can expect is a result that is tolerable to all". 'Beeby VII' would "gauge the tolerability". He reminded delegates it would be "a package deal, some elements of which will inevitably be less acceptable than others" and that "the more one part of the package is attacked from one quarter, the greater the pressure will grow from other quarters to change other parts". Beeby called for stamina and political will as "time is short [and] they will be very long days". He implored delegations to "resist the temptation to fritter away our time tinkering with the text for the sake of perfection" and not to raise issues "only of cosmetic or optical importance".[138] Beeby's pleas fell on sympathetic ears. On 29 May, what seemed to be a procedural provision emerged in just 90 minutes from a group of 11 Parties.[139] It was draft Article 62 which specified the requirements for the regime's entry into force. Perhaps more time should have been given to it: unknown at the time, that provision would ultimately allow the convention to collapse.

[134] Reported by Australian delegate David Lyons, see Bowden, *The Silence Calling: Australians in Antarctica 1947–1997*, 409.

[135] June 1988, B. Doran (compiler) DFAT "Volumes of available documents, Vol 2" (AU-ATADD-4-BB-AQ-266).

[136] 3 March 1988, ASOC information paper 1988-2 "Some solutions to problems with the draft Antarctic minerals convention" (NAA: B1387 87/720 PART 4). 5 May 1988, ASOC Information Paper 1988-3 "Some solutions to the problems with the liability provisions in the draft minerals convention" (AU-ATADD-5-BB-GE-381).

[137] 20 May 1988, AMR/SCM/88/67 "Draft Convention on the Regulation of Antarctic Mineral Resource Activities".

[138] 23 May 1988, INF/09 "Chairman's Plenary statement" (NAA: B1387 87/720 PART 4).

[139] Templeton, *A Wise Adventure II: New Zealand and Antarctica after 1960*, 217.

Key issues remained unresolved. That was the cue for Australia's delegation to trigger the final round of ministerial consultations foreshadowed by Cabinet in March. Instructions were sought on the revenue share and anti-subsidy measures: "several of our original objectives seem clearly unattainable", and "there are no indications that non-claimants are likely to offer anything acceptable". Pursuing such objectives "would leave us isolated and perhaps held responsible for any breakdown in negotiations".[140] Acting Foreign Minister Michael Duffy wrote to relevant ministers emphasising the gains made so far and the need to secure a convention, and advising against pursuing unachievable objectives. He proposed final instructions for the delegation: if Australia becomes isolated on the revenue share issue, Australia should not obstruct proceedings. In the absence of specific anti-subsidy provisions, the delegation should settle on a statement of principle.[141] The Attorney-General and the Environment Minister agreed.[142] Reflecting robust departmental advice, Resources Minister Peter Cook and Treasurer Paul Keating did not—Cook responding with "deep reservations about the need ... to concede two of our key objectives". On subsidised mining he "would not accept, even as a fall-back position, a general statement": even if the delegation became isolated, "we should seek to have the negotiations postponed". He equally insisted on a revenue share as otherwise it could concede a sovereign advantage "without any benefit in return".[143] The following day Paul Keating also responded unambiguously. Fearing that "a convention will mean the internationalisation of Antarctica" his "strong disposition therefore is for Australia to stand firm on the revenue issue".[144]

2 June 1988: A Minerals Convention Is Adopted

Time was running out and Duffy had to decide what instructions to issue. The delegation reported that negotiations had achieved agreement on the "outstanding key issues so far as most participants are concerned". The

---

[140] 26 May 1988, WL33535 "Antarctic minerals negotiations: 12th session: Report no 11—request for instructions from ministers" (NAA: B1387 87/720 PART 4).

[141] For example, see 27 May 1988, letter from Duffy to Cook (NAA: B1387 87/720 PART 4).

[142] For example, see 30 May 1988, letter from Richardson to Duffy (NAA: B1387 87/720 PART 5).

[143] 30 May 1988, letter from Cook to Duffy (NAA: B1387 87/720 PART 4).

[144] 1 June 1988, letter from Keating to Duffy (NAA: B1387 87/720 PART 4).

exceptions were the revenue share and anti-subsidy provisions. On the former, there was no prospect of achieving a "specific percentage share". As claimant cohesion fell away, the United Kingdom, Australia's strongest ally, "made clear to us that, given the other elements of the final package which is emerging, they would accept compromise". Anti-subsidy objectives were equally fraught: other claimants were "leaving the running to us, and most seemed ready to compromise".[145] Australia was isolated and holding up the convention. The United Kingdom and the United States pressured Australia to rely on reference to the issues in the Final Act. It was later observed by the New Zealand delegation that "'the US and British dug Brook, the Australian lawyer, a hole and he jumped into it' while Tormey (the Australian Treasury representative) 'stayed in the wings'".[146]

It was over. Three hours after receiving Keating's letter, and with no time for further consultation, Foreign Affairs confirmed the delegation's final instructions.[147] Whether the delegation was delighted, disappointed or despondent is not recorded—but divided it certainly was. It was suggested that inefficient liaison had delayed resolving departmental and ministers' views.[148] In any event, it was far too late to change course. The following day, 2 June 1988, the Convention on the Regulation of Antarctic Mineral Resource Activities was adopted by consensus.[149] The Final Act was signed, and the Convention itself would open for signature on 25 November that year.[150] Two Australian ministers celebrated the result.[151] And, according to the media, so began the start of "history's slowest gold rush".[152]

[145] 31 May 1988, WL33571 "Antarctic minerals: 12th session: Report no 14—revenue sharing and anti-subsidy" (NAA: B1387 87/720 PART 5).

[146] Tormey, the Treasury representative, appeared particularly dissatisfied with the outcome. Templeton, *A Wise Adventure II: New Zealand and Antarctica after 1960*, 219–20.

[147] 1 June 1988, CE548211 "Antarctic minerals negotiations: Instructions to delegation" (NAA: B1387 87/720 PART 5).

[148] 6 June 1988, DASETT brief to minister "Antarctic minerals convention negotiations" (NAA: B1387 87/720 PART 5).

[149] "Convention on the Regulation of Antarctic Mineral Resource Activities". Antarctic Treaty, *Final Report of the Fourth Special Antarctic Treaty Consultative Meeting on Antarctic Mineral Resources* (Ministry of Foreign Affairs (Wellington), 1988), 43–109.

[150] *Final Report of the Fourth Special Antarctic Treaty Consultative Meeting on Antarctic Mineral Resources*, 36–42.

[151] 2 June 1988, Minister for Foreign Affairs and Trade, news release "Antarctic minerals convention" (NAA: B1387 89/311 PART 1). The release quotes the Acting Foreign Minister Duffy and the Environment Minister Richardson.

[152] 4 June 1988, Peter Ward "South to Antarctica, south the race is on" *Weekend Australian*, 3.

Adoption of CRAMRA appeared to have settled an issue that had not been addressed during the Treaty negotiations, and which had taken innumerable discussions over the 18 years since 1970. A major gap in the Antarctic Treaty System had been filled and mining, if it ever occurred, could be managed by agreed regulations. The compromises embodied in CRAMRA had not appeased everybody, however, and the new-found consensus would be short-lived.

REFERENCES

Antarctic and Southern Ocean Coalition. "Antarctic Minerals Regime: Beeby's Slick Solution." *ECO* XXIII, no. 1, 11–22 July 1983 (1983).

———. "Beeby II: On the Right Track? But in the Wrong Direction?". *ECO* XXVIII, no. 2, 22–31 May 1984 (1984): 4–6.

———. "Let's Hear It for an Antarctic Treaty Park." *ECO* XXXXI, no. 2, 19 May 1987 (1987).

Antarctic Treaty. *Final Report of the Fourth Special Antarctic Treaty Consultative Meeting on Antarctic Mineral Resources.* Ministry of Foreign Affairs (Wellington), 1988.

———. *Report of the Twelfth Consultative Meeting, Canberra, 13-27 September 1983.* Australian Government Publishing Service, 1983.

Antarctic Treaty System: An Assessment. National Academy Press, 1986.

Barnes, James N, and Eliot Porter. *Let's Save Antarctica!* Greenhouse Publications, 1982.

Behrendt, John C. "Are There Petroleum Resources in Antarctica?". In *Antarctic Politics and Marine Resources,* edited by Lewis M Alexander and Lynne Carter Hanson, 191–202: University of Rhode Island, 1985.

Bowden, Tim. *The Silence Calling: Australians in Antarctica 1947–1997.* Allen & Unwin, 1997.

Buckman, Greg. *Tasmania's Wilderness Battles: A History.* Allen & Unwin, 2008.

"Convention on the Regulation of Antarctic Mineral Resource Activities." https://documents.ats.aq/recatt/Att311_e.pdf.

Evans, Gareth. "The Background Politics of the Tasmanian Dam Case." In *The Tasmanian Dam Case 30 Years On,* edited by Michael Coper, Heather Roberts and James Stellios, 11–15: Federation Press, 2017.

Garrett, John N. "The Economics of Antarctic Oil." In *Antarctic Politics and Marine Resources,* edited by Lewis M Alexander and Lynne Carter Hanson, 185–90: University of Rhode Island, 1985.

Haward, M G, and D Mason. "Australia, the United Nations and the Question of Antarctica." Chap. 9 In *Australia and the Antarctic Treaty System: 50 Years of Influence,* edited by Marcus Haward and Tom Griffiths, 201–21: UNSW Press, 2011.

Husseiny, A A, ed. *Iceberg Utilization*: Pergamon, 1978.
May, John, ed. *The Greenpeace Book of Antarctica*: Child & Associates, 1988.
Orrego Vicuña, Francisco, ed. *Antarctic Resources Policy: Scientific Legal and Political Issues*: Cambridge University Press, 1983.
Robson, Lloyd. *A History of Tasmania (Volume 2)*. Oxford University Press, 1991.
Schwerdtfeger, Peter. "On Icebergs and Their Uses." *Cold Regions Science and Technology* 1, no. 1 (1979): 59–79.
Senate Standing Committee on National Resources. "The Natural Resources of the Australian Antarctic Territory." AGPS, 1985.
Stokke, Olav Schram, and Davor Vidas, eds. *Governing the Antarctic*: Cambridge University Press, 1996.
Templeton, Malcolm. *A Wise Adventure II: New Zealand and Antarctica after 1960*. Victoria University Press, 2017.
Tepper, Rohan, and Marcus Haward. "The Development of Malaysia's Position on Antarctica: 1982 to 2004." *Polar Record* 41, no. 2 (2005): 113–24.
Whiticar, M J, E Suess, and H Wehner. "Thermogenic Hydrocarbons in Surface Sediments of the Bransfield Strait, Antarctic Peninsula." *Nature* 314, no. 6006 (1985): 87–90.
Wilderness: Celebrating Australia's Protected Places. The Wilderness Society Tasmania, 2018.
Wolfrum, Rüdiger, and Klaus Bockslaff, eds. *Antarctic Challenge: Conflicting Interests, Cooperation, Environmental Protection, Economic Development: Proceedings of an Interdisciplinary Symposium, June 22nd–24th, 1983*: Duncker & Humblot, 1984.

CHAPTER 4

Doubts About CRAMRA: June 1988 to May 1989

CRAMRA: A Legal Triumph

The date 2 June 1988 may have triggered "history's slowest gold rush", but it also triggered recriminations. The Australian delegation's disappointment was obvious. Greenpeace commented that "some countries had been bludgeoned into the agreement", singling out Australia.[1] The delegation reported that it "found itself alone against a strong onslaught ... Australia can be said to be one of the least satisfied delegations, a perception widely acknowledged".[2] Nevertheless, Chris Beeby's exhortation to find "a result that is tolerable to all" had found a result.

Tolerability, however, fell well short of satisfaction. This was apparent even as the CRAMRA was adopted. Only nine delegations gave closing speeches. Despite relief at ending a five-week meeting and six years of negotiation, celebration was subdued. Many praised Beeby; others were curt.[3] Several mentioned sensitivities like sovereignty, the area of application and liability. With an irony not realised until a year later, France was particularly forthcoming: Jean-Pierre Puissochet observed that

---

[1] 3 June 1988, Murray Williams "Beeby says Antarctic convention historic" *The Dominion* (New Zealand), 3.

[2] March 1989, "Report of the Australian Delegation to the 12th and Final Session of the Antarctic Minerals Negotiations" (NAA: B1387 88/893 PART 2), 3.

[3] Antarctic Treaty, *Final Report of the Fourth Special Antarctic Treaty Consultative Meeting on Antarctic Mineral Resources*, 9.

CRAMRA had "the invaluable effect of strengthening the sense of solidarity between our States. Nothing is more fortunate, and nothing is more promising". As if to emphasise the coming drama, France hoped that CRAMRA would "enter very shortly into force and, consequently, that the period which separates us from its application is as short as possible".[4] Australia did not speak.[5]

CRAMRA was a stunning achievement for Beeby who had invested in diplomacy with remarkable energy. It was also a win for New Zealand, being appointed the Convention's Depositary government and promised the permanent headquarters of the Antarctic Mineral Resources Commission.[6] Advantages for others were less clear. Perhaps a hallmark of consensus was that dissatisfaction appeared equally distributed. Australia reported its disappointments with surprising frankness, criticising "constant disruption [and] emotive outbursts" from one delegate; inflexibility by another; the "irrelevant nuisance" of others and "persistent and obtrusive" attitudes. Equanimity appeared entirely absent, and that was before addressing concerns about the actual substance of what had just agreed.[7]

CRAMRA was nevertheless a legal triumph over political differences.[8] Part of its success was relegating some matters to the Convention's institutions or future discussion. The Convention embodied important principles and detailed prescriptions for achieving them: a priority for environment protection; rules on liability and compliance; an integrated system of decision-making institutions to regulate activities; dispute settlement and arbitration mechanisms.[9] Put it this way: while not perfect,

---

[4] ibid., 8. France appeared keener to support mining than claimant interests. Templeton, *A Wise Adventure II: New Zealand and Antarctica after 1960*, 179.

[5] 3 June 1988, WL33610 "Antarctic minerals: 12th session—report no 18—final plenary" (NAA: B1387 87/720 PART 5).

[6] "Convention on the Regulation of Antarctic Mineral Resource Activities", Art 20(5).

[7] March 1989, "Report of the Australian Delegation to the 12th and Final Session of the Antarctic Minerals Negotiations" (NAA: B1387 88/893 PART 2), 7–8.

[8] Christopher C. Joyner, "The Effectiveness of CRAMRA," in *Governing the Antarctic*, ed. Olav Schram Stokke and Davor Vidas (Cambridge University Press, 1996).

[9] CRAMRA's operation is assessed in: Bush, *Antarctica and International Law: A Collection of Inter-State and National Documents (Looseleaf Volumes)*, Vol III, Booklets AL88D and AL88E. Christopher Beeby, "The Convention on the Regulation of Antarctic Mineral Resource Activities" speech presented to International Bar Association, Auckland, 13 October 1988 (NAA: B1387 88/893 PART 2). Peter J. Beck, "Convention on the Regulation of Antarctic Mineral Resource Activities: A Major Addition to the Antarctic Treaty System," *Polar Record* 25, no. 152 (1989). A. D. Watts, "The Convention on the

CRAMRA was not as bad as its critics portrayed. Given the legal and political issues, and the difficulties and compromises of the negotiations (captured with clarity in delegation reporting), its conclusion was a significant achievement. Australia proudly reported its injection of stringent environmental provisions.[10]

Even on environmental measures there were problems, most notably liability on which differences "were so severe that ... achievement of a Convention appeared in doubt". That issue was deferred to future negotiations. However, anti-subsidy measures were not. Australia's concerns were "restated frequently in the intensive last hours of the 'crunch'" (overnight negotiations on 30 and 31 May 1988), but "Australia was increasingly isolated". The revenue sharing provision was "well outside the parameters of the delegation's instructions" leaving Australia "very disappointed and with a need to carefully review its attitudes".[11] The Environment Department attributed such outcomes not to the difficult negotiations, but to departmental differences that "prevented the delegation from obtaining better results".[12] Beeby's colleague Gerard van Bohemen was more frank, suggesting that "problems within the Australian delegation had been responsible for lack of greater success" and that one had colluded with environmentalists.[13]

Regulation of Antarctic Mineral Resource Activities 1988," *The International and Comparative Law Quarterly* 39, no. 1 (1990). Rüdiger Wolfrum, *The Convention on the Regulation of Antarctic Mineral Resources Activities: An Attempt to Break New Ground* (Springer-Verlag, 1991). Wang, *International Law on Antarctic Mineral Resource Exploitation*, 98–131.

[10] 18 November 1988, "Antarctic minerals negotiations: Achievement of objectives" (NAA: B1387 88/893 PART 1).

[11] March 1989, "Report of the Australian Delegation to the 12th and Final Session of the Antarctic Minerals Negotiations" (NAA: B1387 88/893 PART 2), 74.

[12] 6 June 1988, DASETT brief to minister "Antarctic minerals convention negotiations" (NAA: B1387 87/720 PART 5).

[13] 23 October 1988, Roger Frankel (handwritten notes) "Points arising from discussion with Gerard van Bohemen" (NAA: B1387 88/893 PART 1).

JUNE TO NOVEMBER 1988: MINISTERIAL CORRESPONDENCE

Some Australian delegates carried their disappointments back to Canberra. The robust correspondence between ministers in the negotiation's final days flared again and lasted for weeks.[14] Channelling incensed officials, Treasurer Paul Keating wrote to Acting Foreign Minister Michael Duffy: "I stressed the need to stand firm [but] we have in effect ceded our economic claims over the AAT for virtually nothing". He regretted the "undue haste to agree to the adoption of the Convention", adding that "we need to think seriously before signing the Convention as it currently stands".[15] Resources Minister Peter Cook chimed in, complaining that "we should have made a stronger effort in the closing stages of the negotiations" and that, contrary to understandings "agreed on the evening of 1 June", the delegation did not reserve its position on revenue sharing and anti-subsidy provisions. "We gave away too much, too soon, with little if any real return and the price of consensus was a high one", he said, adding prophetically that "it is by no means certain that this is the direction that Cabinet will wish to go".[16] Cook even mounted a seemingly counter-intuitive environmental argument for not signing, suggesting that anti-subsidy measures "would have prevented uneconomic and, therefore, unnecessary mining".[17]

Foreign Minister Hayden replied that CRAMRA's claimant protections did not fail Australia, and, if Australia objected, the moratorium might collapse further risking sovereign interests. Despite having signed the Final Act, Hayden accepted "the need to think seriously before signing" the Convention itself and thought it not "necessary for Australia to be among the first to sign".[18] While "not entirely satisfactory" to *any* Party, CRAMRA had to be seen in the wider context of protecting the Treaty itself. Optimistically, Hayden invited a "best guess on when the first

---

[14] The 22 letters are catalogued in: 18 November 1988 "Summary of correspondence between ministers on CRAMRA" (NAA: B1387 88/893 PART 1).

[15] 6 June 1988, letter from Keating to Duffy (NAA: B1387 88/893 PART 2).

[16] 20 June 1988, letter from Cook to Hayden (NAA: B1387 88/893 PART 1). The tone of inter-ministerial letters reflected the views of the officials who had been delegates and prepared them. This may explain why the delegation report itself makes no mention of those views—all departments involved would have been expected to sign off on it.

[17] 20 June 1988, letter from Cook to Richardson (NAA: B1387 87/720 PART 4).

[18] 20 June 1988, letter from Hayden to Keating (NAA: B1387 87/720 PART 5).

application to open an area could be expected [to] assist Cabinet in determining its attitude to signature".[19]

The Convention would open for signature from 25 November 1988, but the IDC could not agree when to approach Cabinet. Keating and Cook retained deep reservations about claimant rights.[20] Environmentalists objected to CRAMRA, although for obviously different reasons.[21] With officials not placated, Cook sought an early decision not to sign, arguing with remarkable understatement that rejection of CRAMRA would have "a very strong impact on the deliberations of other Treaty Parties" and might dissuade others from signing.[22] On 21 September, Keating wrote to Gareth Evans (who three weeks earlier had replaced Hayden as Foreign Minister). Keating echoed Cook's views in a strongly worded letter decrying CRAMRA's failures on anti-subsidy and revenue sharing. He argued that Australia should "attempt further to negotiate provisions that better protect our national interests" because it was "forfeiting our sovereignty over Antarctica".[23]

It could be assumed that Cook and Keating were of one mind in objecting to CRAMRA. If so, it did not last long. A few days later, on 30 September, Keating was in Paris. French Prime Minister Michel Rocard raised environmental issues with Keating, who, it was later revealed, expressed his "personal view that Antarctica should be a national park", which was taken to mean "an environmentally protected zone".[24] It is not known precisely when Keating considered arguing against CRAMRA on environmental grounds. It was certainly not in his letter to Evans the previous week.[25] A recent biography on Keating recounts an 'Antarctica deal' done with Rocard at their September 1988 meeting, and that his environmental views were against his officials' advice.[26] Records examined for this book provide no indication that his officials or ministerial colleagues were aware of his environmental view at that time or, if they were aware, why

[19] 4 July 1988, letter from Hayden to Cook (NAA: B1387 88/893 PART 1).
[20] 29 July 1988, DASETT minute "Antarctic minerals convention" (NAA: B1387 87/720 PART 6).
[21] 23 June 1988, Andrew Darby "Hazards ahead in Antarctica" *The Age*, 11.
[22] 10 August 1988, letter from Cook to Hayden (NAA: B1387 88/893 PART 1).
[23] 21 September 1988, letter from Keating to Evans (AU-ATADD-1-BB-AU-193).
[24] Bramston, *Paul Keating: The Big Picture Leader*, 317–19.
[25] 16 November 1988, facsimile DFAT to Antarctic Division "Summary of outstanding correspondence" (NAA: B1387 88/893 PART 1).
[26] Bramston, *Paul Keating: The Big Picture Leader*, 318–19.

they had not reacted to it. His views were not public until April 1989, three weeks before Cabinet met to decide on CRAMRA.[27] Whatever their motives for opposing CRAMRA, unfortunately for Cook and Keating support for CRAMRA among other Parties was growing.

In September 1988, a review conference on the seals convention was held in London along with SATCM VIII to consider applications for Consultative Party status. Sweden and Spain were successful, allowing a last-minute chance to automatically become members of the Antarctic Mineral Resources Commission.[28] A 'round-table' discussion on attitudes to CRAMRA was called, designed to pressure Australia to commit although "if this was the intention it backfired as Australia spoke early and noncommittally". Even Greenpeace no longer argued against signature of CRAMRA, only against its eventual ratification as it would be at that point that the convention became operative.[29]

In October 1988, Cook raised concerns again: this time with Evans, who, as previous Resources Minister, might be sympathetic. Cook recycled the words he had used to Bill Hayden in June: "we gave away too much with little, if any, real return" and CRAMRA should not be signed "in its present form".[30] In New Zealand, Chris Beeby emphasised CRAMRA's environmental provisions, reiterating his refrain of tolerance and cooperation.[31] Such soothing did little to assuage Australian officials still smarting from June. Foreign Affairs thought CRAMRA the best compromise achievable and Attorney-General's lauded it as "the best ever framework agreement in respect of environmental protection". While Graham Richardson and Michael Duffy praised CRAMRA, Keating and Cook held "the faint hope of reopening negotiations". In addition, there was a commitment to table CRAMRA in Parliament to stimulate public discussion.[32] It was time to decide, but there was agreement only to defer

---

[27] This became known to ministers in April 1989. See 27 April 1989, letter from Keating to Hawke (AU-ATADD-1-BB-AU-196). It was publicly revealed a few days later—see 30 April 1989, Alan Fewster "Antarctic park finds an ally in Keating" *Sunday Telegraph*, 122.

[28] "Convention on the Regulation of Antarctic Mineral Resource Activities," Art 18.

[29] September 1988, "Report of the Australian Delegation, 8th Special Antarctic Consultative Meeting" (AAD: B13/198).

[30] 11 October 1988, letter from Cook to Evans (NAA: B1387 88/893 PART 1).

[31] 13 October 1988, Christopher Beeby "The Convention on the Regulation of Antarctic Mineral Resource Activities", speech to International Bar Association, Auckland (NAA: B1387 88/893 PART 2).

[32] 17 October 1988, draft submission to Foreign Minister Senator Evans (NAA: B1387 88/893 PART 1).

the decision. As Evans explained to Cook and Keating, a Cabinet decision just four weeks before the November signing ceremony would not influence other parties as "a number of them are poised to sign". Furthermore, Cabinet consideration should come *after* tabling of the Convention.[33] Cook and Keating reluctantly accepted that nothing else could happen without community consultation.[34]

The government did not need to trigger public discussion. While environmentalists welcomed the Convention's tough environmental provisions, their public position was to object—in their view, CRAMRA's mere existence encouraged mining.[35] ASOC catalogued the flaws and welcomed the prospect of re-opened negotiations.[36] The ACF's Phillip Toyne demanded Australia not sign. Graham Richardson said he was personally against mining.[37] Nevertheless, even though it was "far from perfect", he was inclined to support signature despite describing CRAMRA as unenforceable and "the whole thing is bullshit anyway".[38] Whether Richardson meant that CRAMRA was fake, a falsehood or misleading is unclear.[39] Coprological aversions aside, Richardson was potentially receptive to environmental options. It is therefore odd that AAD's 18 November update to the Environment Minister did not mention Keating's environmental views, of which it had been made aware two days before.[40] However, a leak

---

[33] 21 October 1988, letters from Evans to Cook [and] from Evans to Keating (NAA: B1387 88/893 PART 1).

[34] 26 October 1988, letter from Cook to Evans [and] 3 November 1988, letter from Keating to Evans (NAA: B1387 88/893 PART 1).

[35] 18 November 1988, DASETT (Antarctic Division) submission to minister "Convention on the Regulation of Antarctic Mineral Resource Activities" (NAA: B1387 88/893 PART 1). Others, however, thought that CRAMRA *discouraged* mining—see 2 December 1988, Patricia Birnie "Antarctica" (Ditchley Park Conference Report No D88/15) (AU-ATADD-5-BB-GE-443), 4.

[36] 29 October 1988, ASOC Information Paper 1988-4 "Analysis of the Convention on the Regulation of Antarctic Mineral Resource Activities" (AU-ATADD-5-BB-GE-364), 1–7. 21 November 1988, Greenpeace International "An appeal to the United Nations" (AU-ATADD-5-BB-GE-365).

[37] 20 October 1988, Ross Peake "No Antarctic mining plans: Richardson" *The Age*, p 21.

[38] 11 November 1988, "Antarctic Minerals Convention", unofficial transcript of meeting between Richardson and Peak Conservation Organisations (NAA: B1387 88/893 PART 2).

[39] Harry G. Frankfurt, *On Bullshit* (Princeton University Press, 2005).

[40] 16 November 1988, facsimile DFAT to Antarctic Division "Summary of outstanding correspondence" (NAA: B1387 88/893 PART 1). 18 November 1988, DASETT (Antarctic Division) submission to minister "Convention on the Regulation of Antarctic Mineral Resource Activities" (NAA: B1387 88/893 PART 1).

of Keating's letter to Evans thrust the differing ministerial opinions into public view.[41] Liberal Opposition MP Warwick Smith condemned government disunity, citing the contradictions between statements made at CRAMRA's adoption and the contents of Keating's letter, and accusing the government of secrecy.[42] The leaked correspondence triggered alarm in New Zealand, where Foreign Minister Russell Marshall expressed surprise at Keating's objections. With some understatement, Marshall said, "New Zealand would be pretty disappointed if Australia decided not to sign". ASOC's Cath Wallace suggested that Keating's objections "stemmed directly from Australia's resentment at the way it was treated at the Convention talks in June".[43] None of this hinted at Keating's environmental motives—on the contrary, it was presented as concern about Australia's economic interests.

November 1988: CRAMRA Open for Signature, Open for Discussion

On 22 November, CRAMRA was tabled in Parliament.[44] Evans emphasised that it would not encourage mining but put "a legal framework in place in advance of any pressures" to start, and establish arrangements "to protect the fragile Antarctic environment". He also noted Australia's objective "to derive possible economic benefits from the living and non-living resources of the AAT". Tabling CRAMRA, he said, was "to promote community discussion".[45] It did. Independent Senator Jo Vallentine immediately moved that the government support a world park.[46]

Things were moving fast. On Friday that week, 25 November 1988, CRAMRA opened for signature in Wellington. Marshall sought to dispel

[41] 21 November 1988, Mike Seccombe "Keating warns against signing Antarctic treaty" *Sydney Morning Herald*, 2.

[42] 22 November 1988, Warwick Smith media release "Antarctic minerals policy: Who's in charge? Abysmal government performance" (NAA: B1387 88/893 PART 1).

[43] 23 November 1988, WL35185 "Antarctica: Mineral resources convention" (NAA: B1387 88/893 PART 1). The cable provides the text of an article "Surprise at Keating Treaty opposition" in *The Dominion* (New Zealand).

[44] 22 November 1988, House of Representatives Hansard, 2935-2936; and Senate Hansard, 2476.

[45] 22 November 1988, Minister for Foreign Affairs and Trade news release M200 "Antarctic minerals convention" (NAA: B1387 88/893 PART 1).

[46] 23 November 1988, Senate Hansard, 2578.

fears that CRAMRA opened Antarctica for mining. On the contrary, by filling the "gap in the Treaty system", it would avoid "an unregulated scramble for resources", and CRAMRA was "the best protection for the Treaty system".[47] It was open for signature for one year, after which a state could accede.[48] Nine signed immediately.[49] France almost did—their Ambassador had Full Powers to sign, but an unexplained "departmental hitch" intervened.[50] However, five months later the hitch made it very much easier for France to step back from CRAMRA.

Evans explained that Australia had not signed because "there are different views within the Australian community [but] we will be considering our position, sooner rather than later".[51] Seemingly unaware of this, Australia's permanent representative to the UN, Michael Costello, was giving CRAMRA a rousing defence.[52] Graham Richardson, meanwhile, thought that Cabinet consideration was not urgent and there was "little to be achieved by continuing correspondence between ministers".[53] Not dissuaded, Peter Cook wrote again, asking for a decision by February 1989.[54] The situation was further complicated by US objections to Australian adventurer Dick Smith's audacious Twin Otter flight to the South Pole carrying Greenpeace activists campaigning for a world park.[55] Adding pressure was another Senate motion, this time from Democrats Senator

[47] 25 November 1988, Opening address by Hon Russell Marshall (NAA: B1387 88/893 PART 1).

[48] The benefit of signature (rather than accession) was automatic membership of the Antarctic Mineral Resources Commission.

[49] The Parties that signed on 25 November 1988 were Brazil, Finland, New Zealand, Norway, Sweden, South Africa, South Korea, the USSR and Uruguay. The United States signed separately on 30 November 1988. See https://www.mfat.govt.nz/en/about-us/who-we-are/treaties/convention-on-the-regulation-of-antarctic-mineral-resource-activities/ (accessed 3 February 2021).

[50] Templeton, *A Wise Adventure II: New Zealand and Antarctica after 1960*, 226. 'Full Powers' is the authority granted to officials to legally commit the state to a treaty-level agreement.

[51] 28 November 1988, Senate Hansard, 2967.

[52] 28 November 1988, Sue Neales "Treaty members carve up Antarctic" Financial Review, 13.

[53] 30 November 1988, letters from Richardson to Evans and from Richardson to Cook (NAA: B1387 88/893 PART 2).

[54] 16 December 1988, letter from Cook to Richardson (NAA: B1387 88/893 PART 2).

[55] 25 November 1988, press release "Greenpeace visits South Pole station" (AAD: 84/360-2). The US Antarctic Program reacted that "Australia could not be trusted": 1 December 1988 "Report of events in McMurdo area" (AAD: 84/360-1).

Jean Jenkins proposing an unambiguously intended, but awkwardly titled, "Antarctic Conservation Zone World Wilderness Park".[56] In contrast, the Opposition's Warwick Smith strongly favoured signing.[57]

JANUARY 1989: ANTARCTIC PROBLEMS

Year 1989 would be momentous, not just for Australia's coming decision, but for the future of the Treaty itself. For the AAD, it started with a simple request, but with an odd twist. Richardson's office requested briefing on "the implications of Australia not signing the minerals convention" but that, contrary to normal bureaucratic procedure, AAD "*not* contact DFAT in preparing the paper".[58] On 27 January, the advice outlined the risks of not signing: international credibility would suffer; sovereignty would be weakened; relations with New Zealand would be harmed; UN interest would increase; any replacement regime might not require Australian signature; the moratorium could collapse; and a new convention could be environmentally weaker.[59]

As if to underscore the environmental risk, immediately after lunch the following day, and just as the AAD's advice landed in the minister's office, Argentine Antarctic resupply vessel *Bahia Paraiso* ran aground near Anvers Island. Two days later, at 21:53 on 31 January, the 131 m ship capsized spilling 675,000 litres of fuel and oil into Antarctic waters, killing thousands of seabirds and other marine organisms.[60] Over 300 passengers and crew were evacuated to Palmer Station while a futile attempt was made to contain the spill.[61] It was a timely warning of navigation risks, environmental

---

[56] 30 November 1988, Senate Hansard, 3141. 30 November 1988, media release "Don't lock out science from the Antarctic: Democrats" (NAA: B1387 88/893 PART 1).

[57] 18 January 1989, Warwick Smith letter to the editor "Mining the Antarctic" *The Mercury*, 14.

[58] 4 January 1989, Antarctic Division internal memorandum "Minerals Convention" (NAA: B1387 88/893 PART 2).

[59] 27 January 1989, Antarctic Division minute to ministerial adviser Michael Crawford "Convention on the Regulation of Antarctic Mineral Resource Activities" (NAA: B1387 88/893 PART 2).

[60] May 1989, Argentine document informally circulated at the XV ATCM Preparatory Meeting "Report on the sinking of the Argentine polar ship ARA *Bahia Paraiso*" (AU-ATADD-1-BB-AR-377), part 1. "Argentine Ship Sinks near Palmer Station," *Antarctic Journal of the United States* XXIV, no. 2 (1989). Mahlon C. Kennicutt, "Oil Spillage in Antarctica," *Environmental Science & Technology* 24, no. 5 (1990).

[61] Dave Gallas, *The Last Voyage of the Bahia Paraiso* (Blurb, 2015).

consequences and public alarm. The wreck is still there as a solemn reminder. And this was just the beginning.

Nervousness escalated on 7 February when *HMS Endurance* collided with ice near Deception Island, and alarm bells rang again when Peru's Antarctic ship *BIC Humboldt* struck rocks off King George Island on 28 February.[62] That no pollutants escaped from those two events hardly mattered. The incidents just amplified the chorus criticising France's Dumont d'Urville airstrip and the United Kingdom's Rothera runway;[63] scientists campaigning against CRAMRA;[64] and Greenpeace protests at McMurdo.[65]

Meanwhile, momentum towards CRAMRA continued—by mid-March 1989, there were twelve signatories. In Canberra, buoyed by Australian Mining Industry Council support, Evans wrote that "on balance, signature will best serve Australia's overall interests".[66] In London, the Foreign and Commonwealth Office (FCO) was busy preparing for UK signature and, "God and politics willing", legislation to ratify by mid-year. John Heap was also preparing for May's Preparatory Meeting for the October ATCM. In a letter to the so-called 'Correspondents' Group', he reported that, prompted by *Bahia Paraiso*'s loss, Chile would propose a conference on "international cooperation to conserve the Antarctic environment". Heap also alluded to the French airstrip and Greenpeace activism, but made no connection to CRAMRA.[67] Media made that connection. On 20 March, the prime-time ABC *Four Corners* investigative program broadcast 'Frozen Assets', drawing graphic attention to the minerals debate.[68] It had

[62] 1 March 1989 "Research ship leaking oil in the Antarctic" *The Advocate*, 13. 6 March 1989, TPN Embassy of Peru "Report on the mishap of the Peruvian ship *BIC Humboldt* in Antarctica" (NAA: B1387 1981/468).

[63] 20 January 1989, PA72164 and CE66173 "Antarctica: French airstrip construction" (AAD: 81/346-3). "Britain Plans New Antarctic Airstrip," *New Scientist* 121, no. 1648 (1989).

[64] 20 February 1989 "Scientists urge Antarctic ban on minerals" *Canberra Times*, 2.

[65] 24 February 1989 "A chilly protest on pollution" *Sydney Morning Herald*, 9.

[66] 8 March 1989, letter from Australian Mining Industry Council to Evans (NAA: B1387 88/893 PART 2). 13 March 1989, letters from Evans to Keating and from Evans to Cook (NAA: B1387 88/893 PART 2).

[67] 17 March 1989, letter from John Heap, UK Foreign and Commonwealth Office "XVth Antarctic Treaty Consultative Meeting (NAA: B1387 88/352). The Correspondents' Group comprised representatives of Australia, Federal Republic of Germany, New Zealand, Norway, the United Kingdom and the United States. Letters were addressed by Heap to 'colleagues'.

[68] http://www.abc.net.au/4corners/frozen-asset%2D%2D-1989/2842018 (accessed 3 February 2021).

sent journalist Tony Jones and producer Martin Butler to Antarctica and, as it turned out, to powerful effect.

Meanwhile, officials were iterating drafts of a Cabinet submission on CRAMRA. Without revealing it had already briefed Richardson, AAD advised Department of Foreign Affairs and Trade (DFAT) on the consequences of not signing.[69] By 23 March, DFAT's draft submission was well developed. It recommended signing CRAMRA but deferring ratification. The proposed media release had Evans and Richardson jointly announcing signature.[70] Cook was unimpressed, adamant that Australia not sign. He rejected the submission as unbalanced and, despite 15 explanatory attachments, not fully canvassing the issues. Unlike in December, he now sought *deferral* of a decision pending "a series of comprehensive Cabinet Memoranda on each of these issues". He again argued that "we have consistently underestimated and underplayed our natural negotiating leverage ... we should use it" to extract concessions from others.[71] Evans' rebuttal was prompt. Three more claimants had signed, taking the total to 15—close to the minimum required for entry into force.[72] Evans thought re-opening negotiations "would be legally dangerous", and he saw no value in further exchanges: "the remaining differences need to be resolved in Cabinet soon".[73] Ministerial views seemed counter-intuitive: the Environment Minister wanted to sign a convention that allowed access to minerals in Antarctica; the Resources Minister wanted access to minerals but did not want to sign the Convention that allowed it. Evans' wish that Cabinet resolve the issue would eventually be satisfied, but on the other side of the planet, a completely unexpected calamity of unimaginable consequence had just occurred.

MARCH 1989: ARCTIC PROBLEMS

Joseph Hazelwood had a cordial rendezvous with some colleagues, went shopping, bought a pizza and took a taxi to the port of Valdez. Some four hours later, at nine minutes past midnight on Friday 24 March 1989, his

---

[69] 21 February 1989, facsimile message Antarctic Division to DFAT (NAA: B1387 88/893 PART 3).
[70] 23 March 1989, draft submission for Cabinet "Antarctic minerals convention" (NAA: B1387 88/893 PART 3).
[71] 29 March 1989, letter from Cook to Evans (NAA: B1387 88/893 PART 2).
[72] The new signatories were Argentina, Chile and the United Kingdom.
[73] 12 April 1989, letter from Evans to Cook (NAA: B1387 88/893 PART 3).

whole workplace ground to a shuddering halt as *Exxon Valdez* foundered on Bligh Reef. It rather spoiled the Easter weekend of Captain Hazelwood, his overworked helmsman third mate Gregory Cousins, and his other 18 crew members. It also rather spoiled any further chance of calm discussion about hydrocarbon exploration in Antarctica because, by dawn, over 35 million litres of North Slope crude oil had escaped into Alaska's Prince William Sound.[74] Marine mammals, seabirds, fisheries and reputations were destroyed because the tanker had not been turned into the correct shipping lane. Concerns about the *Bahia Paraiso* impacts mingled with the waves created by the Alaska spill. Argentina protested that media and non-governmental reactions to its problems were "totally out of proportion with the real circumstances of the accident".[75] But it hardly mattered as Arctic and Antarctic disasters were conflated. Reporting of the *Exxon Valdez* slick swept around the world as the $US1.8 billion clean-up got underway. Graphic images ensured acute public alarm at the potential for polar pollution. Environment groups were to go on to make great Antarctic capital from what had happened in the Arctic.[76]

Anti-CRAMRA campaigning accelerated. Jacques Cousteau, lobbying in France, announced plans to confront Australian parliamentarians.[77] French Foreign Ministry officials were pushing for signature, but the Quai d'Orsay's Charley Causeret "painted a rather gloomy picture of the prospects" given the "well publicised (even if ill-informed) anti-minerals convention campaign led by Cousteau". This had increased with Greens successes in French municipal elections and their prospects in forthcoming European Parliamentary polls. Causeret saw part of the problem in CRAMRA's title: "it drew attention to 'emotive minerals exploitation ideas' rather than to the environmental measures." France was rapidly shifting "from 'it's just a matter of time before we sign' to a position of

---

[74] National Transportation Safety Board, "Grounding of US Tankship *Exxon Valdez* on Bligh Reef, Prince William Sound, near Valdez, Alaska, March 24 1989," *Marine Accident Report* NTSB/MAR-90/04 (1990). Alaska Oil Spill Commission, *Spill: The Wreck of the Exxon Valdez* (Oil Spill Public Information Center, 1990).

[75] May 1989, Argentine document informally circulated at the XV ATCM Preparatory Meeting "Report on the sinking of the Argentine polar ship ARA *Bahia Paraiso*" (AU-ATADD-1-BB-AR-377), part 2.

[76] 9 May 1989, ASOC Information Paper No 1 PREP ATCM XV/ASOC INF 1 "Implications of Alaskan oil spill for the Antarctic". 13 May 1989, Greenpeace paper "Second thoughts on CRAMRA" (AAD: B13/192-2).

[77] 3 April 1989, PA73483 "Antarctica and the Cousteau Foundation" (NAA: B1387 88/893 PART 2).

considerable doubt" about whether domestic politics made signature real-istic.[78] This signalled a significant challenge to French officials expecting to sign on 25 November. CRAMRA was at a crucial point. By then, the for-mula for its entry into force now only required participation by *both* Australia and France (as claimants) and *one* of either China or India (as developing states).[79]

Pressures grew in Australia. ALP Caucus Chair Bob Chynoweth cited *Exxon Valdez* to oppose CRAMRA.[80] In Parliament, Senator Vallentine moved a Matter of Urgency on a world park. Despite opposing mining, Graham Richardson still defended CRAMRA: "I, for one, would not like to be the person who started it all again."[81] His view that CRAMRA was the best way to protect the environment reflected Departmental advice.[82] Indeed, the draft Cabinet submission recommended signature for that very reason.[83] However, events in Paris made Australia's decision moot.

APRIL 1989: FRANCE HAS DOUBTS

In a televised interview on 20 April, French Prime Minister Michel Rocard revealed new thinking. Asked on TF1 program *Questions à Domicile* whether he would join 180,000 others in signing Cousteau's petition, he said, "France will not ratify the Treaty in its present state … negotiations must be re-opened." Causeret "did not disguise MFA's 'disappointment

[78] 6 April 1989, PA73569 "Antarctica: Minerals convention: French position" (NAA: B1387 88/893 PART 3).

[79] "Convention on the Regulation of Antarctic Mineral Resource Activities", Art 62. The status of signatures is at: https://www.mfat.govt.nz/en/about-us/who-we-are/treaties/convention-on-the-regulation-of-antarctic-mineral-resource-activities/ (accessed 3 February 2021).

[80] 6 April 1989, House of Representatives Hansard, 1088–1090. Chynoweth had an 'epiphany' in Antarctica the previous summer: Peter Garrett, "Speech to Commemorate the 20th Anniversary of the Hawke Government Initiative to Prevent Mining in Antarctica," (Australian National Maritime Museum, Sydney2009).

[81] 9 April 1989, transcript of Laurie Oakes' interview, National Nine Network (NAA: B1387 88/893 PART 3). 12 April 1989, Senate Hansard, 1424–1443.

[82] 12 April 1989, brief to minister's adviser "Minerals convention" (NAA: B1387 88/893 PART 3).

[83] 12 April 1989, Cabinet Submission "Antarctic minerals convention" (NAA: 14039, 6415).

and embarrassment' at Rocard's comments", and admitted that "Rocard did not know the Antarctic dossier very well, as evidenced by his confusion over 'ratification' and 'signature'". Causeret would recommend 'improvements' to CRAMRA, rather than 'renegotiation', and explain France's new position in the context of developments since CRAMRA's adoption.[84] These included *Exxon Valdez*, but the Dumont d'Urville runway controversy was also up in the air.[85] Adding confusion was a statement to the National Assembly by Thierry de Beauce, secretary of state for International Cultural Relations, which left open France's decision.

France was in an awkward position: it was to host the ATCM in October, starting with the May 1989 Preparatory Meeting. It would be highly unusual for a normally impartial host to preside over a controversy of its own making. French Foreign Ministry officials had been caught unprepared. "A sense of uncertainty and confusion" prevailed in Paris, and Quai d'Orsay official Georges Duquin confirmed that they were still considering Rocard's comments. However, the "reference to 'not ratifying the Treaty *in its current form*' at least gave the MFA something to work with".[86]

Greenpeace was also surprised by Rocard's announcement.[87] ASOC was thrilled—Cath Wallace said that the "sorry saga of the French airstrip is a very good example of why we shouldn't trust the Antarctic countries". She argued that CRAMRA should not be signed, public opinion had moved on and, besides, the moratorium was still in place. Unconvinced, New Zealand Foreign Minister Russell Marshall argued that, while not perfect, CRAMRA's "set of rules is better than no rules at all".[88]

Australian environmentalists considered Rocard's views unambiguous and increased pressure on the government.[89] Departmental officers trying to rationalise France's position suggested that Rocard's statements "do

[84] 21 April 1989, PA73883 "Minerals convention: French position" (NAA: B1387 88/893 PART 3). 20 April 1989 "Antarctic minerals convention: Rocard statement" (AU-ATADD-1-BB-FR-85).

[85] 22 April 1989, Andrew Darby "France calls for new negotiations on Antarctic treaty" *The Age*, 3.

[86] 26 April 1989, PA73944 "French attitude to minerals convention" (NAA: B1387 89/453 PART 1).

[87] 23 February 2020, "Saving Antarctica" *The History Hour* BBC World Service, https://www.bbc.co.uk/programmes/w3csypzz (accessed 6 April 2020), 1:20–10:20.

[88] 24 April 1989, transcript of radio program, Radio NZ *Good Morning NZ* (NAA: B1387 88/893 PART 3).

[89] 25 April 1989, Ross Peake and Andrew Darby "Richardson says no to mining in Antarctica" *The Age*, 6.

not appear to have been thought through" and were "in conflict with the official French position". France, they thought, would not outright veto CRAMRA, just call for stricter liability provisions.[90] New Zealand officials were "disappointed but not despondent", assuming "that Rocard was not very well briefed" and that after "some clarification of the French position" accession would follow.[91] Norway was "not too concerned about Rocard's statement" because re-opening negotiations "would be virtually impossible, as the French will discover".[92] Such optimism would soon evaporate. Decision time for Australia was approaching and opposition to CRAMRA hardening. By month's end, Graham Richardson had received 1793 letters, 2231 postcards and 21 petitions—all opposed.[93] The public campaign was mobilising.

April 1989: Australian Opposition

On 27 April, Paul Keating again wrote to Bob Hawke. Again he objected to CRAMRA, but this time added an entirely new element: the world park alternative. He wrote: "last October I met the French Prime Minister Michel Rocard, and outlined to him both Australia's policy at the time and my personal view of the minerals convention issue. Given all this, I believe we should consider carefully, but soon, the establishment of a world park or at least consider declaring Australia's territory a national park."[94] For some reason, Keating's letter to Hawke did not mention that he had suggested an environmental alternative to Rocard. That claim became public when Keating's world park option found its way into the media in an article based on a departmental official's discussion with a journalist.[95] The article reported that "Rocard thought this sounded like a good idea and that he would look at it [and that] Mr Keating will be briefing the Prime

[90] 24 April 1989, DASETT brief to David Tierney and Michael Crawford (Ministerial advisers) "Antarctic minerals convention—French position" (NAA: B1387 88/893 PART 3).
[91] 24 April 1989, WL36523 "Antarctic minerals convention: French position" (NAA: B1387 88/893 PART 3).
[92] 25 April 1989, ST24548 "Antarctica: Minerals convention: French position" (NAA: B1387 88/893 PART 3).
[93] April 1989, handwritten note to file (NAA: B1387 89/311 PART 1).
[94] 27 April 1989, letter from Keating to Hawke (AU-ATADD-1-BB-AU-196). The reference to a meeting in October 1988 is at odds with a later suggestion it was on 30 September—see Bramston, *Paul Keating: The Big Picture Leader*, 318.
[95] 23 June 2016, anonymous personal communication. The discussion sought to dispel misinformation being put out by competing departments.

Minister on his return" (there is no evidence that such a briefing occurred). The article took the lid off the still-simmering inter-departmental battles, reporting that Treasury and Resources accused DFAT of taking "too soft a line in the negotiations over the convention", maintaining "too tight a level of control", and not allowing other members of the delegation to speak. DFAT's defence was to accuse Resources officials of being "unwilling or unable to make concessions".[96]

Meanwhile, Opposition Leader John Howard had doubts about CRAMRA, citing his shock at the *Exxon Valdez* disaster. He appeared determined to prevent mining: "I'd need a very powerful reason to change my mind on that".[97] Graham Richardson suggested a way out: if France did not sign, then Australia wouldn't have to make up its mind.[98] Howard was more decisive. On 2 May, he declared, with his environment spokesperson Senator Chris Puplick, that Australia should not sign CRAMRA as "mineral activity in the Antarctic poses too great a risk". They called for "a convention to ban mining in Antarctica … we must not let this opportunity pass".[99] That day, an ACF rally in Canberra was addressed by Labor's Bob Chynoweth, the Liberals' Chris Puplick and Democrats Senator Norm Sanders. In the Senate, Puplick railed against government disharmony and pointed to Keating's world park proposal. Gareth Evans debunked the idea and defended CRAMRA as "the best way forward", despite acknowledging that "sovereignty claims are, in effect, continuing to be undermined". It was speculated that Cabinet would defer discussion until the heat from the Opposition cooled.[100] Australian media, however, kept alive the minerals issue and the greening of Keating.[101] Adding pressure to Bob Hawke were assertions that Keating was "attempting to take

[96] 30 April 1989, Alan Fewster "Antarctic park finds an ally in Keating" *Sunday Telegraph*, 122.

[97] 29 April 1989, Ross Peake "Antarctic mining a blue, says Howard, suddenly tingeing green" *The Age*, 3. 29 April 1989, "Look to greenies: Howard" *Canberra Times*, 2.

[98] 30 April 1989, Monitair transcript of SBS *News* (NAA: B1387 88/893 PART 3).

[99] 2 May 1989, media release Senator Chris Puplick, Shadow Minister for the Environment and Arts "Protection of the Antarctic and the climate of planet earth" (AU-ATADD-1-BB-AU-197).

[100] 3 May 1989, Senate Hansard, 1647–1669. 3 May 1989, Keith Scott "Antarctica in delay basket" *Canberra Times*, 4.

[101] 4 May 1989, Keith Scott "Keating backs world park for Antarctica" *Canberra Times*, 10. 5 May 1989, "Keating calls for 'world park' for Antarctica" *Sydney Morning Herald*, 6.

control of the Cabinet debate".[102] Writing to Hawke, Peter Cook used the French and Opposition positions to suggest again that additional factors be assessed, including the world park option which was not canvassed in the draft Cabinet submission.[103]

It was awkward enough having disagreements between ministers, but now the Prime Minister had the Opposition, Democrats and independent Senators wedging him on the environment. Quizzed by journalists, Hawke seemed defensive: "we are totally green, or totally white, as far as the Antarctic is concerned", he thundered, "don't try and conjure up a position that what we're going to have is the Liberals with the Democrats taking up a more appropriate environmental position than this Government. I mean, we haven't reached that peculiar state of affairs".[104] Perhaps Hawke had already made up his mind—it was reported that he was "totally opposed to mining in the Antarctic" after the leaking of Keating's letter calling for a world park.[105] Over the weekend, Foreign Affairs officers added a corrigendum to Evans' draft submission: it would now recommend that Australia "not sign the minerals convention at this stage".[106]

MAY 1989: A NEGATIVE REACTION MAY BE GENERATED

Meanwhile, four Australians were in Paris for the Preparatory Meeting to settle the October ATCM XV agenda. Delegation briefing included the potential for a conference to review the Treaty and instructions to discourage a review that risked "reopening dormant conflicts".[107] The irony was perhaps lost on the delegation whose own actions were shortly to run the risk of precipitating the reviled review. The briefing on minerals was laughably inadequate for what was to unfold. The instruction was simply to

[102] 5 May 1989, Ross Dunn "Hawke wavers on Antarctic treaty" *Australian Financial Review*, 5.
[103] 4 May 1989, letter Cook to Hawke (NAA: B1387 88/893 PART 3).
[104] 5 May 1989, CE712285 "Antarctica: Minerals convention" (NAA: B1387 88/893 PART 3).
[105] 5 May 1989, Susan Houweling "Hawke supports mining ban for fragile Antarctic" *The Australian*, 3.
[106] 7 May 1989, facsimile draft "Recommendations" (NAA: B1387 89/311 PART 1).
[107] "The Antarctic Treaty," https://documents.ats.aq/keydocs/vol_1/vol1_2_AT_Antarctic_Treaty_e.pdf. Art 12.2(a) provides for a possible review conference 30 years after the Treaty's entry into force of the Treaty, that is, any time after 23 June 1991. May 1989 "Brief for the Australian Delegation to the Preparatory Meeting for the XVth Antarctic Treaty Consultative Meeting, Paris, 9–13 May 1989" (AAD: B13/192-2), 9–10.

"ascertain intentions in respect of signature or ratification of CRAMRA …
clarification of the French position … and explain the current Australian
position".[108] It completely missed the point that there *was no* Australian
position: Cabinet consideration was still two weeks away. It also seemed
unaware that Hawke would commit to an environmental position.

On 8 May, Delegation Leader John Burgess received new instructions
by cable for his exclusive attention. He was to test the "likely reaction to
some alternative scenarios to straightforward signature and ratification, and
you are requested to circumspectly canvass opinion accordingly". The cable
pointed to the consequences of Michel Rocard's announcement—no longer would Australia be isolated if it chose not to sign. In addition, domestic
politics made signing unrealistic and passage of implementing legislation
impossible. The four alternative scenarios were to sign CRAMRA but use
Australia's veto to prevent an area being opened; reserve Australia's position until other options had been tested; not sign and, instead, pursue
a comprehensive environmental regime that would prohibit mining; and
finally, campaign for an Antarctic world park. The third option was preferred. Burgess was reassured: "we are very conscious of the negative reaction that may be generated by any suggestion that Australia may be about
to move away from positions already hard won, and you should emphasise
that your proposed discussions are exploratory only."[109] Whatever justifica-
tions were put forward, whatever scenarios canvassed and whatever reassurances offered, such circumlocution was the bureaucratic equivalent of
an exhortation to 'light the blue touchpaper and stand well back'. But no
amount of standing back would ameliorate the fireworks that were to erupt
during the course of the meeting and the diplomatic blowback that Burgess
endured when he proceeded to "circumspectly canvass" opinions. The predicted "negative reaction" was an understatement.[110]

Disdain towards Australia was not diluted by New Zealand Deputy
Prime Minister Geoffrey Palmer suggesting an environment protection
initiative.[111] Nor was it moderated by Chile describing Antarctica as an

[108] May 1989 "Brief for the Australian Delegation to the Preparatory Meeting for the XVth
Antarctic Treaty Consultative Meeting, Paris, 9–13 May 1989" (AAD: B13/192-2), 12.

[109] 8 May 1989, CH538155 "Antarctic minerals convention" (NAA: B1387 89/311
PART 1).

[110] Bowden, *The Silence Calling: Australians in Antarctica 1947–1997*, 413–14.

[111] 8 May 1989, transcript of interview, Radio New Zealand *Midday Report* (NAA: B1387
89/311 PART 1). 9 May 1989 "Palmer plans Antarctic treaty" *The Dominion* (New
Zealand).

"ecological natural park" and calling for "overall measures for the protection of the Antarctic environment".[112] The reason was simple: both proposals assumed CRAMRA's entry into force. Chile's paper, launched early in the meeting, gained enthusiastic support from the United Kingdom. John Heap said that the "Chilean proposal needs distinct attention, at a separate meeting, to do it justice". He suggested a SATCM in 1990 to consider it. Unsurprisingly, this appeared a tactic to defer environmental measures until *after* the deadline for signing CRAMRA as it would allow additional time for accessions and unstoppable momentum towards its entry into force.[113] France, as host, was peeved that Chile's initiative overshadowed its own ideas for an environment charter.[114] Burgess reported being "unable to obtain any very useful, or indeed coherent, statement of the current French thinking on CRAMRA", although Duquin's "bleak, probably personal, view" was that France would now drop any thought of signing and leave a decision on subsequent accession until progress had been made on CRAMRA's liability protocol. Once the heat from Burgess' efforts had subsided, his mid-meeting assessment was revealing: "after a flurry of intense interest in the possibilities of resolving the problems", the atmosphere "is now one of some resignation that the situations in France and Australia have moved into a highly political realm where their course can only be watched … no rancour is evident. There is more a sense of foreboding".[115] Foreboding it was although, of course, at that point neither France or Australia decided against signature.

Meanwhile, Bob Hawke had called Michel Rocard, saying he opposed Antarctic mining and CRAMRA was not the best way to prevent it. He wanted to explore action that "Australia and France might take together to protect the Antarctic environment". This would help inform Cabinet's thinking and, if it rejected CRAMRA, "whether we would be standing

---

[112] May 1989, PREP/WP/1 "Information paper, presented by the Delegation of Chile" (NAA: B1387 89/311 PART 1). Chile was concerned about increasing Antarctic activities and recent accidents.

[113] May 1989, "ATCM XV—Prep" (AWJ personal notes), 46. 9 May 1989, PA74190 "Antarctic minerals convention" (NAA: B1387 89/311 PART 1).

[114] 10 May 1989, PA74208 "Antarctica: Preparatory meeting for ATCM XV Paris 9–13 May" Report No 1" (NAA: B1387 88/352). The competing proposals reflected public concern about the Dumont d'Urville airstrip, the wreck of the *Bahia Paraiso*, waste handling at McMurdo, marine pollution and the impacts of tourism.

[115] 10 May 1989, PA74206 "Antarctic minerals convention" (NAA: B1387 89/311 PART 1).

alone, which may be futile". Hawke suggested that "one option is a world park". They agreed to explore the options.[116] That same day, the Labor Caucus, chaired by Bob Chynoweth, decided to oppose CRAMRA.[117]

MAY 1989: AUSTRALIANS IN PARIS, AT "THE RADICAL END OF THE SPECTRUM"

Alan Brown, head of DFAT's International Legal Division, tasked lawyer Bill Bush with preparing a proposal to put to the meeting still underway in Paris. A working paper was faxed to John Burgess. On the morning of 11 May, the delegation met to discuss it. Burgess said he would sound out other Parties. Lyn Goldsworthy, ASOC representative, expressed reservations about putting around the paper itself rather than canvassing the idea verbally. So did the AAD delegate (this author), who considered the paper too complex and could signal that a decision not to sign CRAMRA had already been made. Burgess, however, believed there was "nothing to lose". It was later revealed that the informal soundings had already happened—and all with negative reactions. Unknown to Goldsworthy and this author, the paper was circulated anyway, raising suspicion that Australia's proposal had been put out on the expectation that it would get demolished and thus convince Cabinet to sign CRAMRA (the then position of DFAT officials).[118] In any event, the paper was out and this time with no tentative testing of scenarios—it went straight to the preferred option: "an integrated catch-all convention to protect the Antarctic environment", which would, over time, subsume existing instruments. It did not say that mining would be prohibited but, in reference to CRAMRA, it included the ominous phrase "should it enter into force", unmistakably revealing Australia's doubts.[119] Burgess suggested the paper be considered on its merits "against the background of the difficulties which have arisen

[116] 11 May 1989, Craig Emerson "Record of conversation between Prime Minister Hawke and French Prime Minister Rocard" (AAD: B13/199). Emerson was Hawke's economics adviser.

[117] 11 May 1989, "Caucus in move for Antarctic mine ban" *The Australian*. 12 May 1989, "ALP turns on Antarctic mining" *The Age*.

[118] May 1989, "Comprehensive environmental protection measures" (AWJ personal notes), 46.

[119] 11 May 1989, PREP/WP/14 (Australia) "A Working Paper concerning a comprehensive scheme of protection for the Antarctic environment" (AU-ATADD-3-BB-AQ-188).

for us on the matter of signing CRAMRA".[120] The reaction was unambiguous.

Undaunted, on 12 May Burgess formally introduced Australia's proposal in Plenary.[121] Apologising for the typographical errors, he described it as an "exploratory paper ... motivated by the wish to explore one possible approach ... to show what a conservation convention might look like". He calmly acknowledged that it "might be interpreted as ambitious" and that other delegations "might find the contents thought provoking".[122] They did.

Other delegations' disappointments were barely disguised in equivalent diplomatic language. Argentina's Alberto Daverede condemned it with impeccable eloquence, noting that it "scales new heights for us [as it] contains many controversial statements that might warrant a more serene reflection ... we ask Australia to reconsider". For the United Kingdom, John Heap gave an impassioned plea in his inimitable measured way. Drawing on his vast ATCM experience, and reflecting on the new focus, he lamented a change "which, if it becomes a habit, will not be helpful to the future of the Antarctic Treaty" because there was a "danger of upsetting the balance that needs to be struck between looking after the environment and getting things done". He argued that "it would be a tragic irony if the Antarctic Treaty itself was to be ... undermined by a distant future threat which we have collectively foreseen and collectively guarded against".[123] Such was the impact of Heap's statement that several Parties requested it in writing.[124] It was not so much what the speech said—it did not even mention CRAMRA. Rather, it was coming from a person of immense experience and who the previous speaker had just referred to as 'Mr Antarctica'.[125] It epitomised Heap's style of making the definitive statement to shape subsequent decisions. It was a particularly awkward discussion. Coming *ahead* of an Australian decision on CRAMRA, it "did little to facilitate sympathy" for the environment convention proposal. To

---

[120] 11 May 1989, PA74240 "Antarctic minerals convention" (NAA: B1387 89/311 PART 1).

[121] 14 May 1989, PA74259 "Preparatory meeting: Antarctic minerals convention" (NAA: B1387 88/352).

[122] 12 May 1989, "ATCM XV—Prep" (AWJ personal notes), 37.

[123] 12 May 1989, "ATCM XV—Prep" (AWJ personal notes), 38–39.

[124] Heap's remarks were subsequently circulated. See 25 May 1989, LH75190 "Antarctica: UK statement at Paris Preparatory Meeting" (NAA: B1387 89/311 PART 2).

[125] May 1989, "ATCM XV—Prep" (AWJ personal notes), 38.

that point, "most delegations appeared to believe that despite French and Australian domestic difficulties (which were regarded as temporary), CRAMRA would come into force". The paper had put Australia "in a difficult tactical position" and was interpreted as signalling that Australia had no intention of signing CRAMRA.[126]

The effect of Australia's proposal was also to overtake an initiative by France, as host of the October ATCM, to find a way out of the dilemma.[127] Prime Minister Rocard's office now considered retaining CRAMRA and taking parallel action, such as lodging a reservation.[128] If Australia was serious, then such a compromise was already redundant. While Australia had seemingly followed France in doubting CRAMRA, it was now taking the lead. It was unclear if France would fall in behind.

Using French indecision on CRAMRA as cover for an Australian decision not to sign was risky. There was a gulf between a decision to sign accompanied by a potentially illegal reservation and a decision not to sign at all. A final French position might not be come until after June's European elections.[129] If France was not on board, Australia would be isolated. Nevertheless, on 12 May Foreign Minister Gareth Evans instructed officials to prepare a new Cabinet submission, for consideration in ten days' time, this time proposing "a full-blown conservation convention".[130] That same day Bob Hawke responded to Paul Keating's 27 April letter advising that officials would "explore the concept of a world park".[131] There was some optimism as Chile's initiative, and the call for a SATCM to discuss it, provided cover for *all* environmental proposals to be considered. A SATCM would only make this possible if its terms of reference, drafted by the United Kingdom, could accommodate Australia's ambitions.[132] By chance, that week there was a state election in Tasmania—a coincidence later seized on by other Parties seeking to explain Australia's actions.

---

[126] 5 June 1989, Andrew Jackson "Report on overseas visit" (NAA: B1387 88/352).

[127] Host governments of international meetings prefer to be seen as neutral.

[128] 12 May 1989, PA74254 "Antarctic minerals convention: French views" (NAA: B1387 88/893 PART 3).

[129] 11 May 1989, PA74238 "Antarctic: Minerals convention" (NAA: B1387 88/893 PART 3).

[130] 12 May 1989, Peter Heyward handwritten minute "Minerals Cab Sub" (NAA: B1387 89/311 PART 1).

[131] 12 May 1989, letter from Hawke to Keating (NAA: B1387 88/893 PART 3).

[132] May 1989, United Kingdom non-paper "Protection of the Antarctic environment" (AAD: B13/192-2). The terms of reference as drafted were limited to reviewing existing measures and gap-filling.

MAY 1989: HAWKE ENGAGES ROCARD

Bob Hawke wasted no time. As the Paris delegation arrived back, he wrote to Michel Rocard pointing out that making a reservation against mining was prohibited by CRAMRA.[133] He also sought to address concerns about a world park.[134] Rocard had moved: he now considered France *should* sign CRAMRA, lest mining be left unregulated, but that there should be a parallel environmental regime. He also noted that there was no urgency on a final decision as CRAMRA would stay open for signature until November that year. A decision could be deferred until after the European elections.[135] Rocard appeared to have accepted the Quai d'Orsay's support for CRAMRA. French officials even denied that Rocard had ever contemplated banning mining.[136]

In Australia, the opposite was occurring. Paul Keating described CRAMRA as "a starter's gun for mining", and media were predicting that Cabinet would decide not to sign.[137] Graham Richardson had received a further 6394 letters opposing CRAMRA and dropped his support for it.[138] The Opposition piled on the pressure with Senator Puplick haranguing the government for "hoping the French, by not signing the convention, will relieve them of their clear moral obligation to make a decision. This

[133] "Convention on the Regulation of Antarctic Mineral Resource Activities," Art 63.

[134] 16 May 1989, letter from Hawke to Rocard. Reproduced in: August 1989, "Australia/France Joint Working Group on the Environment and Antarctica 7–9 August 1989, First Meeting Antarctic Brief" (AAD: B13/199).

[135] 19 May 1989, PA74387 "Antarctica letter from the Prime Minister" (NAA: B1387 89/311 PART 1).

[136] 19 May 1989, PA74390 "Antarctica letter from the Prime Minister" (NAA: B1387 89/311 PART 1). The French officials' denial was odd as Rocard emphatically agreed when Jacques Cousteau said, "industrial development should be banned, purely and simply, and only research permitted". 21 April 1989, PA73883 "Minerals convention: French position" (NAA: B1387 88/893 PART 3).

[137] 17 May 1989, Mike Seccombe "Govt likely to reject Antarctic mine plan" *Sydney Morning Herald*, 3. 17 May 1989, Ross Peake and Caroline Milburn "Cabinet likely to veto Antarctic mining" *The Age*, 5.

[138] 19 May 1989, DASETT submission to minister "Convention on the Regulation of Antarctic Mineral Resource Activities" (NAA: B1387 89/311 PART 1). 15 May 1989, transcript of Radio 2CN "Radio interview with Senator Richardson" (NAA: B1387 89/311 PART 1). 16 May 1989, Pilita Clark "Richardson wavers on Antarctic Treaty" *Sydney Morning Herald*, 4.

cowardice is astounding".[139] Phillip Law had argued humanity's right to use resources and dismissed mining's impact on Antarctica's wilderness values.[140] The Opposition's policy prompted an outburst from Law deriding a world park: "if Australia refuses to sign, she will be utterly discredited among the Treaty nations and will be branded as naïve, ignorant and obstructive ... the campaign for an Antarctic world park is doomed to failure."[141]

MAY 1989: A SUBMISSION TO CABINET

Departmental officers, meanwhile, were getting on with drafting a Cabinet submission recommending that Australia not sign "at this stage".[142] At the same time, Hawke's requested paper on world park options was being completed by Attorney-General's Department (A-G's) lawyer Henry Burmester.[143] It noted the unacceptability of concepts that would internationalise Antarctica and advised that there were no world parks or mechanisms to designate them. Such proposals, it said, were fraught with problems: an undefined concept with no process to establish one—even NGOs had not addressed such issues. The Cabinet submission could hardly recommend a world park. In preparation for Cabinet, AAD provided Richardson with a gloomy assessment of the submission's recommendations. It concluded that pursuing them would "entail considerable effort just to maintain Australia's credibility within the Antarctic Treaty", and, less convincingly, the proposal required the recruitment of an extra staff member. Whether the minister was convinced is not clear, although his office asked that AAD not raise its concerns with DFAT.[144] Meanwhile, Australia's diplomatic posts were advised to make appointments in rele-

[139] 18 May 1989, Chris Puplick media release "Government dragging its flippers on Antarctica" (NAA: B1387 88/893 PART 3).

[140] 26 April 1989, Phillip Law "Developers would but scratch Antarctica" *The Age*, 10–11.

[141] 17 May 1989, Phillip Law, letter to the editor "Proposal for Antarctic World Park is just 'pie in the sky'" *The Age*, 12. 18 May 1989, Phillip Law, letter to the editor "Warning on Antarctica" *The Australian*, 12.

[142] 17 May 1989, draft Cabinet Submission "Antarctic minerals convention" (NAA: B1387 89/311 PART 1).

[143] 18 May 1989, Attorney-General's Department paper "World Park" (NAA: B1387 89/311 PART 1).

[144] 19 May 1989, DASETT submission to minister "Convention on the Regulation of Antarctic Mineral Resource Activities" (NAA: B1387 89/311 PART 1). Whether the Antarctic Division required more staff was addressed in a June 1989 Parliamentary inquiry.

vant capitals for briefings as soon as Cabinet made its decision.[145] The draft decision would be based on Evans' submission, revised two days before the Cabinet meeting to make clear that the government would not raise expectations that a world park was achievable.[146] Speculation that the government would not sign CRAMRA was rife, despite commentators such as Gillian Triggs suggesting that "opposition to the Convention is a tremendous gamble" and David Lyons, one of Australia's negotiators, making a last-minute plea for CRAMRA in the media.[147]

22 MAY 1989: DECISION DAY

Six months to the day from CRAMRA's tabling in Parliament, on Monday 22 May 1989 ministers woke to a Page 1 scoop: a leaked copy of the Cabinet submission, scheduled for consideration that day, would recommend Australia not sign CRAMRA at this stage.[148] Mid-morning, Hawke received a letter from his New Zealand counterpart, Prime Minister David Lange, expressing concern about "an issue of considerable importance to New Zealand". He regretted public misunderstandings generated by CRAMRA, outlined dangers for the Treaty if there were no rules when minerals were discovered, and pointed out that the world park idea would be even less acceptable than it was in 1975.[149]

Lange was too late: Hawke's Cabinet was meeting. It decided that the government would not sign CRAMRA but, instead, "pursue the urgent negotiation of a comprehensive environment protection convention".[150]

Parliament of Australia Joint Committee of Public Accounts, *Report 297: Management of the Antarctic Division* (AGPS, 1989), 44.

[145] 18 May 1989, CH539595 "Antarctic minerals convention" (NAA: B1387 89/311 PART 1).

[146] 20 May 1989, Cabinet Submission corrigendum "Antarctic minerals convention: Further developments" (NAA: 14039, 6506).

[147] 19 May 1989, Robin Bromby "Battle for the last frontier" *The Australian*, 13. Ian Anderson, "Antarctic Minerals Deal Heads for Rocks," *New Scientist*, no. 20 May 1989 (1989). 22 May 1989, D. Lyons, letters to the Editor "Minerals convention is best safeguard" *The Age*, 12.

[148] 22 May 1989, Suzanne Houweling "Cabinet to say no to Antarctic mining treaty" *The Australian*, 1. The leaked copy contained verbatim the recommendations of the 17 May 1989 penultimate draft of the submission. See 17 May 1989, draft Cabinet Submission "Antarctic minerals convention" (NAA: B1387 89/311 PART 1).

[149] 22 May 1989, letter David Lange to Bob Hawke (NAA: B1387 89/311 PART 4).

[150] 22 May 1989, Cabinet Decision 12638 Amended (NAA: 14039, 6415).

Australia would also explore the prospects of "an Antarctic wilderness park, without raising excessive public expectations in Australia that international acceptance of this concept will be achieved".[151] Meanwhile, the government would seek to strengthen the moratorium and consider the matter again "in light of the position expressed by other countries".[152]

Hawke made it clear that his Cabinet was united: "there was (a) no vote, because we don't have votes in cabinet, and (b) there was no expression of opposition to the course of action".[153] There are few records of what actually transpired in Cabinet. Hawke recalls that "with an amused tolerance and almost total scepticism, the Cabinet let me have my head".[154] Graham Richardson recalled, however, that "Keating was the key figure— he was the one who turned it ... and he did it very well". But he also pointed out that Keating's argument against CRAMRA in Cabinet was on *economic* grounds.[155] Richardson, who on departmental advice had previously supported signature, denied that he had been 'rolled' in Cabinet: "we were all in heated agreement", he insisted.[156]

Announcing Cabinet's decision, ministers agreed that "no mining at all ... should take place in and around the continent". While CRAMRA was "very much better than no protective regime", it was "possible to seek stronger protection". Australia would instead pursue a comprehensive environmental convention and "specifically explore the prospects ... of an Antarctic wilderness park", acknowledging this would be "a significant change of approach".[157] Bob Hawke was clear: "we won't be talking about a world park ... we'll be talking about an Antarctic wilderness park"; he ended with both a proposition and a preposition: "You've got to have a process which is capable of being given effect to."

[151] This part of the decision is asterisked as "amended" to reflect officials' advice on world park options and Cabinet's decision not to pursue the concept. See 22 May 1989, Cabinet Minute 12639 "Memorandum No 6507—Antarctica—Possible World Park" (NAA: 14039, 6507).

[152] 22 May 1989, Cabinet Decision 12638 Amended (NAA: 14039, 6415).

[153] 22 May 1989 Prime Minister "Transcript of Joint News Conference" http://pmtranscripts.pmc.gov.au/sites/default/files/original/00007608.pdf (accessed 28 January 2021).

[154] Robert J. L. Hawke, *The Hawke Memoirs* (William Heinemann, 1994), 468–69.

[155] Bowden, *The Silence Calling: Australians in Antarctica 1947–1997*, 414.

[156] 22 May 1989, Parliamentary Library Media Information, Current Awareness and Hansard Service. Transcript of ABC *TV 7.30 Report* (NAA: B1387 89/311 PART 1).

[157] 22 May 1989 Prime Minister "Protection of the Antarctic environment" http://pmtranscripts.pmc.gov.au/sites/default/files/original/00007607.pdf (accessed 3 February 2021).

Hawke was frank about the diplomatic challenge ahead: "Australia has a responsibility to take a lead in this matter [but] we don't underestimate the very considerable difficulties", he said. Gareth Evans was more pointed, and provocative, about the expected "opposition from two or three countries of a predictable kind—US and UK particularly."[158]

The preceding eleven months had been momentous. CRAMRA had been adopted by consensus, yet doubts had immediately surfaced. Several Parties had signed the convention, but two of the Parties holding the key to its survival had not. Inter-departmental arguments had little impact. Public debate about Antarctica, energised by environmentalists, had become established by a media happy to ventilate the issues. Meanwhile, maritime accidents cruelled the prospects of rational public debate. Even conservative Australian politicians had seized the chance to appear environmentally motivated and publicly wedge Hawke. Emboldened by Rocard's hesitation, the Hawke Cabinet had responded decisively.

Initial commentary emphasised the diplomatic challenge and the risks of unregulated mining. There was scepticism about the government's motives, with suggestions that it was driven by popular pressure, a theme picked up by an Opposition "delighted the Government had rejected the convention to account for electoral realities".[159] Others were less charitable, one editorial suggesting that the wilderness park idea was "a utopian notion that was impossibly idealistic" and the decision "has more to do with the next election than any altruistic desire to protect the environment". Borrowing Keating's phrase, it said that "by scuttling the Convention the Government could indeed provide a starter's gun for miners".[160] Irrespective of whether the 'starter's gun' for mining was the adoption of CRAMRA (which would regulate it) or its rejection (which would leave it unregulated), Australia's decision was the starter's gun for heated diplomatic exchange.

[158] 22 May 1989 Prime Minister "Transcript of Joint News Conference" http://pmtranscripts.pmc.gov.au/sites/default/files/original/00007608.pdf (accessed 28 January 2021).
[159] 23 May 1989, Mike Seccombe "Antarctica stand puts Aust out on limb" *Sydney Morning Herald*, 1. 23 May 1989, Ross Peake "Cabinet rejects Antarctic mining" *The Age*, 1.
[160] 24 May 1989, editorial "Greening of Antarctica" *The Australian*, 14.

REFERENCES

Alaska Oil Spill Commission. *Spill: The Wreck of the Exxon Valdez*. Oil Spill Public Information Center, 1990.

Anderson, Ian. "Antarctic Minerals Deal Heads for Rocks." *New Scientist*, no. 20 May 1989 (1989): 3–4.

"The Antarctic Treaty." https://documents.ats.aq/keydocs/vol_1/vol1_2_AT_Antarctic_Treaty_e.pdf.

Antarctic Treaty. *Final Report of the Fourth Special Antarctic Treaty Consultative Meeting on Antarctic Mineral Resources*. Ministry of Foreign Affairs (Wellington), 1988.

"Argentine Ship Sinks near Palmer Station." *Antarctic Journal of the United States* XXIV, no. 2 (1989): 3–12.

Beck, Peter J. "Convention on the Regulation of Antarctic Mineral Resource Activities: A Major Addition to the Antarctic Treaty System." *Polar Record* 25, no. 152 (1989): 19–32.

Bowden, Tim. *The Silence Calling: Australians in Antarctica 1947–1997*. Allen & Unwin, 1997.

Bramston, Troy. *Paul Keating: The Big Picture Leader*. Scribe, 2016.

"Britain Plans New Antarctic Airstrip." *New Scientist* 121, no. 1648 (1989): 27.

Bush, W. M., ed. *Antarctica and International Law: A Collection of Inter-State and National Documents (Looseleaf Volumes)*: Oceana, 1994–2003.

"Convention on the Regulation of Antarctic Mineral Resource Activities." https://documents.ats.aq/recatt/Att311_e.pdf.

Frankfurt, Harry G. *On Bullshit*. Princeton University Press, 2005.

Gallas, Dave. *The Last Voyage of the Bahia Paraiso*. Blurb, 2015.

Garrett, Peter. "Speech to Commemorate the 20th Anniversary of the Hawke Government Initiative to Prevent Mining in Antarctica." Australian National Maritime Museum, Sydney, 2009.

Hawke, Robert J. L. *The Hawke Memoirs*. William Heinemann, 1994.

Joyner, Christopher C. "The Effectiveness of CRAMRA." In *Governing the Antarctic*, edited by Olav Schram Stokke and Davor Vidas, 152–72: Cambridge University Press, 1996.

Kennicutt, Mahlon C. "Oil Spillage in Antarctica." *Environmental Science & Technology* 24, no. 5 (1990): 620–24.

National Transportation Safety Board. "Grounding of US Tankship *Exxon Valdez* on Bligh Reef, Prince William Sound, near Valdez, Alaska, March 24 1989." *Marine Accident Report* NTSB/MAR-90/04 (1990).

Parliament of Australia Joint Committee of Public Accounts. *Report 297: Management of the Antarctic Division*. AGPS, 1989.

Templeton, Malcolm. *A Wise Adventure II: New Zealand and Antarctica after 1960*. Victoria University Press, 2017.

Wang, Runyu. *International Law on Antarctic Mineral Resource Exploitation.* Peter Lang, 2017.

Watts, A. D. "The Convention on the Regulation of Antarctic Mineral Resource Activities 1988." *The International and Comparative Law Quarterly* 39, no. 1 (1990): 169–82.

Wolfrum, Rüdiger. *The Convention on the Regulation of Antarctic Mineral Resources Activities: An Attempt to Break New Ground.* Springer-Verlag, 1991.

CHAPTER 5

Antarctica's Crisis of Consensus: May to October 1989

23 May 1989: Naïve and Impractical, Surprise and Regret

Foreign governments were well aware of Australia's decision but, as a formality, Australia's diplomatic missions circulated Hawke's statement. They were advised to provide context: "unprecedented public interest in Antarctica … the spill resulting from the *Exxon Valdez* [and] the qualitative change which has occurred in international concern about the environment". The overseas missions were reassured that a world park "with its connotations of common heritage and the internationalisation of Antarctica" was not being pursued. Overseas missions were asked to "be assiduous in reporting the reaction of ATCPs".[1] The latter request was hardly necessary. Acerbic reactions were unsurprising. CRAMRA had been adopted by consensus, including by Australia, and 16 Parties had signed—now they were being told that they had got it wrong.

The United States needed no invitation to react. The State Department's Tucker Scully said that the decision misrepresented CRAMRA as an encouragement to mine and expressed surprise that Australia's opposition to mining had not been evident during the negotiations. He pointed to the inconsistency of presuming that mining could never meet CRAMRA's

---

[1] 23 May 1989, CE721590 "Protection of Antarctic environment" (NAA: B1387 89/311 PART 2).

rigorous criteria, while disregarding that CRAMRA provided the process for making that determination. Thwarting CRAMRA, he cautioned, could "destroy the basis on which the moratorium had been established". Failure of the convention, Scully said, would "result in a net loss to environmental protection" and "threaten the Antarctic Treaty as a political mechanism". He said it was unfortunate that Australia had not consulted before its public announcement and the United States would be obliged to make a public statement critical of Australia.[2] Later that day Scully registered his "serious concern" with DFAT Secretary Richard Woolcott, then visiting Washington. "It was a tragic development in that eight years of careful negotiations, in the course of which Australian positions had often been accommodated, were now virtually lost", he said. He again warned that the moratorium could cease and therefore "hoped the Australian decision was not irrevocable". Scully dismissed the wilderness park idea as "seductive in presentational terms" but "naïve and impractical". France, he said, "would sign the convention after a decent period of domestic political window-dressing".[3]

John Heap said that the United Kingdom regretted Australia "stepping back from a text adopted by consensus". CRAMRA represented a balance "properly weighted towards environmental protection", and it was wrong to suggest that all mining was intrinsically unacceptable. Australia's decision threatened UK security as failure of CRAMRA's "timely entry into force" removed the moratorium—any attempt at prospecting in UK territory could precipitate a dispute with Argentina and have "much wider implications".[4] Unsurprisingly, Heap also took issue with Evans' 22 May comment that UK and US objections were predictable.[5]

The British High Commission in Canberra provided a copy of UK instructions listing the points to be made, including that the United Kingdom's CRAMRA legislation was well advanced. It would support strong liability rules and pursue other environmental measures at the October ATCM. Then it noted that Australia had not refused to *"accede*

[2] 23 May 1989, WH104403 "Protection of Antarctic environment" (NAA: B1387 89/311 PART 2).
[3] 25 May 1989, WH104483 "Antarctica: Environmental protection: Minerals convention" (NAA: B1387 89/311 PART 2).
[4] 24 May 1989, LH75039 "Protection of Antarctic environment" (NAA: B1387 89/311 PART 2).
[5] 25 May 1989, letter from Heap to Mason (AHC London) "Prime Minister's press conference, Canberra, 22 May 1989" (NAA: B1387 89/311 PART 4).

to the convention, only that they will not *sign* it".[6] There were grounds for such optimism: Graham Richardson had revealed doubts about the prospects of success, saying that "we've got to reassess our position in 12 months or whatever, and see where we've got to".[7]

Other reactions poured in. Argentina viewed the decision with the "utmost concern"; Belgium expressed "surprise and regret"; Chile and Japan were "disappointed"; Norway considered the decision "threatens the whole Antarctic Treaty System"; Spain thought it would "create tensions"; and the USSR had "serious concerns". Others were ambiguous: Brazil said only that it would defer its own ratification; Denmark had an "open mind"; India "will consider" the issues; the Republic of Korea would study the decision; Sweden thought the decision "causes problems"; and South Africa "noted" it. Only a minority hinted at being more accommodating: Italy was "sympathetic"; Finland "understands"; and Poland took it with "resigned acceptance".[8]

"GOOD TASTE COMPELS US TO FORBEAR QUOTING THE EXPRESSIONS INVOLVED"

Across the Tasman Sea, traditional ally New Zealand would be directly impacted by Australia's decision. New Zealand was strongly invested in CRAMRA having initiated the negotiations, provided the chair, become Depositary and stood to host the Antarctic Mineral Resources Commission. Foreign Minister Russell Marshall said that Australia was seeking "unachievable utopia", warning that Australia would "have a good deal to answer for if, at the end of the day, this venture of theirs fails".[9] His officials displayed "considerable pique". However, Chris Beeby appeared philosophical, suggesting that Australia would investigate the options then reconsider. Australian diplomats reported "we were on the receiving end of some rather tough and bitter words from other Ministry of External Relations and Trade (MERT) contacts ... good taste compels us to forbear quoting some of the expressions involved". Beeby's colleagues, Gerard

---

[6] 26 May 1989, CE723814 "Protection of Antarctic environment" (NAA: B1387 89/311 PART 2).

[7] 22 May 1989, transcript of interview with Paul Lyneham, ABC TV *7.30 Report* (NAA: B1387 89/311 PART 1).

[8] Quotes from a series of cablegrams (NAA: B1387 89/311 PART 2).

[9] 23 May 1989, transcript of interview, ABC Radio *The World Today* (NAA: B1387 89/311 PART 2).

van Bohemen and Frank Wong, "noted that in years gone by New Zealand had been taken to task by the British and others as the 'irresponsible' ATCP [and] with mixed emotions they noted that the mantle would probably now pass to us".[10] Within a day, tempers eased as Marshall "displayed more equanimity than his earlier comments to the media suggested" and Beeby undertook to provide a "considered response".[11] Like Australia, New Zealanders were not united. Opposition Leader Jim Bolger was "calling on the Government to stop whimpering" and said that "outbursts of pique simply make New Zealand stand to look petty and personal. The task was now to build on the widening base of support for a tougher anti-mining convention".[12] Media commentary suggested the government "seriously misjudged New Zealand public opinion" and that the 'sour grapes' stemmed from New Zealand's earlier failed call for a world park.[13] Indeed, David Lange observed, "it's an interesting situation when New Zealand set out … in favour of the world park concept a decade ago, we were actually thwarted in that by Australia".[14] However, he could entertain the world park idea again: "well, Australia is, so we would, undoubtedly would."[15] In the meantime, Lange argued that Australia could stop any Antarctic mining with its veto under CRAMRA. Lange may well have been frustrated that, for a second time, Australia was thwarting New Zealand ambitions.

Australia reassured New Zealand that it was driven by environmental concerns, just as New Zealand had been in its "prophetic proposal of 1975 … in favour of a world park". Australia was "amazed and dismayed" at suggestions that its decision was "motivated by anti-New Zealand feelings … this is ridiculous".[16] New Zealand officials offered measured assessment, albeit prefaced by Beeby admitting that "there was a degree of irritation in New Zealand". Nevertheless, New Zealand recognised public

[10] 24 May 1989, WL36835 "Protection of Antarctic environment: CRAMRA" (NAA: B1387 89/311 PART 2).

[11] 25 May 1989, WL36848 "Protection of Antarctic environment" (NAA: B1387 89/311 PART 2).

[12] 26 May 1989, Oliver Ridell "Pique on ice pact—Bolger" *Christchurch Press.*

[13] 27 May 1989, John Kennedy "NZ's line on Antarctica lacks popular support" *The Age*, 9.

[14] 30 May 1989, "NZ would back polar mining veto" *Canberra Times*, 4.

[15] 29 May 1989, transcript of interview, Radio NZ *Good Morning NZ* (NAA: B1387 89/311 PART 2).

[16] 31 May 1989, "Briefing for visit to Australia by New Zealand Associate Minister for Foreign Affairs and Disarmament, Ms. Fran Wilde, calls on Senator Evans and Mr. Duffy" (NAA: B1387 89/311 PART 4).

concerns and would press for environmental protection, although "we were in major disagreement over the means by which those ends were to be achieved". The risk, they said, was that rejecting CRAMRA raised "the risk of an unregulated scramble" and "nullified the timely entry into force point at which the moratorium would terminate". Beeby "all too readily recalled how long it had taken to negotiate CRAMRA … a comprehensive [environmental] agreement would take five to six times that long to negotiate". It was reported that "for someone who has devoted a large part of the last six years of his life to the negotiation of CRAMRA, Beeby showed considerable equanimity".[17] New Zealand's attitude was crucial, and officials were already reviewing their options. That included an environmental regime to supplement and ultimately subsume CRAMRA but, in the meantime, with a parallel moratorium on mining by New Zealanders.[18] This was just the start of a tortuous process by which New Zealand, which was wedded to CRAMRA, might move. Such a shift was still some time away but, when it came a year later, it was emphatic.

In Australia, the Opposition spokesperson Chris Puplick welcomed the government's decision, but said that "it was made on political grounds and not out of any concern for the environment".[19] Even if that were true, support from environmentalists was enthusiastic.[20] Although it had come as a surprise, the ACF praised the decision for putting Australia "at the forefront in recognising the very special values" of Antarctica. NGO campaigning had paid off at the urging of Graham Richardson who had told them "if they wanted Antarctica to be a wilderness park then they had to make a lot of noise about it". They would also have to take the message abroad. ACF director Phillip Toyne told Bob Hawke that he would mobilise non-government support.[21] ASOC wasted no time: a letter would be sent to US Senator Al Gore promoting an environmental convention and

[17] 29 May 1989, WL36870 "Protection of Antarctic environment" (NAA: B1387 89/311 PART 2).

[18] New Zealand's internal deliberations are related in: Templeton, *A Wise Adventure II: New Zealand and Antarctica after 1960*, 236 ff.

[19] 24 May 1989, Keith Scott "NZ criticism for park decision" *Canberra Times*, 14.

[20] See, for example: 30 May 1989, Phillip Law, letters to the editor "Conservationists have exaggerated the risk" *The Age*, 12. June 1989, Australian Mining Industry Council information sheet "Exploration and mining in Antarctica" (NAA: B1387 89/932 PART 1).

[21] 23 May 1989, Australian Conservation Foundation news release "Antarctic decision is plainly visionary and based on a better view of the world" (NAA: B1387 89/311 PART 2). 29 May 1989, Keith Scott "Breathing space for the last continent" *Canberra Times*, 9.

ASOC's environment paper would be updated by Lyn Goldsworthy and Jim Barnes to include a no-mining position.[22] For once, NGOs were reacting to government needs for support.

JUNE 1989: ANTARCTIC GOVERNMENTS CONSIDER HOW TO REACT

As Australia's proposal had not been completely dismissed, there was a chance that other Parties could be persuaded to support it. The campaign signalled in Hawke's 22 May statement would proceed immediately. Increased diplomatic effort would be required anyway because Australia's opponents would likely mobilise support. Misrepresentation of the decision was also possible, and, if it emerged, Canberra would set the record straight.[23] Coordinated caucusing against Australia was thorough. Within a few days, Belgium received representations from the United States, the United Kingdom, the Netherlands, Chile and New Zealand.[24] Australia appeared tardy with its own requests to its diplomatic posts to canvass reactions.[25] Canberra's request would have been futile anyway as prompt ratification of CRAMRA by other Parties could quickly isolate Australia which had only ruled out signing, *not* subsequent accession. A change of heart was still possible despite bipartisan support in Australia.[26]

UNITED KINGDOM: "THATCHER WILL TURN LIVID OVER THIS"

Doubt about Australia's resolve was picked up by the United Kingdom. Deputy Undersecretary of State David Gillmore emphasised that Australia had not ruled out accession and "probed as to whether the UK should

[22] 31 May 1989, ASOC (Evelyn Hurwich and Jim Barnes) letter to Senator Gore (NAA: B1387 89/311 PART 4). 2 June 1989, AAD handwritten minute "Discussion with Lyn Goldsworthy on ATCM issues" (NAA: B1387 89/311 PART 3).
[23] 1 June 1989, ST24758 and CE726628 "Protection of Antarctic environment" (NAA: B1387 89/311 PART 3).
[24] 8 June 1989, BS47445 "Protection of Antarctic environment" (NAA: B1387 89/311 PART 4).
[25] 7 June 1989, CE729682 "Antarctic minerals convention" (NAA: B1387 89/311 PART 3).
[26] 31 May 1989, CE725451 "Protection of Antarctic environment" (NAA: B1387 89/311 PART 2).

read anything into this". The Australian deputy high commissioner's rather ambiguous response was "not to read any more into our position than the words themselves" and "it would be a mistake to conjecture about any lack of firmness in Australia's determination". The United Kingdom was aware that Australia was attracting sympathy including from India, some Nordic countries and a Green lobby "sufficiently strong to make German signature difficult".[27]

Also gaining a profile in the United Kingdom were the views of Sir Peter Scott (the conservationist son the Antarctic explorer) supporting Australia's stand: "my father would have applauded it, as I do."[28] That did not stop the United Kingdom introducing legislation to implement CRAMRA on the assumption that entry into force was inevitable, and in the hope it would encourage others to do likewise.[29] Nevertheless, comments in the House of Lords acknowledged the "unexpected turn of events" and unease about the moratorium's survival.[30] Whether UK officials' views would be endorsed by politicians would not emerge for some time. In the meantime, media speculated that Prime Minister Margaret Thatcher would not be moved: she had "turned turquoise once already over greenhouse gases, but the betting in some quarters is that she will turn livid over this one".[31]

UNITED STATES: "A TOTAL MINING BAN IS SIMPLY NOT NEGOTIABLE"

State Department officials were resolute: "in the course of a very long discussion, Scully ... showed no disposition to soften US opposition to the Australian decision." Tucker Scully said that the "serious environmentalists" had already expressed concern. Australia's decision, he said, was

---

[27] 1 June 1989, LH75684 "Protection of Antarctic environment" (NAA: B1387 89/311 PART 3). In Bundestag debates, the Greens Party, the Free Democratic Party and the Social Democratic Party supported Australia's decision. 8 June 1989, BO45648 "Antarctica: Environmental protection—FRG" (NAA: B1387 89/311 PART 3).

[28] 6 June 1989, CE728526 "Antarctic: Comprehensive environmental protection: UK position" (NAA: B1387 89/311 PART 3).

[29] 7 June 1989, DFAT facsimile message "CRAMRA: UK legislation" covering a copy of "Antarctic Minerals Bill (HL)" (NAA: B1387 89/311 PART 3).

[30] 9 June 1989, LH76420 "Antarctic minerals convention: UK response to Australian position" (AAD: 76/133–3).

[31] "Antarctic Antics," *New Scientist* 122, no. 1667 (1989).

"motivated solely in response to domestic concerns". He regretted that the issue was "now very public" and that "the environmental lobby, foremost among them Cousteau ... were playing up the issue in the most sensationalist terms". This, he said, would make reasoned debate difficult. Scully was understandably indignant at "Evans' characterisation of US and UK opposition as 'predictable' ... such comments reinforced the fiction that the US was among a group of 'baddies' and 'pillagers'".[32] Like the United Kingdom, the United States was drafting its implementing legislation to create momentum for CRAMRA.[33] This was understandable as some environmentalists had "enthusiastically endorsed the Australian announcement and begun lobbying" and Senator Gore's office was also engaged.[34]

On 8 June, the US Embassy in Canberra handed the head of DFAT's International Legal Division, Alan Brown, an aide-memoire saying that a total mining ban "is simply not negotiable".[35] The presentation was done "in sorrow rather than anger". The Australian decision was "politically, tactically and environmentally" wrong, destabilising the Treaty and threatening the environment. Brown's response "regretted that the US did not appear to understand our position ... and hoped that it [the US] was not characterising our actions to others as seeking to undermine the System".[36] Coming as it did from a highly respected Antarctic player, Tucker Scully's stance revealed the depth of feeling and power of argument that could be employed against Australia. "Continued strong opposition of the United States at official level" caused concern in Canberra as it suggested no appetite for "dialogue on the merits of a comprehensive environmental protection convention". DFAT prepared a strongly worded rebuttal, but

[32] 5 June 1989, WH104900 "Protection of Antarctic environment: Minerals convention" (NAA: B1387 89/311 PART 3).

[33] 7 June 1989, WH105050 "Antarctic minerals convention" (AAD: 84/360–2).

[34] 13 June 1989, WH105287 "Antarctic mineral convention: US: Prime Minister's visit" (NAA: B1387 89/311 PART 4).

[35] 8 June 1989, aide-memoire "The Convention on the Regulation of Antarctic Minerals Resources Activities: The United States view". In: August 1989, "Australia/France Joint Working Group on the Environment and Antarctica 7–9 August 1989. First meeting Antarctic brief" (AAD: B13/199).

[36] 14 June 1989, CE732751 "Protection of Antarctic environment—US views" (NAA: B1387 89/311 PART 4).

not one directed personally at Scully. Rather, it was to be used by all embassies to "correct any misconceptions about our position".[37]

USSR: "IMPOSSIBLE TO GET CONSENSUS TO PROHIBIT MINING"

The USSR was disappointed. The Foreign Ministry's Sergei Karev said that this did not reflect lack of environmental concern—on the contrary, he even asserted that in the 1970s the USSR "had been the first supporters of the idea of a moratorium and a world park". CRAMRA arose because "it would still be impossible to get consensus to prohibit mining forever". A wilderness park "would be the first step towards the renunciation of territorial claims" because economic rights would have to be surrendered, and, accordingly, all claims "would be theoretical rather than practical". It is not clear if Australia took comfort that, by implication, the USSR considered the claims *as they then stood* to be practical rather than theoretical. More alarmingly, Karev regretted "that Australia's decision had been taken on the eve of 1991" and that some countries "may see merit now in a review conference". He added that "in one way or another ... the question of mining in Antarctica would have to be resolved by 1991", lest Malaysia argue the "club was unable to manage properly its affairs".[38] This issue would later turn out to be an important factor in resolving the debate.

INDIA: AUSTRALIA HAD "DROPPED SOMETHING OF A BOMBSHELL"

Unhelpfully, Malaysia's Prime Minister Mahathir Bin Mohamad said that "now Australia, which earlier opposed Malaysia's stand ... was beginning to see our point of view".[39] This played into the hands of those fearing Australia's proposal confused the wilderness park idea with common

---

[37] 16 June 1989, CE734483 "Protection of Antarctic environment: Minerals" (NAA: B1387 89/311 PART 4).

[38] 14 June 1989, MS37598 "Protection of the Antarctic environment" (NAA: B1387 89/311 PART 4).

[39] 5 June 1989, KL117732 "Malaysia: Antarctica" (NAA: B1387 89/311 PART 3).

heritage of mankind arguments.[40] More helpful was sympathy coming from India in the lead-up to Gareth Evans' planned visit.[41] India's receptiveness was confirmed in a joint statement by Evans, Prime Minister Rajiv Gandhi and External Affairs Minister Narasimha Rao. It reported that "India agrees with Australia on the need to protect the environment of Antarctica. India is prepared to join in any ... agreement on Antarctica whose primary aim is to preserve and protect the environment".[42] Evans conceded that "Australia dropped something of a bombshell" with its CRAMRA decision and was delighted that India appeared to be the first to offer support.[43] Evans did not hold back, saying Gandhi was with Australia "all the way" and, with somewhat premature optimism, that "Australia's initiative now has every chance of gaining worldwide support".[44] He had obviously missed that week's announcement by Vinod Gaur, secretary of the Department of Ocean Development, that India's Antarctic program would soon establish a new station to assess Antarctica's minerals potential.[45] What Gandhi had actually said to Evans was, "we are right there with you" but that "things must not be allowed to slip so that we ended up worse off". Evans' reaction was revealing: there would be "a careful assessment of the situation by about September of next year [i.e., 1990], which gave us ample time to swing back if it looked as if we were not likely to succeed. We need, however, to avoid any indication of a willingness ultimately to accede to the mining convention, or this could become a self-fulfilling prophesy".[46]

[40] 8 June 1989, Aide memoire "The Convention on the Regulation of Antarctic Minerals Resources Activities: The United States view". Reproduced in: August 1989, "Australia/France Joint Working Group on the Environment and Antarctica 7–9 August 1989. First meeting Antarctic brief" (AAD: B13/199).

[41] 1 June 1989, ND69064 "Protection of the Antarctic environment: Indian views" (NAA: B1387 89/311 PART 3).

[42] Reproduced in: August 1989, "Australia/France Joint Working Group on the Environment and Antarctica 7–9 August 1989. First meeting Antarctic brief" (AAD: B13/199).

[43] 16 June 1989, CH543717 "Transcript of news conference given by the Australian Minister for Foreign Affairs and Trade, Senator Evans, New Delhi on 9 June 1989" (NAA: B1387 89/311 PART 4).

[44] 10 June 1989, Lindsay Murdoch "India backs plan on Antarctic park" *The Age*, 6.

[45] 6 June 1989, ND69162 "Antarctica: Comprehensive environmental protection: India" (NAA: B1387 89/311 PART 3).

[46] 12 June 1989, ND69271 "India: Minister Evans visit: Conversation with Prime Minister Rajiv Gandhi" (NAA: B1387 89/311 PART 4).

New Zealand: "A Fair Degree of Irritation"

New Zealand's position continued evolving, partly under pressure from the Labour Opposition urging the 1975 world park campaign be re-opened. They would, however, consider CRAMRA an interim safeguard and hoped Australia might agree, even if this implied accession rather than signature.[47] Russell Marshall wrote to Evans thanking him for earlier support for CRAMRA, and noting that New Zealand would have followed Australia's course "but that we crossed that bridge much earlier". He thought an environmental convention too ambitious, but accepted Australia would "have to have a decent crack", adding that "it would be extremely unfortunate if New Zealand and Australia were working against each other". Marshall asked that as it may be necessary to return to CRAMRA, Australia not characterise it as lapsed.[48] MERT officials were "quite frank in admitting that there was still a fair degree of irritation about the Australian decision", but "officials and more moderate ministers felt that there was a lot of common ground" and accepted that the decision was not "for some short-term political gain". They also reported approaches from other Parties to discuss Australia's intentions. Meanwhile, as CRAMRA was an important first step, New Zealand would proceed with its implementing legislation.[49] Bob Hawke sought to build the relationship by responding to David Lange's 22 May letter, inviting New Zealand input on Australia's proposal.[50]

[47] 8 June 1989, WL36986 "Antarctic minerals convention" (NAA: B1387 89/311 PART 3).

[48] 12 June 1989, letter from Marshall to Evans reproduced in: August 1989, "Australia/France Joint Working Group on the Environment and Antarctica 7–9 August 1989. First meeting Antarctic brief" (AAD: B13/199).

[49] 14 June 1989, WL37041 "Protection of the Antarctic environment: Minerals convention" (NAA: B1387 89/311 PART 4).

[50] 15 June 1989, letter from Hawke to Lange reproduced in: August 1989, "Australia/France Joint Working Group on the Environment and Antarctica 7–9 August 1989. First meeting Antarctic brief" (AAD: B13/199).

France: "Faced with a New Ball Game"

Australia found New Zealand's moderate reaction helpful. Equally important would be French attitudes, which appeared indecisive.[51] Georges Duquin revealed that the Foreign Ministry was "disturbed" by Australia's decision. He had been approached by a number of countries with "serious concerns". Some (including Argentina, the United States and the United Kingdom) urged a démarche on Australia to "see if there was anything that could be done to salvage the situation". Duquin was reluctant because France itself "was in state of limbo" and the view that Australia might later accede to CRAMRA was "wishful thinking". A "visibly uncomfortable" Duquin indicated that his personal views overlapped with Australia, but probably more so with the Chilean approach predicated on CRAMRA surviving. In any event, "movement in France's thinking was dependent on Rocard", and Quai d'Orsay relations with the Prime Minister's office were poor.[52]

Complicating French thinking was Jacques Cousteau "waging a systematic campaign" against CRAMRA. His petition had grown to 700,000 signatures, well on track for his one million target—"Cousteau's campaign has been so successful, and his popularity is so great, that he has achieved access at the highest political levels". Indeed, President François Mitterand had commissioned Cousteau to advise on Antarctic environmental measures. Mitterrand's office emphasised "scope for considerable Australian input into French thinking" with Hawke's forthcoming talks with the president.[53] It was still possible that France would sign CRAMRA and, if so, during the August holiday period "to minimise domestic opposition". With all relevant ministries favouring signature, the only major opposition, "and it is a very powerful one", is the environmental lobby "which in France has been virtually incarnated by Cousteau".[54] The Cousteau Foundation's 10 June report to the president was clear. The "ideal solution, one which is no doubt utopian, [is] to make the whole of the Antarctic an international natural reserve". It recommended France

[51] 1 June 1989, DASETT brief to minister "Further response from France on Australia's CRAMRA position" (NAA: B1387 89/311 PART 3).

[52] 6 June 1989, PA74734 "Protection of Antarctic environment—French MFA views" (NAA: B1387 89/311 PART 3).

[53] 6 June 1989, PA74744 "Antarctica: Cousteau" (NAA: B1387 89/311 PART 3).

[54] 8 June 1989, PA74790 "Antarctic minerals convention" (NAA: B1387 89/311 PART 3).

support Australia.[55] Three days later, Mitterrand said that he was "attracted by Cousteau's proposal". Making no mention of minerals, the president asked the government "to examine, along with other countries, the modalities of setting up this reserve". The Foreign Ministry's Charley Causeret "lamented the fact that the Quai d'Orsay had not been fore-warned of Mitterrand's views, let alone their public airing".[56]

AUSTRALIA AND THE DIPLOMATIC CAMPAIGN

Back in Canberra, the Attorney-General's Department refined Australia's proposal and circulated it to other departments.[57] The paper seemed to prevaricate on the government's objectives.[58] A robust argument would be essential for advancing the proposal and dispel the view that Australia was taking "a tactical short-term approach adapted for electoral purposes".[59] The re-write was more forceful, aiming to build on previous measures and directly question ideas that mining was compatible with environment protection. It reinforced that any new measures had to be developed within the ATS.[60]

DFAT needed more resources to run a diplomatic campaign. A dedi-cated group helped, initially headed by John Burgess with advice from the Treaties Section's Bill Bush. He was supported by officers such as Brendan Doran (one of few DFAT staff to have visited Antarctica), Jack Vaughn, Judith Laffan, Jean Page and Marie Kawaja (among others). Senior

---

[55] 10 June 1989, Foundation Cousteau report "Pour la Sauvegarde du Milieu Antarctique. Mission Confiee par le President de la Republique au Commandant Cousteau—Premiers Propositions". Reproduced in: August 1989, "Australia/France Joint Working Group on the Environment and Antarctica 7–9 August 1989. First meeting Antarctic brief" (AAD: B13/199).

[56] 14 June 1989, PA74901 "Antarctica: Mitterrand's support for wilderness reserve". Reproduced in: August 1989, "Australia/France Joint Working Group on the Environment and Antarctica 7–9 August 1989. First meeting Antarctic brief" (AAD: B13/199). 15 June 1989 "Mitterrand supports Antarctic park plan" *The Age*, 8.

[57] 2 June 1989, Attorney-General's Department memorandum "Antarctic environment protection paper" (NAA: B1387 89/311 PART 3).

[58] 6 June 1989, Antarctic Division minute "Comments on the paper by AGS" (NAA: B1387 89/311 PART 3).

[59] 9 June 1989, CE730880 "Protection of Antarctic environment: Minerals convention" (NAA: B1387 89/311 PART 4).

[60] 13 June 1989, Attorney-General's Department paper "Summary of principles underly-ing the Australian proposal for the protection of the Antarctic environment" (NAA: B1387 89/311 PART 4).

diplomats were seconded at crucial times, including Alan Brown and, later, John McCarthy.

It was time for Prime Minister Hawke himself to join the diplomatic effort, making Antarctica a focus during visits to Europe and the United States.[61] On the eve of departure, Hawke sent the revised paper to Michel Rocard. Like all claimants, France had a privileged influence on CRAMRA's future. To Hawke, the *Exxon Valdez* disaster showed that accidents occur "no matter how good the environmental safeguards are on paper".[62] They first met on 17 June at the Paris Air Show, followed by closer discussions at Hôtel de Matignon.[63] Hawke suggested French and Australian officials informally discuss environmental proposals.[64] Hawke told journalists that "we have a good chance of support here in France. Obviously the position of the United Kingdom and United States is more hostile [but] my pitch would be as good as the Americans and the British".[65] On 18 June, Hawke canvassed the Antarctic proposal with Jacques Cousteau at Le Meurice hotel over a "small working breakfast" also attended by Cousteau's son Jean-Michel, Richard Woolcott and Hawke's adviser John Bowan. Cousteau endorsed a mining ban, with the surprising caveat that "in fifty years" the issue might be reconsidered if resources were required.[66]

Officials met the following day and agreed "to work together for a comprehensive environment protection agreement", although there was "concern on the French side to avoid a statement explicitly committing them to not sign the minerals convention". Immediately after these discussions, Hawke met with Prime Minister Rocard, President Mitterrand and Foreign Minister Roland Dumas. It resulted in an agreed statement: "Australia and France call [for] an agreement which would turn Antarctica

[61] 15 June 1989, Victoria Thieberger "Hawke to push stand on Antarctic overseas" *The Age*, 16.

[62] 15 June 1989, CE733362 letter from Hawke to Rocard reproduced in: August 1989, "Australia/France Joint Working Group on the Environment and Antarctica 7–9 August 1989. First meeting Antarctic brief" (AAD: B13/199).

[63] Hawke, *The Hawke Memoirs*, 470. Hôtel de Matignon is the official residence of the French Prime Minister.

[64] 20 June 1989, LH77261 "France: Prime Minister's visit: Antarctica" (NAA: B1387 89/311 PART 4).

[65] 17 June 1989, Prime Minister "Transcript of news conference, Paris Air Show" http://pmtranscripts.pmc.gov.au/release/transcript-7643 (accessed 3 February 2021).

[66] Woolcott, *The Hot Seat: Reflections on Diplomacy from Stalin's Death to the Bali Bombings*, 214. Woolcott, Secretary of DFAT, had led defence of the ATS in the UN. Cousteau's reference to "fifty years" turned out to be prophetic given the Protocol's review provisions.

into an international wilderness reserve. Australia and France will closely cooperate to this end." There was still a caveat: "Mitterand advised the Prime Minister [i.e. Hawke] on a strictly in-confidence basis that France would not sign the minerals convention, although it would be a while before this position was stated publicly." This was in deference to "other friends, especially the UK and the United States". It was also decided to "form an Australia-France Working Group on the Environment" to continue action "on this and other issues".[67] Interviewed on French television, Rocard added confusion by referring to Antarctica as "world heritage … common heritage of mankind".[68]

The situation in France was simultaneously becoming clearer with political engagement, and more clouded with continued prevarication by officials. Inspired by Cousteau, Mitterrand had intervened with a "very direct and personal interest, he is the one who will call the shots on the issues … Rocard is clearly on side, as now is Foreign Minister Dumas".[69] Quai d'Orsay officials were feeling marginalised. Charley Causeret was in a difficult position as "receiver of information from above rather than an integral part of policy-making". As a formal decision on CRAMRA had not been made, officials were receiving forceful representations from other Parties and considered success on the initiative unlikely. That required convincing the United States, which "could well prove the toughest nut to crack".[70]

Hawke proceeded to London and Washington, buoyed by achievements in Paris. In France, Hawke's Antarctic pre-occupation had been "the most visible success". His domestic credentials were boosted by positive media coverage.[71] Hawke's personal intervention, particularly with Rocard, had "acted as a catalyst in the development of French thinking",

---

[67] 20 June 1989, LH77261 "France: Prime Minister's visit: Antarctica" (NAA: B1387 89/311 PART 4. The meeting of officials was attended, on the Australian side, by Woolcott and Hawke adviser Craig Emerson.

[68] 21 June 1989, PA75007 "Antarctica—Rocard comments" (NAA: B1387 89/453 PART 1).

[69] 20 June 1989, LH77261 "France: Prime Minister's visit: Antarctica" (NAA: B1387 89/311 PART 4).

[70] 21 June 1989, PA75005 "Antarctica: French MFA views" (NAA: B1387 89/453 PART 1).

[71] 19 June 1989, Nikki Savva "Australia-France in Antarctic park push" *Adelaide Advertiser*, 1. 19 June 1989, Michelle Grattan "France backs Australia on Antarctic wilderness" *The Age*, 4.

and he had done that by engaging at the highest level.[72] Given Mitterrand's links with Cousteau, and his influence on the French position, it is odd that Hawke described the president as "a most disagreeable man, comprehensively up himself".[73] The affection for Rocard, however, was strong.[74] In all the reporting of the June discussions in Paris, not one mention was made (by Australians or French) of Paul Keating having previously raised with Rocard the idea of protecting Antarctica.

It was all very well securing French sympathy, but momentum would depend on convincing many more. So far, only India and France were attracted to an environmental convention, and then only with caveats. Early support from Greece and Austria meant little as both were NCPs, with no Antarctic programs and limited influence.[75] Support was also found in the European Commission—but the European Union was not even entitled to join the Treaty.[76] The Federal Republic of Germany's Chancellor Helmut Kohl would only "consider" Hawke's proposal. In Stockholm, Australia's Foreign Minister Gareth Evans was told that Sweden saw "some logic" in Australia's proposal, but considered it "perhaps taking too big a risk".[77] Evans argued that Australia had at least two years of the moratorium in which to succeed and, surprisingly, implied that Australia might renounce some claimant interests to secure its wilderness park idea.[78] Most promising was Belgium, which was supportive and argued that no more states should sign CRAMRA before the ATCM.[79] The moratorium's future was crucial. Australia faced accusations that its decision threatened the moratorium and increased the probability of

---

[72] 23 June 1989, PA75041 "The Prime Minister's visit to France, 17–20 June 1989" (AAD: 81/346–3).

[73] d'Alpuget, *Bob Hawke: The Complete Biography*, 803.

[74] The June 1989 meetings in Paris started an enduring close relationship between Hawke and Rocard. 9 July 2016, Nick O'Malley "Clout in the cold together" *The Age*, 25.

[75] 16 June 1989, AT38023 "Antarctic minerals convention" and VI50292 "Antarctic minerals convention: Austria" (NAA: B1387 89/311 PART 4).

[76] 16 June 1989, BS47490 "Antarctic minerals convention" (NAA: B1387 89/311 PART 4).

[77] 17 June 1989, ST24864 "Protection of Antarctic environment" (NAA: B1387 89/311 PART 4). Sweden had already signed CRAMRA, but said it would not ratify it for at least a year.

[78] 29 June 1989, ST24944 "Protection of Antarctic environment: Interview with Senator Evans" (NAA: B1387 89/453 PART 1).

[79] 22 June 1989, BS47544 "Protection of the Antarctic environment: Minerals convention" (NAA: B1387 89/453 PART 1).

mining. Several Parties ran this argument using remarkably similar, probably coordinated, language.[80] Australia had to argue that until at least 15 other Parties had acted to bring CRAMRA into force, Australia "cannot be said to have prevented timely entry into force". Besides, "entry into force would be some years away", and, to that point, "Australia has not formally ruled out accession".[81]

UK: A Ban on Mining "Is Not Negotiable"

The United Kingdom's rejection of Bob Hawke's message was confirmed on 21 June when the FCO circulated a paper coinciding with his arrival in London. It barely mentioned Australia but "in its entirety [was] directed at countering Australia's arguments".[82] A mining ban "is not negotiable", failure of CRAMRA would threaten the environment because "Article IV would go to the wall [and] the ATS would, as a consequence, be fatally undermined".[83] Foreign Secretary Geoffrey Howe put this to Evans, arguing "the perfect, in this case, risked being the enemy of the good, which already existed in the minerals convention". Evans insisted that the moratorium was not at immediate risk: Australia had "forsworn signature and ratification but not the possibility of subsequent accession to the convention … if there is a risk of the moratorium failing, Australia would be prepared to consider its position".[84]

[80] See, for example: Federal Republic of Germany's view in 17 June 1989, BO45798 "Protection of Antarctic environment"; Sweden's views in 17 June 1989, ST24863 "Protection of Antarctic environment"; and Chile's view in 19 June 1989, SC19556 "Protection of the Antarctic environment: Minerals convention" (NAA: B1387 89/311 PART 4).

[81] 16 June 1989, CE734483 "Protection of Antarctic environment: Minerals" (NAA: B1387 89/311 PART 4).

[82] 21 June 1989, David Mason AHC London minute "Antarctic minerals convention: UK views on Australia's initiative" (AAD: B13/199).

[83] 21 June 1989, FCO Polar Regions Section "Antarctic minerals convention: A memorandum" (AAD: B13/199).

[84] 29 June 1989, Cablegram LH77976 "Senator Evans' discussions in London" (NAA: B1387 89/453 PART 1).

US: "IF WE HAVE A DIFFERENCE, LET'S TALK IT OVER"

The United States and the United Kingdom united in resisting Australia. The US State Department worried that press coverage given to Hawke and Evans ran the risk of internationalising the issue beyond the control of the Parties, and was concerned "about the lobbying by environmental groups of Congressmen to support Australia's position".[85] On the eve of arriving in Washington, Bob Hawke received a letter from President George Bush flatly rejecting Australia's proposals.[86] Hawke was sanguine: "it's a relationship of intelligent friendship … if we have a difference, let's talk it over."[87] He was also encouraged by views that US support for mining would assist Australia's case.[88] On 26 June, he met with a number of congressmen, including Bruce Vento, who later enthusiastically took up the cause.[89] Separately, Hawke also met influential Democrat Senator Al Gore who was already well-informed and sympathetic. Gore was surprised that, except for Greenpeace and the Cousteau Foundation, "most environmental groups appeared to be in favour of the minerals convention".[90] As Hawke noted, "in Australia's part of the world" such groups were changing position. Gore's suggestion of signing CRAMRA and then using the veto to stop mining was rejected by Hawke because "such an approach would amount to subterfuge". Hawke also dismissed Gore's middle course of a 25-year mining ban while CRAMRA was strengthened. Gore concluded that if he decided to become engaged, he would work with

---

[85] 21 June 1989, WH105651 "Protection of Antarctic environment: Minerals convention" (NAA: B1387 89/453 PART 1). Lobbying of Congressman *had* occurred, but not at the Australia's instigation. Democrat Congressman Bruce Vento had already "expressed his pleasure at the Australian decision". 21 June 1989, WH105622 "Antarctica: Minerals convention: Congressional interest" (NAA: B1387 89/453 PART 1).

[86] 26 June 1989, Milton Cockburn "US rejects Hawke's Antarctica plan" *Sydney Morning Herald*, 1. The President's reply to Hawke had been strongly influenced by Scott Hajost, a US CRAMRA negotiator. 13 November 1989, UN048479 "Antarctica: Tinker Seminar, New York, 10 September" (NAA: B1387 89/932 PART 1).

[87] 26 June 1989, WH105799 "Transcript of news conference, Blair House, Washington, 25 June 1989" (NAA: B1387 89/453 PART 1).

[88] 26 June 1989, Geoff Keeney "US stand on Antarctic may spur anti-mining option" *Financial Review*, 5.

[89] 6 July 1989, WH106138 "Record of conversation between Prime Minister and Congressman Jones with other members of Congress" (NAA: B1387 89/453 PART 1).

[90] 21 June 1989, TH21638 "Protection of Antarctic Environment—minerals convention" (NAA: B1387 89/453 PART 1).

Australia.[91] Soon Gore was firmly on side. One Australian newspaper, however, reflected on "the futility of the Federal Government's political posturing on Antarctica [and] wooing of the Green vote".[92]

AUSTRALIA: "WE'VE JUST GOT TO WAIT AND SEE"

With Parties' initial reactions clear, the end of June 1989 was an opportunity for Australia to consider the way forward. Early in the campaign, support was uncertain. Bob Hawke, however, was "optimistic that we are going to be able to get the degree of support which persuades people to change their position" and dismissed doubts from diplomats who had invested years of effort in CRAMRA.[93] Hawke's Environment Minister Graham Richardson was less convinced: "we've just got to wait and see".[94] This reflected his remark, in a press conference with New Zealand Deputy Prime Minister Geoffrey Palmer, that it could take six or twelve months to canvass options "and hopefully we will, by the end of that period, be winning and if we are not then we will reconsider".[95] Richardson also floated the idea of enhanced protected areas, "setting the ground for a fall-back position".[96]

Any lack of confidence was understandable given the strong opposition of Australia's traditional Antarctic partner, the United Kingdom. Speaking on the *Antarctic Minerals Bill* in the House of Commons, Secretary of State for Foreign and Commonwealth Affairs Tim Eggar slammed Australia for breaking consensus and taking "a path that could result in the collapse of the Treaty". "A ban on all mineral activity is simply unattainable", Eggar said, "the world needs not a grand gesture, however superficially attractive it might be, but an example of how properly negotiated

---

[91] 6 July 1989, WH106136 "Record of conversation between Prime Minister and Senator Gore" (NAA: B1387 89/453 PART 2).

[92] 28 June 1989, editorial "Hawke's icy reception" *The Australian*, 10.

[93] 5 July 1989, Prime Minister, transcript of news conference. http://pmtranscripts.pmc.gov.au/release/transcript-7669 (accessed 3 February 2021).

[94] 4 July 1989, transcript of interview, Senator Richardson on 7HT radio (NAA: B1387 89/453 PART 1).

[95] 3 July 1989, "Transcript of press conference. New Zealand Deputy Prime Minister & Minister for the Environment, Hon Geoff Palmer. Australian Minister for the Environment, Senator Graham Richardson, Wellington, New Zealand" (NAA: B1387 89/453 PART 1).

[96] 3 July 1989, Rex Moncur file note "Telephone call to Minister in New Zealand" (NAA: B1387 89/453 PART 1).

sustainable development can be pursued".[97] Unexpected was a breakdown in bipartisan endorsement of CRAMRA, attributed to the impact on UK Labour of the large Green vote in European elections.[98] It was also possibly a result of Hawke's meeting with Opposition leader Neil Kinnock in London.[99] Either way, Labour spokesperson George Foulkes supported Australia, giving detailed counterarguments to the official UK position and noting "public outrage" over the *Bahia Paraiso* and *Exxon Valdez* calamities.[100] Heap lamented the way Hawke's visit "had been used to influence the Opposition" and erode bipartisanship.[101]

Australia was firming its position. To forestall claims that Australia was driven by dissatisfaction over claimant rights under CRAMRA, Cabinet amended the statement of Australia's Antarctic policy interests to exclude mining or oil drilling as activities from which Australia could seek resources.[102] A week later, Hawke reiterated his no-mining ambitions in *Our Country Our Future*, a major environment statement.[103] Despite such announcements, Australia's Ambassador in Stockholm reassured Sweden that "Australia had deliberately not ruled out" accession to CRAMRA.[104] Even India, which in June appeared sympathetic, expressed scepticism about "how firmly Australia was committed to its new approach".[105] The United States proceeded with its CRAMRA implementing legislation assuming that "Australia would only pursue its present course … for six to

[97] 4 July 1989, United Kingdom, House of Commons Hansard, 216–218. http://hansard.millbanksystems.com/commons/1989/jul/04/antarctic-minerals-bill-lords (accessed 3 February 2021).

[98] 6 July 1989, LH78414 "Antarctica: An end to bipartisan support for British policy" (AAD: 76/133–3).

[99] 9 July 1989, LH78504 "Antarctica: Environment protection" (NAA: B1387 89/453 PART 1).

[100] July 1989, United Kingdom, House of Commons Hansard, 218–229. http://hansard.millbanksystems.com/commons/1989/jul/04/antarctic-minerals-bill-lords (accessed 3 February 2021).

[101] 11 July 1989, LH78796 "Antarctica: British position" (NAA: B1387 89/453 PART 1).

[102] Andrew Jackson, "Australia Calls for a Wilderness Reserve," *ANARE News*, no. 59 (1989): 6.

[103] Prime Minister, *Our Country Our Future: Statement on the Environment / the Hon R J L Hawke, Prime Minister of Australia, July 1989* (AGPS, 1989), 26–27.

[104] 9 August 1989, ST25146 "Protection of the Antarctic environment: Sweden and Norway" (NAA: B1387 89/453 PART 2). The Ambassador was Ian Nicholson, Australia's leader in the CRAMRA negotiations.

[105] 7 August 1989, CE758073 "Antarctica—Indian views" (AAD: 89/578–1).

nine months more".[106] Some US scientists suggested that Australia's "ulterior motive" was securing exclusive mineral rights, an assertion dismissed when a freedom of information revealed that the US policy had primarily been to obtain property rights for its *own* miners.[107]

AUGUST 1989: AUSTRALIA AND FRANCE, HAWKE AND ROCARD

As Australia feared that it could not succeed alone, locking-in French support was a priority. Bob Hawke had made progress in Paris, and Mitterrand enthused that "if the Antarctic could indeed be fixed, it would be a truly significant event in the history of mankind".[108] That needed France to make a decision on CRAMRA. It was therefore odd that Hawke's letter to Mitterrand on 7 July appeared diffident on this, suggesting only that at the Group of Seven meeting "there may be an opportunity to indicate French views".[109]

A mid-July meeting of the Australian officials' 'Core Group' noted that while President Mitterrand supported Australia, Prime Minister Rocard and his environment minister did not. They still preferred new environmental measures *in conjunction with* CRAMRA. A legal opinion was prepared to reassure France that non-signature of CRAMRA would not automatically end the moratorium.[110] It was also important to activate the Australia/France Joint Working Group agreed between Hawke and Rocard in June. It was proposed that the group would address Antarctica among a range of global issues and meet in Paris before Rocard's August

---

[106] 14 July 1989, WH106442 "Protection of Antarctic environment: US views" (NAA: B1387 89/453 PART 1).

[107] 9 August 1989, Richard Owen "Australia opposed Antarctic treaty through self-interest" *The Australian*, 5. 18 July 1989 "US aims to mine Antarctica" *The Australian*, 8.

[108] 11 July 1989, PA75294 "Prime Minister's meeting with President Mitterrand: Antarctica" (NAA: B1387 89/453 PART 1).

[109] In 1989, the G7 comprised Canada, France, Federal Republic of Germany, Italy, Japan, the United Kingdom, the United States and European Union. France hosted the summit in Paris, 14–16 July. 7 July 1989, CE744793 "Letter from Prime Minister to President Mitterand: Antarctica", in: August 1989, "Australia/France Joint Working Group on the Environment and Antarctica 7–9 August 1989. First meeting Antarctic brief" (AAD: B13/199).

[110] 17 July 1989, "Core Group" (AWJ personal notes).

visit to Australia.[111] Acting Foreign Minister Michael Duffy was tasked with setting it up with a role for Sir Ninian Stephen, Australia's recently appointed environment ambassador.[112] Officials were becoming stretched, having to support Stephen as well as the Joint Working Group, but despite initially inadequate Antarctic briefing, Stephen used his legal credentials to underpin Australia's diplomatic campaign.[113] At first, France was not prepared to commit to Australia's position—a French paper was ambiguous on the mining ban and the moratorium.[114]

Compounding the challenge was a repeat of inter-departmental disagreements, this time on the seemingly clear government decision on Antarctic mining.[115] With officials at odds, it seemed optimistic to expect the Working Group "to prevent any slippage in the French position", especially as French officials "sought to keep alive the option of signing CRAMRA". Sympathy for Australia had come only from Mitterrand and Rocard and "all of the initiative has come from the Australian side".[116] Concerns about the Joint Working Group's viability were alleviated with French officials coming well prepared—well prepared, that is, except for not knowing that Mitterrand had told Rocard that France would *definitely* not be signing CRAMRA. Nevertheless, despite officials' misgivings, there was no backsliding. Instead, the issue became *when* France would reveal its

[111] 19 July 1989, CE749941 "Australia/France Joint Working Group on Environment and Antarctic", reproduced in: August 1989, "Australia/France Joint Working Group on the Environment and Antarctica 7–9 August 1989. First meeting Antarctic brief" (AAD: B13/199).

[112] 24 July 1989, letter from Hawke to Duffy (AAD: 89/578-1). Sir Ninian was Australia's first environment ambassador: 20 July 1989, "Speech by the Prime Minister" http://pmtranscripts.pmc.gov.au/sites/default/files/original/00007687.pdf (accessed 28 January 2021).

[113] 28 July 1989, DFAT memorandum "Australia/France Joint Working Group on the Environment: Briefing requirements" (AAD: 89/578-1). 31 July 1989, author's handwritten notes during inter-departmental meeting (AAD: 89/578-1). Philip Ayres, *Fortunate Voyager: The Worlds of Ninian Stephen* (Miegunyah, 2013), 132–36.

[114] 30 July 1989, PA75679 "Australia/France Joint Working Group on Environment and Antarctica" (AAD: 89/578-1). 3 August 1989, AAD minute "Comments on French draft" (AAD: 89/578-1).

[115] See, for example: 9 August 1989, AAD note to file "Conversation with Mr. Doran, DFAT" and accompanying "Aide memoire"; and related memorandums between 4 and 10 August 1989 (AAD: 89/578-1).

[116] August 1989, "Australia/France Joint Working Group on the Environment and Antarctica 7–9 August 1989. First meeting Antarctic brief" (AAD: B13/199) Antarctic brief" (AAD: B13/199).

rejection of CRAMRA because the public position was still only that it did not support CRAMRA "as it stands".[117] France was concerned that a premature announcement might encourage the United Kingdom and the United States to refuse a special meeting on the environment. The Joint Working Group proceeded to draft a statement for Hawke and Rocard.[118] More importantly, it produced a draft of an ATCM Recommendation calling for a SATCM in 1990 to develop a comprehensive environment regime.[119]

Hawke had written to Rocard in July encouraging cooperation between France and Australia.[120] This was cemented by Rocard's Canberra visit. On 18 August, the two Prime Ministers announced the joint initiative for a convention to turn "the Antarctic into a wilderness reserve". While it would regulate harmful activities, the statement fell short of calling for the mining ban Hawke sought.[121] Rocard agreed only to saying that "both Prime Minsters indicated that mining in Antarctica was not compatible with protection of the fragile Antarctic environment". Going further would have to wait until France made a decision on CRAMRA, something Rocard would not do "on the spot".[122] Questioned by journalists, Rocard dodged the issue, a hesitation not missed by New Zealand.[123] He also dodged the apparent contradiction of France professing environmental concerns while simultaneously blowing up islands in the Pacific and in the

---

[117] 10 August 1989, French Foreign Minister's response to Parliamentary question (NAA: B1387 89/453 PART 2).

[118] 9 August 1989, PA75937 "France/Australia Working Group on Environment: Antarctica" (AAD: 89/578–1).

[119] 17 August 1989, CE763486 "French/Australian Working Group on the Environment: Antarctica" (AAD: 89/578–1).

[120] 28 July 1989, letter from Hawke to Rocard reproduced in: August 1989, "Australia/France Joint Working Group on the Environment and Antarctica 7–9 August 1989. First meeting Antarctic brief" (AAD: B13/199).

[121] 18 August 1989, "Joint Statement on International Environment Issues Agreed by Prime Ministers Hawke and Rocard, Canberra, 18 August 1989. 18 August 1989, CH551922 "Antarctica: Hawke/Rocard joint statement" (AAD: 89/578–1).

[122] 7 September 1989, memorandum from the Department of Prime Minister and Cabinet covering "Record of conversation between the Prime Minister, the Hon RJL Hawke, and the Prime Minister of France, Mr. Michel Rocard: 18 August 1989, 10:15 am, Parliament House" (AAD: 89/578–1).

[123] New Zealand hoped that France might accede to CRAMRA and leave Australia isolated. Templeton, *A Wise Adventure II: New Zealand and Antarctica after 1960*, 249.

Antarctic—the widely condemned nuclear testing at Mururoa Atoll and the increasingly unpopular airstrip at Dumont d'Urville.[124]

AUGUST 1989: NEW ZEALAND AND THE ENVIRONMENTAL HIGH GROUND

While Australia focused on relations with France, across the Tasman Sea pressure was rising in New Zealand. Opposition Leader Jim Bolger demanded that the government "take a clear-cut no mining stance" and promised that "a National [Party] government will not sign the minerals convention, instead it will work with other Treaty nations such as Australia".[125] He was attempting to establish his green credentials and claim "the environmental high ground".[126] It worked. On 9 August, on his first day in office, new New Zealand Prime Minister Geoffrey Palmer tabled a White Paper proposing a binding environmental regime covering issues such as tourism, environmental impact assessment, waste disposal, scientific drilling, marine pollution and use of Antarctic ice.[127] Palmer said that "the international community has now caught up with New Zealand's attitude towards the Antarctic ... in 1975 we formally proposed world park status for Antarctica. This was not acceptable to other Treaty Parties, but it now seems that something like this could be achieved". He added, "we are opposed to mining in Antarctica and we always have been", but with a large caveat: CRAMRA had to remain as "the only instrument that has attracted the necessary consensus". New Zealand would therefore prohibit mining by its nationals in Antarctica and "by anyone in the Ross Dependency".[128] Palmer may have been aiming to retrieve the high ground

---

[124] 18 August 1989, CE764077 "Protection of Antarctic environment: Joint French-Australian initiative" (AAD: 89/578–1). 20 August 1989, editorial "Not yet quite an entente cordiale" *Canberra Times*, 6.

[125] 10 July 1989, WL37297 "Protection of the Antarctic environment: New Zealand Opposition policy" (NAA: B1387 89/453 PART 1). 4 August 1989, Hon J. B. Bolger address to the Environment and Conservation Organisations of New Zealand Conference, Wellington (NAA: B1387 89/453 PART 2).

[126] 8 August 1989, WL37627 "Protection of the Antarctic environment: New Zealand Opposition view" (NAA: B1387 89/453 PART 2).

[127] New Zealand, "White Paper on Antarctic Environment. Laid on the Table of the House of Representatives, August 1989," (Government Printer Wellington, 1989).

[128] 9 August 1989, New Zealand Prime Minister "Press Statement" (NAA: B1387 89/453 PART 2).

from Bolger, but denied trying to do that with Australia.[129] Greenpeace dismissed his use of environmental "buzzwords" and "deliberate ambiguity" in keeping CRAMRA alive.[130] Australia welcomed Palmer's position but "hoped that NZ was not setting its sights too low" by embracing "a *seriatim* negotiation of sectoral agreements that were not really comprehensive".[131] It was also suspected that the seemingly unambitious White Paper had been influenced "by the UK and the US as the language and approach was consistent".[132]

Encouraged by New Zealand's shift and solidifying French support, in mid-August 1989 Hawke wrote to his counterparts in Argentina, Brazil, Chile, China, India, Japan, Spain and Uruguay.[133] Meanwhile, at the Australian mission in New York, representatives of the ATCPs discussed the handling of Antarctica in the UN (where Australia was coordinating the issue). New Zealand took the opportunity to distribute its 'White Paper'. Chile expanded on its May proposal for a series of environmental measures to be considered at the proposed 1990 SATCM.[134] It stayed silent on CRAMRA and was distinct from the Australia/France approach, but it held the tactical advantage of using the October ATCM to obtain a recommendation for negotiations to elaborate binding rules.[135] Australia and France also circulated their paper showing the main elements of an environment regime, along with a draft Recommendation.[136] Importantly,

---

[129] 9 August 1989, New Zealand Prime Minister, transcript of press conference (NAA: B1387 89/453 PART 2).

[130] 9 August 1989, Cath Wallace, "Analysis of the New Zealand Government's White Paper on Antarctic Environment" (NAA: B1387 89/453 PART 2). 10 August 1989 "White Paper disappoints Greenpeace" *Evening Post* (New Zealand).

[131] 11 August 1989, CE760565 "Comprehensive protection of Antarctic environment—NZ position" (NAA: B1387 89/453 PART 2).

[132] 24 August 1989, AAD note to file "Conversation with Brendan Doran DFAT" (NAA: B1387 89/453 PART 2).

[133] For an example, see 18 August 1989, CE764086 "Prime Minister's correspondence: Antarctic initiative" (NAA: B1387 89/453 PART 2).

[134] 22 August 1989, Delegation of Chile "Working paper" ANT./XV./WP./ (NAA: B1387 89/453 PART 2).

[135] 23 August 1989, Department of Foreign Affairs (Bill Bush) "Comments on paper circulated by the Chilean Mission to the United Nations at New York on 22 August" (NAA: B1387 89/453 PART 2).

[136] 22 August 1989, "France-Australian Draft Working Paper on possible components for a comprehensive convention for the preservation and protection of Antarctica"; "A Joint Australian/French proposal in the form of a paper including a draft Recommendation for ATCM XV—Comprehensive measures for the protection of the Antarctic environment and

the United States was prepared to discuss enhanced environmental measures. While useful for testing attitudes, this gathering also saw a Latin American bloc with a "firm and possibly uncompromising resistance".[137] But then came encouraging news: the Swedish Foreign Ministry's Desirée Edmar wanted to be "as helpful as possible to Australia and France".[138] This was significant because, having already signed CRAMRA, Sweden was the first signatory to wobble.

AUGUST 1989: LATIN AMERICA

Shortly after these discussions, possible movement in Chile emerged when DFAT's Alan Brown visited Latin America. Fernando Zegers revealed that Chile had "no real problems with the objective of declaring an Antarctic wilderness reserve or a no-mining provision". The main concern was that an environmental regime not constrain Chilean activities and detract from claimants' rights, which were "of crucial importance". Zegers thought a stand-alone convention unrealistic and, prophetically, suggested a protocol. Chile would offer to host the 1990 meeting to help restore its international credentials in a post-Pinochet government. To further re-establish influence, Zegers also proposed resurrecting the Southern Hemisphere claimants group, an idea having Argentine support.[139] What did *not* have Argentina's support, however, was setting aside CRAMRA to pursue environmental measures—Alberto Daverede challenged the view that Australia and France could propose discussion of an environmental regime, but not support discussion of alternatives "predicated on the existence of the minerals convention". Brown responded that CRAMRA should be put aside while alternatives were explored, and that "it will be important to seek Argentine agreement to this course even if particular enthusiasm on their

its dependent and associated ecosystems"; and "Aide-Memoire: Comprehensive Convention to Protect the Antarctic Environment: Joint Franco-Australian proposal to the Antarctic Treaty Parties" (AAD: 89/578–1).

[137] 22 August 1989, UN047592 "Antarctica: Comprehensive environmental protection initiative" (NAA: B1387 89/453 PART 2).

[138] 23 August 1989, ST25199 "Protection of the Antarctic environment: Sweden" (NAA: B1387 89/453 PART 2).

[139] 29 August 1989, SC19818 "Antarctica—Australian/French initiative: Chilean views" (NAA: B1387 89/453 PART 2).

part may be too much to expect".[140] The best that could be achieved at the October ATCM was agreement to a meeting—not the actual substance of the proposals.[141]

SEPTEMBER 1989: "IT IS ONLY TIME WHICH CAN MODIFY THEIR POSITION"

Foreign Minister Gareth Evans agreed that the priority was securing agreement to a special Treaty meeting in 1990. Only then could environmental options be fully explored. It seemed a long way into the future, and it would need sustained diplomatic effort. Evans conceded that "we have set our sights high … it is going to be neither easy or quick to secure agreement to such a significant change of approach".[142] Alan Brown's visit to Latin America was part of the unfolding diplomatic strategy. Overseas missions were instructed to make representations, alongside French counterparts, to promote the Australian/French proposals. For the first time, approaches would also be made to NCPs in the hope that they might offer support. Belatedly, Spanish versions of the texts were produced.[143] Arrangements were made for Australia's Sir Ninian Stephen and John Burgess to make representations in Moscow, Bonn, London, New Delhi and Brussels—the latter because recent legislation to prohibit Antarctic mining might encourage Belgium to support the initiative.[144]

Australia and France were, of course, not the only Parties consolidating positions. The United Kingdom circulated a document debunking arguments for setting CRAMRA aside. It reprised CRAMRA's development, the Parties' veto power and its consensus adoption. It also reiterated that the moratorium existed only during progress towards CRAMRA's entry into force and the risks if CRAMRA were defeated. It promoted

---

[140] 31 August 1989, BA34047 "Antarctica Australian French initiative" (NAA: B1387 89/453 PART 2).

[141] August 1989, letter from Foreign Minister Gareth Evans to Prime Minister Bob Hawke (AAD: 89/133–2).

[142] 13 September 1989, speech by the Minister for Foreign Affairs and Trade to the National Press Club "The style of Australian foreign policy" (AU-ATADD-1-BB-AU-290), 12–13.

[143] 30 August 1989, CE768728 "Protection of Antarctic environment" (NAA: B1387 89/932 PART 1). 21 September 1989, MA24703 "Protection of Antarctic environment" (NAA: B1387 89/453 PART 3).

[144] 30 August 1989, CE769065 "Environment: Visit of Ambassador Stephen" (NAA: B1387 89/453 PART 2).

CRAMRA's environmental provisions and argued that the threat was not activities in Antarctica but, rather, the "greenhouse effect".[145] Antarctica's environment was robust anyway: John Heap suggested that even if there were oil spills, the circumpolar oceans had "a great capacity to disperse pollution and are most unlikely to bear any detectable impact".[146] Consultations with John Heap and Robin Fearn, assistant undersecretary responsible for Antarctic matters, found little common ground—the United Kingdom rejected any proposal that would "hijack all aspects of the Antarctic Treaty by subordinating them to environmental criteria". All that could be agreed was a SATCM (for which Heap had drafted terms of reference), provided there was no predetermined outcome.[147] French representations to the United Kingdom "prompted a response predictably similar".[148] Heap told environmentalists that any questioning of CRAMRA's credibility "will blow the meeting apart", and "if the Australians refuse to sign CRAMRA then the UK might not sign the Australian environmental convention". Heap did not expect to be able to change Australia's mind quickly: "it is only time which can modify their position."[149] Ultimately, of course, it was time that led both Australia *and* the United Kingdom to modify their positions.

SEPTEMBER 1989: THE UNITED STATES THINKS WE'LL CAVE IN

On the other side of the Atlantic, the US position came under scrutiny. In early September, a US Senate Subcommittee chaired by Al Gore was holding hearings on CRAMRA's future. Tucker Scully's testimony was that "Australia's decision would slow down the Convention and put it at risk

---

[145] September 1989, UK Foreign and Commonwealth Office, "Background brief: The Antarctic minerals convention and its role in protecting the Antarctic environment" (NAA: B1387 1991/55 PART 2).

[146] John A. Heap and Martin W. Holdgate, "The Antarctic Treaty System as an Environmental Mechanism," in *Antarctic Treaty System: An Assessment* (National Academy Press, 1986), 197.

[147] 15 September 1989, LH84221 "Protection of Antarctic environment: Australian and French representations" (NAA: B1387 89/453 PART 3).

[148] 27 September 1989, LH85216 "Antarctica: Franco/Australian representations" (NAA: B1387 89/453 PART 3).

[149] 25 September 1989, Department of Foreign Affairs facsimile covering Dougie Patel's internal report on NGO consultations at the Foreign and Commonwealth Office (AAD: 89/133-1).

to a certain extent" but that ultimately it would enter into force as Australia "would change its position". This view was shared by environmentalist Lee Kimball, representing the World Resources Institute. Gore expressed surprise given Hawke's conviction in June: "I do not know how one can find room in interpreting their statements for alternative understandings." Kimball could not identify any other environmental organisation favouring ratification, and Gore was struck by "the alignment with the Administration of Kimball, whose environmental credentials and expertise on Antarctic issues are well known".[150] Gareth Evans said that the testimony was "no surprise to us", characterising it only as "a demonstration of a policy disagreement".[151] Bob Hawke's reaction was far less diplomatic: "It's reported that one Mr Scully, I think his name is, has deigned to know what the mind of my Government is ... well, I've got news for Mr Scully. He's wrong."[152] Two days later, Hawke wrote to Gore assuring him of Australia's commitment and, that day, Australia and France made joint representations to the State Department.[153] The opportunity was taken to "controvert several assertions ... about Australia's position"—there was "no intention of changing", and the decision "was not linked to domestic political ephemera such as the recent Tasmanian election". The moratorium was not in jeopardy, and soundings with many Parties showed that a "mining ban was not just a pious hope". It was also made clear that "the Australian/French joint initiative was in no way related to territorial claims". Undersecretary of State Richard McCormack reiterated that "substituting an *a priori* ban on minerals activities for the Convention's consensus process of determining their acceptability on an area-by-area basis, is neither environmentally justified nor acceptable to the US". In McCormack's view, the Australian or French representations "are unlikely to bring about a change in the US attitude: only the isolation of the US internationally and continued heightened domestic pressure in the US ...

[150] 12 September 1989, WH108590 "Protection of Antarctic environment: US Senate hearing" (NAA: B1387 89/453 PART 3). 13 September 1989, Deborah Hope "Antarctica: US thinks we'll cave in" *Sydney Morning Herald*, 1.

[151] 13 September 1989, CE776118 "Transcript Senator Evans at the Press Club 13.9.89" (NAA: B1387 89/453 PART 3).

[152] 13 September 1989, Prime Minister, transcript of news conference http://pmtranscripts.pmc.gov.au/sites/default/files/original/00007739.pdf (accessed 3 February 2021).

[153] This was unusual as France was generally reluctant to make joint representations. See 5 September 1989, PA76409 "Protection of Antarctic environment—France" (NAA: B1387 89/453 PART 2).

will do that".[154] While hypothetical, this was a remarkably accurate prediction, although it would take another two years to materialise. Public debate in the United States had barely begun.

Meanwhile, the ATCM discussion had to be tackled, and while the United States did not object in principle to a special meeting in 1990, "whether it would be 'special' with a capital 'S' was another question".[155] What the United States resented was linking minerals to new environmental measures.[156] A week later, however, the State Department's Ray Arnaudo made a despondent observation: "the collapse of the Wellington agreement after so many years of hard work was discouraging."[157] It was revealing that the State Department, one of CRAMRA's strongest champions, was the first to acknowledge its collapse—Australian officials were not so sure.

September 1989: "A Significant Fillip"

The hypothesised domestic pressure on the United States arrived quicker than the State Department anticipated. Jacques Cousteau's Antarctic profile increased while visiting the United States and describing CRAMRA as "an international swindle" and "hypocritical".[158] He was well received by a large crowd.[159] With equal measures of exaggeration and optimism about CRAMRA's fate, Cousteau said that "four nations have refused to sign, that's enough to make it obsolete".[160] After meeting Cousteau, on 26

[154] 15 September 1989, WH108745 "Protection of the Antarctic environment" (NAA: B1387 89/453 PART 3).

[155] 18 September 1989, WH108792 "Protection of Antarctic environment: US views" (NAA: B1387 89/453 PART 3). A formal Special Antarctic Treaty Consultative Meeting (SATCM), with the decision-making authority of a full ATCM, would give the issues significant status.

[156] 19 September 1989, WH108845 "Protection of Antarctic environment: US" (NAA: B1387 89/453 PART 3).

[157] 25 September 1989, Malcolm W Browne "France and Australia kill pact on limited Antarctic mining and oil drilling". *New York Times*, 2. See http://www.nytimes.com/1989/09/25/world/france-and-australia-kill-pact-on-limited-antarctic-mining-and-oil-drilling.html (accessed 3 February 2021).

[158] 20 September 1989, PA76733 "Antarctica—Wellington Convention—interview with Cousteau (NAA: B1387 89/453 PART 3).

[159] 20 September 1989, WH108862 "Protection of Antarctic environment: Cousteau in Washington" (NAA: B1387 89/453 PART 3).

[160] 22 September 1989 "Cousteau wins bid to block Antarctic treaty" *The Australian*, 8.

September Gore declared that just Australia's opposition to CRAMRA was "enough to scuttle the agreement". This statement followed his Senate Resolution that day calling for protection of Antarctica in a "global ecological commons".[161] Gareth Evans described this as "a tremendously important breakthrough … at the highest levels within the US political system, there is a recognition of the need to keep the Antarctic wilderness intact".[162] To Evans, it was a "significant fillip".[163] Maybe, but what was a fillip to Australia was a surprise to the State Department which was reported as having been "put off balance by Gore's move [but] was careful not to foreshadow any counter attack" and "considered the statement and Resolution to be confused, vague and unhelpful".[164] Gore was careful not to gloat, saying it was important to avoid the "political temptation to demonise the convention" as it "represented an effort in good faith on the part of its authors". With CRAMRA in "limbo", he was confident that the United States would not ratify. Gore summed up the administration's competing views: the State Department refused to have mining closed off, while the Environmental Protection Agency (EPA) wanted to ban it. Politically, "Antarctica provided the Administration with a relatively cost-free opportunity to make a grand point on global environmentalism", provided it could be achieved "without doing violence to the institutional constituency in the State Department". Gore could not envisage ever lifting a mining ban, but was more definitive than Cousteau who "didn't insist on an outright ban in perpetuity". In fact, Gore went well beyond what Australia would have found comfortable, musing on "the possibility of Australia making a bold stroke of statesmanship by being the first claimant state to surrender its claim".[165] Australia did not consider *that* element of Gore's thinking a fillip.

---

[161] 26 September 1989, WH109114 "Antarctica—Senator Gore" (NAA: B1387 89/453 PART 3). This was Senate Resolution 206: "A joint resolution calling for the United States to encourage immediate negotiations toward a new agreement among Antarctic Treaty Consultative Parties, for the full protection of Antarctica as a global ecological commons". It achieved presidential signature on 16 November 1989 https://www.congress.gov/bill/101st-congress/senate-joint-resolution/206 (accessed 3 February 2021).

[162] 29 September 1989, CH557600 "Antarctica" (NAA: B1387 89/453 PART 3).

[163] 28 September 1989, Senate Hansard, 1481–1482.

[164] 29 September 1989, WH109247 "Antarctica—US Government views" (NAA: B1387 89/453 PART 3).

[165] 3 October 1989, WH109324 "Antarctica: Call on Senator Gore" (NAA: B1387 89/453 PART 3).

Sir Ninian Stephen's mission as Environment Ambassador was making progress. In Bonn, Foreign Minister Irmgard Adam-Schwaetzer told him that Australia and France could count on support from the Federal Republic of Germany, which would not sign CRAMRA. She promptly dismissed the gentle reminder from the Foreign Ministry adviser Kurt Messer that, actually, the agreed position had been not to make that decision until *after* the ATCM. Environment Minister Klaus Töpfer agreed with Messer, although "FRG's signature … would not be worth the domestic trouble it would bring". Adam-Schwaetzer feared unregulated mining but accepted that no Party considered that the moratorium had actually ended, or "would be prepared to announce or act on it".[166] Japan, however, was concerned about the moratorium and "rather sceptical" of an environmental regime, echoing US views that "there was a substantial difference between the French and Australian positions".[167]

That France and Australia differed was correct: France had still not formally decided to reject CRAMRA, a weakness exploited by opponents of the joint proposals and compounded by French reluctance to participate in joint representations.[168] Canberra instructed overseas posts to emphasise "that the initiative is a joint one".[169] Complicating the quest for unity was the need by France to be *seen* to be separate—as host of October's ATCM, impartial chairing would be expected. Alan Brown visited Paris to discuss tactics for the ATCM. Georges Duquin told Brown that, "as host country, France would be reluctant to be seen as contributing to a breakdown of consensus which could be portrayed … as a diplomatic defeat". What would constitute success was problematic. Some prioritised a 1990 SATCM, others a start on CRAMRA's liability rules.[170] Australia feared that the latter could set back the environmental initiative, yet Duquin argued that liability rules could be transferred to an environmental regime

[166] 8 September 1989, BO46791 "Environment—Antarctica: Visit to Bonn by Sir Ninian Stephen" (NAA: B1387 89/453 PART 3).

[167] 21 September 1989, CE779272 "Protection of Antarctic environment—Japanese views" (NAA: B1387 89/453 PART 3). 2 October 1989, TK65493 "Protection of the Antarctic environment" (NAA: B1387 89/453 PART 3).

[168] 5 September 1989, PA76409 "Protection of Antarctic environment—France" (NAA: B1387 89/453 PART 2).

[169] 21 September 1989, CE779017 "Environment: Antarctic: Joint initiative" (NAA: B1387 89/453 PART 3).

[170] Article 8 of CRAMRA provided for a separate liability protocol, and SATCM IV's Final Act agreed the work should begin "at an early stage". Antarctic Treaty, *Final Report of the Fourth Special Antarctic Treaty Consultative Meeting on Antarctic Mineral Resources*, 36–42.

later. French affection for CRAMRA lingered. On whether or not to sign it, Duquin recalled that "Rocard had asked Prime Minister Hawke not to pressure him on an early announcement" and revealed that some ministers felt CRAMRA "should be given its chance". Brown reassured that "Australia was not waging an active campaign against the Wellington Convention" but was opposed to mining and therefore could not logically support CRAMRA while alternatives were being considered. Duquin suggested a 30-year moratorium would be acceptable in exchange for a special meeting in 1990. He expected agreement to a SATCM on the environment, but was much less confident of an environment convention and mining ban. Speaking frankly, Duquin "could see no way of the US and the UK budging as long as Scully and Heap held their current appointments". He also expected "strong objections" from New Zealand, Norway and Latin American Parties, and backsliding by India and the Federal Republic of Germany. As Brown observed, "we clearly need to keep encouraging [France] at all levels since there is not much enthusiasm among senior officials for a tough battle over the mining issue ... Rocard's influence will be very important."[171]

September 1989: "Regret Our Positions Must Diverge"

Georges Duquin correctly predicted New Zealand objections. Chris Beeby warned that Australia's proposal "could be construed as an attack on the minerals convention".[172] He feared "the legal vacuum that would arise if the Wellington Convention was ignored" and observed, with some satisfaction, that "France had been prudent not to rule out" ultimate accession to CRAMRA.[173] Geoffrey Palmer, too, retained affection for CRAMRA: "we have supported the Australians as much as we can but we have always said that ... the protection offered by CRAMRA is better than none."[174]

[171] 20 September 1989, PA76731 "Antarctica—French views" (NAA: B1387 89/453 PART 3). 22 September 1989, PA76777 "Antarctica—discussions with the French" (NAA: B1387 89/453 PART 3).
[172] 18 September 1989, WL38065 "Protection of Antarctic environment" (NAA: B1387 89/453 PART 3).
[173] 19 September 1989, WL38092 "Protection of Antarctic environment" (NAA: B1387 89/453 PART 3).
[174] 21 September 1989, WL38119 "Antarctic: Australia/New Zealand positions" (NAA: B1387 89/453 PART 3).

New Zealand had "listened to the arguments for abandoning the minerals convention"—it just didn't accept them. Canberra was warned that "New Zealand's position will not be easy to shake now that it has been declared publicly with Prime Ministerial imprimatur".[175]

Palmer's position had not convinced environmentalists, who still called on New Zealand to abandon CRAMRA. Despite being consulted on the New Zealand paper for the forthcoming ATCM, Cath Wallace criticised it as being "more significant for what was missing from it than what was in it". And what was missing from the paper to so enrage environmentalists? Unlike Palmer's 9 August statement, the ATCM paper stepped back from rejecting mining and supporting an Antarctic park.[176] Tactically, this had been done to avoid outright rejection by the United States and the United Kingdom, but doing so left it accused of being identical in substance to the US proposal: a piece-by-piece review of environmental measures and support for the possibility of mining by retaining CRAMRA.[177] New Zealand also argued for liability negotiations to begin, clearly intending to keep CRAMRA alive. Such concerns were anathema to Australia and enough to cause Hawke to write to Palmer expressing his "regret our positions must diverge".[178]

Positions were, however, converging elsewhere. Peru announced that, should it become an ATCP, it would support Australia's proposal for a SATCM.[179] More significant was the 28 September motion in Italy's Chamber of Deputies that Italy oppose CRAMRA and promote a world nature park.[180] Italy was now well ahead of the French political debate, itself well ahead of French bureaucrats. An insight into French officials' attitudes came at hearings in the National Assembly. Quizzed about the development of CRAMRA, "the one question put to everyone holding an

[175] 27 September 1989, WL38182 "Antarctic environmental protection: ATCM XV: New Zealand paper" (NAA: B1387 89/453 PART 3).

[176] October 1989, V/ATCM/WP/4 (New Zealand) "Working Paper on the protection of the Antarctic environment" https://documents.ats.aq/ATCM15/wp/ATCM15_wp004_e.pdf (accessed 16 March 2020).

[177] 5 October 1989, CE785093 "Protection of the Antarctic environment: US paper" (NAA: B1387 89/453 PART 3).

[178] 29 September 1989, CH557712 "Antarctica: Prime Ministerial correspondence" (NAA: B1387 89/453 PART 3).

[179] 6 October 1989, BR12070 "Environment: Peru: Protection of the Antarctic" (NAA: B1387 89/453 PART 3).

[180] 4 October 1989, CE784032 "Environment: Antarctic—Italy" (NAA: B1387 89/453 PART 3).

official position, was whether they had consulted at any stage of the negotiations. The answer was always no".[181]

OCTOBER 1989: ATCM XV, PARIS

It was October 1989. *Bahia Paraiso* still lay capsized, and the *Exxon Valdez* clean-up was nowhere near complete.[182] Also, it had just been revealed that some 200,000 litres of fuel had leaked unnoticed at the US South Pole station.[183] Public attention to polar environmental issues was growing.

In Paris, final preparations were underway for the fifteenth ATCM. Chris Beeby called a Heads of Delegation meeting at the US Consulate on 6 October to urge a start on CRAMRA's liability protocol.[184] Beeby was strongly supported by several Parties.[185] Others were prepared to discuss liability in parallel with environmental proposals. Australia's delegation happily reported that they had blocked the proposed liability debate despite "orchestration of support around the NZ approach". As host, France said that "it only wished to say it would contribute to the search for consensus".[186]

Inability to agree the ATCM's objectives had potentially significant consequences. It would be the last ATCM before the deadline for signing CRAMRA and, ominously, the last before the 30th anniversary of the Treaty after which a review could be requested.[187] Furthermore, criticism of the Treaty in the UN still worried the Parties.

Australia's delegation brief noted the formidable alliance of the UK, US and Norwegian delegation heads. It lamented that a "broader version of this, known as 'John Heap's Correspondents' Group' (including also Australia, New Zealand and the Federal Republic of Germany) has not

---

[181] 3 October 1989, Greenpeace Australia facsimile "Testimony on CRAMRA in France" (NAA: B1387 89/453 PART 3).

[182] Gary Shigenaka, *Twenty-Five Years after the Exxon Valdez Oil Spill: NOAA's Scientific Support, Monitoring and Research* (US Department of Commerce, 2014), 8–10.

[183] 29 September 1989, Keith Scott "Leak fuels hope for a wilderness park" *Canberra Times*, 2. 16 October 1989, Senate Hansard, 1869.

[184] October 1989, "15th Antarctic Treaty Consultative Meeting, Paris, 9–19 October 1989" (AAD: B13/192–1).

[185] These included the United States, the United Kingdom, the Soviet Union, Norway, China and the German Democratic Republic.

[186] 6 October 1989, PA77015 "Antarctica: Pre-ATCM XV meeting" (AAD: 89/133–1).

[187] "The Antarctic Treaty". Art XII.2(a).

met for some time". It postulated that the group's demise (or, more likely, Australia's *exclusion*) was intended to "marginalise Australia because of the ... environmental protection initiative". The brief conceded that the decisions of France and Australia "to depart from the consensus ... has added strains to the system" and, accordingly, ATCM XV "assumes a particular importance". Indeed, it did. The agenda was full anyway, with the added complication of the unprecedented rift in attitudes to resources and the lost CRAMRA consensus. Australia's objective was a SATCM in 1990, with a mandate that would allow consideration of a comprehensive environmental convention "which would establish Antarctica as a wilderness reserve". With that lofty ambition, Australia's proposal for a postage stamp to celebrate the Treaty seemed relatively insipid.[188]

ATCM XV opened on 9 October 1989 with an address from Michel Rocard reflecting on developments since the previous ATCM. He made no mention of CRAMRA—only that the Treaty was "entering a new era" that could be enhanced by more effective environment protection. "Public opinion is being more widely heeded", he said, "the time has come for the politicians to face up to their responsibilities". Rocard specifically raised his joint proposal with Hawke for "a nature reserve, land of science".[189] Applause from the public gallery was led by Cousteau.[190] That Rocard made no mention of minerals was countered by some delegation heads (Brazil, Chile, the German Democratic Republic and the United Kingdom) who reiterated support for CRAMRA and the liability protocol as key elements of environmental measures. Others spoke in more general terms about concern for the environment, and some delegation heads (including the United States) did not speak at all.

Alan Brown, leading for Australia, spoke forcefully for comprehensive environmental measures and called for a meeting in 1990 to examine the proposals. He, too, sidestepped minerals.[191] His opening address was also

[188] October 1989, "15th Antarctic Treaty Consultative Meeting, Paris, 9–19 October 1989" (AAD: B13/192–1).

[189] Antarctic Treaty, *Final Report of the Fifteeenth Antarctic Treaty Consultative Meeting, Paris, 9–20 October 1989* (Imprimerie Nationale, 1989), 124–29.

[190] 10 October 1989, PA77056 "Antarctica: ATCM XV, Paris, 9–20 October—Report No 1 (Opening)" (AAD: 89/133–1). Official opening addresses are the only public session of an ATCM.

[191] Alan Brown, "Antarctic Treaty Meeting in Paris," *Australian Foreign Affairs and Trade: the Monthly Record* 60, no. 10 (1989).

distributed to the media.[192] Beeby reported on the conclusion of SATCM IV, that 16 Parties had signed CRAMRA and six weeks remained for signature. He emphasised that the Final Act agreed to early work on liability.[193] Brown shrugged this off: "other countries are showing the sort of attitude that we are ... time will work with us."[194] He was probably not expecting domestic opposition from Phillip Law lambasting the government that "Australia's refusal to sign the minerals convention has discredited her amongst the Treaty nations and she has been branded naïve, ignorant and obstructive".[195] ASOC summed it up: "we must choose between two paths: we cannot go both ways."[196]

The meeting had 18 environmental proposals which would either supplant CRAMRA (such as by Australia and France[197]) or operate in parallel (for example, Chilean, New Zealand and US papers[198]). Introducing the papers in plenary, Georges Duquin of France emphasised their proposal, made jointly with Australia, was to discuss environmental options at a special meeting. Brown echoed the call for such a meeting in 1990. New Zealand, referring to its 9 August White Paper, stressed that an environmental protection objective was agreed—the differences were only over how to get there. Like other Parties, the United States avoided mention of CRAMRA. Instead, Tucker Scully focused on methodologies for reviewing existing measures, understandably stressing the need to also

[192] 10 October 1989, PA77056 "Antarctica: ATCM XV, Paris, 9–20 October—Report No 1 (Opening)" (AAD: 89/133–1).

[193] Antarctic Treaty, *Final Report of the Fifteeenth Antarctic Treaty Consultative Meeting, Paris, 9–20 October 1989*, 208–10.

[194] Transcript of ABC TV news segment reproduced in: 9 October 1989, CE78616 "Antarctica: ATCM XV" (AAD: 89/133–1).

[195] Phillip Law, "Antarctic Wilderness: A Wild Idea," *The Bulletin* (1989).

[196] Antarctic and Southern Ocean Coalition, "Antarctica at the Crossroads," *ECO* LXXIV, no. 1 (1989).

[197] October 1989, XV ATCM/WP/2 "A Joint Australia/French Proposal in the form of a Paper including a Draft Recommendation for ATCM XV—Comprehensive Measures for the Protection of the Antarctic Environment and its Dependent and Associated Ecosystems" https://documents.ats.aq/ATCM15/wp/ATCM15_wp002_e.pdf (accessed 27 March 2020). October 1989, XV ATCM/WP/3 "Franco-Australia DRAFT Working Paper on Possible Components for a Comprehensive Convention for the Preservation and Protection of Antarctica" https://documents.ats.aq/ATCM15/wp/ATCM15_wp003_e.pdf (accessed 27 March 2020).

[198] October 1989, XV ATCM/WP/7 "Working Paper Submitted by the Delegation of Chile" https://documents.ats.aq/ATCM15/wp/ATCM15_wp007_e.pdf (accessed 27 March 2020).

protect Antarctica's "political ecology". Australia's proposal drew strong support from Belgium, Greece and Austria; sympathy from the Federal Republic of Germany, Bulgaria, India and Poland; and blunt rejection from South Africa and Argentina—the latter concerned about proposals "removed from the spirit of the Treaty". Sweden observed that environmental concerns are "no longer a luxury". Others argued that the only requirement was better compliance with existing measures. With the plenary debate almost concluded, the United Kingdom's John Heap expressed concern about the prospect of over-regulating research, arguing that the focus should be on updating existing measures and developing CRAMRA's liability rules.[199] Chiming-in to support him was Martin Holdgate, the invited IUCN expert and former UK delegate.

OCTOBER 1989: "A RANCID REACTION"

On Friday of the first week, detailed discussions were referred to WG1 to be chaired by Beeby, an appointment criticised privately by some "because of his attachment and association with the minerals convention".[200] John Heap sought to confine debate to draft terms of reference for 1990 discussions, without conceding they could be the 'special' meeting supported by most Parties. His pre-amble catalogued 72 existing environmental measures, including CRAMRA and its future liability protocol.[201] Australia pointed to the proposal's "limited, negative character", and that by listing so many measures it acknowledged the "labyrinthine" structure and need for a comprehensive approach. Brown opposed reference to CRAMRA's liability protocol "in the strongest possible terms" because "in view of known positions this is divisive and deliberately provocative". Argentina regretted that "for some delegations some words, such as 'comprehensive', are magical". France retorted that delegations have long used the word—indeed, it was in the agreed title of the agenda item. Even Chile and New Zealand rejected terms of reference that would exclude available options. Sweden observed that "the Treaty System is at a critical point, a point of no return [but] CRAMRA must not be killed because it keeps the

[199] 11 October 1989, "ATCM XV" (AWJ personal notes), 13–22.

[200] 9 November 1989 "New Zealand sides with the miners" *ASOC Antarctic News*, 1 (AU-ATADD-5-BB-GE-136).

[201] October 1989, XV ATCM/WP/23 (UK) "Draft Recommendation on Protection of the Antarctic Environment and of its Dependent and Associated Ecosystems" https://documents.ats.aq/ATCM15/wp/ATCM15_wp023_e.pdf (accessed 28 March 2020).

moratorium alive". Strong support for the liability discussions came from South Africa, Norway and Japan.[202] Addressing environmental measures was broadly agreed, but the sticking point would be the link with liability under CRAMRA.

With tensions growing, Chris Beeby convened a weekend meeting of 14 key delegation heads to find a way forward on the mandate for work in 1990. It included "many individuals who had been prominent in the minerals negotiations" and Alan Brown reported "it enabled some letting off of steam". John Heap could not accept the word "comprehensive". Fernando Zegers could, but argued for parallel work on liability. Brown could not agree to liability negotiations as "there was no need for any linkage between it and advances on the comprehensive protection front … the Treaty System found itself in a changed political climate and, like it or not, had to adjust". Tucker Scully "regretted that Australia had taken its initiative outside the Treaty System in order to sway public opinion".[203] It was likely, however, that it was public opinion that had swayed Australia to act—similar public opinion was starting to emerge in the United States.[204] Scully rejected an approach which would "set aside or replace CRAMRA [and] could not accept the term 'nature reserve' which prejudiced the question". Norway's Rolf Andersen supported liability discussions and hoped CRAMRA would not be set aside. He supported the UK draft, "but it needed a lot added to it, some of which could be taken from the French-Australian paper". To defuse tensions, Argentina's Alberto Daverede said that the priority was the "need to re-establish consensus". The USSR's Sergei Karev lamented that "this ATCM was the worst he had attended". Discussions concluded with formal positions restated. Beeby offered to draft new terms of reference for a SATCM. At meeting's end, Fernando Zegers offered Chile as host for a 1990 meeting and, rather optimistically, Brown said that if Chile's proposal ran into problems "Australia may be able to make an offer".[205] The discussion had not led to a breakthrough.

[202] 13 October 1989, "ATCM XV" (AWJ personal notes), 35–44.

[203] 16 October 1989, PA77156 "Antarctica: ATCM XV, Paris, 9–20 October—Report No 3" (AAD: 89/133–1).

[204] 16 October 1989, "Antarctica as a park" Los Angeles Times, quoted in 16 October 1989, LO25293 "Antarctic—editorial comment" (NAA: B1387 89/453 PART 3).

[205] 16 October 1989, PA77156 "Antarctica: ATCM XV, Paris, 9–20 October—Report No 3" (AAD: 89/133–1).

Daily reports by the AAD's Rex Moncur recorded the "strong exchange between Australia and the UK [but] our DFAT people are doing well". It was not just the United Kingdom presenting difficulties for Australia. Moncur reported that "a majority of nations are allied against us [and] our DFAT colleagues are working hard behind the scenes to break this alliance".[206] Alan Brown was under great pressure and, in later reflection, recalled "the rancid reaction of the British and Americans, and likened the meetings to four balls being played at once on the squash court".[207]

OCTOBER 1989: AGREEMENT TO HOLD A MEETING, OR TWO

Following the weekend tensions, a more constructive atmosphere developed. Australia and France were still under pressure to agree to liability negotiations "as the price for the environmental meeting". Beeby reconvened the 14 Heads of Delegation on 16 October to discuss two Recommendations—one for a meeting on comprehensive measures, and another on liability. Importantly, "no one spoke against having a meeting on environmental protection in 1990", although Australia and France expressed "extreme disappointment [that] the balance was clearly in favour of the New Zealand, US and Chilean papers". Australia considered it unacceptable for liability negotiations to be held in conjunction with environmental discussions. The United States rejected any reference to a 'nature reserve' as it implied the destruction of CRAMRA. As Brown noted, "it is possible that a meeting on the environment may be vetoed by CRAMRA hardliners ... such an outcome would pose difficulties for a number of countries, not least France which would be worried that ATCM XV would be seen as a diplomatic failure."[208]

The subgroup met again to consider Beeby's revised terms of reference. Brown said that Australia would not be held hostage to the commencement of liability negotiations as it was "tantamount to saying CRAMRA was the top priority". Unsurprisingly, Heap countered that "as Australia had gone along with the consensus on the Final Act of the minerals

[206] October 1989, Rex Moncur, DASETT internal minutes "Antarctic Treaty meeting—Day Five" and "Antarctic Treaty meeting—Day Six" (AAD: 89/133–1).

[207] Jackson and Boyce, "Mining and 'World Park Antarctica'," 256.

[208] 18 October 1989, PA77195 "Antarctica: ATCM XV, Paris, 9–20 October—Report No 4" (AAD: 89/133–1).

negotiations, it had an obligation to allow the liability negotiations to proceed". Scully observed that "Australia had itself made the link between CRAMRA and comprehensive protection by its public presentation that the latter was to replace the former". France regarded as unacceptable "attempts to humiliate the two Prime Ministers".[209] Heap told journalists that the United Kingdom would "consider all proposals"—all proposals, that is, except one implying no mineral development. "The last great wilderness is the size of the United States and Europe put together", he said, asking rhetorically, "is it inevitable that a mine site somewhere in Antarctica would despoil *all* Antarctica? I don't believe it is".[210] It was an impasse.

Australia had worked with France, but now Belgium added support and was "acting as a full partner in the joint initiative". The three Parties agreed to stay united as any Party seeking to veto a 1990 environmental meeting "would attract considerable odium". Brown reported it unlikely that anything could be resolved until the last day: "CRAMRA supporters have got themselves into a difficult position by trying to make this a make-or-break meeting on the future of CRAMRA and to put Australia and France in the dock." He said that "the outcome might put the system under considerable strain". Nevertheless, he complimented Chris Beeby for "chairing the informal group with considerable skill and working for a compromise".[211] Beeby was in a familiar place: trying to engineer an outcome on the future of mining.

Consensus on a 1990 meeting was achieved in the last hours of the ATCM. For Australia and France, it was satisfying: the Recommendation mentioned the Australia/France proposal for an environment convention.[212] The second Recommendation also allowed a meeting "to explore and discuss all proposals relating to Article 8(7)" of CRAMRA—discuss, not negotiate and, crucially for Australia, with no linkage to the

---

[209] 19 October 1989, PA77212 "Antarctica: ATCM XV, Paris, 9–20 October—Report No 5" (AAD: 89/133–1).

[210] Quoted in: 20 October 1989 "United States, Britain defeat Antarctic park plan" *Reuters*. Reproduced in 30 October 1989 DFAT facsimile "British and US press articles on ATCM XV" (AAD: 89/133–1).

[211] 19 October 1989, PA77212 "Antarctica: ATCM XV, Paris, 9–20 October—Report No 5" (AAD: 89/133–1).

[212] Antarctic Treaty, Recommendation ATCM XV-1 (1989) "Comprehensive measures for the protection of the Antarctic environment and Dependent and Associated Ecosystems" https://ats.aq/devAS/Meetings/Measure/170 (accessed 28 March 2020).

environmental meeting.[213] The outcome was praised as a "significant achievement for Australia and France whose proposal met intense opposition from hard-line supporters of the Antarctic minerals convention". CRAMRA's supporters backed down and "had to accept the inclusion of a reference to a 'nature reserve, land of science' … which they had fiercely resisted". France and Australia had "cemented close links which will be essential for the successful carriage of the initiative over the longer term". In return, France "strongly supported Australia" in opposing the liability negotiations and setting CRAMRA aside because Australia would not sign it—a decision that France had still not made.

The outcome was settled at 18:00, on the meeting's last evening, after two days of intense informal consultations led by Chris Beeby, "who did an effective job in very difficult circumstances".[214] Not mentioned in the reporting cablegram was the equally instrumental skill and resilience of Australian delegation head Alan Brown.[215] For France, a diplomatic failure had been avoided. ATCM Chair Michel Combal closed proceedings at midnight on 20 October having adopted 22 Recommendations ranging from commitment to a SATCM on comprehensive environment protection to Australia's proposal for a postage stamp. There were also Recommendations on improvements to waste management, marine pollution, a new protected area scheme and environmental monitoring—evidence that it was, in fact, possible to fill regulatory gaps without a complete overhaul.[216]

Despite the fullest agenda of any ATCM, the bulk of the diplomatic and political energy was expended on Agenda Item 7, which had been front of mind for most delegates and, until consensus was achieved, divisive for many. The Parties had agreed "as a priority objective" the further elaboration of comprehensive environmental measures at a SATCM to be held in 1990 which would consider all proposals. The second Recommendation

[213] Antarctic Treaty, Recommendation ATCM XV-2 (1989) "Comprehensive measures for the protection of the Antarctic environment and Dependent and Associated Ecosystems" https://ats.aq/devAS/Meetings/Measure/171 (accessed 28 March 2020).

[214] 21 October 1989, PA77239 "Antarctica: ATCM XV, Paris, 9–20 October—Report No 6" (AAD: 89/133-1).

[215] October 1989, Andrew Jackson "Antarctic Treaty Meeting, October 1989, Report on Attendance" (AAD: 89/133-1). January 1990, "Report on Overseas Visit—Rex Moncur, 2–27 October 1989" (AAD: 89/133-2).

[216] Antarctic Treaty, *Final Report of the Fifteeenth Antarctic Treaty Consultative Meeting, Paris, 9–20 October 1989*, 43–115.

allowed discussion of CRAMRA's liability protocol. The final report underplayed the meeting's vivid tensions, summarising the proceedings elegantly: "the meeting noted with appreciation the offer of the Government of Chile to host the meetings called for in the above Recommendations."[217]

Distilled to its simplest, after two weeks the signal achievement of ATCM XV had been agreement to hold a meeting—but not a time or place for it.[218] Parties had committed only to a *procedural* outcome. Australia had survived the early dismay at its decision to reject CRAMRA and discussions about what to do next. However, there was still a long way to go, and by far the majority of Parties were antagonistic. Tackling the actual *substance* of the issues would have to wait another year. How this would change the ATS, or the relationship between the Parties, would not be clear for some time. What the Paris meeting meant for mining and the moratorium was unresolved. Meanwhile, there would be almost a year of informal consultations between Parties. In that period, the scope of the battleground would become much clearer. There were many policy, legal and political disagreements to address for an environmental regime to succeed and consensus to be restored.

References

Antarctic and Southern Ocean Coalition. "Antarctica at the Crossroads." *ECO* LXXIV, no. 1 (1989): 1–3.
"Antarctic Antics." *New Scientist* 122, no. 1667 (3 June 1989): 20.
"The Antarctic Treaty." https://documents.ats.aq/keydocs/vol_1/vol1_2_AT_Antarctic_Treaty_e.pdf.
Antarctic Treaty. *Final Report of the Fifteeenth Antarctic Treaty Consultative Meeting, Paris, 9–20 October 1989.* Imprimerie Nationale, 1989.
———. *Final Report of the Fourth Special Antarctic Treaty Consultative Meeting on Antarctic Mineral Resources.* Ministry of Foreign Affairs (Wellington), 1988.
Ayres, Philip. *Fortunate Voyager: The Worlds of Ninian Stephen.* Miegunyah, 2013.
Brown, Alan. "Antarctic Treaty Meeting in Paris." *Australian Foreign Affairs and Trade: the Monthly Record* 60, no. 10 (1989): 586.
d'Alpuget, Blanche. *Bob Hawke: The Complete Biography.* Simon & Schuster, 2019.

---

[217] ibid., 16.
[218] Antarctic Treaty, Recommendation ATCM XV-1 (1989) "Comprehensive system for the protection of the Antarctic environment" https://ats.aq/devAS/Meetings/Measure/170 (accessed 28 March 2020).

Hawke, Robert J L. *The Hawke Memoirs*. William Heinemann, 1994.

Heap, John A, and Martin W Holdgate. "The Antarctic Treaty System as an Environmental Mechanism." In *Antarctic Treaty System: An Assessment*, 195–210: National Academy Press, 1986.

Jackson, Andrew. "Australia Calls for a Wilderness Reserve." *ANARE News*, no. 59 (1989): 6.

Jackson, Andrew, and Peter Boyce. "Mining and 'World Park Antarctica'." Chap. 11 In *Australia and the Antarctic Treaty System: 50 Years of Influence*, edited by Marcus Haward and Tom Griffiths, 243–73: UNSW Press, 2011.

Law, Phillip. "Antarctic Wilderness: A Wild Idea." *The Bulletin* (17 October 1989).

New Zealand. "White Paper on Antarctic Environment. Laid on the Table of the House of Representatives, August 1989." Government Printer Wellington, 1989.

Prime Minister, Australia. *Our Country Our Future: Statement on the Environment/ the Hon R J L Hawke, Prime Minister of Australia, July 1989*. AGPS, 1989.

Shigenaka, Gary. *Twenty-Five Years after the Exxon Valdez Oil Spill: NOAA's Scientific Support, Monitoring and Research*. US Department of Commerce, 2014.

Templeton, Malcolm. *A Wise Adventure II: New Zealand and Antarctica after 1960*. Victoria University Press, 2017.

Woolcott, Richard. *The Hot Seat: Reflections on Diplomacy from Stalin's Death to the Bali Bombings*. HarperCollins, 2003.

CHAPTER 6

Tensions over Antarctica's Future: October 1989 to November 1990

ONE OF THE MOST IMPORTANT MEETINGS

Delegates returned home to reflect. ATCM XV had been every bit as intense as CRAMRA's final session 16 months earlier. *The Times* thundered that pillorying the United Kingdom and the United States as environmental foes was "rendered absurd by the fact that it was they who put forward all the proposals agreed this week".[1] One cheeky Australian official annotated the editorial with "did John Heap write this?".[2] Heap had dismissed "suggestions that intransigence in London and Washington is to blame for the impasse" in Paris: "we are supposed to be the baddies here, but actually our two delegations are the ones doing most of the running with the ball."[3] Environmentalists, however, were scathing of the United States and United Kingdom.[4]

In Santiago, it was reported that Chile mediated "the running clash between Australia and France and the US and UK delegations".[5] Fernando

---

[1] 21 October 1989, "Convention on ice?" *The Times*, 12.

[2] 30 October 1989, facsimile DFAT to AAD "British and US press articles on ATCM XV" (AAD: 89/133-1).

[3] 21 October 1989, Philip Jacobson "Nations split on protecting Antarctic environment" *The Times*, 8.

[4] 23 October 1989 "US, Britain acting like 'dictators' on Antarctica" *The Australian*.

[5] 23 October 1989, *El Mercurio* article reported in: 24 October 1989, SC19989 [untitled] (AAD: 89/133-1).

© The Author(s), under exclusive license to Springer Nature Switzerland AG 2021
A. Jackson, *Who Saved Antarctica?*,
https://doi.org/10.1007/978-3-030-78405-8_6

Zegers "described the ATCM XV as one of the most important meetings in the history of the Treaty because it overcame differences between Treaty Parties".[6] This was rather premature because it actually cemented the *collapse* of consensus as Australia had not backed down. Zegers was, however, pleased that the 1990 meetings would be in Chile, reward for his May 1989 proposal to get comprehensive measures on the agenda and his offer to host. As the primary objective had been to secure a further meeting, irrespective of host, it was therefore odd that France "wondered if some way could be found to change the location".[7] Despite the challenges for France in hosting the ATCM, Sweden thought that the French had made achievement of a 1990 meeting "more difficult". With even more frankness, Sweden observed that the United States had "accused Australia and others of threatening consensus when the United States position was equally making consensus difficult". Unsurprisingly, the United States disagreed. The State Department's Ray Arnaudo said that "but for the 'hoopla' on the minerals convention ... the meeting was an unqualified success" because of the "compromise ultimately reached". "Australia and France should reflect", he said, as there was no increase in the number of countries supporting their proposal.[8] France was nevertheless upbeat as the results "made a significant contribution to consolidating the Antarctic Treaty System".[9] This was immediately contradicted by Henrique Valle of Brazil's Foreign Ministry, who feared that "the Antarctic Treaty System is not as solid as it had previously been ... the agreement to hold an SCM has simply postponed the showdown".[10] Valle was correct.

Although "pleased with the outcome of the Paris ATCM", DFAT considered it essential to maintain "coordination of the French and Australian positions".[11] Georges Duquin wanted to focus on "uncommitted supporters and waverers, rather than on the handful of hard-liners whom he was

[6] 26 October 1989, SC20007 "Chile: Antarctica: Comments by Ambassador Zegers" (AAD: 89/133-1).

[7] 3 November 1989, PA77475 "Antarctica—follow-up to Paris meeting" (NAA: B1387 89/932 PART 1). 9 November 1989, PA77552 "Antarctica: Follow-up to Paris meeting" (NAA: B1387 89/453 PART 3).

[8] 27 October 1989, WH110173 "Antarctica: ATCM XV: US views" (AAD: 89/133-1).

[9] 3 November 1989, PA77482 "Antarctica: ATCM XV: French communiqué" (AAD: 89/133-1).

[10] 2 November 1989, BR12140 "Protection of the Antarctic environment: Brazilian views" (AAD: 89/133-1).

[11] 1 November 1989, CE797312 "Antarctica—follow-up to Paris meeting" (AAD: 89/914-1).

sure would not budge".[12] Sir Ninian Stephen continued campaigning during a visit to the United States where Al Gore was "confident that we would win this battle, although it would take some time".[13] Visiting the State Department, Stephen argued that CRAMRA was "a public relations failure for the Antarctic Treaty", prompting Tucker Scully's reply that "*education* of public opinion was more important than *satisfaction*". Stephen also pointed out that "the Soviet Deputy Foreign Minister had told him that the Soviet Union had never been keen on minerals negotiations, but had proceeded because the US did".[14] Three weeks later, Environment Minister Graham Richardson was told that Moscow "played down any suggestion that the USSR favoured the US or UK positions over the French/Australian".[15]

The US warning about the apparent lack of support for Australia and France began to look shaky. With two weeks left for signing CRAMRA, some Parties were still considering what to do. Spain decided to await the outcomes of the 1990 meetings.[16] Kurt Messer hinted that the Federal Republic of Germany would not sign and its decision would be announced on 25 November, the closing date for signature.[17]

NOVEMBER 1989: FRANCE DECIDES NOT TO SIGN CRAMRA

Then, on 8 November, came long-awaited news: Georges Duquin and Jean-Maurice Ripert (Michel Rocard's diplomatic adviser) reported that France had decided not to sign CRAMRA and announce it on the eve of the signature deadline. There were two caveats: France was only rejecting CRAMRA "in its current form", and "reference might also be made to the

---

[12] 3 November 1989, PA77475 "Antarctica—follow-up to Paris meeting" (NAA: B1387 89/932 PART 1).

[13] 2 November 1989, WH110360 "Call by Sir Ninian Stephen on Senator Gore" (NAA: B1387 89/453 PART 3).

[14] 2 November 1989, WH110359 "Call by Sir Ninian Stephen on US State Department" (NAA: B1387 89/453 PART 3).

[15] 23 November 1989, MS39732 "Visit of Senator Richardson: Antarctica" (NAA: B1387 89/932 PART 1).

[16] 7 November 1989, MA24881 "Antarctica—follow-up to Paris meeting" (NAA: B1387 89/932 PART 1).

[17] 8 November 1989, BO47399 "Antarctica: Follow-up to Paris meeting" (NAA: B1387 89/453 PART 3).

need for the moratorium on mining to continue ... for a specific period, such as 30 years". Australian officials replied that Australia could not leave open "the future possibility of mining". Duquin conceded that "France's position had been 'radicalised' as a result of ATCM XV and the aggressive tactics of the pro-CRAMRA lobby". Australia had "the strong impression that France realised that 'core' solidarity with Australia was the key to long-term success" and that cooperation was essential "both at the political and official levels".[18] Perhaps French officials had come around to Rocard's position and Australia and France did, at last, share objectives. But specifics needed clarifying. Duquin urged that priority be given to defining a 'nature reserve, land of science' to counter accusations of it being vague, and do so by developing a draft environment convention.[19] Australia disagreed and prevaricated on France's wish to expand the supporter group to include Belgium and Italy and, possibly, India and the Federal Republic of Germany. On the one hand, "the French-Australian partnership is in itself a rather unique situation", and there would be problems if it was seen as exclusive; on the other, a wider coalition "would leave it open for hard-line opponents ... to point to differences within the group".[20]

The 'hard-line opponents' aired their objections at a seminar in New York. The 10 November Tinker Foundation seminar was ambiguously titled 'Antarctica: continent at risk' but aimed at defending the minerals convention. Present was DFAT's Brendan Doran, who reported to Canberra that "orchestration by CRAMRA supporters is apparent". US geologist Robert Rutford expressed "strong concern over the campaign against CRAMRA", which, he said, "was essentially a mechanism to prevent environmental damage". The World Resources Institute's Lee Kimball sought to "dispel hype and misinformation ... using arguments which were virtually identical to those used by Tucker Scully of the US State Department", including the call "not to disturb the 'political ecology' of the Antarctic Treaty System at the cost of protecting the environmental ecology". In Kimball's view, "Chile and the UK (by first proposing a special meeting in 1990) were the real architects of the comprehensive protection initiative, not Australia and France who had come with their

[18] 9 November 1989, PA77552 "Antarctica: Follow-up to Paris meeting" (NAA: B1387 89/453 PART 3).
[19] 15 November 1989, PA77649 "Antarctica—French views" (AAD: 89/914-1).
[20] 16 November 1989, CE803620 "Antarctica: Follow-up to Paris meeting" (AAD: 89/914-1).

ideas only later." Bruce Manheim, of the Environmental Defense Fund, said that Kimball had been warned to take "a more neutral position" or risk objections to "continuation as NGO representative with US delegations".[21]

25 NOVEMBER 1989: THE DEADLINE FOR SIGNING CRAMRA

In early November, with one week before the CRAMRA deadline, heated debate continued in Hobart at an Australian Institute of International Affairs conference where, with many familiar faces present, "the atmosphere in some sessions was highly charged". Perspectives were polarised and "those promoting the wilderness reserve proposal were at a serious disadvantage". Jacques Cousteau's participation by satellite precipitated "some very animated exchanges".[22] Bob Hawke made the case for abandoning CRAMRA, which, he said, provided "a dangerous illusion of environment protection". He acknowledged that the joint proposal "has caused considerable anxiety" and sought to disabuse those who assumed opposition to CRAMRA was short term: "let me urge anyone who might still harbour that fantasy to abandon it".[23] Phillip Law was not convinced, dismissing Hawke's environmental cause as "a shrewd vote-catching bit of grandstanding ... but he will do the rounds, suffer the rebuffs, and then announce that he is sorry, he did his best, but was knocked back". Law continued to deride the Antarctic wilderness idea.[24]

Other so-called 'hard-liners' at the conference came out to defend CRAMRA. Chris Beeby outlined its operation and the risk to the moratorium. Unregulated mining, he said, was "the worst possible outcome [which] could do very serious damage to the physical environment of Antarctica, and it could do very serious damage to the political

---

[21] 13 November 1989, UN048467 "Antarctica: Tinker Foundation seminar" (NAA: B1387 89/932 PART 1).

[22] Richard A. Herr, H. Robert Hall, and Marcus Haward, "Introduction," in *Antarctica's Future: Continuity or Change?*, ed. Richard A. Herr, H. Robert Hall, and Marcus Haward (Australian Institute of International Affairs, 1990), 14–15.

[23] Robert J. L. Hawke, "Australia's Policy in Antarctica," ibid., ed. R. A. Herr, H. R. Hall, and M. G. Haward, 19.

[24] Phillip Law, "The Antarctic Wilderness: A Wild Idea!," ibid., 80.

environment as well".[25] Tucker Scully agreed, saying that "we must not, in the face of new theological approaches to Antarctic issues, lose sight of the political, as well as the physical ecology of Antarctica".[26] John Heap added: "it would be a tragedy if CRAMRA, the flower of 30 years of development of the ATS—not just six years of negotiation—were now to be lost. Its survival, like all else in the ATS, will depend on no-one pushing anyone else into an intolerable position."[27] Lord Shackleton (son of the famous 'heroic era' figure who in 1908 discovered Antarctic coal) urged Australia "to think again", saying that undermining consensus would "lead to tensions and instabilities that might not be contained".[28] This shared concern for the Treaty's health was to become a decisive factor in resolving CRAMRA's future—but that was still some time away.

Belgium told New Zealand on 24 November that it would definitely *not* sign CRAMRA.[29] Czechoslovakia and Japan squeezed in signatures just before the deadline. Meanwhile, events of even greater import were taking place as the Berlin wall crumbled, capturing far greater public attention than Antarctic affairs. In Wellington on 25 November 1989, it was a less-eventful spring Saturday and the Foreign Ministry pondered whether any more signatures of CRAMRA would arrive. None did. The total was 19, of which 16 were ATCPs.[30]

New Zealand's position was unenviable. It had green credentials as an early proponent of a world park but also stood to host the headquarters of the Antarctic Mineral Resources Commission. Media listed New Zealand among CRAMRA's supporters: "Mr Beeby, Tucker Scully from the US State Department and John Heap from the British Foreign Office are the minerals convention A-team … now it is they who are under pressure."[31] Whether they would change was moot but, by the end of November, Australia was becoming more optimistic with nine Parties sympathetic.[32]

[25] Christopher C Beeby, "The Convention on the Regulation of Antarctic Minerals and Its Future," ibid., 59.

[26] R. Tucker Scully, "The Antarctic Treaty as a System," ibid., 102.

[27] John A. Heap, "Sovereignty as a Source of Stress," ibid., 187.

[28] 23 November 1989, Lord Shackleton "Cold realism must prevail" *The Australian*, 13.

[29] 1 December 1989, BS48709 "Antarctica" (NAA: B1387 89/932 PART 1).

[30] https://www.mfat.govt.nz/en/about-us/who-we-are/treaties/convention-on-the-regulation-of-antarctic-mineral-resource-activities/ (accessed 3 February 2021).

[31] 8 December 1989, CE813345 "Antarctica: Press article" (NAA: B1387 89/932 PART 1).

[32] States considered sympathetic at the time were Belgium, France, India, Italy (ATCPs); and Austria, Bulgaria, Greece, Hungary, Romania (NCPs). 7 December 1989, DFAT,

With Belgium having decided not to sign CRAMRA, Foreign Affairs official Gérard Surquin appeared mystified as to why Belgium was not accepted as a full partner. He thought the environment initiative could be strengthened with formal cooperation as some support seemed fragile, citing pressure from the United States, which had "told the Greeks in Paris that they would have to pay for their attitude, not in the Antarctic Treaty context but elsewhere".[33]

JANUARY 1990: AUSTRALIA/FRANCE JOINT WORKING GROUP

Australian officials were preparing for the next Australia/France Working Group meeting scheduled for Canberra in January 1990. The IDC agreed to revise the paper on the components of an environmental convention. To appear less radical, it would include elements of other proposals. A goal was to discredit the idea that CRAMRA could operate as a mining ban because it required consensus to open an area. It would also show environmental benefits broader than a mining ban. AAD was requested to prepare advice showing scientists had no reason to fear restrictions on research.[34] This latter issue had traction within a research community "nervous about the implications" of US views that Australia's approach "would include controls on science".[35]

The 'Components Paper' was revised by DFAT's Bill Bush over the Christmas/New Year break, refined in January in consultation with other agencies, and completed in time for the Australia/France Joint Working Group meeting.[36] A "*tour d'horizon*" of other Parties' attitudes suggested that "the logic of the comprehensive approach was becoming more attractive to the large group of undecided countries", including Brazil, India, Chile, Poland and the USSR. Even Norwegian and New Zealand hardliners "seemed more muted since Paris". Sympathy in the US Congress was also increasing. France reported comments made by a senior UK

"Antarctic initiative: running sheet: Overview" (NAA: B1387 89/932 PART 1).

[33] 1 December 1989, BS48709 "Antarctica" (NAA: B1387 89/932 PART 1).

[34] 15 December 1989, "Antarctic IDC—Post-ATCM XV" (AWJ personal notes).

[35] 8 January 1990, WH112169 "Antarctica: US policy on CRAMRA: Keystone meeting" (NAA: B1387 89/932 PART 1).

[36] 16 January 1990, AAD message to Bill Bush, DFAT with comments on "9/1/90 Revised Australian-French components paper" (NAA: B1387 89/932 PART 1). January 1990, briefing notes for "France/Australia—Antarctic talks" (AAD: 89/578-1).

official suggesting "dissatisfaction with John Heap's unilateral handling of the CRAMRA/Antarctic environmental question to date".[37] Nevertheless, French officials still held doubts and were sceptical of developing the components of an environment convention, preferring to focus on political objectives. France needed to "demonstrate to the public that something tangible is achieved at the 1990 meetings". Despite the risk of backsliding, French officials agreed to prepare the next draft of the components paper. Australia came away concerned that French support was "primarily at the political level" and that "Australia will have to put in most of the effort to bring the initiative to fruition".[38]

JANUARY 1990: ENVIRONMENTALISTS ARE ACTIVE

Even if French officials lacked confidence, Sir Ninian Stephen considered Australia in "an imminently winnable position".[39] Jacques Cousteau was equally optimistic, creating publicity and influence—his Foundation had reached 300,000 members, mostly in the United States. Other US environmentalists were united in their campaign to defeat CRAMRA in the Senate.[40] The strategy included building support for the Gore Resolution and rebutting a *Time* magazine cover story promoting CRAMRA.[41] Encouraged by Bruce Mannheim and Jim Barnes, opposing CRAMRA was becoming a priority for US environmentalists. While only just beginning to coordinate, by January 1990 14 US NGOs opposed CRAMRA, leaving the World Resources Institute as "the only environmental organisation actively supporting ratification".[42]

United States momentum for ratification was slowing and the White House had "given no indication that it regards CRAMRA as a priority".

[37] 25 January 1990, CE830446 "Antarctica: French—Australian initiative for comprehensive environmental protection—bilateral consultations, Canberra" (AAD: 89/578-1).

[38] 1 February 1990, DASETT submission to minister "Australian-French Antarctic initiative" (NAA: B1387 89/932 PART 1).

[39] 9 January 1990, John Carruthers "Antarctic ban winnable" *The Herald* (Melbourne), 4.

[40] 4 January 1990, "Cousteau enlists children's help to spread the cold, hard facts" *The Mercury*, 7. January 1990, Cousteau Society "Antarctica in the 1990s: Challenge for a true global environmental policy" (AU-ATADD-5-BB-GE-458).

[41] 10 January 1990, The Wilderness Society (US) memorandum "Notes from 1/10/90 domestic advocacy strategy meeting" (NAA: B1387 90/498 PART 1). Michael D Lemonick, "Antarctica: Is Any Place Safe from Mankind?" *Time* 135, no. 3 (1990).

[42] 11 January 1990, WH112309 "Conservation of the Antarctic environment: United States" (AAD: 84/360-2).

The Gore Resolution's 16 sponsors included "prominent members of the Foreign Relations Committee", and NGOs had lobbied all members of Congress. In addition, Australia's Washington Embassy reported that US industry now appeared to be "generally indifferent to the convention".[43] As the United States was among the strongest CRAMRA supporters, raising domestic awareness would be important. A televised debate between Al Gore and Tucker Scully did just that—nothing new emerged from either side, but it elevated the previously minimal US media attention.[44] Capitalising on the public mood, Representative Silvio Conte introduced a House of Representatives Bill opposing CRAMRA and directing the secretary of state to pursue "permanently banning all mineral development of the continent". According to Conte, "saving a continent is a once-in-a-lifetime chance and we can't afford to miss the opportunity".[45] Environmentalists helped draft the Bill which had Republican and Democrat co-sponsors. Scully "dismissed the Bill as 'posturing' and predicted the Administration would oppose it".[46] What may not have been predicted was that it was part of a coming tide of similar bills.

NGO campaigns ramped up, and diplomats, lawyers and environmentalists began exchanging views. In London, a February 1990 Australian Studies Centre conference informally canvassed differing ambitions for Antarctica with papers by John Heap, John Burgess and Kelly Rigg (Greenpeace), among others.[47] Discussions traversed well-known ground on mining, the importance of consensus, and whether there was a 'moral' position to take.[48] A moral position had been taken by the Soviet Union where General Secretary Mikhail Gorbachev had said that "our grandchildren will never forgive us if we fail to preserve this phenomenal ecological

---

[43] 8 January 1990, WH112132 "Conservation of Antarctic environment: United States" (NAA: B1387 89/417).

[44] 7 February 1990, WH113235 "United States: Antarctic minerals convention" (NAA: B1387 89/932 PART 1).

[45] 8 February 1990, Silvio O. Conte media release "Conte introduces Antarctic protection legislation" (NAA: B1387 89/932 PART 1).

[46] 8 February 1990, WH113303 "United States: Antarctica protection and Conservation Act" (NAA: B1387 89/932 PART 1).

[47] 11 January 1990, conference invitation "Antarctica: An exploitable resource or too valuable to develop?" (NAA: B1387 89/932 PART 1).

[48] David I. M. MacDonald, "Recent Meetings: Antarctica—an Exploitable Resource or Too Important to Develop? Institute of Commonwealth Studies, London. 21 February, 1990," *Antarctic Science* 2, no. 2 (1990). Grahame Cook, *The Future of Antarctica: Exploitation Versus Preservation* (Manchester University Press, 1990).

system".[49] On 14 February, Chairman of the USSR Council of Ministers Nikolai Ryzhkov endorsed "initiatives that cover the survival of the Antarctic" as a global preserve.[50] That the USSR had signed CRAMRA on its opening day was being ignored by Soviet leaders. Bob Hawke lauded Ryzhkov's stance.[51] Hawke had another motive to spruik optimism: on 16 February, he requested Parliament be dissolved for a general election on 24 March. Having come to power in 1983 on the back of a mainland environmental vote, like the 1984 and 1987 campaigns Hawke had to appeal to environmentalists and Tasmanian voters.[52] His platform included an Australian Antarctic Foundation to build support for the Antarctic initiative. In full campaign mode, Hawke announced a visit to Hobart that day with his "good friend" Jacques Cousteau. Leveraging the explorer's popularity, Hawke had invited Cousteau to Australia.[53] During Cousteau's visit, he enjoyed another breakfast with Hawke and was made an Honorary Companion to the Order of Australia.[54]

---

[49] Peter J. Beck, "Antarctica as a Zone of Peace," in *Antarctica's Future: Continuity or Change?*, ed. R. A. Herr, H. R. Hall, and M. G. Haward (Australian Institute of International Affairs, 1990), 220. 26 December 1989, Alexander Bovin "Save the Antarctic" *Izvestia*, translated in: 28 December 1989, DFAT memorandum MS13971, Moscow to Canberra "Antarctica: Soviet press comments on mining" (NAA: B1387 89/932 PART 1).

[50] 22 February 1990, CE842382 "Antarctica: Speech by Ryzhkov" (NAA: B1387 89/932 PART 2).

[51] 14 February 1990, Prime Minister (speech) http://pmtranscripts.pmc.gov.au/sites/default/files/original/00007899.pdf (accessed 1 February 2021).

[52] Hawke's 1983 pledge to protect the Franklin River had cost him votes in Tasmania. See 24 February 1990, Prime Minister, transcript news conference http://pmtranscripts.pmc.gov.au/sites/default/files/original/00007923.pdf (accessed 1 February 2021).

[53] 19 February 1990, Prime Minister, untitled media release http://pmtranscripts.pmc.gov.au/sites/default/files/original/00007913.pdf (accessed 1 February 2021).

[54] "Jacques Cousteau's Visit to Australia," *Australian Foreign Affairs and Trade: The Monthly Record* 61, no. 2 (1990). 21 February 1990, AAD internal minute "Prime Minister's visit to Antarctic Division" (NAA: B1387 1989/1013). Hawke was accompanied by economics adviser Craig Emerson and media adviser Barrie Cassidy.

February 1990: New Zealand Loosens Its Grip on CRAMRA

Across the Tasman Sea, one of CRAMRA's strongest supporters was wavering. Cousteau followed his fêted Australian trip with a visit to New Zealand where a "rethink" had been hinted.[55] The visit happened to coincide with Prime Minister Geoffrey Palmer's surprise announcement on 26 February that Cabinet had that day decided to "set aside the question of ratifying CRAMRA" and, instead, seek a binding moratorium. New Zealand was not abandoning CRAMRA, he said, but seeking to resolve the impasse.[56] Palmer may have been influenced by Bob Hawke during his visit to Auckland to capitalise on advice that a change of New Zealand policy was possible. New Zealand recognised that "CRAMRA was not of itself going to get up, and that new ideas were needed", but had to appease the United States about the "tilt towards Australian policy". Cousteau's visit caused "a great deal of irritation" because "obvious linkages between the Government's decision and the visit would be made".[57] Cousteau's 27 February visit was "rather overshadowed" by New Zealand's decision but, unfazed by being upstaged, he praised the policy shift and "New Zealand's early advocacy of the world park". Cousteau suggested that the proposed environmental regime "should be known as the Wellington Convention in tribute to New Zealand's efforts on CRAMRA" (seemingly oblivious to the confusion this would cause as CRAMRA was already known by that name). He also suggested claimants forego sovereignty to facilitate Antarctica's internationalisation (seemingly oblivious to the threat to the Treaty's stability and, therefore, the success of any environmental regime).[58] Hawke was jubilant at New Zealand's decision which he described as "snowballing support" attributed to "the power of persuasion" (presumably public).[59] *The Dominion* described the decision as "a

---

[55] 14 February 1990, PA79253 "Antarctica—possible evolution in New Zealand position" (NAA: B1387 89/932 PART 1).

[56] 26 February 1990, (New Zealand) Prime Minister "Post-Cabinet press conference, Monday 26 February 1990 2:00 pm" (NAA: B1387 89/932 PART 1).

[57] 26 February 1990, WL39652 "New Zealand: Antarctica" (NAA: B1387 89/932 PART 2).

[58] 1 March 1990, WL39703 "New Zealand: Antarctica" (NAA: B1387 89/932 PART 2). 27 February 1990 "Cousteau suggests end to Antarctic territorial claims" (AU-ATADD-1-BB-NZ-138). 28 February 1990 "Give up Antarctic claims: Cousteau" *Canberra Times*, 16.

[59] 26 February 1990, Prime Minister, media release http://pmtranscripts.pmc.gov.au/release/transcript-7928 (accessed 1 February 2021). Hawke's 'snowball' analogy included

remarkable coup for Mr Hawke" and, sadly for Palmer, characterised it as a backdown and not going far enough.[60] Unconvinced, ASOC's Cath Wallace was suspicious, saying New Zealand was just "trying to work out a deal with the US and Britain that goes some way towards protecting the continent while keeping the options on mining open".[61] Hawke, however, was upbeat: "country after country is responding to public opinion", he said, "which says that it would be an obscenity to allow mining in the Antarctic". He even predicted that on this basis the United States was "unlikely to ratify the minerals regime".[62]

New Zealand's decision was significant—the country standing to gain the most from CRAMRA and having done the most to secure it, now appeared to set it aside. Yet despite seemingly compatible policy, New Zealand was unwilling to embrace fully the Australian and French proposal because, Palmer explained, an environment convention "might not prove universally acceptable". However, "if New Zealand pursued a position which was close to that of Australia … it might be able to be a catalyst which would break the present impasse".[63]

March 1990: Diplomats Call on Capitals

Meanwhile, DFAT's John Burgess continued his European visit, hoping to forestall back-sliding by sympathisers. Gérard Surquin confirmed Belgian support and offered to convene an international symposium in Brussels to generate momentum in the lead up to the SATCM.[64] In Rome, Burgess was told that Italy remained strong.[65] The Federal Republic of

Italy, Belgium and Greece. 26 February 1990, Prime Minister, transcript of interview http://pmtranscripts.pmc.gov.au/release/transcript-7925 (accessed 1 February 2021). Templeton revealed that Hawke beat Palmer to announcing New Zealand's position. See Templeton, *A Wise Adventure II: New Zealand and Antarctica after 1960*, 263.

[60] 1 March 1990, WL39694 "New Zealand: Antarctica" (NAA: B1387 89/932 PART 2).

[61] Stephanie Pain, "New Zealand's U-Turn Threatens Antarctic Mining Treaty," *New Scientist* 125, no. 1707 (1990).

[62] 26 February 1990, Bruce Montgomery "US likely to back ban on Antarctic mining—Hawke" *The Australian*.

[63] 12 March 1990, WL39815 "Antarctica—meeting with Mr Palmer" (NAA: B1387 89/932 PART 2).

[64] 27 February 1990, RO45664 "Antarctica: Consultations by AS ENB: Belgium" (NAA: B1387 89/932 PART 2).

[65] 28 February 1990, BO48598 "Antarctica: Consultations by AS ENB: Belgium" (NAA: B1387 89/932 PART 2).

Germany was being influenced by the Greens highlighting the Antarctic issue, and, in Bonn, the Chancellor's office told him that the Federal Republic of Germany "wished to be helpful". Australia was encouraged by the references to a 'nature reserve, land of science' and the sympathy for either a mining ban or a long-term moratorium. On the other hand, Kurt Messer was proposing a protocol rather than convention and Burgess concluded that such a middle path might not get very far.[66] In France, Charley Causeret was not convinced: the proposal "represented a trap" and he took "a rather cynical view of Messer's motives". Messer appeared to fear that minerals might disrupt the next ATCM, which would be hosted in Bonn in 1991, and, furthermore, his ideas seemed heavily influenced by John Heap. Causeret predicted that "the UK, the US and the Latin Americans would exploit them to argue against the French/Australian proposals".[67] Although the initiative "still has a long way to go", opposition to it nevertheless appeared to be softening.[68]

Burgess then called in to New Delhi. External Affairs official Prakash Shah confirmed Indian support for a mining ban, with a strengthened moratorium until it was achieved. Vinod Gaur of the Department of Ocean Development went further, saying that India will "back you all the way" and "work for total protection of the Antarctic environment until such time as that approach became hopeless". Burgess concluded that "Indian support for our position has in fact firmed".[69] For the moment, it was a positive development.

With strengthening support from known sympathisers, it was time to think about others. The United Kingdom was already "looking to adopt a more accommodating approach", at least by moderating its rhetoric. John Heap considered the "minor differences of approach ... capable of resolution" and accepted the desirability of comprehensive measures. "The real stumbling block", he said, "is whether a new instrument should *replace* CRAMRA". Even so, "ultimately there must be a consensus based on compromise: that was the Antarctic Treaty System way". In a frank

---

[66] 28 February 1990, BO48602 "Antarctica: Consultations by AS ENB: FRG" (NAA: B1387 89/932 PART 2). 22 March 1990, DFAT memorandum "Antarctica: FRG Parliamentary debate 8 February 1990" (NAA: B1387 89/932 PART 3).

[67] 21 March 1990, PA79891 "Antarctica—FRG compromise package—French views" (NAA: B1387 89/932 PART 2).

[68] 1 March 1990, "Park plan support grows" *The Australian*, 12.

[69] 5 March 1990, ND73249 "Antarctica and the environment—Burgess' visit" (NAA: B1387 89/932 PART 2).

exchange with John Burgess and Australian High Commission (AHC) official David Mason, Heap argued for a protocol. It would provide an environmental regime *alongside* the minerals convention. In his view, an environmental protocol should address the weaknesses of both CCAMLR and CRAMRA, but replace neither. Burgess reported that "Heap may be well in advance of US thinking". Heap had "lost none of his zeal for CRAMRA and (against all of the odds) clearly believes that there are still prospects for it getting into place", although it "would be fettered for some time". Heap, still thinking tactics, unsuccessfully requested that Australia and France not circulate the components paper before the May 1990 Nansen Foundation conference, a forum at which powerful voices would be heard.[70] The United Kingdom's preference for a protocol, rather than a convention, was repeated in discussions with France. The Soviet Union, however, preferred a convention.[71] The question the instrument's *form* was to become as critical as its *content.*

US officials were also contemplating a protocol, although comprising only broad principles and a time-limited moratorium.[72] John Burgess considered the US was lagging developments elswehere. However, Antarctica was gaining a profile in Congress where there were now three bills. Representative Conte argued that the risks of mining required the United States to "use our position in the world to negotiate an international agreement ... this is a rare opportunity to leave a lasting legacy".[73] Similar testimony was provided to Congress by the Cousteau Foundation and Jim Barnes. Representative Vento tabled a bill noting the "unwillingness of the Administration to consider seriously alternatives to CRAMRA" and asking it to lead on environment protection.[74] NGO campaigns increased, including requests to meet Secretary of State James Baker, who was believed to "have an open mind on CRAMRA". Environmentalists suggested to

[70] 27 February 1990, RO45663 "Antarctica: Consultations by AS ENB: Heap's views" (NAA: B1387 89/932 PART 2).

[71] 13 March 1990, PA79723 "Antarctica: French discussions with Heap" (NAA: B1387 89/932 PART 2). In 1974, Heap had argued that minerals be addressed in a protocol to the Treaty—see Chap. 2.

[72] Templeton, *A Wise Adventure II: New Zealand and Antarctica after 1960*, 269.

[73] 14 March 1990, "Statement of Honorable Silvio Conte before the Subcommittee on Oversight and Investigations, Committee on Merchant Marine and Fisheries" (NAA: B1387 89/932 PART 2).

[74] 6 April 1990, WH115207 "United States: Antarctica World park and Protection Act" (NAA: B1387 89/932 PART 3).

mining groups that supporting a ban would "improve their environmental credentials ... at little or no cost" and "remove the major pillar from the Administration's argument in support of CRAMRA".[75] Tasmanian environmentalist Bob Brown joined in, co-signing a letter to President George Bush while in Washington on 16 April as one of the inaugural recipients of the Goldman Prize for environmental achievement.[76] Such efforts were rebuffed. Tucker Scully warned Alan Brown that US attitudes had not changed because "CRAMRA was the best environment instrument yet negotiated" and "a ban was unstable because it could be reversed". The United States would, however, put a paper to the Chile meeting proposing "elaboration of the current regulatory approach" but in parallel with CRAMRA. Helpfully, he suggested that the form of future instruments be deferred until there was progress on substantive measures.[77] Consensus was still a very long way off—another year would pass before anything like consensus appeared achievable.

April 1990: "Damaging Tactically to Give Way Now"

Apart from needing to restore consensus, Australia and France had to respond to powerful counterarguments. The problem was relying on *politically* attractive propositions to respond to *legally* persuasive positions— after all, CRAMRA was legally tight, while the environment initiative had no legal framework. DFAT's Bill Bush prepared responses to the issues on which Australia was most vulnerable including the assumption that mining could never be safe; that CRAMRA's environmental provisions were defective; that the need for consensus to open an area amounted to a mining ban; and that CRAMRA was better than an unregulated scramble.[78] This work would support the revised components paper, the drafting of which had required extended negotiation. The 29-page revision was done

---

[75] 30 March 1990, WH114989 "Antarctica: Views of US environmental groups on CRAMRA" (NAA: B1387 89/932 PART 2).

[76] 19 April 1990, WH115539 "Antarctica" (NAA: B1387 89/932 PART 3). See also: https://www.goldmanprize.org/recipient/robert-brown/ (accessed 3 February 2021).

[77] 26 April 1990, WH115847 "Antarctica: United States views on environmental protection" (NAA: B1387 89/932 PART 3).

[78] 15 March 1990, DFAT facsimile "Antarctica: Questions and answers concerning mining and the environmental initiative" (NAA: B1387 89/932 PART 2).

in three languages.[79] France urged early distribution lest it was "distracted by other proposals from the Germans or our opponents".[80] Gérard Surquin agreed that Australia and France "should continue to press forward [as] it would be very damaging tactically to give way now".[81] Australian diplomatic missions were sent instructions to disseminate the paper, with a covering *aide memoire*, to elaborate in "greater detail than attempted hitherto, the possible content of a comprehensive convention".[82]

Australian diplomats reported the non-committal reactions: ministries needed time to study the paper; a response would come as soon as possible; it would be read with a positive spirit; and other classic diplomatic brush-offs.[83] Chile was still rebuilding after the transition to Patricio Aylwin's democracy, but despite the upheaval it still sympathised with comprehensive environmental measures and would host the November 1990 SATCM.[84] Alarmingly, the USSR was not as upbeat as Gorbachev and Ryzhkov had suggested.[85] In the Federal Republic of Germany Foreign Ministry, Deputy Head of the Legal Division Antonius Eitel's sympathy for an environmental convention was quickly overtaken by Messer's advancement of a protocol with a mining ban, while allowing CRAMRA to be revived if agreement could not be reached.[86] Australia regarded the positions as not immediately compatible, but there was a "strong interest in not alienating the FRG".[87] Charley Causeret was unconvinced, jealously concerned that "the proposal is premature and

[79] There was no Russian version. 16 March 1990, "Revised Australian-French paper on the components of a comprehensive regime for the protection of the Antarctic environment and its dependent and associated ecosystems" (NAA: B1387 90/498 PART 2).

[80] 29 March 1990, PA80052 "Antarctica: ATCM XV report and components paper" (AAD: 89/133-2).

[81] 2 April 1990, BS49496 "Antarctica: Belgian views" (NAA: B1387 89/932 PART 2).

[82] 5 April 1990, CE861222 "Antarctic environment initiative: Representations" (NAA: B1387 89/932 PART 3).

[83] Relevant reporting is in NAA: B1387 89/932 PART 3 and NAA: B1387 90/498 PART 2

[84] 26 April 1990, SC20584 "Antarctic environment initiative—representations" (NAA: B1387 89/932 PART 3). 30 March 1990, SC20498 "Chile's Antarctic policy team" (AAD: 89/914-1).

[85] 20 April 1990, MS41600 "Antarctic environment initiative: Representations" (NAA: B1387 90/498 PART 3a).

[86] 11 April 1990, BO49109 "Antarctic environment initiative: Representations" (NAA: B1387 90/498 PART 2).

[87] 3 April 1990, CE859872 "Antarctica: French/Australian initiative" (NAA: B1387 89/932 PART 2).

risks cutting across our own".[88] Australian officials considered this an overreaction to a proposal which gave "CRAMRA a decent burial rather than raising the possibility of its resurrection".[89] Georges Duquin's hesitancy on the Federal Republic of Germany contrasted with his views on "the possibility of associating New Zealand more directly". This appeared to have been inspired by the Cousteau Foundation's Bernard Charrier, who argued that were it "possible to get the New Zealanders on-side ... our position will be almost invincible".[90] Such optimism appeared unduly influenced by NGOs unqualified to determine what would be diplomatically achievable.

Australian NGOs were realistic. Consultations were held to garner their support for the Australia/France components paper.[91] Environmentalists' global campaigning was increasingly coordinated. In the United Kingdom, World Wide Fund for Nature (WWF) spokesperson Cassandra Phillips was confident: "it is never easy to persuade Margaret Thatcher to change her mind, but we are hopeful that we can mobilise enough public opinion". Phillips' optimism was probably justified—thousands had written to UK Parliamentarians calling for a world park. Opinion polls were already showing 60% public support.[92] NGOs simultaneously launched their own proposal, an ambitious 94-page draft.[93] Jacques Cousteau was active again, this time giving testimony before a 2 May US congressional committee where he considered CRAMRA a "lifeless" but well-intentioned "anachronism". By his optimistic count, 13 nations opposed it, and "it would be a great pity", he said, if the United States "was the last country to change its mind". On this, he would prove correct. To the delight of Australia and France, Cousteau spoke strongly for the joint initiative. They would have been less pleased, however, when he repeated his call for the "renouncing

[88] 16 April 1990, PA80320 "Antarctica: French/Australian initiative" (NAA: B1387 89/932 PART 3).

[89] 17 April 1990, CE865006 "Antarctica: French/Australian initiative" (NAA: B1387 89/932 PART 3).

[90] 17 April 1990, PA80337 "Antarctica: French/Australian initiative" (NAA: B1387 89/932 PART 3).

[91] 30 April 1990, DFAT minute "Antarctica: Meeting with NGOs, Tuesday 1 May" (NAA: B1387 89/932 PART 3). 1 May 1990, author's handwritten notes "NGOs briefing" (NAA: B1387 90/498 PART 3).

[92] 10 May 1990, transcript ABC Radio *Early AM* "UK campaign to join Aust in opposing Antarctic minerals convention" (NAA: B1387 90/498 PART 1).

[93] 16 May 1990, James Barnes (Friends of the Earth) "The Convention on Antarctic Conservation—Draft" (AAD: B13/199).

of national claims forever". Greenpeace's Susan Sabella maintained opposition to CRAMRA. The World Resources Institute, however, defended it—after all, it could not be considered "obsolete [as] 17 out of 22 ATCPs had signed" and "even France and Australia had accepted it by supporting the Final Act". The State Department declined to testify "when the sub-Committee decided, against normal practice, to allow Cousteau, rather than the Administration, to appear as first witness".[94] Next day, Cousteau was at the press conference called by Gore and Senator John Kerry to announce the Antarctic environmental bills.[95]

MAY 1990: "RETHINKING THEIR POSITION"

The Australia/France proposal was competing for space with at least six proposals ranging from a program of work to fill gaps in the system, to a new convention subsuming all the existing measures.[96] Without a paper of its own, the United Kingdom pushed for its vision of a protocol rather than a free-standing regime. John Heap described the Antarctic Treaty as "the central pillar on which, like a Christmas tree, other bits could be hung" and argued that a protocol was the appropriate legal form (apparently forgetting that the tree's other hanging bits already included two stand-alone conventions: CCAS and CCAMLR).[97] As the only proponents of a convention, Australia and France needed to mount a strong case. To make progress, someone would have to give ground—but making concessions on environmental options was one thing, conceding precious political positions was altogether different.

New Zealand's February decision had "led to other Parties rethinking their position".[98] Yet just five unambiguously supported a convention containing a mining ban. Sympathy could be heard from six others and,

---

[94] 23 May 1990, WH116817 "US: Antarctica: House Foreign Affairs Committee hearing" (NAA: B1387 90/498 PART 1).

[95] 3 May 1990, WH116126 "Antarctic environment: US Senate legislation" (NAA: B1387 90/498 PART 1). See also the press releases of 3 May 1990 from Congressman Silvio Conte, Senator Al Gore and US Senate (NAA: B1387 90/498 PART 1).

[96] Other proposals came from the United States, Sweden, New Zealand, Chile and environmental groups. 2 May 1990, "Proposals for comprehensive protection of the Antarctic" (NAA: B1387 90/498 PART 2).

[97] 3 May 1990, LH101059 "Antarctic environment initiative: Representations" (NAA: B1387 90/498 PART 1).

[98] 15 May 1990, DASETT brief to minister "Australian/French initiative for Antarctica" (NAA: B1387 90/498 PART 2).

equally, six highly influential Parties were welded to CRAMRA. At best, less than half of the Parties showed sympathy to Australia and France. On the other hand, 22 undecided Parties possibly had room to move. By mid-May, Greece confirmed its support and Denmark followed with the Foreign Ministry's Jørgen Lilje-Jensen considering the Australia/France proposal as the way forward if the "firm no compromises line being touted by Duquin" was relaxed.[99] Support from Greece and Denmark was welcome, but they were NCPs: firm decisions would require ATCPs to be locked-in.

May 1990: "We Are Out of the Bunker"

DFAT's Alan Brown, Ian Nicholson and John Burgess visited Oslo for May's Nansen Foundation symposium. The Foundation had previously provided a forum for informally exchanging views on minerals issues in May 1973. Seventeen years later and with 150 participants from 28 countries, the far larger May 1990 conference addressed the environment.[100] The Australia/France proposals "became the focus of much of the debate, on and off the floor", drawing "charged interventions from CRAMRA supporters" but also "a share of favourable comment". There was still vacillation: Desirée Edmar said Sweden "wished to be helpful, but was not sure how"; Prakash Shah said that India remained "broadly sympathetic" but showed "no readiness to become too closely associated"; and the USSR's Sergei Karev was "strongly critical", revealing "a very wide gap between Soviet responses at the officials' and political level". The United States "took no active part", and Jim Barnes (now representing Friends of the Earth) thought that "there was every indication that the US Congress would not be prepared to ratify the minerals convention". The report to Canberra said that there was "a readiness to recognise the new proposals are a fact of life, here to stay, and have to be addressed seriously"—or, as the French refreshingly summarised it "we are out of the bunker, the initiative has become respectable".[101] Little did they know that in an Oslo

---

[99] 15 May 1990, AT39770 "Antarctic environment initiative: Representations" (NAA: B1387 90/498 PART 1). 31 May 1990, CP14013 "Antarctic environment initiative" (NAA: B1387 90/498 PART 2).

[100] Arnfinn Jørgensen-Dahl and Willy Østreng, *The Antarctic Treaty System in World Politics* (Macmillan/Fridtjof Nansen Institute, 1991), xiii–xiv, xxi–xxii, 1–3.

[101] 24 May 1990, MA25456 "Antarctic: Nansen Institute symposium" (NAA: B1387 90/498 PART 1).

restaurant, at what was later described as a "clandestine" meeting, a select group of CRAMRA supporters was chewing over an alternative: John Heap's proposed protocol.[102]

While in Europe, Burgess visited Madrid, Bonn, Warsaw and Moscow. Spain, a relatively new ATCP, was sympathetic. Burgess reported that while "we can number Spain among our strongest sympathisers outside the core group ... we can count on our critics to pay Spain some further attention".[103] This development proved important because, the following year, Spain would host the meetings that achieved consensus on the environment.

During his 4 June 1990 Moscow visit, Burgess quizzed Sergei Karev on the USSR's position in Oslo which had been highly critical of Australia. Karev, who'd had long involvement in CRAMRA, dismissed the Gorbachev and Ryzhkov statements as they "had not been fully consulted at the expert level". Karev's view was itself dismissed when raised with Deputy Chair of the Supreme Soviet Ecology Committee Alexey Yablokov, the Directorate for International Scientific and Technical Cooperation's Boris Maiorsky, and Head of the Soviet Antarctic Program Artur Chilingarov. All took the view that "Karev and his people would have to change ... we should simply regard the present as a transition period". Burgess considered it "extraordinary that one not so senior officer in the Foreign Ministry [was] defending CRAMRA in consultation with like-minded officials in other countries despite contrary statements at the highest political level".[104] Actually, such disconnects were not unusual. In Wellington, Prime Minister Geoffrey Palmer was also at odds with Foreign Affairs: "it didn't matter what FA officials say, it is what he (Palmer) says that makes policy, and the policy was that NZ did not see itself going back to CRAMRA."[105] Sweden, on the other hand, was unambiguous. It wanted to help Australia and France—it just wasn't convinced about a convention. The Foreign Ministry's Desirée Edmar offered to lobby other Nordic states, but thought it easier to "make an impression" after Rolf Andersen's departure

---

[102] Mike G. Richardson, "John Arnfield Heap, CMG," *Polar Record* 42, no. 3 (2006): 265.

[103] 29 May 1990, MA25473 "Antarctic environment: AS ENB consultations: Spain" (NAA: B1387 90/498 PART 1).

[104] 12 June 1990, CE889356 "Antarctica: AS ENB consultations: Soviet Union" (NAA: B1387 90/498 PART 2).

[105] 19 June 1990, Janet Dalziel (Greenpeace) "Meeting with Prime Minister" (NAA: B1387 90/498 PART 3).

for a new diplomatic posting.[106] In Antarctic affairs, bureaucrats held considerable control over government policy.

Chile was also considering several factors: its own policy interests, its relationship with counterclaimants (Argentina and the United Kingdom), and its wish to facilitate a successful November SATCM. Complicating matters were internal differences between Jorge Berguño and Oscar Pinochet of the Foreign Ministry, and Fernando Zegers (a CRAMRA stalwart and director of the Antarctic Institute), who strongly favoured CRAMRA. On mining, Chile was likely to support a protocol with a moratorium, rather than a convention with a ban. Chile hoped that Argentina would relax its hard-line CRAMRA support and "join forces to act as honest brokers".[107] First, however, the three counterclaimants would meet as they "had agreed to consult closely on all matters which might affect their respective territorial claims".[108] Officials were caught off-guard when, on 25 June, Chile's Foreign Minister Enrique Silva Cimma advised Jean-Maurice Ripert (Michel Rocard's adviser) that Chile supported the joint initiative: the "immediate stifled reaction of the Chilean counsellor accompanying the Foreign Minister indicated that Silva Cimma had gone further than expected".[109] Again, politicians and officials were out of step. The 6 July 1990 trilateral meeting of Antarctic Peninsula claimants did not achieve tripartite agreement and there had been a "worrying" announcement: Argentina's Antarctic territories were "to become provinces of Argentina".[110] Argentina's José Otegui was more accommodating on the environment than on sovereignty and "Argentina and Chile are indeed not only moving along parallel lines but are marching in step".[111] Not so the United Kingdom. John Heap and his legal adviser Ian Hendry insisted that progress on the environment could not proceed without committing

[106] 5 June 1990, ST26555 "Antarctica: Nansen Institute Symposium—a Swedish view" (NAA: B1387 90/498 PART 2).

[107] 15 June 1990, SC20755 "Antarctica: Chile's policy and the SCM" (NAA: B1387 90/498 PART 2).

[108] 19 June 1990, SC20769 "Antarctica: Chile's policy and the SCM" (AAD: 89/914-1).

[109] 27 June 1990, PA81713 "Antarctica: Rocard/Silva Cimma meeting and Santiago SCM" (AAD: 89/914-1).

[110] 20 June 1990, PA81586 "Antarctica—reactions to revised components paper" (NAA: B1387 90/498 PART 2).

[111] 5 July 1990, SC20823 "Antarctica: environment initiative—Chile" (NAA: B1387 90/498 PART 3). 16 July 1990, BA35694 "Antarctica: Australia/France joint initiative: Argentine views" (AAD: 89/914-1). Another revelation was Argentina's willingness to consider a Treaty secretariat.

to CRAMRA's entry into force—a position that Jorge Berguño considered "clever but artificial [as] the UK approach would only lead to further polarisation of the issues".[112] The United Kingdom was setting itself up for a polarised position, and not just diplomatically. Domestically, the traditional bipartisanship on Antarctica had been lost. Shadow Foreign Secretary Gerald Kaufman committed a future Labour government to denouncing CRAMRA, revoking any implementing legislation and promoting Antarctica as a world nature reserve.[113] However, with the Thatcher government endorsing CRAMRA, UK officials continued to argue for an environmental protocol to operate in parallel with CRAMRA.

Unsurprisingly, external factors were influencing some Parties. Peru was keen to show "interest in environmental issues outside the Amazon". Ecuador, however, "does not want to burn its bridges" ahead of the assessment of its bid to be recognised as an ATCP. India's support was waning because of "French involvement in the construction of a nuclear power station in Pakistan" and "Australia's sale of Mirage jets to Pakistan".[114] Despite efforts to quarantine Antarctica from external issues, bilateral problems clearly impinged on policy. Even Australia and France had continuing disagreements. Australia opposed France's wish to circulate a draft convention, preferring to further develop the components paper while Georges Duquin "didn't want to risk boring Antarctic Treaty Parties with a series of revisions of what was a rather turgid paper".[115] Tactics were critical as, by Australia's count, full support had slipped from five to four.[116] The risk of losing the initiative was real.

[112] 11 July 1990, SC20848 "Antarctica: Trilateral meeting between Chile, Argentina and UK" (NAA: B1387 90/498 PART 2).

[113] 1 June 1990, media release "Labour will act to prevent commercial exploitation of Antarctica, says Kaufman: Tory Government licence for mining will be revoked" (AU-ATADD-1-BB-GB-293).

[114] 20 June 1990, PA81586 "Antarctica—reactions to revised components paper" (NAA: B1387 90/498 PART 2).

[115] 14 June 1990, PA81470 "Australia/France Joint Working Group on the Environment" (AAD: 89/578-2).

[116] 27 June 1990, "Antarctic initiative: Running sheet: Overview" (NAA: B1387 90/498 PART 3).

July 1990: "A Helpful Evolution of New Zealand's Position"

New Zealand NGOs reported information from "a confidential source" that environment department officials were seeking to "make the government's position less ambiguous".[117] This coincided with the departure of experienced Antarctic negotiators Colin Keating and Gerard van Bohemen.[118] In addition, for October's coming election the Opposition was supporting a world park, promising to work with Australia on a total mining ban.[119] Palmer was being wedged. On 6 July 1990, he announced New Zealand support for a protocol "to deal comprehensively with environmental protection in the Antarctic". A protocol, he argued, would "overcome the legal pitfalls associated with the idea of a convention" separate from the Treaty. Palmer denied having a "hidden agenda on the minerals convention. That is simply not true ... we have set it aside". New Zealand would also pursue a binding moratorium.[120]

Australia's muted response characterised the announcement only as "a helpful evolution of New Zealand's position".[121] Chris Beeby conceded that it lacked clarity.[122] Palmer may well have been disappointed that his ideas were "notable for the lack of attention they have attracted". Even Greenpeace did not react.[123] However, he was even more disappointed with a bungle by officials. There were discrepancies between Palmer's statement and the version sent to diplomatic posts, a weaker early draft. What really attracted media attention was that it took NGOs to detect the

---

[117] 19 June 1990, Janet Dalziel (Greenpeace) "Meeting with Prime Minister" (NAA: B1387 90/498 PART 3).

[118] 27 June 1990, WL40881 "Antarctic environment: New Zealand policy" (NAA: B1387 90/498 PART 2).

[119] 27 June 1990, WL40887 "New Zealand: National Party's environmental policy" (NAA: B1387 90/498 PART 2). 23 July 1990, CE906809 "Antarctica: New Zealand National Party policy" (NAA: B1387 90/498 PART 3).

[120] 6 July 1990, Prime Minister [New Zealand] press statement "Antarctica environmental policy" (NAA: B1387 90/498 PART 2).

[121] 6 July 1990, "Press points on Mr Palmer's press statement on Antarctica" (NAA: B1387 90/498 PART 3).

[122] 6 July 1990, WL40998 "Antarctica: NZ position on mining and comprehensive protection" (NAA: B1387 90/498 PART 3).

[123] 10 July 1990, WL41022 "Antarctica" (NAA: B1387 90/498 PART 3).

error.[124] Beeby's 10 July visit to Canberra to promote the proposed protocol was received with suspicion. DFAT considered "the term 'protocol' … a focus for those who argue for a minimalist instrument. This reinforces us in our judgement that, for tactical reasons, we should continue to press for a convention". Intriguingly, there was the "striking similarity" between Beeby's protocol and the views of other Parties—it was "clear that there has been considerable caucusing going on".[125] It would be another few weeks before New Zealand would really shift. Meanwhile, another development was underway.

JULY 1990: "MORE FLEXIBLE AND FORTHCOMING"

The United States was also exploring the protocol idea. This "helped explain why Bohlen's evidence to the US Congress, although vague, seemed to suggest a more flexible and forthcoming US position".[126] Curtis Bohlen had recently become assistant secretary of state, overseeing Antarctic issues. Given his previous position as vice president of the World Wildlife Fund (WWF), his appointment by President Bush had been welcomed by NGOs. Bohlen faced a series of Congressional committees examining Antarctica just as his officials were seeking a solution. At Bohlen's maiden appearance before Congress on 12 July, he defended CRAMRA using well-rehearsed arguments about its adoption by consensus and its environmental and economic effectiveness.[127] He also foreshadowed the United States supporting a framework of environmental measures, but only alongside CRAMRA because it was "the best available mechanism for determining whether mineral development activities should ever take place". Quizzed on the Australia-France proposal, Bohlen said that "the problem was it lacked detail". While "the arguments were

[124] 10 July 1990, CE90174 "Antarctica: Australia/French initiative—New Zealand position" (NAA: B1387 90/498 PART 3). 12 July 1990 article in *New Zealand Herald*, 1, reproduced in: 12 July 1990, WL41054 "Antarctica: New Zealand position" (NAA: B1387 90/498 PART 2).

[125] 26 July 1990, CE908892 "Antarctica: Discussion with New Zealand" (AAD: 89/914-1).

[126] 27 July 1990, ST26758, "Antarctic environment Kiel: Informal meeting" (NAA: B1387 90/498 PART 3).

[127] 10 July 1990, US House of Representatives, press release "Hearing on Antarctic minerals policy announced" (NAA: B1387 90/498 PART 3).

all too familiar and repetitious", Bohlen was "decidedly more conciliatory in articulating the Administration's case than some of his subordinates".[128]

JULY 1990: CAUCUSING IN KIEL

Other key players were exchanging views on approaches to the SATCM. On 11 July 1990, Kurt Messer alerted John Burgess to discussions being held privately between a select group in Kiel, knowledge that Messer might not have shared had someone from the Federal Republic of Germany (presumably himself) been invited.[129] The discussions, held without any publicity from 14 to 15 July, involved familiar names from just nine ATCPs, including Chris Beeby, who had gone straight from Canberra to Europe.[130] Australia and France had not been invited but what transpired emerged later. A Universität Kiel Law of the Sea seminar was cover for a side meeting. John Heap circulated a revision of the paper he unveiled in Oslo, outlining an environmental protocol with several annexes. The protocol idea attracted strong support. Apart from becoming integral to the Treaty, it meant that negotiation would be limited to existing Parties. The paper drew no connection with CRAMRA, yet appeared to accept it would be put aside. Neither a mining ban nor moratorium were canvassed. The Kiel developments were significant, not just for the future of the Australian/French proposals, but "more progress may be possible in Santiago than might have been thought achievable ... this is a big but pragmatic step by the US and the UK". The reason for the "striking similarity" with New Zealand's proposal became clear: "Beeby has had a hand in the drafting". It was considered "prudent to have an Australian/French draft for a convention (or protocol) ready, and to show it soon to our close supporters".[131] Perhaps France was right to be concerned about losing the initiative. In Canberra, officials cautiously welcomed developments, provided "we can avoid the discussion becoming bogged down on

---

[128] 13 July 1990, WH118723 "Antarctic minerals: US Congressional hearing 12 July 1990" (NAA: B1387 90/498 PART 2).

[129] 17 July 1990, CE904544 "Antarctic environment: Australian-French proposals" (NAA: B1387 90/498 PART 2).

[130] Participating were Otegui (Argentina), Valle (Brazil), Pinochet (Chile), Rao (India), Beeby (New Zealand), Wetland (Norway), Heap and Hendry (United Kingdom), Scully (United States) and Karev (Soviet Union).

[131] 27 July 1990, ST26758, "Antarctic environment Kiel: Informal meeting" (NAA: B1387 90/498 PART 3).

the question of the form of the instrument".[132] The Kiel meeting also explained Chile's commitment to a protocol and retreat from a mining moratorium. Having been party to discussions in Kiel, Oscar Pinochet was hesitant to move from the understandings achieved. Besides, "Chile's overriding concern was for the SCM to be a diplomatic success and it felt the best means of achieving that was 'to set the bar fairly low'".[133] A protocol with annexes would ultimately succeed as the form of instrument adopted in 1991.

Later that week, Curtis Bohlen appeared before another Congressional committee. His testimony comprised the familiar defence of CRAMRA but, this time, the solution moved from a framework environmental agreement to a protocol.[134] He "vacillated on the minerals exploration issue", unconvinced that "a permanent ban is the best policy".[135] However, for the first time the United States conceded the possibility of a new instrument, rather than just filling gaps in existing measures. In the interval between hearings, the select group had caucused in Kiel to discuss the protocol option. Bohlen's stance was confirmed when he again appeared before the US Senate Foreign Relations Committee.[136] He admitted that "there is no longer international consensus that would bring CRAMRA into force [and] there is no consensus that we can see for the Australian-French proposals … we have to find some middle ground". Possible middle ground, he suggested, was a long-term moratorium, "noting that proposals suggested thus far ranged from 30 years to 99 years". He even accepted Senator Kerry's idea of legislation to prohibit mining by US citizens "so long as it does not imply that it is permanent". It seemed a remarkable turnaround. It was, until Senators' questions revealed that while Bohlen's "written statements have interagency approval, it remains to be seen whether his oral comments are shared by Secretary [James] Baker and senior officials in State, let alone other agencies and the White

---

[132] 31 July 1990, CE910396 "Antarctic environment: Kiel informal meeting" (AAD: 89/914-1).

[133] 20 July 1990, PA82087 "Antarctica—visit by Pinochet de la Barra" (AAD: 89/914-1).

[134] 19 July 1990, "Testimony of Curtis Bohlen before the Subcommittee on Human Rights and International Organizations" (NAA: B1387 90/498 PART 3).

[135] 20 July 1990, WH118916 "Antarctic: Environment: US Congressional activity" (NAA: B1387 90/498 PART 3).

[136] 27 July 1990, "Testimony of Curtis Bohlen before the Senate Foreign Relations Committee" (NAA: B1387 90/759 PART 1).

House".[137] Nevertheless, Australian media gushed a "foreign policy coup for Australia".[138] It would take another year to realise Bohlen's prediction that ultimately "the US will not stand alone in opposing what other countries want".[139]

With a now-evident bloc behind a protocol, coupled with criticisms of the convention proposal, the Australia/France Working Group met in late July to refine its strategy.[140] Despite there being "a lot of support running for a protocol", the Working Group remained firm on a convention because it was what the two Prime Ministers had committed to achieve and, tactically, a 'protocol' had become a "code word for a weak agreement". The options to counter this were to prepare a possible convention, or continue with the components paper but with a draft convention "in the back pocket". Because the United States and United Kingdom were making CRAMRA's entry into force a condition for progress on environmental initiatives, the Working Group even considered, rather counterintuitively, the merits of precipitating an *unsuccessful* SATCM and blaming the United States and the United Kingdom. The Working Group also stressed the need to collaborate with NGOs whose lobbying on behalf of governments was important, despite some considering it too aggressive. Australia and France relied increasingly on NGOs to make contacts that would have been diplomatically provocative to attempt directly, such as engaging the WWF in the United Kingdom and exploiting Bob Brown's environmental credentials to engage Prince Philip, who was International President of the WWF. The Australia/France objectives were to establish a process for developing a comprehensive environmental regime and, in November, obtain a moratorium while negotiations proceeded.[141] A moratorium was critical because, for the United States and the United Kingdom, "the survival of CRAMRA still seemed to be a significant underlying motivation". In view of the "remarkable advance" in the US and New Zealand positions, it was decided to proceed with a revised

---

[137] 31 July 1990, WH119329 "Antarctic minerals: Senate Foreign Relations Committee hearing" (NAA: B1387 90/498 PART 3).

[138] 31 July 1990, Deborah Hope "Bush studies indefinite mining ban" *Sydney Morning Herald*, 8.

[139] 20 July 1990, WH118916 "Antarctic: Environment: US Congressional activity" (NAA: B1387 90/498 PART 3).

[140] 20 July 1990, "Antarctica: France-Australia meeting" (AAD: 89/578-2).

[141] 23–25 July 1990 author's handwritten meeting notes "France-Australia WG" (AAD: 89/578-2).

components paper *and* draft convention. French and Australian leadership would be essential because "those in favour of a protocol were apparently doing so as camouflage for a minimalist regime". Australia would base a draft convention on France's early work and also prepare an aide-memoire to use jointly with Belgium and Italy.[142] Bill Bush would draft the convention, although not call it that. In moving from components to a convention, and in a pleasing nod to French, what appeared was a 'silhouette of a convention'.[143]

AUGUST 1990: AUSTRALIA LEGISLATES TO BAN ANTARCTIC MINING

On 14 August, Cabinet decided to ban all mining in the AAT and by Australians anywhere in Antarctica.[144] This would deflect suggestions that Australia was motivated by disappointment over CRAMRA's treatment of claimant rights and, according to Gareth Evans, "illustrate what we expect collective international action to achieve".[145] It would also subsume the ACT's *Mining Ordinance 1930* which imposed a laughably ineffective £10 penalty for unlicensed mining.[146] Resources Minister Alan Griffiths had to defend objections from the Australian minerals industry.[147] Diplomatic posts were briefed on how to respond to any overseas reactions. Provocatively, the briefing argued that Australia's rights to exercise jurisdiction over its citizens had not been fettered by the Antarctic Treaty, and that extension of Law of the Sea legislation to the continental shelf did not enlarge the AAT—in any event, Australia had asserted its

[142] 14 August 1990, CE916573 "Antarctica: Australian French consultations-23-25 July, Canberra" (NAA: B1387 90/759 PART 1).

[143] 5 August 1990, "Silhouette of a convention for the comprehensive protection of the Antarctic environment" (AAD: B13/199).

[144] 14 August 1990, Cabinet Minute 14,338, Submission 7382 "Legislation to ban mineral activities in Antarctica" (NAA: A14039 7382).

[145] 17 August 1990, speech by Evans "Protecting Antarctica" (NAA: B1387 1990/549 PART 1).

[146] See Section 57 of the Ordinance at http://www.austlii.edu.au/au/legis/act/num_ord/mo1930134/ (accessed 3 February 2021). The ACT Ordinance applied by virtue of Section 6 of the *Australian Antarctic Territory Act 1954* (AAT Act). See https://www.legislation.gov.au/Details/C2004C00099 (accessed 3 February 2021).

[147] 17 August 1990, Alan Griffiths media release "Antarctic decision in perspective" (AU-ATADD-1-BB-AU-820).

continental shelf rights in 1953, long before the Treaty entered into force.[148] Of course, such forthright argument could raise suspicion that Australia *was* in fact motivated by sovereign rights. It did. Chile considered the legislation "not in the spirit of the Treaty" as it relied on unilateral action when Parties should act together.[149] The United States considered it "totally unacceptable" and threatened a formal protest. The USSR resented sovereignty being used to achieve a political outcome and encouraged objections from China.[150] It also urged objection by Poland, but this failed—it was unaware that Poland had just decided to "fully support the French-Australian proposals".[151] AAD and DFAT prepared drafting instructions anyway, and the legislation passed with bipartisan support. It did not last for long—it was repealed a year later after the adoption of the Protocol.[152]

AUGUST 1990: "PERSONAL FACTORS"

Attention turned to the 27 July 1990 US Senate Foreign Relations Committee at which Curtis Bohlen was "more flexible and forthcoming". Australia was concerned that his testimony, that "the French-Australian proposals are imprecise or vague", misrepresented the initiative. Australia considered the components paper "the most detailed set of proposals put forward by any of the Treaty Parties" and that "it is not the *form* of the instrument which will be important but its *content* and workability".[153] Gérard Surquin joined in: it was "the US position that is ambiguous and

---

[148] 22 August 1990, CE920258 "Antarctica: Mining legislation" (NAA: B1387 1990/549 PART 2).

[149] 5 September 1990, SC21084 "Antarctic environment: Chile: Secretary's visit" (NAA: B1387 90/759 PART 2). 26 September 1990, CE935351 "First Latin American NGO workshop on Antarctica" (NAA: B1387 1990/549 PART 2).

[150] 17 September 1990, BJ43393 "Antarctica: Mining legislation—Soviet representation to China" (NAA: B1387 1990/549 PART 2). 25 September 1990, CE934832 "Antarctica: Chinese reaction to Australian anti-mining legislation" (NAA: B1387 1990/549 PART 2).

[151] 24 August 1990, CE921549 "Antarctica: Polish support for French/Australian initiative" (NAA: B1387 90/759 PART 2).

[152] 13 March 1991, House of Representatives Hansard, 1845–1879. 14 March 1991, Senate Hansard, 1870–1880. The *Antarctic Mining Prohibition Act 1991* received Royal Assent on 27 March 1991 and was repealed in 1992 by the legislation implementing the Madrid Protocol.

[153] 2 August 1990, CH592620 "Antarctica: Comprehensive protection—US position" (NAA: B1387 90/498 PART 3).

uncertain" as it assumed a mining convention could protect the environment. In his view, "the minority should move towards the majority, not the reverse".[154] Part of the problem was the apparent disconnection between Bohlen's 27 July support for a mining moratorium and for a protocol parallel to CRAMRA. The State Department's Wesley Scholz put it in context: "the question of a moratorium was very sensitive and there was no agreement among officials in State, let alone *other* US agencies".[155] Internal disagreements aside, in preparing for the Chile meeting the challenge were the links between environmental measures and the mining issue.

On 7 August, France received a US démarche proposing a protocol. Georges Duquin welcomed the US thinking as "leaving open the option of working more closely with the Americans", although Causeret hinted that Duquin "might have overstepped the mark". Duquin was concerned about the US "taking over the running with their own initiative".[156] DFAT thought the US démarche "misrepresented the French-Australian position [and] some of the language was unfortunate". Even James McGlinchey, the US official who delivered it, "seemed uncomfortable with the tone of the US paper".[157] More perplexing were discrepancies between the démarche received by France and that presented to Australia. McGlinchey later admitted that "he had sanitised the first two paragraphs ... as these contained a piece of snottiness about Australian/French views which would really have upset us".[158] The offending mucilage turned out to be the description of French/Australian proposals as "confused and badly drafted". This was revealed after discovering that Belgium had inexplicably received yet another version—a fuller version that had gone to other Parties.[159] Thus, three texts were circulated. Quizzed about this in Washington, the State Department's Ray Arnaudo explained that the troublesome paragraphs had actually been intended only as background to

---

[154] 2 August 1990, BS50356 "Antarctica: Comprehensive protection: US position" (NAA: B1387 90/498 PART 3).
[155] 3 August 1990, WH119515 "Antarctica: Australian/French initiative. US views" (NAA: B1387 90/498 PART 3).
[156] 9 August 1990, PA82384 "Antarctica—possible co-operation with the US" (NAA: B1387 90/759 PART 1).
[157] 8 August 1990, CE914433 "Antarctica: United States position" (NAA: B1387 90/759 PART 1).
[158] 10 August 1990, CE915460 "Antarctica: US views" (NAA: B1387 90/498 PART 3).
[159] 16 August 1990, PA82437 "Antarctica: US views" (NAA: B1387 90/498 PART 3).

its embassies' staff, not part of the démarche itself. McGlinchey "seemed genuinely embarrassed by the glitch". Now less enthusiastic, Duquin forgave the faux pas.[160]

AUGUST 1990: "NO DOUBT ABOUT THE SENSE OF CONGRESS"

Building bridges with the United States was sensible. Curtis Bohlen advised NGOs he was working towards "a long-term ban on mining" and was confident "Baker was in a good position to take a more flexible position". Secretary of State James Baker had said Bohlen was "in charge of the issue". Bohlen, however, was realistic: "having charge of the issue does not guarantee having control of it. One obstacle is the fact that the officials with line responsibility for CRAMRA ... have a diametrically opposed view to his own". He nevertheless expected Baker to allow him to pursue a protocol and an indefinite mining ban at the SATCM. Bohlen would feel even more confident if there was progress on Antarctic legislation in Congress.[161] Seven bills introduced between September 1989 and May 1990 were being considered, with little time to deal with them before the SATCM as Congress would adjourn for October elections. That bills were before Congress at all was positive as it "provided opportunities to air the issues ... and it left the Administration in no doubt about the sense of Congress on protecting the Antarctic environment".[162]

The United States was not alone in considering its position for the November meeting. India swung back to sympathy for Australian/French objectives.[163] In South America again, John Burgess accompanied Richard Woolcott to Lima, Montevideo, Brasilia, Buenos Aires and Santiago. The Peruvian Foreign Ministry's Fortunato Isasi considered "the Australian/ French proposal to be ambitious" and that a 20- to 30-year moratorium

---

[160] 17 August 1990, WH120035 "Antarctica: United States position" (NAA: B1387 90/498 PART 3).

[161] 22 August 1990, WH120222 "Antarctic minerals: US views" (NAA: B1387 90/759 PART 1).

[162] 30 August 1990, WH120480 "US Congress: Antarctica-related legislation" (NAA: B1387 90/759 PART 2). The bills were: HJ Resolution 418 (Owens); HR Bill 3977 (Conte); HR Bill 4210 (Jones); HR Bill 4514 (Vento); SJR Resolution 206 (Gore); Senate Bill S 2575 (Kerry); and Senate Bill S 2571 (Gore).

[163] 7 August 1990, ND75918 "India: Antarctic environment: Australian-French proposals" (NAA: B1387 90/759 PART 1).

was the solution.[164] Uruguay still considered Antarctic mining inevitable, although the priority was consensus.[165] Brazil's Henrique Valle supported "the alternative British proposal which had been gaining momentum" since Kiel. He also revealed that CRAMRA's defenders accepted the price for a protocol "would be agreement to a long-term moratorium on mining and that CRAMRA should be frozen, although not buried".[166] Australia was disappointed that Brazil so quickly aligned itself with protocol approach.[167] Argentina had also adopted the 'minimalist' position.[168] José Otegui said his overriding objective was "to find a new consensus" and told Woolcott and Burgess that Argentina had "suspended or frozen ratification of CRAMRA. This is not because we think it is a bad instrument … but there is no consensus to bring CRAMRA into force". Argentina's "striking departure from its traditionally rigid, sovereignty-dominated approach … could have an important influence on the Treaty System going well beyond the present environment issue". Otegui even said that "Australia and France had done the Treaty System a real service in pursuing the environment issue".[169] Chile's Oscar Pinochet suggested that any differences of view were more to do with form than substance. Woolcott responded off-script: "Australia's strong preference was for a comprehensive convention [but] it was prepared to look at other measures such as a long-term moratorium." In fact, Australia had never considered making that concession, and such a solecism from the Secretary was surprising.[170] With sudden ambiguity about Australia's position, Pinochet

[164] 3 August 1990, BR13133 "Antarctica: Peru" (NAA: B1387 90/498 PART 3).

[165] 3 August 1990, BA35810 "Uruguay: Antarctic environment initiative" (NAA: B1387 90/498 PART 3).

[166] 9 August 1990, BR13159 "Antarctic environment: Kiel meeting: Brazilian views" (NAA: B1387 90/498 PART 3).

[167] 14 August 1990, CE916443 "Antarctica: Brazilian views" (NAA: B1387 90/498 PART 3).

[168] 27 August 1990, CE922212 "Antarctica: Argentine paper on comprehensive protection" (NAA: B1387 90/759 PART 2). Argentina's paper, passed to Australia, was the Kiel Protocol—the first time Australia saw its content.

[169] 3 September 1990, SC21076 "Antarctic environment: Argentina: Secretary's visit" (NAA: B1387 90/759 PART 2).

[170] Woolcott thought a long-term moratorium might buy time to negotiate a convention. 13 September 1990, CE929902 "DFAT Secretary, Richard Woolcott, comments on Antarctica" (NAA: B1387 90/759 PART 1).

deferred further discussion to a separate session with Burgess.[171] Chile's overriding pre-occupation, however, was ensuring a successful meeting in November—that meant giving fair airing of all positions.[172]

Not yet prepared to change position was Norway, seemingly willing to abandon traditional Nordic solidarity in Antarctic affairs and distance itself from Sweden, Finland and Denmark. Norway continued "to align itself closely with the British and American positions" and "no one was going to tell Norway what to do in its own territory".[173] Having promoted a protocol, the United Kingdom continued to "adhere to the fundamentally minimalist position of its approach". John Heap argued that the Treaty "proceeds from the principle that any activity is allowed in Antarctica unless specifically prohibited or regulated", in contrast to the Australian/ French approach characterised as "prohibiting everything unless it was specially permitted". Heap also opposed "moratoriums because they tended to get out of step with reality". Heap's legal adviser Ian Hendry, however, took the opposite view: CRAMRA itself was a moratorium "up to the point when consensus is reached that a specific mineral resource activity could go ahead".[174]

September 1990: New Zealand's Turnaround Was Complete

With the SATCM just two months away, unexpected support for action emerged. Malaysia signalled a U-turn from promoting Antarctic resources as the common heritage of humankind, now suggesting that resources be denied to all. In its statement to the Preparatory Conference for the 1992 United Nations Conference on Environment and Development

---

[171] 5 September 1990, SC21084 "Antarctic environment: Chile: Secretary's visit" (NAA: B1387 90/759 PART 2). 10 September 1990, SC21100 "Secretary's visit to Chile: round table meeting of Foreign Ministry" (NAA: B1387 90/759 PART 1).

[172] 4 September 1990, SC21078 "Antarctica: Santiago SCM: Representations to Chile" (AAD: B13/199).

[173] 4 September 1990, CP14287 "Antarctic environment initiative: Nordic positions" (NAA: B1387 90/759 PART 1).

[174] 13 August 1990, LH108171 "Antarctica: Comprehensive protection—UK views" (NAA: B1387 90/498 PART 3).

(UNCED), Malaysia urged "the international community to support efforts to ban prospecting and mining in and around Antarctica".[175]

More significant was decisive movement in New Zealand. Since meeting Bob Hawke in February, Geoffrey Palmer was keen to move closer to Australia, although "frustrated by a good deal of bureaucratic resistance". Resistance dissolved when he was interviewed during a visit to Wellington by the Greenpeace vessel *Gondwana*.[176] Two months out from an election, Palmer removed any residual affection for CRAMRA: "we aren't going to ratify … we are for permanent bans on mining in Antarctica".[177] One newspaper considered New Zealand's "somersault on the Antarctic minerals convention" inevitable after "suddenly finding a domestically convenient green streak". The editorial chortled about the "chagrin at being led along a six-year path to nothingness … now the government is committed to the world or wilderness park concept, the very point from which a New Zealand Labour government started in 1975".[178] A week later, Palmer's cabinet decided to introduce legislation banning mining in the Ross Dependency and directed officials to prepare a comprehensive Antarctic environment protocol.[179] It would differ from the minimalist protocol promoted by the United Kingdom: it would be a single document and permanently ban mining.[180] Next day, Palmer resigned as Prime Minister, believing he could not win the coming election. However, the new policy was confirmed by Conservation Minister Philip Woollaston on 8 September. New Zealand's vestigial attachment to CRAMRA was erased by Woollaston's commitment to "a total ban on mining within Antarctica … we were talking about this before it became popular".[181] He sought to

[175] 8 August 1990, NA37398 "Environment: UNCED PrepCom: Antarctica" (NAA: B1387 90/703 PART 1).

[176] 24 August 1990, WL41544 "Antarctica: Mining: New Zealand position" (NAA: B1387 90/759 PART 1).

[177] 27 August 1990, CH595660 "Antarctica: NZ position" (NAA: B1387 90/759 PART 2).

[178] 27 August 1990, "Full circle on Antarctica" *New Zealand Herald*, quoted in: 28 August 1990, CE922674 "Antarctica: NZ position" (NAA: B1387 90/759 PART 2).

[179] 5 September 1990, WL41678 "Antarctica: New Zealand position" (NAA: B1387 90/759 PART 2).

[180] 5 September 1990, WL41685 "New Zealand: Position on Antarctica" (NAA: B1387 90/759 PART 2).

[181] 8 September 1990, speech notes "Hon Philip Woollaston—The Antarctic Environment—University of Auckland" (AAD: B13/199).

cement the credentials of new Prime Minister Mike Moore, who had advocated an Antarctic world park in 1981.[182]

Despite moving closer to Australia, New Zealand was keen to make distinct its protocol approach, arguing that a "competing convention would put at risk the Antarctic Treaty itself".[183] Differences were minimal, however, in the anti-mining legislation which closely mirrored Australia's.[184] In New Zealand domestic politics, disagreements with the Opposition were negligible: there was little room left for the Nationals other than urge even quicker pursuit of a protocol.[185] New Zealand's turnaround was complete. It had abandoned CRAMRA's keenest supporters and its affiliation with the Kiel group. It was also more ambitious than Australia and France, who were at least prepared to accept that a mining ban could be reviewed. As the November SATCM approached, the balance had shifted dramatically. Australia was encouraged by New Zealand's move "from the minimalist to the maximalist camp".[186] However, the turnaround caused surprising consternation with Georges Duquin concerned that "New Zealand might try to take the environmental ground from under our feet" and wondering whether it was worth encouraging "NGOs in Australia in favour of our initiative". It was not clear "what provoked this sudden concern on Duquin's part about New Zealand trying to outflank us".[187] Perhaps, in French eyes, the very existence of a competing proposal was more concerning than what it contained.

Australia was sanguine and sought a closer relationship with New Zealand. In Wellington, Chris Beeby admitted that officials' preference for a protocol with annexes "had been overruled and the New Zealand Government had decided to go for a comprehensive protocol". DFAT

---

[182] Mike Moore, *Beyond Today: A Look at a Sustainable Economy, Resource Management and Control and a History of Environmental Politics in New Zealand* (Papanui LEC, 1981), 69–72.

[183] 8 September 1990, speech notes "Hon Philip Woollaston—The Antarctic Environment—University of Auckland" (AAD: B13/199).

[184] 5 September 1990, WL41677 "Antarctica: Mining legislation" (NAA: B1387 90/759 PART 2). 20 September 1990, WL41847 "Antarctica: Australian/New Zealand mining legislation" (NAA: B1387 1990/549 PART 2).

[185] 11 September 1990, WL41755 "New Zealand: Position on Antarctica" (NAA: B1387 90/759 PART 2).

[186] 7 September 1990, DFAT ministerial submission "Antarctica: Silhouette Convention" (AAD: B13/199).

[187] 4 October 1990, CE938196 "Antarctica: French concerns about New Zealand's position" (AAD: B13/199).

considered that "our policies are now very close, even if there may be some risk of them passing in the night'". Visiting Canberra the following day, New Zealand's Frank Wong welcomed closer cooperation because "MERT does not feel comfortable with the directions it has received from Government on what to put in the draft protocol". Wong privately invited representations "to the effect that we believed New Zealand was going down the wrong track", although "MERT would not be particularly happy at having to move to full support of Australia/France". Whether the two countries' policies would align remained to be seen. With both Palmer and Woollaston resigning before October's election, "two prominent architects of the Labour Government policy on Antarctica will be leaving the political arena".[188]

THE SILHOUETTE

Meanwhile, Bill Bush had been progressing the 'silhouette' convention. DFAT sent it to Gareth Evans for approval. His reply suggested that the draft convention "address specifically the question of a ban (or at least extended moratorium) on mining/drilling" and preferred a 'nature reserve' rather than a 'natural reserve'. Evans appeared unperturbed by the French being "taken aback by the complexity and even rigour of the document, in spite of the fact that it was they who pressed us to agree to the development of a full draft convention".[189] France was also keen to develop the revised components paper it had earlier opposed, and what it previously described as "rather turgid" was now "crisper and punchier".[190] The disconnect that previously dogged the Quai d'Orsay re-appeared. Australia's Paris Embassy observed that "the driving force in France for the Antarctic initiative has come from the Prime Minister's office rather than the Foreign Ministry... who are hard-working and committed, but who also have other responsibilities which can distract them". This was compounded by Edwige Avice, the junior minister, "generally regarded as

[188] 3 October 1990, CE937997 "New Zealand position on Antarctica" (AAD: B13/199). 4 October 1990, CE938368 "Antarctic environment: NZ views" (NAA: B1387 90/759 PART 2).

[189] 6 September 1990, DFAT memorandum 1742/12 "Antarctica: Silhouette Convention" (AAD: 91/910-2). 7 September 1990, DFAT ministerial submission "Antarctica: Silhouette Convention" (AAD: B13/199).

[190] 3 October 1990, PA83219 "Antarctica—revised components paper" (NAA: B1387 90/888 PART 1).

carrying insufficient weight in the ministry to be able to give personal impetus to the initiative".[191] Such problems contrasted with DFAT and AAD, where there had been at least a threefold increase in staff working on the initiative. They also had the benefit of keen political engagement. DFAT maintained its diplomatic campaign using Canberra-based officials and a strong network of support in overseas missions. Resources committed to the task included Alan Brown, Australia's High Commissioner in Singapore—the approaching Chile meeting justified bringing in a diplomat of his calibre to lead the delegation.[192]

September 1990: "A Moderating Influence"

Australia was not the only Party lining up influential players. Curtis Bohlen, described as "a moderating influence", was charged with leading the US delegation, possibly as a result of NGO and Congressional pressure "which has brought about a new fluidity in the Administration's position". Bohlen "had read Senator Evans' speech of 17 August [which] had made some impression on him" and "indicated a flexibility on the prospecting issue that was clearly not shared by his staff".[193] His influence would soon be tested. Administration testimony at congressional hearings on 18 September "deflected questions as to the tide of international opinion". Tucker Scully "reiterated the importance of avoiding a situation where ... there was no regulatory regime in place".[194] Two days later, discussions between Bohlen and French officials revealed that he "personally could accept the Australia/France proposal for declaring Antarctica a 'nature reserve, land of science' ... that the Wellington convention was not ratifiable [and] he personally favoured an indefinite ban on mining". However, he also admitted to "some difficulties with the US Administration within which there were significant differences of view".[195]

On 1 October 1990, confirmation that CRAMRA was unratifiable by the United States came with congressional passage of the Owens

[191] 11 September 1990, PA82856 "Antarctic initiative" (NAA: B1387 90/759 PART 1).

[192] 17 September 1990, CE931304 "Antarctica" (AAD: 89/914–1).

[193] 11 September 1990, WH120835 "Antarctic environment: US views" (NAA: B1387 90/759 PART 1).

[194] 18 September 1990, WH121166 "Antarctica environment: Congressional hearing" (NAA: B1387 90/759 PART 1).

[195] 24 September 1990, PA83061 "Antarctica: French MFA discussions with Bohlen" (NAA: B1387 90/759 PART 1).

Resolution. Then, on 4 October, Al Gore's Resolution passed the Senate. Congress was in no mood for CRAMRA. DFAT thought that "the fact that the Administration has accepted the terms of these resolutions marks a very significant turn in US policy".[196] The United States would now put its energy into advancing the protocol proposal of the 'Kiel 5'.[197] In Canberra on 5 October, US Embassy official James McGlinchey outlined it: a protocol with annexes as "a major contribution to the process of restoring consensus among the Parties to the Antarctic Treaty" and, hinting at possible compromise, "ultimately the form of such an agreement is secondary to its substantive provisions".[198] Accordingly, three days later it was safe to include reference to Antarctica in the annual Australia/United States ministerial talks: "the two Governments also expressed support for the negotiation of a new legal instrument … to provide comprehensive protection for the Antarctic environment".[199] The ministerial talks had avoided how a mining ban or moratorium would be handled. Resolving that matter, of the most powerful symbolism, would be essential for political success.

Australia contemplated its tactics. John Burgess noted the pace of developments since ATCM XV in Paris: "had we sought to set our objectives two months ago we would almost certainly have set them too low." He urged flexibility, suggesting a "new prohibition (ban/moratorium) of mining in the Antarctic which improves the prospects that no mining will ever take place". A simple 30-year moratorium expiring automatically was insufficient, and a 50-year moratorium only acceptable if it required consensus to lift, but "any link between a moratorium and bringing CRAMRA into force would not be". An agreement on mining could stand alone or be part of a new regime. Burgess argued the need "to put the minerals issue back on centre stage by writing a full prohibition into the new draft we are now finalising", and suggested that Australia test French views on a convention rather than a protocol. Burgess also identified the risk "that

[196] 12 October 1990, CE942420 "Antarctic environment: US views" (NAA: B1387 90/759 PART 2).

[197] 4 October 1990, WH121918 "Antarctic environment: US proposal" (NAA: B1387 90/759 PART 2). The 'Kiel 5' comprised Argentina, Norway, the United Kingdom, United States and Uruguay.

[198] 5 October 1990, US aide-memoire "Antarctica: US Proposal on Comprehensive Measures—II" (AAD: B13/199).

[199] 8 October 1990, DFAT news release "Australia-United Stated Ministerial Talks—Joint Communiqué" (AAD: B13/199).

the NGOs could desert us for NZ", which was still developing a comprehensive protocol even if "Beeby's heart is not in it".[200]

Australia's position had to be settled. Internal differences needed
addressing, including pacifying scientists concerned about an environmental regime constraining research and lobbying for an influence to
match the NGOs.[201] A-G's put to DFAT that Australia could be on the
wrong path on liability: "while there are good reasons for maintaining a
unified stand with France ... I do not think we can continue to gloss over
these differences". Resources Minister Alan Griffiths warned Foreign
Minister Gareth Evans not to extend a mining ban to Heard Island. Such
correspondence was triggered by DFAT's circulation of draft objectives
"as a basis for discussion".[202] The greatest issue, however, was fundamental: "whether the delegation should continue to seek a permanent mining
ban in keeping with Government public statements, or have the option to
fall back to a long-term moratorium (say 30 to 50 years)".[203] One month
out from the meeting, Australia still had to decide.

OCTOBER 1990: FOUR POWERS

From 8 to 11 October 1990, officials from Australia, France, Belgium and
Italy consulted in Brussels to settle objectives and tactics. The differences
were potentially significant, even on emblematic issues. Australia was committed to a permanent mining ban, including prospecting. France saw "a
ban on prospecting as impossible and, from a tactical viewpoint, not worth
pushing too hard [as] Cousteau himself was not against prospecting".

---

[200] 3 October 1990, John Burgess DFAT "Strategy paper" (AAD: 89/914-2).

[201] 25 September 1990, AAD internal minute Quilty to Moncur "Science input to the new
environmental convention" (AAD: 89/914-1). 5 October 1990, AAD internal minute
Quilty to Moncur "US concerns on 'restraints on scientific research'" (NAA: B1387 90/888
PART 2). 26 October 1990, AAD internal minute Quilty to Moncur "Science contribution
to the environment convention debate" (NAA: B1387 90/759 PART 2). 29 October 1990,
AAD internal minute Quilty to Moncur "Science input to the Australian French environment convention initiative" (NAA: B1387 90/888 PART 1).

[202] 19 October 1990, memorandum Bill Campbell, A-G to Bill Bush, DFAT (NAA: B1387
90/888 PART 3). 19 October 1990, letter from Griffiths to Evans (NAA: B1387 90/888
PART 2). 16 October 1990, CE943562 "Antarctic environment" Australian objectives at
Special Consultative Meeting (Draft 2 of 16.10.90)" (AAD: 89/914-2).

[203] 20 October 1990, AAD brief to minister "Objectives for the Australian delegation to
the SCM" (NAA: B1387 90/888 PART 1).

France could also accept a moratorium.[204] This was anathema to Australia as it implied that ultimately mining was legitimate—just paused for the time being. Such basic issues had to be resolved before Chile as "it would be impossible later to improve on any long-term moratorium adopted. Moreover, an agreement to settle for a long-term moratorium … would be a major concession on our part which it would be unwise to make without extracting some significant concession".[205]

There was also a raft of concerns about the draft convention. These were not trivial. For Australia, it should be "no less rigorous in terms of environmental protection than the minerals convention".[206] It should also be no weaker than proposals from the 'Kiel 5' or New Zealand, nor overshadowed by the 'Barnes draft' prepared for the NGOs. France, however, influenced by the Cousteau Foundation, which had made little substantive contribution since June 1989, preferred a "minimally complex text".[207] Lack of flexibility was "attributable to the fact (as Causeret confirmed subsequently) that the inter-ministerial meeting had, earlier that day, given its formal approval to the French draft".[208] Subsequent efforts were blocked and French intransigence "led to a refusal to accept the silhouette idea … it was even decided there should be no introduction". French determination "encouraged by the Cousteau Foundation [was] quite the antithesis of the approach that Barnes and other environmental groups were urging".[209] Alan Brown admitted that staying close to what NGOs sought was important. His 9 October speech to the concurrent Brussels symposium said that "Australia does not claim to have invented these

[204] 5 October 1990, PA83260 "Antarctica—mining and prospecting issues—French views" (NAA: B1387 90/888 PART 1).

[205] 5 October 1990, "Notes on agenda items on attitudes of other countries" in "Brief for Discussion with the French, Brussels, 8–10 October 1990 (AAD: B13/199).

[206] 9 October 1990, William Bush paper presented at the Colloquium on the Antarctic and the Environment: Future Prospects, Brussels 9–10 October 1990 "The 1988 Wellington Convention: How much environmental protection?" (AAD: B13/199).

[207] 4 October 1990, PA83256 "Antarctica: Cousteau Foundation and Parliamentary Report" (AAD: B13/199).

[208] 7 October 1990, PA83283 "Antarctica: Louvain discussions with French" (NAA: B1387 90/888 PART 1).

[209] 11 October 1990, PA83349 "Antarctica—draft convention—comments" (NAA: B1387 90/888 PART 1).

ideas … the Australian proposal was, of course, influenced by views prevailing among conservationist groups".[210]

A key outcome from Brussels was agreement to Belgium and Italy co-sponsoring a convention to "help match the efforts of our opponents".[211] Brown was "cautious about the development of formal blocs, which often provoked structured confrontation". Belgium's Gérard Surquin understood the concern and agreed that "the Belgian and Italian role could not extend to any drafting. They would simply be co-presenters". Belgium, pleased to be on-board, understood the challenge. Surquin saw the group as "a minority, albeit an effective and active one". Duquin was rather more optimistic: "the Australia/France proposals enjoyed majority support", whereas the 'Kiel 5' paper "was a rather hollow document [and] he thought the tide was turning our way". Even within the group of four differences remained, including on the regime's form. Belgium was flexible, but Italy's Antarctic Affairs Adviser Gianmario Urbini argued strongly for a convention because it was "important to respond to the environmentalists' concerns, and nearly all of them favoured a convention".[212] Further consultations were held in Brussels with a possibly sympathetic wider group including Denmark, Greece, India, the Netherlands and Sweden. Unsurprisingly, there were differences including an altercation between Sweden and France.[213] None in the group were ready to more formally join the initiative.

There were now four Parties supporting a convention containing a mining ban.[214] In Australia, copies were sent to ministers and ASOC.[215]

---

[210] 9 October 1990, Alan Brown, paper presented at the Colloquium on the Antarctic and the Environment: Future Prospects, Brussels 9–10 October 1990 "New proposal—the natural park" (AAD: B13/199).

[211] 7 October 1990, PA83283 "Antarctica: Louvain discussions with French" (NAA: B1387 90/888 PART 1).

[212] 16 October 1990, PA83432 "Antarctica: Meeting in Brussels with Belgium and Italy" (NAA: B1387 90/759 PART 2).

[213] 11 October 1990, PA83350 "Antarctica: Meeting in Brussels with 'like-minded' group" (NAA: B1387 90/759 PART 2). 18 October 1990, ST27119 "Sweden: Protection of the Antarctica (sic) environment" (NAA: B1387 90/759 PART 2).

[214] 16 October 1990, "Draft Convention for the Comprehensive Protection of the Antarctic Environment" (NAA: B1387 90/888 PART 2).

[215] 18 October 1990, DASETT brief to Minister Kelly "Antarctic environment protection convention"; and 20 October 1990, DASETT brief to Minister Kelly "Draft Convention for the Comprehensive Protection of the Antarctic Environment" (NAA: B1387 90/888 PART 1).

No longer a 'silhouette', it became an 'indicative draft' to be distributed to other Parties.[216] Even this stumbled—the covering Third Person Note and aide-memoire still had to be settled, DFAT having found the "French text opaque and repetitive".[217] It was critical to have the proposals circulated before the Chile meeting. On 25 October, Australian diplomatic posts were instructed to commence four-party démarches at "the most senior level possible".[218]

It was not a moment too late. That day, Mike Moore released New Zealand's ambitious protocol. It was, the Prime Minister said, a "comprehensive, binding, international legal instrument to govern all human activity on the continent ... we want real progress to be made in Chile, and New Zealand will be there to make it happen".[219] Apart from the international audience, it was equally a last-minute pitch to a domestic constituency going to an election two days later. In that it failed. Labour lost in a landslide to the Nationals. However, electoral disappointment in New Zealand made little difference in Antarctica—Jim Bolger's Nationals also supported a protocol.

OCTOBER 1990: "A VERY GOOD PIECE OF PAPER"

Illustrating the improved relationship, Australia was the only Party given an advance copy of New Zealand's 89-page proposal and immediately reciprocated with its draft convention.[220] New Zealand was not alone in taking Australia into its confidence. On 23 October, the British High Commission in Canberra slipped DFAT a copy of the Foreign and Commonwealth Office's (FCO's) instructions about an imminent UK paper. The paper would be essentially the 'Kiel 5' document: a protocol of

---

[216] 18 October 1990, CE945106 "Antarctic environment—Australia/France indicative draft convention" (NAA: B1387 90/888 PART 1). 18 October 1990, PA83486 "Antarctica—Italy and Belgium agreement to co-present draft convention" (NAA: B1387 90/888 PART 1).

[217] 19 October 1990, CE945823 "Antarctica: Draft TPN and convention" (NAA: B1387 90/888 PART 1).

[218] 25 October 1990, CE948210 "Antarctic environment: Australia/France indicative draft convention" (NAA: B1387 90/888 PART 2).

[219] 25 October 1990, New Zealand Prime Minister Mike Moore, media release "New Zealand plan to protect Antarctic". Reproduced in: 26 October 1990, WL42195 "Antarctic environment: New Zealand draft protocol" (NAA: B1387 90/759 PART 3).

[220] 19 October 1990, WL42132 "Antarctic environment: 1) New Zealand draft protocol; 2) Aust/French draft convention" (NAA: B1387 90/759 PART 2).

26 articles, one relating to environmental principles and 16 to dispute settlement and arbitration.[221] With New Zealand abandoning CRAMRA, and the United States more flexible, the United Kingdom now appeared to be "the main supporter of mineral and oil exploration". Environment Secretary Chris Patten objected to Britain's image "as the dirty man of Europe" even though its position "has remained virtually unchanged since the minerals convention was signed".[222]

Jacques Cousteau's lobbying of President Bush on 24 October received a sympathetic hearing. The president promised to "do what he could" to help.[223] The understanding that the 'Kiel 5' were not bound to the paper provided room to move. On 29 October, Tucker Scully reassured Australia that the US paper "would be different from John Heap's" and focus on a sectoral approach. He expected little movement on mining but, intriguingly, was "prepared to talk about a moratorium".[224] Next day, Curtis Bohlen received the démarche from the ambassadors of Australia, Belgium, France and Italy on the convention proposal. Bohlen was receptive, observing that positions "seem to be moving closer". On mining, he personally could accept "anything short of a permanent ban" but noted that "inter-agency consultations are not yet complete". In particular, the National Science Foundation and the Department of the Interior were "less enthusiastic than Bohlen about the evolution of US thinking".[225]

On 31 October, New Zealand received the four-party démarche and, in Beeby's view, "it was a very good piece of paper". Although there were several proposals to consider, "there seemed to be an emerging consensus on the possibility of arriving at a single instrument, whatever form this might take". Beeby said that New Zealand could be flexible to avoid "the risk of having to negotiate everything before getting anything". He noted that for both Australia and New Zealand, proposing a mining ban might

[221] 23 October 1990, CE946834 "Antarctica: SCM Chile—draft environmental protocol by Kiel 5" (NAA: B1387 90/759 PART 2). 23 October 1990, facsimile 907/2/5 from David Mason to Antarctic Section DFAT "Antarctica: SCM Chile—draft environmental protocol by Kiel 5" (NAA: B1387 90/759 PART 2).

[222] 28 October 1990, Paul Brown "UK still wants to mine the Antarctic" *The Age*, 12.

[223] 29 October 1990, WH122851 "Antarctica: Call by Jean Cousteau on President Bush" (NAA: B1387 90/759 PART 2).

[224] 30 October 1990, UN50963 "Antarctica: US views" (NAA: B1387 90/759 PART 2).

[225] 30 October 1990, WH122902 "Antarctic environment: Indicative draft convention: US views" (NAA: B1387 90/759 PART 2).

"complicate reaching consensus on the wider instrument".[226] A possible chairing role for Beeby at the SATCM was also discussed, an unexpected idea given his strong association with CRAMRA.

NOVEMBER 1990: "THE DISCUSSION HAD CLEARED THE AIR"

The reaction to the 'Four-Powers' proposal in Wellington was in pleasant contrast to its reception in the London the day before.[227] There, the démarche had been delivered directly to Tristan Garel-Jones, the minister responsible for Antarctic affairs, who said that the British were "most alarmed indeed" at a proposal that "put at risk the consensus that had served all of us so well over the past 30 years". Garel-Jones said restoring consensus was the highest priority, and Australia should know "the claimant states were not going to be a push-over ... the United Kingdom saw a role for itself in holding the claimants together". It seemed oddly contradictory to hold the claimants together by vigorously objecting to what Australia and France (and presumably New Zealand) were doing. But Garel-Jones could explain that: "the UK took comfort in the knowledge that among the *real* Antarctic specialists, scientists and foreign policy experts, its position was well understood and indeed favoured". Garel-Jones seemed incensed that Australia alone proposed legislating to ban mining, strangely overlooking the fact that Belgium and New Zealand had already introduced such legislation. He also thought that public pressure in the United Kingdom was "being orchestrated by or from Australia", rather underestimating the ability of NGOs to think for themselves. David Mason summed up the exchange: There was "more than a whiff of suggestion that we are beginning to get under British skins ... to that degree our message appears to be getting through".[228]

DFAT remarked that "it seems odd to us that the United Kingdom, rather than any other country, is leading the charge against our

---

[226] 1 November 1990, WL42249 "Antarctic environment: Indicative draft convention" (NAA: B1387 90/759 PART 2).

[227] 1 November 1990, WL42269 "Antarctic environment: UK views" (NAA: B1387 1990/549 PART 2).

[228] 31 October 1990, LH114106 "Antarctic environment: Indicative draft convention: UK views" (NAA: B1387 90/759 PART 2).

proposals".[229] Accompanied by Mason, the new head of DFAT's Legal Division John McCarthy called on the FCO's John Heap to clarify Australian thinking. McCarthy pointed out that the United Kingdom's "legislation applying to the British Antarctic Territory stood on the same legal basis" as Australia's and observed that "environmentalist groups were capable of their own lobbying … they did not need Australia to encourage them". Heap rested his arguments on the loss of consensus, reminding McCarthy that the United Kingdom, the United States and Australia had agreed in 1957, before the Treaty, that minerals were Antarctica's "Achilles Heel" and "Australian moves to legislate in the minerals area were, quite frankly, getting up the noses of many Antarctic Treaty partners". Worse than such nasal irritation, following the hard-won consensus on CRAMRA, Australian and French decisions "to renege on the consensus" created a precedent. Nevertheless, Heap acknowledged that "in Chile there might be an unstoppable band wagon in favour of Australia's position … unlikely, but if it occurred the UK would not stand against it". Despite their differences, "Heap was, however, glad that the discussion had cleared the air".[230]

Reporting on the reactions of other Parties flowed into Canberra. Japan supported the United Kingdom, as did Argentina and Brazil. South Korea thought "the Australian-French initiative is jeopardising the international consensus". South Africa considered CRAMRA "an adequate vehicle to protect the Antarctic environment". China feared "upsetting the political balance on Antarctic matters". The USSR warned that Australia and New Zealand "can expect to be taken to task at SCMXI". India would seek to "identify a compromise", as would Spain. The Netherlands worried about "a standoff with essentially no protection". Denmark agreed, declining to be "tied down to any specific instrumental approach". Sweden thought the proposal "could form the basis for consideration" and Poland considered it "very good".[231]

---

[229] 8 November 1990, CE954071 "Antarctica: Consultations with United Kingdom" (NAA: B1387 90/759 PART 3)

[230] 9 November 1990, LH114959 "Antarctica: Consultations with the United Kingdom" (NAA: B1387 90/759 PART 3).

[231] Summaries from cablegrams in NAA: B1387 90/759 PART 2 and PART 3.

November 1990: "Happy with the Lowest Common Denominator"

Finding a path through the plethora of positions on a plethora of proposals would be a major challenge. Chile faced a great challenge: advancing its own version of a protocol and, as SATCM Chair, facilitating a compromise between all the proposals. Preparations for the meeting had started in 1989 after Chile offered to host and Jorge Berguño briefed Parties in September 1990. There would be three meetings, all held in the Santiago. The first would be a special meeting to consider applications by Ecuador and the Netherlands to become ATCPs. The primary meeting was to be the SATCM on the environment, and the third would consider the liability protocol envisaged by CRAMRA's Article 8.[232] As early as November 1989, France had hesitated about Chile hosting.[233] It is not clear whether the concern was the stability of Aylwin's new democratic government, or Chile's ability to run a meeting. Whatever the cause for the concerns, they lingered for months. Just three weeks out from the meeting, the US State Department thought that "organisational arrangements for the SCM left much to be desired".[234] Ironically, it would be US action that would upset those arrangements. At the last minute, Chile had to shift the meeting to Viña del Mar because of a clash with the visit of President Bush to Santiago.[235] The US ambassador had insisted that 700 hotel rooms be reserved for the entourage. In its favour, it was considered that "attendees would be healthier in Viña del Mar" because of Santiago's air quality issues. However, the former's Hotel O'Higgins was already booked for a gastroenterology conference, an irony not lost on the many Antarctic delegates who suffered a complaint that may well have been the subject of the displaced medical conference.[236] The "logistic and communications problems" posed by the move to the coast and the "criticism from several

---

[232] 13 September 1990, SC21127 "Chile: SCM on protection of the Antarctic environment" (AAD: B13/199).

[233] 9 November 1989, PA77552 "Antarctica: Follow-up to Paris meeting" (NAA: B1387 89/453 PART 3).

[234] 30 October 1990, UN50963 "Antarctica: US views" (NAA: B1387 90/759 PART 2).

[235] https://history.state.gov/departmenthistory/travels/president/bush-george-h-w (accessed 3 February 2021).

[236] 26 October 1990, BA36284 "SCM on Antarctic environment"; and 1 November 1990, SC21225 "SCM on Antarctic environment" (AAD: 89/914-2).

delegations" were further complications for Chile to manage.[237] Pinochet indicated that Chile's main objective was now just to have a successful meeting—that meant being an "honest broker at the meeting" to produce a tangible outcome. He thought it immaterial "whether the instrument took the form of a protocol or convention", to which Australia replied "very firmly, that it mattered very much". It was reported that "a good outcome for Chile would be agreement on how to make the next step ... in this sense, Chile would be happy with the lowest common denominator".[238]

The lowest common denominator could mean supporting the 'minimalists'. Sometime, somewhere, someone would have to compromise. New Zealand, having the most ambitious proposal, had considered the need for flexibility.[239] Now the fear was that any flexibility to move from an "all-embracing New Zealand draft protocol" could justify endorsing "the minimalist proposal being put forward by the Kiel 5"—the paper that Chris Beeby himself helped create.[240] Beeby assured that "any shorter New Zealand document would be closer to the Australian/French documents than to the Kiel group".[241] Beeby was prepared to consider something Australia was not: decoupling the mining ban from the main instrument if the minerals issue slowed progress. New Zealand now felt exposed: as Beeby observed, "NZ was the odd man out".[242]

[237] 18 October 1990, PA83483 "Antarctica: Santiago SCM: Procedural questions" (AAD: B13/199).

[238] 5 November 1990, SC21314 "Antarctic environment: Indicative draft convention" (NAA: B1387 90/759 PART 3).

[239] 3 October 1990, CE937997 "New Zealand position on Antarctica" (AAD: B13/199). 1 November 1990, WL42249 "Antarctic environment: Indicative draft convention" (NAA: B1387 90/759 PART 2).

[240] 1 November 1990, CE951278 "Antarctic environment: Indicative draft convention" (NAA: B1387 90/759 PART 3).

[241] 13 November 1990, WL42374 "Antarctic environment: New Zealand position" (NAA: B1387 90/759 PART 3). Frank Wong replaced Beeby on the New Zealand delegation.

[242] 15 November 1990, WL42418 "Antarctic environment: New Zealand position" (NAA: B1387 1991/55 PART 1).

NOVEMBER 1990: "FOR ALL PRACTICAL PURPOSES CRAMRA IS DEAD"

In Washington, Curtis Bohlen had given the 'Four Powers' a sympathetic hearing and noted that once Silvio Conte's Bill had presidential approval, the United States would be only "the second country after Belgium to have in place domestic legislation to ban mining".[243] DFAT was unconvinced: "while Bohlen's views give cause for optimism", the US papers "still place it squarely in the camp of the Kiel minimalists … we find it hard to understand how the United States can claim for itself the leadership role".[244] Signature of Conte's Bill before the 21 November deadline would be a crucial indicator of sympathy for a mining ban.[245] Gore called for the United States to lead: "we must seize the initiative to protect Antarctica's unique, pristine environment." Conte was blunter: "some in the Administration have been playing games with the way this word 'indefinite' is defined", he said, "an indefinite ban means a ban without time limitation, and the Congress certainly did not intend that CRAMRA, or the son of CRAMRA, be part of the agreement … for all practical purposes CRAMRA is dead". Bruce Vento chimed in with a call for Antarctica to be preserved "as the first great world park".[246] He also railed that "Congress would not be satisfied with the lowest common denominator … mining was incompatible with the values Congress was trying to protect". The State Department and Environment Protection Authority (EPA) were unmoved, saying that "while Congress could exhort whatever it wished … final decisions would be taken by the Executive".[247] Next day the president signed the *Antarctic Protection Act*, which provided "an indefinite ban on United States mineral activities in Antarctica".[248]

[243] 30 October 1990, WH122902 "Antarctic environment: Indicative draft convention: US views" (NAA: B1387 90/759 PART 2).

[244] 1 November 1990, CE951496 "Antarctic environment: Indicative draft convention" (NAA: B1387 90/888 PART 2).

[245] 14 November 1990, WH123434 "Antarctica: Action by US Congress" (AAD: 84/360-2).

[246] 15 November 1990, media releases "Gore urges Bush Administration to protect Antarctica"; "Statement of Honorable Silvio O Conte"; and "Statement—Congressman Bruce F Vento" (NAA: B1387 1991/55 PART 1).

[247] 15 November 1990, WH123491 "Antarctic: Congressional and Administration views" (AAD: 84/360-2).

[248] 16 November 1990, White House, Office of the Press Secretary "Protection of natural resources" (NAA: B1387 1991/55 PART 1).

Intriguingly, the White House press release did not actually mention the mining prohibition and sidestepped the ban's duration, adding "another element of unpredictability in the approach of the US delegation to the meetings in Chile".[249] NGOs were disappointed, but Bohlen considered "a long-term moratorium was the likely middle ground where consensus could be reached".[250] The United States had seemingly adjusted its position and yet, on the Friday before the SATCM, there was still confusion about what it would actually seek: a prohibition, indefinite ban, or moratorium.

The United Kingdom was now considered the most firmly wedded to CRAMRA. However, on the eve of the meeting it hinted at possible compromise. Tristan Garel-Jones, briefing NGOs with John Heap, suggested that "Britain now had a degree of flexibility".[251] It is not clear whether this flowed from developments in the United States or 120,000 Britons petitioning for a world park. Garel-Jones said that the United Kingdom was "perfectly prepared to listen to any of the arguments others put forward and try to find a new consensus … the important thing to remember about CRAMRA is that when it came forward it was part of the consensus".[252] The Australian High Commission checked whether the FCO really had softened. David Mason reported "there was in fact no change in the UK position, just an effort to improve presentational aspects" by emphasising the importance of consensus.[253]

Just before the SATCM, Australia did another tally. On the *substance* of the regime, only six ATCPs supported the 'Four Powers'. Eleven, led by the United Kingdom, were considered "minimalists", and the rest undecided. On the *form* of instrument, five supported a convention and ten a Protocol. On mining: 6 accepted a permanent ban, and 13 a long-term moratorium.[254] Whichever way the 24 ATCPs were counted, the 'Four

[249] 16 November 1990, WH123530 "Antarctic environment: US President signs Conte Bill" (NAA: B1387 90/759 PART 3).

[250] 16 November 1990, Charles Campbell "US to urge limited moratorium on Antarctic mining" Associated Press, in: DFAT facsimile 026253 "Antarctic: US press commentary" (NAA: B1387 1991/55 PART 1).

[251] 16 November 1990, Paul Brown "Britain thaws its Antarctic stance" *The Guardian*.

[252] 16 November 1990, transcript of interview, BBC Radio Four *Today* (copy on NAA: B1387 1991/55 PART 1).

[253] 16 November 1990, DFAT AHC London facsimile 015/98 "Antarctica: Press item on UK policy at SCM meeting" (NAA: B1387 1991/55 PART 1).

[254] "Antarctic initiative: Running sheet: Overview, as at 12 November 1990" (AAD: B13/199).

Powers' were a distinct minority. The elevation of the Netherlands and Ecuador to ATCP status on 19 November did nothing to change the balance.[255]

Georges Duquin was positive because most countries were "keeping a reasonably open mind". Whether France itself would be flexible was unclear. In Michel Rocard's office, diplomatic adviser Jean-Maurice Ripert "was not particularly optimistic about the outcome of the SCM". Duquin thought that "it was the British who seemed to be orchestrating the campaign against us" and, accordingly, "France would be placing the bar fairly high and would not yield to the pressure we would inevitably come under". The height of the bar was boosted by France "insisting that the final declaration include reference to a prohibition on mining ... and a convention which designates Antarctica as a nature reserve, land of science".[256]

While Australia's delegation was in the air crossing the Pacific, instructions were sought for a possible compromise on a permanent mining ban. Foreign Minister Gareth Evans gave Alan Brown a fallback position: "a ban on mining which may be reviewed after 30 years, but only with the consensus agreement of all Parties". AAD Director Rex Moncur agreed that it might be "necessary to avoid a break-down of the negotiations" and desirable "to have the flexibility to move" if any of the other 'Four Powers' did. Besides, it represented "an effective long-term ban" as it allowed Australia a veto. Fourteen hours before the meeting commenced, Environment Minister Ros Kelly agreed.[257] And so it was that the delegation's instructions, which had already been printed and were on the way to Chile, were already superseded.

A year had passed, and the Treaty Parties were ready to meet again. CRAMRA lay dormant, and even New Zealand had abandoned it. Australia and France had secured a broader body of sympathisers—but so had their detractors, with many lined up behind a protocol that had become synonymous with 'minimalist' environmental objectives.

---

[255] Antarctic Treaty, *Final Report of the Tenth Special Antarctic Treaty Consultative Meeting, Viña Del Mar, 19 November 1990* (Republic of Chile, 1990).

[256] 15 November 1990, PA84014 "Antarctica-French approach to the SCM" (AAD: 89/914-2).

[257] 16 November 1990, AAD brief to minister "Delegation position on ban on mining"; and 19 November 1990, DASETT note for file "Delegation position on ban on mining" (NAA: B1387 90/888 PART 2).

REFERENCES

Antarctic Treaty. *Final Report of the Tenth Special Antarctic Treaty Consultative Meeting, Viña Del Mar, 19 November 1990.* Republic of Chile, 1990.

Beck, Peter J. "Antarctica as a Zone of Peace." In *Antarctica's Future: Continuity or Change?*, edited by R A Herr, H R Hall and M G Haward, 192–224: Australian Institute of International Affairs, 1990.

Beeby, Christopher C. "The Convention on the Regulation of Antarctic Minerals and Its Future." In *Antarctica's Future: Continuity or Change?*, edited by R A Herr, H R Hall and M G Haward, 47–60: Australian Institute of International Affairs, 1990.

Cook, Grahame. *The Future of Antarctica: Exploitation Versus Preservation.* Manchester University Press, 1990.

Heap, John A. "Sovereignty as a Source of Stress." In *Antarctica's Future: Continuity or Change?*, edited by R A Herr, H R Hall and M G Haward, 181–87: Australian Institute of International Affairs, 1990.

Herr, Richard A, H Robert Hall, and Marcus Haward. "Introduction." In *Antarctica's Future: Continuity or Change?*, edited by Richard A Herr, H Robert Hall and Marcus Haward, 11–16: Australian Institute of International Affairs, 1990.

"Jacques Cousteau's Visit to Australia." *Australian Foreign Affairs and Trade: the Monthly Record* 61, no. 2 (1990): 81.

Jørgensen-Dahl, Arnfinn, and Willy Østreng. *The Antarctic Treaty System in World Politics.* Macmillan/Fridtjof Nansen Institute, 1991.

Law, Phillip. "The Antarctic Wilderness: A Wild Idea!". In *Antarctica's Future: Continuity or Change?*, edited by R A Herr, H R Hall and M G Haward, 71–80: Australian Institute of International Affairs, 1990.

Lemonick, Michael D. "Antarctica: Is Any Place Safe from Mankind?". *Time* 135, no. 3 (1990): 56–62.

MacDonald, David I M. "Recent Meetings: Antarctica—an Exploitable Resource or Too Important to Develop? Institute of Commonwealth Studies, London. 21 February, 1990." *Antarctic Science* 2, no. 2 (1990): 179–80.

Moore, Mike. *Beyond Today: A Look at a Sustainable Economy, Resource Management and Control and a History of Environmental Politics in New Zealand.* Papanui LEC, 1981.

Pain, Stephanie. "New Zealand's U-Turn Threatens Antarctic Mining Treaty." *New Scientist* 125, no. 1707 (10 March 1990): 7.

Richardson, Mike G. "John Arnfield Heap, CMG." *Polar Record* 42, no. 3 (2006): 263–67.

Robert J L Hawke. "Australia's Policy in Antarctica." In *Antarctica's Future: Continuity or Change?*, edited by R A Herr, H R Hall and M G Haward, 17–20: Australian Institute of International Affairs, 1990.

Scully, R Tucker. "The Antarctic Treaty as a System." In *Antarctica's Future: Continuity or Change?*, edited by R A Herr, H R Hall and M G Haward, 95–102: Australian Institute of International Affairs, 1990.

Templeton, Malcolm. *A Wise Adventure II: New Zealand and Antarctica after 1960*. Victoria University Press, 2017.

CHAPTER 7

Negotiating an Environment Protocol: November 1990 to April 1991

NOVEMBER–DECEMBER 1990: SATCM XI OPENS IN CHILE

The Australian delegation arrived early in Viña del Mar for a 'Four Powers' strategy meeting. At the SATCM, Alan Brown would speak first to outline Australia's position, followed by France's Jean-Pierre Puissochet. The convention itself would be introduced later, with a focus on the substance of proposals, rather than the form of instrument.[1] A Heads of Delegation meeting considered the schedule but, completely unexpected, was Chile's Oscar Pinochet adding discussion of a possible 1991 Treaty review conference—a matter so sensitive that the idea was promptly dropped.[2]

SATCM XI opened on 19 November 1990 with 231 delegates. Detailed briefing outlined the challenges facing the six delegates from Australia.[3] The meeting was taking place with "high international interest in environmental issues and a delicate time for the Treaty System", in part because of Australia's actions. It was delicate because the following year, 1991, would see the Treaty's 30th anniversary—the first opportunity for a review conference. Failure to re-establish consensus could be a trigger. The Australians did not underestimate the situation: "the active diplomacy

---

[1] 18 November 1990, "Delegation meeting" (AWJ personal notes).

[2] 20 November 1990, SC21369 "Antarctica: Vina del Mar meetings: organisation" (AAD: 89/914–2).

[3] 1 November 1990, CE951272 "Antarctica: Santiago SCM" (AAD: 89/914–2).

© The Author(s), under exclusive license to Springer Nature Switzerland AG 2021
A. Jackson, *Who Saved Antarctica?*,
https://doi.org/10.1007/978-3-030-78405-8_7

of Australia and France, combined with pressures of public opinion, have seen a remarkable shift in previously entrenched positions" [but] "this has not been tested at the negotiating table where the consensus rule means that it is easy to block and where individual officials can still wield considerable influence". Soberly, it cautioned that "expectations in respect of the Australian-French initiative should not be too high ... a re-run of the tensions of Paris should be avoided".[4] Australia's objectives seemed modest: seek agreement to "start negotiations on a new legal instrument ... to provide a rigorous and workable comprehensive environmental regime". They also seemed timid, only "encouraging moves towards agreement on some form of new prohibition (ban/moratorium)". Australia also wanted "to win the media battle".[5] Any lack of ambition made good sense—it allowed considerable room to move.

In the pigeonholes were just eight working papers. The 'Four Powers' indicative convention secured the coveted spot of Working Paper 1. Others included New Zealand's draft protocol, the 'Kiel 5' protocol and the options submitted by the United Kingdom and the United States. On 20 November Pinochet, as chair, invited opening statements. Twenty-nine Parties spoke. Alan Brown outlined what everybody already knew: Australia was seeking a mining ban in an environmental convention (which he called a 'regime', 'instrument' or 'new arrangement'). Germany's Dietrich Granow pointed to the 300,000 signatures received in the previous week's petition on Antarctica.[6] Curtis Bohlen noted that in the United States "public concern about Antarctica is influencing public policy" and that President Bush had just signed the new US legislation. Welcoming the constructive ideas in other proposals, he confirmed a US "negotiating position that is flexible" and that "to us, form is secondary to substance". That said, he had two papers pushing a protocol. Chilingarov said that the USSR regretted "certain Parties" breaking consensus. Desirée Edmar, however, spoke of Sweden's indebtedness "to Australia and France for their tireless efforts to get support for far-reaching measures" and was particularly pleased with New Zealand's proposal combining form *and* substance. "The world is following our progress", she said.[7]

---

[4] November 1990, "Antarctic Treaty Special Consultative Meetings X and XI, Viña del Mar, Chile 1990. Volume 1" (AAD: B13/199).

[5] November 1990, D.1 Australian objectives in: "Antarctic Treaty Special Consultative Meetings X and XI, Viña del Mar, Chile 1990. Volume 1" (AAD: B13/199).

[6] A unified Germany was at an ATCM for the first time.

[7] 20 November 1990, "XI SCM" (AWJ personal notes).

November 1990: "The Toughest Nut to Crack"

John Heap agreed that "the eyes of the world are upon us", and echoed calls by Finland and China for compromise. He pleaded that "the need for consensus [means] that no Party should put any other Party into an intolerable position. This requires of us all the spirit of mutual forbearance". If not, he said, "before us will be a return to the situation as it was 31 years ago, before the conclusion of the Antarctic Treaty ... unless the system survives there can be no protection of the Antarctic environment". He then turned to "the vexed question of minerals ... the toughest nut to crack". Heap noted "common ground" between the proposals, but "we differ, however, on how best to regulate an activity that is not going on". Consensus required an "agreed mechanism for making decisions about mineral activity in the Antarctic before, and I repeat, *before* the need arises". That mechanism would be CRAMRA. With barely concealed barbs, Heap warned that "we could find ourselves once more in a situation in which support for an agreement reached in this forum is subsequently withdrawn".[8]

New Zealand's Frank Wong welcomed Chile's May 1989 initiative to address environmental measures. He acknowledged New Zealand's proposal was ambitious and, in oblique reference to the 1975 world park idea, said that New Zealand had "put forward bold, sometimes radical, proposals" and "in accordance with that tradition we have tabled a comprehensive proposal, in the form of a draft protocol". Japan's Takahashi Shuhel dug in, calling for CRAMRA's early entry into force and appealing for more accessions. He also demanded that claimants legislating to ban mining explain their actions and the implications for Treaty Article IV. Belgium spoke of the growing "wave of environmental interest" and, of CRAMRA: "it was drafted in good faith, but belongs in a museum".[9] Rolf Andersen said that Norway supported the 'Kiel 5' protocol. Optimistically, he asked: "with all of us wishing to protect the environment, how can we fail?", and warned of "making the best the enemy of the good". To that, the NGOs' Jim Barnes replied: "the best is not the enemy of the good—the best

[8] 20 November 1990, "Opening statement by the Head of the Delegation of the United Kingdom" https://documents.ats.aq/SATCM11_1/ip/SATCM11_1_ip013_e.pdf (accessed 1 February 2021).
[9] 20 and 21 November 1990, "XI SCM Plenary" (AWJ personal notes). See also opening statements in SATCM XI-1 Meeting Documents https://legacy.ats.aq/devAS/ats_meetings_documents.aspx?lang=e (accessed 26 March 2020).

provides inspiration!", and proceeded to argue for the comprehensive measures depicted in ASOC's epic 94-page draft convention.[10] Representing the United States, Bohlen appeared much more flexible than had been suggested by discussions in the corridors. Despite differences remaining, attitudes had shifted over the previous year and Canberra was advised that "it is clear after the first days of this meeting the atmosphere is much better than at the Paris ATCM. The CRAMRA issue has receded to some extent, some old faces are not here". Any criticism expressed was "essentially a venting of frustration at the role Australia has played in crippling CRAMRA".[11]

Each proposal was introduced. France's Jean-Pierre Puissochet presented the 'Four Powers' convention as a framework for all activities with low-risk activities permitted and others, such as mining, prohibited or requiring prior assessment. There would be four institutions but, he reassured, without bureaucratic processes. John Heap introduced the 'Kiel 5' protocol with annexes approach, and Ian Hendry used the United Kingdom's specific proposal to illustrate the legal form. Wong addressed both substance *and* form with New Zealand's protocol, arguing that it responded to public concerns and addressed the mandate of 1989's ATCM Recommendation XV-1. Tucker Scully likewise elaborated on the US preference for a protocol with annexes. Germany, the Netherlands, Norway, China and the USSR also argued for a protocol. Japan argued for CRAMRA, while willing to consider protocol options. France's Jean-Pierre Puissochet could see no logic in a protocol when there were already two conventions in force (CCAS and CCAMLR) and, oddly, one "pending" (CRAMRA).[12]

November 1990: "Hot Potatoes!"

SCAR president Richard Laws joined in the debate by dismissing the premise of a fragile environment and arguing that glacial scouring far exceeds human impacts and fur seals damage far more vegetation. Pointing to the role of SCAR's Group of Specialists on Environment and Conservation (GOSEAC), Laws pleaded for SCAR representation in the

---

[10] November 1990, A.1 Convention on Antarctic Conservation (New Barnes draft, 5/10/90) in: "Antarctic Treaty Special Consultative Meetings X and XI, Viña del Mar, Chile 1990. Volume 2, Supplementary documents" (AAD: B13/199).

[11] 22 November 1990, SC21384 "Antarctic environment: SCM XI: Delegation statements" (NAA: B1387 90/759 PART 3).

[12] 21 and 22 November 1990, "XI SCM Plenary" (AWJ personal notes).

environment debate. Excessive regulation, he argued, would curtail science. Laws ended with an implied threat: "if SCAR's advice was not heeded it would have ways of making its views known". "Hot potatoes!" exclaimed Korea's Yong Hoon Lee, calling for moderation.[13] France's Pierre Jouventin insisted that SCAR's role was to coordinate science, not direct environment debates.[14] Heap came to Laws' defence, pointing out that of the 14 million km^2 of Antarctica, only 50 km^2 (the station precincts) had seen any impacts. He then asked rhetorically: If a protocol is not an appropriate form, why had one just been adopted for the Montreal Protocol?[15]

At the end of Week 1, Australia's delegation reported that "considerable opposition to our views on both minerals and a comprehensive regime remain".[16] A permanent mining ban and a simple moratorium would be rejected: "some creative thinking will be required to devise a proposal which can provide an acceptable solution." Alan Brown's contact with Curtis Bohlen considered the formulation used in US legislation: prohibit mining until there was agreement to lift the ban. Some NGOs were contemplating a moratorium for, say, 30 years with the key question being whether consensus would be required to *extend it* or to *lift it*. Australia, however, was resolute: "insist on a permanent ban and don't peddle any compromises."[17]

NOVEMBER 1990: "GOVERNMENTS DO STRANGE THINGS OCCASIONALLY"

Meanwhile, in Australia, progress was being watched carefully. Prime Minister Hawke was simultaneously pessimistic and optimistic: "we cannot expect that all our objectives will be met at this one meeting", and yet "it is already becoming clear that we have greater reason for confidence than ever before". Pitching to NGOs he said that "the world-wide

[13] 22 November 1990, "XI SCM Plenary" (AWJ personal notes).

[14] Tensions between SCAR, GOSEAC and the Treaty Parties are explored in: David W. H. Walton and Peter D Clarkson, *Science in the Snow* (Scientific Committee on Antarctic Research, 2011), 96–108.

[15] 27 November 1990, SC21410 "Antarctic environment: SCM XI: Plenary" (AAD: 89/914–2).

[16] 25 November 1990, SC21394 "Antarctic environment: SCM XI" (AAD: 89/914–2).

[17] 25 November 1990, SC21393 "Antarctica—SCM minerals issue" (NAA: B1387 90/759 PART 3).

environmental movement, not least the WWF, has played a large part in this". In a six-page Antarctic policy statement, reiterating the case against mining and the illusion created by CRAMRA, he announced that the Australian Antarctic Foundation, chaired by Sir Ninian Stephen, would prepare a conservation strategy for the AAT.[18] The occasion had been the Duke of Edinburgh's meeting with the World Wildlife Fund (WWF) that day. Hawke was asked whether the Chile meeting would sanction mining: "I'd be prepared to take any sort of wager you'd like—I think the Antarctic is safe from mining."[19] Prince Philip, standing alongside, was quizzed about UK attitudes: "I don't mind commenting on this because it's not a party-political issue ... governments do strange things occasionally."[20] As WWF's International president, the Duke called for Parties "to ban any form of prospecting, mining, oil drilling or any other industrial activity within the Antarctic".[21]

In Chile, SATCM XI continued. Working Group 1 (WG1), chaired by Germany's Dietrich Granow, examined matters with political and legal implications. Uruguay's Roberto Puceiro would chair a review of existing measures in Working Group 2 (WG2).[22] It soon emerged that the United Kingdom had "withdrawn its draft protocol from discussion and aligned itself with the US draft".[23] On 28 November, at meeting midpoint, WG1 reviewed progress. Considerable discussion had occurred in a cooperative atmosphere—but also in a vacuum. Puissochet did not conceal French exasperation. Several issues had been examined, but why had "matters of substance" not been addressed? Why had the meeting discussed the UK, US and 'Kiel 5' proposals, but not that of the 'Four Powers'? And was the

[18] 23 November 1990, "Statement by the Prime Minister—Antarctic policy" http:// pmtranscripts.pmc.gov.au/sites/default/files/original/00008211.pdf   (accessed   1 February 2021).

[19] 29 November 1990, CE962474 "Antarctica: Australian Prime Minister's comments" (NAA: B1387 90/759 PART 3), 2.

[20] 23 November 1990, transcript of ABC Radio *PM* reported in: 26 November 1990, CE960802 "Antarctica: Radio report of news conference with Prince Phillip and Prime Minister" (NAA: B1387 90/759 PART 3).

[21] 25 November 1990, letter on WWF letterhead "Open letter to the Special Consultative Meeting of Antarctic Treaty Parties, Viva [*sic*] del Mar, Chile, 19 November to 6 December 1990" (AWJ personal notes).

[22] Antarctic Treaty, *Interim Report of the Eleventh Antarctic Treaty Special Consultative Meeting, Viña Del Mar, 19 November-6 December 1990* (Republic of Chile, 1990), 6–7.

[23] 27 November 1990, SC21409 "Antarctic environment: SCM XI: Working groups" (AAD: 89/914–3).

drafting under way for an instrument, report or communiqué? The United States agreed that SATCM XI would be "a failure if we produce only a report or a communiqué". Australia noted that the mandate was to "explore and discuss all proposals", and this should be done first. Alan Brown's analogy summed it up: "we are manufacturing bricks, but we don't know what we are building!"[24] Also, 12,737 kilometres away in Perth, Bob Hawke had better ideas: "Chile will see the first steps towards the achievement of the position which will ensure that there will never be mining in the Antarctic".[25] The problem was that, in Chile, mining had still not been addressed.

The regime's form had been discussed for weeks, but not resolved. An environment instrument could be either a convention or a protocol. There were obvious political differences: because the 'Four Powers' proposal had been launched by Prime Ministers Bob Hawke and Michel Rocard, a convention had become associated with maximum environment protection. While the 'Four Powers' convention was rigorous, New Zealand's protocol proposal was even more stringent. In contrast, protocols proposed by the 'Kiel 5', United States and United Kingdom were considered less ambitious and, in Australia and France, associated with the 'minimalists'. In legal and practical terms, both a convention and a protocol could be as comprehensive and enforceable as Parties wished. Most Parties argued that the instrument's form was subordinate to its substance but, in Chile, no Parties were attracted to joining the 'Four Powers'. What was accepted, however, was that 'Agreed Measures' would not be used again.[26]

November 1990: CRAMRA's Liability Rules

The meeting paused on 29 November to discuss CRAMRA's liability rules. Chilean lawyer Francisco Orrego Vicuña chaired the meeting.[27] John Heap recalled that in June 1988 liability rules were considered part of environmental protection, and "it was now regrettable ... that governments had turned from CRAMRA" before the full picture was

[24] 23 and 28 November 1990, "XI SCM—WG1" (AWJ personal notes).

[25] 29 November 1990, CE962474 "Antarctica: Australian Prime Minister's comments" (NAA: B1387 90/759 PART 3), 1.

[26] Templeton, *Protecting Antarctica: The Development of the Treaty System*, 10–11.

[27] 7 October 1991, XVI ATCM/INFO 43 "Report to the XVI Antarctic Treaty Consultative Meeting on the Meeting Held Pursuant to Recommendation XV-2" https://documents.ats.aq/ATCM16/ip/ATCM16_ip043_e.pdf (accessed 19 March 2020).

known. Rolf Andersen considered CRAMRA an environmental regime with liability rules so strict as to be a disincentive to mining. Germany cautioned against "taking a totally negative attitude to CRAMRA as it represented years of work and was the most extensive work on the Antarctic environment" and the environmental regime should draw on its liability provisions. Alan Brown did not wish to belittle CRAMRA but Australia could not support elaboration of it. Georges Duquin was forthright: as France had no intention of acceding to CRAMRA (thus preventing its entry into force), there was no point in further discussion. The USSR warned against leaving a legal vacuum, but now was not the time for the debate, a sentiment echoed by the remaining speakers.[28] It was later observed that the desultory discussion was "a last attempt, subsequently proven completely fruitless, to save CRAMRA by expanding and reinforcing its own system of environmental safeguards".[29] With formalities complete, liability under CRAMRA was abandoned.

With little time left, the meeting returned to environmental measures. In WG1, a lively discussion developed on the instrument's institutions and the frequency of ATCMs, issues that would make significant changes to the Treaty's operations. Argentina confirmed its July 1990 hint that it might even consider a Treaty secretariat, a remarkable turnaround given its determined objections since 1961. Many delegations supported an environmental advisory committee for the ATCM and a compliance inspectorate. Burgess seemed sufficiently enthused by discussion of institutional options that he used this example of modernising the ATS to suggest that there was no need to review the Treaty's operation.[30]

Mining, still the most sensitive political issue, remained unresolved. On 26 November the chair met with delegation heads. Pinochet invited them "to speak their minds" but "responses were tentative and reiterated well known positions". They were willing "to seek a solution, but there were few suggestions of optimism … Japan continued to show it will be difficult to move". Bohlen expressed pessimism and the Soviet Union's Artur Chilingarov "urged that no Party take further action that would make an agreement more difficult".[31] The chair then passed around a non-paper to

---

[28] 29 November 1990, "XI SCM—Liability" (AWJ personal notes).
[29] Francioni, "The Madrid Protocol on the Protection of the Antarctic Environment," 50.
[30] 29 and 30 November 1990, "XI SCM—Institutions" (AWJ personal notes).
[31] 27 November 1990, SC21408 "Antarctica—SCM minerals issue" (AAD: 89/914–2).

stimulate thinking.[32] It provided for a mining ban for an undefined period of years, with the ban modifiable by consensus. On expiring, any extension of the ban required a majority decision but, if lifted, a minerals regime adopted by consensus would be required. Thus, the first glimmer of compromise emerged. Informal discussion continued for a week. John Heap helpfully made clear that although the United Kingdom "preferred CRAMRA, it was not apparently opposed to some form of prohibition". Japan's Takahashi Shuhel, however, had no instructions to move beyond voluntary restraint. Alan Brown and Jean-Pierre Puissochet "argued firmly for a ban which could be lifted only by consensus, although a review could take place". Frank Wong responded New Zealand "had problems even with the concept of a review".[33]

DECEMBER 1990: SQUARE BRACKETS

On 30 November, the AAD's Rex Moncur reported that the meeting would likely produce a single text, although much of it "would be in square brackets".[34] Meanwhile, away from the meeting room, an important development was underway. Rolf Andersen was, as a personal initiative, compiling a compromise text. Andersen had led Norway's minerals delegation and wanted to bring Parties together. Norway was one of the 'Kiel 5', and Andersen saw the advantages of a protocol. How he presented the draft would be crucial, as would the handling of mining.

Curtis Bohlen told Alan Brown that "an agreement which he can take back to Washington" needed an agreeable outcome on minerals. Bohlen was seeking instructions for a position acceptable to Australia and its partners—for example, a protocol with a specific reference to a 'nature reserve, land of science'. On minerals, there would be a 30- to 40-year prohibition, with automatic extension by 10-year periods unless a Party objected. Ending the prohibition would require consensus. This caught Japan off-guard: "their position [had] reflected what they understood the US position to be". Brown thought Bohlen's proposal "the best we could hope

---

[32] 'Non-papers' assist discussion, but have limited circulation and are not attributed.

[33] 5 December 1990, SC21441 "Antarctic—SCM—minerals outcome" (AAD: 89/914–2).

[34] 30 November 1990, AAD note for file (NAA: B1387 90/759 PART 3). Square brackets capture words requiring further discussion.

for in the present climate … a later outcome may not be better", and the issue was "whether Bohlen will be able to deliver the US on this".[35]

On 1 December, Andersen's synthesis was shown to a group of just eight. After some amendments, on 3 December it was circulated to all delegation heads as "a personal paper binding on no one". It took the form of a protocol. Australia thought that "while it naturally does not go as far as we would like", it was "a considerable advance on the original proposals of the UK and US". A single sentence dealt with minerals. Entirely within square brackets, it read:

> [ARTICLE 6. PROHIBITION ON MINERAL RESOURCE ACTIVITIES
> Any activities relating to mineral resources, other than scientific research, shall be prohibited]

Puissochet insisted that "there needed to be further discussion of the minerals question". Brown argued that it was "prejudicial to the proponents of a convention", and dealt inadequately with minerals "particularly in the use of discriminatory square brackets", the only article treated that way. Six asked that the square brackets be removed but, importantly, "no speaker advocated the removal of the minerals article from the paper altogether". Bohlen urged Heap "not to hold out hopes for the revival of CRAMRA", but Heap "claimed it was too late to make progress on a prohibition". Progress was faltering and Andersen left early, "obviously disappointed at the course of events". Brown advised Canberra that "it was clear the minerals question was likely to dominate the remaining time of the meeting", and "we will of course be vigilant to preserve Australia's position on this issue".[36] However, he was not convinced of success: "the minerals issue was still a very hard nut to crack", and, he said, "it may not be possible to resolve it at Viña del Mar".[37]

In Canberra, Foreign Minister Gareth Evans regretted "that the United Kingdom, in particular, has failed to recognise this groundswell of national and international opinion". Turning the UK insistence on consensus back on itself, Evans said that "the Treaty System will suffer if this

---

[35] 2 December 1990, SC21431 "Antarctica—SCM—minerals issues" (AAD: 89/914–2).
[36] 4 December 1990, SC21437 "Antarctic environment: SCM XI: minerals" (AAD: 89/914–2).
[37] 4 December 1990, CE964356 "Antarctica: Press release" (AAD: 89/914–2).

procedure—one of its greatest strengths—is misused to oppose changes which reflect these broadly emerging concerns". He appeared unconcerned that it was Australia's reneging of consensus that had precipitated the crisis. Evans concluded optimistically that "it is only a matter of time before the views that we are urging will prevail".[38]

December 1990: "A Piece of Russian Genius"

It seemed that the minerals issue had been taken as far as it would go in Chile. However, progress was made at a 4 December delegation heads meeting: "after many attempts to find an acceptable formula it was decided to remove all the square brackets, but to add three dots after 'prohibited'". It now read:

> ARTICLE 6. PROHIBITION ON MINERAL RESOURCE ACTIVITIES
> Any activities relating to mineral resources, other than scientific research, shall be prohibited . . .

Seemingly small, it was a significant change because it meant the idea was accepted even if the three dots allowed more to be added later. Despite the ellipsis, Alan Brown reported that "the outcome is excellent for Australia and countries proposing a ban on mineral activities". It would "be up to others to propose additions or amendments, a reversal of the situation which would have prevailed if the square brackets had remained". It was later revealed that substituting square brackets with three dots "was a piece of Russian genius that meant exactly the same thing as square brackets". The dots prevailed. The reporting cable summed it up: "the Treaty nations have accepted the assumption of a prohibition of minerals activities". According to Brown, "Australia can claim the Viña meeting has been a great success for its policies ... we sense that the UK is now moving and will not block a new agreement. Japan now appears to be the biggest problem".[39]

---

[38] 4 December 1990, Senate Hansard, 4869.
[39] 5 December 1990, SC21441 "Antarctic—SCM—minerals outcome" (AAD: 89/914–2). 4 January 1991, BO52298 "Antarctica: German views on environmental protection" (NAA: B1387 90/759 PART 3).

With the three-week meeting near the end, formalities for adopting the meeting report could proceed. A final flurry occurred on the last day, 6 December, over paragraph 20 and the minerals issue. The question was how to reflect support for a permanent ban: whether this option was preferred by 'several' or 'many' delegations. Eventually it was agreed to settle on 'a number of'.[40] Further debate concerned the moratorium's status, finally settling on Sweden's formulation that "the present restraint" continues.[41] With the report settled, the meeting adopted the 'Viña del Mar Declaration'. It referred to Antarctica as "an ecological reserve, devoted to peace and science" and, on mining, noted it was "generally accepted that there was a need for prohibiting these activities for a lengthy period". The real substance of the meeting was attached: a draft protocol based on Andersen's text.

Avoiding the political tangles, for three weeks WG2 had attended to many practical matters including updating existing environmental measures. The results appeared in four appendixes to Andersen's text covering marine pollution; waste management; environmental impact assessment; and conservation of fauna and flora. These, too, could not escape square brackets, including around whether sled dogs needed inoculation against canine diseases, an issue that was to come back and bite. All this was only the meeting's interim report.[42] SATCM XI would meet again the following year with Spain offering to host in Madrid.

With debate paused, Australia reviewed attitudes to a mining ban. Of the 26 ATCPs, 10 could accept either a permanent ban or one lifted by consensus.[43] Six retained hopes for CRAMRA, but operating in parallel with an environmental instrument. The rest were uncommitted.[44] Over three weeks, a remarkable shift had occurred.[45]

[40] 6 December 1990, "XI SCM—Plenary, SCM report" (AWJ personal notes).

[41] 8 December 1990, SC21459 "Antarctic environment: SCM XI" (AAD: 89/914-3).

[42] Antarctic Treaty, *Interim Report of the Eleventh Antarctic Treaty Special Consultative Meeting, Viña Del Mar, 19 November-6 December 1990.*

[43] These were Australia, Belgium, Finland, France, Italy, India, New Zealand, the Netherlands, Poland and Sweden.

[44] These were Argentina, Chile, Japan, Republic of Korea, South Africa and the United Kingdom.

[45] 12 November 1990, "Antarctic initiative: Running sheet: Overview, as at 12 November 1990" (AAD: B13/199). 17 December 1990, handwritten list "DANT's assessment of where Parties line up" (AAD: 89/914-2).

The significant shift observed did not satisfy ASOC. Jim Barnes, criticising loopholes in the Andersen text, "was disappointed that the Treaty Parties had not gathered their strength in Chile to resolve the mining issue".[46] Australians, however, returned home delighted that "key points from our proposal … have been included".[47] Evans and Kelly proudly welcomed the reference to a mining prohibition "as an important achievement for Australia, France and our other supporters".[48] Others jostled for credit. New Zealand hailed the result as a New Zealand victory, Foreign Minister Don McKinnon claiming "New Zealand's call for [a] total mining ban in Antarctica is given prominence in the Andersen text. The New Zealand draft protocol … was the main draft document".[49] José Otegui said the meeting was "a great advance" as Andersen had adopted Argentina's preference for a protocol. He saw Japan "as the only Party somewhat outside the convergence" of views.[50] Japan, of course, was quite able to speak for itself: while it thought "positive progress" had been made, it maintained "opposition to a permanent and unconditional ban on mining" and considered that "the *entire* Andersen Paper was still in square brackets". Japan nevertheless recognised that "it is becoming increasingly isolated" and, ultimately, it "would be prepared to be flexible".[51]

January 1991: Manoeuvres to Seize the Initiative

Year 1991 would be momentous for Antarctica. SATCM XI would reconvene in Madrid in April preceded by a Preparatory Meeting for ATCM XVI, and the ATCM itself in October in Bonn. Germany, like all hosts, hoped for a successful meeting, and Dietrich Granow considered "consensus on environmental protection before the October ATCM extremely

[46] 7 December 1990, Paul Hunt and Alexander Smith "Chile meeting drafts plan top to protect the Antarctic" *The Age*, 7.

[47] 14 December 1990, DASETT brief to minister "Outcome of Antarctic Treaty meetings in Chile, November 1990" (AAD: 89/914–2).

[48] 7 December 1990, joint press release "Antarctica: positive move towards mining ban" (NAA: B1387 90/759 PART 3).

[49] 12 December 1990, WL42628 "New Zealand: Antarctic—meeting of Treaty Parties" (AAD: 89/914–3).

[50] 13 December 1990, BA36552 "Antarctic environment: SCM XI" (AAD: 89/914–2).

[51] 31 December 1990, TK70053 "Antarctic environment SCM XI: Japanese views" (NAA: B1387 90/759 PART 3).

important". "If ATS members remained divided on this issue", he said, "there was a real risk that the issue would be decisively hijacked by the UNCED conference". Despite "sympathy for the UK (Heap) view", Andersen's text offered "the best prospects for success".[52] Granow proposed an additional Heads of Delegation meeting on the environment in Bonn in April.[53] France would have none of this, suspecting manoeuvres to seize the initiative. Even though France wanted debate concluded promptly, Charley Causeret "made it clear that France did not wish to see the agreement signed later in the year in Bonn".[54] Georges Duquin thought "the Germans were clearly out to recuperate their image, but should not be rewarded by an HOD meeting … rivalling the importance of the Madrid meeting".[55] Granow's idea was dropped.[56]

Meanwhile, Parties were reflecting on Viña del Mar. While accepting that the Andersen text was the likely way forward, France preferred "not to give up on the idea of a convention, but to save it as a possible concession at a later date". Causeret considered expanding the group of 'like-minded' countries to strengthen support and suggested a wider group include Greece, Romania, Austria, Finland, Denmark and Ecuador—but not Sweden, which he now saw as too close to New Zealand. Australia argued against "briefing the wider group if the position of the four co-presenting Parties was still fluid". To Causeret, any differences "were more likely to emanate from the Italians".[57] In Australia's view, targeting Sweden and New Zealand would help as both were "more influential in the Antarctic context than most of the Like-minded".[58] It was agreed to include Belgium and Italy as full partners. Ironically, France and Australia

[52] 4 January 1991, BO52298 "Antarctica: German views on environmental protection" (NAA: B1387 90/759 PART 3).

[53] 4 January 1991, CE974358 "Antarctica: Meetings in April 1991" (NAA: B1387 91/32 PART 1).

[54] 13 January 1991, PA84984 "Antarctica: Meetings in April 1991" (NAA: B1387 91/32 PART 1).

[55] 7 February 1991, PA85456 "Antarctica: Bonn informal meeting" (NAA: B1387 91/32 PART 1). 6 February 1991, BO52744 "Antarctica: Meetings in April" (NAA: B1387 91/32 PART 1).

[56] 4 March 1991, CE997947 "Antarctica: Schedule of meetings in April" (NAA: B1387 91/32 PART 1).

[57] 3 January 1991, PA84819 "Antarctic environment initiative: Four Party consultations" (NAA: B1387 90/888 PART 2).

[58] 4 January 1991, CE974192 "Antarctic environment initiative: Four Party consultations" (AAD: 89/578–2).

were not particularly like-minded, and there was even disagreement over who else was. Sweden's potential participation was a sore point. Australia "had found the Swedes supportive and helpful", but France did not, although the differences may have stemmed from personal disagreements.[59] Australia thought the exclusion of Sweden counterproductive as they would "not be able to understand why Denmark (a minor player) and Finland would be included".[60] It was, however, unlikely that Norway could be brought around: "despite Andersen's ostensibly 'neutral' role at the Viña del Mar meeting", Norway actually "sided with the minimalists". Eventually France relented on Sweden, but too late for participation in the next 'Like-mindeds' meeting.[61]

How to progress matters would depend on the willingness of Parties to be flexible. Despite having its own proposal in Chile, New Zealand had maintained close contact with Australia. On the other hand, their "relations with the other members of the Four Power group in Viña del Mar were at times tense".[62] The mining issue was of particular concern as Antarctica achieved such a high profile domestically. Chris Beeby thought that "vastly more progress had been made than he anticipated", and "the Madrid meeting in April could possibly fix it"—that is, provided mining's complications and "Japan's intransigence" could be resolved.[63] While New Zealand appeared even more ambitious than Australia, the two countries' positions "are very similar, if not identical", and "the Andersen paper provides a basis for advancing the binding legal instrument". The Australian High Commission in Wellington proposed "a round of consultations with New Zealand to see how much common ground exists".[64] Canberra was surprisingly unenthusiastic. DFAT replied that "it is something of a curiosity that we should enjoy a rather closer cooperative relationship with France than New Zealand ... events which brought about

[59] 18 January 1991, ST27505 "Antarctic environment initiative: Paris consultations" (AAD: 89/914–3).

[60] 1 February 1991, ST27562 "Antarctic environment: Like-minded Group" (NAA: B1387 90/888 PART 2).

[61] 8 February 1991, CE988146 "Antarctic environment—Like-minded Group" (NAA: B1387 1991/56 PART 1).

[62] 4 January 1991, CE974457 "Antarctica: Comprehensive environmental protection" (NAA: B1387 1991/55 PART 1).

[63] 8 January 1991, WL42779 "New Zealand/French relations: Rocard's visit to New Zealand and Antarctica" (NAA: B1387 91/32 PART 1).

[64] 9 January 1991, WL42795 "Antarctic comprehensive environmental protection" (NAA: B1387 90/759 PART 3).

this situation still have their legacy [and] New Zealand was working very actively against our position".[65] Nevertheless, New Zealand was invited to late-January's 'Like-mindeds' consultations.[66]

The 'Four Powers' met on 28 January 1991 and the 'Like-mindeds' the next day.[67] It appeared that "something of a cohesive lobbying bloc is developing around the combination of the four prime movers and the six or seven like-mindeds". Despite DFAT's earlier concern about blocs forming, now it was hoped that "this bloc might gather impetus". Equally, it was acknowledged that "those who either oppose our position, or are lukewarm about it, carry considerable weight". But how minded-alike the 'Like-mindeds' were was moot. On mining, Greece favoured a 50-year prohibition; Italy thought that impossible. Finland could live with a moratorium; Denmark was unsure. New Zealand wanted a permanent ban and India a ban reviewable after 30 years. In fact, these options reflected the spread of views between almost *all* the Parties because, by the end of Viña del Mar, it appeared that only Japan objected to any form of restraint.[68] Australia and France were no longer at the strictest end of the spectrum. The 'Four Powers' had taken a 30-year review option to Viña del Mar, but now the NGOs, which had strongly backed Australia and France, criticised it. While accepting that the Treaty used such a formula, ASOC's Lyn Goldsworthy said a 30-year review was too weak. Consensus to lift a mining ban would be environmentally sound, but the question was really "one of public perception". NGOs now pushed for more than 99 years.[69]

On the nascent environmental instrument, the 'Four Powers' found broad agreement, and it was accepted that "the best approach at the Madrid meeting would be … to seek to amend the Andersen text rather to come up with a new instrument". That would not preclude amendments, and, like Australia, France wanted "to meet the Andersen language at least half the time".[70] On the Article 6 mining prohibition: "our objective will

[65] 14 January 1991, CE977769 "Antarctica: Environment protection" (NAA: B1387 90/759 PART 3).
[66] 17 January 1991, CE979293 "Antarctic environment initiative—New Zealand" (NAA: B1387 90/888 PART 2).
[67] 29 January 1991, PA85274 "Antarctica" (NAA: B1387 90/888 PART 2). At this point, the 'Like-mindeds' were Denmark, Ecuador, Finland, Greece, India, New Zealand and Romania.
[68] 30 January 1991, GE92664 "Antarctic environment" (NAA: B1387 90/888 PART 2).
[69] 8 February 1991, "NGO meeting" (AAD: 91/910–1).
[70] 29 January 1991, PA85274 "Antarctica" (NAA: B1387 90/888 PART 2).

be to eliminate the qualifying dots"—a simple objective masking the challenge of achieving it.[71] Several other areas needed attention including compliance, response action, institutional arrangements and environmental impact assessment.[72] Substantial effort was required to refine the latter.[73] On that there was common ground with New Zealand.

A renewed trans-Tasman relationship was emerging, and bilateral consultations set the scene. New Zealand's Frank Wong raised two issues. One was practical—environmental impact assessment, which he characterised as "the whistle-blowing procedure". The other was political—the question of mining, for which Wong proposed "a brainstorming session". In Wong's view, Japan was at one extreme arguing that CRAMRA was all that was needed. At the other end was New Zealand, which, because of strengthening public opinion, was instructed to seek a permanent prohibition (although Wong wondered "how permanent is permanent?").[74] Technical issues could be resolved, but nothing could be achieved without political agreement between all 26 ATCPs. That was still some way off.

January 1991: The United Kingdom, the United States and Uruguay Are Unconvinced

The United Kingdom still hoped that CRAMRA would complement an environmental instrument. Tristan Garel-Jones noted that only eight countries supported a total mining ban—a policy for which he now associated Australia with New Zealand (rather than France). He claimed that the United Kingdom was "working to find a bridge between the two opposing views among Antarctic Treaty Parties".[75] However, any bridge would have to span much more than two views.

[71] 22 January 1991, DFAT facsimile message "Antarctic environmental protection initiative" (NAA: B1387 90/888 PART 2).

[72] 16 January 1991, Attorney-General's Department memorandum "Preliminary comments on the Andersen draft" (NAA: B1387 90/888 PART 3).

[73] 29 January 1991, PA85274 "Antarctica" (NAA: B1387 90/888 PART 2). 19 February 1991, AAD memorandum "Environmental impact assessment (non-paper)" (AAD: 91/910–1). 21 February 1991, AAD memorandum "Article 7: Environmental impact assessment" (AAD: 91/910–1).

[74] 7 February 1991, WL43003 "Antarctica: Environment protection: ANZ consultations" (NAA: B1387 90/888 PART 2).

[75] 16 January 1991, United Kingdom, House of Commons Hansard, columns 833–836 https://publications.parliament.uk/pa/cm199091/cmhansrd/1991-01-16/Orals-1.html (accessed 3 February 2021).

Just within the United States there were more than two views. Tucker Scully came away from Viña del Mar positive: the atmosphere was "much better than at the Paris ATCM". Others, however, saw the "first two weeks as being very frustrating … delegates from the UK, Japan and some from the US itself having been particularly inflexible". One US delegate thought that "Heap had been unbelievably bad and that the Japanese did not seem to be aware that the US had changed its position at all". Scully admitted that domestically "there were still some differences of emphasis among agencies", a situation others described as "sharp divisions". He conceded, "there was no longer any possibility of consensus on CRAMRA [but] something like CRAMRA would be essential to any new consensus." Environmentalists dismissed this: "Scully still yearns for CRAMRA but has been overridden by senior levels in State."[76] Curtis Bohlen told Australia's John McCarthy that publicly "the reference to prohibition, albeit followed by the three dots, had been especially well received", although he (Bohlen) had been admonished that the "US delegation had gone too far at Viña". Bohlen remarked "that he had a lot more work to do to win round colleagues within State and the Administration [and] he was not optimistic". Agreement to remove the dots seemed unlikely—the maximum US position would "probably be a 20- to 40-year moratorium, plus a mechanism at least as rigorous as CRAMRA".[77]

Uruguay considered a permanent ban unrealistic: "the objective of a permanent prohibition on mining in the quadripartite draft convention would not achieve consensus" because the Treaty "needed to have some regulatory system like CRAMRA in place when Article 6 came up for review".[78] This mirrored USSR thinking and Sergei Karev predicted the "Parties would eventually agree to the Andersen formula in Article 6", although "the Japanese would be opposed". On the other hand, he thought "the Japanese would prefer to avoid being isolated".[79]

[76] 20 January 1991, WH125750 "Antarctica: SCM XI: US views" (NAA: B1387 91/32 PART 1).

[77] 22 January 1991, WH125815 "Antarctic minerals: US policy" (NAA: B1387 1991/55 PART 1).

[78] 29 January 1991, BA36769 "Antarctica: Uruguayan views on next steps" (NAA: B1387 1991/56 PART 1).

[79] 28 January 1991, MS44849 "Antarctica: Soviet views" (NAA: B1387 1991/56 PART 1).

FEBRUARY 1991: A US NON-PAPER INTENDED TO TEST REACTIONS

Despite internal differences, the United States sought to do its own bridge-building. On 4 February, the United States circulated a 'non-paper' intended to test reactions. It did. It set out what it called "the elements of a tolerable middle ground": a binding moratorium of 20 to 40 years with consensus to *extend* the moratorium. That, and the moratorium would be conditional on CRAMRA or its equivalent being in place when the moratorium expires. It expected Parties "to coalesce around such an approach".[80] The failure to coalesce was swift. Australia said the paper took "us backwards rather than towards tolerable middle ground" because it departed from Andersen's 'prohibition' which could only be *lifted* by consensus. Furthermore, minerals were treated in isolation from the environmental regime (of which it made no mention at all).[81] Australia drafted a response expressing "disappointment that it seemed to represent a significant retreat" from the US position in Viña del Mar, from its own legislation, and from the Andersen text. Australia was concerned that "we now had to be pessimistic that an environmental protection instrument could be concluded in Madrid in April or even this year". Given that it was "important that the US paper not go unchallenged", DFAT surprisingly considered the draft response "too heavy handed and counter-productive". However, the gist of it was sent to Paris, bolstering France's response.[82]

Within days it was clear that reactions to the US paper were negative. Its genesis was a factor: there had been little inter-agency consultation—indeed, many agencies had not even known it existed. Some thought it was circulated because the State Department's Economic Bureau was unhappy that the official US position had not been pushed in Viña del Mar. Another view was that officials seeking stronger environmental protection wanted the paper circulated to confirm "that the proposal will be a non-starter [and] compel the Administration to look at other options". US NGOs, having obtained the paper from Greenpeace New Zealand,

---

[80] 4 February 1991, "US Non Paper: The issue of Antarctic minerals resources" (NAA: B1387 1991/55 PART 1).

[81] 4 February 1991, CE986406 "Antarctica: Comprehensive environmental protection—US position" (NAA: B1387 1991/55 PART 1).

[82] 8 February 1991, CE988643 "Antarctica: Australian reaction to US non paper on minerals" (NAA: B1387 1991/55 PART 1). 6 February 1991, PA85425 "Antarctica: Comprehensive environmental protection—US position" (NAA: B1387 1991/56 PART 1).

revealed that Secretary of State James Baker had told them that "there could be a case for taking a 'second look' at it [the minerals issue]". Baker considered Antarctica "a soft environmental issue ... that could be used to reinforce the President's environmental credentials". The State Department confirmed that the paper sought "to resolve (as the Andersen text had been unable to) the impasse on minerals". Ray Arnaudo challenged Australia to "find middle ground".[83] Australia chose not to react, at least not in writing. DFAT asked its Washington Embassy to be subtle: "anything you can do discreetly to expose the position in the US non-paper would be desirable ... please also take every opportunity to make our views known to relevant congressional contacts and NGOs."[84] That would prove unnecessary.

In mid-February Curtis Bohlen admitted that the non-paper hoped "to provoke the sorts of negative responses Australia and others had made, thus reinforcing his own view that the formula contained in the non-paper would not attract support", indeed "only the UK had been somewhat sympathetic".[85] Even Japan seemed to show "room for some movement in their position due to fears of Japanese isolation".[86] Sweden's Desirée Edmar was blunt: the US proposal was "a long way from the middle ground".[87] Pinochet predicted that the compromises in the Andersen text would be the way forward.[88] According to Georges Duquin, Bohlen "acknowledged that his opponents in the Administration had gained ground" but that "the Andersen text should be used as the basis for discussion".[89] Shortly afterwards, Bohlen confidentially passed to DFAT a summary of the lukewarm reactions: consensus was a long way off—of the

[83] 10 February 1991, WH126793 "Antarctica: US non paper on minerals" (NAA: B1387 1991/55 PART 1).

[84] 12 February 1991, CE989529 "Antarctica: US position: Environmental initiative" (NAA: B1387 1991/55 PART 1).

[85] 16 February 1991, WH127318 "Antarctic: US non paper on minerals" (NAA: B1387 1991/55 PART 1).

[86] 1 March 1991, TK70638 "Antarctica: Japanese reaction to the US non-paper on minerals" (NAA: B1387 1991/55 PART 1).

[87] 26 February 1991, ST27675 "Antarctica: Reaction to US non-paper" (NAA: B1387 91/32 PART 1).

[88] 20 February 1991, TPN, Embassy of Chile, covering 28 January 1991 "Considerations on the Viña del Mar meeting by the Chairman of the XIth Antarctic Treaty Special Consultative Meeting" (AAD: 89/914–3).

[89] 26 February 1991, PA85747 "Antarctica-French MFA meeting with Bohlen" (NAA: B1387 1991/55 PART 1).

18 Parties responding, 6 supported a moratorium with a mining regime coming in at the end, and a similar number supported a ban. The USSR thought that "while the US proposal is obviously the best solution, given the unbending positions of those calling for a permanent ban, it may not be obtainable".[90] The non-paper was a non-starter.

NGOs wanted to know if "the Andersen text is *de facto* the informal negotiating text".[91] In their circles it was seen as a "quick and dirty protocol of the type favoured by Norway, USA, UK, Argentina and Chile". Cath Wallace thought that by giving primacy to science it "reflected UK and USA politicking and is designed ... to drive a wedge between environmentalists and scientists". Besides, she said, the amendment provision turned a ban into "a back-door moratorium".[92] Despite progress in Chile, NGOs would demand even more.

The way forward was unclear. For now, the focus was preparations for Madrid in April. Given a possible call for a Treaty review conference, consensus was a high priority for many. The potential trigger, the 30th anniversary of the Treaty's entry into force, was unavoidable—23 June was approaching. Restoring consensus could defuse temptations for a review. But, with April just two months away, negotiations could creep even closer to June. The potential for a symbolic act was not lost on the 'Four Powers' who were considering options for a final meeting. Bonn would host the ATCM. France was anxious, with Jean-Maurice Ripert asking, "why should the Germans get the credit for the environment initiative?" He thought, "Australia might still have a good prospect ... Australia's role in developing an environment treaty would have to be acknowledged." With some understatement, Australia demurred as it was "not wholly popular given the stand we had taken on CRAMRA". Resurrecting Jacques Cousteau's 'Wellington Convention' idea, Australia suggested that New Zealand "would have a certain claim given the CRAMRA history".[93] New Zealand likewise demurred. Chris Beeby "volunteered that New Zealand

[90] 12 March 1991, WH128576 "Antarctica: US non paper on minerals" (NAA: B1387 1991/55 PART 1). Supporters of the United States were Argentina, India, Republic of Korea, the United Kingdom, Uruguay, and the Soviet Union.
[91] 10 February 1991, WH126793 "Antarctica: US non paper on minerals" (NAA: B1387 1991/55 PART 1).
[92] 25 February 1991, Cath Wallace paper "Protocol on environmental protection to the Antarctic Treaty—text prepared by Rolf Trolle Andersen—a critique" (NAA: B1387 1991/56 PART 1).
[93] 30 January 1991, GE92663 "Antarctic environment" (NAA: B1387 91/32 PART 1).

was not interested in hosting a session, having had its fingers burnt in the minerals negotiations". Nevertheless, he was optimistic that the work "could be finished with one more meeting". Apart from the imminent 30th anniversary in 1991, it was desirable "to get this matter out of the way well before UNCED in 1992".[94] This reflected growing external doubts about whether the Treaty was actually *capable* of protecting the environment. UNCED Secretary General Maurice Strong had requested information on the Treaty Parties' intentions as Malaysia was arguing that in UNCED "Antarctic matters would need to be covered in view of the importance of Antarctica to the global environment".[95] Failure to respond convincingly ran the risk of UN intervention. In parallel were the potentially alarming prospects, for the first time, of an expedition to the Antarctic by a state not party to the Treaty.[96] Four months later, the United States, as Depositary Government, was still drafting a reply to Strong, uncertain about what could be achieved.[97]

MARCH 1991: PERSONALITY ISSUES

As April neared, Australia strengthened collaboration with New Zealand as "past difficulties are now behind us". On minerals, Australia argued that Andersen's Article 6 needed only to conclude with a full stop.[98] Australia could, however, accept a review amendable by consensus, but not any form of moratorium. New Zealand could accept a 30-year prohibition with rolling 10-year extensions. On mining, Australia and New Zealand were now close.[99] New Zealand was not, however, close enough to make 'Four Powers' five. Nevertheless, it remained in the 'Like-mindeds'.

[94] 22 February 1991, WL43164 "Antarctica: Consultations with New Zealand" (NAA: B1387 1991/55 PART 1).

[95] 6 March 1991, CE999103 "UNCED: Malaysian views" (NAA: B1387 90/703 PART 1).

[96] Pakistan, which was not a Treaty Party, visited Dronning Maud Land in 1990–91 and planned another expedition in 1991–92. See 4 October 1990, CE938380 "Antarctica" possible Pakistani expedition" (AAD: B13/199).

[97] 7 February 1991, CE987644 "Antarctica: UNCED—reply to letter from Maurice Strong" (NAA: B1387 90/703 PART 1).

[98] 4 March 1991, DFAT facsimile "Australian amendments to the Andersen text" (NAA: B1387 90/888 PART 2).

[99] 22 February 1991, WL43164 "Antarctica: Consultations with New Zealand" (NAA: B1387 1991/55 PART 1). 25 February 1991, WL43169 "Antarctica: Consultations with New Zealand—cable no. 2" (NAA: B1387 1991/55 PART 1).

The 'Four Powers' and 'Like-mindeds' would consult in Rome in March. Australia proposed including Sweden, noting it was "very disappointed not to have been invited to the Paris meeting". France was reluctant because of "Sweden's lack of support for the 4-Power position [and] hoped that Sweden would henceforth adopt a more positive and supportive approach".[100] This seemed an odd way to encourage support, especially as Sweden was already sympathetic and had been for some time. Throughout 1990, it had been clear that Sweden wanted to help Australia and France. Engaging Sweden would have made tactical sense—it was the first Party that had actually signed CRAMRA to become sympathetic to an environmental alternative, and including Sweden might have influenced the other signatories. Desirée Edmar may well have been mystified by French hesitation because "she had received a letter from Lyn Goldsworthy thanking her delegation for its strong environmental position in Viña del Mar". France relented, and Edmar was "very happy to be invited" to the 'Like-mindeds'.[101] This, however, was not for inclusion within the 'Four Powers', a suggestion again raised unsuccessfully on the eve of the Madrid meeting.[102] Italy's Gerardo Carante proposed inviting the Netherlands as "he sensed that the Dutch position was actually very close".[103]

Jean-Pierre Puissochet later admitted that personality issues had influenced French attitudes. Such factors possibly explain DFAT's assessment that Puissochet's "attendance at both the Rome and Madrid meetings will be a great asset given his moderate and pragmatic approach" and that there was now "complete convergence of views between Australia and France with respect to the March and April meetings".[104] That assessment was a little premature. On the crucial mining issue, France wanted a prohibition reviewable after 50 years with amendment by consensus, but "would not die in a ditch if this was reduced to 30–40 years". Australia feared "the French are possibly more prepared than us at this stage to

[100] 26 February 1991, PA85745 "Antarctica: Meetings in March and April" (NAA: B1387 91/32 PART 2).

[101] 26 February 1991, ST27674 "Antarctic environment—Like-minded Group" (NAA: B1387 90/888 PART 2).

[102] 5 April 1991, CP14800 "Antarctic environment" (NAA: B1387 90/888 PART 2).

[103] 1 March 1991, RO48338 "Antarctica: Like-minded Group" (NAA: B1387 90/888 PART 2).

[104] 12 March 1991, PA85950 "Antarctica: Forthcoming meetings: French views" (NAA: B1387 90/888 PART 2).

discuss possible fall-back positions".[105] Australia was standing firm. Back in Canberra, the Senate had, after long delays, just passed the *Antarctic Mining Prohibition Act* 1991. It was fine symbolism but, nine months after its conception, too late for much impact. It could even backfire: in Paris, Charley Causeret warned that "some other ATPs might wish to take up the baton again on the ground that the Australian legislation was not consistent with Article IV of the Antarctic Treaty".[106]

'Four Powers' cohesion would be crucial in April but could not be assumed. At the 25 March consultations in Rome, Italy proposed a new 'Master Text' significantly different from the "agreement reached in Paris that we would work from the Andersen text". In inexplicable diversion from the 'Four Powers' position, Italy's rewrite of Article 6 was tantamount to a moratorium: a fixed duration ban with a mandatory review. "Surprised and concerned", Australia insisted it not be circulated "to the Like-mindeds or any other Party outside the 4P group".[107] France agreed: "the Italian proposal was unacceptable both from a substantive and tactical point of view." Italy argued that it would "catch the public's imagination". Causeret considered it "crucial that there be a unified 4-Power position" and it was necessary to "bring the Italians into line".[108] France and Italy could, however, agree on improving the Andersen text on environmental impact assessment and liability where Australia's proposals were "too detailed".[109] Belgium also proposed problematic amendments.[110] Meanwhile, recognising Rolf Andersen's "experience, common sense and skill", France encouraged Norway to release Andersen to "resume his arbitral/drafting role" in Madrid.[111]

[105] 14 March 1991, PA86015 "Antarctica" (NAA: B1387 90/888 PART 2).

[106] 22 March 1991, PA86166 "Antarctica: Antarctic Mining Prohibition Bill, 1991" (NAA: B1387 1990/549 PART 3). Presumably France, also a claimant, considered the legislation tactically problematic rather than illegitimate.

[107] 21 March 1991, CE5028 "Antarctica: Rome consultations and 4P text" (NAA: B1387 90/888 PART 3).

[108] 21 March 1991, PA86146 "Antarctica: Rome consultations and 4P text" (NAA: B1387 90/888 PART 3).

[109] 21 March 1991, PA86145 "Antarctica: Andersen text: French comments on Australian amendments" (NAA: B1387 90/888 PART 3). 13 March 1991, AAD memorandum to A-G's "Antarctic environment protection instrument—Article 7" (AAD: 91/910–1).

[110] 22 March 1991, CE6753 "Antarctica: SCMXI—Rome consultations, 25–26 March—Italian and Belgian comment on Australian/French texts" (NAA: B1387 90/888 PART 2).

[111] 1 March 1991, ST27693 "Antarctica: Environment—consultations with Norway" (NAA: B1387 1991/55 PART 1). 12 March 1991, PA85950 "Antarctica: Forthcoming meetings: French views" (NAA: B1387 90/888 PART 2).

The 'Four Powers' agreed to circulate amendments to the Andersen text. It was a 'non-paper' described as a "compromise text", although "some drafting sloppiness has inevitably crept in". The form of instrument was studiously avoided as progress would inevitably rely on the Andersen text. It was agreed that the Article 6 mining prohibition required only removing the three dots. Even on this Italy was reluctant, arguing against "making a proposal that had no prospect of being accepted". Alarmed, John Burgess reported that "Italy's readiness to give ground on the mining prohibition and its apparent lack of understanding of the implications of its amendment was the most worrying aspect of the two-day consultations". Duquin also argued against Italy's proposals, but only "on the grounds of tactics rather than substance".[112]

MARCH 1991: "A CURIOUS MIXTURE OF POLITICS, PENGUINS AND SPECULATION"

Apart from keeping the 'Four Powers' united, equally important was keeping the 'Like-mindeds' onside. Greece, Denmark and Finland expressed "unwillingness to lend full support to 4P activities if not kept fully and frankly briefed".[113] Some 'Like-mindeds' "complained about feeling like second class citizens".[114] The 'Like-mindeds' met in Rome on 26 March and the 'Four Powers' reported progress. Compounding its wayward mining proposal, Italy had unilaterally invited Chile and Peru. This was odd because Australia had just warned that Chile wanted to "wind back the progress on the minerals question" and "failed to grasp that we and many others cannot accept any explicit or implicit moratorium".[115] Chile did, however, launch its proposal to have "*peace* added to nature and science as leading values in Antarctica". The 'Like-mindeds' exchanged views "on what was known of changes in the positions of other countries, including the United Kingdom".[116] This was

[112] 27 March 1991, RO48549 "Antarctic environment: Four country consultations: Rome" (NAA: B1387 90/888 PART 3).

[113] 20 March 1991, RO48520 "Antarctica" (NAA: B1387 90/888 PART 3).

[114] 21 March 1991, PA86146 "Antarctica: Rome consultations and 4P text" (NAA: B1387 90/888 PART 3).

[115] 6 March 1991, CE999066 "Antarctica: Minerals prohibition—Chilean views" (AAD: B13/199).

[116] 27 March 1991, RO48549 "Antarctic environment: Four country consultations: Rome" (NAA: B1387 90/888 PART 3). At the Like-minded meeting were: Austria, Chile, Denmark, Ecuador, Finland, Greece, India, Netherlands, New Zealand, Peru, Romania and Sweden.

important to know as, on the basis of "Whitehall sources", media reports postulated a review of the UK position. The FCO's Michael Richardson considered such opinion "a curious mixture of politics, penguins and speculation … no statement has been made".[117] Richardson would have known, however, that a review was indeed underway. Meanwhile, NGOs speculated the United Kingdom would "accept a 20–40 year moratorium on mining"—a position environmentalists would emphatically reject.[118] For the time being, media and NGOs would have to be patient.

Patience was also needed on US thinking. On 5 March, the House Merchant Marine and Fisheries Subcommittee of Congress sought clarification on Administration views. Curtis Bohlen acknowledged that "although the Parties remain far apart on the minerals issue, there appears to be a universal determination to find a workable compromise".[119] He was probed on why the United States was pursuing a 20- to 40-year mining moratorium rather than the Conte Bill's prohibition, and quizzed on distinctions between a 'permanent ban', 'indefinite prohibition' and 'moratorium'. Bohlen responded that "the death of CRAMRA had been evident for some time" but it was "prudent to keep all options open rather than to prohibit mining forever". Bohlen's testimony was "more cautious than he had made at previous hearings and at Viña", although congressional questioning "could also have helped him deal more forcefully with those agencies opposing a more flexible US negotiating position".[120]

Flexibility was necessary because, firstly, 16 senators had written to the president expressing "grave concern" that the United States was shifting from the Conte Bill ban. Secondly, there was disappointment that the US delegation had been instructed to push only for a moratorium of some 20 to 40 years.[121] The State Department was ready to point the finger: "but for the failure of Australia and France to show any willingness to compro-

---

[117] 20 March 1991, LH124064 "Antarctic: UK position on mining" (NAA: B1387 91/32 PART 1).

[118] 21 March 1991, CE5126 "Antarctic: UK position on mining" (NAA: B1387 1991/55 PART 1).

[119] 5 March 1991, "Testimony of Curtis Bohlen, Assistant Secretary of State for Oceans and International Environmental and Scientific Affairs" (NAA: B1387 1991/55 PART 2).

[120] 11 March 1991, WH128559 "Antarctic environment: Congressional hearing 5.3.91" (NAA: B1387 1991/55 PART 1).

[121] 25 March 1991, United States Senate, letter to George Bush (NAA: B1387 1991/55 PART 2). The letter was co-signed by Al Gore, Richard Lugar, Ted Kennedy, Joe Biden, John Kerry, Joe Lieberman and Bill Bradley.

mise on the minerals issue, or to delink it from comprehensive environmental measures, a consensus could indeed be reached". Nevertheless, the United States was "not prepared to dismiss the possibility of reaching agreement" in 1991.[122] To achieve consensus, any US flexibility had to be matched by others.

MARCH 1991: THE TREATY COULD "COLLAPSE IN CHAOS"

Meanwhile, the United Kingdom *had* reviewed its position. NGOs were told first, Minister Tristan Garel-Jones announcing "the UK is now proposing a moratorium [in] a genuine desire to seek compromise". He said British leadership "would remove the threat to the Antarctic Treaty System and enable a return to consensus", and boldly asserted that the British "were founders of the Antarctic Treaty which had provided the framework of consensus over the past thirty years".[123] Writing to Parliamentary colleagues, Garel-Jones said that "only 8 out of 26 Parties" supported a mining ban so "consensus will only lie in the middle ground". That middle ground would be a moratorium ending with "measures to avoid a legal vacuum on minerals".[124] NGOs reported UK fears the Treaty could "collapse in chaos". A moratorium could be "lengthy or substantial", but that "would depend on where consensus can be found". John Heap, one of four FCO officials present at the NGO briefing, was "asked by the Minister if he wanted to add anything, said no, and then proceeded to add a great deal". "The UK's preferred position was support for CRAMRA", Heap said, "but that this was not at present a sellable commodity". On whether a moratorium might be as short as 20 years, "the Minister refused to answer". NGOs were told that "the position adopted by Australia and New Zealand [was] not honourable [and] based on short-term political considerations".[125] For the second time, Garel-Jones had associated Australia with New Zealand rather than France. NGOs were not convinced that it represented serious policy change. Richardson said that

[122] 19 March 1991, WH128885 "Antarctica: ATCM XVI Preparatory Meeting: US views" (NAA: B1387 91/32 PART 1).

[123] 25 March 1991, FCO press release "Antarctic minerals: Towards a solution" (AAD: B13/199).

[124] 25 March 1991, Tristan Garel-Jones letter to Members of Parliament (NAA: B1387 1991/55 PART 1).

[125] 25 March 1991, Greenpeace meeting notes "Meeting with Tristan Garel-Jones" (NAA: B1387 1991/55 PART 2).

"Britain now recognised that the minerals convention could not achieve consensus but felt the same applied to the Australian/French proposal". He left open the moratorium's duration—what was required was a mechanism to "unambiguously show what needed to be done either to end or extend it". Labour Opposition spokesperson George Foulkes was not convinced—a moratorium "requiring consensus to extend it ... would be unacceptable".[126]

On 26 March, UK foreign secretary Douglas Hurd wrote to Gareth Evans promoting replacement words for Andersen's Article 6, a moratorium and an annex detailing provisions to implement it.[127] To Australia it was unacceptable because it assumed that mining was inevitable and kept CRAMRA alive—a fixed-term moratorium, even with a review, "would not attract consensus".[128] Evans' reply to Hurd rejected the proposal politely, but firmly.[129] The FCO briefed UK media that Australia's mineral wealth was "a selfish factor behind [its] decision to oppose Antarctic mining": the fact there were no prospects of consensus on a total mining ban "does not appear to have been registered by Australians".[130]

Nevertheless, the United Kingdom was shifting toward the US-inspired fixed term moratorium, followed by a new mining regime. Australia dismissed the UK position as feeble compromise. Sweden considered the move "a tactical one to reduce its isolation and to seek reciprocal concessions".[131] New Zealand and Poland rejected it.[132] Brazil now decided to support a prohibition, Henrique Valle saying that the UK

[126] 26 March 1991, LH124489 "Antarctica: SCMXI: UK position" (NAA: B1387 91/32 PART 1). 27 March 1991, LH124603 "Antarctica: SCMXI: British Labour views" (NAA: B1387 1991/55 PART 1).

[127] 26 March 1991, British High Commission (Canberra) message covering letter from Hurd to Evans (NAA: B1387 91/32 PART 2).

[128] 27 March 1991, DFAT talking points "Antarctic mining: UK position" (NAA: B1387 1991/55 PART 1).

[129] 5 April 1991, CE10357 "Antarctic—SCM XI—UK position on mining" (AAD: B13/199).

[130] 5 April 1991, CH619259 "Antarctica: UK mining policy and Australian reaction" (AAD: B13/199).

[131] 28 March 1991, ST27838 "Antarctica: UK position on mining" (NAA: B1387 1991/55 PART 1).

[132] 3 April 1991, WL43487 "Antarctica: UK position on mining" (NAA: B1387 1991/55 PART 1). 4 April 1991, WS38790 "Antarctica: UK position on mining—Polish reactions" (NAA: B1387 1991/55 PART 1).

position did not "represent the middle ground [or] a significant advance on British thinking".[133]

Then scientists took a stand.[134] Prominent UK physicist Joe Farman called for a mining ban, saying "save Antarctica now, while we still have a chance".[135] By the Madrid meeting, 300 UK scientists had signed a petition urging a permanent ban.[136] However, scientists were not homogenous. SCAR president Richard Laws weighed in again, saying that "one day we will come to regret rejection" of CRAMRA and "blame for the wrecking of the convention lies with a number of vociferous, well-financed environmentalist groups". Laws dismissed human sewage as negligible compared to the faeces from birds and seals.[137] Whether this was relevant did not matter—more significant was his political activism. Laws later went on to bemoan ASOC promoting a regime "which would conflict with the needs of science" and belittling scientists in its media campaign.[138] Despite his depiction of SCAR as non-political, Laws' contribution symbolised its politicisation and reinforced perceptions of anglocentrism in many aspects of Antarctic science and environment policy. Environmentalists responded by demanding a permanent mining ban, reviewable after 100 years, and requiring consensus to lift.[139] In compromise (or escalation), ASOC then shifted its demand to a 999-year ban, reviewable after 200 years.[140]

[133] 5 April 1991, BR14000 "Antarctica: 2nd session of SCM XI—4 country representations: Brazil" (NAA: B1387 90/888 PART 3).

[134] Jagdish Patel and Susan Mayer, eds., *Antarctica: The Scientists' Case for a World Park* (Greenpeace, 1991).

[135] 28 March 1991, AAP "Call for Antarctic mining ban" *Canberra Times*, 5. Farman's engagement on the environment was potentially embarrassing as the United Kingdom lauded his discovery of ozone depletion as the epitome of British Antarctic science.

[136] 20 April 1991, "Scientists urge Antarctic park" *The Australian*, 16.

[137] R M Laws, "Unacceptable Threats to Antarctic Science," *New Scientist*, no. 1762 (1991).

[138] "Antarctic Politics and Science Are Coming into Conflict," *Antarctic Science* 3, no. 3 (1991).

[139] 2 April 1991, author's handwritten notes "NGOs meeting" (NAA: B1387 91/32 PART 2).

[140] Templeton, *A Wise Adventure II: New Zealand and Antarctica after 1960*, 299.

April 1991: "A Series of Very Tough Meetings"

New Zealand was optimistic. Frank Wong anticipated "the Madrid meeting would bring a lot of work to fruition [and] there could then be another session later in the year to bring everything together".[141] Spain studiously avoided the mining issue—it wanted a diplomatic success and "would play a neutral role".[142] José Candela considered a seven-day session sufficient because "if the will was lacking, agreement would not be reached no matter how long the meeting". Host neutrality was, however, expressed in odd ways. Candela observed that "New Zealand had now firmly aligned itself with the Four" and feared the 'Four Powers' might attract even *more* support. "A sudden shown of strength *en bloc*", he said, might encourage "more rigidly-opposed positions, and this could jeopardise any chance of real progress".[143] He did not, however, discourage any growth in support for the 'Four Powers' *opponents*. Three weeks later, it was clear why— Spain argued that a mining ban was "an unrealistic goal" and urged "further concessions by the Four". Spain's objective was a return to consensus in any form. This was acerbically dismissed by AAD director Rex Moncur, who observed that Spain now "sounds like UK". This was fair comment: it was later revealed that Spanish officials "felt able to support the British position". Candela urged "all participants in the Madrid meeting to work towards a consensus on a text even if it was imperfect, as this would be better than no text at all".[144]

As the April 1991 Madrid meeting approached, Australian officials briefed ministers. On mining, it was proposed to run with Andersen's Article 6, replacing the ellipsis with a full stop. The prohibition could be lifted only by consensus, and reviewable after 60 years. This stance reflected environmentalists' views: "off the record, Greenpeace would not object strongly to 60 years" and "provision for a review conference [was] both a barrier to and a possible catalyst for mining". The 'Four Powers' had differences over the instrument's area of application (with its implications for

[141] 25 March 1991, WL43420 "Antarctica: ATCM XVI Preparatory Meeting—New Zealand views" (NAA: B1387 91/32 PART 1).

[142] 14 March 1991, CE2320 "Antarctica: SCM XI-Spanish non-paper" (NAA: B1387 90/888 PART 3).

[143] 18 March 1991, MA26703 "Antarctica: SCM XI-Madrid, 22–30 April 1991" (NAA: B1387 91/32 PART 1).

[144] 10 April 1991, MA26781 "Antarctica: SCM XI, Madrid—Four country representations" (NAA: B1387 90/888 PART 3).

seafloor mining), liability, and the practicalities of environmental assessment. There were also disagreements with France which advocated "brevity at the expense of clarity", and "the cohesion and potential long-term usefulness to us of the Like-mindeds will be tested". It would be "a difficult meeting" in Madrid: "the US, UK and Japan constitute the weighty opposition to the Four Powers", in part because "the new US and UK positions, regressive and superficially progressive respectively … are very close." DFAT assessed that "the Treaty System can cope with another strained meeting or two, but that there will be a lot of pressure to have the negotiation concluded before UNCED in June 1992".[145] "A series of very tough meetings" was predicted.[146]

Collaboration between the 'Four Powers' continued, but not without a hiccough—Italy had circulated an incorrect version of the 'Four Powers' paper. Alarmingly, the error was misleading on mining, and it had gone to the wrong Parties. All DFAT could do was regret "the confusion which had arisen" and issue revised instructions to its diplomatic posts. This was particularly frustrating given that it was "the last opportunity for discussion with Antarctic contacts before they leave for the Bonn and Madrid meetings".[147]

April 1991: "His Interlocutors Had Gone White"

Despite the 'Four Powers' fumble, Tucker Scully's 8 April 1991 response was forward-looking. "Minerals would remain a difficult issue", he thought, but there should still be "an opportunity to discuss minerals *qua* minerals". In addition, there were practical matters to consider, and the United States would confine its proposals to ideas for the instrument's annexes. Scully reassured that Viña del Mar's 'Five Powers' (Argentina, Norway, the United Kingdom, the United States and Uruguay) were not caucusing and that progress was important as "there were many other fora eager to take up the issue [and] the time to reach agreement was not

---

[145] 4 April 1991, draft DFAT briefing to Evans (NAA: B1387 91/32 PART 2). 15 April 1991, DASETT briefing to Kelly (NAA: B1387 91/32 PART 1).
[146] 9 April 1991, Hugh Lamberton "Tough talks ahead on Antarctic mining ban" *Canberra Times*, 5.
[147] 5 April 1991, CE10239 "Antarctica" 2nd Session of SCM XI, Madrid, 20–30 April—4 country representations" (NAA: B1387 90/888 PART 2).

unlimited".[148] The US State Department was concerned about DFAT's low expectations for Madrid as it was "unhelpful to start the meeting from a position that substantive progress was not likely". While accepting CRAMRA had no future, it reiterated "a permanent ban would not attract consensus". In its view, a minerals regime would be needed to avoid a legal vacuum and that "a better approach would be to remove Article 6 altogether, to de-link minerals from the environment regime and to deal with it separately". The State Department also dismissed suggestions it was "at odds with Congressional views" because they "were not binding on the Administration ... whose negotiating mandate for international treaties derived exclusively from the Executive Power". To DFAT, such views "were neither novel nor surprising", reflecting, as they did, the "harder line US agencies (Interior, Energy and the National Science Foundation)".[149] Whether they were also Bohlen's remained to be seen.

On 15 April, Bohlen advised DFAT's John McCarthy that he had presented Secretary of State James Baker with two options: a 20- to 40-year moratorium, followed by a CRAMRA equivalent; or a prohibition amendable by less than consensus. Most agencies supported the former; Bohlen and the EPA supported the latter. His opponents "had argued for a hard line partly on the basis that France and Australia had shown no disposition to shift". McCarthy replied that a change in Australia's attitude would require "major shifts in the position taken by the US, the British and others". McCarthy reported that "Bohlen did not think much of the latest British proposal" and then added some interesting insights. EPA administrator William Reilly had put it to UK Environment Minister Michael Heseltine that he hoped "the American position on mining in Antarctic would improve". Alarmed at this, John Heap sought reassurance from Tucker Scully, who advised that the United States would not change. McCarthy observed that "the British must be apprehensive at being exposed in the event that the US shifted". Bohlen agreed, remarking that while in Geneva he had similarly speculated about the US position to an FCO official, "at which his interlocutor had 'gone white'". He had also learned of internal differences within the United Kingdom and that "the Environment Ministry favoured a 75-year moratorium". Bohlen hinted

[148] 9 April 1991, WH129563 "Antarctica: SCM XI: Four-country representation to the US" (NAA: B1387 91/32 PART 1).

[149] 15 April 1991, WH129765 "Antarctica: Four-country representations: US views" (NAA: B1387 90/888 PART 3).

that "it would be helpful" if the 'Four Powers' and New Zealand "could move a bit". Baker did not, however, consider the State Department submission before departing for the Middle East, leaving US policy unchanged since Viña del Mar. There was resentment within State Department that the 'Four Powers' and New Zealand had only hardened. Bohlen, however, thought "a stalemate on minerals at Madrid might be what was necessary to force clearer heads to look more closely at what alternative might be acceptable".[150]

APRIL 1991: THE DIFFERENCE WAS "LARGELY PSYCHOLOGICAL"

Other Parties' views were reported to DFAT. The USSR supported a mining prohibition in principle, "subject to eventual review". Sergei Karev, "customarily cautious in his comments", wanted to avoid "endangering in any way the ATS, but the approach presently being taken was one the Soviet Union could accommodate".[151] Poland was backsliding: "the British had been in three days earlier to make representations", the second visit within a week. While sympathetic, Janus Mickiewicz considered "the difference between a fixed-term moratorium and a complete prohibition at this stage was largely psychological", instantly putting at risk Poland's membership of the 'Like-mindeds'.[152] India, too, was now only like-minded to the extent of accepting the need for an environment instrument. It would support a moratorium because, according to Thettalil Sreenivasan, "India would not be the last to stand in the way of a ban ... they were in sympathy with the UK approach".[153] As India might not commit before their May 1991 election, it confirmed DFAT's view that "India continues to be highly erratic".[154]

[150] 15 April 1991, WH129795 "Antarctica: The United States' views" (NAA: B1387 91/32 PART 1). 17 April 1991, WH129881 "Antarctic minerals: US views" (NAA: B1387 91/32 PART 1).

[151] 9 April 1991, MS45655 "Antarctica: Four country demarche" (NAA: B1387 90/888 PART 2).

[152] 9 April 1991, WS38828 "Antarctica: SCM XI—Four country representations" (NAA: B1387 90/888 PART 2).

[153] 12 April 1991, ND 79403 "Antarctica: SCM XI: Four country representations" (NAA: B1387 1991/55 PART 1).

[154] 4 April 1991, draft DFAT briefing to Evans (NAA: B1387 91/32 PART 2).

In Beijing, China's Sun Lin spoke with "guarded optimism" that the 'Four Powers' paper would help consensus. He was even more guarded on China's position, which was "still in the process of elaboration, and it would not be appropriate at this stage for him to speak".[155] South Korea supported only a moratorium.[156] As host of two meetings in 1991, Germany was "reluctant to get out in front and make waves". Being realistic, Dietrich Granow thought that Japan, the United States and the United Kingdom would block the 'Four Powers'. Germany could, however, consider "a full ban on mining for the next decades" (well, for 30 years).[157] He was contradicted on 16 April by Economics Minister Jürgen Möllemann supporting a "complete ban on mining in Antarctica in the forthcoming negotiations of the so-called Consultative States". The statement came as a complete surprise to Granow.[158]

APRIL 1991: STUNG BY JAPAN'S MOVE

Granow considered Japan implacable, but this is precisely where the unexpected occurred. On 9 April, Japan flagged a possible review of its attitude, and, wanting an early return to consensus, its delegation would "be able to support the position which had the largest possible international support".[159] One week later, Canberra received a cablegram from Tokyo with important news: "the Japanese are now prepared to support a prohibition on minerals as per the amended four country text." "The main reason for this about-face", it explained, "was the Japanese fear of international isolation".[160] This was a stunning development, revealed during the

[155] 9 April 1991, BJ45756 "Antarctica: Second session of SCM XI—4 country representations" (AAD: B13/199).

[156] 9 April 1991, SE24496 "Antarctica: SCM XI—Four country representations" (NAA: B1387 90/888 PART 2).

[157] 10 April 1991, BO53504 "Antarctica: SCM XI—Four country representations" (NAA: B1387 90/888 PART 3).

[158] 16 April 1991, BO53602 "Antarctica: SCM XI Madrid, 22–30 April German position on minerals" (NAA: B1387 1991/55 PART 1). 17 April 1991, BO53601 "Antarctica: SCM XI Madrid, 22–30 April—German position on minerals" (NAA: B1387 91/32 PART 2).

[159] 11 April 1991, TK71073 "Antarctica: 2nd session, SCM XI, Madrid, 20–30 April—4 country representations: Japan" (NAA: B1387 91/32 PART 2).

[160] 16 April 1991, TK71138 "Antarctica: ATCP XVI PrepCom, Bonn, 15–19 April—Japanese views" (NAA: B1387 90/888 PART 3).

Bonn Preparatory Meeting, and on the eve of the Madrid session. CRAMRA's supporters were stung by Japan's move.[161]

While ATCM issues were the focus in Bonn, environmentalists dressed as penguins demonstrated outside. Inside were inevitable exchanges on how debate would progress in Madrid when SATCM XI reconvened.[162] On 18 April, Australia's delegation reported "increasing acceptance of a prohibition on mining". Notably, no one was arguing for a moratorium as it was not a "battle [its] proponents wish to fight seriously". When privately put to John Heap that a move was on towards a prohibition, he "accepted that and said that it would not be in the British Antarctic Treaty tradition to become isolated". Attention instead turned to the need for a minerals regime if a prohibition were lifted, and the mechanism for any review: consensus or qualified majority. There was also "talk about not wanting to negotiate another unratifiable instrument". Australia "kept in close contact with the French", held a 'Four Powers' meeting and convened the 'Like-mindeds'. The delegation lamented "the tendency of the French to react negatively to the participation of particular countries", glumly predicting that France "combined with the erratic behaviour of the Italians, will give us at least as many problems in Madrid as those who oppose us on the floor". Nevertheless, despite some way to go, "we can be very satisfied that we are winning the major debate on principle".[163]

APRIL 1991: AUSTRALIA RISKED BECOMING ISOLATED

Such optimism was premature. The following day, the US Embassy in Canberra handed DFAT a 'Reiteration of US Position on Antarctic Minerals'. It was "prepared to be flexible so as to achieve consensus on a position between the two extremes of a permanent ban on mineral activities and the entry into force of CRAMRA". It re-stated the case for a fixed-term prohibition that can be *extended* (rather than *lifted*) by consensus, safeguards to prevent prospecting under the guise science, and a means, such as CRAMRA, to avoid a legal vacuum if the prohibition were lifted. It was essentially a re-run of the 4 February position. However, it was no longer portrayed as the 'tolerable middle ground', probably

---

[161] Jackson and Boyce, "Mining and 'World Park Antarctica'," 264.

[162] 15 to 18 April 1991, "ATCM XVI Prep" (AWJ personal notes).

[163] 18 April 1991, BO53618 "Antarctic: Environmental protection negotiations" (NAA: B1387 91/32 PART 2).

because it was not. As the October 1989 US position was CRAMRA's immediate entry into force, the paper was presented as a significant shift. It was blunt: "the USG sees no reason to alter its present position while others adhere rigidly to their original positions … the flexibility we have shown needs to be matched by those proposing a permanent ban."[164] Delegations had left Bonn hoping that a compromise could be found. The latest US ultimatum had created a cloud of doubt.

Australia went to Madrid with a strong delegation and a hastily prepared brief. By Australia's count, some 16 of the 39 Treaty Parties supported the environmental initiative.[165] Despite that, the briefing was bullish. Wary of defections, the objectives were "to hold the Four Powers and as many Like-mindeds as possible" to the Andersen formula for a mining prohibition. It added that "we now go for a 60-year review period", neatly vindicating the US complaint that Australia's position had hardened. In addition, the delegation would "oppose any moves to remove the minerals question from the instrument". Furthermore, despite basing discussion on Andersen's text, Australia would not be "conceding on form (protocol versus convention)". After minerals, the objective was effective environmental impact assessment procedures but, pre-occupied with minerals, it would "avoid any commitment to finalise the instrument this year". The delegation was also instructed to consult Canberra if it appeared desirable to shift from these positions, or if Australia risked becoming isolated.[166]

April 1991: SATCM XI Second Session, Madrid

The 'Four Powers' met on Sunday 21 April 1991, buoyed by movement towards a prohibition: "we should feel under no pressure to modify our stance." While the "apparent hardening of the US position on the eve of the meeting was disappointing … it would be difficult for them to sustain given the trend in our direction and the lack of unity within the US".

[164] 19 April 1991, CH620593 "Antarctica—SCM XI—Second session—US position" (NAA: B1387 1991/55 PART 1). 22 April 1991, meeting paper XI ATSCM/2/INFO.1 "Position of the United States in the issue of Antarctic minerals resources" (AU-ATADD-4-BB-AQ-198).

[165] 23 April 1991, MA26828 "Antarctica: SCM XI, Second Session, Madrid, 22–30 April—Report No 1" (NAA: B1387 91/32 PART 1).

[166] April 1991, "Antarctic Treaty Special Consultative Meeting XI, Second Session, 22–30 April 1991" (AAD: B13/199).

Australia saw no need to rush negotiations.[167] France was more prepared than Australia "to examine possible concessions or fall-back positions in order to conclude an agreement while the tide of public and government opinion is running in our favour".[168] This was not the only difference: "the rigour of our proposals" for environmental impact assessment "was too much for many, including some of the Like-minded". That afternoon, delegation heads met for the first time, but without the NCPs who were "insensitively and unnecessarily excluded". There was a further surprise: Japan, now a crucial player, had not been at the delegation heads' meeting. The two Working Groups were settled, as well as a coordination role for Oscar Pinochet (Chile's chair in Viña del Mar), whose "precise role (if any) is unclear". Curtis Bohlen restated the demands of the 19 April US démarche. The United States would not move "in the absence from movement from the other side", noting that "two other countries are unlikely to want to make progress in Madrid". Jean-Pierre Puissochet disagreed with that characterisation of positions; Pinochet appealed for a "quick resolution of differences"; and Spain closed the discussion. According to John McCarthy, the US statement "did not go down well".[169]

Australia's delegation reviewed the situation. So far there were few surprises: matters of substance would be handled openly, not in closed discussions (an unrealistic proposition as it turned out) and Bohlen had made it clear that the United States would target Australia in particular.[170] On 22 April 1991, the second session of SATCM XI opened at Madrid's Palacio de Congresos. On the table were Rolf Andersen's Viña del Mar text, and the 'Four Powers' suggested amendments to it.[171] There were eight other proposals, including three from Parties seeking to act as broker (Chile, Japan and the Netherlands).

[167] 21 April 1991, author's handwritten notes "4P meeting" (NAA: B1387 91/32 PART 2).

[168] 19 April 1991, PA86579 "Antarctic: French views" (NAA: B1387 90/888 PART 3).

[169] 23 April 1991, MA26828 "Antarctica: SCM XI, Second Session, Madrid, 22–30 April—Report No 1" (NAA: B1387 91/32 PART 1). 23 April 1991, MA26829 "Antarctica: SCM XI, Madrid—Reporting cable No 2" (NAA: B1387 91/32 PART 1).

[170] 22 April 1991, "Delegation meeting" (AWJ personal notes).

[171] XI ATSCM/8 "Proposed Protocol to the Antarctic Treaty on Environmental Protection" reproduced in: Antarctic Treaty, *Interim Report of the Eleventh Antarctic Treaty Special Consultative Meeting, Viña Del Mar, 19 November-6 December 1990*, 113–25. XI/ATSCM/2/WP.2 "International Instrument Supplementing the Antarctic Treaty and Establishing a Comprehensive Regime for the Protection of the Environment" (AAD: 91/910-2).

It was agreed to examine Andersen's text article by article. Working Group 1 (WG1) would deal with the head instrument, and Working Group 2 (WG2) its four 'appendixes'. WG1 (with Germany's Dietrich Granow back in the chair) tackled the most sensitive issues including minerals, the most sensitive of all. It was therefore odd that, having just agreed to work *seriatim*, the United Kingdom requested that the Article 6 mining prohibition be dealt with promptly because Acting Head of Delegation, Adrian Beamish, had to leave early. Minerals would, however, not be dispatched so efficiently. Round One considered Article 1's designation of Antarctica. Here the 'Four Powers' strongly supported Andersen's "natural reserve, devoted to science". Italy would "accept nothing else". On the other hand, Chile, ostensibly a 'Like-minded', argued for an "ecological reserve devoted to science and other peaceful activities"—sidestepping whether mining is peaceful. Peru insisted on either 'science and peace' together, or neither. The United Kingdom argued for no designation. IUCN representative Martin Holdgate stepped in to assert that as the IUCN was expert in such designations it should decide. No Party responded to the offer.[172]

22 April 1991: "Hard and, for the Moment, Uncompromising"

Round Two tackled Article 2 and 22 April's afternoon session ended with environmental principles intact. The "energetic start" pleased Australia.[173] However, 'energetic' did not mean harmonious—there had been "considerable corridor activity on mining". John McCarthy reported that the United States and the United Kingdom "remain hard and, for the moment, uncompromising". Curtis Bohlen revealed "a view in Washington that because he had been soft on this issue, particularly at Viña, other countries are changing tack away from the US", and he therefore had instructions to "make no concessions unless something significant is received from the other side". The only viable compromise, he said, was "a prohibition

[172] 22 April 1991, "XI SCM (Session II)" (AWJ personal notes), 2–7. Chile's proposal appeared in document XI ATSCM/2/WP14 "Draft Preamble to the Protocol on Antarctic environmental protection and draft proposal for objective (Art. 1) and designation (Art. 2)" (AU-ATADD-4-BB-AQ-178).

[173] 23 April 1991, MA26828 "Antarctica: SCM XI, Second Session, Madrid, 22–30 April—Report No 1" (NAA: B1387 91/32 PART 1).

which is changeable by a qualified majority (say four-fifths)". There were "suggestions that the Four should be more flexible". Alarmingly for Australia, such comments were "also coming from some of the Like-mindeds". McCarthy did not see Australia "as having much flexibility", nor did the French. Italy, however, was "somewhat unpredictable and talked too readily about possible compromises". Germany favoured a permanent ban, but one of its delegates was "talking openly about the need for flexibility". Predictably, NGOs insisted on *no* flexibility. In that evening's 'Four Powers' meeting "there was general agreement that we should stick to our guns". McCarthy summed it up: "things are going our way but opposition, while not extensive, is strong given the US position."[174]

Next day, WG1 breezed through the instrument's relationship with other parts of the ATS and cooperation between Parties. Differences were slight, although the United States wanted a better picture of the overall instrument first, a view immediately echoed by the United Kingdom. Australia suggested that drafting begin and adjustments made later. Norway, however, argued that premature drafting slows progress. Thus, on Articles 3, 4 and 5 the disagreement was on process rather than substance.[175] The same could not be said for Article 6.

23 APRIL 1991: "SEEKING WHAT IS RIGHT FOR THIS GENERATION"

Italy opened discussion on the mining prohibition. Alessandro Vattani proposed to remove any ambiguity by replacing Andersen's ellipsis with a full stop. Brazil's Henrique Valle said that consensus lay in a middle ground not prejudicing the future. The United Kingdom's Adrian Beamish regretted the Treaty becoming "a domestic political football". Replacing CRAMRA with a prohibition was "based on untenable assumptions and is irrational". A return to consensus, he said, required recognition of the future need for minerals and acceptance of facts that the 'Four Powers' ignore. Peter Verbeek spoke to the Netherlands' paper, portraying as compromise an indefinite prohibition where mining could only proceed with consensus and a mechanism in place to regulate it. Chile recalled that in

---

[174] 23 April 1991, MA26829 "Antarctica: SCM XI, Madrid—Reporting cable No 2" (NAA: B1387 91/32 PART 1).

[175] 23 April 1991, "XI SCM (Session II)" (AWJ personal notes), 9–15.

1970 it objected to discussing minerals lest it precipitate a dispute, but now supported a prohibition provided it could be reviewed.[176]

Australia came next, McCarthy confirming that a moratorium was unacceptable as it assumed future mining. Australia, he said, was "not preaching to the future, but seeking what is right for this generation"—a future generation could change the prohibition, but only by consensus because that is how the Treaty works. Australia could not accept an 'indefinite ban' if that were just a mechanism to avoid consensus now. France could not accept a "moratorium or automatic expiry date". Germany supported a permanent ban because it would never be possible to prevent the impacts of mining. For the ban to be amended, it would have to be after at least 50 years. The United States could not accept a permanent ban, however disguised, because requiring consensus to lift it "equals a permanent ban". Ultimately, Bohlen said, "the greed of man may prevail … future generations must be able to make their own decisions". He agreed that the dots at the end of Article 6 could be removed, provided it referred to an annex detailing how the prohibition could be lifted, but controls "at least as stringent as CRAMRA" would have to be in place. Bohlen also said that the United States wanted a "decision by summer" (presumably meaning the boreal summer). Japan joined the chorus for a mining ban, reviewable by consensus. Masaki Konishi said that the ban should be for an indefinite period as it was not possible to predict technological developments and energy needs in the next 20, 40 or 60 years. Argentina proposed a 45-year prohibition with a compulsory review after 40 years. Frank Wong reminded the meeting of New Zealand's call for a permanent ban—just remove the dots at the end of Article 6. He said that "no country has worked harder on this issue in seeking consensus".[177]

Rolf Andersen summarised: with the shared commitment to environment protection, acceptance that CRAMRA would not enter into force, and no imminent interest in mining, it must be possible to find a solution. The task was to "address possible mining if circumstances change [as we] cannot have a legal and political vacuum should a prohibition end". France

[176] 23 April 1991, "XI SCM (Session II)" (AWJ personal notes), 15–17. 23 April 1991, MA26830 "Antarctica: SCM XI: Madrid—Report No 3 (Minerals: WG1 discussion)" (NAA: B1387 91/32 PART 1).
[177] 23 April 1991, "XI SCM (Session II)" (AWJ personal notes), 17–20. 23 April 1991, MA26830 "Antarctica: SCM XI: Madrid—Report No 3 (Minerals: WG1 discussion)" (NAA: B1387 91/32 PART 1). 22 April 1991, XI ATSCM/2/WP9 "Mineral resource activities: Proposed by Argentina" (AU-ATADD-4-BB-AQ-173).

concurred: "pieces of the solution are on the table", Jean-Pierre Puissochet said, and we would not be "taking away the right of future generations to make their own decision". To Artur Chilingarov, what was really being faced was a political problem as the "majority of popular opinion is against mining" and protecting the Treaty was the priority because "there are more important issues than minerals". The USSR, he said, could accept a fixed prohibition for a reasonable period followed by a review conference. Chilingarov also pointed to a potential problem—in 15 to 30 years' time, there could be 50 or more ATCPs: If so, would consensus be possible? And so the *tour de table* continued, with more calls for consensus. Chile noted that the Treaty itself made an exception for consensus at the point of a review conference being called after 30 years—therefore, "the norm is consensus but, in exceptional circumstance like this, a majority could be considered". ASOC sought the last word: Cassandra Phillips welcomed the proposed "adjustment to the Article 6 punctuation" and accepted that a decision was being made "only for this generation". ASOC would insist on consensus to lift a prohibition, but it would never condone mining— no energy crisis would make Antarctic mining acceptable.[178] It was only Day 2, and nearly all ATCPs and many Non-Consultative Parties (NCPs) had spoken. No one objected to a simply expressed mining prohibition. The issue would turn on any review provisions addressing how a prohibition could be lifted or modified. The toughest nut still awaited a cracker.

The landscape was changing. Germany's commitment to a prohibition had been confirmed in a second statement by Environment Minister Jürgen Möllemann.[179] The German delegation, however, "had been astonished" by the statement which "went well beyond the brief for officials that had been cleared interdepartmentally". On the other hand, "it greatly enhanced the flexibility the German delegation had to push their pro-prohibition brief to its limits".[180] Japan locked-in support for a ban and it did not matter whether its move was based on environmental

[178] 23 April 1991, "XI SCM (Session II)" (AWJ personal notes), 20–25. 23 April 1991, MA26830 "Antarctica: SCM XI: Madrid—Report No 3 (Minerals: WG1 discussion)" (NAA: B1387 91/32 PART 1).

[179] 23 April 1991, BO53694 "Antarctica: protection: FRG views" (NAA: B1387 1991/55 PART 1).

[180] 6 May 1991, BO53845 "Antarctica: Madrid SCM" (NAA: B1387 91/32 PART 1). 23 April 1991, XI ATSCM/2/Info 3 "Statement of the Head of the German Delegation regarding the problem on mineral resource activities (Art. 6 of the Andersen draft)" (AU-ATADD-4-BB-AQ-200).

concerns or just avoiding isolation.[181] The United States was becoming marginalised. So was the United Kingdom, its delegation not helped by Shadow Foreign Secretary Gerald Kaufman in the foyer of the Palacio de Congresos, capitalising on media interest and urging the 'Four Powers' not to back down.[182]

By Day 3, draft proposals for a mining prohibition were circulating with various amendment options.[183] Meanwhile, as WG1 had only got to Article 9 the delegation heads reviewed progress. John Heap "raked over the history of discussions in Paris in 1989 and at Viña", criticising "Australia and France, in particular, for getting the Antarctic Treaty System into a rut". His proposal for a small "negotiating group to list and thrash out the key issues" was rejected. WG1 would proceed and the Netherlands Peter Verbeek would convene a drafting group to assemble the text. The following day a UK attempt "to derail these working arrangements" was headed off by Puissochet arguing that they "should be given a chance to work".[184]

On Day 5, WG1 had completed its first run through the head instrument but Australia reported that "overall progress has been slow". The 'Four Powers' had "coordinated well in the presentation and advocacy of their proposed amendments" despite a "pattern of consistent UK/US (and frequently Argentinian) opposition". On the other hand, "support of the 'Like-minded' group on minerals has been variable". New Zealand "generally supported Andersen [and] Sweden is taking an independent line on many issues". However, in the corridors Sweden was being genuinely helpful and had "circulated a paper proposing a compromise": there should be no amendment to a mining ban except at a review conference; a review could only occur after an agreed number of years and if requested by two-thirds of the Parties; and the ban could be lifted by consensus, but

[181] 24 April 1991, CE17408 "Media report on Antarctica" (NAA: B1387 91/32 PART 1).

[182] 23 April 1991, Press Association "UK cold on ice park" *The Mercury*, 7. 23 April 1991, MA26828 "Antarctica: SCM XI, Second Session, Madrid, 22–30 April-Report No 1" (NAA: B1387 91/32 PART 1).

[183] These were the Working Papers provided by the Netherlands (AU-ATADD-4-BB-AQ-174), Japan (AU-ATADD-4-BB-AQ-176) and Chile (AU-ATADD-4-BB-AQ-180).

[184] 26 April 1991, MA26858 "Antarctica: SCM XI, Madrid—Report No 4 (progress report)" (NAA: B1387 91/32 PART 1).

only if an agreed minerals regime were in place.[185] A solution was solidifying.

In the other room, WG2 under Uruguay's Roberto Puceiro was progressing practical provisions and the United States was participating after initially "having refused to do so while debate continued in Working Group 1". Considerable attention was given to environmental impact assessment, marine pollution, waste management and conservation of flora and fauna. Although such matters had been examined in Viña del Mar, "new issues have been raised and old ones reopened".[186]

April 1991: An Unexpected Political Price

While the focus was on a mining ban, in WG2 on 26 April Australian delegates Rex Moncur and Lyn Goldsworthy came under unexpected pressure to ban dogs. It was on an issue for which Australia would pay a high political price. The problem was the incongruity of advocating measures to combat non-indigenous species while allowing the use of dogs which could attack seals and spread distemper. Australia's Mawson Station was one of the few places still using huskies. Rebutting the argument that dogs were a risk was difficult because the other countries using them (by then only Argentina and the United Kingdom) readily supported their removal. It was an awkward fight to have while bigger issues remained unresolved. Environment Minister Ros Kelly said that "some people might be upset by the end of a tradition".[187] She was right. Removal of the huskies enraged a domestic constituency howling at the price seemingly paid for preventing mining.[188] Kelly "received more mail on the Mawson huskies than on any other issue".[189] Although scientists had raised the risk, Phillip Law

[185] 24 April 1991, XI ATSCM/2/WP24 "Swedish non-paper on draft Article 6" (AU-ATADD-4-BB-AQ-188). 26 April 1991, MA26858 "Antarctica: SCM XI, Madrid—Report No 4 (progress report)" (NAA: B1387 91/32 PART 1). 23–26 April 1991, "XI SCM (Session II)" (AWJ personal notes), 25–41.

[186] 26 April 1991, MA26858 "Antarctica: SCM XI, Madrid—Report No 4 (progress report)" (NAA: B1387 91/32 PART 1). 27 April 1991, "XI SCM (Session II)" (AWJ personal notes), 54–55.

[187] 25 May 1991, Katrina Iffland "World pact to put an end to using husky dogs in Antarctica" *Canberra Times*, 1.

[188] Bowden, *The Silence Calling: Australians in Antarctica 1947–1997*, 418–20.

[189] Patrick Moonie, "The Mawson Huskies: The Case for Retention," *Aurora (ANARE Club Journal)* 11, no. 1 (1991): 1. For a typical expression of the sentiment, see 30 May 1991, Christelle Williams "Debate needed on polar dogs" (AU-ATADD-1-BB-AU-351).

barked that the episode was "a sad example of trendy activity by extreme conservation zealots".[190] That said, some dog handlers were sanguine: "their time had come."[191] It was eventually decided that Annex II of the Madrid Protocol would provide that "Dogs shall not be introduced onto land or ice shelves and dogs currently in those areas shall be removed by April 1, 1994".[192] The irony was that it did not prevent dogs being used on the sea ice, precisely where the seals were to be found.[193]

25 April 1991: A Five-Hour Discussion over Dinner

Diplomats were more concerned about mining. On 25 April, John McCarthy reported "a widespread and justifiable appreciation that the prohibitionists have gained ground" after the shifts by Germany and Japan. He observed that "the defection of Japan has been felt keenly by the United States", but with "quiet satisfaction on the part of Bohlen". McCarthy also reported that the United Kingdom continued advocating a moratorium, aided by the USSR, Argentina and South Africa. However, "only New Zealand still uses the phrase 'permanent ban'". He also observed that agreement on minerals would depend on other issues and that "a number of delegations who support us on mining disagree with the Four on some or all other aspects". Although the 'Four Powers' had support, movement was towards a mining ban removable by consensus—that, or a 60-year review period. On the other hand, "the now important array of countries taking a broad prohibitionist approach suggests that the US, Britain and the other hard-liners need to move a good way towards our position". Bohlen, Granow and Puissochet encouraged Andersen to test attitudes to a compromise, and, "if something came of these discussions", Bohlen would put it to Washington. Keen to leave Madrid with

---

[190] Shelagh Robinson, *Huskies in Harness: A Love Story in Antarctica* (Kangaroo Press, 1995), 7. See also: http://www.asoc.org/storage/documents/ECOs/1991/lxxx.3_atcm.pdf (accessed 3 February 2021).

[191] Tom Maggs, personal communication, 20 September 2017.

[192] Antarctic Treaty, *Final Report of the Eleventh Antarctic Treaty Special Consultative, Madrid, 22–30 April 1991; 17–22 June 1991; 3–4 October 1991* (Ministerio de Asuntos Exteriores, 1991), 139.

[193] This anomaly was fixed in 2009. See Antarctic Treaty, Measure 16 (2009) and Article 4 at: https://ats.aq/devAS/Meetings/Measure/433 (accessed 14 March 2020). The exclusion of sea ice derives from the treatment of high seas in the Treaty area. The status of sea ice was a long-standing issue—see, for example: https://documents.ats.aq/ATCM3/att/ATCM3_att001_e.pdf (accessed 14 March 2020).

"meaningful evidence of progress", McCarthy tested Canberra's attitudes to a compromise. Without commitment, and replete with caveats, it could allow Australia to accept a prohibition requiring consensus to amend; after 60 years, a review conference could lift the prohibition with a five-sixth majority; and, if the ban were lifted, new regulations would have to be in place to approve mining proposals and protect claimant interests. McCarthy undertook to call Prime Minister Bob Hawke and Foreign Minister Gareth Evans by week's end because not requiring consensus to lift the mining ban after a review conference would be a major concession. On the other hand, it would address concerns "the US Senate would never ratify an instrument which left open the possibility of one or two countries at some stage preventing the US from mining". Frank Wong said that New Zealand would not want to move from a consensus formula but it "would be unlikely to wish to break ranks with Australia".[194]

That evening, 25 April, Andersen hosted a five-hour discussion by delegation heads over dinner. Only nine were invited (Argentina, Australia, Brazil, Chile, France, New Zealand, the United Kingdom, the United States and the Soviet Union). The discussion focused on a Chilean formula: a prohibition without qualification; after 30 years, a three-quarters majority could call a review conference; and amendments could be adopted by simple majority, but enter into force only with consensus. It would be easier after 60 years: a review conference could be called by just one Party; the prohibition amended by simple majority; and entry into force would require a high majority (four-fifths was suggested), provided all the current 26 ATCPs were included. Horse-trading began: France, New Zealand and Australia argued for a longer period before a review, or no early review at all. The United States replied that would provoke a single 50-year review and accepting any option required "satisfactory solution to the outstanding problems relating to the rest of the instrument". Delegations sought instructions from capitals. After consulting the offices of Hawke and Evans, John McCarthy called ACF director Phillip Toyne. In Madrid, he confidentially approached ASOC representative Lyn Goldsworthy, who recommended a single 50-year period rather than a two-tiered approach "for presentational reasons". Furthermore, "if we do not go for some sort of package on mining ... we could lose ground on other elements". McCarthy also saw risks if the deal were declined: Australia faced

[194] 25 April 1991, MA26853 "Antarctica: SCM XI Madrid: Minerals" (NAA: B1387 1991/55 PART 1).

"acrimony from friends and opponents alike given that the other side may well be seen as having been prepared to move". McCarthy was cautiously optimistic: if the United States moved, "this will amount to a major change". However, he noted that "conservatives in the Administration … will be able to hold out for a very long time". Moreover, "the Americans do have a body of support—we would note that the British are strongly opposed to this arrangement but will probably go along with it". Discussion into the early hours may have found the solution. However, only nine delegations had participated, and Bohlen "stressed the need for the meeting to be kept strictly confidential until the end of the weekend". Participants agreed to "do their best to bluff their way through today [Friday, 26 April] to avoid discussion of possible arrangements leaking out".[195]

26 APRIL 1991: AN ELLIPSIS REPLACED BY A FULL STOP

Later that day, WG1 concluded its first run through the Andersen text. A Heads of Delegation meeting was called, this time with all delegations invited. It was muted by key delegations sidestepping controversy: none of the nine mentioned what had transpired overnight. The Netherlands opened with a report on drafting. Verbeek noted that it "had not been an easy discussion [with] considerable lack of agreement". In addition, "one delegation (US) invited to the drafting group only appeared today", and he was "not sure if they will accept the text". The United States defended its absence "because debates had not been concluded" and "some issues cannot be resolved in the drafting committee". The USSR was alarmed that "progress seems to be being held up by lawyers". Desirée Edmar echoed this, pointing to the challenges of concurrent political and technical issues. Sweden was "ready to discuss Article 6", and the package had to be resolved before UNCED in 1992, and preferably by the Treaty's 30th anniversary. Germany agreed: "we are avoiding addressing the key issues" and "should admit whether or not we want a result from this meeting". Other delegation heads appealed for progress on Article 6. Verbeek observed that progress "depends on the willingness of some Parties to compromise". At that, Spain's chair Carlos Blasco Villa seized the opportunity to directly test the mood of the meeting: "Is there any delegation

[195] 26 April 1991, MA26855 "Antarctic instrument: Minerals" (NAA: B1387 91/32 PART 1).

opposed to a prohibition on minerals activity?". There was no objection. Accordingly, he said, "we have a basis for drafting". Thus the ellipsis in Article 6 was replaced by a full stop.[196] With the punctuation problem resolved, there was a collective sigh of relief. The challenge, however, remained—the chair listed the sticking points: the role of the committee, liability for damage, entry into force of the instrument and provisions for its amendment. Stickiest of all was how any amendment would be linked to the mining prohibition just agreed.

With four days remaining, work accelerated. On Saturday, Verbeek's drafting group reported to WG1 and Roberto Puceiro reported on WG2's efforts on marine pollution, waste management, environmental impact assessment, flora and fauna, protected areas, tourism and alternative energy. It was agreed that Working Groups would finalise their work on Monday. For some, a tour of Toledo's World Heritage would be a weekend highlight. For others, there would be little rest.[197]

Rolf Andersen quietly prepared a revised text. A small group of delegation heads were invited to a dinner on Sunday 28 April to consider it. This time, 11 were present (Argentina, Australia, Brazil, Chile, France, Italy, New Zealand, Norway, Spain, the United Kingdom and the United States). The meal began at 8:00 pm and ended eight hours later. At 4:00 am on 29 April, "it was agreed that the draft was suitable for submission to governments". As only 11 had participated: "any tentative approval by delegations … was premised on other Consultative Parties agreeing". Nevertheless, the achievement was significant: mining in Antarctica would be banned. After 50 years, any Consultative Party could call a review conference, and a decision to amend the prohibition would require a simple majority of ATCPs. However, to enter into force an amendment required three-quarters of the Consultative Parties, including *all* the ATCPs when the instrument was adopted. Crucially, if the ban were lifted, it would remain until there was a regime to regulate mining.[198] McCarthy reported that "most of the discussion on this issue took place between the US and ourselves". The remainder of the time addressed the designation of Antarctica as a 'natural reserve devoted to peace and science'; environmental

---

[196] Note that Article 6 was later re-numbered to become the Madrid Protocol's Article 7, which contains the mining prohibition.

[197] 26 April 1991, "XI SCM (Session II)—HODs" (AWJ personal notes), 53–55.

[198] 29 April 1991, MA26863 "Antarctica: SCMXI, Madrid—Report no. 5 (draft protocol)" (NAA: B1387 91/32 PART 1).

principles; prior environmental impact assessment of activities; the environmental committee; compliance and inspection; and provision for an annex on liability. It was agreed to finalise the text "as soon as possible", and "Bohlen suggested adoption on 23 June, the thirtieth anniversary of the entry into force of the Antarctic Treaty". McCarthy reported that "the US, we think genuinely, said it would do its best to get the deal accepted". Frank Wong received unexpectedly rapid approval from Wellington. France, however, reserved its position on "whether the document should be a protocol or a convention". More strangely, it also reserved its position on whether entry into force required ratification by *all* the Parties. Ironically, that might have allowed one or two Parties to block the regime.[199] Despite last-minute French prevarication, the end appeared to be in sight.

On Monday 29 April, WG1 completed its work, while WG2 proceeded to seal the fate of Antarctica's huskies. A full meeting of the delegation heads meeting that afternoon received the new Andersen text and arranged translation from English into the three other languages. At 7:00 pm, buses collected delegates for a reception where, at last, discussion would be more convivial. The following day, WG2 completed its work except for measures relating to protected areas being relegated to the October ATCM.[200] Plenary convened at 11:00 am with no objections to the final version of the Andersen text. Delegations could proceed to seek approval from governments. A final session of the SATCM was proposed for 17 June, preceded by a legal drafting committee to rectify any textual errors. A linguistics group would harmonise the four languages. It was intended that SATCM IX conclude with a signing ceremony on 23 June 1991, the Treaty's 30th anniversary. McCarthy reported that such haste reflected "a general wish (stressed on Sunday night by Bohlen) to arrange things in such a way as to make it as difficult as possible for the text to unravel".[201]

---

[199] France preferred a requirement of 20 out of 26. 29 April 1991, MA26863 "Antarctica: SCMXI, Madrid—Report no. 5 (draft protocol)" (NAA: B1387 91/32 PART 1).

[200] 30 April 1991, MA26875 "Antarctica: SCM XI, Madrid meeting: Report no. 6 (WG2: Annexes)" (NAA: B1387 91/32 PART 1).

[201] 30 April 1991, MA26874 "Antarctica: SCM XI, Madrid—Report no. 7 (final report)" (NAA: B1387 91/32 PART 1). The form of instrument was still not agreed—the Madrid press release used the terms 'protocol', 'instrument', 'comprehensive measures' and 'document' interchangeably. See Antarctic Treaty, *Final Report of the Eleventh Antarctic Treaty Special Consultative, Madrid, 22–30 April 1991; 17–22 June 1991; 3–4 October 1991*, 33.

The meeting wound up with congratulatory statements: praise for Rolf Andersen, Dietrich Granow and Roberto Puceiro as chairs, and for Spain as hosts. Curtis Bohlen committed to seek US agreement to the text, and was "happy to aim for signing on 23 June". John McCarthy remarked that the "result was welcomed at the highest level in Australia" and "progress had exceeded our expectations". He made special mention of the roles of Chile, the Netherlands and Germany. By now, Jean-Pierre Puissochet had received approval from Paris, and there was no further French equivocation. Nearly every Party spoke. New Zealand added to the chorus of praise. Bohlen took the floor for the last time to suggest the report reflect Andersen's role. John Heap reminded the meeting that a Final Act needed drafting. And, still not satisfied, ASOC's Cassandra Phillips only "welcomed progress *towards* comprehensive protection, especially a long-term prohibition on mining". With no more to discuss, and participants exhausted, that evening's reception was cancelled.[202] Delegates could go home. It appeared the work was done, approval by governments could proceed and the instrument advance to formal adoption. But it would not be quite that simple.

References

Antarctic Treaty. *Final Report of the Eleventh Antarctic Treaty Special Consultative, Madrid, 22–30 April 1991; 17–22 June 1991; 3–4 October 1991.* Ministerio de Asuntos Exteriores, 1991.

———. *Interim Report of the Eleventh Antarctic Treaty Special Consultative Meeting, Viña Del Mar, 19 November–6 December 1990.* Republic of Chile, 1990.

Bowden, Tim. *The Silence Calling: Australians in Antarctica 1947–1997.* Allen & Unwin, 1997.

Francioni, Francesco. "The Madrid Protocol on the Protection of the Antarctic Environment." *Texas International Law Journal* 28, no. 1 (1993): 47–72.

Jackson, Andrew, and Peter Boyce. "Mining and 'World Park Antarctica'." Chap. 11 In *Australia and the Antarctic Treaty System: 50 Years of Influence*, edited by Marcus Haward and Tom Griffiths, 243–73: UNSW Press, 2011.

Laws, R M. "Antarctic Politics and Science Are Coming into Conflict." *Antarctic Science* 3, no. 3 (1991a): 231–31.

———. "Unacceptable Threats to Antarctic Science." *New Scientist*, no. 1762 (31 March 1991b): 4.

[202] 30 April 1991, "XI SCM (Session II)—Plenary" (AWJ personal notes).

Moonie, Patrick. "The Mawson Huskies: The Case for Retention." *Aurora (ANARE Club Journal)* 11, no. 1 (1991): 1.

Patel, Jagdish, and Susan Mayer, eds. *Antarctica: The Scientists' Case for a World Park*: Greenpeace, 1991.

Robinson, Shelagh. *Huskies in Harness: A Love Story in Antarctica*. Kangaroo Press, 1995.

Templeton, Malcolm. *Protecting Antarctica: The Development of the Treaty System*. New Zealand Insitute of International Affairs, 2002.

———. *A Wise Adventure II: New Zealand and Antarctica after 1960*. Victoria University Press, 2017.

Walton, David W H, and Peter D Clarkson. *Science in the Snow*. Scientific Committee on Antarctic Research, 2011.

CHAPTER 8

Antarctic Consensus Restored: April to October 1991

PREMATURE CELEBRATION

The instrument's text had seemingly been settled. In Canberra, Bob Hawke welcomed the "fitting culmination of the intensive diplomatic campaign pursued by Australia and France".[1] However, celebration was premature as governments still had to approve the draft. Australian media blithely reported it a foregone conclusion. So did Environment Minister Ros Kelly, lauding it "one of the most significant agreements ever reached on the environment" and, rather presumptuously, that acceptance by governments was a "mere formality".[2] It wasn't. Even in Australia, not everyone applauded. Lachlan McIntosh of the Australian Mining Industry Council (AMIC) slammed an agreement closing off "sensible options". Praising "a victory for common sense", Resources Minister Alan Griffith rebutted AMIC as "ill-informed and out of touch with national and international sentiment", provoking McIntosh to call the mining ban "a political stunt".[3] Foreign Minister Gareth Evans congratulated John McCarthy

[1] 30 April 1991, Prime Minister "For media" http://pmtranscripts.pmc.gov.au/sites/default/files/original/00008287.pdf (accessed 3 February 2021).
[2] 1 May 1991, "Australia has big win on Antarctic" *The Mercury*, 3; "A 50-year reprieve for Antarctica" *The Age*, 13; and Mike Seccombe "Nations agree to protect Antarctica" *Sydney Morning Herald*, 9.
[3] 1 May 1991, Lenore Taylor "Antarctic agreement angers mining lobby" *The Australian*, 2; and Alan Griffiths media release "Antarctic agreement" (NAA: B1387 91/32 PART 2). 2 May 1991, Lenore Taylor "Miners attack Antarctic ban" *The Australian*, 5.

for his "very significant contribution in leading from the front" and hoped "all officers involved will take real satisfaction from what is undoubtedly an achievement, not just for the Australian Government but for the world community in general".[4] Hawke said that against "formidable opposition our negotiating team did a magnificent job with absolute meticulousness".[5]

Australia was not the only Party to celebrate, and overseas posts reported reactions. Dietrich Granow said that the deal would not be questioned in Germany.[6] New Zealand Foreign Minister Don McKinnon said that the draft represented "a great success". Chris Beeby, however, was not so sure about the NGO attitudes: "as seekers of perfection they would never be totally satisfied".[7] The FCO's John Weston said that "the UK saw the Madrid meeting as a massive step forward".[8] Norwegian Foreign Minister Thorvald Stoltenberg said the "outcome on mining had exceeded his expectations … Norway should have had more faith in the judgement of Australia and France that a prohibition was achievable". In Stockholm, Desirée Edmar was "delighted with the outcome" and praised Japan and Germany for changing position. "In the end", she said, "the UK and US were totally isolated". She was, however, concerned that the length of June's drafting session "might allow time for something to unravel" and, for this, she blamed intransigent delegations.[9] Oscar Pinochet said, "Chile was very happy [and] if all went well, Antarctic Treaty partners would soon be back to the situation of cooperation that existed before their differences on environmental protection."[10]

Success required acceptance by, in particular, the United States and the United Kingdom. The US Administration was under pressure. A 13 May congressional hearing grilled Curtis Bohlen on the position taken in Madrid because it was "inconsistent with the 1990 *Antarctic Protection Act* and resolutions passed by the House and Senate". Senator Al Gore

---

[4] 6 May 1991, letter from Evans to McCarthy (NAA: B1387 91/32 PART 2).

[5] 7 May 1991, House of Representatives Hansard, 3068–3069.

[6] 6 May 1991, BO53845 "Antarctica: Madrid SCM" (NAA: B1387 91/32 PART 1).

[7] 6 May 1991, WL43767 "Antarctic: SCM—second session—Madrid" (NAA: B1387 91/32 PART 1).

[8] 7 May 1991, CE22471 "Antarctica—SCMXI—Second session—UK" (NAA: B1387 1991/55 PART 1).

[9] 17 May 1991, ST28065 "Antarctica: Comprehensive environmental protection agreement" (NAA: B1387 91/32 PART 2).

[10] 20 May 1991, SC22020 "Antarctica: SCM XI—second session—Madrid, Chilean reaction" (NAA: B1387 91/32 PART 2).

slammed the presentation of "a minority opinion put by the ideologues in the Economic Bureau of the State Department". Bohlen defended the delegation's approach as "a genuine attempt at compromise in a situation where other Parties were totally inflexible". Gore was unconvinced: the United States had failed to "take a leadership role" and was "totally isolated among ATCPs".[11] Bohlen also had to deal with divisions between US agencies and, worse, *within* State: "his own Bureau and the Economic Bureau were taking opposing sides". The critical issue was not the mining ban as such, it was the review provisions. NGOs argued that this was "an opportunity for the Administration to add substance to its green credentials ... without engaging significant opposition from domestic oil and mining lobbies". More significant was opposition from resource agencies, "especially Interior, Energy and Treasury".[12] In further complication for the United States, the United Kingdom—once its CRAMRA ally—had just revealed that it would support the new text.[13]

May 1991: "One of the Higher Absurdities"

If the UK position was news to the United States, it also may have been news to some UK officials. Without drawing attention to it, on 10 May Prime Minister John Major had used a written answer to a parliamentary question to "welcome the outcome of the Madrid meeting". He considered it "the basis for the comprehensive protection of the Antarctic environment" and "of particular importance are the provisions for a ban on mineral activity".[14] Media suggested that Major had "outflanked strong Whitehall opposition to the proposed 50-year Antarctic mining ban by the simple but bold expedient of declaring his support for it". It added that "in an unnoticed parliamentary written answer late on Friday, Mr Major expressed the government's unequivocal backing for the ban ... his statement marks the official abandonment of the Government's long-standing

[11] 14 May 1991, WH130900 "Antarctic environment: US congressional hearing" (AAD: 91/226–1).
[12] 16 May 1991, WH131025 "Antarctica: SCMXI second session: US views" (NAA: B1387 91/32 PART 2).
[13] 10 May 1991, WH130827 "Antarctic environment: Madrid SCM: UK views" (NAA: B1387 1991/56 PART 1).
[14] 10 May 1991, United Kingdom, House of Commons Hansard, column 605. https://publications.parliament.uk/pa/cm199091/cmhansrd/1991-05-10/Writtens-1.html (accessed 3 February 2021).

support for the Antarctic minerals convention".[15] How much forewarning officials had is immaterial, the result was the same. An 'FCO spokesman' was hopeful that negotiations would be completed by the Treaty's 30th anniversary and the United Kingdom "was delighted that a return to consensus now looked possible".[16] On hearing Major's decision, Gareth Evans invoked the same past participle: "I was delighted." Evans urged "other Treaty governments to move swiftly so that negotiations can be finalised" and noted the importance that both Australia and the United Kingdom attached to the Treaty system being "strong and flexible".[17]

It wasn't just the Treaty being flexible. UK minister Garel-Jones now reassured Australian high commissioner Richard Smith that the two-year gulf between had been just a "mild disagreement".[18] At officials' level, John Heap also moved to restore the relationship by offering the AAD's Rex Moncur an apology over the huskies. Heap acknowledged that the United Kingdom "left you in the lurch over the dog problem", and then promptly dismissed "the whole argument about dogs as one of the higher absurdities that have marked many aspects of the negotiation of the protocol annexes".[19] Absurd or not, Moncur had already moved on, accepting it was untenable for Australia to push for continent-wide environmental safeguards while maintaining non-indigenous species in the AAT. His focus now was on how to proceed with the huskies' removal.[20] The AAD was seeking $400,000 to support implementation of the new obligations, including environmental assessments, removal of accumulated wastes, development of management plans and drafting legislation. To support its case, the Division argued unconvincingly that lack of "staff motivation is a key issue" and might hinder full implementation of the obligations.[21] The

[15] 15 May 1990, Michael McCarthy "Major adds weight to Antarctic mining ban" *The Australian*, 10.

[16] 14 May 1991, LH127520 "Antarctica: British position and Madrid agreement" (NAA: B1387 91/32 PART 1).

[17] 15 May 1991, Senate Hansard, 3375.

[18] 6 June 1991, LH129301 "High Commissioner's call on Garel-Jones: Antarctica" (AAD: 91/226–1).

[19] 20 May 1991, letter from Heap to Moncur "Sledge dogs" (AAD: 91/226–1).

[20] 23 May 1991, Antarctic Division minute to Departmental Secretary "Minister's interview on 7.30 Report" (NAA: B1387 91/32 PART 2).

[21] 31 May 1991, DASETT brief to minister "Cabinet submission seeking Government approval of Protocol to the Antarctic Treaty" (NAA: B1387 91/290). The loss of staff motivation came from the prospect of the additional workload, not disappointment over the dogs.

funding request was rolled into a Cabinet submission seeking approval to the draft instrument. With Australian bureaucracy now united, no department objected to the mining ban or the instrument as a whole.[22] On 6 June, Cabinet endorsed it, "provided that the texts remain substantially as negotiated in Madrid". Low staff motivation, however, was ignored: any costs would have to be absorbed.[23]

THE FINAL DRAFTING OF A PROTOCOL

There was *still* no decision on the instrument's form. The United Kingdom argued that another issue to address was its area of application because a protocol could apply only to the area defined imprecisely in Article VI of the Treaty. Settling that, however, could thrust sovereignty back into play. McCarthy feared that it "would raise again the question of the existence or not of continental shelves off the Antarctic under national jurisdiction" but "excluding a part of the Antarctic Treaty Area from the effect of the new protocol" would be unacceptable.[24] France agreed. Duquin insisted that "it was not the role of a protocol to the Antarctic Treaty to be challenging or seeking to refine the area of application of the Treaty on which it is dependent".[25] Puissochet considered the environment protection objective should prevail over what he called "secondary considerations" lest it "run the risk of compromising rapid adoption of the protocol".[26] This was understandable as the United Kingdom was proposing "to substantially modify the area of application". Questioning areas of jurisdiction risked "placing in jeopardy the possibility of concluding the negotiations and adopting the protocol by the target date of 23 June 1991".[27] Heap reassured that "if the problem could not be resolved through discussion with the legal experts of its 'friends' (specifically Australia, New Zealand

---

[22] 24 May 1991, DFAT facsimile "Attachment D: Coordination comments" (NAA: B1387 91/290).

[23] 6 June 1991, file note "Precis of CD 15284 of 6 June 1991" (NAA: B1387 91/290).

[24] 20 May 1991, CE28150 "Antarctica: Letter to Beeby on area of application" (NAA: B1387 1991/56 PART 1).

[25] 30 May 1991, PA87283 "Antarctic: 3rd session of SCM XI Madrid, June—draft environmental protocol" (AAD: 91/226–1).

[26] 4 June 1991, PA87355 "Antarctic: 3rd session of SCM XI Madrid, June—draft environmental protocol" (AAD: 91/226–1).

[27] 6 June 1991, CE35484 "Antarctica: SCM XI, Madrid, June—area of application of the environmental protection protocol" (AAD: 91/226–1).

and the United States) then the UK would not 'die in a ditch' over the issue". In Wellington, Wong was worried: "NZ 'did not want the boat rocked' … it all depended on how hard the UK pressed".[28] Legally, the United Kingdom was right to identify a legal vacuum in the operation of the mining ban because it could be argued that seabed mining was a high seas right protected by the Treaty's Article VI. Australia considered a UK proposal to address the anomaly in the Final Act risky: "it would be better to have no interpretative statement in the Final Act than one which made the gap explicit."[29]

Of understandable concern for Tucker Scully and Desirée Edmar was the United Kingdom pressing for a whole week for drafting.[30] A clearly relieved Duquin had considered the Madrid outcome "a minor miracle" but agreed "that the time allocated to the drafting committee might encourage Parties to raise substantive issues and block the adoption of the protocol". Germany, for example, had concerns about the liability provisions. Duquin had other worries, including "the possibility of the US not supporting the revised Andersen text", adding that "the ratification process could virtually be put on indefinite hold".[31]

Almost immediately, this concern was justified by reporting that "there is one big threat to final agreement—the US Government" because both the Department of State and the Department of Interior opposed the length of the mining ban and the provisions for lifting it.[32] The issue came to a head in Madrid at the legal drafting committee in mid-June.[33] While the United States was "well aware of the risks in tampering with the Andersen text", it could not accept the amendment provision because, as drafted, a single Party could exercise a veto. Thus, the United States would insist on allowing a Party to withdraw from the ban if an amendment

[28] 12 June 1991, WL44110 "Antarctica: SCM XI, Madrid, June—area of application of environmental protection protocol" (AAD: 91/226–1).

[29] 12 June 1991, CE37565 "Antarctica: UK views on area of application of environment protection protocol" (AAD: 91/226–1).

[30] 21 May 1991, CE28655 "Antarctica: 3rd session of SCM XI Madrid, June—draft environmental protocol" (AAD: 91/226–1).

[31] 30 May 1991, PA87283 "Antarctic: 3rd session of SCM XI Madrid, June—draft environmental protocol" (AAD: 91/226–1).

[32] 6 June 1991, "What's the hurry in Antarctica?" *New York Times*.

[33] "Report by the Chairman of the Legal Drafting Committee" in: Antarctic Treaty, *Final Report of the Eleventh Antarctic Treaty Special Consultative, Madrid, 22–30 April 1991; 17–22 June 1991; 3–4 October 1991*, 63.

adopted at a review conference did not enter into force within three years.[34] Scully broke the news on 12 June. McCarthy gloomily reported "the Americans are not bluffing". The only scope for flexibility would be a withdrawing Party having to withdraw from the protocol entirely—a politically significant disincentive.[35] In Canberra, Hugh Wyndham said that DFAT would hold off public comment but expected "a howl from NGOs".[36] There was. WWF argued the US proposal was "completely inconsistent with the expressed intent of Congress and the American people". The Environmental Defense Fund pointed to the inconsistency of the United States advocating a legal vacuum, something it had "for more than a decade sought to eliminate". ASOC was "shocked and dismayed by this secret decision of the US Administration ... which cuts to the heart of the new protocol" and is "an embarrassment for our country".[37] Australia feared it would weaken the instrument's "most sensitive elements".[38] Despite the objections, the United States was insistent. Speaking to Michael Cook (Australia's ambassador in Washington), Roger Porter (assistant to the president for Economic and Domestic Policy) described the proposal "as a modest 'out' at the end of the line if commercially viable mining turned out to be possible at an acceptable environmental cost". The United States "did not want the Treaty Parties to lock themselves in a room for the next 50 years having thrown away the key at the outset". Reactions, he said, had come as a surprise "since the proposal had not seemed so big a deal". Rather surprisingly, Cook offered that "if the USA were not prepared to drop it, Australia would prefer to come back to the protocol after a cooling off period", an idea that Porter thought "would

[34] 12 June 1991, WH132107 "Antarctica: US proposal on Antarctic environmental protocol" (AAD: 91/226-2).
[35] 13 June 1991, MA27048 "Antarctica: SCM XI, Madrid—United States position on prohibition of mining" (AAD: 91/226-1). 14 June 1991, CE38959 "Antarctica—SCMXI—US position—Demarche" (AAD: 91/226-1).
[36] 14 June 1991, CE38958 "Antarctica—SCMXI—United States position" (AAD: 91/226-1).
[37] 14 June 1991, WWF letter, James P. Leape to Bohlen. 14 June 1991, Environmental Defense Fund letter, Bruce Mannheim to Robert B. Zoellick. 14 June 1991, ASOC media release "US proposes to undo agreement on 50 year Antarctic minerals ban" (AAD: 91/226-1).
[38] 14 June 1991, CE38960 "Antarctica SCM XI, Madrid: US position on prohibition of mining" (AAD: 91/226-1).

be helpful".[39] Others were less accommodating, expressing alarm that the United States might thwart the April agreement.[40] The United States did not back down.

On 14 June, the legal drafting committee had gone as far as it could. There is no record of the point at which the instrument became a protocol. It appears to have been pragmatic acquiescence by the states arguing for a convention. With no appetite to re-open the question of form, all references to an 'instrument' were dropped and 'protocol' slid into its place.

June 1991: "The Expectations of the International Community"

Spain had a more practical problem: it had been planning for the final session and signature in a few days' time. Until the US amendment surfaced, ten Parties had indicated they would be ready to sign. Four planned ministerial attendance.[41] By 17 June, what was expected to be the final session of SATCM XI was underway in Madrid. It would run to 22 June, with signing of the Protocol scheduled for 23 June. With the last-minute US objections to the length of the prohibition and the review provision, the signing ceremony might not be possible. Parties' reactions to the United States were universally of "disappointment and irritation": Belgium and Italy were described as angry, Germany blunt. France feared the worst: since the 15 May 1991 resignation of Prime Minister Michel Rocard, "there had been a marked decline in interest in the Antarctic in the Matignon ... if agreement was not reached at this meeting there could be serious erosion in the progress made to date". Curtis Bohlen had no flexibility to move, and time was running out.[42] Chile was concerned about "introducing so controversial an amendment at the eleventh hour".[43] Italy pointed out that many Parties "had made considerable compromises in

[39] 17 June 1991, WH132218 "Antarctica SCMXI, Madrid: US position on prohibition of mining" (AAD: 91/226–1).

[40] 18 to 19 June 1991, several reports of Parties' views (AAD: 91/226–1).

[41] 14 June 1991, MA27052 "Antarctica: SCM XI, Madrid: Report No 2—Drafting Committee" (AAD: 91/226–2).

[42] 18 June 1991, MA27066 "Antarctica: SCM XI, Madrid: report no 3—mining issue" (AAD: 91/226–1).

[43] 27 June 1991, SC22159 "Antarctica—SCMXI environment protection protocol—Chilean views" (AAD: 91/226–2).

order to reach agreement". China warned of failing "the expectations of the international community", and New Zealand expressed alarm. With unabashed irony given what it had done to CRAMRA, Australia criticised the United States for walking away from apparent consensus. Japan made it clear "that there was no chance of the Japanese returning to their former position on the minerals issue".[44] The United Kingdom stayed silent as "the Americans are well aware of their position".[45]

Most Parties were not prepared to leave the issue unresolved, citing the risk of the agreement unravelling and the urgency of re-establishing consensus. Again, a select group convened over dinner. Again, Rolf Andersen facilitated. And again, the discussions went into the early hours. On 19 June, delegation heads considered another Andersen proposal. It failed because claimants would not be able to veto future mining. "Discussion adjourned to a back room" where, at 2:00 am on 20 June, a new text emerged—it would allow the United States (or any Party) to walk away from the protocol if a minerals regime adopted by a majority did not achieve consensus to enter into force.[46] The United States had participated in the discussions, but had no authority to agree. John McCarthy reported that "we doubt that we will get anything more out of the Americans if we wait until, say, the meeting in Bonn … they correctly sense that Parties want to settle the matter quickly, even though American actions are widely resented". McCarthy noted that the proposition "permits a nation to mine without controls, Australia no longer had its veto, and the United States has got its way". On the other hand, "most other delegations see it as important to get a result now", and "our strong sense is that the alliance of the four has run its course [as] we were clearly separated at the end of the meeting from the French, the Italians and Belgians [and] are left solely in the company of New Zealand". McCarthy also predicted momentum might be lost: "it is unlikely that Spain would agree to host another

[44] 21 June 1991, TK71897 "Antarctica SCMXI—3rd session: US position—Japanese views" (AAD: 91/226–3).

[45] 18 June 1991, LH129944 "Antarctica SCMXI, Madrid: US position on prohibition on mining: UK views" (AAD: 91/226–1).

[46] 20 June 1991, MA27075 "Antarctica: SCM XI, Madrid" (AAD: 91/226–2), 4. In the "back room" were Argentina, Australia, Belgium, France, Germany, New Zealand and the United States.

session and it might be difficult to find a willing host at short notice".[47] All that could be agreed was referral of the proposal to governments.[48]

June 1991: "The Situation Has Gone from Bad to Worse"

In Australia on 21 June, Foreign Minister Gareth Evans seemed unsurprised "because the United States position up until then had been one of fairly robust enthusiasm for retaining a capacity to engage in mining". He optimistically expected the issue to be "resolved in the next 24 hours".[49] He was wrong. The protocol had been adopted except the review provisions, which were still "subject to agreement by the United States". At the final plenary session on 22 June, Bohlen advised that the Administration needed more time and "he did not know what the likelihood was of the United States eventually agreeing". The United States was not objecting to the prohibition, only the review provisions. There was "sporadic and informal discussion between delegations as to next steps" and then "the British signalled from the floor the possibility that they might need to look at the compromise text anew given the unhappiness in some quarters of Whitehall". There was now a real risk of undoing what had seemed settled. The planned ceremony to sign the Final Act was cancelled.[50] So passed 23 June 1991, the Treaty's 30th anniversary. Now a Party could call a conference to review its operation. The aim of restoring consensus before then had failed.

Back in Canberra, Ministerial offices and departments discreetly disposed of media releases prepared to celebrate adoption of the protocol.[51] In Wellington, the dismayed Foreign Minister issued a statement that "the situation has gone from bad to worse [but] New Zealand is not going to give up".[52] Asked if the United States really wanted agreement, McKinnon put it down to differences of view between US departments. NGOs called

[47] 20 June 1991, MA27075 "Antarctica: SCM XI, Madrid" (AAD: 91/226–2).

[48] 20 June 1991, facsimile Australian Embassy Madrid to DFAT, Canberra (AAD: 91/226–1).

[49] 21 June 1991, Senate Hansard, 5321–5322.

[50] 22 June 1991, MA27089 "Antarctica: SCM XI, Madrid, 17–22 June: Cable no 6—outcome" (AAD: 91/226–2).

[51] Various press statements and media briefing had been prepared. (AAD: 91/226–1).

[52] 23 June 1991, media release "McKinnon deplores collapse of talks on Antarctic environment" (AAD: 91/226–2).

for New Zealand, UK and Australian prime ministers to lobby the White House.[53] Hawke wrote immediately to President Bush regretting that "the Madrid meeting has broken up without being able to conclude the protocol". He urged Bush "to closely consider the merits of the compromise proposal put forward".[54] DFAT urged other Parties to pressure the President.[55] Chile declined, citing the "traditionalist lobby in Chile (including Zegers)" who were receptive to US anxieties, and New Zealand preferred approaching the US ambassador in Wellington.[56] In France, Georges Duquin was "feeling rather depressed about developments in Madrid" but was disappointed with "Australia acting unilaterally and then asking others to follow suit".[57] John Heap also suggested that directly challenging the White House was "neither necessary nor appropriate": all it would take was 25 Parties staying united to show the United States "there was no prospect of them being able to negotiate a better package through, for example, a process of divide and rule". In Heap's view, the problem was simply US inter-agency processes being insufficiently nimble to respond.[58]

3 JULY 1991: "WELL, IT'S NOT MISSION IMPOSSIBLE"

Heap was right. Quizzed about US thinking, Tucker Scully advised that the proposal "had not been rejected, nor had it been accepted". He also recognised the pressure: "the agony should not be prolonged."[59] On 30 June, Bohlen told Australian ambassador Cook that he was "hopeful of a US decision this week, perhaps as early as tomorrow". Remarkably, he also admitted that both he and Scully "thought the Madrid formula better

---

[53] 24 June 1991, transcript, Radio New Zealand *Morning Report* (AAD: 91/226–2).

[54] 24 June 1991, facsimile PM&C to DFAT "Antarctic environment protocol: letter from the Prime Minister to President Bush" (AAD: 91/226–1).

[55] 25 June 1991, CH627864 "Antarctica—SCMXI—environmental protection protocol" (AAD: 91/226–3).

[56] 27 June 1991, SC22159 "Antarctica—SCMXI environment protection protocol—Chilean views" (AAD: 91/226–2). 28 June 1991, WL44253 "Antarctica—SCM XI—environment protection protocol" (AAD: 91/226–2).

[57] 28 June 1991, PA87763 "Antarctica—SCM XI environment protection protocol" (AAD: 91/226–2).

[58] 28 June 1991, LH130774 "Antarctica—SCMXI environment protection protocol—British views" (AAD: 91/226–2).

[59] 27 June 1991, WH132665 "Antarctica: SCMXI: Environment protection protocol" (AAD: 91/226–2).

than the one the USA had taken to Madrid" but that "they were having trouble selling that view to the White House". The president's economic policy adviser Roger Porter was reportedly onside, but not Chief of Staff John Sununu or the Budget Office's Dick Darman. President Bush was aware of Bob Hawke's letter and "a bit testy about it being an issue at all, saying 'I thought this was all wrapped up long ago'".[60] They might not have long to wait. The State Department had prepared a reply to Hawke as a "holding response", itself now on hold.

Two days later, on 3 July, the State Department's Ray Arnaudo advised Australia's Washington Embassy that because "many in Washington take advantage of tomorrow's public holiday to take a long weekend", a decision would emerge the following week.[61] However, the president's decision came that very day. Speaking at Mt Rushmore, Bush announced that the United States would sign the Protocol. He noted that the Protocol's restriction on mining "addresses our concerns and provides effective protection for Antarctica without foreclosing the options for future generations", adding that "I strongly support these measures which are based on a US initiative".[62]

Bob Hawke was jubilant and claimed the result for himself: "my letter to George Bush last week may have been one of the factors." He emphasised his personal role: "you remember when I initiated this process a relatively short time ago, we were treated with almost scorn. It was regarded as mission impossible. Well, it's not mission impossible, and largely as a result of the initiative by Australia and the fact that we've stuck to our guns, that great wilderness in the Antarctic is going to be protected."[63]

Just as effusive as on the adoption of CRAMRA three years earlier, France was also "delighted with the outcome". Georges Duquin

[60] 1 July 1991, WH132790 "Antarctica: SCM XI—environment protection protocol" (AAD: 91/226–2).

[61] 3 July 1991, WH132881 "Antarctica: SCM XI: Environment protection protocol" (AAD: 91/226–2).

[62] George Bush, "Statement on the environmental protection protocol to the Antarctic Treaty, 3 July 1991" http://www.presidency.ucsb.edu/ws/index.php?pid=29657 (accessed 3 February 2021).

[63] 4 July 1991, CE46838 "Antarctica: Environmental protection: United States position" (NAA: B1387 1991/55 PART 2). See also a more formal statement at: 4 July 1991, Prime Minister, for media http://pmtranscripts.pmc.gov.au/sites/default/files/original/00008313.pdf (accessed 3 February 2021). It was later reported that Japan and the USSR had also written to Bush. See 5 July 1991, Greg Austin, "Bush comes around on Antarctic mining ban" *Sydney Morning Herald*, 5.

congratulated Australia on its contribution and said that "the Franco/ Australia initiative had paved the way for this excellent result. He was fulsome in his praise of 'Australia's Antarctic team'".[64] NGOs joined in: while disappointed that ultimately countries could pull out, Greenpeace was "relieved that President Bush has acknowledged the importance of protecting Antarctica". ASOC's Lyn Goldsworthy still had reservations: "the United States is bowing to political and public pressure for the next fifty years but they want to keep their options open."[65] Greenpeace Australia wrote to Environment Minister Ros Kelly praising her "personal support … of new protective measures, including a mining ban, for the Antarctic", despite being only interim steps towards "a 'world park' forever free from the threat of mining".[66] New Zealand, too, saw the protocol as somehow "insufficient, it wanted a permanent ban on mining". Nevertheless, it was "very supportive of the protocol because it returned the Antarctic Treaty System to consensus".[67]

JULY 1991: "WIDESPREAD RELIEF"

With heat taken out of the debate, attention turned to wrapping up SATCM XI. The State Department had suggested a final session held in Madrid back-to-back with Bonn's October ATCM.[68] Shortly afterwards, Spain circulated a Third Person Note proposing just that: a one-day final session on 3 October, followed by a signing ceremony the following day.[69] Tucker Scully was rightly keen to build on "the widespread relief felt at the conclusion of the Protocol". It would now be possible to address protected areas and, possibly, the long-standing impasse over a Treaty

---

[64] 4 July 1991, PA87869 "Antarctica: SCM XI: Environment protection protocol" (AAD: 91/226–2).

[65] 4 July 1991, transcript Radio National *The World Today*. 4 July 1991, Greenpeace Australia media release "Bush overturns decision—US agreed to ban mining in Antarctic", quoted in: 4 July 1991, CE47001 "Antarctica: Environment protocol: Greenpeace position" (AAD: 91/226–2).

[66] 15 July 1991, letter Greenpeace Australia, Lyn Goldsworthy to Kelly (AAD: 91/226–2).

[67] 8 August 1991, WL44458 "Antarctica: SCM XI final session, Madrid, October: New Zealand views" (AAD: 91/919).

[68] 5 July 1991, WH132922 "Antarctica: Environmental protocol: US position" (AAD: 91/226–2).

[69] 16 July 1991, MA27194 "Antarctica: Third period of second session of SCM XI" (AAD: 91/919).

secretariat.[70] Parties could now enjoy consensus and renewed cooperation. Argentina and Chile immediately adopted a bilateral agreement to coordinate environmental management activities.[71] In London, John Heap resurrected the inner-circle Correspondents' Group, which had "passed into a state of desuetude" when, with differences over CRAMRA, it seemed "no longer possible to assume, give or take a bit here and there, that we were all pushing the same barrow". It took 11 pages to outline the content of Heap's resurrected barrow.[72] The reply by DFAT's Hugh Wyndham, equally pally and loquacious, welcomed resumption of "the former habits of informal consultations".[73] Relations had been restored.

External to the Treaty, however, praise was not universal. In the August 1991 third UNCED Preparatory Committee, Malaysia continued arguing for UN intervention in Antarctica, with Hussein Hannif even asserting that some Parties were already mining in Antarctica.[74] ATCP hopes that the Protocol would settle such concerns would have to wait.

An unexpected vulnerability emerged in July when Japan proposed its own amendments to the Protocol's review provisions. While minor adjustments, opening up such a sensitive article risked a cascade of other amendments and re-opened negotiations. Australia thought the suggestions, even if understandable, were unnecessary. Japan acknowledged this, admitting that their proposals had gone to only 11 Parties, "none of which had been very enthusiastic". Although concerned by "the unseemly haste with which the text had been negotiated", in the end Japan "did not want to stand in the way of its signature".[75]

While worried about late suggestions, in September John McCarthy revealed his own proposal that the draft Final Act be amended so that understandings on a mining moratorium could be replaced by an

[70] 24 July 1991, WH133678 "Antarctica: US views" (AAD: 90/111–1).

[71] 2 August 1991 "Specific Additional Protocol on Antarctic Environmental Protection Between the Argentine Republic and the Republic of Chile" (AU-ATADD-1-BB-AR-178).

[72] 26 July 1991, letter from Heap to McCarthy (AAD: 90/111–2).

[73] 6 September 1991, letter from Wyndham to Heap (AAD: B13/193).

[74] 14 August 1991, GE94399 "UNCED: PrepCom III: Antarctica" (NAA: B1387 90/703 PART 2). 15 August 1991, CH63252 "Antarctica: UNCED PrepCom III" (NAA: B1387 90/703 PART 2).

[75] 31 July 1991, TPN Embassy of Japan "Japanese comment on Article 25 of the Protocol on Environmental Protection to the Antarctic Treaty"; 23 August 1991, AAD memorandum to DFAT "Japanese proposal regarding protocol Articles 25 and 26"; and 30 August 1991, TK72711 "Antarctica: SCM XI: Japanese proposal on protocol" (AAD: 91/919).

obligation "not to act contrary to the spirit of a full prohibition".[76] This was because Parties signing the protocol would be obliged by the 1969 Vienna Convention not to defeat its objectives. He also sought commitment to early work on liability.[77] With little time free on SATCM XI's one remaining day, Heap pleaded that "this is clearly going to be a tall order and requires of us considerable forbearance".[78] The State Department was even more hesitant about raising liability, a fear that later proved fully justified.[79]

Tucker Scully's objective was quick acceptance of the Protocol, prompt entry into force, and no further arguments over the environment. He wanted "Madrid and Bonn to be essentially 'snooze' meetings devoid of the political controversy which had prevailed over the two years since the Paris ATCM". He even hoped to avoid any embarrassment over national statements attached to the Final Act, especially if they "had the effect of according any status to idiotic statements". Importantly, there was no retreat from the protocol—in fact, Curtis Bohlen personally wished to sign. Scully was less concerned as to who would sign: "the more important objective was for the US to be one of the original signatories".[80]

4 OCTOBER 1991: SATCM XI FOURTH SESSION, THE MADRID PROTOCOL IS ADOPTED

The Parties re-convened in Madrid on 3 October 1991 for the fourth, and final, session of the 11th Special Antarctic Treaty Consultative Meeting. One day was allowed for editorial corrections and drafting the Final Act. The following day was for a signing ceremony. Australia wanted adoption of the Protocol without changes. For the Final Act, Australia would seek a strengthened moratorium, early work on liability, and provisional

[76] 6 September 1991, letter from McCarthy to Heap (AAD: B13/193).

[77] Vienna Convention on the Law of Treaties, Article 18 http://www.austlii.edu.au/au/other/dfat/treaties/1974/2.html (accessed 3 February 2021).

[78] 19 September 1991, facsimile message FCO to DFAT (AAD: 91/919).

[79] 27 September 1991, CE78682 "Antarctica—liability annex to environmental protocol"; and 30 September 1991, WH136147 "Antarctica: liability annex to protocol: US views" (AAD: 91/919).

[80] 26 September 1991, WH135969 "Antarctica ATCM XVI: Reply to Heap (UK): US views" (AAD: 90/111–2). Idiotic or not, the national statements were attached to Final Report. Antarctic Treaty, *Final Report of the Eleventh Antarctic Treaty Special Consultative, Madrid, 22–30 April 1991; 17–22 June 1991; 3–4 October 1991*, 159–201.

implementation.[81] None of this proved controversial. With "some minor textual changes" the Protocol and its Final Act were completed, as well as the Final Report. On 4 October, all 26 ATCPs ceremoniously signed the Final Act, and 23 signed the Protocol itself.[82]

Spain's Foreign Minister celebrated the Protocol as an "example both of the vitality of the Antarctic system and the spirit of cooperation … demanded of us by worldwide public opinion".[83] For something so significant, the response from ministers and media was muted. NGOs were modest in their praise, some critical that the Protocol "doesn't have a lot of teeth". ASOC's Cath Wallace said the campaign "had been remarkably successful but a lot was still to be done" to strengthen the Protocol "and ensure the minerals ban was made permanent".[84]

Leaving Madrid, delegations went straight to Bonn, where ATCM XVI was about to begin. They took with them the signed *Protocol on Environmental Protection to the Antarctic Treaty*, to which were attached annexes on Environmental Impact Assessment (*Annex I*); Conservation of Antarctic Fauna and Flora (*Annex II*); Waste Disposal and Waste management (*Annex III*); and Prevention of Marine Pollution (*Annex IV*).[85] They were also buoyed by restored consensus.

OCTOBER 1991: "TIME FOR ALL THE WOUNDS TO HEAL"

Twenty years of fractious politics about minerals had ended. There was healthy satisfaction, but no immediate triumphalism. That was to come later. In Australia's view, the Treaty's 30th year had seen the ATS

[81] October 1991, "Final session of SCM XI, Madrid, 3–4 October 1991" (AAD: B13/199).

[82] 4 October 1991, MA27560 "Antarctic environment protocol" (AAD: 91/919). Four ministers signed for their countries and officials signed for the others (McCarthy signed for Australia)—see 4 October 1991 "Final Act of the Eleventh Antarctic Treaty Special Consultative Meeting" (AU-ATADD-4-BB-AQ-239). The outstanding signatures were done the following year. See XVII ATCM/INFO 17 "Status of signatures and ratifications of the Protocol on Environmental Protection to the Antarctic Treaty" https://documents. ats.aq/ATCM17/ip/ATCM17_ip017_e.pdf (accessed 19 March 2020).

[83] Antarctic Treaty, *Final Report of the Eleventh Antarctic Treaty Special Consultative, Madrid, 22–30 April 1991; 17–22 June 1991; 3–4 October 1991*, 105–06.

[84] 5 October 1991, "Mining ban fragile: Antarctic lobbyist" *The Dominion* (New Zealand). 5 October 1991, "Antarctic mining banned for 50 years" *The Age*, 15.

[85] The Protocol and its annexes are at: https://ats.aq/e/key-documents.html (accessed 23 March 2020).

strengthened. It observed that "the return to consensus on mining is particularly important for Australia in view of the antipathy to our initiative", although "it might take some time for all the wounds to heal".[86] Australia aimed to rebuild relationships and not again be considered "unpredictable and demanding". Having abandoned consensus once, "it wanted to be seen as a reliable Party" and "decided to take a low profile on new initiatives, at least for the time being".[87]

Senator Evans' media release announcing Australian signature of the Protocol congratulated France in particular.[88] However, it was at this point that the bond between Australia and France began to weaken. Policy objectives and tactics began to diverge, starting in Bonn where France pushed for tourism regulations. Australia thought that adding new obligations immediately could delay bringing the Protocol into force.

It was important to cement the new stability. Parties praised the key individuals involved. Andersen's contribution was especially mentioned, so too the chairs in Viña del Mar and Madrid. Chile reflected on the "deep divisions" overcome, and Germany lauded the "quick and efficient result". Sweden regarded the Protocol "a significant achievement", and the United States said it was an innovative result which "set a precedent for addressing other pressing global environmental problems".[89] However, it wasn't all positive. SCAR was jealous of ASOC's influence and, in "a rather bitter report", complained about diminution of its role in providing environmental advice. Nigel Bonner lamented SCAR's inadequate funding and uncertain relationship with the new Committee on Environmental Protection (CEP).[90] Such negativity was unexpected when Parties were emphasising harmony. It took until the meeting's end to repair "the damage caused by the insensitive report from SCAR", which would still have "to recover some of its credibility following politicisation of its role". Less controversial was the sole mention of minerals: a US proposal on the free

---

[86] October 1991, overview and objectives, in "Brief for the Australian delegation to the 16th Antarctic Treaty Consultative Meeting, Bonn, 7–18 October 1991" (AAD: B13/193).

[87] Andrew Jackson and Lorne Kriwoken, "The Protocol in Action, 1992–2010," in *Australia and the Antarctic Treaty System: 50 Years of Influence*, ed. Marcus Haward and Tom Griffiths (UNSW Press, 2011), 301–02.

[88] 4 October 1991, Minister for Foreign Affairs and Trade news release "Australia signs agreement to protect the Antarctic environment" (AU-ATADD-1-BB-AU-353).

[89] 9 October 1991, "ATCM XVI—Plenary" (AWJ personal notes), 14–21.

[90] 8 October 1991, BO55764 "Antarctica—ATCM XVI—Bonn—7-18 October" (AAD: 90/111–2). 7 October 1991, "ATCM XVI—Plenary—Reports" (AWJ personal notes), 5.

exchange of marine seismic data to avoid any suspicion that such data might have commercial value.[91]

The priority at ATCM XVI was provisionally implementing the Protocol, including establishing the Committee on Environmental Protection (temporarily achieved through the Transitional Environmental Working Group) and handling environmental impact assessments. There were also discussions on the Protocol's implications for the frequency of Treaty meetings; public availability of documents; and growing calls for a Treaty secretariat.[92] Also raised in Bonn was whether to commence work on environmental liability. That was referred to a Group of Legal Experts for advice thus sidestepping, for the time being, one of the most problematic environmental and legal issues.[93]

The Parties promptly addressed the protected area system. Discussion was led by UK and US papers.[94] The proposals were combined and adopted as Annex V.[95] This was a major development, becoming one of the most productive areas of the CEP. That said, achieving Annex V was unexpectedly "fraught with seemingly intractable sticking points". These had been introduced by France, Australia's closest collaborator on the environmental initiative. France essentially held the meeting to ransom by insisting "there can be no protected areas annex without a tourism annex". Possibly still smarting at Greenpeace activities at Dumont d'Urville, France had already flagged its wish for stricter regulation of non-governmental activities. This

[91] 18 October 1991, BO55868 "Antarctica: ATCMXVI: Final report and recommendations" (AAD: 90/111–2).

[92] 14 October 1991, BO55789, "Antarctica—ATCM XVI: Report no 2—SCM XI and working groups" (AAD: 90/111–2). 7–18 October 1991, "ATCM XVI"(AWJ personal notes). The move to annual meetings reflected agreement that activities subject to a Comprehensive Environmental Evaluation not be held up by more than 15 months.

[93] The legal experts met from 1993 to 1997, and subsequent formal negotiations resulted in the 2005 adoption of the Protocol's Annex VI. See https://ats.aq/devAS/Meetings/Measure/331 (accessed 27 March 2020). Antarctic Treaty, *Antarctic Treaty Consultative Meeting: Final Report of the Twenty-Eighth Meeting, Stockholm, Sweden, 6–17 June 2005* (2005), 33–39.

[94] 7 October 1991, XVI ATCM/WP 1 "Area protection and management in the Antarctic" https://documents.ats.aq/ATCM16/wp/ATCM16_wp001_e.pdf   (accessed   27 March 2020).

[95] Antarctic Treaty, Recommendation ATCM XVI-10 "Annex V of the Environmental Protocol (Area Protection and Management)" https://documents.ats.aq/keydocs/vol_1/vol1_9_AT_Protocol_Annex_V_e.pdf (accessed 27 March 2020). Antarctic Treaty, *Final Report of the Sixteenth Antarctic Treaty Consultative Meeting, Bonn, 7–18 October 1991* (1991), 24–25.

was addressed in a paper which, surprisingly, it said had been developed with Australia. ASOC "enraged France" by arguing against it.[96] There then ensued a "long and at times bitter debate" with France seeking maximum regulation of tourism and the United States rejecting anything mandatory.[97] France seemed to miss the point that having just adopted a Protocol applying comprehensive environmental measures to *all* activities, it was incongruous to suggest that measures (which France itself had proposed) did not adequately regulate one of Antarctica's major activities. Furthermore, many issues relating to tourism and non-government activities were about safety and self-sufficiency—matters unrelated to environment protection and thus outside the Protocol's scope. After celebrating consensus on the Protocol, arguing over such activities seemed odd. Australia was surprised that its "French colleagues adopted a very inflexible stance and obstructed sensible progress in consideration of the issues".[98] Greenpeace was not concerned about the possible regulation of non-governmental activities: protests at Dumont d'Urville had concluded, and World Park Base would be removed from Ross Island immediately as direct action was no longer necessary.[99] The priority for Greenpeace was for national Antarctic programs to implement the new obligations.[100] Regulation of tourism and non-governmental activities was referred to future ATCMs, where nothing ever came of proposals for a stand-alone annex.[101]

[96] 14 October 1991, BO55789, Antarctica—ATCM XVI: Report no 2—SCM XI and working groups" (AAD: 90/111–2). October 1991, 16th Antarctic Treaty Consultative Meeting "Summary of delegation reports and action arising" (AAD: B13/193). The French paper is at https://documents.ats.aq/ATCM16/wp/ATCM16_wp002_e.pdf (accessed 27 March 2020).

[97] 18 October 1991, BO55868 "Antarctica: ATCMXVI: Final report and recommendations" (AAD: 90/111–2). 10–11 October 1991, "ATCM XVI—WG1" (AWJ personal notes), 27–32, 34–37.

[98] 11 November 1991, Antarctic Division minute, Rex Moncur "Report on overseas visit" (AAD: 91/919).

[99] Antarctic and Southern Ocean Coalition, "Leading by Example," *ECO* LXXXI, no. 1 (1991): 4. France's subsequent abandonment of the Dumont d'Urville runway was not solely due to NGO objections—before being commissioned, the runway was destroyed by storm damage. See Tara Patel, "Waves Smash Antarctic Airstrip," *New Scientist*, no. 1914 (1994).

[100] Michael Szabo, *State of the Ice: An Overview of Human Impacts in Antarctica* (Greenpeace International, 1993), 2–21.

[101] Mike G Richardson, "Regulating Tourism in the Antarctic: Issues of Environment and Jurisdiction," in *Implementing the Environmental Protection Regime for the Antarctic*, ed. Davor Vidas (Kluwer, 2000).

A TREATY REVIEW

The Bonn meeting also adopted a declaration, drafted by Australia, to celebrate the Treaty's 30th anniversary. It made no mention of minerals, the one issue which had dogged the Parties for two-thirds of the Treaty's existence. It did, however, declare a 'Decade of International Antarctic Cooperation, 1991 to 2000'. The declaration neither required, nor resulted in, any specific actions. Nevertheless, it was symbolic confirmation of a restored status quo in Antarctic affairs and recognised that the Protocol was "a fitting tribute to the thirtieth anniversary of the Antarctic Treaty", neatly setting set aside any suggestion that a Treaty review was a live option.[102] On the contrary, dealing with mining and the environmental issues, and re-establishing consensus, was a de facto review.[103]

The protocol became known as the Madrid Protocol, in recognition of the city in which it was adopted. Fittingly, Spain became the first state to ratify it, doing so on 1 July 1992.[104] Other Parties soon followed. On 14 January 1998, with all the ratifications complete, the Protocol entered into force. Antarctica was saved. From what, exactly, Antarctica was 'saved' is discussed in Chap. 10.

REFERENCES

Antarctic and Southern Ocean Coalition. "Leading by Example." *ECO* LXXXI, no. 1 (1991): 4.

Antarctic Treaty. *Antarctic Treaty Consultative Meeting: Final Report of the Twenty-Eighth Meeting, Stockholm, Sweden, 6–17 June 2005.* 2005.

———. *Final Report of the Eleventh Antarctic Treaty Special Consultative, Madrid, 22–30 April 1991; 17–22 June 1991; 3–4 October 1991.* Ministerio de Asuntos Exteriores, 1991a.

———. *Final Report of the Sixteenth Antarctic Treaty Consultative Meeting, Bonn, 7–18 October 1991.* 1991b.

[102] Antarctic Treaty, *Final Report of the Sixteenth Antarctic Treaty Consultative Meeting, Bonn, 7–18 October 1991*, 133–39.

[103] Invoking the Article XII review provision has never been subsequently considered and Parties have made several declarations confirming commitment to the Treaty.

[104] XVII ATCM/INFO 17 (USA) "Status of signatures and ratifications of the Protocol on Environmental Protection to the Antarctic Treaty" https://documents.ats.aq/ATCM17/ip/ATCM17_ip017_e.pdf (accessed 27 March 2020).

Jackson, Andrew, and Lorne Kriwoken. "The Protocol in Action, 1992–2010." Chap. 13 In *Australia and the Antarctic Treaty System: 50 Years of Influence*, edited by Marcus Haward and Tom Griffiths, 300–19: UNSW Press, 2011.

Patel, Tara. "Waves Smash Antarctic Airstrip." *New Scientist*, no. 1914 (26 February 1994).

Richardson, Mike G. "Regulating Tourism in the Antarctic: Issues of Environment and Jurisdiction." In *Implementing the Environmental Protection Regime for the Antarctic*, edited by Davor Vidas, 71–90: Kluwer, 2000.

Szabo, Michael. *State of the Ice: An Overview of Human Impacts in Antarctica*. Greenpeace International, 1993.

CHAPTER 9

Influences and Influencers in Antarctic Affairs

UNDERSTANDING WHAT HAPPENED

The story began with the first interest in Antarctic minerals and ended with the Madrid Protocol which prohibited their use. Access to government records and the inner working of the Antarctic Treaty System (ATS) help describe *what* occurred, but they do not explain *why*. The events were made possible by pre-existing conditions and events that were concurrent or serendipitous.[1] What followed was not *inevitable* but was made *possible* when individuals took advantage of those circumstances. This chapter assesses the influential events and participants.

PRE-EXISTING CONDITIONS

Pre-existing circumstances include the Antarctic Treaty, territorial sovereignty, consensus decision-making, the stability of the ATS, Antarctica's mineral potential, the diplomatic investment made in CRAMRA, the mining moratorium, existing environmental concerns, national Antarctic policy, domestic politics and aspirations for a world park.

---

[1] Some historians call these factors *contingence, conjuncture* and *accident*. Marks, *The Origins of the Modern World*, 10–17.

© The Author(s), under exclusive license to Springer Nature Switzerland AG 2021
A. Jackson, *Who Saved Antarctica?*,
https://doi.org/10.1007/978-3-030-78405-8_9

The Antarctic Treaty System

The Treaty brought States together for cooperative Antarctic governance. Progressive expansion of the instruments and institutions, and parallel maturation of the Treaty's operating norms, resulted in the governance framework known as the Antarctic Treaty System. Negotiation of the Treaty itself demonstrated how problems could be solved, such as exchanging views informally outside formal negotiations—a 'no surprises' approach.[2] Such approaches provided confidence to tackle resources and other complex issues as initial doubts about the Treaty's longevity evaporated. Australian fears of legal inflexibility dissipated, as did UK views that the Treaty was an expedience pending internationalisation.[3] It was logical that minerals issues be contained within the ATS and its established practices. Addressing problematic issues early, such as the 1972 Seals Convention (CCAS) and the 1980 Convention on the Conservation of Antarctic Marine Living Resources (CCAMLR), gave confidence to address the more sensitive minerals issue. By the 1982 commencement of the minerals debate, the number of Parties had more than doubled.[4] Eleven more acceded *during* the CRAMRA negotiations, motivated by the prospect of gaining access to potential minerals and becoming members of the Antarctic Mineral Resources Commission. Whatever the motives, it further legitimised the ATS. Inviting non-Consultative Parties (NCPs) to the meetings improved transparency.[5] Increased legitimacy meant stronger commitment to the Treaty's principles without which the minerals debate would have been even more highly contested.

Territorial Sovereignty

Seven Parties maintain territorial claims, and two assert a basis of claims. None enjoy universal recognition. Handling this is at the Treaty's core. Article IV requires acceptance not of the claims themselves, but that they

---

[2] This has also been called "pre-negotiation". Hall, *International Regime Formation and Leadership: The Origins of the Antarctic Treaty*, 65–67 and 153.

[3] October 1970, "Sixth Antarctic Treaty Consultative Meeting, Brief for the Australian delegation" (NAA: B1387 1991/640 PART 3).

[4] https://ats.aq/devAS/Parties?lang=e (accessed 15 March 2020).

[5] The rapid growth in Treaty Parties between 1982 and 1988 is illustrated in Daniela Liggett et al., "Is It All Going South? Four Future Scenarios for Antarctica," *Polar Record* 53, no. 5 (2017): 461–62. Antarctic Treaty, *Report of the Twelfth Consultative Meeting, Canberra, 13–27 September 1983*, 14–15, 122–23

exist—it does not set aside the claims, but seeks to set aside disruptive argument *about* them.[6] One way this is achieved is through 'bifocalism' which allows differing views to be described in language capable of different, but equally valid, interpretation.[7]

Sovereignty concerns had been accommodated in CCAS and CCAMLR, various Treaty measures and ATCM practice. For claimants, sovereignty was routinely demonstrated by occupying stations; enacting legislation; issuing postage stamps and assigning place names. Minerals showed that something more tangible was at stake: resources with quantifiable value, exclusive rights and strategic potential.[8] The territorial claims problem became unavoidable in the minerals negotiations and, as Chris Beeby put it, "differences about sovereignty have [become] a large part of the reason for embarking on them in the first place".[9] Thus, the minerals negotiations

---

[6] In brief, Article IV protects the interests of states that maintain a territorial claim and those that do not, and allows cooperation to proceed unhindered by the differences of view. Watts, *International Law and the Antarctic Treaty System*, 126–36. Joyner, *Governing the Frozen Commons*, 57–58.

[7] The term emerged in March 1978 during the CCAMLR negotiations. UK Head of Delegation Donald Logan remarked that the Parties seemed to be looking at a draft article on jurisdiction through bifocal glasses. The solution accepted was "non-claimants would interpret references to coastal state jurisdiction as applying solely to areas of undisputed national jurisdiction north of 60 degrees South and claimants would interpret such references as applying both to north and south of that latitude". March 1978, Australian delegation report, Antarctic marine living resources (AAD: B13/197). The importance of bifocalism is examined in: Martin L Lee, "The 1959 Antarctic Treaty, the "Freezing and Bifocalism" Formula," *Australian International Law Journal* (2000). Bush, *Antarctica and International Law: A Collection of Inter-State and National Documents*, Vol I, 406. Marcus Haward and Nicholas Cooper, "Australian Interests, Bifocalism, Bipartisanship, and the Antarctic Treaty System," *Polar Record* 50, no. 1 (2014). R. Tucker Scully, "The Development of the Antarctic Treaty System," in *Science Diplomacy: Antarctica, Science, and the Governance of International Spaces*, ed. Paul Arthur Berkman, and others (Smithsonian Institution, 2011), 31. James N. Barnes, "The Emerging Antarctic Living Resources Convention," *American Society of International Law Proceedings* 73 (1979): 279–81.

[8] For the sovereignty challenge posed by minerals, see Hambro, "Some Notes on the Future of the Antarctic Treaty Collaboration." Roberts, "International Co-Operation for Antarctic Development: The Test for the Antarctic Treaty," 111–13. Auburn, *Antarctic Law and Politics*, 109–10. Finn Sollie, "Jurisdictional Problems in Relation to Antarctic Mineral Resources in Political Perspective," in *Antarctic Resources Policy: Scientific, Legal and Political Issues*, ed. Francisco Orrego Vicuña (Cambridge University Press, 1983), 317–35.

[9] Christopher C Beeby, "The Antarctic Treaty System: Goals, Performance and Impact," in *The Antarctic Treatgy System in World Politics*, ed. Arnfinn Jørgensen-Dahl and Willy Østreng (Macmillan/Fridtjof Nansen Institute, 1991), 7.

were as much about safeguarding sovereignty as about accessing the resources themselves. The effectiveness of CRAMRA's sovereignty safeguards is moot, but its regulatory committees had to include the relevant claimant. CRAMRA thus provided for its demise: if a claimant state reneged, the institutions could not operate. CRAMRA gave sovereignty unintended potency.

Despite differences between the claimants, protecting sovereignty was a shared matter of principle. Even if not sharing identical positions, they often acted en bloc. Norway, described as "a fairly dispassionate claimant", retained its claim "because it serves as a ticket to a first-class ride".[10] Once minerals gained attention the United Kingdom overcame its hesitations and resumed its robust claimant stance.[11] Chile thought that "one of the weaknesses of the Treaty had been that the claimant States had claimed too little rather than too much". Argentina had wanted sovereignty concerns addressed before agreeing to even *discuss* minerals.[12] On the other hand, both Latin Americans "were terrified of the prospect of raising discussions of sovereignty [and] very relieved to have Australia lead the charge, very relieved".[13]

Australia was described as a "hard claimant". Accomplished diplomat John Rowland considered Australia an "assertive claimant" because "although the claim may be too big to be credible internationally … it is too big to surrender".[14] Australia was not always robust on sovereignty, but it was on mining. For Keith Brennan, Australia's rights "were not negotiable" but an outcome on minerals "could not be essentially destructive of the position of either the claimant or non-claimant states".[15] He considered "sovereignty over resources, and the right to collect revenue from the exploitation of resources, inseverable concomitants of

[10] Stokke, "The Making of Norwegian Antarctic Policy," 387–89.

[11] 21 January 1976, Memorandum AHC London "Antarctic Policy" (NAA: B1387 1996/864 PART 1). It was ventured that "it might be best for the United Kingdom to look upon itself as a non-claimant state". Roberts, "International Co-Operation for Antarctic Development: The Test for the Antarctic Treaty," 112.

[12] 26 April 1976, O.BA3430 "Antarctica—Paris preparatory meeting" (NAA: B1387 1991/708 PART 1).

[13] 12 January 1977, "Note for file" (NAA: B1387 1991/748).

[14] Stokke, "Domestic Politics and ATS Change: Introductory Assessment," 324. Rowland, "The Treaty Regime and the Politics of the Consultative Parties," 21.

[15] July 1976, Report of the Australian Delegation to the Special Preparatory Meeting of Antarctic Treaty Consultative Parties on the Exploration and Exploitation of the Mineral Resources of Antarctica, Paris, 28 June–10 July 1976 (AAD: B13/197), 3–4

sovereignty".[16] Australia, aware of the risks, noted that "protection of sovereignty will be continuous and could be a long-term source of irritation and expense".[17] In 1981, Brennan warned that "we have to be continually on our guard" that non-claimants might leave us a "clause that is a *de facto* surrender of all relevant rights".[18] Ceremonial speeches were normally noted for their inspiring blandness but, in Hobart, Australia's Science Minister Barry Jones opened a minerals meeting by demanding a claimant share of minerals revenue.[19] Treasury's obsession with revenue overshadowed Australia's credibility on environmental provisions.[20] Unsurprisingly, when Australia rejected CRAMRA on environmental grounds, its motives were questioned. Australia's vigour benefited other claimants unwilling to be so bold. By hosting the negotiations, New Zealand would not have to take head-on the United States, which wanted access to Ross Sea resources—it could rely on Australia to fight for claimant entitlements.[21]

The CRAMRA debate raised potent sovereignty issues that the Treaty itself had sidestepped. As shown in the narrative, non-claimants were keen to avoid accommodating claimant interests. Japan even warned that if a regime "led to too many special privileges for territorial claimants or superpowers", it would walk away from the Treaty.[22] Parties otherwise close on policy were opposites on sovereignty. Australia had wanted to

---

[16] Keith Brennan, "Criteria for Access to the Resources of Antarctica: Alternatives, Procedure and Experience Applicable," in *Antarctic Resources Policy: Scientific, Legal and Political Issues*, ed. Francisco Orrego Vicuña (Cambridge University Press, 1983), 224.

[17] 18 April 1977, draft by the Legal Adviser "Antarctica" (NAA: B1387 1991/697 PART 4).

[18] 24 August 1981, BU7082 "Antarctica—Draft recommendation on mineral resources" (NAA: B1387 96/894).

[19] 14 April 1986, "Opening address by the Hon Barry O Jones" (NAA: B1387 1985/889 PART 2). Contrast this with Jones' earlier view that if resource shortages made Antarctica attractive "it was time we looked for another planet": 6 April 1983, "Antarctica should be a peace zone, says Jones" *The Australian*.

[20] In 1986, New Zealand was disappointed that Australia put great weight on economic interests. Templeton, *A Wise Adventure II: New Zealand and Antarctica after 1960*, 186–87, 206 and 14.

[21] Alternatively, New Zealand leadership on minerals was "self-interest"—a regime with favourable terms because it had no domestic oil reserves. Ibid., 114–19. In CCAMLR negotiations, Australia benefitted from vigorous French advocacy of sovereignty over islands in the CCAMLR area.

[22] Robert Friedheim and Tsuneo Akaha, "Antarctic Resources and International Law: Japan, the United States, and the Future of Antarctica," *Ecology Law Quarterly* 16, no. 1 (1989): 144–46.

support CRAMRA and take advantage of minerals—but not in a way that created disagreements with traditional allies. The Madrid Protocol saved the Parties from such dilemmas. Both claimants and non-claimants needed to protect the integrity of Article IV. Thus, maintenance of the sovereignty status quo was a fortunate consequence of abandoning CRAMRA. In neat irony, Australia used the special rights of a claimant to defeat CRAMRA, the regime it saw as derogating from those rights.

Sovereignty's relevance was threefold: providing the conditions to precipitate dissatisfaction with CRAMRA; allowing claimants to block CRAMRA by defeating its institutions; and Treaty Article IV had facilitated Antarctic cooperation in the first place.

Consensus Decision-Making

Consensus is a well-embedded ATS practice originating in the fundamental differences over sovereignty. The consensus 'rule' is not codified as such, only a provision that measures "shall be adopted by the Representatives of all Consultative Parties".[23] Achieving consensus requires diplomatic skills, creative problem-solving, compromise and forbearance.[24] The United States argued for regulation "through negotiation and consensus, not sovereign control".[25] The closest that Parties came to defining consensus was in CRAMRA itself, where it meant the absence of formal objection.[26] This is an essential characteristic.[27] After unanimity, consensus has been described as "the most demanding decision rule there is [as] collec-

[23] Antarctic Treaty, *Rules of Procedure of the Antarctic Treaty Consultative Meeting and the Committee for Environmental Protection* (Secretariat of the Antarctic Treaty, 2017). Consensus avoided the prospect of a claimant being outvoted and prevented from taking an action that it considered a sovereign right. In the Treaty's early years, consensus prevented the claimants outvoting non-claimants.

[24] Jackson, "Politics, Diplomacy and the Creation of Antarctic Consensus."

[25] US Congress Office of Technology Assessment, *Polar Prospects: A Minerals Treaty for Antarctica* (US Government Printing Office, 1989), 6.

[26] "Convention on the Regulation of Antarctic Mineral Resource Activities", Article 22.5. The same definition was adopted for the Council in Article 161.8(e) of the 1982 Law of the Sea Convention. See http://www.un.org/depts/los/convention_agreements/texts/unclos/unclos_e.pdf (accessed 3 February 2021).

[27] Some authors suggest that unanimity is implied. See, for example: Myhre, *The Antarctic Treaty System: Politics, Law, and Diplomacy*, 42. M. J. Peterson, *Managing the Frozen South: The Creation and Evolution of the Antarctic Treaty System* (University of California Press, 1988), 93. Beck, *The International Politics of Antarctica*, 155.

tive action will be limited to those measures that are acceptable to the least enthusiastic Party".[28] The United Kingdom's John Heap captured it eloquently: "don't ask me to say yes, and I won't say no."[29]

The consensus challenge compounded as Parties increased during the minerals debate and the Protocol negotiations.[30] Consensus is required just to place an issue on the agenda, let alone settle its substance. Next, entry into force of a measure required domestic legislation which could be blocked. CRAMRA went further than any previous instrument in moving away from the consensus requirement.[31] Yet it still contained another stage: consensus to open an area for mining.[32] John Heap emphasised this in advocating CRAMRA (despite the incongruity of promoting a mining regime on the basis that it could be used to *prevent* mining). It was thus argued that CRAMRA actually contained a mining ban, a view resisted by others.[33] The proposition that a Party could use CRAMRA to veto mining was unconvincing—signing up while planning to defeat its purpose would contravene the Vienna Convention on the Law of Treaties.[34]

CRAMRA created unprecedented opportunities to renege on expectations. The risk of the consensus failing was probably underestimated. Had it been recognised, it is unlikely that CRAMRA would have provided the

[28] Underdal, "One Question, Two Answers," 25.

[29] 26 April 1991, "XI SCM (Session II)" (AWJ personal notes), 52.

[30] Beeby, "The Antarctic Treaty System: Goals, Performance and Impact," 13–15.

[31] Consensus was also abandoned in the Protocol's Article 25 requirement for "a majority of the Parties" to adopt a modification to the Protocol. This qualified majority ensures the Protocol would not suffer the same fate as CRAMRA. Francioni, "The Madrid Protocol on the Protection of the Antarctic Environment," 69.

[32] CRAMRA did not require consensus to open an area for prospecting.

[33] John A. Heap, "The Political Case for the Minerals Convention," in *The Future of Antarctica: Exploitation* Versus *Preservation*, ed. Grahame Cook (Manchester University Press, 1990), 45–46. Beeby, "The Convention on the Regulation of Antarctic Minerals and Its Future," 56, 58. John Burgess, "Comprehensive Environmental Protection of the Antarctic: New Approaches for New Times," in *The Future of Antarctica: Exploitation* Versus *Preservation*, ed. Grahame Cook (Manchester University Press, 1990), 63–64.

[34] A counterargument was that the Vienna Convention prevented CRAMRA's signatories supporting a mining ban as that would have defeated the convention's purpose. That viewpoint was dismissed when *all* Parties to CRAMRA agreed to depart from it: Watts, *International Law and the Antarctic Treaty System*, 287. It has also been argued that an *individual* Party can drop support without contradicting the Vienna Convention: J. G. Podehl and D. R. Rothwell, "New Zealand and the Convention on the Regulation of Antarctic Mineral Resource Activities (CRAMRA): An Unhappy Divorce?" *Victoria University of Wellington Law Review* 22 (1992): 44–45.

mechanism to sink it. Nevertheless, there it was: regulatory committees had to include the relevant claimant, and CRAMRA required participation by "*all* of the States necessary in order to establish *all* of the institutions of the Convention in respect of every area of Antarctica".[35] Each Party could have vetoed CRAMRA at its adoption, but nine states could veto its entry into force (the claimants plus the USSR and the United States).[36] A regime had been adopted allowing a minority to renege on the consensus of the whole—legally, this proved to be a fatal flaw. The assumption was that having been negotiated in good faith, and adopted by consensus, the deal would not be broken. Equally surprising was the speed with which consensus evaporated.[37]

The last reason consensus helped provided the right circumstances for a decision is because the loss of consensus raised such concern. Was that anxiety over a failed convention or over wider implications for the ATS? When CRAMRA was rejected, much was made about the moratorium's stability and the legal void created. However, there were still no economic minerals and no suggestion that anyone wanted to go looking. Even so, the situation was seen as a crisis of consensus taking the Treaty "to the brink of collapse".[38] The concern was for the tradition of Antarctic cooperation, rather than grief for a legal vacuum over hypothetical activities. The loss of the CRAMRA consensus created a precedent for reneging on other agreements. Worse, it could weaken commitment to some of the Treaty's most enduring principles (including peaceful use, priority for science and the accommodation of differences over sovereignty), because without such commitment there would be no Antarctic cooperation.

Failure to *reach* consensus was common, as were delays in implementing agreements already made. However, abandoning consensus *afterwards* was unheralded until Australia and France reneged. Australia's defection also undermined its reputation as a Treaty stalwart, and the one who was concurrently leading ATCPs in the UN. Australia dramatically illustrated

[35] "Convention on the Regulation of Antarctic Mineral Resource Activities", Articles 29, 62.

[36] The veto power was also held by others because of the requirement that at least 16 Parties participate in CRAMRA. At the time of Australia's decision not to sign CRAMRA, to fulfil the prescribed formula the Convention also required participation by either of India or of China (as developing States). China signed.

[37] See, for example: Elliott, *International Environmental Politics: Protecting the Antarctic*, 162, 71.

[38] Chaturvedi, *The Polar Regions*, 141, 229.

the ability of one Party to wilfully override the will of many.[39] The shock of losing consensus contributed to calls for its urgent restoration and implied threats about the consequences if not.[40]

Some Parties appeared ambivalent about the debate's substance, concerned more for re-establishing consensus. It has been described as "the backbone of the Treaty System".[41] For minerals, the impetus was to resolve differences before commercial interest emerged.[42] After six years of enervating debate, Chris Beeby implored Parties to find solutions "tolerable to all". Even then fatigue did not provoke departure from the consensus model. Similarly, with impasse in Madrid, no delegations canvassed alternative decision-making processes. Australia's own pessimism recognised that the obstacle to success was the consensus requirement. Being isolated on the environment had not worked for New Zealand in 1975, and would have been even harder after CRAMRA's adoption.

Stability in Antarctica

The stability of the ATS as a whole provides confidence. While the minerals and environment debates dominated proceedings for some years, Antarctic affairs had never been a single issue. There were key principles to protect, including allowing scientific freedoms, protecting the territorial status quo, and preserving non-militarisation. Quarantining Antarctic affairs from other issues made it possible for states otherwise in dispute to maintain harmony—for example, during the Cold War and cooperation with South Africa despite anti-apartheid sanctions.[43] Argentina and the United Kingdom squabbled over South Atlantic islands during the minerals debate but, as Beeby recalled, "neither of those two delegations, nor any other, spoke a single word about the Falklands/Malvinas".[44] Despite

---

[39] Argentina's sustained objection to an Antarctic Treaty Secretariat was another example.

[40] Beeby, "The Antarctic Treaty System: Goals, Performance and Impact," 18–19. Rolf Trolle Andersen, "Negotiating a New Regime: How CRAMRA Came into Existence," in *The Antarctic Treaty System in World Politics*, ed. Arnfinn Jørgensen-Dahl and Willy Østreng (Macmillan/Fridtjof Nansen Institute, 1991), 108.

[41] Kjell Magne Bondevik, "Foreword," ibid., ed. Arnfinn Jorgensen-Dahl and Willy Ostreng, xxi.

[42] Rolf Trolle Andersen, "Negotiating a New Regime: How CRAMRA Came into Existence," ibid., ed. Arnfinn Jørgensen-Dahl and Willy Østreng, 95–96.

[43] 1 August 1986, Bob Beale "South Africa uses Antarctic Treaty to keep doors open" *Sydney Morning Herald*, 12.

[44] Beeby, "The Antarctic Treaty System: Goals, Performance and Impact," 4.

the hostilities, they protected the Treaty's integrity and their influence as ATCPs.[45] States sympathetic to Malaysia in the UN remained committed to the Treaty.[46] Maintaining stability provided a safe environment for handling difficult problems and the resilience necessary to deal with the most significant challenges.[47]

Such resilience had to be earned. Fear of instability was one reason why minerals were avoided in the Treaty, and then deferred for so long. With the issue simmering since the 1958 Continental Shelf Convention, avoiding it was no oversight.[48] Unresolved sovereignty explained why the 1982 UN Convention on the Law of the Sea (UNCLOS) did not tackle the Antarctic waters problem, deferring it to the ATCPs.[49] Before the IGY, minerals had been seen as one of Antarctica's nine key issues.[50] Most were tackled, but not minerals.[51] Mining raised sensitive problems such as sovereignty, jurisdiction and confidentiality of scientific results.[52] John Heap thought the minerals problems were underestimated and "the most explosive issue ... the thing most likely to tear the Antarctic Treaty apart".[53]

[45] Joyner describes this as 'political pragmatism'. Joyner, "Anglo-Argentine Rivalry after the Falklands/Malvinas War: Law, Geopolitics, and the Antarctic Connection," 499–500.

[46] Many authors have assessed the impact of the UN consideration of Antarctica: Tepper and Haward, "The Development of Malaysia's Position on Antarctica: 1982 to 2004." Joyner, *Governing the Frozen Commons*, 235–51. Haward and Mason, "Australia, the United Nations and the Question of Antarctica."

[47] The resilience of the ATS has been assessed in: Mel Weber, "The Strength to Continue: A Case Study Approach to Examining the Robustness of Polar Governance in the Era of Environmental and Energy Security" (PhD thesis, University of Tasmania, 2011).

[48] Bush, *Antarctica and International Law: A Collection of Inter-State and National Documents*, Vol I, 288.

[49] Bernard H. Oxman, "Antarctica and the New Law of the Sea," *Cornell International Law Journal* 19 (1986). Morell, *The Law of the Sea: An Historical Analysis of the 1982 Treaty and Its Rejection by the United States.*

[50] C. Wilfred Jenks, "An International Regime for Antarctica?" *International Affairs* 32, no. 4 (1956): 418.

[51] Wolfrum suggests that mining *was* brought up at the Antarctic Treaty conference: Rüdiger Wolfrum, "The Exploitation of Antarctic Mineral Resources: Risks and Stakes," in *The Antarctic Environment and International Law*, ed. Joe Verhoeven, Phillipe Sands and Maxwell Bruce (Graham & Trotman, 1992), 27.

[52] Lewis M. Alexander and Lynne Carter Hanson, eds., *Antarctic Politics and Marine Resources* (University of Rhode Island, 1985), 18. Elliott, *International Environmental Politics: Protecting the Antarctic*, 108–09.

[53] 18 October 1972, ANT/17 "Antarctic resources of effects of mineral exploration: draft Recommendation submitted by the United Kingdom" https://documents.ats.aq/ATCM7/wp/ATCM7_wp017_e.pdf (accessed 10 March 2020). John A. Heap, "The Treaty and the

The Treaty negotiators could have banned mining, as they did for military manoeuvres, weapons testing and radioactive waste disposal. Being a peaceful use with potential economic benefit, presumably they wanted the option left open. Eventually, despite the sensitivities, Parties felt confident that minerals could be addressed. Even the idea of prohibiting mining threatened stability because mining might proceed anyway (although it was never suggested that weapons testing and radioactive waste disposal would occur contrary to the prohibitions).[54]

Further potential destabilisation came from the 1991 opportunity for a Treaty review to be called. Realistically, it is unlikely that the Treaty could have been re-negotiated or that a more effective regime would result.[55] That was no comfort, however, if stability were to be lost at the very time a review was called.

Deciding to tackle mining *before* minerals were found is also evidence of the importance attached to stability—had exploration been underway, the destabilising effects would have been even worse. There was a succession of ironies: initially, stability was achieved by *not* addressing minerals. Then, a minerals regime was negotiated lest the *absence* of one destabilise the Treaty. Finally, the regime itself precipitated instability when it was rejected. Throughout, the overriding objective was maintaining stability—ultimately restored by the Protocol.

Prospects of Mineral Wealth

Antarctica's minerals potential was a factor because of the possibility that resources might be found. The prospects of an Antarctic *El Dorado*, and fear of missing out, were potent. There was no evidence of viable resources, but no one said that nothing would ever be found. Had a fruitless search occurred, there would be need for neither regime nor prohibition. However, with belief that minerals *could* be found, the Parties acted as if they *would*. In addition, 1970s technology was allowing Arctic mining.[56]

Protocol," in *Antarctica: The Environment and the Future*, ed. G Mudge (International Academy of the Environment and International Peace Research Institute, 1992), 37.

[54] Burgess, "Comprehensive Environmental Protection of the Antarctic: New Approaches for New Times," 63.

[55] Alexander and Hanson, *Antarctic Politics and Marine Resources*, 97.

[56] Chaturvedi, *The Polar Regions*, 30–34.

While the Antarctic hazards are more challenging, technological progress was expected to make Antarctic mining more viable.[57]

The aspirations of Douglas Mawson and Lord Casey were strong motives for establishing Australia's first Antarctic station in 1954.[58] IGY turned up nothing, despite some considering it essentially an economic survey.[59] Subsequent expeditions found little, but that did not deter Dufek's optimism that resources would be discovered, or Law's optimism that they would be found in abundance and soon, although both ignored the fact that minerals had to be economically viable. Eventually, attitudes changed and even industry did not campaign to keep CRAMRA.

CRAMRA as Diplomatic Investment

The diplomatic investment in CRAMRA was important because major issues were addressed for the first time. The minerals problem was tackled because of the political risks of a major discovery in the absence of rules. Regulations would give miners legal security and encourage investors.[60] Sensitivities could be minimised if regulations were agreed in advance, a so-called "prophylactic provision" because a legal vacuum would be difficult to fill once a 'gold rush' occurred.[61] Accordingly, the diplomatic capital invested removed political, legal and environmental uncertainties, although the slow negotiations meant the moratorium's dependence on 'timely' progress was at risk. Nevertheless, CRAMRA's eventual achievements were lauded as a major contribution to international law.[62] Adoption by consensus "left everybody a little unhappy [and] probably meant that

[57] R. A. Cook and F. J. Davey, "Hydrocarbon Exploration and Potential," in *The Antarctic Sector of the Pacific*, ed. G P Glasby, Elsevier Oceanography Series (Elsevier, 1990), 182–85.

[58] Martijn Wilder, *Antarctica: An Economic History of the Last Continent* (Department of Economic History, the University of Sydney, 1992), 57. Swan, *Australia in the Antarctic: Interest, Activity and Endeavour*, 347–48.

[59] Adrian Howkins, *Frozen Empires: An Environmental History of the Antarctic Peninsula* (Oxford University Press, 2017), 19.

[60] US Congress Office of Technology Assessment, *Polar Prospects: A Minerals Treaty for Antarctica*, 19.

[61] Watts, *International Law and the Antarctic Treaty System*, 224. Christopher C Beeby, "The Antarctic Treaty System as a Resource Management Mechanism—Nonliving Resources," in *Antarctic Treaty System: An Assessment* (National Academy Press, 1986), 271.

[62] "The Convention on the Regulation of Antarctic Minerals and Its Future." Watts, *International Law and the Antarctic Treaty System*, 221–51. Elliott, *International Environmental Politics: Protecting the Antarctic*, 135–61.

the negotiators had managed to strike the necessary balances".[63] CRAMRA removed legal uncertainty, and mining was neither promoted nor prohibited. To that extent, it was neutral. But it did provide the means to judge whether mining, if it occurred, would be acceptable. Despite its deficiencies, it also protected the Treaty by avoiding conflict.[64]

CRAMRA was more controversial *after* its adoption than during its negotiation.[65] Its detractors said that by allowing the possibility of mining, it implied that mining could be environmentally safe—in other words, it was *not* neutral. This argument came from Australia, a Party that had strengthened CRAMRA's environmental provisions. It is ironic that CRAMRA's title (also suggested by Australia) was a weakness because it neglected the environmental controls. As John Heap put it, "the care that CRAMRA expressed for the Antarctic environment was seen by some as not being innovative enough".[66] This proved a significant political flaw.

Rejection of the regime was galling for diplomats accused of having got things so wrong. There was understandable reluctance to abandon a diplomatic success—especially as the hard-won consensus to fill a regulatory gap was replaced by a vacuum. Some delegates had committed years of their diplomatic careers to Antarctic affairs. By 1989, Chile's Fernando Zegers had been involved in ATCMs for 14 years, and Tucker Scully of the United States for 12. Their service was dwarfed by John Heap, who started in 1966, 23 years earlier. Chris Beeby chaired all the CRAMRA negotiations, committing considerable personal energy. Many Antarctic careers (including those of Australians) spanned multiple meetings over more than a decade. Substantial effort had been invested by individuals but, even though CRAMRA did not succeed, the diplomatic investment was not entirely wasted. For a start, the negotiations thoroughly traversed an issue not resolved in the Treaty—had it not been done, the issue would still niggle. Secondly, negotiation of the Protocol drew directly from CRAMRA. Thirdly, the Protocol's review provisions require that lifting of the mining ban would have to include a regulatory regime, allowing for

---

[63] Andersen, "Negotiating a New Regime: How CRAMRA Came into Existence," 106–07.

[64] Alan Brown, "The Design of CRAMRA: How Appropriate for the Protection of the Environment," ibid., 113–14. Christopher C. Joyner, "CRAMRA: The Ugly Duckling of the Antarctic Treaty System?" ibid., 171–73. James N. Barnes, "Protection of the Environment in Antarctica: Are Present Regimes Enough?" ibid., 191–94.

[65] Watts, *International Law and the Antarctic Treaty System*, 5.

[66] Antarctic Treaty, *Final Report of the Sixteenth Antarctic Treaty Consultative Meeting, Bonn, 7–18 October 1991*, 197.

something like CRAMRA to be resurrected.[67] In addition, the techniques to wrangle complex issues strengthened the Treaty by proving that the Parties could tackle the most challenging problems.

The Mining Moratorium

The moratorium provided stability because it disadvantaged no one and allowed negotiations to proceed without distortion.[68] Despite being a pressure-relief mechanism, the moratorium added some uncertainty because of the implication that time was not unlimited. The Final Act of SATCM IV reaffirmed the moratorium pending CRAMRA's entry into force but, of course, that never happened.

While no one sought to exploit the breakdown of CRAMRA for mining, some exploited the *threat* of the moratorium's collapse to advocate for CRAMRA.[69] Pro-CRAMRA Parties argued that despite regulating mining the convention contained a potent mining ban, implying that the moratorium was less effective at inhibiting mining than CRAMRA itself. The argument rested on a Party's right to prevent opening an area—exercising that veto was as good as any mining ban in an environmental regime. Andersen argued "the consensus provision would prove to be an obstacle of such monumental proportions that such activity would for all practical purposes not take place".[70] Whether or not it was intended to operate that way, CRAMRA contained another obstacle: no mining could occur without liability rules, a requirement needing years to satisfy.[71] Even Chris

---

[67] "Protocol on Environmental Protection to the Antarctic Treaty", Article 25.5(a).

[68] Calling it a 'moratorium' was misleading as an activity not occurring could hardly be paused. Although the language gained popularity, the moratorium was actually cast more subtly, such as 'urging states to refrain'.

[69] Heap, "The Political Case for the Minerals Convention," 51. In May 1989, the United States threatened that if CRAMRA failed, it would no longer feel bound to observe the moratorium. 24 May 1989, WL36835 "Protection of Antarctic environment: CRAMRA" (NAA: B1387 89/311 PART 2).

[70] Andersen, "Negotiating a New Regime: How CRAMRA Came into Existence," 107.

[71] "Convention on the Regulation of Antarctic Mineral Resource Activities", Article 8(9). Rüdiger Wolfrum, "The Unfinished Task: CRAMRA and the Question of Liability," in *The Antarctic Treaty System in World Politics*, ed. Arnfinn Jørgensen-Dahl and Willy Østreng (Macmillan/Fridtjof Nansen Institute, 1991). The 'liability' annex under the Protocol took 13 years to develop and, at the time of writing, is yet to enter into force. It can be argued that Annex VI does not even address liability for environmental damage, providing only an obligation to respond to emergencies, or compensate those who do.

Beeby, a champion of CRAMRA, doubted that mining would ever be approved. This begged the question that if CRAMRA really acted as a ban, why not ban mining outright? The difference between a 'ban' under CRAMRA and a ban under an environmental regime was that if mining did nevertheless proceed, at least under CRAMRA it could be regulated.[72] CRAMRA's opponents were unconvinced. For a start, objections to opening an area did not prevent prospecting; it applied only to exploration and development. Australia considered this a "slippery slope" argument: if prospecting proved promising, it would be difficult to stop it proceeding to exploration and development.[73] In any event, promoting CRAMRA as a mining ban meant that any Party wanting to mine could simply prevent its entry into force. Alternatively, if Parties actually intended a mining ban, there was no reason for CRAMRA at all. Why, then, would CRAMRA advocates accept a ban implicit in the convention, but reject a ban explicit in an environmental regime? The difference was that CRAMRA's 'ban' was conditional: a Party could only veto opening an area if doing so was consistent with the convention.[74] More likely, by appropriating the language of a mining ban, the argument was used to improve the chance of CRAMRA surviving its critics.

That said, attachment to the moratorium remained strong. Even after CRAMRA was scuttled, taking with it a moratorium conditional on its timely entry into force, the moratorium survived. Chile proposed extending the moratorium during the impending environmental negotiations.[75] Thus, using a moratorium to encourage negotiations worked again, allowing time for the environmental debate to conclude. Even that did not end the moratorium idea. The Protocol perpetuated it one last time: Article 25 requires that if the mining prohibition is amended, the ban must continue "unless there is in force a binding legal regime on Antarctic mineral resource activities".[76]

---

[72] Beeby, "The Convention on the Regulation of Antarctic Minerals and Its Future," 57.
[73] 15 December 1989, "Antarctic IDC—Post-ATCM XV" (AWJ personal notes).
[74] "Convention on the Regulation of Antarctic Mineral Resource Activities", Article 41.2.
[75] 13 October 1989, "ATCM XV" (AWJ personal notes), 37.
[76] "Protocol on Environmental Protection to the Antarctic Treaty", Article 25.5(a).

Existing Environmental Concerns

Environmental concerns were prominent in the first two ATCMs and became an ongoing priority. SCAR achieved early attention to issues that led to the 1964 Agreed Measures.[77] The 1972 Seals Convention showed it possible to regulate something that was not happening, and completely protect certain species. CCAMLR showed it possible to prioritise conservation. Multiple other measures were then adopted. Internal inconsistencies and patchy implementation encouraged calls for their rationalisation, including Australia's seemingly premature call in 1983 for an environment convention.[78] IUCN proposed an Antarctic conservation strategy, as did the Australian Antarctic Foundation.[79] Such developments paralleled rising global environmental awareness which washed through the Treaty System, with concerns raised about compliance with the various obligations. Australia was criticised for environmental practices in Antarctica.[80] By May 1989, prompted by the *Bahia Paraiso* incident, Chile was calling for comprehensive environmental measures. Whatever happened to CRAMRA, the Parties had already agreed to review existing requirements.

Environmental concerns were embedded in CRAMRA, including obligations in Article 8 and the Final Act relating to response action and liability. So substantial were the hurdles that some characterised CRAMRA as an environmental regime. If so, its title was unfortunate—criticisms might have been thwarted had it reflected the environmental objectives.[81] David Lyons suggested that if CRAMRA's title had include the environment

[77] Martin J. Riddle and Paul M. Goldsworthy, "Environmental Science and the Environmental Ethos of Anare," in *Australian Antarctic Science: The First 50 Years of Anare*, ed. Harvey J. Marchant, Desmond J. Lugg and Patrick G. Quilty (Australian Antarctic Division, 2002), 564–66.

[78] 26 September 1983, ANT/XII/6/CORR 1 "Man's impact on the Antarctic environment" (AU-ATADD-3-BB-AQ-644). Senate Standing Committee on National Resources, "The Natural Resources of the Australian Antarctic Territory," 98–122.

[79] IUCN—The World Conservation Union, *A Strategy for Antarctic Conservation* (IUCN, 1991). Walton, "The Scientific Committee on Antarctic Research and the Antarctic Treaty," 80–81.

[80] 10 February 1984, "Australia neglecting Antarctic environment" *Canberra Times*, 9. 18 February 1986, Bob Beale "The Antarctic: our icy rubbish dump" *Sydney Morning Herald*, 1 and 7.

[81] Concerns about the implications of CRAMRA's title emerged early. 6 April 1989, PA73569 "Antarctica: Minerals convention: French position" (NAA: B1387 88/893 PART 3). 13 November 1989, UN048467 "Antarctica: Tinker Foundation seminar "Antarctica: Continent at Risk, New York, 10 November" (NAA: B1387 89/932 PART 1).

"it'd still be around ... although you joke about the titles of things, they are actually terribly important". ASOC's Lyn Goldsworthy agreed, saying that "a name change would certainly have made the convention more difficult to reject".[82] CRAMRA was thus a public relations failure as much as a political one.[83]

National Policy

National Antarctic policies informed negotiations within the ATS. Australian delegation briefing reflected the broad national interests which had evolved over many years. Douglas Mawson emphasised Antarctica's proximity, resource potential and scientific opportunities.[84] The interests later expanded to include peace, influence and environment protection.[85] Even if priorities changed, some elements remained consistent. The perennial sovereign interest was especially advanced during the minerals negotiations, with other claimants similarly motivated. It was not unusual to see tensions between objectives, such as between resource benefit and environment protection. National policies can evolve to reflect or influence developments within the Treaty, or respond to public opinion. On tabling CRAMRA in Australia's Parliament in November 1988, it was specifically noted that it would be assessed against resource benefit interests. Eight months later, on 13 July 1989, Cabinet deliberately excluded minerals from such benefits. New Zealand also saw policy reversals: it contemplated renouncing its territorial claim, then proposed a world park,

[82] Bowden, *The Silence Calling: Australians in Antarctica 1947–1997*, 409. Bowden quotes David Lyons (an Australian delegate to CRAMRA negotiations), who, in turn, credits Sweden. Ironically, CRAMRA's unfortunate title came from an Australian proposal—see Chap. 3.

[83] CRAMRA's public relations problem is explored by others: Brown, "The Design of CRAMRA: How Appropriate for the Protection of the Environment," 115. Scully, "The Development of the Antarctic Treaty System," 35–36. John Heap in: Antarctic Treaty, *Final Report of the Sixteenth Antarctic Treaty Consultative Meeting, Bonn, 7–18 October 1991*, 197.

[84] Mawson argued that "the geographical position of this land [Antarctica] privileges Australians in taking advantage of its products and renders the collection of scientific data therefrom obligatory upon us". 20 January 1911 'Lecture by Dr. Mawson: Appeal to Australians', *The Press*, 9.

[85] The changing priorities are explored in Jan Morgan, "Australia's Antarctic Policy: Theory and Practice" (University of Tasmania, 1996). Marcus Haward and Andrew Jackson, "Australia's Antarctic Future," in *Australia and the Antarctic Treaty System: 50 Years of Influence*, ed. Marcus Haward and Tom Griffiths (UNSW Press, 2011).

then championed CRAMRA, and then sought environmental provisions stronger than all other proposals.

Domestic policy-making processes were also relevant. Successive shifts of responsibility for Australian Antarctic policy from Foreign Affairs, to Science, to Environment reflected (and precipitated) policy changes. Even so, tensions between agencies arose—for example, arguments between the Foreign Affairs, Resources and Environment portfolios during the minerals debate.[86] Archival records reveal that arguments within delegations provided grounds for politicians to express doubts about CRAMRA. Likewise, the United States saw conflict between resources agencies, the National Science Foundation and the State Department (and, sometimes, between different parts of the State Department). Ministers occasionally intervened to the surprise of relevant agencies.[87] It is unclear what influence the resources industry had on UK policy but, at the height of the minerals debate, both Esso and BP International sponsored a British Antarctic Survey promotional book.[88]

Delegations took established positions into the minerals and environment debates, sometimes with considerable flexibility, or with instructions so rigid that instructions were sought during debates. Self-evidently, consensus is easier if every delegation has flexibility. As government representatives, officials were expected to advance national policy, although, on occasion, distinctions between personal and national interests blurred.

Domestic Politics

Domestic politics were a factor because of the influence on national positions. For most Parties, Antarctic affairs had a low profile. In countries with deep Antarctic traditions, policy was generally uncontroversial and enjoyed bipartisan support. But not always—in 1989, the then Opposition Leader John Howard and environment spokesperson Chris Puplick called for a mining ban. A conservative Opposition taking an environmental line

---

[86] Richard A. Herr and Bruce W Davis, "ATS Decision-Making and Change: The Role of Domestic Politics in Australia," in *Governing the Antarctic*, ed. Olav Schram Stokke and Davor Vidas (Cambridge University Press, 1996), 338–44.

[87] Consider interventions by Möllemann in Germany; Major in the United Kingdom; and Bush in the United States.

[88] "Antarctica: A Continent for Science," (British Antarctic Survey, 1987), 32.

was embarrassing to Hawke, adding a domestic political imperative.[89] Hawke denied Opposition policy influenced his thinking, but Howard celebrated wedging Hawke.[90]

Environmentalists had even greater impact. In Australia, environmentalists happily capitalised on Hawke's 1983 environmental credentials, and Hawke happily accommodated them. Craig Emerson (Bob Hawke's economics adviser) recalls that "every time we talk about the environment, our vote goes up".[91] NGO campaigns stirred public interest which politicians could not ignore. By 1990 Ministers had received over 4000 letters opposing mining and some 20,000 signatures on 21 petitions. Within a year, petitioners had reached 58,441.[92]

Germany's 300,000 signature petition was dwarfed by the more-than-one-million signatures on Cousteau's.[93] Cousteau achieved early traction in French domestic politics, Rocard responding in part to redeem France's environmental credentials after years of Pacific nuclear testing. Cousteau's Antarctic campaign, and Michel Rocard's reaction, provided cover for Hawke—although France had not formally opposed CRAMRA, Hawke could argue that the convention was in doubt and shift responsibility to France if necessary. Environmentalists also influenced New Zealand, the United Kingdom and the United States, and Parties that derided countries flirting with environmentalists also began to feel the pressure. Internationally, NGOs collaborated through ASOC, an umbrella group whose influence had strengthened in the minerals debate.[94] ASOC represented an amicable face, leaving Greenpeace to run provocative direct action at Dumont d'Urville airstrip and on Ross Island. Antarctica was no longer a low-profile area of diplomacy where NGO demands could be

---

[89] 24 May 1989, Keith Scott "NZ criticism for park decision" *Canberra Times*, 14. 24 May 1989, "A risky strategy on Antarctica" *The Age*, 13.

[90] 25 February 1990, Prime Minister (Hawke) "Transcript of debate with Andrew Peacock, Leader of the Opposition, ABC Studios, Sydney" (AU-ATADD-4-BB-AQ-109). 6 March 1991, House of Representatives Hansard, 1419. 17 August 1990, Senator Fred Chaney media release "Antarctic mining ban" (AU-ATADD-1-BB-AU-335).

[91] Emerson, *The Boy from Baradine*, 184.

[92] 8 July 2010, AAD email to author "FW: Enquiry from NAA re Antarctic mining".

[93] 19 November 1990, "XI SCM" Opening statements (AWJ personal notes), 3. 23 February 2020, "Saving Antarctica" *The History Hour* BBC World Service, https://www.bbc.co.uk/programmes/w3csypzz (accessed 6 April 2020), 7:12.

[94] ASOC's history is summarised at: https://www.asoc.org/about/history (accessed 3 February 2021).

dismissed as minor irritations, fuelled by misinformation and timed to influence elections.

Side–stepping suggestions that he was hostage to environmentalists, Bob Hawke saw rejecting CRAMRA as assisted by a "rising tide of public opinion which the bureaucrats and their political masters would not be able to withstand".[95] Environment Minister Richardson denied Hawke was "buying votes for any election".[96] Nevertheless, facing a 1990 election the government needed to re-assert its environmental credentials when the Opposition appeared greener on Antarctica. Bob Hawke and John Howard found the Antarctic issue attractive given strong public opinion and no industry to disappoint. Diplomats and lawyers resented the misleading campaign material, but politicians could not ignore the mood, however ill-informed. NGOs were consulted and increasingly represented on Treaty delegations and, once started, became impossible to stop. Greater transparency increased public attention, and thus even greater government responsiveness.

World Park Aspirations

The world park idea formed the prime conceptual alternative to a minerals regime, although, with no such thing as a 'world park', it was only ever an intangible concept. However vague, it conveyed an image that, for some, avoided the problems of managing resources. Without such an option, it was easy to suggest that the only alternative to a minerals regime was unregulated chaos. With appealing images of Antarctic wildlife and wild landscapes, it was a potent message for bumper stickers, banners and books.[97]

Despite the world park idea being attributed to New Zealand by many authors, its genesis was well before New Zealand gave it short-lived legitimacy in 1975. The concept had surfaced in 1961 with Robert Carrick's nature reserve proposal, echoed by Robert Cushman Murphy's 1962 call

[95] Hawke, *The Hawke Memoirs*, 467–68.

[96] 9 April 1989, transcript of Laurie Oakes' interview, National Nine Network (NAA: B1387 88/893 PART 3).

[97] See, for example: Barnes and Porter, *Let's Save Antarctica!* Barney Brewster, *Antarctica, Wilderness at Risk* (Sun Books, 1982). J. G. Mosley, *Antarctica, Our Last Great Wilderness* (Australian Conservation Foundation, 1986).

for an international sanctuary.[98] Thus, the concept's originators were scientists, not environmentalists. Later, it was championed primarily by environmentalists and, perhaps *because* it was promoted by NGOs, Parties dismissed it as unrealistic. Support by some scientists did not improve its prospects.[99] The best it achieved was relegation as a premature idea.[100] Nevertheless, it became emblematic of an environmental regime. ASOC acknowledged that the idea could be interpreted in many ways.[101] Some argued for CRAMRA operating alongside a world park.[102] This may have been anathema to purists but even some NGOs essentially abandoned world park ideals, preferring to strengthen CRAMRA's environmental provisions. The Fund for Animals' Annette Horsler conceded that "a world park was not feasible and unlikely to achieve the Fund's objectives".[103]

Inconsistent and sometimes nonsensical nomenclature did not help: it looked like environmentalists did not know what they wanted. As Hildebrand observes, "naming, as any explorer knows, is as much about controlling a landscape as describing it".[104] Failure to find a clinching title did not help sell a world park as a way of controlling the environment. Over 20 options were proffered, ranging from the loftily inspired to the

[98] Carrick, "Conservation of Nature in Antarctica," 534. This built on his earlier ideas in: "Conservation of Nature in the Antarctic," ibid., no. 66 (1960). Robert Cushman Murphy, "Antarctic Conservation: Only by Careful Planning and Cooperation Can We Save This Primeval Region from the Ravages of Man," *Science* 135, no. 3499 (1962): 195.

[99] J. G. Mosley, "The Natural Option: The Case for an Antarctic World Park," in *Australia's Antarctic Policy Options*, ed. Stuart Harris (Australian National University, 1984). W. A. Budd, "Scientific Research in Antarctica and Australia's Effort," ibid., 246. 21 April 1986, ANT SCM/8 ASOC Paper no. 4 "The World Park option for Antarctica". (NAA: B1387 1985/889 PART 2).

[100] Elliott, *International Environmental Politics: Protecting the Antarctic*, 169.

[101] 21 April 1986, ANT SCM/8 ASOC Paper no. 4 "The World Park option for Antarctica". (NAA: B1387 1985/889 PART 2).

[102] 21 December 1988, House of Representatives Hansard, 3920.

[103] Senate Standing Committee on National Resources, "The Natural Resources of the Australian Antarctic Territory," 119.

[104] John Hildebrand, *A Northern Front: New and Selected Essays* (Borealis, 2005), 27.

gratingly inelegant.[105] Even 'wilderness' was ill-defined.[106] Hawke himself was baffled: "evocative images of rapturous wonder are not sufficient to sustain public policy, particularly in areas of international relations."[107] While Antarctica's wilderness and aesthetic values have been recognised, quantifying them is hard.[108]

The world park concept, nevertheless, captured public attention and formed an important backdrop to the minerals debates by providing a vision, albeit clouded, of an alternative. Ironically, the Protocol embodied the practical effect of a world park with a mining ban in a binding environmental regime. It included a unique designation (Natural Reserve, Devoted to Peace and Science), although one of such dubious euphony it is never used. But in an important distinction from earlier concepts, the Protocol forms part of the ATS, alleviating perennial confusion with world heritage, the common heritage of humankind and other United Nations connotations.

COINCIDENTAL AND CONCURRENT EVENTS

Parallel events influential in the Antarctic debates included technological developments; resource scarcity concerns; rising environmentalism and domestic politics; developments in international law; growing UN interest

[105] The nomenclature used included: nature reserve (1962); international park (1962); international sanctuary (1962); international nature reserve (1963); special conservation area (1964); world park (1972); international reserve (1975); international park (1975); national park (1975); world preserve (1979); world natural heritage (1979); Antarctic world park (1985); Antarctic Treaty park (1987); Antarctic conservation zone world wilderness park (1988); wilderness park (1989); wilderness reserve (1989); world heritage park (1989); world nature park (1989); Antarctic global commons (1989); world wildlife park (1990); global preserve (1990); ecological reserve (1990); international wilderness preserve (1990); global ecological commons (1990); natural reserve, land of science (1990); and natural reserve, devoted to peace and science (adopted in 1991).

[106] Joyner, "CRAMRA: The Ugly Duckling of the Antarctic Treaty System?" 174–77. James N. Barnes, "Protection of the Environment in Antarctica: Are Present Regimes Enough?" ibid., 210–11.

[107] Robert J. L. Hawke, "Australia's Policy in Antarctica," in *Antarctica's Future: Continuity or Change?*, ed. R. A. Herr, H. R. Hall, and M. G. Haward (Australian Institute of International Affairs, 1990), 17.

[108] T. J. Tierney and G. W. Johnstone, "Conserving Australia's Wilderness: Antarctica as Wilderness," in *Australia's Wilderness: Conservation Progress and Plans*, ed. Geoff Mosley (Australian Conservation Foundation, 1978). Rupert Summerson and Ian D. Bishop, "Aesthetic Value in Antarctica: Beautiful or Sublime?" *The Polar Journal* 1, no. 2 (2011).

in Antarctica; impending challenges to the future of the ATS; and developments in bilateral relations.

Technological Developments

The 1968 discovery of Alaska's Prudhoe Bay oil field precipitated serious interest in polar minerals. Arctic mining technologies rapidly developed, but Antarctica presented greater technical challenges, riskier environments and much greater distance to refining facilities and markets. Nevertheless, as Arctic expertise grew, so did optimism about solving Antarctica's technical problems, at least for seafloor resources. At least one study was confident that new technology would made Antarctic mining plausible.[109]

Iceberg harvesting was also contemplated when the question of their ownership attracted attention in the 1970s. One entrepreneur applied to capture icebergs to "provide a solution to a freshwater problem in Perth".[110] The idea was floated again to solve South Africa's drought and trials were proposed for Western Australia, but the idea sank when environmental, regulatory and technical hurdles were queried.[111] An entire conference examined technical solutions to an activity that has never occurred.[112]

[109] De Wit, *Minerals and Mining in Antarctica: Science and Technology, Economics and Politics*, 8–42. US Congress Office of Technology Assessment, *Polar Prospects: A Minerals Treaty for Antarctica*, 155–70, 71–80.

[110] 6 October 1977, "Aust may rule the icebergs" *West Australian*. 8 November 1977, House of Representatives Hansard, 3124. 20 November 1978, letter from A. H. Perry to Minister for Science (NAA: B1387 80/456).

[111] 30 April 2018, Lucinda Dordley "Could an iceberg help Cape Town's water crisis?" http://www.capetownetc.com/news/icebergs-help-city-water-crisis/ (accessed 3 February 2021). 11 July 2019, "United Arab Emirates entrepreneur's $80m plan to drag Antarctic iceberg to Perth" https://thewest.com.au/business/water/united-arab-emirates-entrepreneurs-80m-plan-to-drag-antarctic-iceberg-to-perth-ng-b881255618z (accessed 3 February 2021). 14 August 2019, "Why a Middle Eastern business thirsty for water can't just tow an iceberg from Antarctica" https://www.abc.net.au/news/2019-08-14/why-a-middle-eastern-business-cant-just-tow-antarctica-iceberg/11318638 (accessed 3 February 2021).

[112] Husseiny, *Iceberg Utilization*. Technical options are still examined—see Bruno Spandonide, "Iceberg Water Transportation from Antarctica to Australia" (PhD thesis, University of Tasmania, 2012).

Resource Scarcity

Antarctic minerals discussions pre-dated the October 1973 OPEC oil embargo, the issue having been aired in 1970 Treaty meetings and listed on the 1972 Treaty agenda. The June 1973 Nansen Foundation conference also preceded the 'oil shock'—it had been proposed before the *Glomar Challenger* discoveries in the Ross Sea and therefore, while easily misinterpreted, was not a response to them.[113] Nevertheless, speculation grew about Antarctic oil filling future shortfalls. Meanwhile, the Trans-Alaska Pipeline was commissioned as Arctic production accelerated.[114] The coincidence of the oil shock coming so soon after *Glomar Challenger*'s February 1973 discoveries, and oil security fears, provided an important incentive for Antarctic minerals discussions.

This book does not further explore the global concerns about resource security for hydrocarbons and other minerals. The key point is that the Treaty consideration of minerals and, later, the oil embargo echoed broader concerns about resource sustainability and the Club of Rome report on the 'limits to growth'.[115]

Rising Environmentalism and Domestic Politics

Debate about Antarctica's future reflected the global environmentalism of the 1970s and 1980s. CRAMRA had strict provisions—its institutional decision-making processes and environmental requirements were significant disincentives to mining.[116] Nevertheless, global environmental concern impinged on CRAMRA's acceptability. Governments witnessed rising domestic environmentalism embrace Antarctica, starting in Australia and France, then playing out in other constituencies. France already had Jacques Cousteau campaigning on marine and nuclear issues and, in

---

[113] Auburn, *Antarctic Law and Politics*, 244–45.

[114] https://history.state.gov/milestones/1969-1976/oil-embargo (accessed 3 February 2021). https://aoghs.org/transportation/trans-alaska-pipeline/ (accessed 3 February 2021).

[115] Donella H Meadows et al., *The Limits to Growth: A Report for the Club of Rome on the Predicament of Mankind* (Universe Books, 1972). This assessment of global resource sustainability had its origins in 1968.

[116] Beeby, "The Convention on the Regulation of Antarctic Minerals and Its Future," 52–56. Watts, *International Law and the Antarctic Treaty System*, 267–76.

Australia, state-based issues had attracted national political attention when electoral success was at risk. Hawke, conscious of the fate of leaders ignoring public demands, invoked Federal powers to override a Tasmanian hydroelectric scheme.[117] This proved potent in a place where political positions are prompted by parochial problems. Tasmania delivered no seats to Hawke's 1983 election victory but established his national reputation as an environmental politician. Both Hawke and Environment Minister Richardson deny that Tasmanian politics had any influence on rejecting CRAMRA.[118] Richard Woolcott disagreed, attributing Hawke's motives as "essentially political and related to the green vote" in Tasmania.[119] Quite apart from election timing, environmentalists strongly influenced Australian politics.[120] By coincidence, the Antarctic minerals question arose just as campaigning concluded on the Tasmanian dams issue. Emboldened by success in Tasmania, within days NGOs turned to Antarctica for another campaign.[121]

From the mid-1980s, Australian parliamentarians and journalists were invited to Antarctica in the hope of increasing public awareness.[122] At the time of Australia's CRAMRA decision, the government faced a hostile Senate with pro-environment independents and Democrats holding the balance of power and Labor likely unable to pass CRAMRA's

---

[117] There was international dismay at the flooding of Lake Pedder National Park to divert water to an adjacent catchment. D. A. Lowe, *The Price of Power: The Politics Behind the Tasmanian Dams Case* (Macmillan, 1984). B. Galligan, "The Dams Case: A Political Analysis," in *The South West Dam Dispute: The Legal and Political Issues*, ed. M. Sornarajah (University of Tasmania, 1983), 110–14.

[118] 29 May 1989, transcript of interview, Radio NZ *Good Morning NZ* (NAA: B1387 89/311 PART 2).

[119] Woolcott, *The Hot Seat: Reflections on Diplomacy from Stalin's Death to the Bali Bombings*, 214. Hawke and Rielly, *Wednesdays with Bob*, 47–48. Just before the Hawke government decision, five Greens candidates succeeded in Tasmanian state elections, increasing the Greens' Federal prospects.

[120] Ton Bührs and Peter Christoff, "'Greening the Antipodes'? Environmental Policy and Politics in Australia and New Zealand," *Australian Journal of Political Science* 41, no. 2 (2006): 227–36.

[121] 4 July 1983, "Antarctica to be new target for conservation" *Canberra Times*, 5. The Tasmanian dams case had been resolved in the high court three days before, on 1 July 1983, see Michael Coper, *The Franklin Dam Case* (Butterworths, 1983).

[122] Bowden, *The Silence Calling: Australians in Antarctica 1947–1997*, 412–13. Stephen Murray-Smith, *Sitting on Penguins: People and Politics in Australian Antarctica* (Hutchinson, 1988).

implementing legislation.[123] It gave confidence to other Parties that "Australia would eventually draw back … after the Australian elections".[124]

Domestic politics in other Parties played an equivalent role. For example, the success of Green parties in Europe and increased activism in New Zealand, the United Kingdom and the United States, contributed forcefully to changing policy.[125] Public sympathy for environmental campaigns influenced governments in ways that diplomacy could not. NGOs supported the Australian government with campaigns targeting media or politicians overseas, provoking the United Kingdom's Garel-Jones' displeasure "that Australia might be orchestrating these pressures".[126] Environmentalists influenced with a timeliness and impact that would be impossible using regular diplomatic channels. By allowing NGOs to act as agents for government policy, environmentalists acted as both antagonists and protagonists.[127]

Concurrent Developments in International Law

Other developments in international environment law informed Antarctic debates. The 1982 UN Convention on the Law of the Sea was concluded just as the minerals debate got under way. Various other instruments addressed global and regional environmental issues—such as agreements on ozone depletion, marine pollution, fisheries, migratory animals, transboundary movement of wastes, nuclear energy and environmental liability. Such parallel developments provided a broader context for the Antarctic debates.

---

[123] Grahame Cook, "Possible Future Developments," in *The Future of Antarctica: Exploitation* Versus *Preservation* (Manchester University Press, 1990), 100. Three weeks before the government decided to reject CRAMRA, the Senate had called on the government not to sign it: 3 May 1989, Senate Hansard, 1647–1669.

[124] 8 January 1990, WH112169 "Antarctica: US policy on CRAMRA: Keystone meeting" (NAA: B1387 89/932 PART 1).

[125] See, for example: 27 August 1990, WL41558 "New Zealand: environmental groups" (NAA: B1387 90/759 PART 2). 11 September 1990, WH120835 "Antarctic environment: US views" (NAA: B1387 90/759 PART 1).

[126] 9 November 1990, LH114959 "Antarctica: consultations with the United Kingdom" (NAA: B1387 90/759 PART 3).

[127] 30 April 1990, DFAT minute "Antarctica: meeting with NGOs, Tuesday 1 May" (NAA: B1387 89/932 PART 3). 1 May 1990, author's handwritten notes "NGOs briefing" (NAA: B1387 90/498 PART 3). 12 February 1991, CE989529 "Antarctica: US position: Environmental initiative" (NAA: B1387 1991/55 PART 1).

Developments in International Relations

Coinciding with the Antarctic minerals debate were growing challenges to the Treaty in the United Nations General Assembly, erupting in 1983 with Malaysia pursuing the 'Question of Antarctica' and timed to disrupt the minerals negotiations.[128] The annual debates had amplified impact in a global forum where Antarctic states were in the minority. Malaysia's challenge rested on the common heritage of humankind concepts developed ahead of Law of the Sea negotiations. Prime Minister Mahathir asserted that Antarctica was locked up by wealthy Western nations' colonial attitudes.[129] Treaty Parties were accused of securing exclusive benefits from Antarctica's presumed mineral wealth. The Parties' response, that the Treaty was open to any UN member, was tempered by the knowledge that participation in decision-making required the means to establish an Antarctic station, essentially confirming privileged access for wealthy nations.[130] The ATCPs had to develop a regime sufficiently attractive that new players might be persuaded to participate, or risk them operating outside CRAMRA's regulatory controls.

Australia led defence of the Treaty in the UN, a role championed so successfully by Richard Woolcott as Permanent Representative that for many years no other Party would take it on.[131] Australia's work to keep the ATCPs united amplified the shock when it reneged on CRAMRA: an Antarctic stalwart had turned its back on the system it had defended. That effort had to be directed to re-establishing unity in the ATS lest it legitimise assertions that the Treaty could not be trusted to manage Antarctica.

Other parallel developments in international relations, including moves towards the reunification of Germany and the impending dissolution of the Soviet Union, had scant impact on the Antarctic environment debate.

---

[128] The criticisms originated in India's 1958 attempt to have the UN discuss Antarctica and Sri Lanka's initiative at the 1976 Non-Aligned summit. Bush, *Antarctica and International Law: A Collection of Inter-State and National Documents*, Vol I, 245–46.

[129] Beck, *The International Politics of Antarctica*, 270–99. Tepper and Haward, "The Development of Malaysia's Position on Antarctica: 1982 to 2004."

[130] India (also in the Group of 77, the main critics of the Treaty) acceded to the Treaty and met the requirements of becoming an ATCP. Possibly to Malaysia's surprise, it did so in 1983, the first year of the UN Question of Antarctica. Brazil (in 1983) and China (1985) also became ATCPs, somewhat blunting Malaysia's accusations of exclusivity.

[131] Woolcott, *The Hot Seat: Reflections on Diplomacy from Stalin's Death to the Bali Bombings*, 210–13. Haward and Mason, "Australia, the United Nations and the Question of Antarctica."

However, Malaysia's sustained criticisms led to suggestions that if the resources questions were removed, tiresome UN debates would abate.[132] There is no evidence that Australia's 1989 decision was influenced by international events—Australia, and other Treaty governments, appeared far more sensitive to domestic pressure.

Internal and External Challenges

One significant challenge was built into the Treaty itself: 30 years after its entry into force a Party could request a review conference.[133] The earliest it could be requested was 23 June 1991. With some understatement, Chris Beeby described this a "less than happy coincidence".[134] That coincidence amplified the implied threat: on the eve of the opportunity for a disaffected Party to request a review, consensus had been lost on one of the most fractious issues. There was no obligation for a review and, if triggered, did not mean the Treaty would change or end. Furthermore, a 'cooling-off' period was provided. Impetuosity was intentionally impeded.[135] Ultimately, no Party requested a review—on the contrary, effort was redoubled to restore consensus before 23 June 1991, and the Parties almost achieved it. The declaration adopted at the October 1991 ATCM confirms that the debate to restore consensus on the environment *became* the review.[136] Avoiding a review was in every Party's interest: all had something to lose if the delicate balances of the Treaty were upset.

A further imperative for restoring consensus was the impending June 1992 'Earth Summit'. The risk was that, in Rio, any disunity would reveal a Treaty incapable of managing a globally significant environment. Restoring consensus well before 1992 was urged.[137] Just as Antarctica had been quarantined from UNCLOS, so it was kept out of UNCED.

---

[132] Burgess, "Comprehensive Environmental Protection of the Antarctic: New Approaches for New Times," 65. Marie Jacobsson, "Building the International Legal Framework for Antarctica," in *Science Diplomacy: Antarctica, and the Governance of International Spaces*, ed. Paul Arthur Berkman, et al. (Smithsonian Institution Scholarly Press, 2011), 10.

[133] "The Antarctic Treaty", Article XII(2)a.

[134] Beeby, "The Antarctic Treaty System: Goals, Performance and Impact," 17.

[135] Daniels, "The Antarctic Treaty," 15.

[136] Antarctic Treaty, *Final Report of the Sixteenth Antarctic Treaty Consultative Meeting, Bonn, 7–18 October 1991*, 133–39.

[137] "Item 21: Any other business (A) UN/UNCED matters" in: October 1991, Australia "Brief for final session of SCM XI, Madrid, 3–4 October 1991" (AAD: B13/199). 14 October 1991, BO55790 "Antarctica—ATCM XVI—UN issues (NAA: B1387 90/703

Developments in Bilateral Relations

Bilateral developments also had influence. Australia's cooperation with France capitalised on both being original Treaty signatories, being claimants with shared Antarctic boundaries and enjoying mutual recognition of their claims. Dumont d'Durville was the closest Antarctic station to Australia. Even so, collaboration had been modest—occasional shared logistics and research projects. On environmental policy, there were sharp differences: for example, Australia vigorously opposed the French nuclear testing underway during the minerals debate.

In 1982, Australia was invited to join long-term French research at Dome C, deep within the AAT. While costly, this could have facilitated greater Australian access to the inland areas of its territory and boost scientific and logistic cooperation. The invitation was declined and Concordia was established with Italy. A complication was France flattening Îles des Pétrels to construct a rock runway. Australia considered supporting its construction and using the airfield itself.[138] Vigorous protests ensued and several Parties had reservations.[139] The United Kingdom accused France of breaching the Agreed Measures, and Greenpeace criticisms discouraged Australia.[140] Coming on top of France's environmental reputation in the Pacific, it was potentially awkward for Australia to collaborate in disrupting CRAMRA.[141] During the environment debate, Australia's relationship with France was close at the political level. At the level of officials, the relationship was patchy, with tactical disagreements and personality differences. Although the Antarctic environment initiative was forged by two Prime Ministers (Bob Hawke and Michel Rocard), it was often described as Australian. After becoming a 'Four Powers' proposal, Australia was still considered leader; Italy was new to Antarctica with a nascent scientific

PART 2). 19 November 1990, "XI SCM Plenary" (AWJ personal notes), 4–5. 26 April 1991, "XI SCM (Session II)—HODs" (AWJ personal notes), 50.

[138] 18 February 1982, Department of Science minute "Contact with the French regarding Antarctic air transport" (AAD: 81/346–1).

[139] 26 April 1985, BS20929 "Antarctic: French airstrip" (NAA: B1387 88/159).

[140] 4 June 1987, AAD submission to minister "Request from French for assistance to transport personnel from Antarctica (AAD: 81/346–2). 2 September 1987, AAD submission to minister "Transport of equipment for French Antarctic program on *Nella Dan*" (AAD: 81/346–3).

[141] Prime Minister Michel Rocard defended France's environmental credentials when the Antarctic initiative was developed. See 18 August 1989, CE764077 "Protection of Antarctic environment: Joint French-Australian initiative" (AAD: 89/578–1).

program; and Belgium had no program at all. The absence of a deep history of these Parties collaborating was an impediment—launching a major proposal without being confident of support from traditional allies appeared risky and some officials were pessimistic.

The situation was different with New Zealand. Well-established policy cooperation struggled after Australia reneged on CRAMRA, but differences evaporated when New Zealand itself abandoned the Wellington Convention.[142] More problematic for Australia were relationships with Norway, the United Kingdom and the United States. Strong bonds had been manifested, for example, in the Correspondents' Group run by the United Kingdom's John Heap. Abandoning CRAMRA jeopardised cooperation on *any* Antarctic issue if Australia were to be seen as disloyal or unpredictable. Restoring the Correspondents' Group post-Protocol allowed relationships to be restored.

Unexpected Circumstances

Some key influences in the Antarctic debate were entirely unanticipated, and the most obvious were maritime accidents. Despite causing harm, they occurred at a time when they could have maximum impact on environmental politics. Their importance is that they could not have been foreseen or orchestrated, yet their timing had undoubted influence on the minerals debate. Other serendipitous timing included the detection of Antarctic hydrocarbons.

Maritime Casualties

Had they come at another time, the 1989 run of accidents may been considerably less dramatic. Ship casualties in the Antarctic were not unusual, and several occurred during the development of CRAMRA: *Gotland II* sank in 1981; *Southern Quest* in 1986; and *Nella Dan* in 1987.[143] All were

---

[142] 7 February 1991, WL43003 "Antarctica: Environment protection: ANZ consultations" (NAA: B1387 90/888 PART 2).

[143] Klaus Strübing, "The Sinking of the German *M/V Gotland II* in Dec 1981 at the Oates Coast, Antarctica" (paper presented at the International Ice Charting Working Group, Hobart, 26 September 2017). Daniela Liggett, "Destination Icy Wilderness: Tourism in Antarctica," in *Exploring the Last Continent*, ed. Daniela Liggett, et al. (Springer, 2015), 389. Australian Transport Safety Board, *Report on the Preliminary Investigation in the Grounding of MV Nella Dan at Macquarie Island on 3 December 1987* (ATSB, 1988).

avoidable but did nothing to deter CRAMRA's negotiators. By the late 1980s, it could be argued that the spate of 'accidents' simply reflected increased Antarctic activity.

Marine pollution risks were already appreciated, and ATCM had begun addressing vessel construction standards and cooperation in hydrographic charting. Further incidents were inevitable—and they occurred with compelling impact. As governments considered signing CRAMRA, *Bahia Paraiso* ran aground off Palmer Station in January 1989. It had struck a rock not marked on Argentine charts.[144] The volume of fuel spilled was unprecedented for Antarctica and precipitated a multiparty clean-up and cooperative research into ecosystem impacts.[145] February's incidents involving the United Kingdom's *HMS Endurance* and Peru's *BIC Humboldt* had lesser consequences but further highlighted environmental risks.[146] In New Zealand, Geoffrey Palmer conceded that "there may have to be restrictions on who can sail into Antarctic waters".[147] John Heap reported Lord Shackleton saying that "it's not the best time to be asking Parliament to look at Antarctica with ships sinking and Greenpeace raising Cain". Heap also reported that "environmentalists have been on to us asking what means we had in the Antarctic of coping with such an accident. 'None', we said. 'Tut, tut' they said!".[148] Such dismissiveness would not last—within a week *Exxon Valdez* ran aground in Alaska. Immediately, a connection between polar mining and maritime safety was unavoidable. Several authors have noted the barely credible coincidence with the post-CRAMRA debate.[149]

---

[144] The United Kingdom asserted that the rock was marked on UK charts, underscoring calls for better cooperation on hydrographic charting.

[145] 12 May 1989, "Argentine presentation" (AWJ personal notes). 12 May 1989, "The sinking of the Bahia Paraiso—supplemental information provided by the United States government" (AU-ATADD-1-BB-AR-378).

[146] 20 February 1989, "Scientists urge Antarctic ban on minerals" *Canberra Times*, 2. Mary Lynn Canmann, "Antarctic Oil Spills of 1989: A Review of the Application of the Antarctic Treaty and the New Law of the Sea to the Antarctic Environment," *Colorado Journal of International Environmental Law and Policy* 1 (1990).

[147] 1 March 1989, transcript, Radio New Zealand *Morning Report* (NAA: B1387 1981/468).

[148] 17 March 1989, letter Foreign and Commonwealth Office "XVth Antarctic Treaty Consultative Meeting (NAA: B1387 88/352).

[149] Elliott, *International Environmental Politics: Protecting the Antarctic*, 165. Howkins, *The Polar Regions: An Environmental History*, 1–5, 154, 62–66. Jackson and Boyce, "Mining and 'World Park Antarctica'," 247–48.

Thus, an Arctic event shaped Antarctic history. Only those who could exploit the *Exxon Valdez* disaster to shift public attitudes to Antarctic minerals could consider it fortunate timing. The disaster, Joyner said, "paradoxically became a media bonanza for Antarctic environmentalists" and that it was "the best thing ever to happen" to them.[150] NGOs were not ashamed to exploit *Exxon Valdez*, even if misleading that Antarctic crude oil extraction was imminent, would use giant tankers, and oiled penguins and seals were inevitable (assuming, of course, that resources were in Antarctica, accessible, economic and used). It was a powerful message supported by real-time reporting of ruined fisheries and the agonising clean-up. Arctic images of oiled beaches, seabirds and marine mammals were far more effective than any Antarctic images of Ross Island waste or Dumont d'Urville bulldozers. The timing was perfect for illustrating what NGOs portrayed as certainty. Antarctic Treaty Parties could not deny the possible impacts of mining. Nor could they guarantee that CRAMRA's environmental controls and liability rules would be adequate if Antarctic mining was, one day, to proceed and an oil tanker were to founder.

The incident was not used by bureaucrats to inform Australia's 22 May 1989 Cabinet decision on CRAMRA, nor was it used in Hawke's media release.[151] Curiously, it was not until the following day that it was cited to justify Cabinet's decision: "the spill resulting from the *Exxon Valdez* has been perceived by the Australian community as demonstrating that it is impossible to prevent major accidents occurring".[152] Subsequently, it was drawn on repeatedly, its impact undeniable as it both illustrated and distorted the issues.

Unexpected Detection of Antarctic Hydrocarbons

Glomar Challenger's February 1973 excursion into the Ross Sea unexpectedly encountered traces of methane and ethane, of itself not extraordinary. Not anticipated was it triggering breathless speculation of vast oil reserves, or various corporations approaching governments about the

---

[150] Joyner, *Governing the Frozen Commons*, 150. "The Effectiveness of CRAMRA," 163.

[151] 12 April 1989, Cabinet Submission "Antarctic minerals convention" (NAA: 14039, 6415). 22 May 1989, Prime Minister "Protection of the Antarctic environment" http://pmtranscripts.pmc.gov.au/sites/default/files/original/00007607.pdf (accessed 3 February 2021).

[152] 23 May 1989, CE721590 "Protection of Antarctic environment" (NAA: B1387 89/311 PART 2).

prospects of further Antarctic surveys. The surprise arises because the voyage was not actually looking for resources.[153] Denying the evidence of resources, however, did not dull the expectation that they existed.

The accidental discovery further stimulated the Antarctic minerals debate and influenced the decision to adopt a moratorium. Had *Glomar Challenger* not encountered gas traces, the debate may not have proceeded with such vigour, or it may have been further deferred. On the other hand, deferring discussion may have allowed the long-feared scenario of an economic resource being confirmed before it could be regulated. After all, well into the CRAMRA debate, *Polarstern*'s Bransfield Strait voyage recovered marine sediments reeking of hydrocarbons—minerals discussions commenced after that may have proceeded with a quite different set of imperatives.

Leaders and Influencers

Explaining what happened requires more than identifying prior circumstances, concurrent or serendipitous events. The narrative also reveals the presence of individuals with distinct personalities and experience and who took advantage of such circumstances.

Antarctic Forums as a Platform for Leadership

We now turn to how leadership was demonstrated to achieve consensus, the end point of Antarctic diplomacy. To provide context, we will start by examining the ATCM and SATCM. Templeton and O'Reilly are among the very few authors to describe some of the otherwise opaque procedures of a normal ATCM, where established practices allowed diplomatic leadership to be exercised.[154] Given the sensitivities involved, discussing minerals triggered unusually stressful negotiations. It proved a "herculean task" on an "esoteric subject". Consensus was the objective: "no one was forced to positively say yes to an outcome, whilst all had the opportunity to say no", yet "all the delegations wanted to succeed". There was widespread use of

---

[153] As the objectives were seafloor geomorphology and plate tectonics, the voyage was instructed to stop drilling if gases were encountered.

[154] Templeton, *A Wise Adventure II: New Zealand and Antarctica after 1960*. Jessica O'Reilly, *The Technocratic Antarctic: An Enthnography of Scientific Expertise and Environmental Governance* (Cornell University Press, 2017), 113–14.

casual 'contact groups' on specific issues, drafting groups and impromptu 'corridor' consultations.[155] Such processes continued in the environment debate. The effectiveness of 'backroom' meetings was revealed by Georges Duquin's resentment of their use by opponents of a comprehensive regime (the reverse was undoubtedly true as well).[156] In addition, there was inter-sessional use of quasi-academic sessions to explore options—often 'invitation-only' events involving the same individuals, but ostensibly presenting personal views.[157]

Chairs enhanced proceedings with several techniques including consulting an 'inner circle', or circulating a chair's personal text to test ideas.[158] Continuity of chairing was crucial—notably Chris Beeby in CRAMRA and Rolf Andersen on the Protocol's mining ban. Continuity of delegates and strong interpersonal relationships complemented traditional diplomatic communications. Some commentary dismisses such connections between civil servants as "incestuous discussions with their counterparts".[159] It is certainly true that a distinct 'clubbiness' was evident with privileged delegates referred to by their given name, and others as 'the distinguished delegate'. Personal friendships used to foster common ground could lead to others feeling excluded. Nevertheless, meeting-to-meeting continuity provided invaluable 'institutional memory'.[160]

Another influence was the dominance of English despite there being four official languages.[161] As decisions and reports were almost invariably first drafted in English, native speakers sought to influence the result subtly by reinforcing a point or diluting by ambiguity. English speakers often

---

[155] Andersen, "Negotiating a New Regime: How CRAMRA Came into Existence," 94–96, 104–05.

[156] 26 February 1991, PA85745 "Antarctica: Meetings in March and April" (NAA: B1387 91/32 PART 2).

[157] These included the June 1973 Nansen Foundation meeting of experts; January 1985 Beardmore Glacier workshop; November 1989 Antarctica's Futures conference; April 1990 Australian Studies Centre conference; May 1990 Nansen Institute conference; July 1990 Kiel meeting; and October 1990 Louvain University symposium.

[158] The Whangaroa sessions illustrate Beeby convening an 'inner circle'.

[159] Garth Paltridge and Julia Jabour, "Antarctica and the Madrid Protocol," *Institute of Public Affairs Environmental Backgrounder*, no. 23 (1996): 2.

[160] Examples include Heap (United Kingdom), Scully (United States), Wolfrum (Germany) and Beeby (New Zealand). Joyner, *Governing the Frozen Commons*, 104.

[161] English, French, Russian and Spanish are official languages. The 29 ATCPs use at least 18 national languages. CRAMRA was the only time a fifth language, Chinese, was recognised: "Convention on the Regulation of Antarctic Mineral Resource Activities", Article 67.

sought to lead the drafting of decisions, and control the policy outcome by accepting or declining amendments and influence the words used to record the making of the decision.[162] Such language factors provided a privilege for English speakers and reinforced perceptions of the anglocentric character of the minerals and environment debates.

Also relevant was the operation of blocs to advance (or frustrate) developments.[163] The 'Four Powers' constituted a distinct bloc (although uncomfortable with the description), just as the United Kingdom and the United States operated as a pro-CRAMRA bloc. Such collaboration was particularly effective in meetings hosted in English when the 'Uniteds', often of compatible policy view, sat physically adjacent.[164] While advantageous for collaboration, blocs were neither formal nor applied to every issue. Sometimes it took temporary caucusing to advance an argument, even to the point of choreographing the sequence of interventions. Blocs, such as the 'Four Powers' and the 'Kiel 5', would also agree to endorse a particular position and employ identical language to promote it.

A less-obvious factor was a Party's offer to host a meeting. Prestige flows from a successful meeting and hosting could impact on a Party's approach to policy. For the minerals negotiations, Chile encouraged New Zealand to offer, which it willingly did.[165] In the environment debate, France was antagonistic towards CRAMRA but, in 1989, it was scheduled to host ATCM XV. France moderated its approach, Georges Duquin saying that "as host country, France would be reluctant to be seen as contributing to a breakdown [and] a diplomatic defeat for the ATS and France".[166] France was prepared to settle on a procedural outcome, in lieu of policy

---

[162] Consider debate over words like "agreed", "welcomed" or "noted" concerning a proposition, and debate over "most", "many", "several" or "some" to describe the level of support for it. Such perennial debates reflected "the mood of the room" or "the sense of the meeting". 6 December 1990, "Plenary (SCM report)" (AWJ personal notes), 74–76.

[163] Examples of blocs included the claimant states, the Southern Hemisphere Parties, European or Latin American Parties.

[164] The Parties sit in order of their name in the language in which the ATCM is hosted—most often this is English which allows the United Kingdom and United States to sit together.

[165] Chile appeared keen for a Southern Hemisphere claimant, other than Argentina, to chair. Templeton, *A Wise Adventure II: New Zealand and Antarctica after 1960*, 115.

[166] 22 September 1989, PA76777 "Antarctica—discussions with the French" (NAA: B1387 89/453 PART 3).

victory.[167] As host of the November 1990 SATCM XI, Chile held no ambition beyond "honest broker".[168] Similarly, Germany was concerned to avoid acrimony lest it disrupt the Bonn meeting.[169] France *also* wanted the Protocol resolved before the Bonn meeting because it resented the prospect of Germany getting credit for the environment initiative.[170] Hungry for diplomatic success, Spain urged compromise to secure agreement in Madrid and won the enduring cachet of the Madrid Protocol. A handbrake on engagement in policy debates came from chairing negotiations. New Zealand, for example, "avoided positions on many issues because of the need to protect Beeby's position". The neutrality of chairing could be advantageous if it allowed others to take the heat for unpopular positions. Chris Beeby, however, was confident that he could distinguish "between the role of a chairman and that of being an advocate for a New Zealand position".[171]

Interactions between individual participants relied on diplomatic conventions. While there can be a sense of performance, the participants were still individuals with differing personalities. At times, personalities revealed a national character. Without judging their effectiveness, it is undoubtedly the case that many styles were on display. Progress depended on the interactions of individuals and the minerals/environment debate became a story of individuals, political and diplomatic, government and non-government, and their personalities.

Elliott refers to key officials involved in the environment debate as the "bureaucratic elite".[172] Some of these led the delegations. Others were in the Foreign, Resources or Environment Ministries developing national policy. There was also a political elite, NGO elite and scientific elite. What has not been addressed here is the role of women in the debates. Antarctic environmental diplomacy, like Antarctic exploration, was male-dominated

[167] 18 October 1989, PA77195 "Antarctica: ATCM XV, Paris, 9–20 October—Report No 4" (AAD: 89/133–1).

[168] 5 November 1990, SC21314 "Antarctic environment: Indicative draft convention" (NAA: B1387 90/759 PART 3).

[169] 10 April 1991, BO53504 "Antarctica: SCM XI—Four country representations" (NAA: B1387 90/888 PART 3).

[170] 30 January 1991, GE92663 "Antarctic environment" (NAA: B1387 91/32 PART 1).

[171] 18 June 1984, WL19815 "Antarctica minerals meeting" (NAA: B1387 1981/343 PART 2). New Zealand's pursuit of its interests seems to have been held back in deference to Beeby's role. Templeton, *A Wise Adventure II: New Zealand and Antarctica after 1960*, 185 and 251. ibid., 251.

[172] Elliott, *International Environmental Politics: Protecting the Antarctic*, 125–26.

(it still is). At the time of the minerals and environment debates, women were in the minority in delegations and, with a few marked exceptions, even more in the minority as delegation heads. In the minerals negotiations, some 9% of delegates were women, but none were delegation heads. In the environmental negotiations, some 11% were women and just one led a delegation.[173] Women were far more prominent in the NGOs.[174]

Leadership

With consensus on the goal, leadership must be exercised to overcome objections or inertia. In Antarctic affairs, the problems in finding consensus were seen at various levels. The higher-level obstacle was how to agree on a vision for Antarctica's future, that is, the change from CRAMRA to the Madrid Protocol. A lower-level obstacle was, for example, finding an agreeable formula for reviewing the Protocol's mining ban. Either way, leadership was required to set directions and find solutions in a situation where, whatever the magnitude of the challenge, consensus was always the measure of success. By implication, the ultimate measure of leadership success was that others followed.

In international bargaining for regime formation, effective leadership comes from the thinkers who use the power of ideas; the agenda-setters and those who exercise negotiation skills to solve problems; or the structural leaders who exploit institutional or positional power.[175] Each form was in evidence during the minerals and environment debates, and often in combination. This book argues a special case for positional power where an individual's capacity for such leadership was enhanced by their affiliation with a particular Treaty Party. In fact, it goes further than that—within Antarctic forums, the power relationships of a *Party* can demonstrate influence independently of the individuals who might from time to time represent that Party—in other words, the simple fact that an individual (of any calibre) represents a particular Party may be sufficient to imbue that individual with a high degree of influence. In Antarctic affairs, such leader-

---

[173] The proportion of women on delegations had since risen to 25%.

[174] Emma Shortis, "'In the Interest of All Mankind': Women and the Environmental Protection of Antarctica," in *Feminist Ecologies*, ed. L Stevens, P Tait, and D Varney (Palgrave Macmillan, 2017).

[175] These have also been described as *intellectual* leaders, *entrepreneurial* leaders or *structural* leaders. Young, "Political Leadership and Regime Formation: On the Development of Institutions in International Society," 284–85, 303.

ship is inherently powerful and often the default form of influence. However, because of the Treaty's consensus operation, on many occasions in this story other forms of leadership were necessary to overcome obstacles.

LEADING WITH IDEAS

Intellectual leadership played an instrumental role and was often exercised at the level of officials who did not have to rely on the power of their positions to get their ideas heard. For example, initiative on the world park concept came from scientists, based on the early thinking of Robert Carrick. Such concepts formed the basis of the talismanic ideals championed by New Zealand in 1975 and environmentalists from the 1980s. These ideas were ahead of their time because they were objective proposals, rather than solutions to an existing negotiation problem. Nevertheless, they provided creative options for addressing the future of Antarctic resources, a matter not resolved by the Treaty.

The idea of a mining moratorium pending regulation was introduced by the United Kingdom's Brian Roberts in 1972, and given substance by Edvard Hambro at the Nansen Foundation in 1973.[176] It enabled careful pursuit of a minerals regime without the threat of negotiations being derailed by precipitate action. At the other end of the debate, Sweden's Kjell Anneling proposed that CRAMRA's title reflect its environmental provisions, generating "a few chuckles around the room".[177] Such reaction should not be used to belittle the idea—failure to adopt the suggestion spoiled the public acceptability of CRAMRA and contributed to its rejection, thus precipitating the 'crisis of consensus'.

Chileans had a history of providing intellectual leadership. Julio Escudero's proposed accommodation over the territorial claims later became the heart of the Antarctic Treaty.[178] In 1989, Fernando Zegers proposed a stand-alone environmental regime to update existing measures

---

[176] 11 October 1972, letter from FCO to AHC London "Seventh Antarctic Treaty Consultative Meeting, Antarctic Resources—effects of mineral exploration" (NAA: B1387 1991/462 PART 3). 29 May 1973, "Prepared remarks by Ambassador Edvard Hambro" (NAA: B1387 1991/370).

[177] Bowden, *The Silence Calling: Australians in Antarctica 1947–1997*, 409.

[178] Bush, *Antarctica and International Law: A Collection of Inter-State and National Documents*, Vol II, 383–86. Hall, *International Regime Formation and Leadership: The Origins of the Antarctic Treaty*, passim.

at risk of not being implemented. As an agenda-setter, Zegers offered Chile as host for a 1990 meeting to develop ideas, triggering a wave of support for his idea as a substitute for Australia's more ambitious objectives.

Political leaders achieved influence by relying on positional power. It could be argued that intellectual leadership was exercised by their staff. Bob Hawke's economics adviser, Craig Emerson, brought the minerals issue to the Prime Minister's attention shortly before the matter was to go to Cabinet. Emerson has revealed he was "shocked that a proposition as momentous as this could have made it through the system without the Prime Minister or his office being aware of it". Seeing the opportunity for "the fifth icon" (key environmental decisions of the Hawke government), he raised with Hawke the idea of putting a stop to CRAMRA and, behind the scenes, encouraged collaboration with France.[179] Such thinking did not come without risks and audacity does not correlate with intellectual leadership. While having domestic political appeal, it was not directed at problem-solving in the Antarctic debate—it actually served to create division internationally. It would take other skills to bring the Parties together in consensus.

Like Emerson's intervention, officials generating creative ideas were not necessarily present at negotiations but, rather, operating within government agencies. In Australia's case, after the Hawke Cabinet decision, the Foreign Ministry's Bill Bush developed the content of a comprehensive environmental regime between May 1989 and December 1990. His components paper, and subsequent iterations, were intellectual solutions to the international problem. Any solution proffered by Australia to a problem of its own making might immediately have been seen as self-serving. However, by setting a high benchmark, the Bush proposals forced others to think through the options. Most of the Bush structure and principles were adopted, even if not the specific language.

The United Kingdom's John Heap exercised influence in mid-1990 as the heat rose in the environment debate. It has been suggested that because Heap promoted a protocol as the *form* of regime, it necessarily means that he solved the regulatory problem.[180] At that time, however, the question of *form* was subordinate to the substantive content of the environmental measures. Whether this constituted intellectual leader-

---

[179] Emerson, *The Boy from Baradine*, 182–89. The other 'icon' issues were the Tasmanian wilderness, Kakadu, Queensland rainforests and Shelburne Bay.

[180] Richardson, "John Arnfield Heap, CMG," 265.

ship is moot: it was equally an attempt to prevent Australia and France being politically rewarded for their actions in 1989. In this book, John Heap's leadership is founded on positional power.

Some leaders were both intellectually creative and practical problem solvers. New Zealand's Chris Beeby stands out as Chair of the minerals negotiations guiding complex negotiations by creating the opportunities for solutions to emerge. He set the timetable, insisted on maintaining momentum and urged compromise. Beeby's effectiveness was greatly enhanced by circulating personal suggestions that drew on his understanding of meeting dynamics and the personalities involved, knowledge of the issues and insights into where common ground might be found.[181] Much of the creativity came in his choice of language to express complex ideas, supported by a willingness to abandon personal attachment to any particular formulation, and the use of refined interpersonal skills to maintain momentum.

AGENDA-SETTERS AND PROBLEM-SOLVING LEADERS

Agenda-setting leaders sought to have issues tackled collaboratively. An early example of this was the 1973 Nansen Foundation's meeting of experts to explore the scope of the minerals issue. Participation was limited to individuals with personal expertise, rather than representing the views of their states. Even if complete separation of state and personal views was unrealistic, it provided a safe environment for airing problems and posing solutions. Norway's credentials in convening such discussions stemmed from leading the minerals Working Group at ATCM VII the previous year. The Nansen Foundation and other academic forums repeated the process during the environment debate.

As noted above, Chris Beeby's agenda-setting leadership fostered productive negotiations. His approach refined the techniques that Australia's Keith Brennan and Tucker Scully from the United States had used during the CCAMLR negotiations. Beeby's use of informal discussions based on personal drafting was particularly successful. Progress on minerals was facilitated by informal meetings during SATCM IV, or inter-sessionally at Whangaroa, with 'Beeby Drafts' to focus debate. While Beeby formally chaired the negotiations in 1988, Norway's Rolf Andersen led the main

---

[181] See, for example, the use of personal drafts 'Beeby I' to 'Beeby VII' to construct a minerals regime. Templeton, *A Wise Adventure II: New Zealand and Antarctica after 1960*, 146.

committee.[182] Andersen's leadership continued into the 1990 environmental deliberations where he stimulated debate using similar techniques, demonstrated most effectively in the critical discussions in Madrid in April 1991 on provisions to review the mining ban.

Sweden's Desirée Edmar exercised influence in Madrid in April 1991 by independently circulating ideas for a formula to address a review of the mining ban. Germany's Rüdiger Wolfrum applied similar leadership in discussions on the vexed liability issues under CRAMRA (and, later, under the Protocol).

Environmentalists might argue that they exercised agenda-setting and problem-solving leadership by forcing a debate on environmental protection. However, objecting to something (such as CRAMRA) and demanding an alternative, *created* the negotiation problem rather than solved it. In many ways, environmentalists were followers rather than leaders, latching onto existing world park ideas or submitting drafts of an environmental instrument in response to work undertaken by the Parties. Thus, NGOs created the opportunity for leadership by others to flourish, and encouraged this by lobbying for progress.

LEADERSHIP BY POSITION AND POWER

Structural leaders apply leverage in negotiations by exploiting the 'power resources' flowing from positions they occupy. In the events covered in this book, such structural power often embraced several elements. For example, power might come from representing an original signatory to the Treaty or a claimant state (or both), command of English, prior experience and the reputation it generates, and so on. In Antarctic affairs, many exercising leadership do so as agents of the Parties, seeking outcomes that advance the interests of the states they represent—the leadership form most visibly exercised. This was done by many participants, including officials (such as diplomats, lawyers and advisers), and representatives of institutions or non-government organisations. Domestic politicians who directly engaged in the debate also provided influence. In addition to the leadership of individuals, the action of collective entities (such as Parties) is also relevant.

---

[182] Antarctic Treaty, *Final Report of the Fourth Special Antarctic Treaty Consultative Meeting on Antarctic Mineral Resources*, 4.

Diplomats as Structural Leaders

Diplomats represent their governments internationally, either bilaterally or in multilateral forums. In Antarctic affairs, delegation heads are typically career diplomats, supported by officials from relevant government agencies. Some delegation heads rotate through the position, but others park their careers on an Antarctic plateau, exchanging promotion for personal influence in a specialised area of diplomacy.

There is a degree of 'performance' in the work of diplomats, with theatrical skills employed to add emphasis or to persuade. In Antarctic affairs, credibility also attaches to polar experience, international legal expertise, and familiarity with the ATS itself. In the minerals and environment debates, experience in these last two areas gave some participants distinct advantages. Influence also came from an individual's association with a Party having a long connection to the Treaty, especially if that Party was an original signatory with all the respect conferred by long-term commitment and deep knowledge of Treaty norms.

It would be meaningless to rank diplomats in terms of their effectiveness in the minerals and environment debates. Nevertheless, it is possible to point to outstanding examples of diplomats exercising structural leadership. Some employed (or were bestowed) significant influence by virtue of power accrued from great intellect, personal presence and persuasive powers. A participant may have years of experience in Antarctic affairs and detailed knowledge of the subjects and participants. Adding value is fluency in English and the comfort of representing an original signatory with any of the assumed status it implies. And deeper still may be the satisfaction of being among the Antarctic territorial claimants, who often command attention. The participant's power is therefore more than personal; it is inherited from the fortunate heritage of their Antarctic 'citizenship'.

Chris Beeby is a good example: half his life was spent as a career diplomat. He previously represented New Zealand at the International Court of Justice in the *Rainbow Warrior* case, and was appointed as Ambassador to France.[183] His Antarctic diplomatic involvement commenced in 1981 as delegation head, leading to appointment as chair of the minerals negotiations. His leadership role was enhanced by being a native English speaker from an original signatory and claimant state. Coupled with his intellec-

---

[183] 21 March 2000, media statement, Foreign Minister "Passing of distinguished diplomat Chris Beeby" https://www.beehive.govt.nz/release/passing-distinguished-diplomat-chris-beeby (accessed 3 February 2021).

tual and entrepreneurial abilities, he achieved celebrated status as patient leader of the negotiations, a structural leadership role strengthened each time his appointment as chair was endorsed.

There are similarities with Rolf Andersen, a career diplomat with experience in negotiations for the Law of the Sea and CCAMLR. He first led Norway's delegation in 1982. By 1990, he was lead facilitator on the most sensitive issues in the environmental negotiations, his effectiveness enhanced as a fluent English speaker.

Leadership of a meeting can be achieved without chairing. John Heap carried considerable experience in Antarctic diplomacy with a remarkable recall of past practice, all conveyed with a characteristic gravitas. Heap stands out, starting his Antarctic career as a scientist, becoming a UK delegate in 1966 and, later, as head of the FCO Polar Regions Section representing the United Kingdom in numerous Antarctic forums and leading the delegation from 1983 to 1991. In Treaty meetings, the description of Heap as an "urbane and accomplished speaker" was understated.[184] He was the master of oratory, with interventions that demanded attention. His timing was impeccable, often coming at the end of a round of speakers, with many delegates unsure where debate would head until Heap had spoken. His impassioned speech at the ATCM XV Preparatory Meeting on 12 May 1989 was of such resounding impact that other delegations, impressed as much by the delivery as the words themselves, asked that it be circulated in writing.[185] Heap's influence relied on ownership of the paper being debated, being prepared to defend it and, by his own admission, "after all that, well it is all just theatre".[186] Heap's mastery of tactics not only dominated Treaty meetings, he also was adept at nurturing relationships inter-sessionally, most notably through the Correspondents' Group of like-minded 'old hands', invariably with the chummy sign-off, "yours ever, John".

Heap had been mentored by Brian Roberts, his equally well-regarded predecessor with structural power. Occasional differences between them did not diminish their influence. Heap's exercise of power was facilitated by the respect accorded him by others, sometimes tantamount to awe: his

---

[184] 18 March 2006, obituaries "John Heap" https://www.telegraph.co.uk/news/obituaries/1513269/John-Heap.html (accessed 3 February 2021).
[185] 12 May 1989, "ATCM XV—Prep" (AWJ personal notes), 38–39. 25 May 1989, LH75190 "Antarctica: UK statement at Paris Preparatory Meeting" (NAA: B1387 89/311 PART 2).
[186] Richardson, "John Arnfield Heap, CMG," 265.

minister, Tristan Garel-Jones, described Heap as "a figure of epic proportions, towering over the Antarctic scene".[187] Andersen referred to Heap as "Mr Antarctica".[188] Behind this was Heap's good fortune: a mastery of English with outstanding powers of persuasive speech; an unmatched ability to recall previous debate in precise detail; the cachet of being from an original signatory; and the weight of a representative of a claimant state not afraid to wield it. All these were material attributes of influence in Antarctic diplomacy. Yet it was not all seen positively: "Heap revealed himself as someone locked in a time zone … the political realities of the 1980s and 1990s needed to be looked at differently from those of the 1950s, 1960s and 1970s."[189]The last day of ATCM XVI, 18 October 1991, was also the last day of Heap's unmatched Treaty presence.[190] ASOC reported that many "appeared openly happy that John Heap's imminent retirement may end the power wielded by the UK and USA … he received endless accolades, not the least of which was a standing ovation at the close of the meeting".[191] What delegates witnessed was an unusual tribute to a remarkable individual, which Heap happily enjoyed as part of the 'theatre' he himself had created.

Another individual with such influence was Tucker Scully from the US State Department who had served on US delegations to Law of the Sea negotiations. Although a career diplomat, he was able to forego overseas posting and stay in Antarctic affairs.[192] He "survived some four Presidents" to retain his role.[193] Scully established a reputation as a leading force in

[187] 25 March 1991, Greenpeace meeting notes "Meeting with Tristan Garel-Jones" (NAA: B1387 1991/55 PART 2).

[188] Illustrating the depth of mutual admiration, Heap's reply was "Thanks, Rolf!". 12 May 1989, "ATCM XV—Prep" (AWJ personal notes), 38.

[189] November 1990, B.1 Overview in: "Antarctic Treaty Special Consultative Meetings X and XI, Viña del Mar, Chile 1990, Volume 1" (AAD: B13/199).

[190] Heap later found success as director of the Scott Polar Research Institute, but not his ambition of becoming head of a future Treaty Secretariat. Richardson, "John Arnfield Heap, CMG," 265–66. 23 October 1988, Roger Frankel (handwritten record of conversation) "Points arising from discussion with Gerard van Bohemen" (NAA: B1387 88/893 PART 1).

[191] October 1991, ASOC "Report of the XVI Antarctic Treaty Consultative Meeting, Bonn" (AU-ATADD-5-BB-GE-124).

[192] Christopher C. Joyner and Ethel R. Theis, *Eagle over the Ice: The US in the Antarctic* (University Press of New England, 1997), 232 at fn66.

[193] 25 October 1989, ST25515 "Antarctica: ATCM XV: Informal Swedish reaction" (NAA: B1387 89/453 PART 3).

CCAMLR negotiations, demonstrating structural leadership.[194] Apart from dealing with complex resource management and legal issues, in the minerals debate he faced conflicting national objectives and handled the "complicated agenda with considerable finesse".[195] During the environment debate, Scully was justifiably described as "America's most experienced Antarctic diplomat".[196] Like Heap, Tucker Scully was endowed by other Parties with power by virtue of his Treaty experience. Like Heap, he also represented an original signatory and exploited his command of English and outstanding ability to communicate a viewpoint. He was similarly persuasive in advancing issues concerning the United States, including on sovereignty and access to resources.

Heap and Scully could multiply their power by working in tandem with compatible policy positions and collaborating in their interventions. On one occasion, this resulted in a revealing (and presumably inadvertent) contribution when one delegation took the microphone to "agree with what John Scully said"[197]! Of course, representing different governments, they had their differences, but their individual influence made them formidable in partnership. The records suggest that the influence of 'the Uniteds' was such that some delegations were prepared to shelter behind Scully and Heap, who could do a more convincing job in advancing a case or withstanding objections. Such power blocs were obviously helpful for sympathetic delegations. As Australia's October 1989 delegation brief noted: "the considerable influence of the long serving representatives Heap, Scully and Andersen ... who caucus to organise the agenda, continues to be a feature of all Treaty System meetings."[198] This comment probably reflected some envy of their impressive experience and inimitable skills. A year later it was noted that "individual officials still wield considerable influence" but "the CRAMRA issue has receded to some extent [and] some old faces are not here".[199]

---

[194] Young, "Political Leadership and Regime Formation: On the Development of Institutions in International Society," 292.

[195] Templeton, *A Wise Adventure II: New Zealand and Antarctica after 1960*, 135.

[196] 9 January 1991, National Science Foundation media alert "Protecting Antarctica: Progress in Chile" (AAD: 89/914–2).

[197] 17 October 1991, "WG1" (AWJ personal notes), 65.

[198] October 1989, "15th Antarctic Treaty Consultative Meeting, Paris, 9–19 October 1989" (AAD: B13/192–1).

[199] November 1990, B.1 Overview in: "Antarctic Treaty Special Consultative Meetings X and XI, Viña del Mar, Chile 1990, Volume 1" (AAD: B13/199). 22 November 1990,

Curtis Bohlen, also from the United States, was another a structural leader.[200] While having less ATCM experience than Tucker Scully, he nevertheless occupied an influential position. At the Viña del Mar meeting, Bohlen "played an important part ... although not an expert in Antarctic matters, he left others in no doubt that the US position was changing".[201] Those 'others' included his subordinates in the State Department.[202] Bohlen was exercising a more conventional power, flowing from the influence afforded a high-level political appointment.

Australia also had structural leaders, typically career diplomats rotating through DFAT's legal division every two or three years between overseas postings. The environment debate drew in people such as John Burgess (with CCAMLR experience) and Brendan Doran (with ATCM experience). Eminent international lawyer Bill Bush was excused from overseas postings and led the Treaties Section. In the environment debate, the political profile of the issues, and the resistance encountered, saw very senior diplomats brought in. These included Alan Brown and, later, John McCarthy, who was praised by Foreign Minister Evans for "leading from the front".[203] Despite relatively short-lived involvement in Antarctic affairs, diplomats of such calibre deployed the skills essential for mounting a strong case. This was not easy—Australia had blocked CRAMRA and weakened the credibility it had established under Keith Brennan, John Rowland, Richard Woolcott, Ian Nicholson and others. Instead of being a champion of consensus, it now had to defend breaking it. DFAT added considerable resources to the effort, temporarily boosting the number of staff to strengthen the diplomatic campaign. Australia's deputy delegation head, Australian Antarctic Division Director Rex Moncur, brought much-needed direct Antarctic experience to the debate.

SC21384 "Antarctic environment: SCM XI: Delegation statements" (NAA: B1387 90/759 PART 3).

[200] Young cites Bohlen's structural leadership in the 1973 Agreement on the Conservation of Polar Bears. Young, "Political Leadership and Regime Formation: On the Development of Institutions in International Society," 292.

[201] 5 December 1990, SC21441 "Antarctic—SCM—minerals outcome" (AAD: 89/914-2).

[202] 11 September 1990, WH120835 "Antarctic environment: US views" (NAA: B1387 90/759 PART 1). 24 September 1990, PA83061 "Antarctica: French MFA discussions with Bohlen" (NAA: B1387 90/759 PART 1).

[203] 6 May 1991, letter from Evans to McCarthy (NAA: B1387 91/32 PART 2).

France applied diplomatic resources to the campaign but was sometimes overwhelmed. Jean-Pierre Puissochet's involvement as delegation head added stability to French campaigning, with Alan Brown observing that "Puissochet played a very important personal role and under his leadership the French were much more effective in supporting our joint position".[204]

Politicians as Structural Leaders

Domestic political figures rely on structural leadership—they seek it and are endowed with it by a constituency that elects them to exercise positional power. On most occasions, it was played to a domestic audience. In the Antarctic minerals and environment debates, that power was occasionally employed personally in the negotiating forums to directly influence institutional bargaining.

Bob Hawke's demonstration of structural leadership has been well covered, including its frequent exploitation by environmentalists. Occasionally, Hawke directly engaged in diplomacy, taking Australian proposals to other national leaders including UK Prime Minister Margaret Thatcher, US President George Bush and others. Most significant was his early contact with President François Mitterand and Prime Minister Michel Rocard of France. Hawke's personal representations did not suggest that his foreign ministry was unable to mount a campaign. Rather, it was recognition that controversial initiatives required support at the highest political level. This was an astute move, making use of personal connections with world leaders to underpin Australia's conviction and circumvent the filtering inherent in bureaucratic mechanisms to advise governments.

Hawke was by no means the only Australian political figure to join the environment debate. His Treasurer, Paul Keating, exercised considerable influence in various ways, although taking an ambiguous position between opposing CRAMRA on economic or environmental grounds. Hawke himself was influenced by others. Bob Chynoweth, chair of the Australian Labor Party caucus, was instrumental in advancing environmental issues within the Hawke government.[205]

---

[204] 5 December 1990, SC21441 "Antarctic—SCM—minerals outcome" (AAD: 89/914–2).

[205] Bergin, "The Politics of Antarctic Minerals: The Greening of White Australia," 226.

There was also earlier leadership on the Antarctic by Opposition Leader John Howard who opposed CRAMRA before Hawke. Howard may in turn have been influenced by the even earlier Senate motion by the Australian Democrats' Jo Vallentine. Howard's move surprised Hawke in the lead up to Cabinet's May 1989 decision, by which point he had seized the policy lead as Prime Minister. Shortly after the decision, Hawke appointed Sir Ninian Stephen to advocate protection of Antarctica as environment ambassador.[206]

Other political leaders exercised influence at critical times. As Prime Minister, Geoffrey Palmer made the decision to move New Zealand away from CRAMRA. US senator Al Gore was active in promoting the Antarctic environment in Congress, along with colleagues such as Silvio Conte and Bruce Vento. In May 1991, Prime Minister John Major intervened to ensure UK support for the draft protocol, possibly to the surprise of officials. Ultimately, on 3 July 1991, President Bush secured the Protocol by announcing US commitment.[207]

Institutional Representatives as Structural Leaders

Institutions affiliated with the Antarctic Treaty (including SCAR and Council of Managers of National Antarctic Programs (COMNAP)) also exercised influence. SCAR's conduct in the environment debate raised questions about its role being politicised, undermining its reputation for impartial scientific advice.[208] SCAR's establishment preceded the Treaty. Its role was to "encourage and assist in the dissemination of scientific knowledge" and, unless invited, SCAR would "abstain from involvement in political and juridical matters".[209] Despite having no formal environmental role SCAR was, however, requested to provide advice on the possible impact of minerals activities.[210] From 1987, SCAR was regularly invited to observe Treaty meetings, and it did not take long for SCAR to influence political debate, potentially putting itself at odds with its original purpose.

[206] Ayres, *Fortunate Voyager: The Worlds of Ninian Stephen*, 132–35.

[207] Jackson and Boyce, "Mining and 'World Park Antarctica'," 265.

[208] Walton and Clarkson, *Science in the Snow*, 96–108.

[209] Bush, *Antarctica and International Law: A Collection of Inter-State and National Documents*, Vol I, 6.

[210] Scientific Committee on Antarctic Research, *A Preliminary Assessment of the Environmental Impact of Mineral Exploration/Exploitation in Antarctica (EAMREA)*.

Although not particularly politically active on the minerals question, SCAR became very active on environmental measures, especially on protected areas. This engagement amplified in 1989 when proposals for an environmental regime emerged. SCAR seemed jealous of NGOs and appeared to fear that its capacity to influence would diminish in new institutional arrangements. In addition, it assumed that an environmental regime would restrict research. Alan Brown objected to misinformation that the convention proposal was anti-science and wanted support from Australian scientists for the government's objectives.[211] Some scientists, however, continued airing their fears, revealing a disconnect between practising scientists and the SCAR Executive.[212] The large cohort of scientists supporting new environment measures must have come as a surprise.[213]

Those most vocal were in powerful positions, epitomised by SCAR President Richard Laws. Previously director of the British Antarctic Survey (BAS), Laws was well imbued with UK policies given the connections between the FCO and BAS. The presence of both BAS and SCAR in Cambridge contributed to perceptions of anglocentrism of Antarctic affairs, as both the United Kingdom and SCAR enjoyed considerable influence. The FCO was probably pleased with Laws' forthright criticism of environmental proposals.[214] Laws' remarks were presented as the considered position of all Antarctic scientists, a view on which he was emphatically disabused in Viña del Mar. His denigration of ASOC did not help, nor threats to more widely publicise criticism of the proposed environment regime.[215] Such outbursts revealed the politicisation of SCAR which harmed its relationship with the Parties and environmentalists.[216] In SCAR's case, its institutional role had been effectively commandeered by its leadership. Representatives of Antarctic institutions can exercise considerable power, but squander that influence by failing to respond if their reputation is compromised.

[211] 15 December 1989, "Antarctic IDC—Post-ATCM XV" (AWJ personal notes).

[212] Elliott, *International Environmental Politics: Protecting the Antarctic*, 183.

[213] 20 April 1991, "Scientists urge Antarctic park" *The Australian*, 16.

[214] Laws, "Unacceptable Threats to Antarctic Science." "Antarctic Politics and Science Are Coming into Conflict."

[215] 22 November 1990, "XI SCM Plenary debate" (AWJ personal notes), 16 and 19.

[216] John A. Heap, "Antarctic Politics and Antarctic Science: Are They at Loggerheads?" *Antarctic Science* 3, no. 2 (1991). Walton, "The Scientific Committee on Antarctic Research and the Antarctic Treaty," 82–83.

In some ways, SCAR was outperformed by the Council of Managers of National Antarctic Programs, which represented Antarctic operators. It also had close links with individual Parties, yet conducted itself largely immune to accusations of politicisation. That does not mean it was ambivalent in the environment debate—like scientists, operators could attract greater scrutiny and regulation. However, they appeared less confrontational. One exception is, perhaps, Phillip Law. While no longer an active program manager, he often spoke as if he were.[217] However, such commentary from the sidelines of the debate went largely ignored by the Parties and COMNAP itself.

IUCN's engagement in the environment debate was another lost opportunity for institutional leadership. IUCN embarked on an Antarctic conservation strategy which could have provided useful independent guidance on contemporary practice.[218] It failed for several reasons, including its late delivery in the environment debate.[219] It also ran the risk of politicisation by including in its drafting team strongly pro-CRAMRA individuals.[220] Further confounding the perception was IUCN's location in the United Kingdom and leadership by a previous member of the UK Treaty delegation.

Environmentalists as Structural Leaders

Unlike the IUCN and other institutional players, activist NGOs *wanted* politicisation—that was their raison d'etre. Environmentalists exerted influence within Treaty forums, collectively as invited experts and individually in national delegations achieving a privileged position leveraged for considerable public awareness. Foreign Minister Gareth Evans acknowledged environmentalists' power, warning that any backsliding on Australia's part "would invite strong criticism from NGO and community groups".[221] New Zealand environmentalists were proud of their ability to influence national policy.[222] The great advantage held by NGOs was the

---

[217] Law, "The Antarctic Wilderness: A Wild Idea!."
[218] IUCN—The World Conservation Union, *A Strategy for Antarctic Conservation*.
[219] Walton, "The Scientific Committee on Antarctic Research and the Antarctic Treaty," 81.
[220] Mosley, *Saving the Antarctic Wilderness*, 75.
[221] 24 April 1991, CE17582 "EC—SVP—Brinkhorst—discussions on Antarctica" (NAA: B1387 90/888 PART 3).
[222] 27 August 1990, WL41558 "New Zealand: Environmental groups" (NAA: B1387 90/759 PART 2).

capacity to communicate quickly to a receptive public audience, without the constraints on government communications which normally sought to avoid hyperbole, distortion and disinformation.

Initially, NGO involvement was measured. The ACF, for example, did not oppose mining in 1974, asking only that it "must not be allowed to endanger the ... environment of Antarctica" and, in 1986, reassuring that "a world park won't lock up minerals forever".[223] Engagement with environmentalists came about, in part, because of John Heap's early suggestion that delegations include "a top-level active environmentalist". The objective was not stakeholder engagement, but getting advice on environmental standards.[224] Environmentalists focused on maximising CRAMRA's environmental provisions by "plugging the gaps".[225] While environmentalists preferred a world park, they would "support a [minerals] convention to the extent that it would ensure stringent environmental protection".[226] By 1988, environmentalists outnumbered industry representatives on Australia's delegations to minerals negotiations.[227] To that point, NGOs had only been present *within* delegations: not until the environment debate could NGOs attend meetings in their own right, when ASOC participated as an observer.[228]

ASOC had been established as a coalition of environmental groups interested in Antarctica.[229] Apart from demonstrating stakeholder engagement, admitting ASOC to ATCMs encouraged NGOs to coordinate the views of its constituent organisations. While invited on the ATCPs' terms, ASOC was free to run its own media commentary, opening Antarctic

[223] 14 October 1974, letter from J. G. Mosley (ACF) to Minister for Science (NAA: B1387 1991/531 PART 1). 1986 ACF Briefing Paper "Antarctic – the world park and world heritage options" (AU-ATADD-5-BB-GE-174), 3–4.

[224] 22 September 1982, Department of Science memorandum "Evolution of draft paragraphs for inclusion in the report of the first sessions of the 4th Special Antarctic Treaty Consultative Meeting (AMR/SCM/11)" (NAA: B1387 1982/230 PART 2).

[225] 16 March 1987, Lyn Goldsworthy (Ecofund) letter to Ian Nicholson (DFAT) (NAA: B1387 87/720 PART 1).

[226] 27 April 1987, Cabinet Minute, Submission 4757 "Australian objectives in Antarctic minerals negotiations" (NAA: A14039 4757).

[227] 21 December 1988, House of Representatives Hansard, 3963–3964.

[228] Antarctic Treaty, *Interim Report of the Eleventh Antarctic Treaty Special Consultative Meeting, Viña Del Mar, 19 November-6 December 1990*, 5 and 96.

[229] Among others, ASOC included Friends of the Earth, the World Wildlife Fund, and the Australian Conservation Foundation. ASOC was the only means for Greenpeace to access the ATCM.

negotiations to wider public scrutiny. ASOC thus exercised structural power as the lead communicator of public opinion, with far more influence than IUCN, an institutionalised environmental body.

Prominent in ASOC was Jim Barnes, enjoying a credibility earned from years as a measured campaigner.[230] Many campaigners were vocal in environmental groups within and outside Treaty forums.[231] Others actively included individuals not normally regarded as environmentalists but who commanded respect.[232] Several groups were drawn to the Antarctic cause, and NGOs generally promoted compatible objectives.[233] Those present in Treaty forums necessarily acted in moderate ways lest they jeopardised future invitations. Others were less restrained: Jacques Cousteau, for example, was described as "a one-man assault force", normally charming, but ruthless "when the occasion and cause demand".[234] Presumably he was well aware of Greenpeace campaigns, but had no idea of CRAMRA until it was adopted or how it worked.[235] Nevertheless, by leveraging his public profile, Cousteau rapidly mobilised an extraordinarily effective anti-CRAMRA campaign. Even the French government, which could not ignore him, ignored the fact that he "didn't even understand how the Antarctic Treaty System worked".[236] In some quarters, obstreperous

[230] Antarctic and Southern Ocean Coalition "Some farewell thoughts from some of Jim's longtime colleagues" https://www.asoc.org/about/history/1118 (accessed 3 February 2021).

[231] Key individuals include Janet Dalziel, Lyn Goldsworthy, Bruce Manheim, Beth Marks, Doug Nicol, Cassandra Phillips, Maj de Poorter, Cath Wallace, Barry Weeber, Roger Wilson and many others. 15 November 1990, The Wilderness Society media release "Antarctica world wilderness urged" (NAA: B1387 1991/55 PART 1).

[232] For example, Sir Peter Scott and Prince Phillip; and adventurers Will Steger and Robert Swan.

[233] The Wilderness Society identified 11 groups affiliated in Antarctic campaigning (ASOC, Defenders of Wildlife, Environmental Defense Fund, Friends of the Earth, Greenpeace, Humane Society of the United States, National Audubon Society, National Wildlife Federation, Natural Resources Defense Council, Sierra Club, the Antarctica Projecti and the Wilderness Society).

[234] 11 October 1989, Philip Jacobson "Fight to save Antarctica: Cousteau draws battle lines" *The Times* (United Kingdom), 9.

[235] Shortis, ""Who Can Resist This Guy?" Jacques Cousteau, Celebrity Diplomacy, and the Environmental Protection of the Antarctic," 372. Templeton, *A Wise Adventure II: New Zealand and Antarctica after 1960*, 226–28.

[236] *A Wise Adventure II: New Zealand and Antarctica after 1960*, 260.

NGOs were considered unhelpful because of their campaigning against public policy. On the other hand, Australia depended on NGOs to advance environmental concerns using methods unavailable to governments. Gareth Evans praised NGOs for their role in "consciousness raising".[237] In that sense, a symbiotic relationship served both government and NGO objectives, strengthening the structural leadership of environmentalists. That said, the relationship with NGOs was not invariably harmonious—in New Zealand, some environmentalists hectored officials to the point of exasperation.[238]

The Parties as Providers of Structural Leadership

In some models, 'structural leadership' is exercised by individuals. In many situations discussed in this book, such leadership is made possible simply through their affiliation to a particular Party. Accordingly, Parties facilitating such behaviour can exercise structural leadership irrespective of the representatives it deploys. The leadership potential of a Party was enhanced by longevity of participation, reputation, being an original signatory, being a claimant, use of English, consistency of representatives and willingness to join blocs.

The United Kingdom exercised such structural power. By the start of the minerals debate, it was influencing debate in all Treaty forums, with a reputation as a Treaty stalwart. This was a distinct about-turn from considering the Treaty a temporary expedient pending internationalisation, an idea abandoned as the Law of the Sea and minerals issues emerged. The United Kingdom's capacity to exercise influence transcended its representatives, but was enhanced by the long retention of key individuals who used personal knowledge of past practice to steer debate, and maintain the meeting traditions. Bush points out that Brian Roberts' (and his protégé John Heap's) combination of "continuity and scientific credibility at the highest level of national policy direction of Antarctic affairs is unrivalled in

---

[237] 4 October 1991, speech by Senator Gareth Evans "Antarctica: An international environment win for Australia" (AU-ATADD-1-BB-AU-354), 1–2.

[238] Templeton, *A Wise Adventure II: New Zealand and Antarctica after 1960*, 180–81, 97 and 295.

any country".[239] The United Kingdom enjoyed leading by example. It was the first to pass legislation to implement CRAMRA and, later, the first to sign the Protocol.[240] Such practice sought to stamp UK authority on the proceedings, reinforcing a sense of UK 'stewardship' of the ATS. The capacity of the United Kingdom to act within blocs was demonstrated, including the advantages of being in 'the Uniteds'. On occasions, the United Kingdom appeared dependent on the United States taking a consistent position although, in counterpoint, it was observed that "the British sometimes tended to act for US positions in Antarctica".[241]

The United States similarly exercised considerable structural power. It also had longevity in the ATS and retained experienced delegates over consecutive meetings. Some Parties sharing US sentiments on resources and environmental issues (such as Japan, Korea, the USSR and others) let the United States lead in these debates because of its command of the subject and capacity to influence.[242] Japan, in particular, was seen as the most intransigent on minerals.[243] CRAMRA supporters were therefore shocked when the normally low-profile Japan abandoned its support for them on the eve of the April 1991 Madrid meeting.

New Zealand had a history of structural leadership in contentious issues including its short-lived 1975 'world park' proposal, and its 1977 interest in exploring the "scope for compromise" between the United States and Australia on Antarctic resources issues.[244] That interest extended into the minerals negotiations where, by chairing, it appeared to take a lower profile on its national interests with a view to facilitating an outcome for all.

Australia's structural leadership weakened after rejecting CRAMRA, its reputation as a Treaty defender severely compromised by upsetting the hard-won consensus. Previously it enjoyed a standing equal to that of other original signatories, representing them in the UN and leading CCAMLR's development. In blocking CRAMRA, Australia contradicted

---

[239] Bush, *Antarctica and International Law: A Collection of Inter-State and National Documents (Looseleaf Volumes)*, Vol III, Booklet AT/Rev. 1992–94, 6.

[240] Redgwell, "Antarctica: Wilderness Park or Eldorado Postponed?" 139.

[241] 19 June 1990, SC20769 "Antarctica: Chile's policy and the SCM" (AAD: 89/914–1).

[242] 2 December 1990, SC21431 "Antarctica—SCM—minerals issues" (AAD: 89/914–2).

[243] 8 January 1991, WL42779 "New Zealand/French relations: Rocard's visit to New Zealand and Antarctica" (NAA: B1387 91/32 PART 1). 7 February 1991, WL43003 "Antarctica: Environment protection: ANZ consultations" (NAA: B1387 90/888 PART 2).

[244] 14 July 1977, CH542725 "ANZUS: Antarctica" (NAA: B1387 77/176 PART 1).

its wish to be "an effective middle power", especially in "resources diplomacy".[245] Its unpredictable behaviour squandered the effectiveness it had achieved in CCAMLR and CRAMRA. Restoring Australia's reputation required considerable effort, long-term recovery requiring a period of consolidation to re-establish its credentials and "allow all the wounds to heal".[246]

Australia sought to enhance its structural leadership in the environment debate by entering into a bloc with sympathetic states. Any value in the weight of numbers seemed moot in the face of almost overwhelming opposition. The real value came from French support, because CRAMRA could only survive with all the claimants aboard. Even so, France did not finally reject CRAMRA until November 1989, after considerable momentum had developed and Australia had attracted much of the opprobrium. In some ways, the leadership value of Australia associating with France, Belgium and Italy was at least odd, optimistic at best. Belgium was an original signatory to the Treaty and yet in 1989 had scarcely been involved in Antarctica since the IGY—activity so low that France suggested Belgium no longer qualified as an ATCP.[247] Italy was a relative newcomer. Furthermore, Australia was at odds with France over Pacific nuclear testing and construction of the Dumont d'Urville airstrip. Several other issues troubled the relationship, leading to the observation it would "remain an odd blend".[248]

Later, such observations appeared justified. Despite the close Antarctic political cooperation there were many differences in tactics, stemming from policy being driven by Prime Minister Rocard's office, while the Foreign Ministry was significantly under-resourced.[249] Australian and French officials diverged on environmental policy—for example, on impact assessment and liability.[250] On tactics, Australia was bemused by tensions between France and other Parties (such as New Zealand and Sweden) and its surprising reluctance to expand the 'Four Powers' while Australia

[245] Evans and Grant, *Australia's Foreign Relations in the World of the 1990's*, 322.
[246] Jackson and Kriwoken, "The Protocol in Action, 1992–2010," 301.
[247] 17 September 1985, PA41352 "Antarctica" (NAA: B1387 85/997).
[248] 14 November 1989, CH563488 "Future relations with France" (AAD: 89/578–1).
[249] 11 September 1990, PA82856 "Antarctic initiative" (NAA: B1387 90/759 PART 1).
[250] 19 October 1990, memorandum Bill Campbell, A-G's to Bill Bush, DFAT (NAA: B1387 90/888 PART 3). 21 March 1991, PA86145 "Antarctica: Andersen text: French comments on Australian amendments" (NAA: B1387 90/888 PART 3).

sought to build support.[251] France seemed willing to concede policy objectives too readily.[252] At times, such differences extended within the 'Four Powers' and brought to a head by Italy's surprise proposal, without consultation, of a major concession on the mining ban in April 1991.[253] On this, Australia had sympathy from France, but only on tactics, not the proposal itself.[254] Sulikowski presents a more agreeable picture of French engagement in Antarctic affairs more broadly and recognises that there is a national character in the way France conducted itself which sometimes added uncertainty to its relationships.[255] Thus, structural leadership can be demonstrated by Parties operating individually or as a bloc, and success can turn on subtleties in interactions with other Parties.

The final observation on structural leadership considers difficulties in isolating the national character from individual performance. There are legion examples of disconnections between national political objectives and officials' attitudes. The differences were between political ambitions and the intuition of officials tasked with achieving them. Such dissonance can be explained by Antarctic affairs not being domestically controversial: Antarctica rarely troubled politicians who trusted officials to resolve any controversy. Many officials had considerable personal investment in Antarctic policy, often with little political or public scrutiny. Careers depended on it. Officials were often inclined to present papers with the caveat that their views were not necessarily representative of government—yet there was, in fact, little distinction between the positions because political leaders often accepted the advice of experienced officials without question.[256] This changed when Antarctic minerals issues became contested, fuelled by contemporary public concern for the global environment and exacerbated by spectacular maritime accidents. With media attention galvanised, politicians intervened, officials were overruled and

---

[251] 4 January 1991, CE974457 "Antarctica: comprehensive environmental protection" (NAA: B1387 1991/55 PART 1). 13 January 1991, PA84985 "Antarctic environment initiative: Paris consultations" (NAA: B1387 91/32 PART 1).

[252] 19 April 1991, PA86579 "Antarctic: French views" (NAA: B1387 90/888 PART 3).

[253] 21 March 1991, PA86146 "Antarctica: Rome consultations and 4P text" (NAA: B1387 90/888 PART 3).

[254] 27 March 1991, RO48549 "Antarctic environment: Four country consultations: Rome" (NAA: B1387 90/888 PART 3).

[255] Sulikowski, *France and the Antarctic Treaty System*, 131–24 and 371–73.

[256] Sollie, *Antarctic Resources: Report from the Informal Meeting of Experts 30 May-9 June 1973*, 2. Heap, "The Political Case for the Minerals Convention," 44. Beeby, "The Convention on the Regulation of Antarctic Minerals and Its Future," 47.

policy leadership transferred to politicians.[257] New Zealand Prime Minister Geoffrey Palmer encapsulated this in June 1990, saying that *he* made policy, not MFAT officials.[258] The April 1991 intervention by Economics Minister Jürgen Möllemann similarly caught Germany's Foreign Ministry by surprise.[259] No longer could officials act as though they personally owned Antarctic policy and contain the debate within the comfort zone of familiar power relationships and conventional Antarctic diplomacy.

References

Alexander, Lewis M, and Lynne Carter Hanson, eds. *Antarctic Politics and Marine Resources*: University of Rhode Island, 1985.

Andersen, Rolf Trolle. "Negotiating a New Regime: How CRAMRA Came into Existence." Chap. 7 In *The Antarctic Treaty System in World Politics*, edited by Arnfinn Jørgensen-Dahl and Willy Østreng, 94–109: Macmillan/Fridtjof Nansen Institute, 1991.

"The Antarctic Treaty." https://documents.ats.aq/keydocs/vol_1/vol1_2_AT_Antarctic_Treaty_e.pdf.

Antarctic Treaty. *Final Report of the Fourth Special Antarctic Treaty Consultative Meeting on Antarctic Mineral Resources.* Ministry of Foreign Affairs (Wellington), 1988.

———. *Final Report of the Sixteenth Antarctic Treaty Consultative Meeting, Bonn, 7–18 October 1991.* 1991.

———. *Interim Report of the Eleventh Antarctic Treaty Special Consultative Meeting, Viña Del Mar, 19 November-6 December 1990.* Republic of Chile, 1990.

———. *Rules of Procedure of the Antarctic Treaty Consultative Meeting and the Committe for Environmental Protection.* Secretariat of the Antarctic Treaty, 2017.

"Antarctica: A Continent for Science." British Antarctic Survey, 1987.

Auburn, F M. *Antarctic Law and Politics.* Hurst, 1982.

Australian Transport Safety Board. *Report on the Preliminary Investigation in the Grounding of MV Nella Dan at Macquarie Island on 3 December 1987.* ATSB, 1988.

Ayres, Philip. *Fortunate Voyager: The Worlds of Ninian Stephen.* Miegunyah, 2013.

[257] For example: Hawke's decision on CRAMRA contradicted advice from his Foreign Ministry and Environment Department; John Major intervened to support the mining ban; and President Bush announced that the United States would sign the Protocol.

[258] 19 June 1990, Janet Dalziel (Greenpeace) "Meeting with Prime Minister" (NAA: B1387 90/498 PART 3).

[259] 17 April 1991, BO53601 "Antarctica: SCM XI Madrid, 22–30 April—German position on minerals" (NAA: B1387 91/32 PART 2).

Barnes, James N. "The Emerging Antarctic Living Resources Convention." *American Society of International Law Proceedings* 73 (1979): 272–91.

———. "Protection of the Environment in Antarctica: Are Present Regimes Enough?". In *The Antarctic Treaty System in World Politics*, edited by Arnfinn Jørgensen-Dahl and Willy Østreng, 186–228: Macmillan/Fridtjof Nansen Institute, 1991.

Barnes, James N, and Eliot Porter. *Let's Save Antarctica!* Greenhouse Publications, 1982.

Beck, Peter J. *The International Politics of Antarctica*. Croom Helm, 1986.

Beeby, Christopher C. "The Antarctic Treaty System as a Resource Management Mechanism – Nonliving Resources." In *Antarctic Treaty System: An Assessment*, 269–84: National Academy Press, 1986.

———. "The Antarctic Treaty System: Goals, Performance and Impact." In *The Antarctic Treatgy System in World Politics*, edited by Arnfinn Jørgensen-Dahl and Willy Østreng, 4–21: Macmillan/Fridtjof Nansen Institute, 1991.

———. "The Convention on the Regulation of Antarctic Minerals and Its Future." In *Antarctica's Future: Continuity or Change?*, edited by R A Herr, H R Hall and M G Haward, 47–60: Australian Institute of International Affairs, 1990.

Bergin, Anthony. "The Politics of Antarctic Minerals: The Greening of White Australia." *Australian Journal of Political Science* 26, no. 2 (1991): 216–39.

Bondevik, Kjell Magne. "Foreword." In *The Antarctic Treaty System in World Politics*, edited by Arnfinn Jorgensen-Dahl and Willy Ostreng, xxi–xxii: Macmillan/Fridtjof Nansen Institute, 1991.

Bowden, Tim. *The Silence Calling: Australians in Antarctica 1947–1997*. Allen & Unwin, 1997.

Brennan, Keith. "Criteria for Access to the Resources of Antarctica: Alternatives, Procedure and Experience Applicable." In *Antarctic Resources Policy: Scientific, Legal and Political Issues*, edited by Francisco Orrego Vicuña, 217–27: Cambridge University Press, 1983.

Brewster, Barney. *Antarctica, Wilderness at Risk*. Sun Books, 1982.

Brown, Alan. "The Design of CRAMRA: How Appropriate for the Protection of the Environment." In *The Antarctic Treaty System in World Politics*, edited by Arnfinn Jørgensen-Dahl and Willy Østreng, 110–19: Macmillan/Fridtjof Nansen Institute, 1991.

Budd, W A. "Scientific Research in Antarctica and Australia's Effort." In *Australia's Antarctic Policy Options*, edited by Stuart Harris, 217–53: Australian National University, 1984.

Bührs, Ton, and Peter Christoff. "'Greening the Antipodes'? Environmental Policy and Politics in Australia and New Zealand." *Australian Journal of Political Science* 41, no. 2 (2006): 225–40.

Burgess, John. "Comprehensive Environmental Protection of the Antarctic: New Approaches for New Times." In *The Future of Antarctica: Exploitation Versus*

Preservation, edited by Grahame Cook, 53–67: Manchester University Press, 1990.

Bush, W M, ed. *Antarctica and International Law: A Collection of Inter-State and National Documents*. Oceana, 1982.

———, ed. *Antarctica and International Law: A Collection of Inter-State and National Documents (Looseleaf Volumes)*: Oceana, 1994–2003.

Canmann, Mary Lynn. "Antarctic Oil Spills of 1989: A Review of the Application of the Antarctic Treaty and the New Law of the Sea to the Antarctic Environment." *Colorado Journal of International Environmental Law and Policy* 1 (1990): 211–21.

Carrick, Robert. "Conservation of Nature in Antarctica." *Polar Record* 10, no. 68 (1961): 532–40.

———. "Conservation of Nature in the Antarctic." *Polar Record* 10, no. 66 (1960): 299–306.

Chaturvedi, Sanjay. *The Polar Regions*. Wiley, 1996.

"Convention on the Regulation of Antarctic Mineral Resource Activities." https://documents.ats.aq/recatt/Att311_e.pdf.

Cook, Grahame. "Possible Future Developments." In *The Future of Antarctica: Exploitation Versus Preservation*, 95–103: Manchester University Press, 1990.

Cook, R A, and F J Davey. "Hydrocarbon Exploration and Potential." In *The Antarctic Sector of the Pacific*, edited by G P Glasby. Elsevier Oceanography Series, 155–85: Elsevier, 1990.

Coper, Michael. *The Franklin Dam Case*. Butterworths, 1983.

Daniels, Paul C. "The Antarctic Treaty." *Bulletin of the Atomic Scientists* 26, no. 10 (1970): 11–15.

De Wit, Maarten J. *Minerals and Mining in Antarctica: Science and Technology, Economics and Politics*. Oxford Science Publications. Oxford, 1985.

Donella H Meadows, Dennis L Meadows, Jørgen Randers, and William W Behrens. *The Limits to Growth: A Report for the Club of Rome on the Predicament of Mankind*. Universe Books, 1972.

Elliott, Lorraine M. *International Environmental Politics: Protecting the Antarctic*. Macmillan, 1994.

Emerson, Craig. *The Boy from Baradine*. Scribe, 2018.

Evans, Gareth, and Bruce Grant. *Australia's Foreign Relations in the World of the 1990's*. Melbourne University Press, 1992.

Francioni, Francesco. "The Madrid Protocol on the Protection of the Antarctic Environment." *Texas International Law Journal* 28, no. 1 (1993): 47–72.

Friedheim, Robert, and Tsuneo Akaha. "Antarctic Resources and International Law: Japan, the United States, and the Future of Antarctica." *Ecology Law Quarterly* 16, no. 1 (1989): 119–54.

Galligan, B. "The Dams Case: A Political Analysis." In *The South West Dam Dispute: The Legal and Political Issues*, edited by M Sornarajah, 102–23: University of Tasmania, 1983.

Hall, H Robert *International Regime Formation and Leadership: The Origins of the Antarctic Treaty.* PhD thesis, University of Tasmania, 1994.

Hambro, Edvard. "Some Notes on the Future of the Antarctic Treaty Collaboration." *The American Journal of International Law* 68, no. 2 (1974): 217–26.

Haward, M G, and D Mason. "Australia, the United Nations and the Question of Antarctica." Chap. 9 In *Australia and the Antarctic Treaty System: 50 Years of Influence*, edited by Marcus Haward and Tom Griffiths, 201–21: UNSW Press, 2011.

Haward, Marcus, and Nicholas Cooper. "Australian Interests, Bifocalism, Bipartisanship, and the Antarctic Treaty System." *Polar Record* 50, no. 1 (2014): 60–71.

Haward, Marcus, and Andrew Jackson. "Australia's Antarctic Future." Chap. 15 In *Australia and the Antarctic Treaty System: 50 Years of Influence*, edited by Marcus Haward and Tom Griffiths, 334–45: UNSW Press, 2011.

Hawke, Bob, and Derek Rielly. *Wednesdays with Bob.* Macmillan, 2017.

Hawke, Robert J L. "Australia's Policy in Antarctica." In *Antarctica's Future: Continuity or Change?*, edited by R A Herr, H R Hall and M G Haward, 17–20: Australian Institute of International Affairs, 1990.

———. *The Hawke Memoirs.* William Heinemann, 1994.

Heap, John A. "Antarctic Politics and Antarctic Science: Are They at Loggerheads?". *Antarctic Science* 3, no. 2 (1991): 123–23.

———. "The Political Case for the Minerals Convention." In *The Future of Antarctica: Exploitation Versus Preservation*, edited by Grahame Cook, 44–52: Manchester University Press, 1990.

———. "The Treaty and the Protocol." In *Antarctica: The Environment and the Future*, edited by G Mudge, 35–40: International Academy of the Environment and International Peace Research Institute, 1992.

Herr, Richard A, and Bruce W Davis. "ATS Decision-Making and Change: The Role of Domestic Politics in Australia." In *Governing the Antarctic*, edited by Olav Schram Stokke and Davor Vidas, 331–60: Cambridge University Press, 1996.

Hildebrand, John. *A Northern Front: New and Selected Essays.* Borealis, 2005.

Howkins, Adrian. *Frozen Empires: An Environmental History of the Antarctic Peninsula.* Oxford University Press, 2017.

———. *The Polar Regions: An Environmental History.* Polity, 2016.

Husseiny, A A, ed. *Iceberg Utilization*: Pergamon, 1978.

IUCN—The World Conservation Union. *A Strategy for Antarctic Conservation.* IUCN, 1991.

Jackson, Andrew. "Politics, Diplomacy and the Creation of Antarctic Consensus." *Yearbook of Polar Law* 9 (2018): 243–61.

Jackson, Andrew, and Peter Boyce. "Mining and 'World Park Antarctica'." Chap. 11 In *Australia and the Antarctic Treaty System: 50 Years of Influence*, edited by Marcus Haward and Tom Griffiths, 243–73: UNSW Press, 2011.

Jackson, Andrew, and Lorne Kriwoken. "The Protocol in Action, 1992–2010." Chap. 13 In *Australia and the Antarctic Treaty System: 50 Years of Influence*, edited by Marcus Haward and Tom Griffiths, 300–19: UNSW Press, 2011.

Jacobsson, Marie. "Building the International Legal Framework for Antarctica." In *Science Diplomacy: Antarctica, and the Governance of International Spaces*, edited by Paul Arthur Berkman, Michael A Lang, David W H Walton and Oran R Young, 1–15: Smithsonian Institution Scholarly Press, 2011.

Jenks, C Wilfred. "An International Regime for Antarctica?". *International Affairs* 32, no. 4 (1956): 414–26.

Joyner, Christopher C. "Anglo-Argentine Rivalry after the Falklands/Malvinas War: Law, Geopolitics, and the Antarctic Connection." *University of Miami Inter-American Law Review* 15, no. 3 (1984): 467–502.

———. "CRAMRA: The Ugly Duckling of the Antarctic Treaty System?". In *The Antarctic Treaty System in World Politics*, edited by Arnfinn Jørgensen-Dahl and Willy Østreng, 161–85: Macmillan/Fridtjof Nansen Institute, 1991.

———. "The Effectiveness of CRAMRA." In *Governing the Antarctic*, edited by Olav Schram Stokke and Davor Vidas, 152–72: Cambridge University Press, 1996.

———. *Governing the Frozen Commons*. University of South Carolina Press, 1998.

Joyner, Christopher C, and Ethel R Theis. *Eagle over the Ice: The US in the Antarctic*. University Press of New England, 1997.

Law, Phillip. "The Antarctic Wilderness: A Wild Idea!". In *Antarctica's Future: Continuity or Change?*, edited by R A Herr, H R Hall and M G Haward, 71–80: Australian Institute of International Affairs, 1990.

Laws, R M. "Antarctic Politics and Science Are Coming into Conflict." *Antarctic Science* 3, no. 3 (1991): 231–31.

———. "Unacceptable Threats to Antarctic Science." *New Scientist*, no. 1762 (31 March 1991): 4.

Lee, Martin L. "The 1959 Antarctic Treaty, the "Freezing and Bifocalism" Formula." *Australian International Law Journal* (2000): 200–14.

Liggett, Daniela. "Destination Icy Wilderness: Tourism in Antarctica." In *Exploring the Last Continent*, edited by Daniela Liggett, Bryan C. Storey, Yvonne Anne Cook and Veronika Meduna, 379–98: Springer, 2015.

Liggett, Daniela, Bob Frame, Neil Gilbert, and Fraser Morgan. "Is It All Going South? Four Future Scenarios for Antarctica." *Polar Record* 53, no. 5 (2017): 459–78.

Lowe, D A. *The Price of Power: The Politics Behind the Tasmanian Dams Case.* Macmillan, 1984.

Marks, Robert B. *The Origins of the Modern World.* 3rd ed.: Rowman & Littlefield, 2015.

Morell, James B. *The Law of the Sea: An Historical Analysis of the 1982 Treaty and Its Rejection by the United States.* McFarland & Company, 1992.

Morgan, Jan. "Australia's Antarctic Policy: Theory and Practice." University of Tasmania, 1996.

Mosley, J G. *Antarctica, Our Last Great Wilderness.* Australian Conservation Foundation, 1986.

———. "The Natural Option: The Case for an Antarctic World Park." In *Australia's Antarctic Policy Options,* edited by Stuart Harris, 307–26: Australian National University, 1984.

———. *Saving the Antarctic Wilderness.* Envirobook, 2009.

Murphy, Robert Cushman. "Antarctic Conservation: Only by Careful Planning and Cooperation Can We Save This Primeval Region from the Ravages of Man." *Science* 135, no. 3499 (1962): 194–97.

Murray-Smith, Stephen. *Sitting on Penguins: People and Politics in Australian Antarctica.* Hutchinson, 1988.

Myhre, Jeffrey D. *The Antarctic Treaty System: Politics, Law, and Diplomacy.* Westview, 1986.

O'Reilly, Jessica. *The Technocratic Antarctic: An Enthnography of Scientific Expertise and Environmental Governance.* Cornell University Press, 2017.

Oxman, Bernard H. "Antarctica and the New Law of the Sea." *Cornell International Law Journal* 19 (1986): 211–47.

Paltridge, Garth, and Julia Jabour. "Antarctica and the Madrid Protocol." *Institute of Public Affairs Environmental Backgrounder,* no. 23 (1996).

Peterson, M J. *Managing the Frozen South: The Creation and Evolution of the Antarctic Treaty System.* University of California Press, 1988.

Podehl, J G, and D R Rothwell. "New Zealand and the Convention on the Regulation of Antarctic Mineral Resource Activities (CRAMRA): An Unhappy Divorce?". *Victoria University of Wellington Law Review* 22 (1992): 23–50.

"Protocol on Environmental Protection to the Antarctic Treaty." https://documents.ats.aq/keydocs/vol_1/vol1_4_AT_Protocol_on_EP_e.pdf.

Redgwell, Catherine. "Antarctica: Wilderness Park or Eldorado Postponed?". *Environmental Politics* 1, no. 1 (1992).

Richardson, Mike G. "John Arnfield Heap, CMG." *Polar Record* 42, no. 3 (2006): 263–67.

Riddle, Martin J, and Paul M Goldsworthy. "Environmental Science and the Environmental Ethos of Anare." In *Australian Antarctic Science: The First 50 Years of Anare,* edited by Harvey J Marchant, Desmond J Lugg and Patrick G Quilty, 561–71: Australian Antarctic Division, 2002.

Roberts, Brian. "International Co-Operation for Antarctic Development: The Test for the Antarctic Treaty." *Polar Record* 19, no. 119 (1978): 107–20.

Rowland, J R. "The Treaty Regime and the Politics of the Consultative Parties." In *The Antarctic Legal Regime*, edited by Christopher C Joyner and Sudhir K Chopra, 11–32: Martinus Nijhoff, 1988.

Scientific Committee on Antarctic Research. *A Preliminary Assessment of the Environmental Impact of Mineral Exploration/Exploitation in Antarctica (EAMREA)*. Edited by J H Zumberge. SCAR, 1977.

Scully, R Tucker. "The Development of the Antarctic Treaty System." In *Science Diplomacy: Antarctica, Science, and the Governance of International Spaces*, edited by Paul Arthur Berkman, and others, 29–38: Smithsonian Institution, 2011.

Senate Standing Committee on National Resources. "The Natural Resources of the Australian Antarctic Territory." AGPS, 1985.

Shortis, Emma. "'In the Interest of All Mankind': Women and the Environmental Protection of Antarctica." In *Feminist Ecologies*, edited by L Stevens, P Tait and D Varney, 247–61: Palgrave Macmillan, 2017.

———. "'Who Can Resist This Guy?' Jacques Cousteau, Celebrity Diplomacy, and the Environmental Protection of the Antarctic." *Australian Journal of Politics & History* 61, no. 3 (2015): 366–80.

Sollie, Finn, ed. *Antarctic Resources: Report from the Informal Meeting of Experts 30 May-9 June 1973*: Fridtjof Nansen Foundation, 1974.

———. "Jurisdictional Problems in Relation to Antarctic Mineral Resources in Political Perspective." In *Antarctic Resources Policy: Scientific, Legal and Political Issues*, edited by Francisco Orrego Vicuña, 317–35: Cambridge University Press, 1983.

Spandonide, Bruno. "Iceberg Water Transportation from Antarctica to Australia." PhD thesis, University of Tasmania, 2012.

Stokke, Olav Schram. "Domestic Politics and ATS Change: Introductory Assessment." In *Governing the Antarctic*, edited by Olav Schram Stokke and Davor Vidas, 323–60: Cambridge University Press, 1996.

———. "The Making of Norwegian Antarctic Policy." In *Governing the Antarctic*, edited by Olav Schram Stokke and Davor Vidas, 384–408: Cambridge University Press, 1996.

Strübing, Klaus. "The Sinking of the German *M/V Gotland II* in Dec 1981 at the Oates Coast, Antarctica." Paper presented at the International Ice Charting Working Group, Hobart, 26 September 2017.

Sulikowski, Chavelli. *France and the Antarctic Treaty System*. PhD thesis, University of Tasmania, 2013.

Summerson, Rupert, and Ian D Bishop. "Aesthetic Value in Antarctica: Beautiful or Sublime?". *The Polar Journal* 1, no. 2 (2011): 225–50.

Swan, R A. *Australia in the Antarctic: Interest, Activity and Endeavour.* Melbourne University Press, 1961.

Templeton, Malcolm. *A Wise Adventure II: New Zealand and Antarctica after 1960.* Victoria University Press, 2017.

Tepper, Rohan, and Marcus Haward. "The Development of Malaysia's Position on Antarctica: 1982 to 2004." *Polar Record* 41, no. 2 (2005): 113–24.

Tierney, T J, and G W Johnstone. "Conserving Australia's Wilderness: Antarctica as Wilderness." In *Australia's Wilderness: Conservation Progress and Plans,* edited by Geoff Mosley, 118–26: Australian Conservation Foundation, 1978.

Underdal, Arild. "One Question, Two Answers." In *Environmental Regime Effectiveness: Confronting Theory with Evidence,* edited by Edward L Miles, and others, 3–43: MIT, 2002.

US Congress Office of Technology Assessment. *Polar Prospects: A Minerals Treaty for Antarctica.* US Government Printing Office, 1989.

Walton, D W H. "The Scientific Committee on Antarctic Research and the Antarctic Treaty." In *Science Diplomacy: Antarctica, Science, and the Governance of International Spaces,* edited by Paul Arthur Berkman, Michael A Lang, D W H Walton and Oran R Young, 75–88: Smithsonian Institution, 2011.

Walton, David W H, and Peter D Clarkson. *Science in the Snow.* Scientific Committee on Antarctic Research, 2011.

Watts, Arthur. *International Law and the Antarctic Treaty System.* Grotius, 1992.

Weber, Mel. "The Strength to Continue: A Case Study Approach to Examining the Robustness of Polar Governance in the Era of Environmental and Energy Security." PhD thesis, University of Tasmania, 2011.

Wilder, Martijn. *Antarctica: An Economic History of the Last Continent.* Department of Economic History, the University of Sydney, 1992.

Wolfrum, Rüdiger. "The Exploitation of Antarctic Mineral Resources: Risks and Stakes." In *The Antarctic Environment and International Law,* edited by Joe Verhoeven, Phillipe Sands and Maxwell Bruce, 27–31: Graham & Trotman, 1992.

———. "The Unfinished Task: CRAMRA and the Question of Liability." Chap. 9 In *The Antarctic Treaty System in World Politics,* edited by Arnfinn Jørgensen-Dahl and Willy Østreng, 120–32: Macmillan/Fridtjof Nansen Institute, 1991.

Woolcott, Richard. *The Hot Seat: Reflections on Diplomacy from Stalin's Death to the Bali Bombings.* HarperCollins, 2003.

Young, Oran R. "Political Leadership and Regime Formation: On the Development of Institutions in International Society." *International Organization* 45, no. 3 (1991): 281–308.

CHAPTER 10

Conclusions

It is undoubtedly true that by examining the past we can better understand the future.[1] This chapter examines from what Antarctica was 'saved'
and who did it. It also considers two matters that, despite all the diplomatic effort expended, have not been finally settled: will mining ever occur
in Antarctica, and will there ever be an Antarctic world park?

ANTARCTICA 'SAVED'?

Multiple authors refer to 'saving' Antarctica and Greenpeace says that
Antarctica was "saved from a deadly threat".[2] Such hyperbole reveals deep
passions, but begs the question of from what Antarctic was saved. Various
synonyms have been used, but it is more than semantics: it suggests specific threats demanded immediate responses. Many previous
environmental issues needed attention, but the impetus to 'save' Antarctica
arose only in the context of mining, even though there were no known
economic minerals.[3] A century of geological research has not turned up

---

[1] History as a tool for prediction is explored in: Carr, *What Is History?*, 66–70.

[2] Murphy, "Antarctic Conservation: Only by Careful Planning and Cooperation Can We
Save This Primeval Region from the Ravages of Man." Barnes and Porter, *Let's Save
Antarctica!* Mosley, *Saving the Antarctic Wilderness.* http://www.greenpeace.org/new-
zealand/en/about/history/how-we-saved-antarctica/ (accessed 3 February 2021).

[3] Several geologists were emphatic on this. See, for example: John C. Behrendt,
"Geophysical and Geological Research in Antarctica Related to the Assessment of Petroleum

anything to trigger serious interest in the prospects of winnable minerals. It can hardly be argued that Antarctica was saved from something unlikely to occur. If mining was the threat, at best Antarctica was protected from a theoretical threat. But that treats the Protocol only as a solution to a notional problem—a regime *regulating* hypothetical activities replaced by a regime *prohibiting* hypothetical activities.

CCAMLR arguably had a greater role in 'saving' Antarctica when the greatest threat came from marine resource harvesting which *was* occurring. Krill is the centre of the food chain and CCAMLR's rules protected an entire ecosystem. However, the language of 'saving' Antarctica has been particularly linked to the Madrid Protocol.

Various polar maritime accidents (particularly the *Bahia Paraiso* and *Exxon Valdez* disasters) were seized upon as triggers for the environmental debate. Yet the Protocol did not Antarctica from maritime accidents—in fact, such incidents increased.[4]

Another view is that the Protocol 'saved' Antarctica from weak adherence to the then existing environmental measures. Under this argument, assembling measures into a comprehensive regime achieved improved compliance and new Parties would better understand their obligations. That existing measures were not presented in an integrated form seems weak ground for arguing the Protocol 'saved' Antarctica.

It could also be argued that consolidating environmental measures allowed them to be strengthened. That argument also fails as there was not a *regime-wide* strengthening of measures. The real change was expressing the existing measures in binding form and making acceptance of them (but not compliance) a condition of becoming an ATCP.

It is further possible to argue that the greatest risk to Antarctica's environment comes from events outside the Treaty area, rather than within—for example, the Antarctic impacts of increasing global atmospheric carbon dioxide and oceanic pollution.[5] In that case, the Protocol did not 'save'

and Mineral Resources and Potential Environmental Hazards," in *Antarctic Challenge III*, ed. Rüdiger Wolfrum (Duncker and Humblot, 1988), 165.

[4] Maritime incidents immediately after the Protocol included: *Lyubov Orlova* (2006); *Explorer* and *Nordkapp* (2007); *Ushuaia* (2008); *Ocean Nova* (2009); *Clelia II* and *Insung No 1* (2010); *Polar Star* (2011); and *Mar Sem Fim* (2012); *Fram* (2013). At least 15 other incidents damaged tourist vessels in that period. See Liggett, "Destination Icy Wilderness: Tourism in Antarctica," 389–91.

[5] 31 May 2019, XLII ATCM/IP 136 (SCAR) "Antarctic Climate Change and the Environment—2019 Update" https://documents.ats.aq/ATCM42/ip/ATCM42_ip132_e.doc (accessed 11 January 2021).

Antarctica at all as it does not regulate activities *outside* the Treaty area. In any event, until such impacts are averted then Antarctica is not 'saved'.

If it is accepted that Antarctica did not have to be protected from mining itself (as distinct from its theoretical possibility), and that other environmental risks were not significant (except for maritime accidents which were not prevented anyway), then we must look at other ways in which the Protocol may have 'saved' Antarctica. In this view, there are several substantial achievements:

- Consensus around the Protocol saved the Treaty Parties from years of further speculation and divisive debate about the future use of Antarctica's mineral resources (although CRAMRA also had this ambition). It did this by simply prohibiting such activities, and affording unambiguous priority to environment protection. Giving priority to science as the region's primary use reinforced this. While the Protocol may be reviewed at any time (provided there is consensus), the likelihood is that debate on the issue has been forestalled for at least two generations.
- Adoption of the Protocol saved the Treaty from dealing with the tensions over Antarctic sovereignty which had re-emerged with the prospect of minerals. Furthermore, accommodations made over sovereignty may have set useful precedents for future consideration of such issues—if differences could be handled on something as sensitive as minerals, it should be possible for any other issue.
- The Protocol avoided the diversion of Antarctic research effort from science to prospecting (at least, this is assumed).
- The Protocol sidestepped a public relations problem—a problem that might have been avoided in the first place with more deft handling. This includes the problematic title which presented CRAMRA as facilitating mining, rather than protecting Antarctica from its effects.
- By emphasising the environment, the Protocol defused external criticism of the Treaty, especially in the United Nations where objections were raised about the perceived exclusivity of access to minerals. It did this ahead the 1992 First Earth Summit, which held the prospect of increasing UN interest in Antarctic affairs. Under this argument, the Parties saved the existing governance system by protecting the integrity of the Treaty itself.

Such benefits may have been conscious or unconscious motivations. Either way, the essential status quo of the Antarctic Treaty System was preserved, even if it took considerable time, resources and diplomatic capital to achieve it.

Who 'Saved' Antarctica?

Within the raft of concurrent events and public policy issues, and amid a cacophony of public outrage, were the diplomats, lawyers, scientists and environmentalists seeking to extract an outcome acceptable to themselves and to others. Re-establishing consensus achieved that. Many individuals and organisations stood up to celebrate success and claim responsibility. Others were credited with responsibility whether or not they sought recognition.

In examining the claims by individuals to have saved Antarctica, it is helpful to recall the context of their actions. This includes existing territorial claims and a stable Antarctic Treaty that dealt with them; proven operational practices of the Treaty, including adherence to consensus; latent interest in mining and the diplomatic investment in a regime to regulate it; an existing moratorium; national policy and domestic politics; existing environmental measures and calls for a world park. In addition, there were significant serendipities, notably maritime casualties. Concurrently, there were promising technological developments in Arctic mining; fears of resource scarcity; rising global environmentalism and public expectations; external scrutiny, including from the UN; and a special opportunity to debate Antarctica's future in the lead up to the June 1991 opportunity for a Treaty review conference to be called. Such elements may well have facilitated the outcome, but none made it inevitable: it was necessary for individuals to act by taking advantage of such circumstances.

Claiming Credit

Australia was often blamed for CRAMRA's demise. After the environment debate, Australia was often credited for pursuing the environmental initiative to replace it.[6] 'Australia' is a short-hand disguising many individuals.

---

[6] Sometimes credit is shared with France. See, for example: Elliott, *International Environmental Politics: Protecting the Antarctic*, 162–66. Joyner, *Governing the Frozen Commons*, 150. 30 May 2016, Evan Bloom "The history, vision behind and impact of the

It is impossible to ignore former Prime Minister Bob Hawke. Hawke himself claimed credit, promoting his personal role and asserting that saving Antarctica was one of the greatest achievements of his time as Prime Minister.[7] The achievement "really was mine", he said in 2003.[8] Hawke's triumphalism did not subside over time, nor the accolades.[9]

Hawke's claim of priority has been disputed, most notably by his Treasurer Paul Keating. Keating claims that he came up with the idea of making Antarctica an "environmentally protected zone" and had suggested this to French Prime Minister Michel Rocard on 30 September 1988.[10] Much later (in 1995), Keating recalled telling Rocard in the 1988 Paris conversation that "I'd have to convince Bob (Hawke) about this, but if you give him a suitably flattering letter, we might get him into it".[11] Perhaps Keating's conversion to an environmental option emerged on the

Protocol on Environmental Protection to the Antarctic Treaty" (25th Anniversary Symposium, Santiago) https://2009-2017.state.gov/e/oes/rls/remarks/2016/258286. htm (accessed 3 February 2021).

[7] 10 November 2014, transcript "Just call me Bob" (part 1) ABC TV *Australian Story*. https://www.abc.net.au/austory/just-call-me-bob/5869580 (accessed 3 February 2021).

[8] March 2003, Michael Gordon "Bob Hawke on his loves, legacies and life after politics" *The Age* http://www.theage.com.au/articles/2003/02/28/1046407750547.html (accessed 3 February 2021).

[9] Ryan and Bramston, *The Hawke Government: A Critical Retrospective*, 419. 14 December 2009, media release "20th anniversary of the Hawke government's action to protect Antarctica" http://www.antarctica.gov.au/news/2009/20th-anniversary-of-the-hawke-governments-action-to-protect-antarctica (accessed 3 February 2021). 14 December 2009 "Hawke honoured for Antarctic mining fight" http://www.abc.net.au/news/stories/2009/12/14/2771530.htm?section=justin (accessed 3 February 2021). 9 July 2016, Nick O'Malley "Bob Hawke: There is not one outstanding leader in the world" http://www.theage.com.au/nsw/bob-hawke-there-is-not-one-outstanding-leader-in-the-world-20160708-gq1kgf.html#ixzz4DrHwk4mM (accessed 3 February 2021). 4 October 2016, Tim Stephens "Australia proved it was an environmental world leader with the Antarctic agreement" *Sydney Morning Herald*. Hawke and Rielly, *Wednesdays with Bob*, passim. 18 February 2018, ABC TV "Hawke: the larrikin and the leader" (Series 1, Episode 2), at 42:15 http://www.abc.net.au/tv/programs/hawke-the-larrikin-and-the-leader/ (accessed 3 February 2021). 3 July 2019, House of Representatives Hansard, 4–82. 3 July 2019, Senate Hansard, 6–41.

[10] 1 January 2015, Troy Bramston "Cabinet Papers 1988–1989: Hot under collar at who saved Antarctica" *The Australian*. Day, *Paul Keating: The Biography*, 322–23. Bramston, *Paul Keating: The Big Picture Leader*, 318–19.

[11] Bush, *Antarctica and International Law: A Collection of Inter-State and National Documents (Looseleaf Volumes)*, Vol IV, Booklet AU88–89, 21 at footnote 6. Bowden, *The Silence Calling: Australians in Antarctica 1947–1997*, 410–12. 3 March 1995, Tony Vermeer "Keating tells how he helped save Antarctica" (ATADD-1-BB-AU-718). Keating

road to Paris because, just a few days earlier, his 21 September letter to Foreign Minister Gareth Evans offered no environmental reason for objecting to CRAMRA—his objections had been its poor protection of sovereign and economic interests.[12] These issues included a special share of revenue and anti-subsidy provisions, precisely the concerns he had raised in correspondence immediately after CRAMRA's adoption. This exactly matched Treasury's position. It is not clear whether Keating and Resources Minister Peter Cook had collaborated in opposing CRAMRA, but they certainly wrote to Hawke with their objections within a week of each other.[13] If environmental concerns had become Keating's primary motive for opposing CRAMRA, his Treasury officials ignored it at the time of the 12 April 1989 final draft of the critical Cabinet submission.[14] Peter Cook has not claimed to have influenced Hawke's position on Antarctica, but Keating gave Cook credit anyway.[15]

Evans was responsible for the Cabinet submission and recommended signing CRAMRA, supported by Environment Minister Graham Richardson. Australia appeared on track to sign. However, on 20 April Rocard announced his reservations about CRAMRA, attracting considerable media attention. A week later, on 27 April, Keating wrote to Hawke making the case for a world park (or, failing that, declaring the AAT a national park), but without revealing he had suggested such options to Prime Minister Rocard in 1988.[16] It is not clear when Hawke received Keating's letter, but he denied being influenced by it anyway. Keating's opposition to CRAMRA on environmental grounds possibly strengthened in the last few weeks before the 22 May 1989 Cabinet meeting. His delay

went on to say that Rocard did write to Hawke, "and it was the Bob and Michel show from there on". If Rocard wrote to Hawke, this author has not seen it.
[12] 21 September 1988, letter Keating to Evans (AU-ATADD-1-BB-AU-193). 16 November 1988, facsimile DFAT to Antarctic Division "Summary of outstanding correspondence" (NAA: B1387 88/893 PART 1).
[13] 27 April 1989, letter Keating to Hawke (AU-ATADD-1-BB-AU-196). 4 May 1989, letter Cook to Hawke (NAA: B1387 88/893 PART 3).
[14] 12 April 1989, Cabinet Submission "Antarctic minerals convention" (NAA: 14039, 6415). Treasury's objections to CRAMRA refer only to revenue and anti-subsidies: 24 March 1988, AAD brief to minister "Antarctic minerals convention—Cabinet Submission" (NAA: B1387 87/720 PART 2).
[15] 3 March 1995, Tony Vermeer "Keating tells how he helped save Antarctica" *AAP* (AU-ATADD-1-BB-AU-718), 2.
[16] Keating's letter said only that he had outlined to Rocard Australia's policy his personal views on minerals. 27 April 1989, letter Keating to Hawke (AU-ATADD-1-BB-AU-196).

in revealing support for a world park remains unexplained—Peter Boyce's quizzing of Keating on this in October 2010 shed no light on the matter.[17] Also unexplained is the contradiction with Graham Richardson's recollection that, in Cabinet, Keating "argued strongly on economic rather than environmental grounds ... and he did it very well".[18]

A further gap in the records is exactly when Bob Hawke became aware of the Cabinet submission—the timing is critical to his claim to priority. Hawke suggests that he realised the significance of the issues on seeing the submission. Hawke's biographer says it was "one weekend". His economics adviser, Craig Emerson, says it was in April.[19] This could well have been the very same 29–30 April 1989 weekend that John Howard's objection to CRAMRA was reported and Keating's letter appeared in the media.[20] This timing would explain why delegation briefing for the Preparatory Meeting in Paris did not reflect these developments. Several factors may have been in play for Hawke. He may have felt wedged by Opposition Leader Howard being ahead of him on an environment issue. Although Hawke denied it, he may also have felt wedged by Keating who had long held ambitions to become Prime Minister and, it was later revealed, wished to have "more than just an economic dimension to his political persona".[21] After all, Hawke's electoral success was founded on bold environment decisions. Hawke also took pride in the Antarctic dimension to his relationship with the French Prime Minister, Michel Rocard. In Hawke's later claims to priority on the ideas, the revelation that Keating had raised Antarctica with Rocard matters months in advance of Hawke may also have irritated. The documents examined for this book are inconclusive so, for the time being, the conflicting accounts remain unresolved.

Former Science Minister Barry Jones has supported Bob Hawke's view, praising his achievement and saying that "saving Antarctica from mining

---

[17] Jackson and Boyce, "Mining and 'World Park Antarctica'," 251–52. ibid., 251.

[18] Bowden, *The Silence Calling: Australians in Antarctica 1947–1997*, 414.

[19] Hawke later said it was as late as May 1989. 9 July 2016, Nick O'Malley "Clout in the cold together" *The Age*, 25.

[20] 29 April 1989, Margo Kingston "Libs likely to oppose Antarctic mining" *Sydney Morning Herald*, 6. 30 April 1989, Alan Fewster "Antarctic park finds an ally in Keating" *Sunday Telegraph*, 122.

[21] The Hawke/Keating rivalry included the November 1988 Kirribilli Agreement, which addressed succession arrangements: Bramston, *Paul Keating: The Big Picture Leader*. d'Alpuget, *Bob Hawke: The Complete Biography*. Day, *Paul Keating: The Biography*, 323.

was a major achievement and all his own work".[22] Other than Paul Keating, Hawke's colleagues have not sought to take credit. Despite his portfolio responsibilities for Antarctic and environment policy, and despite the domestic political significance and global impact of Australia's decision, Graham Richardson does not seek credit—surprisingly, his memoirs make no mention at all of Antarctica.[23] Richardson had supported the draft Cabinet submission which, until Gareth Evans' last-minute amendments, recommended that Australia sign CRAMRA.[24] There was an apparent paradox: in the lead-up to the May 1989 Cabinet decision Richardson, as Environment Minister, supported signature of the minerals convention while Peter Cook, the Resources Minister, opposed. Evans' overwhelming interest as foreign minister had been the stability of the Antarctic Treaty and maintaining good relations with Treaty partners. That is probably why, after the Cabinet decision, he held open the prospect that Australia might one day sign CRAMRA.[25] Evans' support for CRAMRA, however, did not mean that he was unsympathetic to environmental causes.[26] As Foreign Minister, Evans had a low profile in the diplomatic campaign but it must be recognised that Iraq's 1990 invasion of Kuwait led to Evans cancelling his proposed tour of South American capitals to campaign for the Antarctic initiative. The ensuing Gulf War became a continuing pre-occupation.[27] Evans can, however, take credit for changing his recommendations to Cabinet two days before the May 1989 meeting and resourcing his officials to advance the outcome. He later proudly reflected on the Antarctic decision and subsequent diplomatic achievement.[28] More

[22] Ryan and Bramston, *The Hawke Government: A Critical Retrospective*, 419.

[23] Graham Richardson, *Whatever It Takes* (Bantam, 1994). Richardson opposed mining but accepted Departmental advice to support CRAMRA. 12 April 1989, brief to minister's adviser "Minerals convention" (NAA: B1387 88/893 PART 3). 12 April 1989, Cabinet Submission "Antarctic minerals convention" (NAA: 14039, 6415).

[24] Evan's submission was amended on the Saturday, two days before the Cabinet meeting. See 20 May 1989, Cabinet Submission corrigendum "Antarctic minerals convention: further developments" (NAA: 14039, 6506).

[25] 12 June 1989, ND69271 "India: Minister Evans visit: conversation with Prime Minister Rajiv Gandhi" (NAA: B1387 89/311 PART 4). 29 June 1989, LH77976 "Senator Evans' discussions in London" (NAA: B1387 89/453 PART 1).

[26] Evans achieved infamy in the Tasmanian dams issue by commissioning RAAF surveillance over the state. Evans, "The Background Politics of the Tasmanian Dam Case," 14.

[27] Bill Bush, personal communication, 4 December 2020.

[28] Evans and Grant, *Australia's Foreign Relations in the World of the 1990's*, 156–58.

recently, Evans gave due credit to Hawke and did so colourfully: "you bugger, you were right!"[29]

As noted above, in 1989 Bob Hawke's principal adviser on the issue was Craig Emerson. Several accounts crediting Hawke also cite Emerson's role. Emerson himself graciously cedes credit to Hawke.[30] There is evidence, however, that it was Emerson that first seized on the significance of the imminent CRAMRA decision.[31] Given the close relationship between ministers and advisers, it is legitimate to give some credit to Emerson for his role in 'saving' Antarctica. If so, it is also reasonable to recognise others who may have influenced Hawke. They include Bob Chynoweth (ALP Caucus chair who announced opposition to CRAMRA in April 1989); independent senator Jo Vallentine (who launched a motion against CRAMRA in November 1988); and Democratic senator Jean Jenkins (who the same month proposed an 'Antarctic conservation zone world wilderness park'). Opposition Leader John Howard can also take some credit. His objection to Antarctic mining was publicly announced on 29 April 1989, at least a week before Hawke. On 2 May 1989, his environment spokesperson, Chris Puplick, rallied and railed against CRAMRA. Even though it became bipartisan policy, Howard relished being ahead of Hawke on an environmental issue.[32]

In France, Michel Rocard had already questioned CRAMRA at a critical point in Australia's domestic debate, showing the potential for using public opinion to defy the Antarctic status quo. Rocard's questioning of CRAMRA had been made easier by the departmental mis-communication which prevented the French Ambassador signing CRAMRA on 25 November 1988.[33] Had France signed, it would have been very much harder to step back. The impact on Rocard of his discussion with Keating in September 1988 is not clear, and, unsurprisingly, there is no reference to a pre-existing 'Antarctica deal' in the account of Hawke's meetings with

[29] Gareth Evans, *Incorrigible Optimist: A Political Memoir* (Melbourne University Press, 2017), 131. Evans spoke in similar terms at the National Press Club in October 2017: http://iview.abc.net.au/programs/national-press-club-address/NC1706C037S00#playing at 34:55 (accessed 3 February 2021).

[30] Emerson, *The Boy from Baradine*, 186–97.

[31] 18 February 2018, "Hawke: The larrikin and the leader" (Series 1, Episode 2) ABC TV, at 42:15 http://www.abc.net.au/tv/programs/hawke-the-larrikin-and-the-leader/ (accessed 3 February 2021).

[32] 6 March 1991, House of Representatives Hansard, 1419.

[33] Templeton, *A Wise Adventure II: New Zealand and Antarctica after 1960*, 226.

Rocard in 1989. If Rocard had an environmental option in mind since 1988, and had revealed the Keating discussions, then French officials might have been less surprised by him rejecting CRAMRA in April 1989. In any event, Rocard was influenced by environmentalists, including Jacques Cousteau whose petition had attracted thousands of signatures. Whatever motivated Rocard, the April 1989 announcement of French concerns about CRAMRA were instrumental. For Bob Hawke, it provided cover for breaking consensus as both Australia and France were required for CRAMRA to enter into force—Hawke could argue it was France, *not* Australia, that put CRAMRA in doubt. Hawke and Rocard went on to enjoy a very close relationship. After his death in 2016, Rocard was credited with being the "father of the Madrid Protocol".[34]

If Not Just Hawke, Who?

The problem with giving all the credit to Bob Hawke (or Paul Keating, or Michel Rocard) is that doing so does not recognise that, ultimately, achievement of both the mining ban and the Protocol required the consensus of 26 ATCPs. Consensus is crucial to Antarctic decision-making, and it is remarkably easy to block—all it takes is one objection. To give credit to Hawke, it is straightforward to recognise his undoubted influence over Cabinet's decisions that led to CRAMRA being scuttled. That took immense international political courage and precipitated a crisis to be resolved. However, giving credit for scuttling the regime that allowed mining does *not* equate to giving credit for the consensus to establish the regime that would prohibit it. That would conflate two distinct processes. Creating consensus is considerably harder than blocking it—one Party cannot impose its will to achieve it, let alone one person. At the time, 26 Parties were required to achieve consensus and the narrative shows that was not simple. After a decade of informal discussion, CRAMRA took six years of formal negotiations to achieve consensus. The liability annex took 13 years.[35] The Treaty Secretariat took 32 years.[36] By comparison, the

[34] Yuri Rubinsky, "Arctic Interests and the Policy of France," *Arctic and North* 24 (2016).

[35] Antarctic Treaty, Measure 1 (2005) "Annex VI to the Protocol on Environmental Protection to the Antarctic Treaty: Liability Arising from Environmental Emergencies" https://ats.aq/devAS/Meetings/Measure/331 (accessed 27 March 2020).

[36] Antarctic Treaty, Measure 1 (2003) "Secretariat of the Antarctic Treaty" https://ats.aq/devAS/Meetings/Measure/294 (accessed 27 March 2020).

two-year period to re-establish consensus after the rejection of CRAMRA was remarkable. However, it was neither the work of one person, nor one Party.

So we need to look outside the circle of domestic politicians to see who else can take credit for bringing an end to CRAMRA and building consensus around the Madrid Protocol. The field of players is large, involving diplomats and the officials who advise them; scientists; the media; as well as political leaders and the environmentalists who influenced them.

Diplomats and Officials

Woolcott calls the Antarctic environment debate a diplomatic 'event' and securing the Protocol as "one of the most successful exercises in Australian diplomacy".[37] As an international forum, the ATCM was the primary theatre for diplomatic skills. Because of the operation of consensus, each delegation head can take credit for the Protocol, but getting to that point was where most of the effort was expended.

Australians particularly active included Ambassadors Alan Brown and John McCarthy. Brown took the heat in Paris in October 1989, using great diplomatic skill to keep Australia's objectives alive when they were at their most vulnerable. He went on to lead the delegation at Viña del Mar in late 1990. McCarthy led in the crucial Madrid sessions which concluded the Protocol. Gareth Evans gave him special praise and, through him, acknowledged the delegation as a whole.[38] In response, McCarthy especially recognised contributions by DFAT's John Burgess and Jean Page.[39] The delegation was also praised by Bob Hawke and Senator Evans in Parliament.[40] Such praise, however, ignores the work of those in Canberra and Hobart providing much of the intellectual effort required. For example, particular recognition belongs to DFAT lawyer Bill Bush, who drafted the environmental convention and established principles which carried through the negotiations. Henry Burmester of the Attorney-General's Department also provided legal support and AAD's Rex Moncur

---

[37] Richard Woolcott, "Foreword," in *Australia and the Antarctic Treaty System: 50 Years of Influence*, ed. Marcus Haward and Tom Griffiths (UNSW Press, 2011), xiv.

[38] 6 May 1991, letter Evans to McCarthy (NAA: B1387 91/32 PART 2).

[39] 8 May 1991, letter McCarthy to Evans (NAA: B1387 91/32 PART 2).

[40] 7 May 1991, House of Representatives Hansard, 3068–3069. 7 May 1991, Senate Hansard, 2769.

ran Australia's negotiation of practical environmental measures. It is also important to recognise Keith Brennan, who, instrumental in developing CCAMLR, helped establish Australia's Antarctic environmental reputation and gave Australia considerable confidence in advancing sovereign interests. One DFAT official, Brendan Doran, was awarded a 1992 Public Service Medal[41] for "outstanding work" in the Antarctic campaign.[42]

Sir Ninian Stephen, former governor general and inaugural Australian environment ambassador, was nominated for France's *Commandeur de la Legion d'Honneur* in recognition of his role in pursing Antarctic protection.[43] While the environment initiative is often attributed to Australia it was, of course, led jointly with French officials (and then the 'Four Powers') who equally share credit. Within the ATCMs, France was represented by Georges Duquin, in turn supported by Charley Causeret. Jean-Pierre Puissochet, France's delegation head, was particularly credited with playing "a very important personal role".[44]

New Zealand also had prominent participants, notably Chris Beeby and Frank Wong. Beeby's influence stemmed from his chairing role on minerals and, as Joyner observes, Beeby's "personal influence, political credibility, and diplomatic skill had been instrumental in securing agreement".[45] The environment principles he embedded in CRAMRA were drawn on for the Protocol. He later facilitated New Zealand's change of heart on CRAMRA, done with considerable equanimity given rejection of his efforts on minerals. Replacing him was Frank Wong, another player with considerable personal influence.

A key player in the Protocol negotiations was Rolf Andersen, the Norwegian diplomat who generated the 'Andersen Text'. In Madrid, Andersen convened key players to resolve the mining prohibition, using personal connections to break the deadlock.[46] His predecessor, Edvard

---

[41] The Public Service Medal is part of the Australian honours system.

[42] https://honours.pmc.gov.au/honours/awards/868972 (accessed 3 February 2021).

[43] 8 July 1993, letter Evans to McMullan, Minister for the Arts and Administrative Services (AAD: 81/346–3). Ayres, *Fortunate Voyager: The Worlds of Ninian Stephen*, 133–36.

[44] 5 December 1990, SC21441 "Antarctic—SCM—minerals outcome" (AAD: 89/914–2).

[45] Christopher C. Joyner, "1988 Antarctic Minerals Convention," *Marine Policy Reports* 1, no. 1 (1989): 81.

[46] 4 December 1990, SC21437 "Antarctic environment: SCM XI: Minerals" (AAD: 89/914–2). 26 April 1991, MA26855 "Antarctic instrument: Minerals" (NAA: B1387 91/32 PART 1).

Hambro, initiated the crucial moratorium idea in 1973.[47] That moratorium survived the negotiations and its legacy lingers in the Protocol's Article 25.

Chile's Fernando Zegers also played an important role. At the May 1989 ATCX XV Preparatory Meeting, he proposed that Parties strengthen existing environmental requirements, initially in response to maritime accidents.[48] After Australia flagged the possibility that Australia might not sign CRAMRA, this resulted in comprehensive measures being placed on the ATCM agenda for referral to a special meeting. This served two purposes—it bought time for Australia to canvass support for its proposals and, for others, time for CRAMRA to continue attracting signatures.[49] Inclusion of Zegers' proposal on the ATCM agenda turned out to be the key for having environmental measures discussed at all.

Being historically influential in Treaty forums, the United States could be expected to influence the environment debate. US priorities were protection of the Treaty itself, vigorous advancement of its national interests and the enforceability of any measures adopted. While the United States withheld consensus on the Protocol until it stood alone in resisting, this does not suggest uniform opposition. The appointment of Curtis Bohlen, previously vice president of the WWF, to lead the United States in Viña del Mar and Madrid indicated the importance attached to an environmental regime's integrity. Bohlen's engagement helped the United States shift position on CRAMRA. Tucker Scully, whose Antarctic diplomatic experience commanded considerable respect, is nevertheless the most-mentioned US figure in the Australian documents. Scully's United Kingdom equivalent was John Heap, also a career diplomat and Antarctic specialist with years of uninterrupted ATCM experience.[50] Heap and Scully were formidable when collaborating. Belgium's Gérard Surquin described Scully as "strong and likely to remain so", and suggested that "without Scully, Heap would be a relatively insignificant force".[51] Fair or not, such frank-

[47] 29 May 1973, "Prepared remarks by Ambassador Edvard Hambro" (NAA: B1387 1991/370).

[48] May 1989, PREP/WP/1 "Information paper, presented by the Delegation of Chile" (NAA: B1387 89/311 PART 1). 9 May 1989, PA74190 "Antarctic minerals convention" (NAA: B1387 89/311 PART 1).

[49] May 1989, "ATCM XV—Prep" (AWJ personal notes).

[50] Andersen, "Negotiating a New Regime: How CRAMRA Came into Existence," 96–97.

[51] 1 December 1989, BS48709 "Antarctica" (NAA: B1387 89/932 PART 1). This contrasts with later observations that the British tended to act for the United States. See 19 June 1990, SC20769 "Antarctica: Chile's policy and the SCM" (AAD: 89/914–1).

ness revealed influence coming as much from powerful personalities as from the policy positions proposed, and the ability to control debate from the floor or through personal connections. Influence exercised on the basis of experience should not be underestimated. Figures such as Scully and Heap invested considerable diplomatic capital in CRAMRA and then in the Protocol. Personal pride was potentially at stake when the convention was challenged. Heap had been unashamedly pro-CRAMRA, justifiably pointing to the risks to the environment, and the Treaty itself, if minerals activities remained unregulated. The United Kingdom was the first Party to introduce CRAMRA legislation.[52] Being first to sign the Protocol underscored the United Kingdom's U-turn, restoring the United Kingdom's image as a leader in Antarctic affairs. As a staunch defender of CRAMRA, some on the Australian and French side might have found it somewhat disingenuous that the United Kingdom later gave John Heap credit for the Protocol, a claim made on the grounds that Heap was the first to propose a protocol as the *form* of environment instrument (although his proposal was for it to operate alongside CRAMRA).[53]

Scientists

Several scientists helped 'save' Antarctica. These include SCAR specialists who advised on environmental matters triggered by CRAMRA and, earlier, influenced the 1964 Agreed Measures by reflecting the concerns of Robert Carrick and Robert Cushman Murphy.[54] Scientists such as Murphy and Australia's Don McMichael had promoted an international park, later adapted to become calls for a world park.[55] Credit also goes to geologists, including John Behrendt, whose insistence that there were no economic resources removed urgency from the minerals debate.[56]

[52] 7 June 1989, DFAT facsimile message "CRAMRA: UK legislation" covering a copy of "Antarctic Minerals Bill (HL)" (NAA: B1387 89/311 PART 3).

[53] Richardson, "John Arnfield Heap, CMG," 265.

[54] Robert Carrick, "Conservation of Nature in Antarctica," ibid.10, no. 68 (1961). Murphy, "Antarctic Conservation: Only by Careful Planning and Cooperation Can We Save This Primeval Region from the Ravages of Man."

[55] Elliott, "Recommendation 5: Establishment of Antarctica as a World Park under United Nations Auspices," 443–44. Murphy, "Antarctica: The Urgency of Protecting Life on and around the Great Southerly Continent," 22.

[56] Behrendt published eight such papers between 1981 and 1991, all concluding there are no known petroleum or mineral resources. For example: John C. Behrendt, "Recent Geophysical and Geological Research in Antarctica Related to the Assessment of Petroleum Resources and Potential Environmental Hazards to Their Development," in *Mineral*

SCAR's criticisms of the environment debate were overcome as the feared constraints on science did not materialise. While SCAR had become politicised, eventually science became a major beneficiary of the Protocol and scientific research prospered to play a crucial role in improving environmental measures. In that sense, the Protocol strengthened SCAR and the Treaty's priority for science.

National Political Leaders

The claims of Bob Hawke and others for 'saving' Antarctica have been examined above. Intriguingly, other notable political leaders have since given Antarctica little attention. Biographies of key Australians such as Graham Richardson and John Howard make no mention of the Antarctic events, nor the biographies of New Zealand Prime Ministers David Lange and Geoffrey Palmer.[57] Palmer's strongly pro-environment approach to CRAMRA was reinforced by Conservation Minister Philip Woollaston and by Palmer's successor, Mike Moore, who had advocated a world park as early as 1981.[58] New Zealand Labour Prime Minister Bill Rowling had endorsed such an idea in 1975, in turn building on the 1956 proposal of his predecessor Walter Nash.

Other national leaders also played an important role. French Prime Minister Michel Rocard's early role was crucial. US Senator Al Gore was particularly prominent, and congressmen Silvio Conte, Bruce Vento and John Kerry generated momentum by sponsoring various bills and resolutions. Later, Prime Minister John Major intervened to ensure UK support for a mining ban, reportedly without consulting Cabinet or officials' support.[59] This may well have influenced President George Bush who, on 3 July 1991, announced US support for the Protocol, even asserting the Protocol was "based on a US initiative".[60] Even so, Bush must be credited

---

Resources Potential of Antarctica, ed. John F. Splettstoesser and Gisela A. Dreschhoff, Antarctic Research Series 51 (American Geophysical Union, 1990), 163.

[57] Richardson, *Whatever It Takes*. John Howard, *Lazarus Rising: A Personal and Political Autobiography* (HarperCollins, 2011). David Lange, *My Life* (Viking, 2005). Geoffrey Palmer, *Reform: A Memoir* (Victoria University Press, 2013).

[58] Moore, *Beyond Today: A Look at a Sustainable Economy, Resource Management and Control and a History of Environmental Politics in New Zealand*, 72.

[59] 15 May 1990, Michael McCarthy "Major adds weight to Antarctic mining ban" *The Australian*, 10.

[60] George Bush, "Statement on the environmental protection protocol to the Antarctic Treaty, 3 July 1991" http://www.presidency.ucsb.edu/ws/index.php?pid=29657 (accessed 3 February 2021).

with his role in 'saving' Antarctica as, given the consensus system, the United States was the last to remove objections.[61]

Environmentalists

Political leadership was, in part, driven by environmentalists whose influence stirred enough public concern to force governments to act.[62] Several authors credit NGO campaigns for the turnaround on CRAMRA.[63] Many groups were active.[64] Geoffrey Palmer conceded the influence of NGOs and Tucker Scully described the environmental movement as "irresistible".[65] In Australia, Environment Minister Ros Kelly praised NGOs for supporting government objectives.[66] Foreign Minister Gareth Evans paid "particular tribute" to ASOC's Lyn Goldsworthy, who was more formally recognised by appointment as a Member of the Order of Australia in 1993.[67]

Policy positions were not necessarily consistent among NGOs. For example, NGO views ranged from accepting CRAMRA as the best

[61] Hawke asserted that he influenced Bush's decision by writing to him the previous week—this is impossible to verify as US hesitation triggered representations from several Parties and NGOs. See 5 July 1991, Greg Austin, "Bush comes around on Antarctic mining ban" *Sydney Morning Herald*, 5.

[62] This was described as "the Cousteau method". See 20 September 1989, PA76733 "Antarctica—Wellington Convention—interview with Cousteau" (NAA: B1387 89/453 PART 3).

[63] Bergin, "The Politics of Antarctic Minerals: The Greening of White Australia," 222–25. Francioni, "The Madrid Protocol on the Protection of the Antarctic Environment," 49. Elliott, *International Environmental Politics: Protecting the Antarctic*, 194–95. Chaturvedi, *The Polar Regions*, 212. Templeton, *A Wise Adventure II: New Zealand and Antarctica after 1960*, 270–96. Clark, "The Antarctic Environmental Protocol: NGOs in the Protection of Antarctica."

[64] Apart from ASOC, Australian groups included the Antarctic Defence Coalition, Fund for Animals, Project Jonah, Greenpeace Australia, Australian Conservation Foundation, Ecofund and World Wildlife Fund. United States groups included Defenders of Wildlife, Environmental Defense Fund, Friends of the Earth, Greenpeace, Humane Society, National Audubon Society, National Wildlife Federation, Natural Resources Defense Council, Sierra Club, The Antarctica Project, and The Wilderness Society.

[65] 27 August 1990, CH595660 "Antarctica: NZ position" (NAA: B1387 90/759 PART 2). Scully, "The Development of the Antarctic Treaty System," 36.

[66] 14 October 1992, House of Representatives Hansard, 2156.

[67] 4 October 1991, speech by Senator Gareth Evans "Antarctica: An international environment win for Australia" (AU-ATADD-1-BB-AU-354), 2. https://honours.pmc.gov.au/honours/awards/878250 (accessed 3 February 2021).

solution achievable, to calls for a permanent mining ban in a world park (or even a World Heritage area outside the Treaty System[68]). Some environmentalists considered the Protocol fell well short of expectations but were not shy in taking credit, with Cath Wallace openly proud of NGO influence.[69] Wallace, a co-founder of ASOC New Zealand, was awarded the Goldman Prize in 1991 for her role in protecting Antarctica.[70] Other prominent environmentalists also take credit for 'saving' Antarctica. Cassandra Phillips, herself a leading campaigner (who claimed that it had been WWF that changed Australia's mind[71]), said of Jim Barnes that "I doubt whether anyone has done more to ensure Antarctica is saved".[72] Greenpeace's Kelly Rigg says that she led and won the campaign to save Antarctica.[73] Geoff Mosley has written about the part played by himself and the ACF.[74] Other prominent environmentalists include the ACF's Margaret Moore, David Westlake and Phillip Toyne; the Sierra Club's Beth Marks; Janet Dalziel of Greenpeace; Maj de Poorter, Bruce Manheim, Doug Nicol, Barry Weeber, Roger Wilson and more. Some would say that all of them were outdone by Jacques Cousteau.[75] As a so-called "celebrity environmentalist", he attracted considerable accolades for the Antarctic

[68] J.G. Mosley, "Antarctica: The Case for a World Wilderness Park," in *Fighting for Wilderness*, ed. J G Mosley and J Messer (Fontana/ACF, 1984).

[69] 27 August 1990, WL41558 "New Zealand: environmental groups" (NAA: B1387 90/759 PART 2).

[70] Antarctic and Southern Ocean Coalition, "Congratulations, Cath," *ECO* LXXX, no. 1 (1991). See also: https://www.goldmanprize.org/recipient/cath-wallace/ (accessed 3 February 2021).

[71] 10 May 1990, transcript ABC Radio *Early AM* "UK campaign to join Aust in opposing Antarctic minerals convention" (NAA: B1387 90/498 PART 1).

[72] https://www.asoc.org/about/history/1118 (accessed 3 February 2021). Barnes, who founded ASOC in 1978, had an extraordinarily long association with Antarctic campaigns. See https://www.asoc.org/about/history (accessed 3 February 2021).

[73] https://www.huffingtonpost.com/kelly-rigg/we-saved-antarctica-or-di_b_5344635. html (accessed 3 February 2021). Credit is also given to Kelly Rigg in: 23 February 2020, "Saving Antarctica" *The History Hour* BBC World Service, https://www.bbc.co.uk/programmes/w3csypzz (accessed 6 April 2020), 1:20–10:20.

[74] Mosley, *Saving the Antarctic Wilderness.*

[75] Clark Lee Merriam, "The Cousteau Society/Foundation Cousteau: Retrospective of 1990 Activities," *Colorado Journal of International Environmental Law and Policy* 2 (1991): 326–28.

campaign, his "crowning achievement".[76] Hawke described him as a "magnificent human being" and made him a Companion of the Order of Australia.[77]

Media

Without access to the media environmentalists would have had difficulty attracting attention. Sometimes, however, the media made up its own mind. In 1989, ABC *Four Corners* visited Antarctica for a story presented by Tony Jones.[78] It aired on 20 March 1989, unaware that four days later, in exquisite coincidence, the *Exxon Valdez* calamity would inflame the public mood even more. In a 22 August 2011 retrospective on *Four Corners*, Jones claimed to have put Antarctica "on the political agenda", adding that "we always like to say that Martin Butler, the producer, and myself, if we do nothing else in our lives at least we saved Antarctica". Butler agreed, reflecting that the Antarctic experience showed "journalists really could make a difference".[79] He has a point: John Howard said that "I think it was an excellent story. It did have an impact on me ... not long after that program I declared opposition to mining in Antarctica ... and the Government followed pretty soon thereafter".[80]

[76] Shortis, ""Who Can Resist This Guy?" Jacques Cousteau, Celebrity Diplomacy, and the Environmental Protection of the Antarctic," 366–67.

[77] 11 July 1989, PA75294 "Prime Minister's meeting with President Mitterrand: Antarctica" (NAA: B1387 89/453 PART 1). "Jacques Cousteau's Visit to Australia," 81. See also: https://honours.pmc.gov.au/honours/awards/878276 (accessed 3 February 2021).

[78] http://www.abc.net.au/4corners/frozen-asset—1989/2842018 (accessed 3 February 2021). The program later achieved a gold award at the New York Film and Television Festival: Robert Raymond, "Frozen Assets," *Panorama: Ansett Airlines inflight magazine*, no. 92 [April] (1990): 32.

[79] http://mpegmedia.abc.net.au/news/fourcorners/50years/video/4c_50yrs_ TonyJones_frozenassets_288p.mp4 (accessed 3 February 2021). 25 February 2017, Martin Butler "Five places that made me" *The Age* (Traveller section), 5.

[80] http://iview.abc.net.au/programs/four-corners-55th-anniversary/ NC1627H003S00#playing (accessed 3 February 2021).

Parties

Rather than pointing to individuals, some credit certain Parties with 'saving' Antarctica. The ACF regarded it "an Australian initiative".[81] So, too, the USSR.[82] Giving sole credit to Australia is odd given the effort put into emphasising the proposals were equally French (with later support from Belgium and Italy). It is possibly explained by Australia being ahead of France by some months in formally deciding not to sign CRAMRA. In addition, Australia appeared to lead promotion of the initiative and applied more resources to it, with France occasionally reluctant to participate in joint representations.[83] Ironically, Australia had only felt free to reject CRAMRA after France had thrown its future into doubt.[84] Australia largely declined triumphalism at the Protocol's conclusion, instead preferring a lower profile with the focus on compliance and the Protocol's early entry into force.[85] France argued that success should be celebrated equally by all Parties.[86]

New Zealand earned strong credit. Its dramatic shift from CRAMRA in 1990 resulted in the most ambitious environmental proposals. It had been able to leverage the credibility it had earned leading the CRAMRA negotiations to pressure other Parties to adopt effective environmental measures. It seems odd, however, that Sweden received little recognition for being the first signatory to CRAMRA to abandon it—and, at the time, little was done to capitalise on that. Sweden had earlier revealed its environmental sympathies by suggesting in 1988 that CRAMRA's title should refer to the environment.

The United Kingdom directly put its claim on the Protocol by promoting the fact that it was the first Party to sign it. Despite its long advocacy of CRAMRA, it subsequently emphasised its role in advocating a protocol with annexes as the regime's form, and celebrated that the United

[81] 7 August 1991, DFAT minute "Antarctic environment treaty—Australian Conservation Foundation" (AAD: 91/919).

[82] 1 August 1991, CE57547 "Antarctica: SCM XI final session, Madrid, October: USSR views" (AAD: 91/919).

[83] 5 September 1989, PA76409 "Protection of Antarctic environment-France" (NAA: B1387 89/453 PART 2).

[84] 29 May 1989, transcript of interview, *Good Morning* NZ Radio NZ (NAA: B1387 89/311 PART 2).

[85] Jackson and Kriwoken, "The Protocol in Action, 1992–2010," 300–01.

[86] Antarctic Treaty, *Final Report of the Eleventh Antarctic Treaty Special Consultative, Madrid, 22–30 April 1991; 17–22 June 1991; 3–4 October 1991*, 173.

Kingdom had been an early supporter of Chile's idea for a special meeting to negotiate it.[87] Chile deserves recognition for its May 1989 proposal for a meeting to discuss comprehensive environmental measures, thus buying time for the issues to be fully aired.[88] It was Chile's unheralded proposal that enabled Parties to put a review of environmental measures on the agenda.

Others

Of course, multiple others were involved in 'saving' Antarctica, even if there is no clear record in the archives. Some had a vicarious role. For example, the suggestion at the 1972 Second World Conference on National Parks to make Antarctica a world park seems to have come from US alpinist Nicholas Clinch. In another forum, Law of the Sea negotiators excluded the Antarctic sea floor—had that not occurred, sea floor mining would have been possible, and it would have been too late to do anything about it within the ATS. Public petitioners and anonymous private correspondents helped gain Antarctica political attention. In France, public pressure may have been motivated by the need to make amends for the bombing of *Rainbow Warrior*.[89] But if there was a singular event to enrage the public, it was probably *Exxon Valdez* foundering at the other end of the world at a critical time in Antarctic affairs. Several authors point to the impacts of this disaster on the Antarctic minerals debate.[90] Accordingly, on those grounds, it would be remiss not to recognise the inadvertent influence of Captain Joseph Hazelwood and his helmsman Gregory Cousins that fateful night.

---

[87] February 1993, UK Foreign & Commonwealth Office brochure "Britain's role in Antarctica" (AAD: 94/55), 12. 7 December 2016, speech by Alan Duncan MP "The UK's leading role in protecting the Antarctic" https://www.gov.uk/government/speeches/the-uks-leading-role-in-protecting-the-antarctic (accessed 12 December 2016).

[88] Jacobsson, "Building the International Legal Framework for Antarctica," 10.

[89] 23 February 2020, "Saving Antarctica" *The History Hour* BBC World Service, https://www.bbc.co.uk/programmes/w3csypzz (accessed 6 April 2020), 7:05.

[90] Elliott, *International Environmental Politics: Protecting the Antarctic*, 165. Joyner, "The Effectiveness of CRAMRA," 163. Howkins, *The Polar Regions: An Environmental History*, 16–17.

'How' Rather than 'Who'

Clearly, no person or Party can claim exclusive credit for the demise of CRAMRA, or for the environment Protocol which replaced it. No list can do justice to the number of participants involved in 'saving' Antarctica. The archival records reveal some, but not all, and a simple catalog of famous, infamous or obscure names is probably irrelevant anyway. The more important question is *how* Antarctica was 'saved'. In the absence of insight into the political and diplomatic processes, it is easy to focus on the 'who' rather than the 'how', and tempting for prominent individuals to fill the gaps by offering their own names. The answer lies in consensus.

What is also now clear, therefore, are the broader circumstances for the essential consensus to be constructed. That consensus could only be formed by the Parties at an ATCM. On 4 October 1991, the Final Act of the 11th Special Antarctic Treaty Consultative Meeting was signed in Madrid, thus adopting the Madrid Protocol. Not one Party objected. All those Parties proceeded to ratify the Protocol. With a consensus criterion, *all* the Parties share equal credit for 'saving' Antarctica.

Even then, Antarctica could not truly be considered saved until the Protocol's obligations were implemented and with full compliance.[91] That involves another cohort of players altogether: legislators, national Antarctic programs, tour operators, scientists and more. Their work is still being done. The Protocol's Committee for Environmental Protection continues to find ways to improve environmental measures.

Some Reflections

This book shows that it is unrealistic to identify a single individual or Party responsible for the events. As noted in Chap. 1, research for this book used the Australian archival record. Other historians may have to enter other archives for further insights. This author would be happy to be proven wrong in the conclusions drawn here, and delighted if others come to a better answer. This book, however, shows what archival records can reveal about the shift from CRAMRA to the Madrid Protocol. Australian

---

[91] Davor Vidas, ed. *Implementing the Environmental Protection Regime for the Antarctic* (Kluwer, 2000). C. J. Bastmeijer, *The Antarctic Environmental Protocol and Its Domestic Legal Implementation*, International Environmental Law and Policy Series: V. 65 (Kluwer, 2003). Jackson and Kriwoken, "The Protocol in Action, 1992–2010." Lorne Kriwoken and Tom Maggs, "Environment," ibid.

records inform a narrative richer than that provided in many existing accounts, and more complicated than popular understanding might have us believe.

There was surprise at the speed with which the CRAMRA consensus was broken in a system where change is normally at glacial pace.[92] If it was so easy to unpick after its adoption, why not during its development? The policy reversal adopted a regime that prohibited mining and comprehensively protected the environment, an idea previously dismissed as unachievable. The difference is explained by public and political engagement. CRAMRA encountered public relations deficiencies, including its possibly misleading title—in retrospect an obvious flaw. Some stakeholders complained that the minerals negotiations had been concealed.[93] CRAMRA's strict regulations failed to appease Malaysia and other UN critics.[94] Joyner explains the poor understanding of CRAMRA's environmental safeguards.[95] UK official Michael Richardson summed up CRAMRA as "an appalling piece of marketing", and Tucker Scully of the United States considered it went too far in admitting the possibility of mining.[96] CRAMRA's protagonists accepted that mining could be prevented, but wanted to retain the possibility. CRAMRA's antagonists *also* accepted that mining could be prevented, but wanted to remove even the possibility. But that was not the point. In 1988, the Parties decided to accept the possibility of mining, even if remote. Thus, there was a failure to publicise CRAMRA's significant hurdles to mining, including the veto on opening an area, the absence of agreed liability rules, and the absence of economic minerals—hurdles such that mining may never have occurred.[97] Given that there were no known economic resources, public fear that mining was inevitable was unfounded. The convention may never have been activated—just like the Seals Convention.

[92] Elliott, *International Environmental Politics: Protecting the Antarctic*, 162.

[93] 3 October 1989, Greenpeace Australia facsimile "Testimony on CRAMRA in France" (NAA: B1387 89/453 PART 3). Templeton, *A Wise Adventure II: New Zealand and Antarctica after 1960*, 145 and 97.

[94] 8 September 1989, BO46791 "Environment—Antarctica: Visit to Bonn by Sir Ninian Stephen" (NAA: B1387 89/453 PART 3).

[95] Joyner, "CRAMRA: The Ugly Duckling of the Antarctic Treaty System?"; and "The Effectiveness of CRAMRA," 165.

[96] These remarks were made at a 2001 Wilton Park conference (AAD: 01/616C).

[97] Christopher Beeby, speech presented to International Bar Association, Auckland 13 October 1988 (NAA: B1387 88/893 PART 2).

It was undoubtedly hard to explain CRAMRA's environmental safe-guards, and it was easy for NGOs to portray the convention as ruinous despite its environmental controls. Considerable "time, energy and intel-lectual effort" produced a "highly sophisticated legal instrument contain-ing environmental protection provisions that ranked among the strongest, most comprehensive of any international agreement ever concluded".[98] Indeed, CRAMRA was itself mined for concepts useful for other regimes.[99] Accordingly, it can be argued that despite developing a doomed instru-ment, the ATS is considerably better off. Negotiating CRAMRA was a political and legal exercise executed elegantly. As a diplomatic exercise, it showed how consensus and compromise combine in the most contentious circumstances. It was entirely necessary at the time discussions started. Without encouraging mining, it successfully addressed resources and sov-ereignty issues while protecting the environment. The resource manage-ment, sovereignty and environmental problems appeared resolved. Nevertheless, in all the self-congratulation, CRAMRA had in Joyner's words become "politically bankrupt".[100] It was a product of its time and its people, who were swamped by a sudden tsunami of scepticism.

Immediately after the Madrid Protocol was adopted, John Heap under-standably observed that "for democratically expressed reasons within their own countries, the care that CRAMRA expressed for the environment was seen by some as not being innovative enough. The consequence of that difference of view was signed by many of us in Madrid three days ago".[101] After later reflection, he suggested that the Protocol was *not* a direct con-sequence of the breakdown of consensus over CRAMRA: "its roots lie elsewhere."[102] This book shows that the causes were many. However, what

---

[98] Joyner, "The Effectiveness of CRAMRA," 165.

[99] For example, the requirement for sufficient information to make environmental assess-ments: Scully, "The Development of the Antarctic Treaty System," 35. It established prin-ciples for Antarctic environmental liability and found ways to manage resources in the absence of universally recognised sovereignty: Jacobsson, "Building the International Legal Framework for Antarctica," 10. CRAMRA's lessons for the International Seabed Authority are discussed in: Nicholas R. Kirkham, K. M. Gjerde, and A. M. W. Wilson, "Deep-Sea Mining: Policy Options to Preserve the Last Frontier—Lessons from Antarctica's Mineral Resource Convention," *Marine Policy* 115 (2020).

[100] Joyner, "The Effectiveness of CRAMRA," 171.

[101] Antarctic Treaty, *Final Report of the Sixteenth Antarctic Treaty Consultative Meeting, Bonn, 7–18 October 1991*, 197.

[102] John A. Heap, ed. *Handbook of the Antarctic Treaty System*, 8th ed. (US Department of State, 1994), 2002. Heap may be suggesting that the ideas originated in Chile's May 1989 proposal for a separate consolidation of environmental measures.

is clear is that without CRAMRA there may have been less pressure to address comprehensive environmental measures in a binding form.

Re-establishing consensus on minerals became inseparable from consensus on an environmental regime. CRAMRA could have been rejected without taking further action on the environment, accepting the risk that no one would start prospecting without evidence of resources and legal certainty about access. But the urgency for simultaneous consensus on mining and the environment included the imminent 1991 opportunity for a Treaty review conference to be called, ongoing scrutiny of the Treaty within the UN and the looming 1992 UNCED conference. Haste resulted in the Protocol embedding unintended ambiguities, inconsistencies and omissions.[103] It did not even specify the area to which it applies.[104]

Therefore, like CRAMRA, the Parties had adopted an imperfect regime. The process for amending the Protocol presented considerable hurdles, and it is only a little better for updating the Annexes. On the other hand, the Protocol generated considerable political will towards improved environmental protection, made adherence to the Protocol mandatory for the ATCPs and new entrants and, significantly, made recognition of ATCP status no longer contingent on establishing scientific stations.[105] Furthermore, the Treaty inspection provisions rapidly grew into a de facto system of monitoring environmental compliance.

Unfortunately, also like CRAMRA, the Protocol's reputation is weakened by misrepresentation of its achievements. Consider, for example, the odd suggestion that "Antarctica has become one of the world's *least* environmentally protected continents", using the flawed metric of the area covered by zones protected under the Protocol's Annex V.[106] Such interpretations miss the point that the entire continent has been designated as a protected area by the very existence of the Protocol. Others more

[103] Francioni, "The Madrid Protocol on the Protection of the Antarctic Environment." Francisco Orrego Vicuña, "The Protocol on Environmental Protection to the Antarctic Treaty: Questions of Effectiveness," *Georgetown International Environmental Law Review* 7 (1994). Chaturvedi, *The Polar Regions*, 206–12. Joyner, *Governing the Frozen Commons*, 163–74. Templeton, *A Wise Adventure II: New Zealand and Antarctica after 1960*, 317–18. Jackson, "Politics, Diplomacy and the Creation of Antarctic Consensus."

[104] The Protocol and its mining ban apply to the Treaty area defined in Article VI, which leaves unresolved the Antarctic high seas.

[105] Serge Pannatier, "Acquisition of Consultative Status under the Antarctic Treaty," *Polar Record* 30, no. 173 (1994).

[106] Doaa Abdel-Motaal, *Antarctica: The Battle for the Seventh Continent* (Praeger, 2016), 213–14.

astutely observe that the Protocol "establishes Antarctica as one of the *most* protected environments anywhere on the planet".[107] Equally concerning is the common mischaracterisation of the mining prohibition as a moratorium.[108] More misleading is perpetuation of suggestions that mining is inevitable after 2048.[109] Or even 2041.[110]

UNANSWERED QUESTIONS

After years of addressing minerals and debating environment protection, two issues remain unresolved: Will mining ever occur in Antarctica? Will Antarctica ever be a world park?

Will Mining Ever Occur in Antarctica?

The Protocol is imperfect, but repeated misrepresentation of the Protocol is unhelpful. It is more than a mining ban, although, politically, that was the headline achievement. In reality, the prospect of Antarctic mining is

[107] Howkins, *The Polar Regions: An Environmental History*, 167. Joyner, *Governing the Frozen Commons*, 179–80.

[108] Interpretations vary. For the view that a moratorium is intended, see Redgwell, "Antarctica: Wilderness Park or Eldorado Postponed?" 137. For the view that a moratorium is time-limited, see Philippe Sands et al., *Principles of International Environmental Law*, Third ed. (Cambridge University Press, 2012), 586–87. For suggestions that a review conference is likely, see Ben Saul and Tim Stephens, eds., *Antarctica in International Law* (Hart, 2015), lxvi. For the interplay between permanent prohibition, prohibition, permanent moratorium and moratorium, see Donald Rothwell and Ruth Davis, *Antarctic Environmental Protection: A Collection of Australian and International Instruments* (Federation Press, 1997), 30–32.

[109] In addition, numerous media articles and websites conflate the Protocol and the Treaty, asserting that the Treaty itself expires in 2048. See, for example: 28 August 2015, Adam Lockyer "A cold war on Australia's doorstep" https://www.huffingtonpost.com.au/adam-lockyer/a-cold-war-on-australias-doorstep_b_8046812.html (accessed 8 September 2015).

[110] Robert Swan, *Antarctica 2041: My Quest to Save the Earth's Last Wilderness* (Broadway, 2009). The reference to 2041 derives from a misunderstanding of Protocol Article 25. The special review provision becomes available in 2048, 50 years after the Protocol's 1998 entry into force, not its 1991 adoption. The name of an entire organisation is based on this error: https://2041foundation.org/about-us/ (accessed 6 January 2021). See also: "Robert Swan: Let's save the last pristine continent" https://www.ted.com/talks/robert_swan_let_s_save_the_last_pristine_continent/transcript?language=en at 1:38 (accessed 4 May 2015); and "Protecting Antarctica beyond 2041: an interview with Robert Swan" https://news.mongabay.com/2019/07/protecting-antarctica-beyond-2041-an-interview-with-polar-explorer-robert-swan/ (accessed 26 July 2019).

unchanged since 1991 when it was prohibited (or even since 1959 when the Treaty feared the issue might erupt). Yet the possibility of mining remains subject to speculation, and the question is whether it really has been prevented.

There is a perennial difficulty in predicting resource interests, technological viability and economic potential. The 1960 Dufek and 1964 Law predictions testify to overenthusiasm.[111] Year 1989 saw more sober predictions that any interest would be at least 30 years away, if ever.[112] With over 30 years now having passed that was obviously optimistic, but in 2016 it didn't stop Australian politician Barnaby Joyce talking up the AAT's minerals prospects: "there's minerals there, there's gold, there's iron ore, there's coal ... do I turn my head and allow another country to exploit my resource? Or do I position myself in such a way as I'm going to exploit it myself before they get there?"[113] But ambitious language does not make exploitation economically viable. In 1988, it was suggested that oil would need to exceed $US50 per barrel to make Antarctic exploration attractive.[114] By 2006, Iranian energy expert Ali Samsam Bakhtiari put the threshold at $US200–300.[115] Four years later, it appeared that 'peak oil' had passed—or deferred by unconventional resources—putting the prospect of economic Antarctic oil even further away.[116]

Economics alone suggest that interest in Antarctic resources will remain low, especially while other sources are more readily available in a worldwide market. A global price on carbon, were it to be introduced, and growing divestment in fossil fuels put Antarctic hydrocarbons even further out of reach. It would be enormously expensive to go mining simply for a perceived strategic value. That said, rare earth elements have increasing strategic value globally and, if discovered in Antarctica, could be economic

[111] Dufek, *Through the Frozen Frontier*, 171–86. Law, *Antarctica 1984*.

[112] US Congress Office of Technology Assessment, *Polar Prospects: A Minerals Treaty for Antarctica*, 3.

[113] 1 May 2016, transcript of ABC TV *Australian Story* "The polariser" http://www.abc.net.au/austory/the-polariser/9173734 (accessed 15 June 2015).

[114] 28 November 1988, Sue Neales "Treaty members carve up Antarctic" *Australian Financial Review*, 13.

[115] 11 July 2006, Senate Hansard, Rural and Regional Affairs and Transport References Committee "Australia's future oil supply and alternative transport fuels", 4–6. 14 July 2006, Andrew Darby "Oil hungry world may turn to Antarctica" *The Age*.

[116] International Energy Agency, "World Energy Outlook 2010: Executive Summary," International Energy Agency. 14 November 2010, John Collins Rudolph "Is 'peak oil' behind us?" New York Times.

if accessible (such as on the sea floor). It is therefore possible that geological research might one day inform interest in future exploration. Article 7 of the Protocol specifically allows for scientific research, but its drafters did not anticipate prospecting as envisaged in CRAMRA.[117] Some commentators question geologists' motives, raising fears that some Parties might harbour aspirations for future benefit.[118]

Of course, the prohibition on minerals activities applies only to Parties to the Protocol—states not party to it are not constrained (including the Treaty Parties not party to the Protocol). There are, however, no signs such states have an interest in Antarctic minerals and, were that to change, they could expect considerable diplomatic and public objections. While the minerals prohibition could fail, that provision is no less stable than the Treaty's other absolute prohibitions (such as military manoeuvres or nuclear waste disposal). Accordingly, minerals activities are likely to proceed only if the existing prohibition is removed, a move highly unlikely before the calling of a review conference, which could not be contemplated before 2048.[119] Without a review conference the mining ban cannot be lifted with less than consensus.

Templeton suggests that it is no coincidence that the opportunity for a review coincides with when resources might be required.[120] Even if the

---

[117] Unlike CRAMRA, the Protocol does not define mineral resource activities. The distinction between science and prospecting is important—the former is subject to the Treaty's provision for free exchange of scientific results. Prospecting usually implies the non-disclosure of commercially sensitive data.

[118] See, for example: Lebedeva and Petukhov, "Russia Decides to Return to the Antarctic with Serious Intentions and for Long." 4 November 2010, "Ukraine to look for oil, gas in Antarctic" http://www.kyivpost.com/news/nation/detail/88645/#ixzz14LszFKUO (accessed 5 November 2010). Russia denies it has disguised prospecting—see, for example: XXV ATCM IP-014 (Russian Federation) "Russian scientific geological research in Antarctica in context of Article 7 of the Madrid Protocol" https://ats.aq/devAS/Meetings/Documents/56 (accessed 23 March 2020). Russian intentions continue to the subject of speculation, for example: https://jamestown.org/program/is-russia-preparing-to-challenge-the-status-quo-in-antarctica-part-two/ (accessed 3 February 2021). For speculation about China's intentions, see Anne-Marie Brady, *China as a Polar Great Power* (Cambridge University Press, 2017), 201–07. Clive Hamilton, *Silent Invasion: China's Influence in Australia* (Hardie Grant, 2018), 252–54.

[119] "Protocol on Environmental Protection to the Antarctic Treaty", Article 25.

[120] Templeton, *Protecting Antarctica: The Development of the Treaty System*, 50. *A Wise Adventure II: New Zealand and Antarctica after 1960*, 316.

prohibition were lifted, strict conditions need to be satisfied.[121] These include there being "in force a binding legal regime on Antarctic mineral resource activities" which would also have to "fully safeguard the interests of all States referred to in Article IV of the Antarctic Treaty". In other words, sovereignty concerns would have to be traversed again. CRAMRA was not obliterated and could be resurrected.[122] A future regime, however, would likely be quite different because, unlike CRAMRA, it would be developed knowing there was interest in minerals. Whether a new regime could be developed quickly is moot especially if, like CRAMRA, it required strict liability provisions. Of course, a review conference, if called, could *extend* the minerals prohibition—some regard this as simply deferring the decision to another generation.[123] It is true that one generation cannot constrain the next, precisely the point George Bush made in his 3 July 1991 presidential announcement that United States would endorse the Protocol. Indeed, this may explain predictions that in 2058, with oil at $US450 per barrel, it will be extracted from Antarctica.[124] However, that argument assumes that price will drive demand, rather than domestic scarcity. In late 2020, Australia had just 33 days oil in its national reserve—self-sufficiency in oil from a nearby source could be a driver, rather than the global price.[125] On the other hand, a future generation will also be guided by social licence, the same social licence that sealed CRAMRA's fate.[126]

[121] A. J. Press, "The Antarctic Treaty System: Future Mining Faces Many Mathematical Challenges," in *The Yearbook of Polar Law*, ed. Gudmundur Alfredsson, Timo Koivurova, and Julia Jabour (Brill Nijhoff, 2015). Sean Coburn, "Eyeing 2048: Antarctic Treaty System's Mining Ban," *Columbia Journal of Environmental Law* 42, no. 2 (2017).

[122] Joyner, "The Effectiveness of CRAMRA," 171. See also: https://www.mfat.govt.nz/en/about-us/who-we-are/treaties/convention-on-the-regulation-of-antarctic-mineral-resource-activities/ (accessed 22 July 2015).

[123] Redgwell, "Antarctica: Wilderness Park or Eldorado Postponed?" 141.

[124] Mahlon C. Kennicutt, "Looking to the Future: The Poles in 2058," *Antarctic Science* 21, no. 2 (2009): 97.

[125] Department of Industry Science Energy and Resources Australia, "Australian Petroleum Statistics," (2020), Table 7. https://www.energy.gov.au/sites/default/files/Australian%20Petroleum%20Statistics%20-%20Issue%20292%20November%202020.pdf (accessed 4 February 2021).

[126] Claire Mason et al., "Charting the Territory: Exploring Stakeholder Reactions to the Prospect of Seafloor Exploration and Mining in Australia," *Marine Policy* 34 (2010). Social Licence exists when industry activity or government policy has "ongoing approval within the local community and other stakeholders". http://socialicense.com/definition.html (accessed 30 September 2019).

Some might argue that a Party might walk away if sufficiently dejected by the failure of a modification made at a review conference to enter into force. Whether such a defection would ever eventuate is unknown. Article XII of the Treaty itself contains a walkout provision. Its use has never been contemplated even though, arguably, there are even greater issues at stake than minerals. The Protocol is probably no weaker than the Treaty to which it is attached.

As the narrative has shown, at the debate's height during 1989 and 1990 there were many proposals for a mining moratorium to be set at 30 years. This was, in part, on the assumption that there would be no interest in minerals for at least that time (in addition, 30 years would defer the issue for a full generation and avoid the then negotiators of having to deal with the problem again). Well, with over 30 years since the mining debate there is still no interest in the resources. Coincidentally, 2020 was the year it was predicted that oil would reach $US200–300 per barrel and make Antarctic exploration economically viable.[127] What seemed like a very distant future has arrived, and without the feared pressure on the Parties to relax the mining prohibition.

There are no indications of interest in Antarctic minerals and no activities that threaten the integrity of the Protocol. In fact, the evidence is exactly the opposite. Accessions to the Treaty and the Protocol continue.[128] Development of environmental measures still dominates the annual meetings. Treaty inspections occur with increasing frequency and emphasise environmental compliance. Importantly, with the adoption of the Santiago Declaration to mark the Protocol's 25th anniversary, the ATCPs dispelled any doubts about commitment to the Protocol.[129] This was reit-

---

[127] 11 July 2006, Senate Hansard, Rural and Regional Affairs and Transport References Committee "Australia's future oil supply and alternative transport fuels", 4. At the time of writing, oil was around $US60 per barrel.

[128] Antarctic Treaty, *Final Report of the Thirty-Fourth Antarctic Treaty Consultative Meeting, Buneos Aires, 20 June – 1 July 2011* (Secretariat of the Antarctic Treaty, 2011), 19–20. Antarctic Treaty, Resolution 1 (2011) "Strengthening support for the Protocol on Environmental Protection to the Antarctic Treaty" https://ats.aq/devAS/Meetings/Measure/494 (accessed 10 March 2020). *Final Report of the Thirty-Fifth Antarctic Treaty Consultative Meeting, Hobart, Australia 11–20 June 2012* (Secretariat of the Antarctic Treaty, 2012), 23–24.

[129] Santiago Declaration on the 25th Anniversary of the signing of the Protocol on Environmental Protection to the Antarctic Treaty, in: *Final Report of the Thirty-Ninth Antarctic Treaty Consultative Meeting, Santiago, Chile 23 May-1 June 2016* (Secretariat of the Antarctic Treaty, 2016), 183–84.

erated in 2019 when celebration of the Treaty's 60th anniversary reaffirmed commitment to the Protocol and the mining prohibition.[130]

There is no reason to suggest that the Protocol is at risk if Antarctic governance continues to adapt. Key stakeholders will continue to keep the Parties on track, especially environmentalists active in the CEP and ATCM. NGOs led a concerted campaign to engage public interest and influence governments. Public attention was a novelty for the Treaty which had allowed lawyers and diplomats to determine policy outcomes with little political oversight. During the period for signing CRAMRA, NGOs were able to direct more public attention to it than they could during its negotiation. Had they attracted public attention *during* the negotiations, they might have achieved stronger environmental provisions and then been disinclined to reject it, thus allowing CRAMRA to survive. Protests at Dumont d'Urville and Ross Island gained little traction but NGOs capitalised on external events, such as 'fortuitous' maritime accidents and French doubts about CRAMRA. Mobilisation of public opinion by NGOs, even with cherry-picked information, helped drive Parties' commitment to the environment. The security of the Protocol was made stronger by their scrutiny, rather than weakened by their criticism.

Diplomatic events and processes are often opaque to the public, and even to politicians. Political leaders deal with multiple issues simultaneously. The complexities of a niche policy area like Antarctica may never need to be grasped by politicians; it is the political messaging that counts. The minerals debate made Antarctica a mainstream public concern, coinciding with contemporary environmental issues such as ozone depletion and climate change. Antarctica, for a time, was no longer a narrow topic for specialists interested in science, territoriality or heroic tales.

Antarctic law (like international law generally) is, in effect, the codification of diplomatically negotiated policy, and considerable Antarctic policy is determined by bureaucrats.[131] They were not immune from criticism that they "develop policy almost entirely in the light of incestuous discussions with their counterparts at international meetings of the Antarctic

---

[130] 8 July 2019, "Prague Declaration on the Occasion of the Sixtieth Anniversary of the Antarctic Treaty" in: *Final Report of the Forty-second Antarctic Treaty Consultative Meeting*, Volume 1, 209–211 https://documents.ats.aq/ATCM42/fr/ATCM42_fr001_e.pdf (accessed 26 March 2020).

[131] Templeton, *A Wise Adventure II: New Zealand and Antarctica after 1960*. Rowland, "The Treaty Regime and the Politics of the Consultative Parties," 12. Trachtenberg, *The Craft of International History: A Guide to Method*, 75–76, 97–99.

Treaty System".[132] Antarctica remains a peripheral issue in domestic politics, and few governments include Antarctica in their policy platforms.[133] Ministers seldom engage on issues which have bipartisan support and bureaucrats can run 'safe' issues.[134] Officials do not always agree: the CRAMRA debate saw many inter-agency disagreements and rivalries— bitter differences between Australian departments erupted in the final sessions of the CRAMRA negotiations. New Zealand experienced similar issues.[135] The US State Department was also at odds with other agencies, or even at odds internally.[136] In France, the same occurred in the Quai d'Orsay during the environment debate. Such bureaucratic politics could impinge on the establishment of coherent, unified national positions.[137] Officials do not always get their own way or get it right—the environment debate showed several instances of politicians stepping in to overrule bureaucrats. Ministers intervened when the political costs became too high: "national governments, long accustomed to regarding Antarctic Treaty matters as wholly arcane and best left to the technicians, simply had to start giving instructions."[138] The long-established cosy way of operating could no longer be taken for granted, and 'old hands' had to accept the intrusion of political leaders into their domain. By 1991, the Treaty system settled back into its more comfortable routine. Individuals resumed their trade of diplomacy, international law and environmental management, and their careers flourished. Despite the implied misjudgements, no Antarctic bureaucrat lost their job as a result of political interventions in the mining and environment debates. On the contrary, through the upheaval they defended the Treaty and its principles.

Sovereignty is a case in point. The Treaty effectively distanced management of the Antarctic from the fractious issues of sovereignty. This is not to say, as some do, that it somehow suspends sovereign actions.[139] It

---

[132] Paltridge and Jabour, "Antarctica and the Madrid Protocol," 2.

[133] *Antarctic Treaty System: An Assessment*, 285.

[134] Stokke, "Domestic Politics and ATS Change: Introductory Assessment," 327–28.

[135] Templeton, *A Wise Adventure II: New Zealand and Antarctica after 1960*, 279–81.

[136] 3 August 1990, WH119515 "Antarctica: Australian/French initiative. US views" (NAA: B1387 90/498 PART 3). 15 April 1991, WH129765 "Antarctica: Four-country representations: US views" (NAA: B1387 90/888 PART 3). 16 May 1991, WH131025 "Antarctica: SCMXI second session: US views" (NAA: B1387 91/32 PART 2). 1 July 1991, WH132790 "Antarctica: SCM XI—environment protection protocol" (AAD: 91/226–2).

[137] Bergin, "The Politics of Antarctic Minerals: The Greening of White Australia," 232–33.

[138] Evans and Grant, *Australia's Foreign Relations in the World of the 1990's*, 157.

[139] Klaus Dodds and Mark Nuttall, *The Scramble for the Poles* (Wiley, 2016), 81.

doesn't.[140] One of the challenges presented by mineral resources was the link it created between management and sovereignty, a connection that has since abated.[141] Rowland argues that the existence of the claims justified the minerals negotiations.[142] However, CRAMRA could not 'solve' the sovereignty issues, and, by accommodating claimants, it made them give something away.[143] For some Australian officials, that 'something' was more than they could stomach. On the other hand, it can be argued that CRAMRA *strengthened* the claims by recognising their existence— outright denial could not be sustained because it was accepted as legitimate to maintain a previously asserted claim. Thus, claimants achieved something to satisfy their interests, even if not what Brian Talboys considered "the real stuff of sovereignty".[144] Having claimant status gave Australia a sovereign power not previously contemplated: it used its position to thwart a convention whose operation required claimant participation. That was a sovereign decision as influential as any. Australia and the other claimants came out of the minerals and environment debates without their sovereignty diminished. In fact, some went on in other areas to capitalise on their claimant status.[145] Yet the Treaty's accommodation of sovereignty, expressed in Article IV, had also not been diminished. The Treaty remained intact.

Will Antarctica Ever Be a World Park?

All this praise for the Protocol does not mean that it is without critics demanding even more. Throughout this book, calls for an Antarctic world park (or equivalent terminology) have emerged, ranging from the first airing of the concepts in the 1970s and the progressive evolution, lukewarm

---

[140] Article IV of the Treaty provides only that such actions cannot later be used to assert, support or deny sovereignty.

[141] Daniel Bray, "The Geopolitics of Antarctic Governance: Sovereignty and Strategic Denial in Australia's Antarctic Policy," *Australian Journal of International Affairs* 70, no. 3 (2016).

[142] Rowland, "The Treaty Regime and the Politics of the Consultative Parties," 26–27.

[143] Andersen, "Negotiating a New Regime: How CRAMRA Came into Existence," 99–102. Peter J Beck, "The Antarctic Resource Conventions Implemented: Consequences for the Sovereignty Issue," ibid., 246–55.

[144] 13 August 1977, Letter from Brian Talboys, Minister for Foreign Affairs, Wellington to Andrew Peacock, Minister for Foreign Affairs (NAA: B1387 77/177).

[145] For example, submissions to the Commission on the Limits of the Continental Shelf with respect to shelves extending from Antarctic claims.

reception and ultimate rejection of such proposals throughout the 1980s. After conclusion of the minerals convention, world park ideas were floated with more vigour, and, following the 1989 rejection of CRAMRA, hopes rose again.[146] Such optimism was unfounded: the language of world park had already been rejected as implying a regime outside the ATS. The concept, however, was not dismissed completely and, ultimately, the Protocol delivered the same environmental outcomes through comprehensive binding measures, but wholly within the ATS.[147] Joyner considers Antarctica tantamount to a world park.[148] The 'park' concept was not helped by the inability of its various proponents to settle on an appropriate name. Sadly for its proponents, the adopted title of 'Natural Reserve, Devoted to Peace and Science', while descriptive, resonated with no-one and was never used. The phrase had little recognition outside Antarctica and has not been emulated. Adoption of the Madrid Protocol in 1991 did not end calls for a world park. In 1993, Greenpeace simultaneously called for prompt ratification of the Protocol *and* designation of a world park by 2010.[149] Calls for a world park continued intermittently and then almost faded away.

Failure to achieve a world park in name has not discouraged criticism of what was achieved in practice. In fact, it stimulated an even more ambitious objective: inscription of Antarctica on the World Heritage list.[150] This has been proposed by environmental stalwarts such as Bob Brown and Geoff Mosley.[151] For them, it is not an academic issue; it is one of powerful symbolism. That is why the issue remains alive and appeals, once again, to social licence. In March 2018, the Bob Brown Foundation

---

[146] J.G. Mosley, "World Park for Antarctica," *Habitat Australia*, no. 4 (October) (1989). 29 April 1991, World Wildlife Fund, Press Information "Major progress towards world park for Antarctica".

[147] Howkins, *The Polar Regions: An Environmental History*, 166.

[148] Joyner, *Governing the Frozen Commons*, 180.

[149] Szabo, *State of the Ice: An Overview of Human Impacts in Antarctica*, 44–45.

[150] Article 11(2) of the Convention Concerning the Protection of the World Cultural and Natural Heritage 1972 https://whc.unesco.org/archive/convention-en.pdf (accessed 11 April 2018).

[151] Bob Brown, *Memo for a Saner World* (Penguin, 2004), 153–54. J. G. Mosley, Antarctica: Securing Its Heritage for the Whole World (Envirobook, 2007). *Saving the Antarctic Wilderness*, 77–100.

surveyed supporters on whether it should campaign for Antarctic World
Heritage and, in December 2020, appointed its campaigners.[152]

Given the public affection for world heritage, it is surprising that the
proposal has been poorly articulated with respect to how it would be
implemented, whether it would make any practical difference and, most
importantly, how the listing could be negotiated. Listing would likely
make no difference on the ground as all nations active in Antarctica are
Parties to the Protocol. By far the most thorough analysis of the option is
understandably optimistic.[153] There will be institutional resistance by
Treaty governments which, through the ATS, have already judged that the
best way to achieve the environment protection objective is through the
Protocol. There would be little appetite to re-open such issues. Accordingly,
the World Heritage idea is probably futile given the unlikely prospect of
being able to convince even the Parties most supportive of strong environmental measures. Despite the popular appeal of Antarctic issues, Australian
political parties no longer entertain the Antarctic World Heritage idea.[154]
An adviser to the Australian government specifically recommends that
World Heritage not be pursued as the proposal could backfire by re-
opening the minerals debate. This is particularly pertinent as World
Heritage designation does not preclude mining.[155]

[152] Bob Brown Foundation, "Supporter Survey" https://www.surveymonkey.com/r/
X2QZFG2 (accessed 18 March 2018). https://www.bobbrown.org.au/mr_07_12_2020
(accessed 16 December 2020). October 2014, Geoff Mosley "The next big step: gaining
World Heritage recognition for Antarctica" https://www.bobbrown.org.au/gaining_
world_heritage_recognition_for_antarctica (accessed 5 March 2020)

[153] Mosley's strategy relies on every Treaty Party endorsing a nomination, without amending the World Heritage Convention. Mosley, *Antarctica: Securing Its Heritage for the Whole
World*, 17–22. More provocatively, Australia would nominate the AAT and encourage other
claimants to act likewise. Keith D Suter, *World Law and the Last Wilderness*, 2nd ed. (Friends
of the Earth, 1980), 64–65.

[154] 18 June 2012, Andrew Darby "Antarctica must go on heritage list—Coalition" https://
www.smh.com.au/environment/conservation/antarctica-must-go-on-heritage-list-coali-
tion-20,120,617-20i5r.html (accessed 11 April 2018). 18 June 2012, "Coalition calls for
Antarctica world heritage listing" http://www.news.com.au/travel/travel-updates/coali-
tion-calls-for-antarctica-world-heritage-listing/news-story/a65c33810ee76491c69048f7
9b90ca75 (accessed 11 April 2018).

[155] 16 June 2012, Tony Press "An own goal in political ice hockey? World Heritage listing
for Antarctica could reopen minerals debate" http://theconversation.com/an-own-goal-in-
political-ice-hockey-world-heritage-listing-for-antarctica-could-reopen-minerals-
debate-7683 (accessed 19 June 2012).

An Antarctic World Heritage nomination would have great symbolic value and, if successful, engage many more nations in recognising Antarctica's environmental values.[156] The overriding obstacles, however, are the sovereignty issues.[157] Inscription of an Antarctic property as World Heritage would re-open those problematic issues in the Treaty, or require amendments of the World Heritage Convention to allow for areas to be nominated in the absence of universally recognised sovereignty. Neither option is likely to succeed, and trying to get there could be counterproductive. It was therefore surprising that, in 2012, UN Secretary General Ban Ki-Moon announced that he would "work with States to make Antarctica a World Nature Preserve".[158] Global options continue to emerge and possibly concerns persist about Antarctica's future under the Treaty. Perhaps, again, there has been a failure to communicate an achievement of the ATS. The diplomatic energy required to address such issues again would probably be far better expended on better promoting the Treaty's achievements, encouraging more accessions to it, improving compliance with existing environmental measures, and efforts to reduce the impact *within* the Antarctic Treaty area of activities *outside* it.

THE HEROIC ERA OF ANTARCTIC DIPLOMACY

Over half of the world's population has been born since the Madrid Protocol was adopted.[159] If they have any understanding of Antarctica, they are likely to have no expectation of the Antarctic other than as a region where mining is prohibited and the environment has priority. While this could now be taken for granted, it might not have turned out that way. The early years of the ATS may have given it a "congealed

---

[156] With 193 Parties to the World Heritage Convention, inscribing Antarctica on the world heritage list could increase the number of nations recognising Antarctica's values almost fourfold. Note, however, that the Antarctic Treaty Parties already represent some 64% of the global population http://worldpopulationreview.com/countries/ (accessed 11 April 2018).

[157] A Party to the Convention can only nominate properties "situated on its territory". A successful Antarctic nomination implies improbable scenarios of states not recognising claims accepting a claimant's right to nominate its territory. Bray, "The Geopolitics of Antarctic Governance: Sovereignty and Strategic Denial in Australia's Antarctic Policy," 270–71.

[158] 26 January 2012, "UN Secretary-General outlines 'The Future We Want'" http://unohrlls.org/news/un-secretary-general-outlines-%C2%93the-future-we-want%C2%94/ (accessed 13 April 2018).

[159] https://population.un.org/wpp (accessed 6 January 2020).

appearance".[160] It has now coagulated around environment protection. Remarkable circumstances allowed a vast part of the globe to be protected in a stable regime. The entry into force of the Protocol marked the start of new priorities in Antarctic affairs.

In 1988, CRAMRA was considered "the most important political development in the regulation of Antarctica".[161] By the end of 1989, the rejection of CRAMRA presented the ATS "with as severe a test as any it has dealt with", raising the risk of unregulated mining and re-opening sovereignty arguments.[162] By the end of 1990, the world park vision of the NGOs, the Antarctic wilderness park idea of Australia and the wilderness reserve sought by France had not been achieved. CRAMRA's political accommodations had dissolved and no one was happy. Established relationships between Treaty partners had been shaken, and doubts had been raised about once-trusted colleagues. But, by the end of 1991, the "crisis of consensus" was over. Adoption of the Protocol ended a period of great turmoil that "brought the ATS to the brink of collapse".[163] Parties were determined to maintain stability in the Antarctic Treaty System and chose consensus on the environment ahead of consensus on access to notional resources. The result was "among the most comprehensive, far-reaching multilateral environmental instruments ever promulgated".[164]

Bob Hawke may have underestimated how his Cabinet's May 1989 decision would undermine traditional Antarctic partnerships—or he may have been untroubled about that—but he seemed jubilant in achieving "the impossible dream".[165] It stood in contrast to Evans' willingness to consider a fallback in June 1989, Alan Brown's pessimism in December 1990 and the doubts of many officials.[166] Hawke's Science Minister Barry Jones later observed that such pessimism "only made Hawke all the more determined".[167] It may also be true that the Protocol "exceeded even the

[160] Chaturvedi, *The Polar Regions*, 121.
[161] Beeby quoted in: Templeton, *A Wise Adventure II: New Zealand and Antarctica after 1960*, 222.
[162] Beeby, "The Antarctic Treaty System: Goals, Performance and Impact," 17.
[163] Chaturvedi, *The Polar Regions*, 132 and 229.
[164] Joyner, *Governing the Frozen Commons*, 78–79.
[165] 7 May 1991, House of Representatives Hansard, 3068.
[166] 29 June 1989, LH77976 "Senator Evans' discussions in London" (NAA: B1387 89/453 PART 1). 5 December 1990, Ross Peake "Ban on mining unlikely in Antarctic pact" *The Age*, 5
[167] 17 May 2019, Peter Hannam, "'Penguins can't vote': Bob Hawke took the long view on the environment" https://www.smh.com.au/environment/conservation/penguins-

most optimistic prediction".[168] If so, it begs the question of whether Antarctica would have been saved anyway, even if Australia and its supporters had not taken action. It could be argued that, on this issue, political courage alone was not enough as other occasions of political courage in Antarctic affairs had failed. If not Australia, another Party may have stepped in to take advantage of the public mood to prevent mining. Alternatively, Parties might have relied on CRAMRA's liability annex never being resolved, allowing the minerals convention to lapse by legal logjam. Or, a Party may have vetoed the opening of any area for minerals activities and withstood any opprobrium. Had an alternative to CRAMRA not been proposed (or not been agreed), it is not at all clear that taking the ATS "to the brink of collapse" would have tipped it over the brink. After all, the evident commitment of Parties to keep the Treaty intact in the face of mounting external criticism seemed unbreakable. That is what drove the search for compromise and consensus.

By solving the political dilemma over minerals, it was possible for the Parties to make progress on more practical issues. At the debate's peak, Alan Brown observed that the minerals issue would be "a very hard nut to crack".[169] But a neat piece of bifocalism delivered the solution: two alternative readings were equally legitimate. Article 7 met the objective of those wanting a permanent mining ban—they could come away announcing vindication of their position (just as Prime Minister Hawke did). Article 25 precisely met the objective of those *not* wanting a permanent ban—they could come away arguing that it was a decision for future generations (just as President Bush did). Creativity on the link between Article 7 and Article 25 became the key to the successful compromise required to allow consensus on the entire Protocol.

As noted earlier, consensus was a product of all the Parties. The need to re-establish it arose because the rejection of CRAMRA by Australia and France, and later by others, presented an immense challenge to the ATS. It raised considerable risks, and, worse, was potentially destructive. In the lead up to 1991, there was the possibility for a Treaty review conference being called and, in 1992, external scrutiny by the UNCED Earth Summit. In addition, Australian action marked unprecedented departure from the

can-t-vote-bob-hawke-took-the-long-view-on-the-environment-20190517-p51oev.html (accessed 17 May 2019).

[168] Evans and Grant, *Australia's Foreign Relations in the World of the 1990's*, 157.

[169] 5 December 1990, Ross Peake "Ban on mining unlikely in Antarctic pact" *The Age*, 5.

hard-won consensus on an issue contentious for years. Furthermore, the action smacked of sovereign motives previously subdued in the interests of mutual tolerance. Remarkably, no Party now openly resents those debates—on the contrary, they are celebrated. Evan Bloom of the US State Department, speaking at the Protocol's 25th anniversary, observed "the daring, perhaps heroic, decision by leaders of countries like Australia and France, we must admit, led to something better. With the benefit of hindsight, the wisdom of that change of course is now quite evident".[170] Why the decisions were daring, or even heroic, is now a little clearer.

As it turned out, no one was actually wedded to Antarctic mining. Any lingering affection for CRAMRA was insufficient to justify the political capital to sustain it. If there had been serious mining interest, the environmental regime would never have prevailed: hence, no one really regrets the outcome. For all the effort that Australia and France put into the environment initiative, equivalent effort was put in by other Parties to keep the System intact while the issues were debated. This was entirely legitimate even if, at the time, it was presented as anti-environment. It would be wrong to suggest that Australia or France had more honourable aspirations for Antarctica—they had just as much to gain from a stable Treaty.

This book shows that the minerals and environment debates were the result of remarkable circumstances that probably could not have been predicted or orchestrated. It is unlikely that such a coalescence of circumstances could ever be recreated. Consider, for example, the following:

- Adoption of a Treaty instrument not requiring consensus to enter into force, but creating an unprecedented opportunity for the few Parties whose support was essential to renege on expectations
- The title of CRAMRA being an inept piece of public relations for a convention with strong environmental controls
- Differences between Australian ministers on basic Antarctic policy interests
- Differences within the disgruntled Australian minerals negotiating team, providing cover for ministers to express doubts about

---

[170] 30 May 2016, ATCM39 AD010 (25th Anniversary Symposium) Evan T. Bloom "Remarks on the history, vision behind and impact of the protocol on environmental protection" https://documents.ats.aq/ATCM39/ad/ATCM39_ad010_e.pdf (accessed 26 March 2020).

CRAMRA even if they didn't particularly want an environmental alternative

- An Australian government facing an election in 1990 and needing to reinforce its environmental credentials after John Howard, leader of the conservative Opposition, wedged the government by appearing to be greener than Bob Hawke
- An Australian government without a Senate majority, facing the prospect of being unable to pass any CRAMRA implementing legislation
- A procession of polar maritime accidents at a critical time, culminating in the loss of a polar crude oil tanker, ensuring saturation media coverage of oil-soaked wildlife
- New Zealand, the architect of the CRAMRA negotiations, reverting to an environmental proposal it first proposed in 1975 and ending up with the most ambitious environment proposals
- Predictions of a strong showing for the Greens in forthcoming European elections coupled with the influence of an activist septuagenarian on the French Prime Minister
- Increasing UN interest in the Treaty System's attitude to resources and the Parties' shared concern that they might lose influence in Antarctic affairs
- The imminent arrival of the June 1991 option for a Treaty review conference, on the eve of the 1992 UNCED First Earth Summit
- A public mood at the peak of concern for global environmental issues, inspired by environmental campaigns and thrilled by dreams of wilderness purity

This book shows that the shift from a resource management to an environmental view of Antarctica was the result of multiple circumstances and events. Many of the pre-existing circumstances provided the conditions for what was to occur. These were supplemented by several seemingly serendipitous and coincidental events. Even in combination, these circumstances and events did not make the Madrid Protocol outcome inevitable. That required deliberate human input.

Between 1988 and 1991, there were remarkable people dealing with these circumstances and events. Policies may have been at odds, but not the individuals involved. In the contest of ideals for Antarctica's future, there was a human story. Away from harsh politics, people had to get on with each other. Ultimately that human story was about the influence exercised by the participants—irrespective of whether that influence derived from personality, charisma, intellect, power, position or tradition or whether the exercise of that power was deliberate or unconscious, overt or subtle. In the institutional bargaining to re-establish consensus, Young's typology of structural, entrepreneurial and intellectual leadership was demonstrated. There was undoubtedly leadership by domestic politicians, policy leadership in the crafting of proposals and leadership by the brilliant diplomats representing governments to negotiate outcomes. There was also the influence of lobbying done by non-government organisations and the domination of communications to a public constituency.

Chapter 1 opened with a domestic debate between Prime Minister Bob Hawke and Treasurer Paul Keating over who saved Antarctica. This book concludes that it was neither. If we give Keating a role, it was because in September 1988 he may have had some influence over Rocard's thinking. If we give Hawke a role, it was because he led his Cabinet to refuse signature of CRAMRA in May 1989. That was a 'daring' decision in its own right and one that accelerated the change of attitudes already under way. Of itself, the Hawke Cabinet decision neither stopped Antarctic mining nor create consensus on a new environmental regime. Rebuilding consensus was crucial for many reasons, including reasons that go to the heart of the Antarctic Treaty. As this book has shown, the restoration of consensus was achieved by many individuals and nations working equally decisively to protect both the environment and the Antarctic Treaty System.

Antarctica is a vast and remote continent, late to be discovered and still visited by relatively few. It hides behind a barrier of distance, storms and ice, and, for much of the year, is inaccessible to those who might seek to exploit it. It generates awe in those who see it and passion in those who cannot. Perhaps it can be argued that Antarctica has helped saved itself—at least, that is, while the ice remains.

References

Abdel-Motaal, Doaa. *Antarctica: The Battle for the Seventh Continent.* Praeger, 2016.

Andersen, Rolf Trolle. "Negotiating a New Regime: How CRAMRA Came into Existence." Chap. 7 In *The Antarctic Treaty System in World Politics*, edited by Arnfinn Jørgensen-Dahl and Willy Østreng, 94–109: Macmillan/Fridtjof Nansen Institute, 1991.

Antarctic and Southern Ocean Coalition. "Congratulations, Cath." *ECO* LXXX, no. 1 (1991): 3.

Antarctic Treaty. *Final Report of the Eleventh Antarctic Treaty Special Consultative, Madrid, 22–30 April 1991; 17–22 June 1991; 3–4 October 1991.* Ministerio de Asuntos Exteriores, 1991a.

———. *Final Report of the Sixteenth Antarctic Treaty Consultative Meeting, Bonn, 7–18 October 1991.* 1991b.

———. *Final Report of the Thirty-Fifth Antarctic Treaty Consultative Meeting, Hobart, Australia 11–20 June 2012.* Secretariat of the Antarctic Treaty, 2012.

———. *Final Report of the Thirty-Fourth Antarctic Treaty Consultative Meeting, Buneos Aires, 20 June–1 July 2011.* Secretariat of the Antarctic Treaty, 2011.

———. *Final Report of the Thirty-Ninth Antarctic Treaty Consultative Meeting, Santiago, Chile 23 May-1 June 2016.* Secretariat of the Antarctic Treaty, 2016.

Antarctic Treaty System: An Assessment. National Academy Press, 1986.

Australia, Department of Industry Science Energy and Resources. "Australian Petroleum Statistics," 292, (2020).

Ayres, Philip. *Fortunate Voyager: The Worlds of Ninian Stephen.* Miegunyah, 2013.

Barnes, James N, and Eliot Porter. *Let's Save Antarctica!* Greenhouse Publications, 1982.

Bastmeijer, C J. *The Antarctic Environmental Protocol and Its Domestic Legal Implementation.* International Environmental Law and Policy Series: V. 65. Kluwer, 2003.

Beck, Peter J. "The Antarctic Resource Conventions Implemented: Consequences for the Sovereignty Issue." Chap. 7 In *The Antarctic Treaty System in World Politics*, edited by Arnfinn Jørgensen-Dahl and Willy Østreng, 229–76: Macmillan/Fridtjof Nansen Institute, 1991.

Beeby, Christopher C. "The Antarctic Treaty System: Goals, Performance and Impact." In *The Antarctic Treatgy System in World Politics*, edited by Arnfinn Jørgensen-Dahl and Willy Østreng, 4–21: Macmillan/Fridtjof Nansen Institute, 1991.

Behrendt, John C. "Geophysical and Geological Research in Antarctica Related to the Assessment of Petroleum and Mineral Resources and Potential Environmental Hazards." In *Antarctic Challenge III*, edited by Rüdiger Wolfrum, 165–78: Duncker and Humblot, 1988.

———. "Recent Geophysical and Geological Research in Antarctica Related to the Assessment of Petroleum Resources and Potential Environmental Hazards to Their Development." In *Mineral Resources Potential of Antarctica*, edited by John F Splettstoesser and Gisela A Dreschhoff. Antarctic Research Series 51, 163–74: American Geophysical Union, 1990.

Bergin, Anthony. "The Politics of Antarctic Minerals: The Greening of White Australia." *Australian Journal of Political Science* 26, no. 2 (1991): 216–39.

Bowden, Tim. *The Silence Calling: Australians in Antarctica 1947–1997.* Allen & Unwin, 1997.

Brady, Anne-Marie. *China as a Polar Great Power*. Cambridge University Press, 2017.

Bramston, Troy. *Paul Keating: The Big Picture Leader*. Scribe, 2016.

Bray, Daniel. "The Geopolitics of Antarctic Governance: Sovereignty and Strategic Denial in Australia's Antarctic Policy." *Australian Journal of International Affairs* 70, no. 3 (2016/05/03 2016): 256–74.

Brown, Bob. *Memo for a Saner World*. Penguin, 2004.

Bush, W M, ed. *Antarctica and International Law: A Collection of Inter-State and National Documents (Looseleaf Volumes)*: Oceana, 1994–2003.

Carr, E H. *What Is History?* 2nd ed.: Penguin, 2008.

Carrick, Robert. "Conservation of Nature in Antarctica." *Polar Record* 10, no. 68 (1961): 532–40.

Chaturvedi, Sanjay. *The Polar Regions*. Wiley, 1996.

Clark, Margaret L. "The Antarctic Environmental Protocol: NGOs in the Protection of Antarctica." In *Environmental NGOs in World Politics*, edited by Matthias Finger and Thomas Prince, 160–85: Routledge, 1994.

Coburn, Sean. "Eyeing 2048: Antarctic Treaty System's Mining Ban." *Columbia Journal of Environmental Law* 42, no. 2 (2017): 1–6.

d'Alpuget, Blanche. *Bob Hawke: The Complete Biography*. Simon & Schuster, 2019.

Day, David. *Paul Keating: The Biography*. First printing, 1st ed.: HarperCollins, 2015.

Dodds, Klaus, and Mark Nuttall. *The Scramble for the Poles*. Wiley, 2016.

Dufek, George J. *Through the Frozen Frontier*. Brockhampton, 1960.

Elliott, H. "Recommendation 5: Establishment of Antarctica as a World Park under United Nations Auspices." In *Second World Conference on National Parks 1972*, edited by H Elliott, 260, 443–44: IUCN, 1974.

Elliott, Lorraine M. *International Environmental Politics: Protecting the Antarctic*. Macmillan, 1994.

Emerson, Craig. *The Boy from Baradine*. Scribe, 2018.

Evans, Gareth. "The Background Politics of the Tasmanian Dam Case." In *The Tasmanian Dam Case 30 Years On*, edited by Michael Coper, Heather Roberts and James Stellios, 11–15: Federation Press, 2017a.

———. *Incorrigible Optimist: A Political Memoir*. Melbourne University Press, 2017b.

Evans, Gareth, and Bruce Grant. *Australia's Foreign Relations in the World of the 1990's*. Melbourne University Press, 1992.

Francioni, Francesco. "The Madrid Protocol on the Protection of the Antarctic Environment." *Texas International Law Journal* 28, no. 1 (1993): 47–72.

Hamilton, Clive. *Silent Invasion: China's Influence in Australia*. Hardie Grant, 2018.

Hawke, Bob, and Derek Rielly. *Wednesdays with Bob*. Macmillan, 2017.

Heap, John A, ed. *Handbook of the Antarctic Treaty System*. 8th ed: US Department of State, 1994.

Howard, John. *Lazarus Rising: A Personal and Political Autobiography.* HarperCollins, 2011.

Howkins, Adrian. *The Polar Regions: An Environmental History.* Polity, 2016.

International Energy Agency. "World Energy Outlook 2010: Executive Summary." International Energy Agency.

Jackson, Andrew. "Politics, Diplomacy and the Creation of Antarctic Consensus." *Yearbook of Polar Law* 9 (2018): 243–61.

Jackson, Andrew, and Peter Boyce. "Mining and 'World Park Antarctica'." Chap. 11 In *Australia and the Antarctic Treaty System: 50 Years of Influence,* edited by Marcus Haward and Tom Griffiths, 243–73: UNSW Press, 2011.

Jackson, Andrew, and Lorne Kriwoken. "The Protocol in Action, 1992–2010." Chap. 13 In *Australia and the Antarctic Treaty System: 50 Years of Influence,* edited by Marcus Haward and Tom Griffiths, 300–19: UNSW Press, 2011.

Jacobsson, Marie. "Building the International Legal Framework for Antarctica." In *Science Diplomacy: Antarctica, and the Governance of International Spaces,* edited by Paul Arthur Berkman, Michael A Lang, David W H Walton and Oran R Young, 1–15: Smithsonian Institution Scholarly Press, 2011.

"Jacques Cousteau's Visit to Australia." *Australian Foreign Affairs and Trade: the Monthly Record* 61, no. 2 (1990): 81.

Joyner, Christopher C. "1988 Antarctic Minerals Convention." *Marine Policy Reports* 1, no. 1 (1989): 69–85.

———. "CRAMRA: The Ugly Duckling of the Antarctic Treaty System?". In *The Antarctic Treaty System in World Politics,* edited by Arnfinn Jørgensen-Dahl and Willy Østreng, 161–85: Macmillan/Fridtjof Nansen Institute, 1991.

———. "The Effectiveness of CRAMRA." In *Governing the Antarctic,* edited by Olav Schram Stokke and Davor Vidas, 152–72: Cambridge University Press, 1996.

———. *Governing the Frozen Commons.* University of South Carolina Press, 1998.

Kennicutt, Mahlon C. "Looking to the Future: The Poles in 2058." *Antarctic Science* 21, no. 2 (2009): 97–97.

Kirkham, Nicholas R, K M Gjerde, and A M W Wilson. "Deep-Sea Mining: Policy Options to Preserve the Last Frontier – Lessons from Antarctica's Mineral Resource Convention." *Marine Policy* 115 (2020).

Kriwoken, Lorne, and Tom Maggs. "Environment." Chap. 14 In *Australia and the Antarctic Treaty System: 50 Years of Influence,* edited by Marcus Haward and Tom Griffiths, 320–33: UNSW Press, 2011.

Lange, David. *My Life.* Viking, 2005.

Law, Phillip. *Antarctica 1984.* Sir John Morris Memorial Lecture 1964. Adult Education Board of Tasmania, 1964.

Lebedeva, Kira, and Sergei Petukhov. "Russia Decides to Return to the Antarctic with Serious Intentions and for Long." *Commersant* 8 (22 January 2003).

Liggett, Daniela. "Destination Icy Wilderness: Tourism in Antarctica." In *Exploring the Last Continent*, edited by Daniela Liggett, Bryan C. Storey, Yvonne Anne Cook and Veronika Meduna, 379–98: Springer, 2015.

Mason, Claire, Gillian Paxton, Joanna Parr, and Naomi Boughen. "Charting the Territory: Exploring Stakeholder Reactions to the Prospect of Seafloor Exploration and Mining in Australia." *Marine Policy* 34 (2010): 1374–80.

Merriam, Clark Lee. "The Cousteau Society/Foundation Cousteau: Retrospective of 1990 Activities." *Colorado Journal of International Environmental Law and Policy* 2 (1991): 325–36.

Moore, Mike. *Beyond Today: A Look at a Sustainable Economy, Resource Management and Control and a History of Environmental Politics in New Zealand*. Papanui LEC, 1981.

Mosley, J G. *Antarctica: Securing Its Heritage for the Whole World*. Envirobook, 2007.

———. "Antarctica: The Case for a World Wilderness Park." In *Fighting for Wilderness*, edited by J G Mosley and J Messer, 165–84: Fontana/ACF, 1984.

———. *Saving the Antarctic Wilderness*. Envirobook, 2009.

———. "World Park for Antarctica." *Habitat Australia*, no. 4 (October) (1989): 6–7.

Murphy, Robert Cushman. "Antarctic Conservation: Only by Careful Planning and Cooperation Can We Save This Primeval Region from the Ravages of Man." *Science* 135, no. 3499 (1962): 194–97.

———. "Antarctica: The Urgency of Protecting Life on and around the Great Southerly Continent." *Natural History* 76, no. 6 (1967): 18–31.

Palmer, Geoffrey. *Reform: A Memoir*. Victoria University Press, 2013.

Paltridge, Garth, and Julia Jabour. "Antarctica and the Madrid Protocol." *Institute of Public Affairs Environmental Backgrounder*, no. 23 (1996).

Pannatier, Serge. "Acquisition of Consultative Status under the Antarctic Treaty." *Polar Record* 30, no. 173 (1994): 123–29.

Press, A J. "The Antarctic Treaty System: Future Mining Faces Many Mathematical Challenges," *The Yearbook of Polar Law* 7, (2015): 623–31.

"Protocol on Environmental Protection to the Antarctic Treaty." https://documents.ats.aq/keydocs/vol_1/vol1_4_AT_Protocol_on_EP_e.pdf.

Raymond, Robert. "Frozen Assets." *Panorama: Ansett Airlines inflight magazine*, no. 92 [April] (1990): 30–34.

Redgwell, Catherine. "Antarctica: Wilderness Park or Eldorado Postponed?". *Environmental Politics* 1, no. 1 (1992).

Richardson, Graham. *Whatever It Takes*. Bantam, 1994.

Richardson, Mike G. "John Arnfield Heap, CMG." *Polar Record* 42, no. 3 (2006): 263–67.

Rothwell, Donald, and Ruth Davis. *Antarctic Environmental Protection: A Collection of Australian and International Instruments*. Federation Press, 1997.

Rowland, J R. "The Treaty Regime and the Politics of the Consultative Parties." In *The Antarctic Legal Regime*, edited by Christopher C Joyner and Sudhir K Chopra, 11–32: Martinus Nijhoff, 1988.

Rubinsky, Yuri. "Arctic Interests and the Policy of France." *Arctic and North* 24 (2016): 145–52.

Ryan, Susan, and Troy Bramston, eds. *The Hawke Government: A Critical Retrospective*: Pluto Press, 2003.

Sands, Philippe, Jacqueline Peel, Aguilar Adriana Fabra, and Ruth Mackenzie. *Principles of International Environmental Law*. Third ed.: Cambridge University Press, 2012.

Saul, Ben, and Tim Stephens, eds. *Antarctica in International Law*: Hart, 2015.

Scully, R Tucker. "The Development of the Antarctic Treaty System." In *Science Diplomacy: Antarctica, Science, and the Governance of International Spaces*, edited by Paul Arthur Berkman, and others, 29–38: Smithsonian Institution, 2011.

Shortis, Emma. ""Who Can Resist This Guy?" Jacques Cousteau, Celebrity Diplomacy, and the Environmental Protection of the Antarctic." *Australian Journal of Politics & History* 61, no. 3 (2015): 366–80.

Stokke, Olav Schram. "Domestic Politics and ATS Change: Introductory Assessment." In *Governing the Antarctic*, edited by Olav Schram Stokke and Davor Vidas, 323–60: Cambridge University Press, 1996.

Suter, Keith D. *World Law and the Last Wilderness*. 2nd ed.: Friends of the Earth, 1980.

Swan, Robert. *Antarctica 2041: My Quest to Save the Earth's Last Wilderness*. Broadway, 2009.

Szabo, Michael. *State of the Ice: An Overview of Human Impacts in Antarctica*. Greenpeace International, 1993.

Templeton, Malcolm. *Protecting Antarctica: The Development of the Treaty System*. New Zealand Insitute of International Affairs, 2002.

———. *A Wise Adventure II: New Zealand and Antarctica after 1960*. Victoria University Press, 2017.

Trachtenberg, Marc. *The Craft of International History: A Guide to Method*. Princeton University Press, 2006.

US Congress Office of Technology Assessment. *Polar Prospects: A Minerals Treaty for Antarctica*. US Government Printing Office, 1989.

Vicuña, Francisco Orrego. "The Protocol on Environmental Protection to the Antarctic Treaty: Questions of Effectiveness." *Georgetown International Environmental Law Review* 7 (1994): 1–13.

Vidas, Davor, ed. *Implementing the Environmental Protection Regime for the Antarctic*: Kluwer, 2000.

Woolcott, Richard. "Foreword." In *Australia and the Antarctic Treaty System: 50 Years of Influence*, edited by Marcus Haward and Tom Griffiths, xii–xv: UNSW Press, 2011.

APPENDIX: TIME LINE OF KEY EVENTS

1912	Douglas Mawson's 1911–1914 Australasian Antarctic Expedition makes the first collection of geological samples found to contain Antarctic gold and silver.
1908–1946	Antarctic territorial claims formalised. Australian Antarctic Territory officially proclaimed in 1933.
1959	Antarctic Treaty negotiations sidestep the issue of mineral resources. Treaty adopted on 1 December 1959 and enters into force on 23 June 1961.
10–24 July 1961	First Antarctic Treaty Consultative Meeting (ATCM I) held in Canberra with the 12 original Antarctic Treaty Consultative Parties (ATCPs).
2–13 June 1964	ATCM III (Brussels). Antarctica designated as "Special Conservation Area" in the Agreed Measures for the Conservation of Antarctic Flora and Fauna.
1970	Minerals issue first broached within the Antarctic Treaty Consultative Meeting (ATCM) and placed on the agenda for the 1972 meeting.
11 February 1972	Convention for the Conservation of Antarctic Seals (CCAS) adopted.
18–27 September 1972	Second World Conference on National Parks (Yellowstone) recommends establishment of Antarctica as a 'World Park'.
30 October–10 November 1972	ATCM VII (Wellington). Norway offers to host a meeting of experts to informally discuss minerals in 1973.

(continued)

© The Author(s), under exclusive license to Springer Nature
Switzerland AG 2021
A. Jackson, *Who Saved Antarctica?*,
https://doi.org/10.1007/978-3-030-78405-8

411

(continued)

3–5 February 1973	*Glomar Challenger* encounters traces of gases in the Ross Sea during the Deep Sea Drilling Project.
30 May–9 June 1973	Nansen Foundation hosts an informal conference in Oslo on Antarctic minerals and explores a wide range of issues. Considers a moratorium on minerals activities until basic rules are developed.
October 1973	OPEC oil crisis triggered by Arab-Israeli War.
9–20 June 1975	ATCM VIII (Oslo). On 12 June 1975, New Zealand informally proposes an Antarctic 'international park' or 'international reserve' (later to be described as its 'world park' proposal).
28 June–10 July 1976	Special Preparatory Meeting on minerals (Paris).
29 July 1977	First Special Antarctic Treaty Consultative Meeting (SATCM I) recognises Poland as a Consultative Party, making it the first ATCP to be added since the Treaty's entry into force and taking the number of ATCPs to 13.
1976–1981	Discussions within the ATCM and related forums on options to progress the minerals issue.
20 May 1980	Convention on the Conservation of Antarctic Marine Living Resources (CCAMLR) adopted.
23 June–7 July 1981	ATCM XI decides to refer the minerals issue to a Special Antarctic Treaty Consultative Meeting. Moratorium confirmed.
14–25 June 1982	First session of the Fourth SATCM (SATCM IV) held to negotiate a regime to regulate Antarctic mineral resource activities (Wellington).
5 March 1983	Bob Hawke appointed Australian Prime Minister after Labor Party was successful in an election heavily influenced by environmental issues.
6–9 October 1982	Minerals discussed at the Conference on Antarctic Resources Policy held at Chile's Teniente Marsh Base, the first international conference held in Antarctica.
17–28 January 1983	SATCM IV second session (Wellington).
11–22 July 1983	SATCM IV third session (Bonn).
12 September 1983	SATCM V (Canberra). Brazil and India recognised as ATCPs.
18–27 January 1984	SATCM IV fourth session (Washington).
23–31 May 1984	SATCM IV fifth session (Tokyo).
7–13 January 1985	Beardmore Glacier workshop, discusses minerals informally.
26 February–8 March 1985	SATCM IV sixth session (Rio de Janeiro).
23 September–4 October 1985	SATCM IV seventh session (Paris).

(*continued*)

(continued)

7 October 1985	SATCM VI (Brussels). China and Uruguay recognised as ATCPs.
March 1986	Beeby convenes informal discussions at Whangaroa (New Zealand).
14–25 April 1986	SATCM IV eighth session (Hobart).
26 October–12 November 1986	SATCM IV ninth session (Tokyo).
March 1987	Beeby convenes further informal discussions at Whangaroa (New Zealand).
11–20 May 1987	SATCM IV tenth session (Montevideo).
5 October 1987	SATCM VII (Rio de Janeiro). Italy and German Democratic Republic recognised as ATCPs.
9–20 November 1987	Beeby holds further informal discussions with select delegation heads at Auckland.
11–29 January 1988	SATCM IV 11th session (Wellington).
2 May–2 June 1988	Final session of SATCM IV (Wellington). Convention on the Regulation of Antarctic Mineral Resources (CRAMRA) adopted by all the then Antarctic Treaty Consultative Parties. Final Act signed.
June 1988–May 1989	Australian Prime Minister Bob Hawke, Environment Minister Senator Richardson and Foreign Minister Senator Evans receive thousands of representations calling for Australia not to sign CRAMRA. Extended run of correspondence between Australian ministers.
30 September 1988	Australian Treasurer Paul Keating meets French Prime Minister Rocard and discusses Antarctica.
22 November 1988	CRAMRA tabled in Australian parliament with the objective of "promoting community discussion". This is followed by a series of parliamentary discussions as well as community debate.
25 November 1988	CRAMRA opens for signature for one year.
28 January 1989	Argentine ship *Bahia Paraiso* capsizes in Antarctica, spilling oil and fuel.
7 February 1989	The United Kingdom's HMS *Endurance* collides with ice near Deception Island.
28 February 1989	Peru's BIC *Humboldt* strikes rocks off King George Island.
24 March 1989	*Exxon Valdez* disaster in Prince William Sound Alaska.
20 April 1989	French Prime Minister, Michel Rocard, announces that France will not sign CRAMRA in its current form.
27 April 1989	Treasurer Keating writes to Hawke supporting a 'world park' or 'national park'.
28 April 1989	Australian Opposition Leader John Howard announces opposition to Antarctic mining.

(*continued*)

(continued)

9–13 May 1989	Preparatory Meeting for the 15th Antarctic Treaty Consultative Meeting (Paris). Australia signals that it might propose an alternative to CRAMRA. Chile proposes development of comprehensive environmental rules in parallel with CRAMRA. Decision to discuss all options at a SATCM in 1990.
22 May 1989	Hawke cabinet meets to consider CRAMRA. The Australian government announces Cabinet's decision not to sign, but instead promote a regime that would prohibit mining and establish an 'Antarctic wilderness park'.
May–October 1989	Period of intense diplomatic activity as other Treaty Parties react to the Australian position.
June 1989	Prime Minister Hawke visits Europe and meets French Prime Minister Michel Rocard and Jacques Cousteau.
30 June 1989	Belgium amends its Antarctic laws to prohibit Belgian mining in Antarctica—the first such law by an Antarctic state
7–9 August 1989	First meeting of Australia/France Working Group.
18 August 1989	Mr Hawke and Mr Rocard agree, in Canberra, to promote a joint initiative for comprehensive Antarctic environment protection in a regime that would establish a 'wilderness reserve'.
9–20 October 1989	ATCM XV (Paris). Treaty Parties agree to refer the question of the Australian/French proposal to a SATCM to be held in Chile the following year.
9 November 1989	France formally decides not to sign CRAMRA.
18–19 November 1989	Australian Institute of International Affairs conference in Hobart.
October 1989–November 1990	Further intense diplomatic activity results in increased support for the Australia/French position. Belgium and Italy become co-sponsors of the proposal.
21–23 May 1990	Informal discussions held in Oslo at the Nansen Institute conference on 'The Antarctic Treaty System in World Politics'
14–15 July 1990	Small group meeting in Kiel to develop idea of a protocol.
23 August 1990	New Zealand abandons all support for CRAMRA.
19 November–6 December 1990	First session of the 11th Special Antarctic Treaty Special Consultative Meeting (SATCM XI) held in Viña del Mar. Andersen text compiled in a difficult and tense meeting.

(*continued*)

(continued)

December 1990–April 1991	Further intense diplomatic activity results in the core group of supporters being joined by an increasing body of 'like-minded' countries.
27 March 1991	Royal Assent for Australia's *Antarctic Mining Prohibition Act*. The act prohibited mining in the AAT, and by Australians anywhere in the Antarctic to demonstrate commitment to the no-mining option.
16 April 1991	Japan drops its support for CRAMRA, unwilling to be isolated.
22–30 April 1991	SATCM XI second session (Madrid). Protocol language largely agreed, and four annexes developed.
17–21 June 1991	SATCM XI third session (Madrid). Protocol text and annexes virtually finalised, but the United States unable to agree to the formula for reviewing the mining prohibition.
23 June 1991	Thirtieth anniversary of the entry into force of the Antarctic Treaty (the first date at which a review conference could have been called).
3 July 1991	Consensus restored when President Bush announces that the United States accepts the draft Protocol, including the mining prohibition.
3 October 1991	SATCM XI fourth session. Protocol on Environmental Protection to the Antarctic Treaty (Madrid Protocol) adopted, along with four annexes.
4 October 1991	Final Act of the SATCM signed by all Treaty Parties and Protocol opened for signature for one year. All except three Consultative Parties sign the Protocol itself that day. Parties agree to ratify the Protocol as soon as possible.
7–18 October 1991	ATCM XVI (Bonn). At the 16th Consultative Meeting the Parties agree to a fifth annex to the Protocol on area protection and management, but reject the idea of a tourism annex.
14 January 1998	Entry into force of the Madrid Protocol.
17 June 2005	ATCM XXVIII (Stockholm). Sixth annex to the Protocol adopted on liability arising from environmental emergencies.
14 January 2048	The first date at which the environmental protocol, including the mining prohibition, can be modified if there is less than consensus.

INDEX

417

Printed by Books on Demand, Germany